South African Review 4

South African Review 4

Edited and compiled by
Glenn Moss and Ingrid Obery
for the Southern African Research Service (SARS)

Ravan Press　　　　Johannesburg

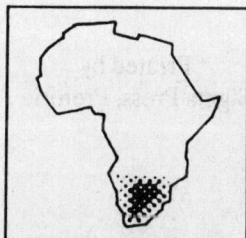

Southern African Research Service

Published by
Ravan Press (Pty) Ltd
PO Box 31134, Braamfontein 2017, South Africa

First Published 1987

Cover Design: Ingrid Obery

ISBN 0 86975 335 5

Printed by
Sigma Press, Pretoria

Indiv. chaps. on cards

Contents

urban political economy.

Contents

prosecutions decline - Pressure from press, business and
political parties - Urban authorities urge poltical reforms -
Hopes for change dashed.

Preface

The fourth *South African Review* had its origins in a meeting of potential contributors, held in Johannesburg at the beginning of February 1987. Since then, over 60 authors and editors have been involved in producing the *Review*.

The co-operative and collective nature of the *Review* is one of its main features. Most articles have been extensively discussed, reformulated and re-written. Section co-ordinators have attempted to create a coherence in each of the six sections, and SARS and Ravan Press staff have edited contributions with a view to readability and accessibility for non-specialist readers.

While SARS bears responsibility for the overall nature and form of the book, contributors are responsible for the views expressed in their own articles.

Special thanks are due to the section co-ordinators: Daryl Glaser, David Kaplan, Alan Mabin, David Webster and Eddie Webster. They commented extensively on draft articles, ran seminars with contributors, and generally assisted the editors in structuring the book.

Apart from the contributors themselves, thanks are also due to Susan Brown and Isabel Hofmeyr, who edited sections of the book, and Ravan Press's Ivan Vladislavic, who was most efficient and helpful in final editing and proof reading of the *Review*.

The assistance of Daphne Chalmers, who both typeset the book and trained SARS staff in the use of desktop publishing systems, is also gratefully acknowledged.

Glenn Moss and Ingrid Obery
October 1987

Usages and Abbreviations

In this *South African Review*, the term 'black' refers collectively to all racially oppressed groups in South Africa, ie Africans, Indians and coloureds. These racial categories reflect part of the reality of apartheid society and their use is accordingly necessary in contemporary writings. But the editors of the *Review* reject the racism implicit in such categorisation.

Most abbreviations used in the text of the *Review* are spelled out in full on first usage. Newspapers referred to in the text are abbreviated in the following way:

BD	*Business Day*
Cit	*Citizen*
CP	*City Press*
CT	*Cape Times*
DD	*Daily Dispatch*
DFA	*Diamond Fields Advertiser*
DN	*Daily News*
EPH	*Eastern Province Herald*
EPost	*Evening Post*
FM	*Financial Mail*
FT	*Financies en Tegniek*
FW	*Finance Week*
Lead	*Leader*
NM	*Natal Mercury*
NW	*Natal Witness*
OL	*Oosterlig*
Pat	*Patriot*
PN	*Pretoria News*
RDM	*Rand Daily Mail*
SAO	*South African Observer*
SE	*Sunday Express*
Sow	*Sowetan*
ST	*Sunday Times*
S.Star	*Sunday Star*
STrib	*Sunday Tribune*
WA	*Weekend Argus*
WM	*Weekly Mail*
WP	*Weekend Post*

General Introduction

Reforming the Contradictions: Crisis and the State

When imposing the state of emergency in June 1986, government acknowledged that the previous emergency from July 1985 to March 1986 had failed to suppress resistance to apartheid. This exposed the contradiction at the heart of the state's much-touted reform policy: the stability necessary for reform is impossible without repression, while repressive measures deepen the crisis to which reform is a response.

The fourth *South African Review* raises important questions about current South African society. What opportunities are presented by state attempts to reform apartheid? How does the changing nature of the state affect reform, crisis and struggle? Is reform failing because of limitations and contradictions in its formulation, or is it by definition incapable of producing the results state and capital desire? What is the relationship between crisis and reform? The answers to these questions lie in analysis of the crisis, in the nature and content of reform, and in the relationship between the two.

In 1981, John Saul and Steven Gelb described the developing South African crisis as 'organic'. An organic crisis, they argued, is characterised by incurable structural contradictions deeply embedded in society; by its extreme duration; and by the efforts of competing forces to overcome these contradictions.[1] Though somewhat vague, this conceptualisation makes a useful distinction between the present crisis and previous South African crises as well as those cyclical crises to which capitalism is subject. An organic crisis differs from others in that it pervades society, influencing economic, political, ideological, social and juridical relations and structures. It is more than a cyclical economic crisis; more than a recession and different from a depression, although it displays characteristics of both.

Organic crisis is also more than a structural crisis, which results from economic conditions either inherent in capitalist production or structured into the economy over time.

In reality, of course, it is impossible to make clear-cut distinctions between various 'levels' of society. Political, ideological and legal factors continually interact with those in the economy, shaping them and being shaped in turn. Thus in the political economy of apartheid, which is characterised by a relative 'overpoliticisation', political and ideological aspects have come to constitute barriers to capital accumulation.

Two 'incurable structural contradictions' of the current crisis have their origins in the earliest days of capitalist development. They are the migrant labour system and the structural imbalance between mining and manufacturing - the primary and secondary sectors of production. By the early 1970s these were defining features of the social relations which make up society.

Contradictions of migrant labour

At the turn of the century, mining companies forced Africans down the mines through the contract, compound and pass systems. These became the foundations on which segregation and later apartheid were constructed. Mine owners and governments of the time forced only those Africans whose labour they required into towns. They paid 'bachelor' wages to African miners on the grounds that their families had sufficient means of subsistence in the rural 'reserves', and barricaded Africans whose labour they did not require in the 'reserves'. This laid the foundation for the bantustans, which in turn provided the basis for the forced migrant labour system.

But migrant labour has become contradictory for capitalism. Certainly the cost of migrant labour is generally cheaper than that of a permanent urban proletariat, and a migrant labour force is less cohesive and more open to exploitation. But a migrant labour force also has an extremely high turnover, which is detrimental to capital's need for stable, reliable labour that can provide the skills necessary for economic expansion. And the necessary political controls over the movement of the labour force between bantustans and the urban areas have been extremely costly - both politically and economically - and highly inefficient.

Once the economy demanded a higher level of skilled and semi-skilled labour for its continued expansion, the migrant labour system became counterproductive. No longer is it only the cheapness of labour which is important, but the cheapness of skilled labour. Trapped in the contradictions of the migrant labour system inherited from mining, capitalism in South Africa has a history of successive failures to overcome these contradictions. The effect of this institutionalised oppression and exploitation on the contemporary crisis cannot be overemphasised. It is now a significant barrier to accumulation, though in its time it greatly facilitated the development of capitalism.

The migrant labour system and the legal and political superstructures it gave rise to involve a major structural contradiction. Though basic to capitalist development, their very existence in time proved a historical trap from which capital has been attempting to escape for decades.

South Africa and the world economy

Migrant labour is not, however, the only 'accident' of history which limits the ability of the state and capital to resolve the crisis. For South Africa is a semi-industrialised country with a peripheral position in the world economy.

Mining companies minimised costs by purchasing locally produced commodities. This, combined with government policies designed to foster an indigenous secondary sector by redistributing surplus extracted from mining, was crucial to secondary industrialisation. Manufacturing owed its existence and continued development to the primary sector's needs and fortunes, and so developed within comparatively narrow parameters. It was therefore severely disadvantaged in its ability to compete for the international markets on which its growth depended.

The imbalance between mining and manufacturing was structured into the economy as a result. As a peripheral country internationally, South Africa has a relatively open economy which is highly dependent upon foreign investment, trade, technology and capital goods. This dependency reinforces the relative uncompetitiveness of manufacturing and restricts the growth potential of the economy as a whole.

Demand for consumer goods manufactured by secondary industry is limited by the size of local and regional markets. The internal market is also limited by low black wages and whites' bias towards imported luxury consumer goods. The narrow market in the sub-continent is a result of underdevelopment caused by South Africa's regional sub-imperialist role and the reluctance of independent black states to trade with apartheid. This lack of demand reinforces the manufacturing sector's limited ability to compete on the international markets vital to its development. Small markets and the country's dependence on imported capital goods and technology combine to preclude the economies of scale which might otherwise boost competitiveness.

During upturns in the economy, manufacturing firms tend to make the capital investments necessary to increase competitiveness. This provokes balance of payments problems because of the narrowness of the country's export base, and chokes off expansion within the manufacturing sector. Only the pivotal role of gold has made the economy viable. Gold has facilitated secondary industrialisation through the redistribution of the surplus extracted from the mining sector, by indirectly financing expansion and by preventing a permanent balance of payments crisis.

From the late 1970s government fiscal policy aimed at curbing inflation. Steeply rising state expenditure, necessitated by the rising costs of defending apartheid, was a major cause of inflation. Taking its lead from monetarist policies adopted in Britain and the United States, government decided that controlling the money supply was the best way of reducing inflation.

Here yet again government policies were more a problem than a solution. For the manufacturing sector they were disastrous. In 1985 inflation reached its highest level in 66 years. The rise in interest rates precipitated monetarist policies, choked off new investment and combined with inflation to increase wage costs. Numbers of bankruptcies rose dramatically, while those firms still in business attempted to ride out the recession by retrenching workers. The already excessive centralisation of the economy increased with a rash of takeovers and mergers, as firms sought to rationalise production without committing themselves to costly investment. In three of the four years between 1982 and 1985, there was negative growth in real gross domestic product. Between 1981 and 1985 the average ratio of capital to output rose, indicating a decline in productivity. Capitalism was suffering a crisis of accumulation as apartheid became increasingly dysfunctional.

Throughout the economy, output and investment declined. Interest rates rose along with inflation and the currency weakened. This culminated in the debt crisis which manifested itself dramatically in the collapse of the rand, closure of the stock exchange and the default on debt repayments which exacerbated the balance of payments problem. The economy was locked into a downward spiral, which limited the scope for political reform.

As the economy moved into the worst recession in 50 years, the manufacturing sector showed signs of stagnation and declining profitability. It needed reform of the system of control and exploitation of African labour, to rationalise the supply of migrant labour and make the system less costly and inefficient. But at no time did the state seriously contemplate steps aimed at removing the problem. Its aim, and its new buzzword, was 'reform'.

From then onward almost every reformist initiative compounded the contradictions at the heart of the crisis rather than resolving them. Reform itself became a crucial element of the crisis. The theoretical incoherence of reform and its contradictory effects caused the final element of the organic crisis to emerge: the gradual political and ideological disintegration of the ruling class, leading to significant changes within the state itself.

The content of reform was thus determined by three main factors: the structural crisis in the economy, the rising tide of internal and international resistance to apartheid, and changes in the state. They combined to limit the options available to the state. John Vorster, prime minister at the time, heading an increasingly corrupt and moribund administration and almost paralysed by the class conflict within Afrikanerdom, reluctantly and haltingly began the process of restructuring. In 1977 he put forward a set of constitutional proposals which ultimately formed the basis for the tricameral constitution, and he appointed the Wiehahn, Riekert and De Kock commissions. At the same time, the power and influence of the military were growing steadily under PW Botha's stewardship. For Botha and his generals the context of reform was set in the form of Total Strategy.

Total Strategy did not merely favour the centralisation of command structures and organisation, it dictated them. When General Magnus Malan, chief of the Defence Force, became minister of defence it symbolised the blending of the political and military spheres. Policies were conceived and ratified in the State Security Council, composed of key cabinet ministers, police and military leaders, which virtually usurped the role of cabinet government. The tentacles of the military and the police spread throughout South African society through the structures connecting the State Security Council with the local-level Joint Management Centres.

In the militarisation of the state and society, the generals came to exercise growing influence over political and economic policies. Behind the veneer of white democracy a silent coup was taking place. This culminated with Botha's assumption, under the 1984 tricameral constitution, of sweeping executive powers as state president, which put him at the head of a de facto military dictatorship. The state had secured an alternative power base.

Necessary reform, the generals argued, could only take place in a context of stability provided by military dominance. In the subcontinent, destabilisation tactics aimed at neutralising the African National Congress and reproducing the dependency and underdevelopment of the frontline states. Inside South Africa, political resistance had to be neutralised, while economic resistance was to be co-opted.

Reform itself was therefore based upon repression from the start. Its ideological and theoretical roots in military strategy cut it off from the economic and political roots of the crisis, so it was anti-democratically conceived and imposed from above. The reform programme lacked historical perspective or a dynamic element: government believed that gradual changes in specific spheres would allow apartheid to continue in a slightly modified form. But every reform compounded existing contradictions rather than resolving them.

Rising internal resistance meant that the time and scope necessary if reform was to succeed were limited and that ever-greater repression was necessary if changes were to be imposed.

A fundamental contradiction was that reform in the late 1970s and early 1980s was still firmly based on the continuation of 'grand apartheid': the illusory economic viability of the bantustans continued to be the theoretical basis for proposed political solutions. Accepting the permanence of the urban African labour force, government still hoped that African workers could be stripped of citizenship, and that the minority coloured and Indian communities could be co-opted by being given a stake in apartheid, capitalism and stability.

In the absence of legitimate areas for political expression, the trade unions slowly but inevitably became quasi-political bodies as grassroots pressure expressed itself in the links between life under apartheid in and away from work. The centrepiece of reform - industrial relations - had simply served to increase the pressure for further reform, this time at the political level.

Intent on dividing the black population on both class and racial lines, on halting growing international condemnation of apartheid, and above all on maintaining white domination, the ideologues of reform came up with the tricameral parliament and the Koornhof Bills. This attempted political solution simply reinforced the spiral of crisis. The United Democratic Front was formed to fight the new dispensation. Impoverishment increased as the economic crisis deepened and resistance intensified to the point at which states of emergency were necessary to maintain order. But this added to the cycle of crisis. The emergencies intensified resistance and magnified economic problems by precipitating a major debt crisis, sanctions and the further erosion of the economic base necessary for the salvation of white domination.

The states of emergency amounted to an admission that government had lost control, that the township community councils - designed to provide a form of political representation for urban Africans - had been destroyed, that the townships were indeed ungovernable, and that repression was the only solution possible. Reform had collapsed after deepening rather than resolving the crisis.

By failing to address the fundamental issue of political representation for Africans, the new constitution - the jewel in the reformist crown - was condemned to failure. Its rejection forced the state to recognise that it was in a dead end, and marked the end of the first phase of reform dominated by Wiehahn, Riekert and the new constitution. Phase two was about to begin.

State planners began to abandon the illusions of 'grand apartheid' and seek new ways to secure favourable conditions for accumulation and white domination. 'Orderly urbanisation', the concept laid out in a government White Paper adopted in 1986, was the basis of this new attempt to resolve the crisis. Departing from the orthodoxies of separate development, it accepts the permanence of African urbanisation. It shifts the terrain of reform towards economic development regions which cut across the old spatial divisions of the bantustans. These regions will be run by Regional Services Councils composed of municipal representatives of the various racial groupings defined by apartheid.[2]

More coherent and sophisticated than the first phase of reform, 'orderly urbanisation' attempts to deracialise limited aspects of South African society and shift the focus of control from race to class. But on closer analysis it is apparent that most of the contradictions of Reform Mark I are replicated in the new version. It is yet another attempt to reform rather than remove apartheid, in that racial segregation remains intact.

The state has resolved to withdraw from the lower reaches of the economy, hoping to remove the barriers to accumulation now constituted by orthodox influx control, forced removals and decentralisation based on the bantustans. This is a tacit admission that apartheid has failed to meet the labour needs of capital. The proposed use of fiscal measures to encourage the deconcentration of capital fits neatly into the monetarist policies pursued during the 1980s. In Thatcher's Britain, another country subject to long-term economic decline, the effects of similar policies are clear. There, the lethal combination of monetarism and the crusade to minimise the role of the state in the economy has resulted in massive unemployment, the destruction of the welfare state, and an assault on the working class. This overt class war has been accompanied by rising authoritarianism and the ideology of free enterprise, individualism and rabid anti-socialism. The South African government could hardly ask for more.

Thatcherism ultimately deepened Britain's decline, and the prospects look no better in South Africa. With the costs of defending apartheid steadily rising, the state intends through 'orderly urbanisation' to shift many of the costs of labour reproduction (for health, housing and education, for example) onto the working class. The sheer inefficiency of the current system and the country's critical foreign debt situation dictate the need for a less costly system and a less interventionist state. It is no accident that so much is being heard about privatisation as the 'solution' to the current crisis.

By removing some immediate causes of resistance, such as the pass laws, the state hopes to suppress the unrest and restore stability to the townships. However, the repeal of the pass laws, though a positive step removing an immediate grievance and source of conflict, cannot get rid of the need for a disguised form of influx control as long as there is an unfree labour market. The social and political risks of uncontrolled urbanisation are simply too great. The legacy of dependency on migrant labour, reformed though it now may be, is still a central feature of the crisis.

This highlights the contradiction of attempting to reduce state intervention while maintaining as much control as before. If urbanisation is to be 'orderly', it must be imposed from the top down, implying a range of controls at variance with rule by market forces. With resistance and industrial conflict endemic and the crisis constantly deepening, the options available to the state and capital continually become narrower.

Shifting the costs of the reproduction of the labour force onto the working class is likely to increase the costs of the system: economically because of the increasing unemployment, ill-health and poverty which must follow, and politically because of the resistance it will provoke. Moreover, if the main source of Regional Services Councils' revenue is to be a tax on the turnover and wages of firms in each region, the rise in labour costs which must accompany such a process will be a source of conflict between the state, trade unions and capital.

Finally, 'orderly urbanisation' aims at securing the very stability it depends on to succeed. With the destruction of the community councils envisaged as the third tier of government for Africans, the concept is in danger of being stillborn. Without increased repression it cannot succeed - but every turn of the repressive screw deepens the organic crisis.

Exploiting the contradictions

The militarised state was forced by class and national struggle to resort to ever-growing repression. With a diminishing political power base, the state has lost a great measure of control over South African society. It can impose its rule in the townships only at gunpoint. Increasing tensions between the state and capital and within Afrikanerdom reveal the ideological and political fragmentation of the ruling class.

However, while the state may no longer hold the degree of control to which it has become accustomed under apartheid, it has not mobilised all the repressive weapons at its disposal yet. The state of emergency under which it now rules has not succeeded in destroying resistance - but there can be little doubt of its effectiveness in undermining it. The emergency has dictated new forms of organisation. But progressive forces face not only the state but the reactionary force of Inkatha, vigilantes and divisions over strategies and tactics. And the emergency is not only aimed at smashing resistance. Under its umbrella the state actively promotes reactionary interests while attempting to smash progressive initiatives.

The latest state initiatives demand more than a knee-jerk response. More subtle and sophisticated than before, they will present new problems and new opportunities. The contributions which make up the fourth *South African Review* survey those areas crucial to an understanding of the South African crisis, and its resolution: resistance and struggle, state policy, labour and trade unions, repression, South Africa's interventions in Southern Africa, the economy, militarisation and privatisation.

Reform cannot work because it is part of an organic crisis which demands solutions as fundamental as the problems. Reform, by its very definition, cannot resolve the contradictions. But it provides opportunities to exploit the contradictions hitherto absent in the struggle to create a new society.

The structure of this *Review* breaks down many of the major areas of conflict and policy into sections and articles. But there are important connections between sections and articles. Resistance and the state of emergency cannot be analysed as separate entities in society. Nor can they be viewed without reference to developments in the economy and state policy. And South Africa's relationship to the rest of the sub-continent both reflects and affects internal political and economic developments.

The sections and articles making up this *Review* describe and analyse a general social process. Their points of intersection are as important as their separation into different areas for analysis. At the same time, the *Review* is silent on a number of crucial themes. The role of organisations like the United Democratic Front and some of its affiliates; school boycotts, student and youth politics; and the changing relationship between the state and international financial institutions are just some of the areas where the *Review* remains silent. But the *Review* is not meant to be a comprehensive description of every event or issue of importance. Silences are imposed by the necessity of keeping the book a manageable length, as well as the difficulties of writing about some issues under emergency conditions.

The intersections between areas that are presented as separate; the silences on some areas of social importance; and the authors' attempts to analyse and describe a social process rather than specific events must be borne in mind when reading the fourth *South African Review*.

Notes

1   John Saul and Steven Gelb, *The Crisis in South Africa - Class Defence, Class Revolution,* Monthly Review Press, 1981, chapter 1.

2   For more detail on 'orderly urbanisation' see for example William Cobbett et al, 'South Africa's Regional Political Economy: A Critical Analysis of Reform Strategy in the 1980s', *South African Review 3,* Johannesburg, 1986; Doug Hindson, 'Urbanisation and Influx Control', *Work In Progress,* 40, February 1986; and Doug Hindson, 'African Urbanisation: Creating New Controls', *Work In Progress,* 41, April 1986.

Section 1: Resistance

Introduction

Alan Mabin

Anti-apartheid forces in South Africa pass through a continuing cycle of euphoria and depression. When the state appears on the retreat and resistance organisations seem strong, great optimism prevails as to the longed-for end of apartheid. But during periods of crushing repression, when state resources seem unlimited and the weaknesses of resistance apparent, a pessimistic atmosphere develops. Broadly, the 1950s were a period of optimism, followed by a wave of gloom during the repressive 1960s. From the early 1970s a more optimistic tone developed. During the past decade there have been rapid swings between hope and despair as the forces of resistance and the state have continually altered the balance of South African politics.

In mid-1987, there can be no doubt which phase of this cycle the consciousness of resistance has entered. Anglican Archbishop Desmond Tutu speaks of the country entering its 'darkest age'. During May 1987, a prominent anti-apartheid activist remarked that organisations of resistance should prepare for a 30-year struggle. The mood contrasts starkly with that prevailing at the time of publication of *South African Review 3,* the previous volume in this series. The two states of emergency - and especially the current one, declared on 12 June 1986 - are in part responsible for this change. Unprecedented numbers of political activists and ordinary people have been detained without trial, freedoms of speech and association have been viciously attacked, and anti-apartheid organisation has been severely affected. But it is not adequate simply to blame the difficulties of resistance organisations on state repression. The articles in this section are concerned with assessing the progress and setbacks experienced within broad resistance to the apartheid state over the past year or two.

The formation of the United Democratic Front in 1983 and its subsequent growth paralleled both deepening recession and an immense upsurge of popular political activity. The degree to which the national organisation and substantial resources of the UDF were key elements in the rise of popular resistance, or products of that resistance, is a question which cannot yet be answered satisfactorily. This section contains no national overview, and part of that silence is the absence of a piece on the UDF as a central organisation of resistance. But the activities of many organisations and groupings affiliated to, or closely associated with the UDF, are subjected to scrutiny. And the second section of this book, covering the state of emergency, comments on the curtailment of UDF and other national political activities.

The first theme which emerges is that of boycott strategies developed in a variety of contexts - among school students, consumers and township rent payers. The most widespread and enduring boycotts have been in education, in particular the boycotts of black education. Black schools became the object of pervasive student boycotts, leading to the recognition of a crisis situation in education generally. To provide a national summary of this complex situation is impossible here. Johan Muller's piece in this section takes as its starting point the existence of widespread boycotts and explores responses to that situation on the part of black communities. The creation by early 1986 of the National Education Crisis Committee and the evolution of the idea of people's education form the focus of his analysis of responses to the boycotts. He looks at what was achieved in the light of the constraints under which the NECC operated.

The next article, by an Eastern Cape group which monitored

consumer boycott action, takes up the issue of a tactic which proved immensely successful in some situations over the past two years, but failed to achieve significant demands in other cases. The image of community leaders forcing Chambers of Commerce to negotiating tables is a powerful memory of 1985. But the growing intransigence of the state in 1986 made the achievement of boycott goals increasingly difficult. With the second state of emergency from mid-1986, many community organisations lost their more experienced leadership, and since then few consumer boycotts have been successful in significantly denting trade in the 'white' towns, accomplishing the release of detainees or ending the emergency. Both the internal dynamics of community organisations and the attitude of the state, as well as local questions of politics and geography, are explored in this article.

If consumer boycotts have attracted less support during 1987, township rent boycotts continue to prove intractable for the state. Chaskalson, Jochelson and Seekings examine the developing history of rent and service-charge boycotts since the Vaal uprising of September 1984. They locate the origins of contemporary rent boycotts in the state's determination to finance the townships from revenue raised within them. Although they do not explicitly raise the question, their article provides much food for thought on the persistence of the rent boycott tactic in a period of massive repression and the failure or abandonment of other boycott tactics. The connections between different forms of organisation and resistance thus become central issues, and focus the second theme of this section.

Georgina Jaffee explores some aspects of those connections by studying the struggles waged by women in trade unions and townships. Jaffee shows that individuals involved in both union and community organisations are important carriers of ideas about women's rights between the two. She demonstrates that the incorporation of African women into the industrial workforce has raised specific issues in both community organisations and trade unions. The extent of this development is further explored by a second article which raises similar concerns, that of Beall, Friedman, Hassim, Posel, Stiebel and Todes. These authors argue that the involvement of women in organisation and struggle has the potential to transform their roles, and that the experience of African women in Durban during 1985-86 has already resulted in some changes. But while their social construction as women draws them into struggle and makes movement beyond traditional roles possible, the same social construction also limits that possibility. In this context the authors of the article express concern that gains won in this area through struggle may slip away. That concern is one which troubles all the authors mentioned so far, for there is a general feeling that the hard-won advances of the recent past may be driven back under the current difficulties faced by oppositional organisations in South Africa.

Laurie Nathan, in a reflective piece on the first three years of the End Conscription Campaign, shares exactly those fears. After much hard work, ECC - which differs from the organisations scrutinised by other authors mentioned in its focus on resistance among white South Africans - has established itself as a real factor in the struggle to end apartheid. With the massive entry of troops into the townships during 1985 and 1986, the 'border' came into the cities and towns of South Africa, and the role of the ECC became a serious problem for a state dependent on conscripts for the maintenance of its rule in the townships. Whether the ECC will be able to maintain and expand its role under these new circumstances is not yet clear.

If uncertainty clouds the campaign to end conscription, a wide variety of other forms of resistance have also been affected by unpredictable events. Nowhere is this more so than in the bantustans. Realignment of classes, brought about by the creation of bantustan structures and the strains of economic crisis, has created new possibilities for resistance. The defeat, even if only temporary, of Kwandebele 'independence' plans was only one dramatic illustration of this. But, as Jeremy Keenan points out in his contribution to this section, there has also been massive state repression in the bantustans. Nevertheless, he argues that the long-term political significance of resistance in the bantustans should not be underestimated. Out of sight of the media even prior to emergency restrictions, the struggle in the bantustans forms an important component of national politics which urban events have often obscured.

The struggle in the townships has diminished somewhat in intensity (and has all but disappeared from the columns of the censored press). But reflection on the relationship between that on-the-ground struggle and the activities of African National Congress cadres continues - not least in the offices of the ANC itself. Tom

Lodge provides this section of the book with a review of ANC thinking and action since the Kabwe Conference, in military, diplomatic and ideological terms. Many of the issues which are raised by the other contributions in more detail surface in Lodge's contribution, which for that reason opens this section.

This selection of articles on resistance does not provide a complete review of the state of anti-apartheid action in the country. But some of the major features of resistance in the past few years are addressed, and some of the consequences of the major styles of organising and action are discussed. A more thorough assessment of the grounds for current pessimism about the ending of apartheid will have to rely on extensive research. Although the contributors to this section differ in their views of recent gains and setbacks, all share a measure of pessimism on immediate prospects. But none suggests that the struggle against apartheid will ultimately fail, nor that it should be allowed to flag now.

The African National Congress after the Kabwe Conference

Tom Lodge

It is nearly two years since the African National Congress held its second consultative conference in Zambia. Then, with unprecedented accompanying publicity, the organisation reassessed its military strategy, debated ideological principles and elected fresh leaders as well as re-electing many old ones. The atmosphere of the conference was exuberantly confident. Had the preceding decade not witnessed the ANC's renaissance as a political force in South Africa? Was it not apartheid's most morally impressive opponent in the arena of international politics? Let us go to battle, vowed the assembled delegates, voting in their resolutions in favour of an insurrectionary 'people's war'. The phase of selective and inspirational 'armed propaganda' was over. Umkhonto we Sizwe's saboteurs had won the battle of the headlines. Now was the time to prove their supremacy in the battle for the streets, to build an organised army out of the spontaneous insurrectionary movement which had evolved since the 1984 Vaal uprising.

The traditional National Executive anniversary statement on 8 January designated 1986 'The Year of Umkhonto we Sizwe'. It called for a 'military offensive that (would) put the enemy into a strategic retreat'. Umkhonto we Sizwe should be massively expanded to the point where it, together with the self-organised youth fighters (in ANC phraseology 'mass combat units'), could constitute a vast army. Military activities should increase so that 'mass insurrectionary zones' covered the country 'in its entirety'. Guerilla forces, while continuing to defend the townships, must extend their activities 'to mount a continuous assault on the economy'.

Meanwhile the ANC in expanding its underground structures

should encourage the 'broadest possible united offensive' linked to the abolition of passes and the demand for non-racial municipalities. In the countryside people should be mobilised against bantustan structures and white 'soldier-farmers', and prepare for the 'central task of seizing the land'.[1]

Sixteen months and two states of emergency later the expectations aroused by such a message seem in retrospect a little premature. The state has yet to be confronted with a military threat which seriously stretches its resources. The repression unleashed with the second state of emergency appears, at least for the time being, to have checked the tide of insurrection. Though Umkhonto attacks increased significantly in the last two years, the ANC's most conspicuous gains have been diplomatic rather than military.

The scope of Umkhonto insurgency

A conservative estimate of the scope of Umkhonto insurgency can be put together from press reports of violent actions involving weapons regularly used by the ANC. Though it is likely that some of these incidents can be attributed to rival guerilla organisations or to the state's surrogates, it still seems reasonable to argue that the ANC and its followers are responsible for most of them. Possibly not all incidents are reported in the press, and certainly they are described in an increasingly distorted and cryptic fashion. But there is no evidence to indicate large-scale suppression of such information.

According to the barometer of press reportage, then, the 18 months which followed the June 1985 Kabwe Conference did feature a striking increase in guerilla activity. A total of 88 attacks were recorded in the second half of 1985, making a record annual total of 136. In 1986, guerillas struck 228 times, towards the middle of the year almost daily. Many of these operations, though, were very simple; hand grenade attacks account for almost a third of them. Altogether 160 guerillas were either killed or captured, more than one-third of the ANC's casualties since it opened the campaign in 1977.

Though the increased frequency of attacks may suggest the presence of larger numbers of Umkhonto soldiers, it is more probably the result of a wider distribution of weapons. Press reports suggest that 'comrade' groups which are only loosely under

Umkhonto guidance sometimes have grenades and small arms. One of the intentions of the 'people's war' strategy was that the war should become less dependent on exports from Unkhonto's Angolan camps, that guerillas should train people locally and arm them appropriately.

This may explain the absence of complicated and elaborate operations comparable with, for example, the 1980 rocket attack on the Sasolburg refinery. It may also be the reason for the continuing tendency to bomb such targets as shopping arcades, invariably inflicting civilian casualties. This seems an issue about which there are differences of opinion within the ANC, possibly within its leadership. Trial evidence suggests that neither all trained Umkhonto people nor their local recruits share Joe Slovo's view that attacks on soft targets are 'blemishes' and 'diversions'.[2]

The largest proportion of guerilla attacks took place in the Transvaal and Natal. Though the Reef and Durban remain the areas of most extensive Umkhonto activity, it appears to have a presence in small rural towns as well. With the introduction of landmines in Transvaal border areas in November 1985, Umkhonto seemed set to open up a new theatre of rural insurgency. Nearly 40 landmines have so far been detonated, mainly, though not exclusively, in border areas. The ANC argues that farmers in such regions are indistinguishable from soldiers because of the extent of their participation in South African Defence Force civil defence networks.

The removal of a friendly administration in Lesotho and the increasing nervousness of the Botswana authorities added to the difficulties of maintaining command, communication and supply links between the external hierarchy and guerilla units in South Africa. The escalation of the guerilla offensive occurred *despite* the emergency regime which has immobilised so many thousands of political activists. But Umkhonto's campaign falls well short of representing a major threat to the physical security of apartheid's beneficiaries, to the operation of government outside the townships or the day-to-day functioning of the economy. It is directly responsible for only a minor proportion of the political violence since September 1984. For every weapon deployed by Umkhonto cadres, the police claim to have discovered another four in arms caches (*Cit*, 22.05.86).

Trials indicate considerable police success in locating even

Table 1:

Incidents involving use of Soviet or Eastern European weaponry*

Attacks/exchanges of fire on police and state witnesses	68
Attacks/exchanges of fire on municipal police	10
Attacks/exchanges of fire on SADF personnel	7
Attacks resulting in civilian casualties (mainly grenade or limpet mine)	
a. community councillors	23
b. in central business districts during working hours	19
c. in other built-up areas	52
d. in rural areas (landmines)	7
Sabotage of railway installations	3
Sabotage of government buildings	9
Sabotage of power installations	13
Sabotage of fuel storage facilities	4
Explosions in central business districts with no civilian injury	8
Limpet mine on domestic premises - no injuries	1
Limpet mine under motor car - no injuries	1
Sabotage of water pipes	3
Armed robbery	1
	229

* Not necessarily always attributable to the ANC

Table 2:

Classification of attacks according to types of weaponry used

Hand grenades	76
Limpet mine	64
RPG7	1
Land mines	
a. exploded	12
b. discovered	13
Others (mainly AK47)	76

Source: Figures in both tables are from press reports compiled by Wim Booyse at the Institute of Strategic Studies, University of Pretoria.

experienced Umkhonto units.[3] Such evidence also suggests that a large number of major incidents are the work of a fairly small body of men and women. With an estimated 400 or so trained combatants operational at any one time, Umkhonto's strength and capacity is comparable with that of, say, the Zimbabwean African National Liberation Army in the first half of the 1970s. But Umkhonto confronts a much more formidable opponent than the Zimbabweans faced. In South Africa, therefore, the role of guerilla warfare is likely to remain chiefly inspirational and psychological, important mainly to the extent that it can help the ANC exercise political leadership over constituencies it is unable to organise directly.

In contrast with the sense of impending triumph in public statements issued early in the year, the ANC's assessment of its achievements in a document circulated to national command centres in October 1986 was soberly critical.

'Despite all our efforts', it argued, 'we have not come anywhere near the achievement of the objectives we set ourselves'. ANC underground structures remained weak and unable to supply reliable support for Umkhonto cadres. Umkhonto units still operated largely in isolation from 'mass combat groups'. The document expressed concern about attacks on shops as well as the casualties inflicted by landmines. These it called 'political setbacks'. Organisation had to be dismantled and people withdrawn from Lesotho and Botswana. Internal organisational shortcomings had hindered the ANC from exploiting the 'revolutionary preparedness' in certain communities.[4]

Growth in ANC international stature

In the light of this evaluation, it is reasonable to have reservations about the extent to which the last two years have seen military advances for the ANC. There is no question, though, about the dramatic growth in its international stature. The meetings between ANC officials and the Eminent Persons Group (EPG) in the first half of 1986; between Oliver Tambo and the British foreign minister in September 1986; Tambo's visit to Moscow in November 1986; his talks with US Secretary of State George Schultz in Washington in January 1987; and most recently his tours of Japan and Australia - all confirm a general tendency among concerned foreign governments to recognise the ANC as an indispensable element in any settlement of Southern African political conflict.

Increasingly the ANC is viewed, to quote US Undersecretary of State Armacost, as the 'legitimate voice of the black community'.[5]

The importance of ministerial-level meetings with Western administrations does not lie in the actual content of the discussions. These apparently involve formal rehearsal of positions already mutually well understood. There are instead a number of dimensions to their significance. First, they do have an impact on white South African opinion - not so much on the general public as in those elite circles most anxious for restoration of South Africa's international respectability. The meetings help to strengthen the position of those inside South Africa who advocate negotiation with the ANC.

Second, contact with the ANC lessens the possibility of Western backing for Inkatha. Such meetings were at least partly the result of domestic pressure on Western governments by parts of their own constituencies. As such they reflect the declining credibility of Inkatha even among Western conservatives. Chief Buthelezi's tour of the United States in late 1986 was notable for its failure to attract more than a sprinkling of black notables to his addresses.

Third, international recognition of the ANC boosts the morale of black South Africans. Fourth, official contact with the West brings fresh opportunities to raise the question of the South African government's continued legal legitimacy.[6] Finally, in the course of such talks the ANC is increasingly under compulsion to clarify its intentions for post-apartheid reconstruction.

ANC responses to the EPG mission were initially cautious and tentative. Leaders' anxiety not to alienate Commonwealth sentiment was tempered by reluctance to commit the ANC to negotiations which they believe would be fruitless at this stage. The ANC is probably aware of the limits to its own capacity for leverage at the negotiation table. There would also be the difficulty of keeping the support of its more youthful and volatile supporters during the extended processes of compromise any negotiations would inevitably involve.

The implications, though, of the EPG proposals were attractive - especially the prospect of being able once again to organise legally in South Africa during negotiations. However barren any meeting with the South African government might prove, the ANC would benefit from the opportunity to entrench its organisation powerfully. Hence ANC preconditions for negotiation appeared to soften, and leaders indicated they would be willing to suspend (though not renounce) violence.

The official British belief is that the South Africans deliberately scuttled the EPG mission as it was nearing acceptance by the ANC, with the raids on supposed ANC guerilla facilities in Zambia, Zimbabwe and Botswana. The ANC emerged from the EPG episode with considerably enhanced prestige; its response to the mission probably contributed to the British decision to extend the implicit recognition of ministerial-level meetings with Tambo.

Tambo's visit to the Soviet Union in November 1986 saw the first meeting between an ANC official and the general secretary of the Communist Party of the Soviet Union. This signalled the prospect of much stronger Soviet support for the ANC in future. Tambo said that the Soviet Union had agreed to supply more arms. These may possibly be of a more sophisticated variety than those Umkhonto customarily deploys; up to now the ANC's weaponry seems to have largely comprised old Warsaw Pact surplus. In fact, in 1986 Umkhonto units may have been affected by an arms shortage. ANC leaflets exhorted people to 'obtain arms from the enemy' and from other sources within South Africa.[7] Aside from improving the supply of munitions, the visit to the Soviet Union may have been intended to offset the effects of frequent contact with Western administrations.

Gains within South Africa

ANC diplomacy is not confined to governments. Since Kabwe, it has welcomed a succession of delegations to Lusaka or Harare from a broad cross-section of South African interest groups: students, teachers, university administrators, businessmen both black and white, trade unionists, churchmen, white politicians and journalists. The ANC has become much more accessible and informative to the left as well.

In 1986 it emphasised a conciliatory image, directed at white businessmen in particular and the white public in general. For example in November the ANC telexed the Federated Chamber of Industries asking it not to send representatives to the summit meeting between industrialists and State President PW Botha. The telex said that it would be 'most unfortunate...if concerned businessmen were to allow themselves to be diverted from the path towards a democratic society' (*Star*, 06.11.86). The National Executive statement of 8 January 1986 called upon white businessmen to join the 'mighty anti-pass campaign'. The 1987 statement committed the ANC to protecting basic civil liberties, including freedom of the press, assembly, speech, language, association, and the right to join political parties.[8] Other aspects of the ANC's broader diplomacy include the series of discussions with representatives of multinational corporations,[9] and its observers' conscientious attendance at academic gatherings and international conferences.

On the whole ANC diplomacy is sophisticated and astute. ANC people usually employ low-key language and are sensitive to etiquette and conventional courtesies. The favourable public impression they make in many Western countries is strengthened by sympathetic media coverage - for example a recent succession of British television documentaries.

Nevertheless, diplomatic success brings problems in its wake. In the last two years the ANC has acquired two constituencies which it seeks to influence more energetically than before. These are the Western public and the white South African community. It needs to cultivate support within both, for the prospects of outright military victory are slight. Its eventual ascendancy is most likely to come from an erosion of morale and commitment among supporters of minority rule both *inside* and *outside* South Africa.

Nevertheless the ANC's political priority must remain the extension of its active support base within the black community and maintenance of unity within its own organisation. It is confronted with a very radical popular political culture which informs the actions and hopes of township youth. ANC spokesmen have already told journalists of their worry that if the ANC fails to keep pace with the expectations of its younger street supporters, these may begin to look elsewhere for leadership.[10]

Presenting a conciliatory image to white businessmen - or black businessmen for that matter - could also increasingly conflict with the need to retain the trust and backing of South African trade unionists. Unlike liberation movements in most anti-colonial struggles, the ANC has to inspire a well organised, independently mobilised and politically sophisticated industrial working class. A South African Communist Party document summed up the diplomatic dilemma succinctly: 'Premature speculation about possible compromises in order to tempt broader forces such as the bourgeoisie onto our side may serve to blunt the edge of the people's revolutionary militancy'.[11]

The SACP's particular concern was quite understandable; an explicit motive behind the official American policy shift towards the ANC is to weaken the left within the organisation.[12]

In its diplomacy and public appeals the ANC has to maintain a delicate balance between the relative importance of its different constituencies. The reluctant and ambivalent response of its spokesmen to the issues of necklacing and soft targets was symptomatic of the difficulty of doing this. Whatever their private feelings about such matters (and within the ANC there appear to be differences about both),[13] if ANC leaders had condemned such practices in absolute terms many loyal and committed ANC supporters would have felt betrayed. More generally - and in the long term more important, given the strategic emphasis on building the broadest possible social unity, on cultivating the widest range of supporters and exploiting whatever lines of fission exist in white South African politics - it is very difficult for the ANC to clarify or debate in public the details of post-apartheid society. Yet there is a growing need to do this.

Insurrection vs negotiation: two routes to power

There seem to be two strategic conceptions within the ANC as to how it will eventually attain power. Both understand victory as the consequence not of the ANC's military effort alone, but as the outcome of a generalised political, social and economic crisis brought about by civil unrest, labour insurgency, economic recession and external isolation. The ANC's role in such a situation would be to supply the decisive element of leadership. In the words of a senior ANC member,

> It is not the duty of a revolutionary to make the revolution because the ingredient out of which a revolution is made does not depend on the revolutionary moment, on what we do in our agitation, on our preparation.[14]

Revolutions are not made, they happen. All ANC activities, military, diplomatic, organisational and cultural, should be orchestrated to provide the paramount influence at the appropriate time. In the end war becomes politics.

The strategists appear to differ, though, as to what happens during the insurrectionary crisis itself. In one view the insurrection (a greatly magnified version of what is happening at present) provides the pressures which compel government to negotiate and persuade it to concede power - but to concede it nonetheless through *negotiation*. In such a scenario both sides would have some leverage and a measure of bargaining strength. The other strategic approach understands the transfer of power in terms of seizure, of dismantling and destroying the state apparatus. This conception seems stronger within the lower echelons of the military. It may reflect a rank-and-file perception, but is not currently stressed by ANC leaders.[15]

In line with what seems a dominant commitment by ANC leaders to a negotiated victory is their current emphasis on the retention of a mixed economy, at least in the initial post-apartheid stage. An especially forceful advocate of this is Joe Slovo.[16] Of course, this could be interpreted as a mere tactic - a ploy either to win over or at least to ensure the passivity of potentially hostile social groups. But it is likely that the arguments favouring a lengthy 'transitional' stage before the attainment of socialism reflect sincere convictions.[17] ANC leaders have been able to evaluate from direct experience unsuccessful rapid 'transformationist' policies by radical African governments - notably that of Mozambique.[18] In their contacts with multinational companies ANC representatives indicate an apparent desire for the continuation of existing foreign trade links.[19]

Does this necessarily imply that socialists within the Congress camp will begin to transfer their allegiance? This is most unlikely. Quite apart from the lack of a visible popular alternative, there is a strong socialist discourse within the ANC. In this context it is important to begin a much more careful discussion of the implications of nationalisation than has been the case up to now. The ANC's acknowledgement of the independent role of the Congress of South African Trade Unions and its altered conception of SACTU's functions [20] seem to imply recognition of the need for the autonomy of working-class organisations. The ANC's constant insistence that the Freedom Charter is not a socialist document, that its nationalisation provisions aim to correct national wrongs rather than class injustices, should reassure socialists rather than alienate them. If the Charter claimed to be socialist it would be difficult to defend the independence of working-class organisation.

But quite apart from these considerations, the enormous disparity in strength and resources between the ANC on the one hand and the state on the other provides no sensible alternative to a strategy of broad social alliances.

Notes

1   African National Congress, *Attack, Advance, Give the Enemy No Quarter*, Message of the National Executive Committee, 08.01.86, Lusaka, Zambia.

2   BBC World Service, 04.07.86.

3   ANC sources recently conceded police successes in penetrating its organisation in Botswana and Swaziland (*WM,* 08.05.87). One of several Umkhonto members affected by police penetration was Vusmuzi Sindane, who was responsible for maintaining communications between Swaziland and units inside South Africa. In August 1986 he was arrested during a journey across the border to bring weapons to a contact operating from Soweto. The South African authorities had advance knowledge of his mission and set up two roadblocks manned by members of the security police. Three of the four men travelling in a kombi were killed. Sindane, a former Umkhonto camp chief of staff in Angola, was sentenced to 17 years imprisonment in Ermelo Regional Court on 7 May 1987.

4   '1987: What Is To Be Done', document distributed by the Politico-Military Council to regional command centres, October 1986. Later released to South African journalists at a government press conference.

5   *Sow,* 22.12.86. This statement was later glossed over by a State Department official who said: 'It has long been our policy that the ANC is one authentic voice of South Africa's black community, though not the only one...' (*Star,* 20.01.87).

6   See for example the condemnation of Western governments' treatment of the South African state as legitimate in Oliver Tambo, 'Economic and Political Perspectives of the ANC for a Liberated South Africa', Bonn, 08.04.86, 7.

7   ANC, 'From Ungovernability to People's Power', Lusaka, May 1986, 3.

8   ANC, 'Advance to People's Power', statement of the NEC, Lusaka, 08.01.87, 4.

9   See for example chapter 13, 'Tycoons and Revolutionaries', in Anthony Sampson, *Black and Gold: World Capitalism and the Apartheid Crisis*, London, 1987.

10 Peter Sullivan, 'ANC Keeps Wary Eye on its Left', *Star,* 08.06.86; Alister Sparks, 'Brutalised, Bitter and Beyond Control', *Star,* 17.09.86.

11 Working document allegedly circulated by the SACP Politburo, released by the Office of the State President, 12.06.86.

12 US State Department Report on 'Communist Influence in South Africa', submitted to the US Congress in fulfilment of section 509 of the Comprehensive Anti-Apartheid Act of 2 October 1986. See discussion of US policy in *Star,* 17.07.86 and 08.02.87.

13   For a report of apparent endorsement of necklacing by Alfred Nzo see *Star*, 15.09.86. The complexities of the ANC's views on attacks on soft targets are well illustrated in the text of the press conference which accompanied the printed version of the 1986 NEC message 'Attack, advance ...', 16-17. The US State Department Report supports the view that most SACP members together with 'old guard' christian ANC leaders reject indiscriminate terrorist tactics.

14   David Coetzee, 'The Struggle Goes On', *Africa Asia*, 33, September 1986, 16.

15   For the 'seizure' approach see Ronnie Kasrils, 'People's War, Revolution and Insurrection', *Sechaba*, May 1986. For the 'negotiation' position see 'Attack, advance...', 16; and 'Advance to People's War', 5.

16   'Communist Blueprint for South Africa', *Guardian Weekly*, 17.08.86.

17   See for example the argument by HJ Simons 'that most peasant workers, who form the bulk of the working class under apartheid, are not yet class conscious enough or ready for the adoption of a socialist solution', in Anon, *Selected Writings on the Freedom Charter, 1955-1985*, London 1985, 103.
      Clearly, though, there are different views within leadership. Oliver Tambo, for example, understands the public ownership clauses as creating 'the situation in which it will be possible for all business people to compete on an equal basis', Bonn, 08.04.86, 2. Pallo Jordan though, does not rule out the possibility that neither the 'class' revolution, nor the 'national' revolution 'takes precedence', that the two may be 'coterminous'. See Pallo Jordan, 'Socialist Transformation and the Freedom Charter', *African Journal of Political Economy*, 1(9), 1986, 160.
      For an unusually emphatic recent depiction of the revolution as a process of *stages* (a term the SACP tends to use less often than in previous years) see 'Stages of our Revolution', *Umsebenzi*, 2(1), 1986, 10-11.

18   For a SACP view on post-revolutionary Mozambique see 'Scorpio', 'Mozambique: The Long Haul to Socialism', *The African Communist*, 103, 1985, 99-109. In the same issue, 'Nyawuza', in 'New "Marxist" Tendencies and the Battle of Ideas in South Africa', argues: 'The problem with people advocating "socialism now" is that they expect those blacks who cannot read or write to run socialist industries and mines. The danger here is that we find ourselves depending on the expertise of the very forces we want to defeat: people who are against our socialist principles. The result would be economic chaos'.

19   Where in any case could a majority administration find alternative export markets and sources of foreign investment? Winrich Kuhne, one of the leading experts on the evolution of Soviet African policy, believes economic cooperation with the West will continue under majority rule. See also Phil van Niekerk, 'A Soviet Eye on the White South', *WM*, 09.01.87.

20   Rob Davies on nationalisation is illuminating: 'None...of the likely immediate priorities of a transformation process would, however, necessarily be enhanced if the available cadre were absorbed in taking over the day-to-day management of the large number of existing enterprises as a result of premature nationalisation - either forced or willed by a conception that socialism depends on an immediate far-reaching change in property relations. It is precisely here that the question of shop-floor workers' organisation will be of crucial importance', *South African Labour Bulletin*, 12(2), 1985, 48.

People's Education and the National Education Crisis Committee

Johan Muller

The notion of people's education has acquired wide political currency in South Africa. To ordinary black South Africans, it describes a promised liberation from an inferior and disabling education system. Conversely, the state considers it a threat to law and order that must be curtailed. To academics it is a concept to be dissected, defined and given an academic lineage.[1] To the National Education Crisis Committee (NECC), its patron organisation, it has become the focus of an increasingly complex strategy of contestation and challenge. For all, people's education is less a concept with precise semantic content than the symbol of a national educational and political movement in the making.

People's education and the emergence of the NECC mark the shift of oppositional strategy in education from simple boycott to the construction of alternatives. This dialectic between disruptive and creative tactics is common to all meaningful social movements. People's education articulates a common vocabulary of hope and protest for educational aspiration. This leads in turn to a collective search for a new range of opposition tactics. The projected long-term goal is to form new educational rules for South Africa.

NECC priorities represent a curious amalgam of struggles for conventional rights (such as demands for free textbooks) and more radical struggles such as that for student participation in school management. This duality results from the authoritarian character of the South African state and the consequent absence of a liberal public domain, where in liberal capitalist societies conventional educational issues are contested. This causes in turn the unresolved tension between liberal and radical tendencies that lies at the heart of people's education and the NECC. The state reacts by conflating the tendencies and reacting harshly to any educational challenge, so the duality makes both people's education and the NECC especially vulnerable to state action. All this helped to shape the responsive, co-ordinating and non-directive role that the NECC executive came to assume, which gave the organisation the character of a consultative network.

The NECC operates across a number of constituencies, embracing a multiplicity of groupings. People's education began at the initiative of Soweto parents. It was powerfully shaped by student participation and is likely to be influenced by the unions, to name three major groupings influential in the NECC. The strategic direction of people's education depends on which of the major constituencies is in the ascendancy within the movement at a given time. State restriction prevents the emergence of intermediate-level structures and has removed many credible individuals who were able to give direction to the more militant elements in the movement. The degree of students' influence in the NECC will be decisive to the nature of its strategies.

The formation of the Soweto Parents Crisis Committee

Significantly, people's education emerged in the 'Year of Remembrance' ten years after the Soweto uprising, which was also the 'Year of Umkhonto we Sizwe'. The continuous discontent in schools, especially those non-bantustan black schools under the authority of the Department of Education and Training (DET), mounted as 1985 drew to a close. The partial state of emergency declared in July, which was extended to Cape Town in October, put the South African Defence Force in many schoolyards. This produced a fraught learning environment and constant confrontation and provocation. As a parents' memorandum to the DET in October expressed it: 'The presence of the army in the township is a situation of conflict and war. No normal community life can reign with the army in our midst'.[2]

In August 1985 the Congress of South African Students, the largest umbrella student organisation and the single largest affiliate of the United Democratic Front was banned. Students, especially those in the Transvaal, Natal, Free State, Eastern Cape and Border, where COSAS was well established, were left without organisation and direction. The Azanian Students Movement, a smaller National Forum-orientated grouping committed to a stridently non-collaborationist policy, added to rather than mediated in the escalating conflict. The situation worsened daily. Students were being shot or detained at the slightest provocation, the authority of school principals was seeping away and teachers lapsed into defensive apathy. The Detainees Parents Support Committee's October figures estimated that 25% of emergency detainees were students, who, with other youth groups, comprised up to 60% of all emergency detainees.[3]

Especially after the COSAS banning, student frustration focused inwards onto student-student and student-teacher conflicts. Teaching and learning virtually ceased. It seemed likely that the slogan 'Liberation first, education later' might become a student strategy for 1986. By October it had become clear to many teachers and parents that final examinations in areas of major disturbance like Soweto would be a fiasco. Growing disillusionment in 1985 is reflected in the matriculation figures. At the beginning of the year 25 584 students registered for Standard 10 classes in DET schools. A total of 10 523 eventually wrote the examination. Of those originally enrolled, 19,1% passed at the ordinary grade,[4] while 5,2% obtained university entrance qualifications.[5] A group of Soweto parents decided to try to intervene.

There is a long history of not very successful parent-teacher association intercessions with the authorities on educational issues. In Soweto itself, a parents' committee chaired by Winnie Mandela operated briefly in 1976 before being banned. In the early part of 1985, a national parents' committee tried to establish itself, but was stillborn, disbanding in the face of DET intransigence.

The Soweto Civic Association moved into the vacuum. It called a meeting in early October, which was banned. Two of its organisers were briefly detained. Although the prospect looked bleak, the civic persevered, and on 13 October it held a large meeting in Diepkloof. The meeting mandated a Soweto Parents' Crisis Committee (SPCC) to arrange a meeting with the DET, among other things to seek an urgent postponement of the November examinations in Soweto. Negotiations dragged on inconclusively. On the day exams were to be written, Soweto school principals unilaterally decided to call them off. Presented with this fait accompli, the DET found there was only one representative body with which to negotiate, the SPCC.

Although the SPCC was the product of a specific issue, within four weeks it managed to organise an event of national importance, the first National Consultative Conference at the University of the Witwatersrand on 28 and 29 December 1985. That conference signalled a decisive change in opposition educational politics.

The first National Consultative Conference

The idea of a national conference on education struck a responsive chord across the country despite differences between political organisations and in regional priorities, and despite the fact that it originated in Soweto. The state of emergency, SADF occupation of the townships, the banning of COSAS and the struggle for 'proper' education were indisputably national issues.

With the help of students, the SPCC managed to draw 145 organisations to the conference.[6] These were sorted into parent, teacher or student delegate blocs. Both the Azanian People's Organisation and the UDF were present, as were their union and education affiliates. The overriding concern was to resolve the school boycott issue. The African National Congress sent a message urging a return to school. The motion in favour of return was carried on condition that various, mostly student, demands were met within three months: the unbanning of COSAS; release of detainees; recognition of student representative councils; postponement of exams; restoration of damaged school buildings; reinstatement of teachers; and lifting of the state of emergency. Of these, the campaign for democratic students' representative councils pioneered by COSAS was probably the most important and was certainly the most long standing.

The decision marked the beginning of a shift in attitude and strategy away from purely boycott politics. Concluding from a review of past attempts at alternative education that schools themselves were important sites not to be abandoned in boycott, Smangaliso Mkhatshwa, secretary of the South African Catholic Bishops' Conference, articulated the new position in his keynote address: 'Current schools must be taken over and transformed (from) within'.[7]

Lulu Johnson, a past president of COSAS who spoke for the students, echoed this conclusion: 'At the moment, making use of the apartheid structures to our favour becomes a burning question'.[8]

The conference theme - People's Education for People's Power - was embodied in intent if not in detail in a number of resolutions. Although people's education remained relatively undefined, its course was set as an initiative within the existing educational system.

The situation in schools at the beginning of the 1986 school year continued to be unstable and confused. It appeared to community organisations that the state was making no real attempt to address the grievances articulated by the conference, though it did provide free stationery and lift the partial state of emergency in early March. On the other hand, Minister of Education and Development Aid Gerrit Viljoen was of the opinion that the only condition which had not been met was the unbanning of COSAS.

At a meeting early in March, the National Education Crisis Committee was finally constituted, as mandated by a conference resolution. The SPCC with three representatives, and one representative from each of the eight national regions, formed the first executive, which also had the power to co-opt additional members. Its first action was to call the second National Consultative Conference for 29-30 March in Durban.

Despite a series of report-backs across the country to consolidate support for the call to return to school, notably the 40 000-strong Zwide meeting, students had been slow to respond. When they did turn up, they often refused to enter class. Local grievances about school fees, automatic promotion, 'inferior' free stationery and detained colleagues sparked off boycotts in a number of schools in the Transvaal and the Eastern Cape.

In the organisational vacuum left by the COSAS banning, student frustration increasingly focused on local single-issue grievances. The well organised Western Cape, which had 26 parent-teacher-student associations (PTSAs) by the end of 1985, was an exception (*Star*, 16.05.86). A new and disturbing feature of the state's response to boycotts was to close schools indefinitely where there was no 'effective attendance or discipline'.

The second National Consultative Conference

In this highly volatile atmosphere the second conference was called. It was to take place at the University of Natal, but moved to the Rajput Hall in Chatsworth when the politically timid university administration withdrew its facilities at the last minute. Once again, teacher, parent and student delegates from more than 200 organisations demonstrated the breadth of national concern, although National Forum affiliates chose to attend their own annual congress, scheduled for the same weekend. While registering, delegates were attacked by busloads of men widely believed to be sent by Inkatha. The disruption was such that the conference sat for one night only.

This severely curtailed time for discussion, which led to some student dissatisfaction. Nevertheless, the 'back to school' motion was carried again. It was buttressed by a further strategic shift. The student slogan 'Liberation first, education later' assumed that national liberation was imminent. This assumption was not shared by the ANC, and certainly not by the unions. The fact that the unions were much in evidence in Durban was therefore not insignificant. Keynote speaker Zwelakhe Sisulu spelt it out: 'We are not poised for the immediate transfer of power to the people. The belief that this is so could lead to serious errors and defeats'.[9]

The educational struggle was therefore likely to be a protracted one 'from within', as Mkhatshwa had suggested at the first conference. While duly complimentary about the achievements of the 'young lions', Sisulu suggested that the time had come for the students to pull back from the forefront of the struggle and lend their support to the larger community effort: 'The struggle for people's education is no longer a struggle of the students alone'.

The conference did not clarify people's education further, apart from charging the ad hoc People's Education Commission to report within three months. The conference also resolved on the return to school to 'implement alternate people's education programmes immediately'. From the outset it was unlikely that either resolution could be achieved in the time set. But by the end of the second conference the NECC had managed to formalise a network of parent, teacher and student bodies, and, where possible, PTSAs, for consultation.

If there was a word which described people's education at this stage, it was probably consultation or 'process'.[10] While never exactly defined, 'process' connotes practical grassroots democracy and an emphasis on evolving the strategy and content of people's education in the process of mass participation. It received a serious setback when a state of emergency was reimposed on 12 June 1986, effectively preventing the township meetings necessary for consultation.

The difficult birth of people's education

School attendance had not improved in the wake of the Durban conference. By April an estimated 100 000 students were boycotting[11] and the DET continued closing schools. In addition, the cautiously cordial relationship which had been developing between the SPCC and certain DET officials had begun to cool.

There are several reasons for this. The state, by its lights, had been making an effort to address the problem. A ten-year plan for education was announced in April. It involved substantial increases in expenditure for black schooling, but at the same time renewed the commitment to segregated education. As Minister of National Education FW de Klerk was later to affirm: 'The great danger of a single department with one minister being politically responsible is that it creates the opportunity for exploitation of minorities and abuse of power' (*Star*, 12.12.86).

The NECC predictably criticised the plan. But it managed to negotiate a change in the date for an examination deferred from the end of 1985, from the sensitive 1 May to 2 May. This was probably its last successful negotiation with the DET. Although the state initially regarded people's education in a cautiously neutral light, probably it was the increasingly bold and challenging public stance of the NECC and its People's Education Commission which by midyear forced a reconsideration.

Clearly the socialist - in its view 'revolutionary' - aims of people's education had begun to alarm the state. The first crop of state of emergency detentions therefore unsurprisingly included as many top NECC officials as could be found.

The state's attitude perceptibly hardened as the military gained the ascendancy within it, making the initially sympathetic DET ineffectual in the state hierarchy. The NECC continued to try to set up meetings with the DET, to no avail. When Northern Transvaal NECC executive member Joyce Mabudafasi was sent to the Eastern Cape to fill the gap left by the detention of Ihron Rensburg, who was the local representative on the NECC, she too was detained. When the third school term started in July, various regulations - notoriously the compulsory re-registration of all students and introduction of identity cards - brought immediate reaction. Some 30 000 students failed to re-register, and were summarily dismissed. The NECC challenged the dismissals in the Rand Supreme Court, and lost.

Mystery pamphlets were distributed by helicopter in Soweto, blaming the NECC for necklacing, arson and other acts of intimidation. Meanwhile the state continued to close schools. A total of 73 were shut by the end of the year: 60 in the Eastern Cape, 10 in Soweto, two in Katlehong and one in Lamontville (*Star*, 21.01.87). A stalemate was reached in areas like Soweto and the Eastern Cape. The National Students Crisis Committee (an organisation trying to fill the vacuum left by the COSAS banning, which is now known as the National Students Co-ordinating Committee) had called for a continued stayaway in October, and by the end of the year there was serious disruption in 70% (230 of 328) of DET secondary schools.[12] Estimates suggest that about 250000 students who enrolled at the beginning of 1986 were out of school by the end of the year.[13]

Much more now depended on the promised appearance of the NECC's alternative people's education materials. By October subject committees in History and English had undertaken to produce 'teaching packages' to be introduced in 1987. The committees understood their brief to mean producing supplementary material for Standard 10 students to be used on no more than two afternoon periods a week. But understandably the public and the press expected the impossible: 'alternative English and History syllabuses' (for example *Star*, 07.01.87). With this prospect in mind, major organisations and unions across the political spectrum called for a return to school in 1987.

The state also shared this misapprehension. Nothing else explains the extraordinary restrictions imposed on the NECC in the wake of its press conference on 27 November to announce the third National Consultative Conference. This was to be held at the University of the Witwatersrand on 29 and 30 November. The conference was promptly banned. Among the press restrictions announced on 12 December was the prohibition of publication of information about education boycotts or stayaways. On 27 December, regulations in terms of the Public Safety Act of 1953 empowered the director general of Education and Training to prohibit all non-approved syllabuses, courses, pamphlets and books. According to Director General Joe Schoeman this was designed to create 'a healthy climate' in the schools (*Star*, 30.12.86). On 9 January 1987 regulations issued in terms of the Public Safety Act of 1953 prohibited all gatherings by or on behalf of the NECC to discuss unauthorised school courses or syllabuses. All prominent NECC officials who could be found were also detained.

The harshness of this reaction made the state's attitude to people's education and the NECC unambiguously clear. The NECC was left running its operation from hiding, since its offices were regularly raided by the police. By the beginning of 1987, progress had slowed to a snail's pace.

The challenge of people's education

With the advent of people's education, the educational struggle in South Africa moved from protest to challenge. This, together with evolving UDF policy, indicates an intention to shift away from mass popular front politics to a more consolidated, disciplined strategy. [14] The nature of this challenge requires careful consideration.

For many, the evolution of people's education through the two consultative conferences can be understood as a shift from 'Liberation first, education later' to 'Education for liberation'. It marked the change from a strategy of potentially militant struggle which was temporarily willing to forfeit education, to a strategy of emancipatory education as an *alternative* to militant struggle - a last-ditch attempt to avoid the proverbial bloodbath. This argument (also applied to sanctions and disinvestment), was used effectively by Archbishop Desmond Tutu and others in the NECC to swing international support and finance behind people's education.

This understanding of the challenge leads the liberal group

within the people's education movement to perceive a large middle ground occupied by those interested in getting on with the normal business of schooling - the ANC, the NECC and the DET. To this group, the harshness of the state's response to the NECC is completely inexplicable.[15]

Their line is not persuasive to the more militant youth who help to take many of the important political decisions within the NECC network. To these, education and militant struggle are not necessarily alternatives, but may be complementary tactics in the overall struggle for people's power. The students have certainly not eschewed legal options. As late as September 1986, COSAS challenged its banning in the Natal Supreme Court, and lost. But to the extent that students accede to the 'back to school' call, they are likely to agree with the Victorian socialist William Morris when he says:

> I want an educated movement. Discontent is not enough, though it is natural and inevitable. My belief is that the old order can only be overthrown by force; and for that reason it is all the more necessary that the revolution should not be ignorant, but an intelligent revolution.[16]

How far this constituency is mobilised behind people's education depends upon the degree to which people's education is clearly linked to an overall strategy of winning people's power. And to the extent that this occurs, it will attract the full might of the state, which in any case already sees people's education as coterminous with the 'Liberation first, education later' tactic.[17]

Another major constituency in the urban townships might also act as a brake on the liberal view. It is often assumed that education is good for all people equally. This is not necessarily so. In class societies, it produces educational casualties. Not least among these are the roughly 250 000 DET dropouts since 1976. Considering that less than 20% of urban youths under 25 have full-time employment,[18] it remains to be seen whether this vast urban army of unemployed will accede to a 'back to school' strategy. From their point of view it can only give others a leg-up at their expense. To mobilise this group behind the common purpose of people's education will require that people's education hold out the promise of some kind of second chance to them, perhaps in the form of night schools or adult education centres.

People's education will also have to face the challenge of

bantustan education. In 1985 the number of Standard 10 graduates in all DET schools (4 897) was smaller than the number of such graduates in the Transkei (5 149), Bophuthatswana (6 009), Kwa-Zulu (7 149) and Lebowa (6 933). Indeed, bantustan high school graduates outnumbered their urban counterparts in 1985 by more than seven to one.[19]

Urban black education is degenerating even as education in the rural areas is accelerating sharply. This is a unique situation, quite different from other countries where popular education movements have been successful. Guinea Bissau, Nicaragua and Zimbabwe, for instance, all have large uneducated peasantries in the countryside. The converse will soon be true in South Africa. The NECC can therefore not afford in the long run to restrict people's education to DET schools, although the political risk in dealing with the bantustans will be great.

Education and politics

Education and politics cannot usefully be considered separately, though they should not be conflated. The central strategic question is how to balance political and educational imperatives. The NECC is aware that it needs to pay due attention to political accountability - popular control over education - as well as to educational canons, which should influence decisions about the content and methods of education.[20]

People's education was in its origins a response to a political crisis. Understandably, political considerations loomed larger than educational ones at the outset. Educational criteria, for example, would dictate that educational restructuring begin with primary education, but since the crisis occurred at the matric level, the first curricular packages will be directed at matrics in those two most political of subjects, History and English. There is nothing wrong with dealing with political exigencies promptly, provided that there are appropriate structures to balance educational and political needs in the long term.

The bodies targeted for this task are the PTSAs. The NECC sees them as shadow school management committees, and as the bodies which will vet curricular proposals and materials. It is imperative that PTSAs be able to make knowledgeable decisions about disciplinary content, appropriate teaching methods, appropriate learning strategies and the like. These criteria cannot take a permanent back seat to political ones, although the latter can never be ignored.

A much-neglected constituency, the teachers, will be crucial to this, as Mkhatshwa emphasised at the first consultative conference. Not only must they be involved in producing curricula, but they must be part of the vetting procedure and will have to be trained in using the new material if people's education is to be implemented widely. Up to now, academics have produced material because of the urgent need for it, and students, because of their political clout, have done the vetting. But without appropriate procedures for ensuring educational validity - and without teacher participation - these packages cannot succeed.

The teacher issue has been enormously complicated by antagonism between the large, conservative African Teachers Association of South Africa (ATASA) and smaller, newer and more progressive bodies like the National Education Union of South Africa and the Western Cape Teachers Union. If the NECC works with ATASA, it often cannot work with the other two. Until one union is somehow forged out of these bodies, in accordance with COSATU's policy, the NECC will have to find ways of achieving some measure of collaboration between them, perhaps by means of teacher workshops.

'What was won must be judged by what was possible'[21]

State restrictions could spell the end of people's education. But it is possible they will merely halt its immediate implementation, creating a moratorium that could provide time for the necessary processes of clarification and consultation to take place, even if clandestinely. Certainly the breakneck pace of events in 1986 left the NECC with very little time for reflection. Either way, the fear of frustrated expectations should not be allowed to drive the people's education initiative at a faster pace than it accountably can go. This means that there must be the opportunity for effective participation by all interested groups and regions, and time for adequate educational evaluation.

The NECC executive's effectiveness will depend on its continuing to act more as a co-ordinating network than as a body which dictates policy. This will involve creating a forum for meetings not only between its constituent groups, but also between other divided educational domains. Prominent among the latter are academic and popular knowledge. Initiatives currently being negotiated with some universities look promising in this regard.

Nevertheless, networks like the NECC are exceedingly vulnerable in their developmental phase. The NECC will become as flexible as it needs to be and able to defend itself only when it moves from dependence on key individuals towards structures which do not rely on personalities for their continued operation. It is hard to guess what will happen if the two full-time NECC organisers, who at the beginning of 1987 are running a minimal but vigorous operation, are detained.

The strongest element in the people's education prospectus is likely to be the insistence on 'process'. Politically, this has meant an emphasis on grassroots participation by student and youth groups and by civic and street committees. Academics and universities need to be brought more systematically into this process too. Lessons from the union experience about discipline, strict accountability to membership and regular consultation will also deepen the sense of process.

Insistence on process while developing curricula means emphasis on the development of critical skills rather than exclusive stress on alternative content. But it is hardly surprising that many students still expect from people's education the unvarnished 'truth', given some of the more extravagant public claims put forward in its name, for example: 'to recover and comprehend the past *in full*'.[22] A campaign will be needed to co-ordinate student expectations with the way curricula are taking shape.

A further implication of the focus on process is that the teaching packages will have to be learner-driven 'learning packages' which can be used even where there is no knowledgeable teacher or tutor in charge. A combination of poorly trained teachers, restrictions on distribution in the schools and the continuing cornerstone role of student organisation within the NECC will dictate this. Dealing with the large numbers of teachers threatened by people's education will be yet another challenge for the consultative resources of the NECC.

The continuing importance of student groups, along with other youth groups, in the larger picture of urban township politics no doubt means that students will remain the key constituency in the

NECC for the foreseeable future. There is some indication from the student representative councils being elected in Soweto in 1987 that a pro-education, pro-militant leadership is emerging. It seems to reject both ultra-left ('Liberation first, education later') and liberal (education instead of militant struggle) strategies. Certainly the 1987 school year has started off with more scholastic determination than any of the past three years, though it is too early to judge whether effective learning has resumed.

The upshot may well be a strong leftwards pull on the NECC, despite moderate groups' efforts to curb the student influence. The effect of this on the liberal centre in the NECC is uncertain. There is bound to be some measure of estrangement between the students and parent-teacher and perhaps even church groups. This will test the diplomatic powers of the NECC executive to the full.

Even if people's education is barred from state schools, the state will not be able to prevent it from moving into private community schools. Indeed, it may not legally be able to prevent people's education from being taught in schools built with private money. It is certain that the NECC will continue in 1987 to contest the limits of state restrictions, and the state will continue its efforts to keep the lid on popular initiatives. It is likely to provide a stern test of the resilience of people's education for people's power.

Notes

1 People's education is discussed in a burgeoning corpus of texts. The central ones are the keynote addresses at the two consultative conferences: Smangaliso Mkhatshwa, 'Keynote address', in *Report on the National Consultative Conference on the Crisis in Education,* Johannesburg, December 1985; and Zwelakhe Sisulu, 'People's Education for People's Power', *Transformation,* 1, 1986.

   Also important are the three statements released to the press on 27 November 1986: the statement on 'People's English', the statement on 'People's History'; and the official NECC statement, 'The Road to People's Education'. Besides these, a number of academic analyses, at least one completed dissertation, and two Human Sciences Research Council-supported research investigations all add to the clamour about people's education.

2 'Memorandum to be presented to the Deputy Ministers of Education and Training, Law and Order and Defence on 19 October 1985', in *Report on the National Consultative Conference,* Appendix 3, 4.

3 Max Coleman and David Webster, 'Repression and Detentions in South Africa', Southern African Research Service (ed), *South African Review 3,* Johannesburg, 1986, 127.

4 KB Hartshorne, 'Post-Apartheid Education: A Concept in Progress',

McGraw Hill seminar paper, Johannesburg, September 1986, 9.

5 KB Hartshorne, 'African Matric Results: The Disintegration of Urban Education', *Indicator SA*, 4(2), 1986, 55-56.

6 Estimates vary widely. *Race Relations Survey, 1985* puts the number at 160. Debbie Quin in *Indicator SA*, 3(4), 1986, puts it at 312. The official conference report lists 145 organisations.

7 Mkhatshwa, 'Keynote Address', 13.

8 L Johnson, 'Students' Struggles', *Report on the National Consultative Conference,* 19.

9 Sisulu, 'People's Education', 78.

10 See Ihron Rensburg in 'People's Education: Creating a Democratic Future', *Work in Progress,* 42, 1986.

11 Hartshorne, 'African Matric Results', 58.

12 D Quin, 'A National Civil Disorder', *Indicator SA,* 4(2), 1986, 12.

13 Hartshorne, 'Post-Apartheid Education', 9.

14 See 'UDF Plans Tighter Organisation', *Southscan,* 16, January 1987.

15 See for example Auerbach in H Zille, '"People's Education": A Lost Opportunity', *Die Suid Afrikaan,* 9, 1987, 27.

16 William Morris quoted in D Widgery, *Beating Time: Riot 'n Race 'n Rock 'n Roll,* London, 1986, 47.

17 SABC News Comment, 31.12.86.

18 Hartshorne, 'Post-Apartheid Education', 10-11.

19 Hartshorne, 'African Matric Results', 55.

20 'The Road to People's Education', 4-6.

21 F Piven and R Cloward, *Poor People's Movements,* New York, 1979, xiii.

22 'People's History', press statement, 27.11.86.

'Asithengi!'*
Recent Consumer Boycotts

Kirk Helliker, Andre Roux and
Roland White**

South Africa's rulers face deepening social crisis. Central to this is intensifying nation-wide opposition to apartheid. During 1984-85 near consensus about national political demands and militant modes of struggle developed in African townships throughout the country. Political morale was high and confidence often euphoric. This manifested itself in massive stayaways, school and rent boycotts and extensive action against state-created institutions like black local authorities and the tricameral parliament. This was accompanied by the growth and consolidation of mass-based organisations which provided national and regional co-ordination and local direction and leadership.

But the upsurge in resistance provoked severe repression. By mid-1985 the state had banned the meetings of many organisations, sent the South African Defence Force into the townships and declared the first state of emergency, detaining many thousands of activists. This had contradictory effects. On the one hand it increased the anger and resentment of its victims, facilitating the politicisation and mobilisation of a wide spectrum of township residents. On the other, it limited the political space in which popular organisations could operate, compelling them to respond with creative new methods of struggle.

This was the context which gave rise to the consumer boycotts.

---

* In Xhosa, this means 'We do not buy!'

Township mobilisation, unity and morale were necessary conditions for sustained mass involvement in boycott action. At the same time boycotts were seen by organisations as *relatively* resilient in the face of repression. As one observer put it:

> The state can ban organisations and meetings, it can clear the streets and change the dates of funerals, it can detain people and it can even shoot them dead, but it cannot force people to buy if they do not want to do so.[1]

From early 1985 to the end of 1986 the consumer boycott became a central resistance strategy of the oppressed in much of South Africa.

Consumer boycotts, like Afrikaner boycotts of Indian traders in the early 1940s and selective boycotts of Wilson Rowntree and Fatti's & Monis in the early 1980s, have occurred periodically in South Africa. But two features distinguish the recent boycotts. They generally consisted of a multi-class alliance of African consumers withholding its purchasing power from the white, and sometimes coloured and Indian, retailers of an entire city or town. The main, most consistent boycott demands were national political, usually including the lifting of the state of emergency and withdrawal of troops from the townships. Socio-economic demands were less prominent.

Tactically, a key aim of recent boycotts involved pressurising white commercial interests to use their political influence to extract concessions from the state. But boycott action also had strategic objectives: to weaken the state's social base by further alienating business from apartheid, and to deepen the politicisation and unity of the oppressed classes.

National overview

Consumer boycotts began in the Eastern Cape in March 1985 and soon engulfed the region. By August at least 23 centres were affected, including the Port Elizabeth-Uitenhage industrial complex. The second half of 1985 saw initiation of boycotts in other parts of the country. None of the major centres - Johannesburg, Pretoria, Cape Town and Durban - were untouched. But it was the emergence of boycotts in scores of smaller towns in all provinces which indicated that the strategy was truly a nation-wide phenomenon.

This does not mean that boycotts were nationally co-ordinated. It was not unusual for a boycott in one centre to be winding down just as one began in a nearby town. But there certainly was regional pressure on organisations to move with the flow of events. In certain cases local organisations were asked by activists from other towns to follow a regional line. Sometimes local activists felt obliged to launch a boycott because surrounding towns had down so. The number and duration of boycotts also varied greatly from town to town. Thus Queenstown had one eight-month boycott lasting from August 1985 to April 1986, while Grahamstown experienced five during 1985 and 1986, the longest lasting about three months. In many areas boycotts continued into 1986, although by that year's end they had all but died out.

Boycotts also differed from region to region. The Eastern Cape was the epicentre. In most of its towns boycotts had massive support and were often tenacious and durable, usually lasting three to six months. In major metropolitan centres they were more sporadic and shortlived. Thus the boycott in Durban only lasted one month. The Cape Town boycott focused on a mere 19 chain stores, while in Johannesburg the call met with little success and the East Rand seems to have been more or less unaffected. Only in Pretoria and certain small towns in the Transvaal and the Western Cape did boycotts rival those in the Eastern Cape.

Business and the boycotts

Economic effects

Consumer boycotts were intended to mobilise commerce against apartheid by their economic effects. But the economic impact of boycotts on retailers is a complicated matter, as the example of Grahamstown shows. A study of retailers in Grahamstown[2] found that African customers accounted for 36% of the sample group's total clientele. But this figure probably slightly overestimates the value of African trade, since only about 25% of the total pre-tax income earned in Grahamstown accrues to Africans. It seems reasonable to conclude that African consumption amounts to between 25% and 36% of the total.

So the effects of a total boycott on average turnover would be fairly substantial. Net trading income would show an even greater decline in percentage terms because of fixed overheads. If for instance we assume that fixed costs amount to a third of net trading income, a 30% decline in sales would lead to a 40% decrease in income. However, the total annual decrease in incomes was usually substantially less, since the boycotts only lasted for part of the year.

We estimate that in 1985 and 1986, when boycotts were in force for about three months in each year, the average annual income of Grahamstown white retailers declined by slightly over 10%. If these estimates are reasonably representative of other centres in the Eastern Cape, retailers were significantly affected while a resolute boycott was in force. But limits to the lifespan of boycotts significantly blunted their final effects. It seems that from a longer-term perspective the economic impact was on average bearable.

Economic effects of boycotts varied considerably from shop to shop, depending among other things on product lines and ownership structure. The study of Grahamstown retailers suggests that there is a fairly clear division between shops which are 'largely white' (with less than 20% African custom) and those which are 'largely African' (with more than 50% African custom). A substantial 45% of Grahamstown retailers fall into the former category and 25% into the latter. Food-related outlets like grocers, cafes, bottlestores and supermarkets, as well as clothing and furniture stores, tended to be harder hit. Service, gift, sports and video shops are virtually immune to an African boycott. Chain stores of course have the capital resources to limit the economic impact of boycotts. As Pick 'n Pay's chief, Raymond Ackerman, said: 'Unfortunately it is the small businessman who is vulnerable. The big guys can look after themselves. Although hurting, they can survive' (*BD*, 02.12.85).

But retailers sometimes adapted to cope. In Queenstown and East London, for example, they successfully approached the minister of manpower for certain financial concessions, including permission to cut wages by up to 80%. And several retailers invented schemes to maintain their African trade, such as finding alternative markets and taking unmarked vehicles into townships. On the other hand, for many retailers the experience was clearly traumatic. Many shopowners nearly went bankrupt, while others closed their doors permanently.

Business responses

The political response of commerce to the boycotts was not an automatic result of economic losses. In fact, in the Eastern Cape the economic damage caused by boycotts did not on the whole make a response imperative. In other parts of the country where the boycotts were less comprehensive, the economic factor was even less important. Overall, the retailers' responses depended more crucially on their political and ideological views about South Africa.

Organised commerce was markedly upset about the boycotts and 'concerned at white business being singled out for such action'.[3] But there was no unified political response. There were variations between and within centres as a result of local conditions and dynamics. Some chambers of commerce and shopowners adopted a liberal stance. They claimed that the root cause of boycotts was apartheid and racial domination, and that the boycott strategy was a legitimate form of protest with large-scale support in African communities.

The Port Elizabeth Chamber of Commerce, for instance, developed a high-profile reformist line. It issued a memorandum calling for a variety of urgent reforms, publicly criticised government's handling of the boycotts and put pressure on the authorities to meet some of the political demands. It was backed by the initiatives of several ordinary retailers. Seventy Port Elizabeth traders sent telegrams to the state president, calling on him to negotiate with African leaders. A group of retailers began canvassing support for a charter pointing towards a non-racial society.

However, other organisations had a more reactionary attitude, showed little sympathy for African grievances and opted to believe that the boycotts were the work of agitators. This seemed to be the case in Pretoria, where to counter the boycott the chamber of commerce had pamphlets dropped on the townships which read: 'Goodwill and peace for all. Tomorrow and all day Saturday you people of Mamelodi will be able to do your Christmas shopping freely and in peace' (*ST,* 15.12.85). The president of the chamber claimed that this pamphleteering was a response to widespread complaints of intimidation.

Nor was there necessarily a unified response within centres. Though the Grahamstown Chamber of Commerce adopted a reformist line, some 'militant individuals' argued for a more hard-line approach and others took a pragmatic stance, 'superficially' going along with the Chamber line because they did not want to 'cut their own throats' by antagonising African residents.[4]

Despite these variations, retailers throughout the country seemed to believe that the national political demands, which they recognised as the driving force behind the boycotts, were beyond their sphere of influence. In many instances commerce shied away from the demands either by refusing to discuss them or agreeing to act only as a channel of communication between the townships and the authorities. Although chambers of commerce often expressed concern about the consequences of state repression for resolving the boycotts, it was indeed rare for them to apply forceful public pressure on the state. It is therefore hardly surprising that so few of the political demands were met. On the other hand, retailers were willing to discuss and address socio-economic grievances and suggested that the prospects for real progress on this front were good. But to the townships the political objectives were pre-eminent, which precluded such progress. Conditions for an impasse between commerce and the townships were thus ever-present.

But the boycott strategy was not purely concerned to achieve specific demands. Embodied in it was the attempt to weaken the state's support base by alienating white business from apartheid. For this reason the boycotts were directed at a wide spectrum of commercial interests. Big business may have clout with the state and may thus be a worthwhile target for a boycott aimed solely at achieving specific demands. But it made sense, in trying to exacerbate divisions between the state and a wide range of white middle-class interests, to include small and vulnerable retailers in boycott action.

The actual efficacy of boycotts in reshaping white business views is uncertain. The Grahamstown Chamber of Commerce president,[5] while warning that business attitudes hardened as boycotts continued, also spoke of intangible benefits, including increased knowledge and understanding of local Africans' problems among retailers. Yet the survey of Grahamstown retailers[6] found little clear evidence of changing political attitudes. Staunch Progressive Federal Party or National Party supporters did not shift their positions in the face of boycotts. On the other hand, some shopowners began to raise critical questions about government intransigence, while others indicated that the pace of reform ought to be accelerated. But boycott action did not turn any retailers in the survey sample into *active* opponents of the state: shopowners claimed that resolving the boycott issue required national political processes, and felt isolated and alienated in the face of a seemingly all-powerful central state.

This reaction is in part a result of the long association between business and apartheid. South African business has a history of political passivity and an ideology that distances it from open and active involvement in politics. It often acquiesced even when apartheid conflicted with specific business interests. The boycotts, through their vivid demonstration of the close connection between economics and politics, may have exposed how untenable business apathy was. However, any shift in this ideology would initially be slight and tentative.

But boycott tactics were rarely, if ever, geared to maximising changes in business attitudes. In Port Elizabeth and Port Alfred, where fairly complex relationships developed between township and commerce, there was more ideological ferment. Business opposition to current forms of local government and attempts to move towards non-racial municipalities received their clearest expression in these towns. In most other centres contact between boycott leaders and retailers often ended in an early collapse of negotiations, thereby slowing any change in business perceptions.

Generally, however, a significant political gap opened between white business and the state during 1985 and early 1986. There was significant loss of confidence in the state's ability to resolve political conflict and provide a stable economic environment. But how far consumer boycotts contributed to this is unclear; they played a role, though international pressures and generalised internal resistance were probably more important. Judging by business reactions to the second emergency and to the advent of international sanctions, it is clear that it will take much more than consumer boycotts on the scale of 1985-86 to effect a real breach between business and the state.

Townships and the boycotts

Mobilisation and politicisation

Different kinds of organisation started consumer boycotts in different areas. In the Eastern Cape, community-based organisations affiliated to the UDF played the crucial role; elsewhere, for example in Pietermaritzburg, trade unions were more involved. In most cases the leadership and organisations that guided and co-ordinated boycotts represented all sectors of the community. In Port Elizabeth a consumer boycott committee representing all township organisations was formed; and in Port Alfred the civic organisation, made up of the executives of worker, youth and other organisations, became the organising and negotiating body during the boycotts. The structures which co-ordinated consumer boycotts emerged from existing community organisations.

The boycotts were usually organised in the townships since consumption takes place in the residential environment. The boycotts could be effectively organised and sustained because of the residential patterns enforced by apartheid. The concentration of Africans in specific areas enormously facilitated the task of organising and monitoring boycotts.

The hegemony of the UDF and its affiliates in the Eastern Cape townships was also important. Unity among boycott leaders greatly reduced indecision and allowed for rapid development of a consistent strategy. The UDF's ability to project itself as a worthy opponent of apartheid inspired confidence and simplified mobilisation. But in certain areas, usually outside the Eastern Cape, tensions arose between organisations. In Pietermaritzburg, for instance, reinstatement of dismissed workers was an important issue. While the unions argued that the boycott should be directed towards achieving this demand, the UDF claimed that more political demands, such as lifting of the emergency, were necessary to maximise public support. In Cape Town there was debate as to whether a blanket or selective boycott was desirable.

Boycott demands were primarily political in nature. Repression-related issues, such as the lifting of the emergency, release of detainees and withdrawal of the SADF from the townships were emphasised. The boycotts were in many respects a specific response to state repression. But political demands also reflected more general concerns, ranging from general calls for the abolition of apartheid to demands for a non-racial municipality and the resignation of town councillors.

A range of socio-economic demands which varied from place to place were also often included. Housing and rents, or the upgrading of township facilities, were frequent issues. A survey of attitudes[7] in Grahamstown showed that the demands put forward by the local boycott committee reflected the concerns and grievances of the African community reasonably accurately. The results clearly demonstrate that there was consensus in the township about the legitimacy and importance of both the socio-economic and political demands. Two socio-economic demands were ranked first and third in importance by respondents, while repression-related demands were accorded second, fourth and fifth place among the options offered.

This demonstrates a certain paradox about the boycott strategy. There was strong support for it as a pressure on local authorities and business to achieve limited socio-economic gains. But the genesis of the boycotts lay in heightened mass resistance. They were part of a national protest against the state and the apartheid system. Boycotts were thus intrinsically political and were organised and supported accordingly. The more limited socio-economic demands could not be isolated from the broader political ones. The boycotts could not be used solely to achieve limited local socio-economic gains, an area in which they could conceivably be highly effective.

Community support for boycotts in the Eastern Cape was phenomenal. When they were at their height the Port Elizabeth Chamber of Commerce regularly reported a 100% boycott. Research in Grahamstown indicated a 94% boycott rate. Other reliable figures are hard to come by, but unquestionably in many areas - and not only in the Eastern Cape - a very large proportion of township residents actively supported the boycott call.

Why? Anti-boycott proponents often claimed that such support was a result of coercion and intimidation by a small and militant minority. While intimidation did occur, reports and rumours about it are generally exaggerated. The Grahamstown research, the most scientific attempt to measure support, indicates that a very small proportion of the boycotting community was coerced, and 92% of respondents said they supported the boycott because they 'wanted some changes' rather than 'because town goods will be confiscated'. The vast majority of residents embarked on boycott action because they viewed it either as a worthwhile tactic to achieve their demands or as a strategy to facilitate opposition to apartheid. While they knew the costs involved in boycotting, residents viewed them as necessary sacrifices. Although Grahamstown is a single example, our overriding impression is that in boycotts throughout the country coercion was not a significant factor in generating support.

There is in fact a strong, but not necessarily predominant, feeling in African townships that a limited degree of coercion during boycotts is justified. This does not mean assent to an 'anything goes' policy. But it does reflect a belief that an illegitimate state has no moral claim to monopoly on the use of coercion, and that if individuals wish to do something against the interests and wishes of the majority in the community they should be prevented from doing so, forcibly if necessary. Thus confiscation of goods bought in town by a boycott-breaker would be regarded as legitimate action to protect the community at large.

Methods of mobilisation varied in time and from community to community. The April 1986 Port Elizabeth boycott was launched by tight, extensive organisational structures. But generally the mobilisation process was less structured, often because organisations were weak or repression curtailed full organisational activity. Pamphlets, word-of-mouth and mass meetings were used extensively to publicise boycott calls. Many residents needed no further persuasion. Others were convinced to join boycott action by the activist networks, often informal, which extended throughout townships.

This system worked efficiently as long as the message was simple and a groundswell of support existed. Its limitations emerged when more complex tactics and strategies were needed. It was difficult, for instance, for the leadership to deploy subtle tactics in negotiation or in suspending and reimposing boycotts. Likewise it inhibited fuller development of political awareness and understanding among many residents. Finally, the informal mobilisation process restricted organisers' ability to resolve and respond to tensions in communities about issues like when to end a boycott. While these problems should not be underestimated, neither should they be exaggerated. Many boycotts, even those that ground to a halt under controversial circumstances, left a community more united and committed than at the outset.

Township youth played a key role in organising and monitoring the boycotts, but did not dominate them unduly. In most places the youth were only partially responsible for the boycotts. The strategic prerogative of guiding boycott action was kept firmly in the hands of representative community structures. Where excessive coercion did occur, the youth were usually responsible. But in general they acted within parameters set by the wider community. Their mobilising role was carried out in tune with rather than in antagonism to their communities.

Organisational developments

The consumer boycotts took place under conditions of heightened politicisation and mobilisation. Political consciousness intensified greatly and a culture of resistance grew in the course of the boycotts. They are a mode of political action that involves nearly every member of the community. Boycotts demonstrated the power of united action, extended participation in the struggle to hitherto passive residents, and focused attention on political demands and long-term national democratic objectives.

The boycotts' connection to extension of organisation is important. One of the most significant developments during 1985-86 was the organisation of residents in many townships throughout South Africa into street and area committees. The basic principle of such organisations is the involvement of every resident in democratic grassroots structures. They are forums to which people bring their everyday problems to be discussed, considered and acted on. But they also have a far more directly political dimension, being the units through which major political issues and strategies, such as boycotts, are democratically discussed and organised.

These embryonic organs of people's power emerged most widely in the Eastern Cape and parts of the Transvaal. In Port Elizabeth and several other centres, street and area committees took off during the boycotts in the latter half of 1985. Although boycotts were not in themselves responsible for the development of the committee system, they often provided the context in which such initiatives were able to take place. The fact that boycotts involved practically every resident in the townships for a protracted period, that they intensified politicisation and mobilisation and that any significant change required widespread support from township residents, facilitated the development of grassroots structures. The imperative to develop decentralised, resilient organisations capable of sustaining boycott action in the face of severe repression gave added impetus.

But these processes were in many ways limited. In the face of repression politicisation sometimes suffered from the often loose methods of mobilisation adopted and the lack of coherent educational programmes. And in many townships the extension of organisation to the street level was never carried through.

Alliances

An important feature of the boycotts was the attempt to develop alliances within oppressed communities. Boycott strategy relies on support from all sectors of the community. The Grahamstown survey showed astonishing unity and support for boycotts, irrespective of economic status, age, sex and education. Typically the youth, males, the more educated and the employed were more militant. But such differences are of only marginal significance. It seems that in Grahamstown, and probably many other small towns, forces promoting unity dominated factors like social differentiation which generate tension. The boycotts often facilitated alliances between different social groupings. But this was not necessarily always the case. In communities more strongly differentiated along political and economic lines, a boycott can be divisive.

Another significant feature of the boycotts was their effect on the African commercial petty bourgeoisie. The boycotts pushed township retailers into a position of support for the boycotts and of resistance to apartheid in general. The increase in township trade resulting from the boycott of white shops provided an obvious economic motive. But in areas like Port Elizabeth and Alexandria, where traders were subject to state repression and harassment, the economic motive was often transformed into a commitment to the aims and objectives of the democratic movement. This manifested itself in such traders lowering prices, providing material resources for political work and becoming involved in civic organisations. There were exceptions, like the Inkatha-dominated African Chamber of Commerce in Pietermaritzburg which opposed the boycott, and community and town councillors whose shops were often boycotted.

Generally the boycotts exacerbated African traders' alienation from the state and made them more inclined to identify their interests with those of the oppressed. Problems may arise in consolidating this alliance. But the fact that the boycotts involved entire communities in direct conflict with the state minimised the chance of traders becoming dominant in the alliance. There were no instances of traders controlling the course of boycotts.

Relations between African, coloured and Indian communities were also important to the course of boycotts. Coloured and Indian communities did not participate fully in boycotts. This may be understandable, but raises important questions about the extent of political cross-fertilisation between racially divided oppressed communities in South Africa.

In many places - particularly in the Eastern Cape - coloured and Indian shopkeepers were in fact boycott targets. In Grahamstown boycott pressure on Indian traders involved a specific political demand: that they dissociate themselves from the tricameral parliament. In the end, after unsuccessful attempts to evade the issue, the Indian Association released a statement to this effect. The boycott of their shops was then lifted. In Port Elizabeth Indian and coloured shops were boycotted more by default, since it was extremely difficult to organise and monitor the boycott of white shops unless coloured and Indian traders were included.

Results of targeting coloured and Indian traders were ambiguous. In Grahamstown and Port Elizabeth shopowners issued statements sympathising strongly with the plight and struggle of the townships. So on the one hand parts of the Indian and coloured population were pushed into increasing opposition to apartheid, which potentially inhibited the state's programme of co-option. On the other hand, boycotts of Indian and coloured shops were often difficult to lift once they were under way. This generated frustration among such traders, which could in time threaten any gains originally made.

Townships, business and the state

Negotiations

Negotiations between business, various branches of the local state and boycotting communities became a central feature of consumer boycotts, particularly in the Eastern Cape. Boycott leaders perceived negotiations as essential to the boycott process. The Grahamstown study indicated popular support for such negotiations. While certain respondents had reservations about the details of the process in Grahamstown, an overwhelming 85% were in principle positive. In many centres, commerce also expressed a willingness to negotiate and in certain cases this enabled the townships to win concessions.

In Port Alfred, for example, the negotiation process was soon relatively advanced. The Employers' Federation was committed to negotiating from the outset, and the township responded by lifting the boycott as soon as negotiations commenced. The federation arranged meetings between township leaders and various government bodies. As a result the township achieved the scrapping of rent arrears, the release of detainees and a say in the upgrading of the township.

In Port Elizabeth, negotiation between local business, the local state, the PFP and township leaders began in late 1985. This followed sustained boycott pressure, while at the same time the ineffectiveness of the first emergency in quelling militant resistance had become apparent. The upshot was a notable victory for residents: the police and SADF were withdrawn from the townships and those in hiding were free to re-emerge. Several minor demands were also met.

After both victories, massive reorganisation immediately began. The release of township leadership and the withdrawal of the police and SADF allowed the militancy and mobilisation of 1985 to be organisationally consolidated. Commenting on the highly organised state of the townships in early 1986, a member of the Port Elizabeth boycott committee said: 'It is doubtful that we would have come to where we are now if the boycott had not won us the breathing space that we got after our negotiations with the authorities in November'.

From the point of view of the democratic movement, the

negotiation process is a marriage of the tactical imperative of winning demands and the strategic imperative of long-term organisation. The most important gains won by negotiation were often those that helped organisation. It thus served both short- and long-term interests of community and leadership.

Not all negotiations were problem-free. In Grahamstown, where organisation was weaker than in many other Eastern Cape communities, they quickly collapsed. Boycott leaders in many areas lost interest in negotiation, frustrated at claims by commerce that its power to satisfy demands, particularly political ones, was limited. Moreover, the negotiation process was subject to pressures resulting from the dynamics of struggle at a national level. This made it very difficult for local boycott leaders to tailor their tactics to local conditions and achieve specific local demands. Instead boycotts were often suspended and reimposed with disregard for negotiations under way, and these negotiations suffered as a consequence.

But the state was the real problem. Repression severely hindered negotiation. The detentions of boycott leaders and the banning and disruption of meetings restricted the possibility of democratic negotiations. Thus in Cradock, where business was willing to negotiate but community leaders were detained, the civic's president said that they could not negotiate until their leaders were released. And in Adelaide the president of the youth congress said: 'We are the voice of the people, not puppets like the community councillors were, and we have to consult with residents and obtain a mandate' for negotiation (*EPH*, 18.07.85). In fact dialogue, the process the state claimed to be interested in, was hindered by its coercive acts. Thus negotiations bore fruit in isolated cases, but by and large did not achieve much in concrete terms, either in the Eastern Cape or nationally.

State strategy

The state was a crucial 'actor' in the consumer boycotts. Its repressive action provoked them in the first place, but its response to them was also important. The state's approach to consumer boycotts can be divided into two periods. In the first, which lasted until the declaration of the state of emergency in June 1986, its approach was complex and sometimes contradictory: it seemed to vacillate between obstruction and indifference.

This allowed some space for accommodation at the local level. The boycotts had a strong local dimension, as commerce was expected to bring concerted pressure to bear on local authorities. The Port Elizabeth experience, where business successfully approached the local security forces to effect the release of detainees and the withdrawal of the police and SADF, illustrates the potential local influence of business. More important, it demonstrates that local authorities may to some extent act autonomously of the central state, particularly when the latter does not have a uniform policy. Some demands met in Port Elizabeth and Port Alfred transcended strictly local affairs, but were nevertheless issues over which local authorities had discretionary powers or could influence the central state. However, it was exceptional for the pressure network from township to business to local government to work effectively.

The role of the central state was decisive. As well as refusing to grant national political demands, it tried to obstruct local negotiations. Central state officials sometimes actively tried to dissuade chambers of commerce from participating in negotiations. There is ample evidence that the state tried to foster an apathy among retailers. The minister of trade and industry, for example, refused any major aid to commerce in the Eastern Cape, and merely advised retailers to adapt to the new conditions.

At times the state resorted to open repression, detaining boycott leaders or harassing township traders. But repression in this period before the second emergency did not have a depressive effect on the boycotts. In fact, it probably strengthened the resolve of the boycotters and prolonged boycotts. Detentions, phoney pamphlets and security force action did cause problems. But generally even where large numbers of leadership were detained, boycotts were solidly in place and needed only a little monitoring by the remaining township activists to keep going. This failure of the repressive approach created a climate in which now and again the state conceded to some demands.

Before the second emergency the Botha government might have been more accommodating had boycotts been few, isolated and concerned with local issues. But the central state was typically intransigent as the boycotts' national dimension came to dominate their local aspects. Boycotts were projected by boycott organisers as primarily a national protest against apartheid. This raised the stakes immeasurably for the state and it responded accordingly. At this stage the state may have been comparatively uncertain and tentative about many of its programmes, but it never intended to make major political concessions. Further, while government did experience considerable pressure, the boycotts were not very successful as a concerted form of national opposition. In the three major metropolitan centres and in many small towns they were sporadic, partial or shortlived, which made it easier for the state to resist making concessions.

A major shift in the state's approach to consumer boycotts came in mid-1986 as it undertook a more concerted and systematic onslaught on extra-parliamentary resistance. The declaration of the national emergency in June meant an all-out attack on progressive organisations and strategies, which ended any latitude for local authorities to compromise with boycotting communities.

Boycotts which had carried over from 1985 or which were started in response to repression collapsed because of the huge leadership vacuum and organisational weaknesses. A boycott in Grahamstown launched by an inexperienced leadership in late 1986 soon fizzled out. Port Elizabeth saw a more organised retreat as the boycott committee officially called off the boycott just after New Year in 1987. In a public statement the committee claimed that this was 'not a sign of weakness', but clearly it was. The committee had no choice. The state's intransigence and repression had taken their toll. Communities became demoralised as the possibility of making concrete gains became ever more remote. The groundswell of euphoria and support died away. At all levels organisation and leadership were severely battered.

Repression was central to the demise of the boycotts. The boycott strategy, for all its resilience, was not able to withstand the onslaught launched against it under the second emergency.

Evaluating the boycotts

The recent consumer boycotts were largely unsuccessful in realising their specific tactical objectives. Few concrete demands were met. The negotiation process tended to falter for a number of reasons: the contradiction between local tactical and national strategic requirements; the dispute between townships and commerce over the feasibility and importance of national political versus socio-economic demands; and disruption by the state along with the constraints it placed on democratic decision-making. The boycotts also did not have the brute economic pressure necessary to compel commerce and the state to make concessions. Business was able to withstand their limited long-term economic effects. Nor did the state ever face a solid nationally co-ordinated effort. This made the state's intransigence, and its ability to maintain it, practically inevitable.

The boycotts fared a little better with their effects on business. Because there were many political pressures on business at the time it is difficult to identify the specific effects of the boycotts. But overall it seems that commerce reacted to the boycotts in a contradictory and ambiguous manner, showing a range of reformist, apathetic or reactionary responses. There were marked variations between centres, but in general it seems that while boycott action sharpened political tensions in the ranks of business, no fundamental disunity emerged.

While a significant sector of commerce took a reformist line, this did not translate into a consistent or active rejection of apartheid by the sector as a whole. Boycotts played a part in widening the gap that opened up between business and the state in 1985, but this did not become a final split. Though the boycotts may have helped to awaken certain retailers to the interconnection between politics and business and the need for a less passive political approach, this trend has yet to gain momentum.

The most enduring achievement of the boycotts was mobilisation and organisation within communities. Under highly repressive conditions boycott action evolved as a mode of resistance which sustained direct confrontation with the state and extended the militancy, politicisation and unity of African communities. Boycotts generated dynamic organisational developments with significant long-term political implications. And they indicated that solid and durable organisation most often develops during direct political action.

Consumer boycotts are likely to be used again. The three aims of the boycotts - to gain local concessions, alienate business from the state and mobilise African communities - were not always tactically reconcilable. This is particularly evident in relation to the achievement of specific and limited demands, where local tactical responses were greatly constrained by the boycotts' national political character. Limited and local boycotts, coupled with a sensitive tactical approach, could be effectively used in future to attain specific socio-economic concessions.

Further, boycott tactics were rarely tailored to the strategic aim of weakening the state's social base. It is unlikely that this dimension of the strategy will ever become the primary focus of consumer boycotts, whether national or local ones. The central objectives of the democratic movement are mobilisation and organisation, which will be pursued at the expense of alienating business from the state. Nevertheless, there is scope to refine tactics to intensify the impact of boycott action on business and white ideology. To be successful, such an approach would have to be part of a more general strategic intervention by the democratic movement as a whole in the ideological arena of white politics.

The boycotts, though most successful in mobilising African communities, were not necessarily conceived and planned with this in mind. For instance in some Eastern Cape centres township unity was threatened when boycotts were reimposed or prolonged merely to stay in line with the rest of the region. But the need to maintain community support for boycotts tended to limit the potential mismatch between the tactical requirements of mobilisation and the achievement of national political demands. Consumer boycotts, especially shorter ones, will in future probably be used specifically to mobilise communities. There is still scope for this despite the level of repression.

The South African state can in the short term crush a popular uprising which is limited to the resistance strategies and organisational forms dominant until now. Future deployment of the consumer boycott weapon should be assessed with this in mind. National political consumer boycotts are likely to be significant only if they are one of several strategies brought to bear in a climate in which the central issue is the transfer of political power. The experience of 1984-86 indicates that consumer boycotts, like rent boycotts, were simply not enough. They do exert pressure on the state, but even where organisation is very solid it is not enough to effect the transfer of power. The democratic movement will have to bear this in mind when it considers the future use of such measures, and their relation to an overall strategy of national liberation in South Africa.

Notes

** Emergency restrictions prevented one author, Andre Roux, from participating in the actual writing of this article. Its content is in part based on a prior publication that he co-authored and on informal discussions among the authors. He shares responsibility for the broad thrust of the arguments and it therefore seemed appropriate to include his name here. However, he wishes to disclaim responsibility for details.

1   J Pieres, *Rhodeo* (Rhodes University student newspaper), June 1985.
2   C McMurtry and M Tomlinson, 'Echoes From High Street', Industrial Sociology III research project, Rhodes University, 1986.
3   Association of Chambers of Commerce statement, *WM*, 23.08.85.
4   Authors' interview with Steve Birt, president of the Grahamstown Chamber of Commerce and Industry, December 1985.
5   Interview with Steve Birt.
6   McMurtry and Tomlinson, 'Echoes'.
7   A Roux and K Helliker, 'Voices From Rini', Institute of Social and Economic Research working paper no 23, Rhodes University, 1986.

Rent Boycotts
and the
Urban Political Economy

Matthew Chaskalson, Karen Jochelson
and Jeremy Seekings

Rent boycotts in the northern Orange Free State, the Pretoria-Witwatersrand-Vaal (PWV) area, and the Eastern Transvaal have been widespread since September 1984.

A 'rent' boycott involves refusal to pay both rent and service charges. These are in practice indistinguishable to township residents as they are billed and paid together. The state, however, attaches great importance to the theoretical distinction. Rents in principle are made up of site and house rent for state housing tenants. Service charges cover the cost of township capital development and provision of services.

Service charges constitute most of the 'rent' in many townships, and rose markedly in proportion to site and house rents in the early 1980s. In Sebokeng, for example, service charges comprised 83% of proposed total 'rent' for 1984-85. The 'rents' referred to in this article include service charges unless otherwise specified.

The first rent boycott of the current phase of resistance started during September 1984 in the Vaal Triangle townships of Sebokeng, Sharpeville, Evaton, Boipatong and Bophelong. In 1985, boycotts began in northern Free State townships which, like the

Vaal Triangle, are administered by the Orange Vaal Development Board (OVDB). The first of these, beginning in April, took off in Tumahole near Parys; later boycotts spread to Vredefort, Kroonstad, Bothaville, and Viljoenskroon.

In the Eastern Transvaal township of Ethandukukhanya (Piet Retief), many residents did not pay rent after January 1984. This was not at first a formal boycott, but developed into one over the next 18 months. Boycotts began in other Eastern Transvaal townships in mid-1985, encouraged by the success of the Ethandukukhanya boycott. Townships involved were: Silobela (Carolina), KwaThandeka (Amsterdam), KwaZanele (Breyten), Wesselton (Ermelo), and Umgwenya (Waterval Boven).

Residents of Mamelodi (Pretoria) boycotted rents after the 'Mamelodi Massacre' of 21 November 1985, when police killed 13 while brutally dispersing a mainly female crowd of rent protesters.

A later wave of boycotts swept townships on the Rand during 1986. In most cases boycotts were already under way in certain areas of each township. By mid-1986 boycotts had spread throughout the townships. In Alexandra, the boycott was generalised during April. In Soweto, boycotts began in Chiawelo and Jabulani in March, and spread through the townships in June. In Tembisa, rents were widely boycotted from May. Boycotts also started in mid-1986 in Vosloorus and Tsakane and by February 1987 national township rent arrears officially stood at R177,6 million (*Star*, 11.02.87).

Origins of the rent boycotts

Rent boycotts reflect fundamental contradictions in the urban political economy which had been intensifying during the early 1980s.

From the mid-1970s the South African state's response to chronic political and deepening economic crises was to alter the constraints and opportunities affecting black South Africans. This involved significant changes in many urban policies, including reform of influx control, rising state investment in and deregulation of township housing and infrastructure, opening up more business opportunities in townships, and restructuring local government. The local state sought to provide more extensive housing and public services. But the central state remained committed to the

principle that township administration and development should
continue to be funded through township-raised revenue.

By the early 1980s most administration boards were accumulating colossal deficits. Their aggregate deficit for 1982-83 was estimated at R32 million.[1] While expenditure was rising, several sources of income were falling, especially profits from beer and liquor
sales used to subsidise housing and services. The state increased
rents and service charges rather than increase taxes on capital or
central state subsidies. Large increases were required to raise rents
to the 'economic' levels which would completely pay for the
provision of housing and services.

Raising revenue from rents was a political problem. Restructuring township local government was, at least in part, designed to
resolve it. But this restructuring caused unanticipated political
changes in the townships, transforming the relations between councillors and their supposed constituents. Councillors were increasingly seen as corrupt, unaccountable and irresponsible. Dependent
on rents to finance township development, councillors more and
more frequently presided over rent hikes and resorted to coercive
measures against squatters. In short, they attempted to resolve the
financial problem at the expense of their political credibility.

The outbreak of rent boycotts represented a new stage in the
ongoing political mobilisation around rents, housing, and local
government. The trigger was both economic and political. Many
households found it increasingly difficult to pay rents that continued to rise in real terms while incomes were eroded by inflation.
At the same time residents were less and less motivated to pay
rents because of the apparent lack of promised township development, the scale of corruption among councillors, the councils' illegitimacy, and (later in most cases) rising levels of repression.

The inability to pay

A major factor in mass support for boycotts was many households'
growing inability to pay rising rents. Local authorities' attempts to
achieve economic rentals coincided with deepening economic
recession.

Surveys of the PWV townships carried out by the UNISA
Bureau of Market Research (BMR) indicate that the proportion of
households below constantly defined minimum and supplementary

living levels, and of households earning below R4000 a year, increased between 1980 and 1985. Employment rates also fell dramatically. The BMR data, conservatively interpreted, suggest that at least 25% of PWV households had falling real income between 1980 and 1985.[2]

The OVDB's determination to achieve economic rentals caused Vaal rents to rise by more than 400% between 1977 and 1984. When the August 1984 rent increase of R5,90 was announced, the average rent of R62,56 was already more than R10 higher than any other township, and more than double the national metropolitan average.[3] In Tumahole, the community council announced in mid-1984 that rents would be increased from R26,25 to R37 as of 1 July. Other northern Free State townships under the OVDB's jurisdiction faced similar increases.

Rents had also increased steadily in the Eastern Transvaal during the early 1980s. In Carolina's Silobela township, for example, rents increased by 300% between 1981 and 1984. In July 1985 the Eastern Transvaal Development Board (ETDB) announced rent increases in all the townships under its jurisdiction. Rents in Silobela, Umgwenya, Ethandukukhanya, KwaZanele, Emjindini and KwaThandeka rose to over R40.

Inability to pay rent was reflected in growing rental arrears. For example, the Mamelodi Council was allegedly owed R0,9-million in late 1984 (*RDM Extra,* 05.11.84); amounts owed to the Katlehong Council were said to be R2-million in January 1985, and R5-million just over one year later (*Star Africa,* 24.01.85; *Sow,* 20.02.86).

But the transition to an actual rent boycott requires additional explanation. Widespread hostility to rent increases and an inability to pay do not necessarily lead to a boycott.

In some cases rent boycotts simply evolved out of an uncoordinated mass non-payment of rent. Elsewhere they began with a definite collective decision. Such decisions were in some cases an expression of popular moral outrage at the local authorities, and in others were explicitly adopted as a tactical or strategic weapon.

Boycott by default

In Piet Retief's Ethandukukhanya township, residents were moved to a newly built area after the destruction of their shacks by

Cyclone Demoina in January 1984. The ETDB did not inform residents of their new rent for five months. In June, they were told that rents were to be higher than they had been in the Old Location and that they would now be determined according to the Pay-As-You-Earn (PAYE) system.[4] The new rents were backdated to the date of occupation, so households were immediately faced with considerable arrears. Some residents continued not to pay rent.

During late 1984 and early 1985, other Ethandukukhanya residents became involved, adding their grievances. A further R5 rent increase in February, together with a deadlock in rent negotiations and the ETDB's recourse to evictions, led to a general boycott. The Ethandukukhanya boycott, therefore, came about more by default than design.

In the rest of the Eastern Transvaal rent boycotts evolved in response to the July 1984 increases. Residents initially did not consider a total boycott of rents. Some continued to pay the old rent; others decided to pay a reduced rent; others paid nothing at all. When the ETDB and the councils insisted on the new rentals a total rent boycott began.

Boycott in outrage

Before 3 September 1984, Vaal residents did not intend boycotting rent. Anti-rent meetings focused on the increase and resolved to continue paying the old rent. On 3 September residents marched through Sebokeng in protest against the increase. Sixty-six people were killed in clashes with police in the next week. Only after this did residents stop paying rent.

Events in Mamelodi followed a similar pattern. The trigger for the boycott was the 'Mamelodi Massacre' of 21 November 1985. At an earlier meeting residents had decided to march to the mayor to discuss rent increases, the presence of the SADF in the township, and police brutality. The marchers were dispersed when police fired into the crowd without provocation. 'The crowd scattered running back into a column of people. As they ran they shouted for people not to pay rent because the councillors and police preferred to shoot rather than talk'.[5] Thirteen marchers were killed.

In Tumahole, the rent boycott was a response to a series of incidents in which popular frustration with the administration board had accumulated. After lengthy and unsuccessful negotiations, residents decided that they would boycott rent from 1 April 1985 unless the board listened to their grievances at a public meeting and reduced the rent. The board cancelled the meeting, and the boycott began.

Strategic boycotts

Activists claim that northern Free State boycotts (other than in Tumahole) began after a strategic decision early in 1985 by representatives in the Rent Action Co-ordinating Committee (RACC). The RACC resolved to start rent boycotts in Vredefort, Viljoenskroon, Bothaville and Kroonstad as a way of strengthening - or in some cases initiating - organisation in these townships. It is unclear, however, whether participants in the boycotts saw them in the same way, and to what extent boycotts should be attributed to activists' intentions.

The strategic use of rent boycotts really took off in mid-1986. UDF had failed to develop a co-ordinated response to the first wave of rent boycotts in 1984-85. In the first few months of 1986, however, the UDF convened national meetings of civics that resolved to use rent boycotts as a general weapon of protest. By June, rent boycotts had broken out in several PWV townships. Most of these boycotts were started by UDF activists and were organised around national demands but they took place in areas where local rent struggles were already being waged (*WM*, 20.02.87).

Organisation and inception of boycotts

In the Vaal, opposition to rent increases was led by the Vaal Civic Association (VCA) and the Sharpeville Anti-Rent Committee. These organisations had held meetings in Sharpeville, Sebokeng and Boipatong to protest the increases. After 3 September 1984 all meetings were banned. Most VCA and anti-rent committee leadership went into hiding. Those who did not were arrested by the end of September. The rent boycott thus started at a time when there was very little organisational presence in the Vaal.

In Tumahole the situation was different. The boycott followed the breakdown of lengthy rent negotiations between the civic association and the development board. The civic was formed in

October 1984 in response to the rent issue and confined its activities to organising rent protests. Elsewhere in the northern Free State rent boycotts pre-dated any significant township organisation. Indeed, activists saw boycotts as a means of stimulating organisation as rent protests had done in Tumahole.

Ethandukukhanya served as an epicentre for the rent protests and boycotts in the Eastern Transvaal. The Paper, Wood and Allied Workers Union (PWAWU) organised the first protests. The presence of the union was crucial. Though PWAWU was only established in the Piet Retief area in 1983, it provided a coherent organisational alternative to the community council. There were no similar pre-existing structures like the unions in other Eastern Transvaal townships. The Ethandukukhanya rent issue was discussed in factories, and shop stewards went from house to house in the township canvassing it. Residents decided to form a representative Committee of 13. Several committee members belonged to PWAWU, and the chairperson was also head of the Mondi factory's shop stewards committee.

Opposition to rent increases in other Eastern Transvaal townships was encouraged by newspaper and word-of-mouth reports of the apparent success of the Ethandukukhanya boycott. Activists from the different townships met through lawyers in Nelspruit, and thereby heard of successful legal action against evictions.

The very gradual transformation from mass non-payment to rent boycott can probably be attributed to the small and relatively isolated nature of the townships, and the absence of strong traditions of either union or township organisation. Councils seem to have retained some legitimacy until 1985. In Umgwenya, for example, discontent with a rent increase in 1984 was limited to unsuccessful attempts to take up the issue with councillors and the township manager. No formal organisation existed until July 1985. An action committee was finally formed in response to police requests that representatives be elected. The action committee was larger than such committees elsewhere in the Eastern Transvaal, with 26 members made up of parents, 'ordinary people' (workers and unemployed), teachers and businessmen, but not students.

In Soweto, the general rent boycott that began in June 1985 was organised through the network of street committees built up in conjunction with the 13 branches of the Soweto civic. The committees enabled the boycott call to be widely relayed at a time when mass meetings were prohibited, and helped strong support to develop throughout Soweto. In both Alexandra and Tembisa, unions and individual unionists were centrally involved in the inception of rent boycotts.

State responses

The state does not appear to have formulated any overall plan to counter rent boycotts. Emergency press regulations prohibiting unauthorised reports about rent boycotts indicate that some elements within the central state are concerned about them. But there is no evidence that this has been translated into directives for dealing with boycotts. For the most part it seems that state responses have been determined by the local state, with central state policy limiting its choice of options. The Joint Management Committees (JMCs) might well have played an important part in state responses to boycotts, but it seems likely that *de facto* power within JMCs rests with the board and council officials and not with the military or police.

Even individual development boards lacked any coherent strategy to counter boycotts for a long time. The first and only known formulation of such a strategy was approved by the Lekoa Town Council in November 1985.

Two contrasting approaches by the local state are identifiable:

* discussion or concession, in the belief that rent increases are justified and need only to be explained, coupled with a concern to avoid violent conflict; and

* coercion, aimed at crushing rent boycotts with evictions and deployment of force.

The state displayed an unusual reluctance to adopt the second approach, especially during 1984-85. The Lekoa Town Council only started to explore repressive responses in November 1985. Its first evictions took place in August 1986, almost two years after the boycott started. In both the Eastern Transvaal and Tumahole, officials waited 15 months before evicting tenants for non-payment of rent. In all these cases the authorities have suspended evictions pending the outcome of cases testing their legality, and as at May 1987 the boycotts were continuing.

Three   factors   influenced   these   responses: officials misinterpreted boycotts; they were concerned to avoid violent confrontation; and their legal position was weak.

Initial state analysis of boycotts

Despite the long history of intensifying opposition to rent increases and the housing shortage, nearly all state officials publicly blamed protests - including the new boycotts - on agitators and intimidation. They failed to recognise that economic rents are beyond the means of most township residents.

Soweto Deputy-Mayor Jwara contended that 'people in general are keen to pay, but they fear victimisation from instigators...(being) necklaced or having their homes burnt by comrades' (*WM*, 25.07.86). Nic Louw, the Lekoa town clerk, testified in court in October 1985 that Vaal residents were contented and that agitators bussed in from Soweto were responsible for the events of 3 September and the rent boycott.

Intimidators were contrasted with the mass of 'reasonable' residents who would, officials believed, recognise that paying rents was in their own interest. Officials could not understand why there might be mass opposition to rent increases. Increases were seen as 'necessary' to provide the housing and services residents demanded. At the beginning of the rent boycott in Silobela, for example, the ETDB stated that rent increases could not be reconsidered because they were 'necessitated due to certain capital projects'; the board called on

> ...every responsible and thinking person to approach an increase in service charges in a positive way and to realise that it is done to ensure a more comfortable life for everybody... It is obvious that each and every member of the inhabitants of this town has a responsibility in paying for what they receive.[6]

This misinterpretation of the nature of protest led the state to underestimate the potential for rent boycotts to continue. For a long time the state responded to boycotts in the belief that the township public would happily pay rent if they were neither intimidated nor misinformed. The state therefore sought to set up ways for residents to pay rent without intimidation, engaged in lengthy negotiations and constantly used the press to explain the 'necessity' of rent increases.

To facilitate 'safe' payment of rent, the Soweto council opened an office in Johannesburg and arranged that rent could be paid by post. Particularly in the Vaal, the state's initial response was to negotiate. The council met with the Vaal Trade Union Co-ordinating Congress (VTUCC) between October 1984 and December 1985. Negotiations, however, could not resolve the contradictory positions of state and residents. The VTUCC took residents' incomes as its starting point; officials took the council budget as theirs. Yet the authorities clearly expected negotiations to end the rent boycott because they took no steps to evict rent defaulters until November 1985.

Fear of conflict

Fear of provoking further violent conflict was also a factor in the state's reluctance to respond coercively. Most of the rent increases announced in mid-1984 were suspended in the immediate aftermath of the Vaal uprising.

Fear of provoking resistance also restrained the state's attempts to break boycotts through the courts. Evictions could easily provoke confrontation. The OVDB's legal director warned that evictions do 'not solve the problem of social riots', and his reservations proved well founded.[7] In January 1986 Breyten youths threatened to destroy the administration offices if electricity supplies to the township were cut off to break the boycott. The ETDB ignored the threat and suffered the consequences - their offices and two councillors' houses were burnt down on the day electricity was switched off.

When the Soweto Council began evicting families in late August 1986, it started very tentatively, limiting evictions to just seven families. Further, according to the council's controversial housing director, Del Kevan, 'They were the incorrigibles - people who had not paid for months, not the rent boycotters who stopped paying in June' (Star, 06.09.86).

Similarly the Tembisa Council stressed that the first families to be evicted were (they thought) long-standing defaulters. Officials believed - or hoped - that action against these criminalised families would serve as an example, but not provoke the other 'reasonable' residents.

The Soweto evictions led to the 'White City war', immediately after which Kevan said that 'it will be provocative to carry out evictions when there is such trouble in the townships' (*Sow*, 28.08.86).

Elsewhere, the likelihood of bloody resistance to evictions must have occupied the minds of officials considering ways of resolving their rent crises.

Legal weaknesses

The state's reluctance to face confrontation also stemmed from lack of success in using the courts to enforce evictions. But it seems unlikely that local state officials were aware of the weakness of their legal position before they found eviction orders being contested in court. This does not explain why there were often such long delays before boycotters were evicted; but it does help explain why the state's moves towards a more confrontational approach were often tentative and inconclusive.

None of the local authorities affected by the pre-1986 rent boycotts were legally able to reclaim rent arrears or enforce consequent evictions through the courts. To effect rent increases, development boards or town councils are legally obliged to advertise the proposed increase in at least two newspapers, provide a 30-day period for lodging objections to the increase, consider the objections, submit the increases to the minister for approval, and then gazette the increases if they are still deemed necessary. None of the 1984-85 increases that sparked off the boycotts complied with these requirements. Indeed, many local authorities are alleged to have failed to gazette rent increases since the late 1970s.

Even when rent boycotts began, local authorities were remarkably slow to rectify their legal position. Thus the Lekoa Town Council's 'Strategy for the Collection of Arrear Rentals and Service Charges', dated 1 November 1985, included the directive:

> 1.14 Arrange for tariffs of rented houses in the area of jurisdiction to be approved by the Minister.
> - investigate the legality of declared rental and the necessity for declaration.[8]

Legal weaknesses in the state's position were exploited by lawyers representing evicted residents. Thus the potential intimidatory effects of legal action against residents were negated by the evident success (at least to date) of lawyers in delaying or preventing eviction or imprisonment.

The shift in state approach

The eventual shift to coercion was inevitable, given officials'
obstinate adherence to their misinterpretation of boycotts and
boycotters. Indeed, the shift does not seem to have involved any
fundamental change in officials' analyses of the causes of boycotts,
but rather a recognition that new responses were required.

The Lekoa Town Council and OVDB finally abandoned their
conciliatory approach to boycotts in November 1985. The 'Strategy
for the Collection of Arrear Rentals and Service Charges' was
adopted at a meeting of the Lekoa Town Council executive committee on 7 November 1985. Its first objective was to 'collect outstanding tariffs without delay'. It called for a repressive attack on
boycotters with the help of the police and the courts. Civil proceedings against boycotters were to be accompanied by a sustained
hearts-and-minds campaign to encourage payment of rent and
promote the image of local authorities.[9]

A number of factors explain the council's shift in attitude. The
rent boycott had been in progress for over a year and the council
must finally have realised that simple explanations of the capital
budget would not move residents to start paying rent again. While
the council still made its mandatory references to 'revolutionary
groups or organisations', it acknowledged that residents were not
going to start paying rent unless they were forced to. The OVDB
and the council also felt secure enough by late 1985 to contemplate
the use of force against residents. The first state of emergency, with
mass detentions and a sustained police and army show of strength,
had led to relative peace in the Vaal townships.

In Soweto, the council changed its approach much sooner, in
the second month of the Soweto-wide boycott. The council executive resolved on 7 July 1986 that boycotting residents should be
threatened with eviction. On 9 July municipal police began serving
eviction notices under section 65 of the Housing Act, ordering residents to pay their rent within seven days or vacate their premises
(*BD*, 09.07.86; *Sow*, 10.07.86).

This changing approach was reflected in a subtle but significant
shift in official rhetoric. Council officials immediately made much
more threatening public announcements. Instead of 'sympathising'

with residents, officials began emphasising the waiting-list for housing in Soweto. For example, Kevan said:

> Please, Sowetans, be warned - if you don't pay your rents, no matter what excuse you make, you are going to lose your house or flat and you'll wait for many long years before you get another one (*Sow*, 09.07.86).

However, the key reason for the shift in approach went unstated in most public announcements. After a month of near-total boycott, Soweto's town clerk finally recognised that swift action was required 'because it's more difficult to pay off arrears when the amounts have accumulated over several months' (*Star*, 21.07.86).

While officials continued to interpret the boycott in terms of intimidation, a new response was quickly needed if it was not to achieve a momentum of its own.

The Tembisa Town Council seems to have changed its approach at about the same time. Defaulters were evicted, and the town clerk announced that the council would get tough and ensure that rent was paid 'even if this means getting the whole of the South African Defence Force to Tembisa' (*Star*, 16.07.86, 28.07.86). It is not clear whether there was any organisational link between these changes in approach or if they were coincidental, given that boycotts were now one or two months old, and the heightened repressive atmosphere of the state of emergency.

Coercive approaches have not to date been any more successful than the state's earlier responses. In the Vaal and Tumahole, residents ignored the rent summonses issued in November and December 1985. When defaulters were arrested in April 1986 for contempt of court, a group of women marched on the administration offices in Sebokeng demanding their release. Elsewhere in Sebokeng state property was attacked. Wary of another Vaal uprising, the council released the arrested residents and did not implement eviction plans for four months.

When the council finally evicted 31 families in August 1986 it again encountered resistance and promptly stopped. The most recent action was the January 1987 Sebokeng confiscation of furniture from households in arrears; when this provoked violent confrontation, officials abandoned the measure.

Events in the northern Free State followed a pattern almost identical to those of the Vaal. Aggressive steps by the OVDB have twice been abandoned in the face of resistance.

In Soweto, however, officials ignored signs of imminent confrontation. On 16 July 1986, police raided houses in Naledi Extension 2, demanding to see rent receipts and serving eviction notices. Over 1000 women and students marched to the council offices in Jabulani in protest, and the Bureau of Information reported clashes elsewhere (*Star, NN, Cit,* 17.07.86). On 26 August, 21 people were killed and 98 injured - according to official accounts - in clashes with security forces in the 'White City war' over evictions.

Continued official determination despite the lack of results reflected the local state's limited alternatives as much as the prevailing atmosphere of repression. Administrators recognised that the longer the boycott went on, the harder it would be to break. Yet there was nobody with whom they could negotiate, given the state of emergency and the fact that they found it impossible to consider negotiating with the Soweto Civic Association or the Soweto Youth Congress.

Different state approaches

Local state analyses of boycotts were not homogeneous. Rather, different groups of officials interpreted boycotts in different ways and developed their responses accordingly. Political interpretations by hardline councillors, government and police, contrast with the more technocratic interpretations of many local officials. Only a few perceptive councillors recognised what was at issue, and they for the most part heeded residents' call to resign. The overall state response reflects the relative importance of these different groups.

For the most part it seems that the blindly technocratic approach of professional officials in both development boards and councils determined the nature of the state's response. Officials' approach, as Malan put it, was that payment of rent should be apolitical, 'but it has been turned into a political issue' (*WM,* 05.09.86), and that counter-boycott strategies are essentially technical and apolitical. For example, Kevan justified evictions, saying: 'There is no housing authority in the world who will not evict tenants who do not pay rent' (*Star,* 06.09.86).

Many councillors have been less conciliatory, seeing the boycott as a political attack on themselves. Their response was therefore more explicitly political. Soweto councillor Letsatsi Radebe, the chairman of the management committee and a former Magotla leader, blamed the rent boycott on intimidation by 'comrades'. In mid-June 1986 he led an armed group which abducted and assaulted youths in Naledi. Over 1 000 protesting local residents confronted Radebe at his home, secured the release of the youths, and called for his resignation (*CP*, 15.06.86). Radebe's approach was clearly shared by other councillors, because the council later resolved unanimously to establish vigilante groups.

Elsewhere councillors served as a brake on state aggression. In Tembisa, for example, the collapse of the council can be attributed to its unhappiness with evictions, which increased councillors' unpopularity and the threat to their property and lives. Nowhere, however, have councillors had an obviously major impact on state responses.

Relations between the state and capital

The authorities received little support from employers over rent boycotts. This is best illustrated by events in the Vaal, where capital's involvement in the rent boycott has been longest. The Vaal Chamber of Commerce and Industry was drawn into the rent issue in October 1984 when the council first tried to break the boycott with stop-order rents.

At no stage did the chamber accept the legitimacy of ('stop order') Proclamation R186. It instructed its members not to make stop-order facilities available to the Lekoa Town Council. Then from June 1985 to January 1986, the chamber hosted negotiations between the council and the VTUCC. In the course of negotiations, chamber delegates repeatedly sided with the VTUCC. So much so, in fact, that the council eventually demanded that the chamber chairman cease to chair the negotiations because he was not impartial.

Union pressure influenced the chamber's role in negotiations. Its members began to apply their minds to the 'rent problem' after receiving the following advice from the VTUCC:

> It is incumbent upon you to be seen to be practically involved in the present rent and other related matters presently taking place in the whole Vaal area. It is suggested therefore that you have a duty to intervene in this matter and your failure to do so is and will be construed by all and sundry as an unforgivable and gross dereliction of your important duty.[10]

This moral censure was accompanied by the threat of industrial action if there was no suitable response by employers within the next month. The unions also explained to the chamber that residents could not afford to pay the current rents; accordingly, if rents did not decrease workers would have no option but to demand higher wages.

However, a crude reading-off of employers' responses from their fears and interests is inadequate. In the course of the Vaal negotiations the chamber became increasingly sympathetic to residents' demands and increasingly frustrated by the intransigence of the town council.

There was also strain between employers and local authorities outside the Vaal. Generally, the crucial point of conflict between employers and town councils was the issue of deducting rents from wages. The councils saw stop-order rents as a simple way of ending the rent boycotts; employers saw them as a way of transferring the rent conflict from the township to the factory floor. In April 1986, Constitutional Affairs Minister Chris Heunis tabled the Black Local Authorities Amendment Bill in parliament. The bill included a new stop-order clause to circumvent the legal opposition to Proclamation R186. It was strongly opposed by capital as damaging to labour relations. According to Vincent Brett of the Association of Chambers of Commerce (ASSOCOM), the financial problem in the townships 'is very much a political problem rather than an economic one, and requires a political answer' (*BD*, 14.05.86). In May the clause was dropped.

The campaign against stop orders was spearheaded by ASSOCOM. After this success ASSOCOM's policy has been to avoid being caught up in the rent conflict as far as possible. An ASSOCOM circular, 'Rent Boycotts', distributed in July 1986, advised all members: 'Do not become directly involved with the local town council over the collection of rents and service charges'. The rest of the circular made it clear that employers would do best to keep a distance from the rent controversy.[11]

Rent boycotts and changes in township politics

Rent boycotts have informed township politics and have also been shaped by them. Though it is difficult to distinguish the political impact of the boycotts themselves from related or even coincidental events, it is worth trying to identify their direct and indirect effects on township politics.

Rent boycotts easily develop their own momentum. They involve immediate material benefits to participants, and as arrears escalate the cost of ending the boycott rises. Not only do residents have a direct financial stake in its continuation, but past a certain point they do not have the financial resources even to consider breaking the boycott. Once initiated, therefore, a rent boycott requires relatively little organisation to continue, and frequent detentions of 'organisers' have not markedly affected boycotts.

The very factors that foster the success of a rent boycott may also weaken organisation. The Tumahole Civic Association was established to deal with the rent crisis, specifically to negotiate with the OVDB. There was no perceived need for organisation around rents in the period between the time the OVDB broke off negotiations and the first eviction orders. The boycott itself resolved the issue as far as residents were concerned, and the civic atrophied.

Rent boycotts may also directly influence political culture and consciousness. Participation in a successful boycott may radicalise previously passive residents. Even the first rent boycotts, which responded to specifically local grievances, involved organisers linked to national or regional political structures. National political themes were thereby incorporated into local political consciousness. In addition, residents' conception of their rights may be redefined or extended to include notions of a 'just rent'. In the Vaal there was general consensus in favour of a rent of R30 (including service charges).

Crucially important to the interaction of boycotts and township politics was the state's response. The state's initial negotiation-based approach accelerated organisational formation in many townships. The Sharpeville, Bophelong, and Boipatong Civic Associations and the Umgwenya Action Committee were formed to negotiate with officials over rent boycotts. In Tumahole and some Eastern Transvaal townships, organisations were formed in the course of negotiations over the rent issue before the boycott. Organisations involved in negotiation were generally made up of older residents, often conservative professionals, rather than younger activists.

In Mamelodi the council responded to the boycott by discontinuing refuse removal. Activists set up street and section committees responsible for cleaning programmes in each area. These were seen as the foundation of a future civic organisation. The state's response to the rent boycott also strengthened street committee organisation in Soweto. The council's threat to evict rent defaulters there prompted the formation of defence committees increasing participation in grassroots structures.

Elsewhere, however, eviction threats had a very different effect on organisation. In the Vaal, Eastern Transvaal and northern Free State, activists concentrated on opposing evictions and contesting the legality of rent increases through the courts. But dependence on extra-township resources like lawyers can disrupt organisational structures originally developed for different purposes. The Tumahole Civic, for example, was elected to negotiate with the development board about rents. Its representatives were chosen by the community because of their popular standing rather than for their political commitment. Committed or more educated activists tended to be involved in the youth congress. Lawyers' need for articulate individuals as intermediaries meant that they dealt with youth congress activists rather than the civic's leaders. And the unemployed activists, not workers, had the time to spend at lawyers' offices in Johannesburg. But the youth congress had no mandate to deal with the rent issue. Unlike the civic it was an organisation of self-conscious political activists which did not have mass participatory structures. The heightened role of such individuals strained existing relations of accountability, leading to breakdowns in co-ordination between activists, and between activists and residents. The civic began to atrophy when negotiations stopped and the rent boycott began, and youth congress activists became still more dominant.

When local authorities did try to evict families, support for boycotts was often strengthened rather than weakened. Eviction was necessarily seen as illegitimate, given belief in the justice of the boycott. Such perceived illegitimacy was increased by the violence of its enforcement. Not surprisingly, residents resisted eviction. Heavy-handed reactions by the security forces, as in the 'White City war', provoked further moral outrage.

Eviction or the threat of eviction may cause tension between those who can afford to pay their debts and rent, and those who cannot. Losing a home is a serious threat in the present housing shortage, but boycott breakers face retribution. In August 1986, for example, an evicted Tumahole resident agreed to pay his arrears so he could be reinstated. The day after he moved back into his house, it was set alight. A more constructive approach resulted in defensive structures. Soweto street committees extended their activities from arbitration and crime prevention to protecting residents from eviction. Street committee networks could muster residents quickly to resist an eviction.

State repression, intransigence or provocation during the course of boycotts often created new conditions in which existing organisations and forms of protest seemed to lose relevance. The state's shift to a coercion-based approach reduced the appeal of more conservative organisational responses in the townships. The radicalisation of township politics was something the former organisational leadership was often anxious to avoid. At a mass meeting in Umgwenya in 1985, residents demanded resolution of the rent dispute, fearing school children might otherwise cause a riot which they did not want. Likewise the Umgwenya Action Committee had emphasised that residents 'want peace, stability or understanding and mutual co-operation' with the administration board. 'We insist that we as a community do not want violence but violence is forced down our throats by circumstances beyond our control'.[12]

In January 1985 youths took to the streets in several townships stoning and burning municipal buildings, threatening councillors or police and forcing them to leave the townships.

In some townships rent boycotts were a major factor contributing to the resignation of councillors and collapse of elected black local government. Daveyton Mayor Tom Boya reportedly claimed that 32 community and three town councils had collapsed because of rent boycotts (*Cit, BD*, 25.07.86), though he subsequently denied having said this. Councillors, he said, resigned because 'they were victimised by their radical opponents who use violence and intimidation' (*WM*, 01.08.86). Tembisa and Alexandra councillors' resignations were clearly related to the crisis surrounding the rent boycott.

Councillors in the Vaal and Soweto remained in office. In the Vaal, however, most went into exile to an army camp. In Soweto, after the 'White City war' when one councillor was killed, most fled to Fordsburg. No doubt their flight lost them whatever residual support they might have had, especially as 'exiled' councillors expected the council to foot their bills.

Rents and the urban political economy

Rent boycotts are the manifestation of fundamental conflict between township residents and the local state over urban policy. The
state sought to ensure the social reproduction of the black urban
population in a fiscal and political framework that both contradicts
residents' ideas of political justice and legitimacy and is beyond
their financial resources. Implicit in residents' participation in rent
boycotts is the demand that urban policy be determined by their
needs rather than the state's requirements.

In similar conditions elsewhere, states have resolved such conflict (at least temporarily) by subsidising social reproduction. Indeed, in South Africa such a strategy was a key element in the
state's response to white working class militancy in the first half of
the twentieth century. In the 1980s, however, the state was unwilling to compromise with even limited subsidisation, since any concession violates the ideology and political basis of reformist apartheid.

The need for significant state subsidies is implicit in township
residents' demands. These are recognised by capital but ignored or
side-stepped by the state. Negotiations between officials and residents have therefore inevitably resulted in deadlock. In the Vaal
negotiations, as previously mentioned, residents' delegates took
local income as their starting point; officials took the council
budget as theirs. The state in any case did not see such talks as
negotiation, but rather as an opportunity to persuade residents'
delegates that paying rising rents was necessary. Residents,
however, see no reason to accept the local state's principle of financial self-sufficiency. Negotiations could not resolve the conflict of
interests; coercion could only suppress it.

The state's immediate responses to the rent crisis were based
on refusal to recognise any fundamental change in the fiscal
relationship of residents and councils. Officials constantly warned
that a continued boycott would 'compel' them to cut public services. In fact, there has been little apparent deterioration in
provision of services. Local authorities have continued to provide
services by a combination of cost cutting (including shelving some
capital expenditure), drawing on their reserves and arranging

bridging loans. But, as Soweto's acting town clerk warned, 'ulimately the residents are going to have to pay interest on the outstanding money' (*BD*, 06.01.87). The Soweto Council has stressed that it is not bankrupt: 'At the moment our debtors outnumber our creditors. The people still owe us some money, and once they pay, our problems will be over' (*Star*, 14.01.87).

Local state officials have on several occasions sought central state funds as a temporary measure. The central state has not been publicly forthcoming. But it seems likely that local authorities have drawn on central government funds during the rent boycott. The reserves of the Lekoa Town Council, for example, would not have covered its arrears of over R100-million. Nor could commercial loans have been arranged without state guarantees.

In the long term, the state appears to be planning to wash its hands of the rents problem. The White Paper on Urbanisation released late in 1986 provides for the further commercialisation of township housing and introduces the basis for increased private sector township development. The state will only accept responsibility for providing welfare housing for families with monthly incomes of less than R150.

In short, the state envisages that the private sector will resolve both its financial and political contradictions. While private capital sees state contracts as lucrative, it is very unlikely to contemplate assuming responsibility for wholesale black township development. It has no reason to believe that tenants will respond any more positively to private landlords than they have to the state.

Notes

1   Simon Bekker and Richard Humphries, *From Control to Confusion: The Changing Role of the Administration Boards in South Africa, 1971-1983*, Pietermaritzburg, 1984, 132.
2   University of South Africa Bureau of Market Research, 'Income and Expenditure Patterns of Urban Multiple Households in Pretoria/the West and East Rands/Johannesburg/Vaal Triangle, 1980/1985', Research Reports nos 94.1/.3/.4/.7, Pretoria, 1981; and 130.2/.8/.9/.13, Pretoria, 1986. The 25% estimate for the Vaal is conservative.
3   UPE Fact Papers, 22, October 1977, and 53, March 1984, table 45.
4   PAYE (Pay-As-You-Earn) tied rents to income on a sliding scale. In Ethandukukhanya, for example, the rents announced in 1984 ranged from a minimum R30,31 for households with income below R50 per month (that is, rent as approximately 78% of income), to R36,64 for households earning R150 160 (about 24,2%), to R50,09 for households earning R400-410 (about

12,5%).

5   Interview with Mamelodi activist, 11.08.86.
6   GL James, ETDB Chief Director, to Messrs Phosa, Mojapelo and Partners (lawyers), 08.07.75.
7   'Strategy for the Collection of Arrear Rentals and Service Charges', annexure to the agenda of the second special meeting of the executive committee of the Town Council of Lekoa, 07.11.85, 12, 6A.
8   'Strategy for the Collection', 7.
9   'Strategy for the Collection', 12, 6A.
10   P Thom and P Masia, 'VTUCC memorandum', undated.
11   GAV Brett to secretaries of all Chambers, Members of the Manpower Committee, Affiliated Members, Senior Associate Members and Associate Members, 'Rent Boycotts', 25.07.86.
12   Undated memorandum, 'Complains (sic) of the Umgwenya Community'.

Women in Trade Unions and the Community

Georgina Jaffee *

Since 1960, increasing numbers of black working-class women have been employed in the manufacturing, commercial and service sectors of the South African economy. Between 1960 and 1980 there was an increase in the number of economically active women of all racial categories. African women currently constitute almost two-thirds (65%) of the economically active female workforce, while coloured women make up 12%, Indians 2% and whites 21%.[1] In the last 20 years the proportion of women workers rose from 15% to 25% in manufacturing and from 24% to 34% in commerce. This change reflects a huge increase in numbers of economically active African women.[2]

The government's policy of industrial decentralisation was implemented more systematically after 1982, following the new accord between business and the state. Its effect was to incorporate large numbers of African women into the labour force. Many industries in the industrial deconcentration areas have a majority female workforce.[3] The decreasing demand for domestic labour and the low wages paid in this sector, the increasing impoverishment of the rural areas and the collapse of subsistence agriculture

* Some of the research for this article on women and the community was contributed by Collette Caine

all provided a ready-made cheap labour force for expansion of industry in areas close to or within bantustans.

The incorporation of women into the industrial workforce explains the emergence of a set of women-specific demands from the shop floor. Such demands include higher wages, maternity benefits, childcare facilities and an end to sexual harassment in the workplace. Women have contributed actively to trade union growth and militancy despite their reproductive responsibilities. Their widespread demands address aspects of their oppression as women workers.

The growth of the trade union movement provided the impetus for increasing organisation of women in previously non-unionised sectors. Domestic workers, who number 800 000, have started organising along trade union lines. In November 1986, the South African Domestic Workers Union (SADWU) was launched. This brought together a number of small domestic workers' unions in the Western and Eastern Cape, the Transvaal and Natal. SADWU, with 60 000 members, is affiliated to the Congress of South African Trade Unions. COSATU has also committed itself to organisation of agricultural workers, where 16% of economically active African women are employed.

The increasing numbers of women entering the workforce and becoming part of organised labour will enable the issue of women's oppression to be raised within the struggle for working-class rights.

African working-class women have also emerged as a powerful force for change within their communities. As popular resistance intensified in the past few years, working-class women increasingly formed and participated in women's organisations which played a major role in progressive politics. From 1980 onwards, women's political organisations re-emerged in most South African black communities.

Local women's groups have initiated projects concerned with childcare, adult literacy and co-operative buying.

Women have participated in campaigns against the increase in general sales tax, in struggles concerned with education, consumer boycotts, rent boycotts, and the demand that troops get out of the townships. In the last three years repression has continually disrupted popular organisation, and worked against the growth of grassroots organisation necessary to advance the specific interests of working-class women. 'It is difficult to organise creches when our children are being shot by the soldier-boys', explained one woman.[4]

Intellectual debate and analysis of the 'women's question' and how it fits into the politics of national liberation has been lacking. Debates about the relationship between working-class hegemony and national liberation have not seen women's oppression as central to distinctions between the 'politics of liberation' and the 'politics of transformation'.[5] According to this distinction, the latter secures the interests of the working class and changes in the relations of production, while the former serves to end apartheid.

In contrast, a younger generation of women activists feels the need to address the oppression of women as part of the struggle for national liberation. They have started a debate about the relationship between the affiliates of the United Democratic Front and the newly constituted women's organisations. Questions are being asked about the lack of women in leadership positions in the UDF; how women's issues can be taken up within its affiliates; and the special problems faced by women workers in the factory and in their relationships with men. Women in both trade unions and community organisations are beginning to address the question of women's oppression as integral to the struggle for national liberation.

According to the Federation of Transvaal Women's (FEDTRAW) education officer, speaking at a recent workshop:

> Our understanding of the special disabilities faced by women is that they are rooted in exploitation, racial oppression and sexism. The battle against capitalism, racism and sexism cannot be fought as part of a three stage plan - the struggle must be waged simultaneously at all these levels. We are committed to building women's organisations; to uniting women; to raising the voice of women in the national-democratic struggle led by the working class. It is our task to develop working-class leadership amongst women and to allow working-class interests to dominate our women's organisations.[6]

Although embryonic, the struggle working-class women are beginning to wage both on the shop floor and within communities opens up a crucial area of debate on the politics of transformation. The struggle to change patriarchal attitudes, share the double shift, and achieve higher wages and better working conditions, is being forced onto the agenda of trade unions and popular organisations.

Shop-floor demands

Women's demands from the factory floor reflect the increasing strength of the organised working class in the post-Wiehahn period. The Wiehahn Commission aimed to curb the growth of shop-floor unionism which gathered strength from the early 1970s. It recommended state recognition of African trade unions and provided for their incorporation into established industrial relations structures. The achievement of enforceable rights in the workplace allowed trade unions to enter negotiations on all aspects of work conditions, including women's rights and health and safety. Gains on the factory floor allowed for greater organisational initiatives: in the past seven years the independent trade union movement has grown significantly and now has over 800 000 members.[7]

Unions with large numbers of women members face a set of demands linked to, but different from, the demands of African male members. These include righting the problem of low pay for 'women's work' and unequal pay for the same job, the inclusion of demands for maternity rights and childcare facilities in negotiations, taking up occupational health problems specific to women, and ending sexual harassment.

Low wages and unequal pay

It is now illegal to set separate wage rates for women. The 1981 Labour Relations and Wage Acts, following the recommendations of the Wiehahn Commission, abolished discrimination based on sex in minimum wage agreements. But this is unlikely to make any substantial difference to the income of African women in general, as most work in the lowest-paid, least skilled 'women's jobs'.

As many African women workers are sole breadwinners or support extended families, the fight against low wages and 'women's work' is a central issue of union organisation. Unions have resisted attempts by management to impose percentage increases which widen the wage gap between low and high grades. Instead they have tried to negotiate for flat-rate increases in an attempt to narrow the gap.

There has been an attempt to fight for a 'living wage' for all workers, rather than a 'family wage' based on the notion that women's wages are supplementary to those of a male breadwinner.

A recent example of success in equalising wages involved negotiations between the Chemical Workers Industrial Union and the Vulco Latex rubber company, which resulted in a R30 a week raise for women. Male workers in a higher grade received a R20 per week increase.

Equal pay for equal work is only an effective policy if it is combined with equal access to promotion. Trade unions are also fighting management's tendency to invent new job titles for women which have lower status and benefits compared to those of men who perform the same duties.

Overtime

In 1985, legislation was changed to allow women to work the same amount of overtime as men.[8] This equalisation placed an extra burden on women workers. Women start a second shift - cooking, cleaning and childcare - at the end of the work day. Overtime means a triple shift.

The removal of the protective clause for women workers has placed the issue of overtime firmly on the agenda of unions with large numbers of women workers. While women workers suffer most from overtime, they are also most in need of the extra money. Overtime is at present being dealt with through the demand to reduce the working week to 40 hours for all workers. But fighting overtime will only be viable once a living wage is won for all workers in the country.

Job security and maternity benefits

Job security is a crucial demand for women in the unions. For workers who are also mothers, job security is further threatened by lack of paid maternity leave. Bird argues that 'without job protection, women can find that maternity leave becomes retrenchment'.[9] The struggle for maternity benefits was central to women's demands. Unions such as the Commercial, Catering and Allied Workers Union (CCAWUSA) met with considerable success in getting these met.

CCAWUSA's growth exemplifies the expansion of women into the retail sub-sector. Seventy percent of the 40000 paid-up members of CCAWUSA are women. In 1985 CCAWUSA signed the

most comprehensive maternity agreement to date with a national
retailer, Metro Cash and Carry. This agreement allows for 12
months' maternity leave with a guaranteed right to return to work;
seven of the 12 months are paid leave at 33% of salary. With Unemployment Insurance Fund payments, this amounts to 78% of
salary for six months and one month at 33%. There is paid paternity leave of three days for the biological father, and time off to
facilitate breast feeding and attend ante-natal and post-natal
clinics. Other clauses in the agreement involve health and safety,
prevention of discrimination against pregnant job applicants and
flexibility about leave. Early in 1987 the first industry-wide national
maternity agreement between unions and employers in the metal
industry was signed. This allowed for six months' paid absence from
work, guaranteed re-employment after confinement, and was widely welcomed as a major breakthrough for women workers on the
issue of maternity benefits.

A number of other maternity agreements were signed by affiliates of both COSATU and the Council of Unions of South
Africa (CUSA). Although not as comprehensive or as far-reaching
as the Metro agreement, they generally include 12 months' leave,
six months' paid leave and job security.

The recession intensified the focus on women's job security as
companies retrenched large numbers of workers. Unions adopted
the last-in, first-out principle, and forced employers to investigate
alternatives to retrenchment in consultation with workers' representatives. Although the battle to save jobs has been hard, where
attempts to negotiate met with success they helped prevent women
from bearing more than their share of the burden of job loss.

Health

Health and safety has become an important component of worker
demands. In most union recognition agreements, health and safety
clauses are included which consider the special conditions women
workers need especially when they are pregnant. Education and information on health and safety have limited management attempts
to impose certain forms of family planning on female workers.

Some unions have started looking at the relationship between
shift work, health and family life. The effect of shift work on health
and family responsibilities of women workers is currently being

researched by trade union service organisations, and introduced into educational programmes. Education on contraception has also been started within union courses.

Childcare

As increasing numbers of African women enter the labour market, there is a growing need for childcare services either in the townships or at the workplace. This has not been met by the state or capital. Recent studies show that black working-class women have to rely on family members or informal child-minders to look after their children.[10] Of a population of four million pre-school African children, only 0,3% were looked after in creches. These creches are predominantly funded by fees and subsidies from private welfare groups rather than the state.[11]

The demand for childcare has started to feature in negotiations. BMW, for example, has agreed to finance a creche at its factory in Rosslyn. This will be jointly administered by management and the union, the National Automobile and Allied Workers Union. In the Programme for Women developed by CUSA in 1984, there is a demand for the establishment of creches, nurseries and after-school centres. The demand for childcare will certainly feature in negotiations in the near future. Unions intend forcing the private sector and the state to provide childcare facilities in the townships and, when convenient, at the place of work. The fact that most workers in South Africa live a long way from their homes generally makes childcare at the point of production impractical.

Sexual harassment

Sexual harassment is another problem specific to women workers, and they are organising to fight it. In the last few years there have been several strikes because of this issue, with the men responsible for harassment being dismissed. At Unilever in 1983 a white employee was sexually harassed by a manager; this led to a one-day stoppage of the black workforce which demanded that the man be fired. In the end he was transferred to another plant.

Women's rights on the agenda

> COSATU believes that women workers should take first place in our struggle. Women workers suffer the most under the bosses and the system.[12]

COSATU's December 1985 launch saw women's rights placed firmly on the agenda of the country's major trade union federation. COSATU, representing more than half a million workers, wrote into its constitution a resolution on women which commits it to fight for women's rights at work, in society and in COSATU itself. The COSATU resolution on women states that it is:

* Against all unequal and discriminatory treatment of women at work, in society and in the federation;
* For the equal right of women and men to paid work as an important part of the broader aim to achieve full and freely chosen employment;
* For equal pay for all work of equal value - the value of work must be determined by organised women and men workers themselves;
* For the restructuring of employment to allow women and men the opportunity of qualifying for jobs of equal value;
* For childcare and family facilities to meet workers' needs and make it easier for workers to combine work and family responsibilities;
* For full maternity rights, including paid maternity and paternity leave and job security;
* For protection of women and men from all types of work proved to be harmful to them, including work which interferes with their ability to have children;
* Against sexual harassment in whatever form it occurs; and
* For adequate and safe transport for workers doing overtime and night work.

Its constitution also commits COSATU to finance and set up a sub-committee to monitor progress in implementing these resolutions and to promote understanding of the specific discrimination suffered by women workers.

Acceptance of this resolution signifies a definite advance in formally recognising working-class women's needs, but for many working women the fight for equality within the trade union movement is likely to be long and hard. Such policies have not yet been implemented. But with the increasing numbers of women becoming active in the trade union movement there is now a material basis for their implementation.

The COSATU resolution developed from a growing awareness within a small group of women in the Federation of South African Trade Unions (FOSATU), a precursor of COSATU. One of the group's aims was to achieve equal rights for women within FOSATU. A member explained:

> We wanted our presence to be felt. There are just about no women in union leadership - men are in control and we felt our silence within the federation was proving the inferiority of women. It proved the thinking in traditional African society that the dignity of women is lower than that of men.[13]

In 1986 CUSA had 12 union affiliates with a total membership of 200 000, 30% of which was female. In 1987 it merged with the Azanian Confederation of Trade Unions to form the National Council of Trade Unions (NACTU). CUSA resolved in 1982 to establish a Women's Unit; to redouble efforts to stamp out discrimination in all aspects of employment; to increase the number of childcare services in the community; and to encourage women's full participation in unions and politics.

In 1984 the women's unit was set up with the objective of investigating all issues of concern to women workers in CUSA. It is very active educationally, producing documents on health and safety, equal pay, maternity and paternity leave and sexual harassment. The unit also publishes a women's news digest which contains articles on women in South Africa and other parts of the world.

The unit recently ran a number of seminars for women shop stewards and women members and adopted a programme for women. It is proving most successful in drawing attention to the specific plight of working women and is making far-reaching demands on both capital and the state regarding the specific burden carried by women workers.

Referring to the rich tradition of women in resistance in South Africa, CUSA's information officer argues: 'It is now incumbent on women in the trade union movement to organise and mobilise themselves to press for their own special interests and thereby contribute to the struggle to fight for the rights of all workers'.[14]

With state repression and the demands of other union business, it is a struggle to get women's issues included among the many issues that require action. Despite this, officials are confident that women's issues will continue to be taken up and given due recognition at all levels in the future.

Women in community and political organisations

South African Women's Day, 9 August 1986, marked the thirtieth anniversary of the Federation of South African Women's (FSAW) 20 000-strong march to Pretoria to protest the extension of passes to women. FSAW drew up the Women's Charter in 1954, articulating women's demands for inclusion in the Freedom Charter. It dealt with the right to vote, full opportunities for employment and equal pay, equal rights with men in relation to property and marriage, maternity benefits, welfare, clinics and creches. It demanded the removal of all laws restricting free movement of women and committed itself to building and strengthening the women's section of the national liberation movement.

The anniversary of the march was to have been celebrated by the launch of a national women's organisation, but disruption of progressive organisation by the state of emergency declared on 12 June 1986 forced a postponement. A new federation will be launched in the course of 1987, to co-ordinate national women's campaigns. It will bring together a broad spectrum of women's groups, dealing with a wide range of women's issues.

The United Democratic Front Women's Congress was formed on 25 April 1987. This brought together eight regional women's organisations affiliated to the UDF, including the Natal Organisation of Women (NOW), FEDTRAW, the Port Elizabeth Women's Organisation, and the Western Cape-based United Women's Congress (UWC). The UDF Women's Congress is a concerted attempt to assert women's leadership, bring women's issues into the UDF in a more forceful way, and ensure that women's struggle is an integral part of political struggle. The congress intends working closely with COSATU and working-class women, building organisation on a grassroots level.

The massive impact of the 1976 student rebellion and the generalised resistance that followed set the stage for the mobilisation and organisation of African women. This is rooted in spontaneous local protest against the harshest manifestations of the crises of the apartheid state and the South African economy: the fight against Bantu Education, housing shortages, high rents, the soaring cost of living and the lack of social services.

In the Western Cape, the United Women's Organisation (UWO) was initially formed to support students in the education struggle. As a UWO executive member explained:

> 1976 showed parents that they were not able to support their children and that there was something wrong in our society. We had fought Bantu Education when it was started in 1954, yet many parents became their children's enemy when they stood up against that education in 1976. We saw that we had no voice to speak for us or our children. We knew that as women we were oppressed both in our houses and at work, and that we needed to work towards changing things as women with both short- and long-term goals.

The UWC was formed in the Western Cape in March 1986. It brought together the UWO and the Women's Front. Both were formed in 1980, but organised and campaigned separately until 1986.

FEDTRAW was established in December 1984 to unite women in common action for the removal of political, legal, social and economic disabilities. FEDTRAW claims to be active in 22 areas in the Transvaal. It has participated in campaigns for an end to military conscription, for the withdrawal of troops from the townships, for free and equal education in South Africa, and for the abolition of apartheid. FEDTRAW sees itself following in the tradition of 1950s women's organisation under the leadership of FSAW.

NOW was formed in 1983. It has about 20 branches in the Durban area, and is expanding to rural areas. Its aim is to organise women around issues that most affect their lives - the high cost of living, poor housing, maternity benefits and childcare. NOW sees the participation of women in trade unions and community organisations as important.

There are many other women's organisations. Not all have progressive potential, in particular those linked to bantustan structures of administration.

There are also a number of women's service organisations which provide resource material. *Speak* magazine was started during 1982 in an attempt to expose the problems that face women. It is widely used in trade union education. In 1983 the Women's Centre was set up in Durban and is mainly involved in providing literacy seminars, resource material and other educational services for women. The Johannesburg Democratic Action Committee (JODAC) women's group is involved in issuing a booklet for working women.

During 1984 the Vaal Organisation of Women (VOW), a FEDTRAW affiliate, became very active in those Vaal triangle townships where the nation-wide revolt of that year began. A small group of women came together to discuss problems with education and childcare. Once established, the group's involvement quickly broadened to embrace high rents, inadequate housing and low wages. Boycotts against high rents and the government-sanctioned community councils which administer them are one of the major campaigns in the current phase of mass resistance. According to a VOW member:

> The problem is that people in the Vaal get low wages and can't afford a rent of R65 or R78.[15] As mothers we cannot afford the rent. When a child is hungry, the mother is affected and she cannot afford to educate her children because the rent is high.[16]

Townships throughout the country boycotted rents during 1986-87. In sustaining these boycotts, women faced harsh state repression. Recently troops and township council staff started to evict rent defaulters. In at least two cases, hundreds of women marched in protest against evictions, only to meet with violent beatings by troops and police. In Naledi, Soweto, more than a thousand women and youths marched on the administration board offices in early July 1986 to protest these raids (*Star,* 17.07.86). In Tembisa, near Johannesburg, scores of mothers, some carrying their babies, were severely beaten by police while protesting against police raids, troops in the township and restrictions on funerals (*Sow,* 29.05.86).

Brutal attempts by the state to crush such campaigns brought more women into organisations. According to one women: 'Mothers see their children shot outside their homes; troops patrol the streets day in and day out'. This mobilised women to participate in one of the campaigns undertaken since the 1985 emergency, the demand for troops to get out of the townships.

In the wake of attacks on residents of Durban's Chesterville township by vigilantes known as the A-Team, allegedly backed by township police, local women formed a township watch. They guard the two entrances to the township every night. Unarmed and with no support from the authorities, they have succeeded in preventing further 'A-Team' attacks.

Despite the substantial increase in the numbers of women active in resistance groups, they have as a rule been unable to break into the male-dominated hierarchies of popular organisations. In the same way that women are largely excluded from union leadership, so they are in the main absent from decision-making positions in the political movement.

But in the Western Cape women are strongly represented in local community organisations. The UWO was an early forerunner of the current phase of resistance and organisation; its members actually helped initiate community organisations. As a result, women maintained their positions in such organisations. In the rest of the country, though, women usually still find themselves excluded from leadership. In the words of one woman activist: 'Even when you have worked 12 or 14 hours a day for the struggle and earned your place within it, you still have to continue fighting for affirmation'.[17]

This exclusion weakened a number of the recent consumer boycotts used as tactics to enforce political demands. In areas where women were under- or unrepresented on local boycott committees, tensions developed between the mainly male organisers and the largely female boycotters. Women, after all, do the shopping and cooking to feed families.

Excluding women from decision-making when they are primarily responsible for sustaining the campaign further alienates them from political and community organisation. While no boycotts actually broke down under this tension, the exclusion of women did not promote democratic grassroots organisation.

Exclusion and alienation of women increases the tendency to use violence in enforcing such campaigns and has an overall disorganising effect on the politics of the community. By contrast, women activists point to a clear link between women's representation on local boycott committees and a stronger sense of unity within the community.

Women's participation is important for the success of broad political campaigns. However, although these campaigns address issues of vital importance to women, they do not confront their oppression. Women are appealed to and mobilised as mothers, although the issues around which they are being mobilised concern everyone in the community. Such stereotyping of women in the course of mass mobilisation is double-edged. On the one hand it is a real rallying point which reflects the genuine concerns of women as mothers; on the other hand it serves to perpetuate the narrow image of women as nurturers rather than workers or activists. This tends to reinforce subordination of women's interests to the broader struggle, instead of integrating them into it.

In isolated instances some tentative steps have been taken to change the circumstances which prevent women from pursuing more active political lives. In the Eastern Cape, grassroots political organisation is commonly regarded as more developed than elsewhere, and there is a long tradition of community and popular organisation. In this region there have been experiments aimed at releasing women from domestic labour. Young comrades are helping to run creches and to form housework and laundry co-operatives, in order to free women from the tasks which tie them to their homes. In turn, these women are able to participate in street committees and other community programmes.

Port Alfred, a small town between Port Elizabeth and East London, is well known for its high degree of community organisation. Local affairs are run by a civic association; schools are run by teacher-parent-student committees; and students and pensioners are organised into representative bodies. In this small community, women's specific interests have been incorporated into broader political demands and campaigns.

The Port Alfred Women's Organisation (PAWO) was formed in March 1986, primarily to discipline and run projects with the youth. Two months after its launch PAWO successfully organised a stayaway of the township's entire female workforce. This was in protest against the rape of an elderly resident and police refusal to charge the rapist. Every African woman worker in Port Alfred stayed away from work for a week. The vast majority are domestic workers, who demanded that their white women employers help to get the rapist prosecuted. The rest of the community supported this initiative and helped enforce their decision to banish the rapist from the township. The domestic workers' action in this incident also enabled them to open up communication with employers through PAWO.

Women are playing a fundamental role in the reorganisation of communities and in the politics of protest. Their organisations are beginning to be influenced by unionised women and trade union officials. FEDTRAW sees a definite link between the level of politicisation and consciousness of women in certain areas and the presence of women with union experience.

Already women have been mobilised in support of worker conflicts with employers. In a recent wave of sit-in strikes, support from women made it possible for workers to sit it out until their demands were met. At the Bosch factory in Brits in the Transvaal, 300 male and female Metal and Allied Workers Union (MAWU) members staged a sit-in after they were dismissed during a wage strike. Women (and men) in the communities organised to bring food and blankets to the factory for the striking workers.[18]

In a strike at Haggie Rand, a metal factory on the East Rand close to Johannesburg, women organised food and raised money for striking workers. For two weeks they supported a sit-in by 2 100 MAWU members who were demanding a 40-hour working week, an across-the-board wage increase and May Day as a paid holiday.[19]

The big picture is that women are participating in organisations which are beginning to address their triple oppression as blacks, women and workers. The incorporation of African women into important unionised sectors of the economy, and the commitment of the trade union movement and women's organisations to women's equality, provide potential to address the interests and needs of working-class women.

The oppressive conditions under which women live and work led to specific demands on management from the shop floor. At the same time women are struggling for representation in leadership positions in the trade union movement. Women workers are beginning to develop a consciousness which identifies the link between economic exploitation and gender oppression. This consciousness is slowly beginning to affect the views of male workers too. Some recognise the divisiveness of women's inequality for the working class as a whole. For example, at a 1983 FOSATU workshop on women workers, a male shop steward said:

It's high time that we surrendered brothers... This is the struggle and for the sake of the struggle we should be hand in hand (with the women). If we are both in the struggle - my wife and I - and we are both working, then when I get home I must not rest while my wife carries on for 24 hours.
Women are now doing a double job. We say we are the oppressed nation, but women are more oppressed. They go to work and then start again at home. We should put aside the whisky and make the fire if the wife is not yet home.

And also carry the child. After all it is the man's child also. We must appeal to our bosses. Pregnant women's jobs must be protected. If not, we are oppressing our women. And bosses will see to it that they can pay low wages to women - and some time they will chuck us out. Then we will cry! So it is high time that we showed the bosses we're equal.[20]

There is a growing awareness that women do not win their emancipation only in the politics of mass mobilisation. They struggle for it in organisations which address the specific needs of women within the overall struggle for national liberation.

After we have thrown in our lot with the struggle for democracy, we may find that on the day when freedom comes we are in fact not so free... This is precisely why we struggle today, and why we need to plant the seeds of the new society in the womb of the old so that it grows and develops in the direction we would like it to go.[21]

The organisation of women both within trade unions and community organisations makes it possible to confront traditional patriarchal values. As Volbrecht argues: 'For black working-class women, the realisation that conditions in the home must change flows from their political involvement and discussion around questions of political power and democracy'.[22]

Molyneux has shown that in post-revolutionary societies the political, social and economic needs of women were met more often in societies which made some attempt to make the transition to socialism. In societies like China, South Yemen, Cuba and the USSR, the realisation that there is an inextricable link between class oppression and the subordination of women meant that there has always been a commitment in principle to the emancipation of women as part of the commitment towards a more egalitarian society.[23]

Despite the many shortcomings of existing socialist societies, they appear to provide the necessary conditions for the formal emancipation of women. Women in these societies have achieved a degree of equality in education and law, and have benefited from the extension of social services. Such formal equalities can provide the springboard to extend the struggle against women's oppression to other spheres of inequality. In the South African context if changes are made to accommodate the specific needs of working-class women on all levels, they will benefit all women in the society.

If a post-apartheid state is committed to addressing inequality in all spheres, then the question of working-class interests in general and the needs of women workers in particular becomes central. The degree to which women's demands are integrated into programmes and accepted by popular democratic organisations struggling for national liberation, and the strength of women's organisations involved in the process of change, will be crucial to the depth of the transformation of South African society.

Notes

1   Calculated from *South African Statistics*, 1968, 1980 and 1982; and Development Bank of Southern Africa, *1980 Census Reports on Transkei, Bophuthatswana and Venda*, reproduced in Pundy Pillay, 'Women in Employment: Some Important Trends and Issues', *Social Dynamics*, 11(2), 1985, 23.

2   *Population Census Reports, 1980*; and Development Bank of Southern Africa, *1980 Census Reports*, reproduced in Pillay, 'Women and Employment', 25.

3   VM Martin and CM Rogerson, 'Women and Industrial Change: The South African Experience', *South African Geographical Journal*, 66(1), 1984.

4   Authors' interview with woman worker, Brits location, 1986.

5   This distinction was first made by Alec Erwin, 'The Question of Unity in the Struggle', *South African Labour Bulletin*, 11(1), September 1985.

6   Leila Patel, speech given at United Democratic Front workshop on women, Johannesburg, February 1985.

7   J Lewis and E Randall, 'Focus: State of the Unions', *South African Labour Bulletin*, 11(2), 1985, 75.

8   See the Basic Conditions of Employment Act 1983, discussed in Jonny Myers and Malcolm Steinberg, 'Health and Safety: An Emerging Issue on the Shop Floor', Southern African Research Service (eds), *South African Review 2*, Johannesburg, 1984, 146.

9   Adrienne Bird, 'Organising Women Workers', *South African Labour Bulletin*, 10(8), 1985, 82.

10 J Cock et al, 'Childcare and the Working Mother: A Sociological Investigation of a Sample of Urban African Women', paper no 115 presented at the Carnegie Conference, Cape Town, 1984.

11 CUSA, 'Women's Unit Paper', 1985, 11.

12 COSATU News, 1(1), August 1986.

13 Authors' interview with ex-member of FOSATU women's group, 1986.

14 Dale Tifflin in the CUSA newspaper *Izwilethu*, October 1984.

15 Barrett et al, *Vukani Makhosikazi*, Johannesburg, 1985, 242.

16 According to the Bureau of Market Research, the average monthly wage in the Vaal in 1983 was R296,23.

17 Authors' interview with Leila Patel, FEDTRAW's education officer, July 1986.

18 'Strike at Bosch', *Work In Progress*, 39, October 1985.

19 Authors' interview with MAWU's Transvaal education officer, June 1986.

20   'Workshop on Women', *South African Labour Bulletin,* 9(3), December 1983, 14.

21   Leila Patel, speech given at United Democratic Front workshop on women, Johannesburg, February 1985.

22   Dinny Volbrecht, 'Marxism or Feminism', unpublished paper presented to conference of the Association of Sociologists in Southern Africa, University of Natal, Durban, July 1986.

23   Maxine Molyneux, 'Socialist Societies Old and New: Progress towards Women's Emancipation?', *Monthly Review,* July-August 1982.

African Women in the Durban Struggle, 1985-1986: Towards a Transformation of Roles?

Jo Beall, Michelle Friedman,
Shireen Hassim, Ros Posel,
Lindy Stiebel and Alison Todes

Victoria Mxenge was shot by unknown assassins at her Umlazi home on 2 August 1985. This murder came four years after the slaying of her husband, respected civil rights lawyer and political figure Griffiths Mxenge. To many township residents the second attack on the Mxenge family seemed an act of extreme cowardice. It was not only Victoria's status as Griffiths' widow which provoked the widespread and powerful reaction to her death, but her position as a United Democratic Front executive member in her own right and her symbolic status as 'mother of the nation'. This peculiar knot of gender constructions explains the extent of reaction to her murder. As one woman put it:

> People felt particularly strongly because she was a woman, even people who
> were not politicised. She was a mother with children, and her husband had

already been murdered...and also because she had been killed by men in a cowardly manner. With our traditional culture, women are never killed. Even during the old war times, any leader who killed women and children was looked down upon.[1]

Ironically, it was the fact that she stepped out of her traditional role as a woman that made Victoria such a high-profile figure.

At the time there were already simmering tensions in the greater Durban region. Economic recession, rising levels of unemployment, increased costs of social services and political restructuring marked the first half of the 1980s. In the formal townships of Durban, there had been protracted battles over education, transport costs, rents and incorporation into Kwazulu. The informal settlements had been affected by worsening material conditions and increased pressure on already scarce resources, coupled with insecurity of land tenure in a number of areas.

These tensions manifested themselves politically in ethnic clashes, and as a battle for hegemony in the townships. The antagonists were the UDF, the state and Inkatha. The latter dominates the political arena in the Kwazulu areas of Durban, partly because of its relationship to the Kwazulu administration and control over material resources. Immediately before Victoria Mxenge's death the townships were simmering over the imposition of the first state of emergency (despite Natal's exemption from its restrictions), the murder of four popular Eastern Cape leaders and the national education crisis.

Three forms of settlement

The impact of the troubles on African women in the greater Durban region, and the impact of women on struggle, are examined in this article. Contradictions in the role and perception of women in struggle are discussed. Contrary to the orthodox feminist view that women are written out of history, women are being rendered visible in contemporary records, but in a particular way. The dominant ideology reflected in the media does not see women as active political subjects, but as victims and peacemakers. If they are accorded any role at all, it is a conservative one, obscuring their valuable contribution and undermining their impact on struggle.

Interviews are our main sources of information. This has its limitations, especially under state of emergency restrictions. But

although certain generalisations had to be made about women's experience, we were particularly wary about regarding 'women' as a
monolithic category, and tried to be sensitive to variations in class,
age, and individual political history.

The article's focus on locality allows for exploration of these
variations. Given the degree of state intervention in the construction of locality in South Africa, and particularly in Durban, important differences between areas exist.[2] Three broad types of settlements are examined: informal areas, Kwazulu townships and Natal
townships. Each has been racked by conflict of a specific type.

In informal areas like Inanda and Umbumbulu, politics has
been about survival. Struggles have been localised over scarce
material resources, most often land and water. Usually struggles
take an ethnic form and women are not *directly* involved. In Natal
townships, by contrast, struggle took the form of direct battles
against the state, for example against incorporation into bantustans
and against Bantu Education.

In the Kwazulu townships, the major cause of unrest has been
education, but conflict spread to other issues as well. The battle for
hegemony between the UDF and Inkatha resulted in increasing
violence as people on opposing sides became victims of house
burnings, assassinations and abductions.

The Natal townships have a longer history of resistance to the
state and its allies than Kwazulu townships and informal settlements. Unrest in these Natal townships over the past few years
focused on issues like high rents, inadequate education and opposition to incorporation into Kwazulu. The result was the growth of
organisational structures which later affiliated to the UDF, notably
the Joint Rent Action Committee and the Natal Organisation of
Women (NOW).

The murder of Victoria Mxenge in full sight of her children
sparked off a dramatic sequence of events. Progressive organisations immediately responded to her death with calls to boycott
schools and organise commemoration services. This evoked
response from both the state and Inkatha, which saw a threat to
their hegemony in these events. In the wave of violence that followed, schools and commemoration services became battlefields.

It is difficult to establish a direct link between Victoria's death
and the events in Inanda during the following week. Attempts to
analyse the Inanda unrest have focused on three aspects: the

material roots of the conflict, the widespread but unorganised politicisation in Durban's black townships and the conflict between factions of the local petty bourgeoisie.[3] Sitas points to Inkatha's reconstitution of and reliance on traditional forms and symbols of Zulu culture.[4] Since these are patriarchal,[5] women were not surprisingly excluded from direct participation. In media accounts of the Inanda conflict, women are portrayed as victims, usually fleeing or being sent to 'safe' areas by their husbands. Although in Inanda these images primarily referred to Indian women, representation of African women in conflicts in other informal settlements has been similar. Our research into women's participation and conflict in informal settlements has not contradicted this media image. Nevertheless women in these areas should not only be seen as victims as it is likely that they have significant investments in and are highly dependent on resources in the informal areas. Whether women *control* these resources needs further investigation.

Unlike the formal townships where women were frequently drawn into politics as mothers, that is as *protectors* of their children, there were few compelling reasons for women in informal settlements like Inanda to become involved as women. There are a number of reasons for this, for example, no obvious organised presence of youth;[6] and women's organisation, whilst present, was not politically focused. This was because the fight did not directly involve protecting home and community from the state. Moreover, the main protagonists on either side of the ultimate conflict draw almost exclusively on men when gathering their troops. Perhaps the fact that in the informal settlements women were perceived, and indeed perceived themselves as victims, is to be expected. As one victim said, 'Women and children fled the township in tears not knowing where to go next and bewildered by the removal of their menfolk'.[7]

However, women were active in the restoration of the community after the conflict. One informant said of the Bambayi situation: 'It is the women who must do all the talking and running around... The men were there but the women were spokespeople'.[8] This aspect of women's strength was neglected in the media and needs documentation.

A clearer link can be seen between Victoria Mxenge's death and the unrest in the formal townships. In the Natal townships the state stepped in directly with troops to restore control, establishing a permanent base in Lamontville. This changed the tenor of the unrest. Opposition to the presence of troops mounted and, with increasing vigilante attacks on the homes of progressives, in particular by the infamous A-Team, township residents began to accuse the state of providing cover for criminals. The majority of adults drawn into opposition against the troops and vigilantes were women. In the Kwazulu townships, Inkatha rather than the state intervened to restore control, intensifying its conflict with the UDF.

Organisation of women in Inkatha and the UDF

There is a history of formal women's organisation in the townships, since both Inkatha and the UDF saw the need for it. The Inkatha Women's Brigade has a central role in Inkatha's attempt to reconstitute traditional patriarchal family relations. This is a necessary part of Inkatha strategy. On the one hand, it serves to legitimate the hierarchical structure of the organisation, and on the other it provides a basis for social control. Inkatha is rigidly structured, with men in positions of greatest power while women 'make sure the youth are on the right track'.[9] 'The women wear uniforms: black skirt, black beret, khaki shirt. They march like scouts'.[10] Since its formation in 1976 the Women's Brigade has been a subordinate structure. When in 1979 it came under the 'direction and control of His Excellency the President of Inkatha',[11] this was not questioned by the executive committee of the Women's Brigade. On the contrary, minutes of the annual general meeting record its warm support for the move.

Until recently, the Women's Brigade seldom participated publicly in politics, leaving this to men and especially Inkatha's central committee. Even those members of the Women's Brigade who are community councillors appear to take their direction from the central committee rather than from the brigade. The only time in recent years that the brigade made a public stand on an issue was in 1985, when it censured Fatima Meer for her criticism of Inkatha: 'We say to her, how can you as a woman and mother participate in the escalation of black violence in which our children are being killed?' (*DN*, 21.10.85).

This censure is couched in the traditional terms of womanhood and motherhood. The incident reflected both the relatively conservative definition of women's role in Inkatha, and Inkatha's narrow definition of women's role in society. While a stratum of women in Inkatha has moved from traditional female spheres into business, local politics and wage labour, Inkatha's dominant ideology remains preservation of the family and its structures of control. Within Inkatha these traditional roles remain unchallenged and unaltered. There has been no shift in women's domain or in the definition of that domain, so women's involvement in the organisation remains within the conservative parameters defined by its hierarchy.

By comparison, the UDF is both less structured (in the formal sense) and less hierarchical. This greater democracy creates space for women to formulate local responses to issues and to direct strategy. Within the UDF, Natal women as a group are organised by NOW, which was formed as an autonomous body in 1983.

During 1984-85, after affiliation to the UDF, NOW went through an internal crisis during which women's issues were subordinated to the national question. The tension between NOW's status as a women's organisation and its position as a UDF affiliate was reflected in the funeral of Victoria Mxenge, where her UDF membership was the focus, rather than the fact that she was an executive member of NOW. Nevertheless, central to the meeting was praise of Victoria as an example of womanhood. That she was *exceptional* was stressed: the transcendence of her traditional role was seen as progressive, contributing to the advance of the struggle. In effect, the UDF's definition of women's role in struggle and society, produced in the process of actual struggle by women, allows women greater potential for liberation.

With the increasingly severe restrictions on mobilisation imposed by the state, the struggle has become locally organised and more community based. Since the home, community and children are effectively managed by women, attacks on these by the SADF and vigilantes precipitated women's greater involvement in politics. This has shifted struggle more firmly onto women's terrain.

NOW has come into its own as a women's organisation, consolidated its position and drawn larger numbers of women into its ranks. Importantly, it drew in a previously unorganised group of young women who had tended to regard NOW as a 'gogos' (grandmothers') organisation.[12]

Apart from the growth and consolidation of NOW, women also

created new structures in which they have moved into positions of dominance in certain townships. These were in the main crisis committees set up to deal with local issues like detentions, troops in the townships, support for pupils and so on. Such committees tended to be managed by women. In some instances, women placed men on committees to secure their involvement. Significantly, these committees have only been formed in the Natal townships. In the Kwazulu townships, formation was impeded by the presence of Inkatha and the lack of political coherence - itself the result of the differences in the histories of the Natal and Kwazulu townships.

Women as mothers

The role of women as mothers can be interpreted in either a progressive or a conservative way. Hazel Carby has argued that the black family functioned as a site of resistance during slavery and colonialism, and under authoritarian regimes.[13] This is borne out in some areas of Durban. Women in townships like Lamontville and Chesterville are acting in essentially traditional roles - the defence of their families - but these actions can be seen as radical and perhaps revolutionary.

Being a mother in Chesterville, for example, means facing Casspirs and troops with machine guns. Contrary to the media image of a generation gap between adults and the youth, our interviews reveal that women supported their children and that this support resulted in the mothers' politicisation. Their position as women provided the basis for politicisation. As N put it, 'If people talk about the gap between mothers and sons, this may be in the long term, but if there is a crisis the first people to get there are the women and they help their sons'.

This is not to suggest that women have no prior politicisation; indeed, the events of the past few years make this unlikely. In fact their response is specific and sometimes more manifest than that of men. This may be attributed to their position as *women* in one particular political tradition or another. Thus, for example, women in Chesterville held all-night vigils to protect their children from attacks by troops and vigilantes, whereas Inkatha women in Umlazi were responsible for the discipline of children. While Inkatha retains a traditionalist definition of women and their domain, the UDF's definition of women's role contains the potential (sometimes realised) to empower women and transcend traditional roles.

The movement of troops into the townships and the activities of the vigilantes touched women in a particular way. The site of struggle shifted to the home and the community, into a sphere in which women have particular responsibility and which they feel particularly obliged to defend. Clearly these perceptions are socially constructed: the home is traditionally regarded as the women's domain, and the care of children is 'women's work'.

The women we interviewed saw these roles in communal, rather than individual, terms. Biological parenthood is not the only kind of parenthood in the townships. Women feel a social obligation as mothers to all children in the neighbourhood. This may in part be explained by material conditions in the townships, where women who work entrust their children to the care of relatives and neighbours. This sense of communal responsibility provided an imperative for women's active involvement.

The social construction of femininity drew women into the struggle in other ways as well. The view that women are physically weak and vulnerable (held both by reconstituted Zulu culture and the SADF) created an immunity which women exploited in the defence of their terrain.[14] N tells of an incident in Lamontville in which teachers decided to confront the SADF with women in the front and men behind. 'It was felt they would not shoot if we did this... This works if women are in front. We believe it works'.

Such tactics forced women to take positions in the front line of the battle and allowed them to assume leadership roles, laying the basis for a transformation of women's role and position in society. This points to a classic contradiction in the role of women in struggle: they are drawn in to defend their terrain but in so doing are forced to move beyond narrowly conceived notions of their roles.[15]

This is epitomised by the position of detained women. Unlike men, women, by virtue of the responsibility they feel as mothers, must make more considered choices about the extent of their involvement in struggle. In the process they render themselves vulnerable to manipulation by both police and media. As M explained: 'The security police implied that women who were involved in political activity have very low morals'. This is not just an attempt to undermine women's political activity, but is part of the reaction against the movement of women out of their traditional roles.

The security police also manipulate women's maternal concerns in the bargaining process. Women are caught in a double bind: while they are determined to construct a better future for their children, it is at their children's expense in the present. According to one woman,

> I feel a total failure as far as taking care of my children is concerned. I was terribly worried about them when I was in detention. I haven't been able to support them or given them enough love or guidance. They understand to some extent. They are growing up with a hatred of a government which detains their mother and so many others.[16]

The media responds to detained mothers by sentimentalising them, albeit sympathetically. By focusing on their role as mothers, it legitimises social constraints on women.

These developments must be seen against the background of an ongoing battle over the form of the family. Among African households in South Africa the nuclear family is the exception rather than the rule.[17] In explaining the prevalence of youth violence the state seized on this absence of effective nuclear families as structures of socialisation (*FM*, 04.07.86). Thus current discussions about fostering nuclear family relations may be part of the state's attempt to establish the family as a foundation for social control. While African women in the townships struggle to maintain family relations, these are different from family relations characterised by discipline as proposed by the state.

Family relations as they exist in the townships are potentially subversive. Support given by mothers to their children is directly political. Contrary to the way the cultural role of mothers has been theorised, mothers in areas like Chesterville and Lamontville are not transmitters of dominant ideology: rather, they 'were carrying stones in their pinafores to give to the youth'.[18]

While women's nurturing role as mothers led them to be actively supportive of their children, it also involved them as mediators. This role takes many forms. Female teachers tend to mediate in conflicts between children, and between children and troops when troops enter the school grounds. In Lamontville, women intervened to prevent the 'comrades' from taking violent revenge on girls who were sleeping with soldiers. This role as community mediators points to an important part women can and have played in reducing potential violence arising out of people's courts.

While women's position as mothers and mediators in the

community brought them into the forefront of struggle, the same cannot be said for young girls. Socialisation and their greater responsibility for household labour militate against girls playing a leading role. One informant said: 'With the youth the boys dominate events... The girls do not participate as much as the boys because they have to cook and do housework, and cannot attend meetings late at night because parents worry and think they will get pregnant'.[19] While mothers are creating space for themselves, they may be limiting it for their daughters. Further, girls have at times found themselves in the crossfire: they are seen as impressionable and unreliable. In Chesterville, for example, girls were suspected of spying for the A-Team and the police.

Gender and township violence

Indisputably, the national struggle has become violent. But the extent of women's participation in the violence is unclear. In Natal at least, it seems that violence was generalised among men and exceptional among women. However, women on both sides were increasingly involved in supporting, directing and organising violence of various kinds. Nevertheless, Inkatha's attacks on opponents were overtly male in style. Attacks by amabutho (tribally defined warriors) were based on traditional patriarchal structures. Men were recruited and warrior-like symbols (spears, shields, skins) used.[20]

Women in Durban are active subjects in the historical process, challenging the dominant conception of women as passive victims. This article's description of them will hopefully contribute to the practice of women's liberation, highlighting the contradictions experienced by women in struggle. While their social construction as women draws them into struggle and makes it possible to move beyond traditionally defined roles, this very social construction limits that possibility. It is important that this space be explored and articulated to preserve and extend the gains women are making: belief that their personal oppression is unimportant means that women do not take up struggle for themselves, even if they do so for their children.

The link between women's personal and political oppression needs to be made not only in theory but in practice. This political dimension is vital, given that women's hard-won gains in other struggles have often been lost when 'home and hearth' are restored.

Notes

The authors wish to thank the women interviewed. Without their experience and help, this article could not have been written. It was produced under difficult circumstances, in particular the detention of Jo Beall, who was still held by security police at the time of writing.

1 Interview with N, 12.11.86.
2 For a discussion of this issue see AM Schofield, 'Chasing the Wind: Unrest, Space, Place and Time in Durban: 1982-1986', unpublished BA Honours dissertation, University of Natal, Durban, 1986.
3 Ari Sitas, 'Inanda, August 1985: "Where wealth and power and blood reign worshipped gods"', *South African Labour Bulletin*, 11(4), 1986; Heather Hughes, 'Violence in Inanda, August 1985', paper presented to the Institute of Commonwealth Studies, London, 1986.
4 Sitas, 'Inanda, August 1985'.
5 JD Beall, 'Class, Race and Gender: A Political Economy of Women in Colonial Natal', unpublished MA thesis, University of Natal, Durban, 1982.
6 It is intriguing that demographic research on Inanda indicates a much lower proportion of children than is the norm. See Michael O Sutcliffe and Paul A Wellings, 'Attitudes and Living Conditions in Inanda: The Context for Unrest?', Built Environment Support Group, University of Natal, Durban, 1985.
7 Interview with resident of Folweni, 05.12.86. Quote from *NM*, 24.01.86.
8 Interview with P, 24.11.86.
9 Interview with A, 10.12.86.
10 Interview with J, 26.11.86.
11 Resolutions of the the Third Conference of the Women's Brigade, 15-17.12.79.
12 This was at November 1986. The situation may have changed since then.
13 Hazel V Carby, 'White Women Listen! Black Feminism and the Boundaries of Sisterhood', in Centre for Contemporary Cultural Studies, *The Empire Strikes Back: Race and Racism in '70s Britain*, London, 1982.
14 The relatively greater immunity enjoyed by white women was also exploited as a tactic in Chesterville where Black Sash women joined the vigils.
15 This is discussed in another context by EN Chinkanda, 'Black Woman: Mother and Revolutionary?', paper presented to the Association of Sociologists of Southern Africa congress, University of Natal, Durban, 1986.
16 *WM*, 06-12.06.86. Although this detainee is not a Durban woman, her guilt is typical of many detained mothers.
17 See for example Virginia van der Vliet, 'Staying Single as a Strategy for Survival', paper presented to the Carnegie Conference on Poverty and Development in Southern Africa, University of Cape Town, 1984.
18 Interview with N, 12.11.86.
19 Interview with N, 12.11.86.
20 While this was true for Durban during the period under discussion it may not be true for other areas or an accurate reflection of clashes since.

Resistance to Militarisation: Three Years of the End Conscription Campaign

Laurie Nathan

In 1967 Minister of Defence Jim Fouche introduced white male conscription to the South African Defence Force (SADF). Opposition to this move seemed highly unlikely from a largely conservative and racist community whose monopoly of power and 'way of life' was increasingly threatened. Yet by the late 1970s there were conscripts so strongly opposed to military service that they chose exile or jail instead. In 1983 the End Conscription Campaign (ECC) was formed to co-ordinate and give direction to the growing opposition to conscription. By 1986, the ECC enjoyed a breadth of support and capacity to mobilise people in the white community that posed a significant challenge to the state.

The history of war resistance in South Africa is that of the relationship between the intensifying struggle for liberation, the state's attempts to control it by military means, and the white community's reaction to these developments. By compelling white men to take up arms against black opposition, government has made itself vulnerable to dissension within the ruling group and its army. Conscription is of paramount concern in the white community, and has provoked a life crisis for thousands of conscripts.[1]

This article examines opposition to conscription and reviews the ECC's features and development in the context of black resistance and the militarisation of South African society. It looks at war resistance prior to the ECC's formation, the character and content of the ECC's campaigns, and the response of the state and right wing. It assesses the reasons for the ECC's growth and the intensity of state action against it, and considers the future of the ECC and war resistance.[2]

Debate about participation in an 'unjust war' emerged in the English churches and universities during the mid-1970s, and several conscripts were imprisoned for refusing to do military service. The state's attempts to stifle this debate ironically led to the ECC's formation at the end of 1983.

In 1984 the ECC focused on Namibia and the call-up, and began building regional and national structures. The continuous and extensive use of the SADF against black resistance from October that year stimulated the ECC's development. In June 1985 it established a national presence through its multi-cultural Peace Festival. In August it presented arguments to the Geldenhuys Committee which was set up by the SADF to investigate various aspects of defence force policy. In September the 'Troops Out' campaign highlighted the call for the SADF's immediate withdrawal from the townships. The 'Working for a Just Peace' campaign of May 1986 demonstrated constructive alternatives to military service.

By June 1986, the ECC had taken the war resistance movement beyond the traditionally radical sectors of the English-speaking universities and churches. A range of different constituencies and over 50 organisations were involved in its campaign. The ECC had raised the white community's awareness of military issues, powerfully expressing white opposition to conscription and the SADF's role. It had nine branches around the country and committees on five university campuses. But the state of emergency in June 1986 put a sudden brake to its momentum, growth and plans for the rest of the year. The ECC has since then experienced a level of repression that makes the future of war resistance in South Africa uncertain.

Early resistance to conscription

Pressure on government grew in the 1960s and 1970s, with mass uprisings in 1960 and 1976, the intensification of armed struggle by SWAPO and the ANC and the liberation of Angola and Mozambique. Accordingly, the SADF began playing an increasingly central role in the management of conflict.

Its operations included the occupation of Namibia, destabilisation of neighbouring countries and policing apartheid laws. Between 1960 and 1983, a relatively obsolete army became a technologically sophisticated institution, and military expenditure rose from 6% of government spending to approximately 20%.[3] The SADF's standing operational force increased from 11 500 soldiers to 180 000 and its total available manpower grew from 78 000 to half-a-million.

Compulsory military service for white men was introduced in 1967; its duration was gradually extended to the current two years' continuous service plus 720 days of 'camps' spread over 12 years, and a further 12 days per year up to the age of 55.

From 1978, the SADF became a key participant in both military and non-military state policy formation once its representatives were placed on the State Security Council. Its rise to power reflected its desire to develop 'militarily defensible policies' and a 'total strategy' that co-ordinated the state's response to a situation of 'total war'.

The earliest incidents of war resistance involved Jehovah's Witnesses and other 'peace church' members refusing military service on the grounds of opposition in principle to fighting in any war. Their stand was strictly apolitical and they shunned publicity about their imprisonment in army detention barracks.

The first public and explicitly political opposition to participation in the SADF was expressed at the South African Council of Churches' 1974 conference. In the context of a debate about the church doing something practical to change the status quo, the conference stated that the army was defending 'a fundamentally unjust society', and urged its members 'to consider becoming conscientious objectors'.

Conservative and even liberal sectors of the white community condemned the resolution as 'criminal', 'defeatist' and 'a threat to national security'. Government's response indicated how seriously it viewed opposition to military service. It amended the Defence Act. Section 121 (c) makes it an offence punishable by a maximum fine of R6000 or six years' imprisonment to encourage or assist anyone to refuse or fail to render military service.

The amendment inhibited public support for the SACC stand, but the 1976 Soweto uprising and doubling the length of military service the following year heightened war resistance. Between 1975 and 1978 an estimated 5 900 conscripts either went into exile or evaded the authorities while remaining in South Africa.

Public resistance took the form of high-profile campaigns around the nine conscientious objectors imprisoned between 1979 and 1983. The objectors argued from various philosophical perspectives, but all opposed the SADF's role 'in defending the violence of apartheid' against people 'who are generally not foreigners but South African citizens'. Their objection challenged other conscripts to consider seriously their own positions, and led to the formation of the Conscientious Objector Support Group (COSG) in 1980.

In 1983 government reacted to mounting pressure by amending the Defence Act, broadening the category of conscientious objectors to include religious pacifists outside the 'peace churches'. If their bona fides were accepted by a Board for Religious Objection, they could apply for non-combatant status in the SADF or community service in a government department. The amendment increased the jail sentence for other objectors to a maximum of six years.

Government had made an important concession by introducing the option of community service, but its intention was to co-opt the churches, divide the war resistance movement and make the cost of political objection prohibitive. The results were quite the reverse. The churches reiterated their belief that all objectors should be recognised, and some denominations refused to be represented on the Board for Religious Objection. Military advice bureaux were formed around the country under COSG's auspices, and the emerging war resistance movement reassessed its direction.

The positive response of English-speaking churches and universities to objectors created the potential to advance the movement in a more effective and far-reaching way, but the increased jail sentence meant it could no longer depend on individual objectors. The movement required a co-ordinated campaign with a clear focus and an independent programme of action. Its inspiration came from the 1983 Black Sash conference which demanded that government 'abolish all conscription for military service'. At the fourth annual COSG conference in Durban later that year, delegates decided to launch a national campaign against conscription.

Conscription and the white community

Conscription is one aspect of the apartheid regime that imposes a real burden on the white community. Two years of military discipline and authority are for many young men a waste of time at best, and at worst a psychologically disturbing experience. Behavioural scientists have found that violence, drunkenness and sexual frustration in returning national servicemen are 'inevitable consequences of the intensifying border war' (*WA*, 28.03.81). Case studies of soldiers who have done township duty reveal similar aggressive and violent tendencies and an 'acute sense of alienation and meaninglessness'.[4] After their initial service, many soldiers have difficulty adjusting to civilian life and finding employment.[5] They still have to do two years of service in the form of annual 30- and 90-day army camps, whatever the consequences for their jobs and families.

The permanent use of the army in the townships politicised military service and heightened the moral dilemma of liberal conscripts. The arena of conflict was not just far away in Namibia against SWAPO guerillas and 'the Cubans'; it was now close and easy to understand, and 'the enemy' were ordinary black South Africans. In the experience of the ECC and the military advice bureaux, an increasing proportion of young people opposed to apartheid automatically oppose conscription.

This opposition developed in a period of increased political consciousness and acceptance of extra-parliamentary struggle. The white community had united behind the 'new constitution' in 1983, but was deeply polarised by the growth of popular organisations, mass resistance and state repression in the next three years. The Progressive Federal Party, English-speaking business and the church took relatively more radical positions, while white democratic organisations experienced greater legitimacy. Within the liberal white community many people were filled with despair about the future, but others were motivated to become involved in

anti-apartheid work. The issue of conscription focused these tendencies, as more conscripts emigrated and more supported and
joined the ECC.

It is difficult to measure accurately the extent of war resistance.
In 1981 it was sufficiently serious to warrant the formation of the
South African Army Non-Effective Troops Section to 'locate men
who attempt to evade service by means of subterfuge'. Before October 1984 an average of 1 500 men failed to report for duty at each
call-up.[6] In the first call-up after troops were used in townships, this
number rose by 500%, according to figures released by the minister
of defence.[7] The SADF subsequently claimed that this figure was
'incorrect', and the minister has refused to release figures for subsequent call-ups. Court cases and sources in the SADF indicate
that attendance at army camps is generally between 40% and 60%.[8]

Other statistics confirm this trend. From 1984 to 1985, almost
1 000 conscripts applied to the Board for Religious Objection (*DN*,
26.08.86). When the South African Citizenship Amendment Act
was passed in 1984, 600 immigrants refused South African citizenship to avoid military service (*Star*, 10.04.85). There are currently
an estimated 7 000 South African war resisters in Europe and the
United States (*Cit*, 28.08.84).

Military service is depicted by government and SADF as a
conscript's 'patriotic duty', but the fact remains that it is compulsory and not voluntary. The psychological, material and moral
problems associated with it have caused widespread dissatisfaction
among conscripts and their families, and laid the basis for the
ECC's development as a mass movement.

The character of the campaign to end conscription

The ECC's success was due to its developing a political style that
captured the breadth of opposition to conscription. Its public activities and constituency work, and its structure as a coalition
around a single range of issues, contributed to the character and
growth of the campaign.

The primary objective was to put white community pressure on
government to end conscription. In doing this, the ECC aimed to
raise awareness and build opposition to militarisation and the
SADF's role in defending apartheid. A further aim was to involve
as many people as possible in its sub-committees. By mobilising,

educating and organising around military issues in the community
from which soldiers are drawn, the ECC hoped to contribute to the
broader struggle against apartheid and build non-racialism.

The ECC's role was clear. It existed to campaign in the white
community, and did this energetically and creatively. Traditional
political events like public meetings and seminars were comple-
mented by 'creative actions' like fun runs, fairs and building sand
castles. Cultural projects included concerts, cabarets, film festivals
and art exhibitions, and tens of thousands of stickers, badges and T-
shirts were produced. These activities contributed to the development of an anti-war culture and consciousness in the white community. They broadened the ECC's appeal and put across its
message in ways appropriate to different groups of people. Sensitivity to the differences between various constituencies characterised the ECC work. School, student, church and cultural sub-
committees systematically consolidated the ECC's general
activities.

National campaigns centred on activities with mass appeal in
the white community. During the 'Troops Out' campaign in 1985,
several conscientious objectors fasted for three weeks. In Cape
Town, over 2 000 people signed the visitors' book in St George's
Cathedral where Dr Ivan Thoms was fasting, and 4 000 attended
the final rally in the city hall. In all centres there was a high level of
public participation in the 24-hour 'peace fast' that concluded the
campaign. For the first time, jewish, hindu and muslim groups were
involved in war resistance, and christian involvement went beyond
church hierarchies and activists to include ministers and congregations.

The 'Working for a Just Peace' campaign in 1986 involved
about 600 ECC members and supporters working on community
projects for a month in black areas. These demonstrated constructive alternatives to military service. Over 6 000 people attended
mass meetings at the end of the campaign.

New ECC branches in Pretoria and at Stellenbosch University
in 1985-86 transformed the war resistance movement's
predominantly English-speaking character. The ECC wanted to go
beyond having two Afrikaans branches to develop a bilingual campaign. It took an Afrikaans name, 'Aksie Teen Konskripsie', and
distributed Afrikaans pamphlets in all centres. The process was
hampered when the Stellenbosch branch was banned on campus by

university authorities within a month of its formation, and by anti-ECC propaganda widely distributed in Afrikaans-speaking areas.

The ECC's character was shaped by its structure as a coalition of church, student, women's and human rights organisations. The coalition reflected the unity and diversity of a war resistance movement made up of different political and theological perspectives - liberal and radical, religious and secular, pacifist and those specifically opposed to an unjust war. Over 50 organisations were involved in the campaign, taking it to their constituencies and adding weight and credibility to the call to end conscription. The coalition functioned smoothly because no one perspective or organisation attempted to assert its control over the campaign. The organisational emphasis on democracy and accountable leadership was also important.

The coalition's unity was based on an opposition to militarisation, conscription and the SADF's internal and external role. Because it is a single-issue campaign, the ECC's policy and focus did not extend to other aspects of apartheid.

Content of the ECC's campaigns

The ECC's opposition to conscription was the central theme of its public work. As its reading of the changing situation in South Africa developed, new arguments and themes were introduced.

The ECC explained its opposition to compulsory military service in early pamphlets: conscription
* is used to implement and defend apartheid policies;
* maintains South Africa's illegal occupation of Namibia;
* destabilises neighbouring states;
* increases the financial costs of the war;
* conditions people to accept militarisation; and
* violates the internationally recognised right to freedom of conscience in relation to military service.

The ECC Declaration of October 1984 summarised these arguments and called for 'a just peace in our land'. In motivating the call, the ECC contrasted 'the government's notion of securing peace by preparing for war' with its own belief in 'achieving peace through justice'. Although there was no policy on exactly what was meant by 'a just peace', the ECC speakers generally demanded as necessary preconditions the dismantling of apartheid and security legislation, unbanning organisations and the release of detainees and political prisoners.

The 'peace' sub-theme was an important reason for the ECC's appeal. It balanced its protest and criticism, offering a positive vision to a community increasingly frightened about the future.

The launch of the declaration coincided with the start of widespread and continuing troop deployment in black areas. This became the key factor in the ECC's opposition to conscription, and the call for immediate withdrawal of troops from townships became a central theme of its activities.

The ECC argued that the escalating cycle of violence could only be ended by removing the root cause, apartheid. The use of the army raised the level of violence and was strongly opposed by township residents. These arguments were backed up in ECC literature by township residents' and occasionally soldiers' descriptions of troop actions.[9]

The ECC aimed, in building white support for the withdrawal of troops, to increase pressure on government and stand in solidarity with black communities increasingly hostile to whites as a result of security force behaviour.

The ongoing focus on the SADF's internal role culminated in the 'Troops Out' campaign. The campaign reflected a change in the ECC's attitude to soldiers when it demanded that troops should have the right to refuse deployment in a township. The ECC had realised that in some of its media and arguments for the withdrawal of troops, it portrayed the individual soldier as 'the enemy'. This was insensitive to the dilemma of conscripts who opposed conscription and township duty, but for whom the alternatives of jail or exile were unrealistic. The ECC therefore attempted to project itself clearly 'as opposing conscription, not conscripts'. It was 'with and on behalf of conscripts' that the campaign was conducted. This was a significant shift from the early war resistance movement's approach of urging conscripts to conscientiously object.

The ECC's concern for the rights of conscripts was also expressed in its interim demands for the broadening of community service options while conscription remained. It proposed to the Geldenhuys Committee that the 1983 Defence Amendment Act be changed, making community service:

* available to 'all who in good conscience cannot serve in the SADF', and not limited to religious pacifists;

* the same duration as military service rather than one-and-a-half times as long; and

* available in religious and welfare organisations, not confined to government departments.

The 'Working for a Just Peace' campaign aimed to illustrate these demands in a symbolic but practical way. The campaign demonstrated that there are constructive alternatives to military service, and that 'real national service' involved volunteers entering townships 'with tools and not guns' after thorough consultation with the community. The notion of working for a just peace was supported by some sections of the white community in the period of intensifying conflict between the two states of emergency.

The second state of emergency declared in June 1986 substantially affected the ECC's focus on conscription. Emergency regulations prohibited making 'subversive statements' that 'undermine or discredit the system of compulsory military service'. The ECC was on the defensive for the first time, campaigning for 'the right to speak' and the release of the ECC detainees. Other campaigns focused on militarisation. Parents were encouraged to buy their children Christmas toys 'for peace and not war', and the 'War Is No Solution' campaign raised questions about 'the physical, economic and psychological costs of the war'.

State and right-wing response to the ECC

Whereas many European governments see war resistance as apolitical, the South African government branded it 'subversive' and reacted with punitive legislation. Hundreds of Jehovah's Witnesses were imprisoned from the late 1960s, and political opposition to military service was dealt heavy blows by Defence Act amendments in 1974 and 1983. South Africa's position on conscientious objection is amongst the harshest in the world.

The ECC's growth was matched by the development of relatively sophisticated and increasingly well co-ordinated smear campaigns. SADF and government representatives repeatedly accused the ECC of breaking the law, of being linked to banned organisations and assisting 'terrorism'. Right-wing groups and conservative newspapers regularly 'exposed the ECC's hidden agenda', and soldiers were lectured about it during basic training.

In an effort to counter the propaganda, the ECC complained to the Media Council about libellous allegations made by *Rapport* and the ultra-right *Aida Parker Newsletter*. The council found in the ECC's favour on both occasions, but the cumulative effect of the smears was damaging.

The propaganda aimed to undermine and criminalise the ECC, thereby legitimising direct repression against it. Such repression generally coincided with high-profile ECC activity, beginning with the detention of four of its members during the 'Troops Out' campaign. In the following months, activists were assaulted, their vehicles tampered with and their houses raided. Publications and meetings were banned, and in some regions Departments of Education barred the ECC from white schools.

Repression peaked under the second state of emergency, with over 60 ECC members detained and more than 90 homes raided. Police action and legislative restrictions were so severe in the first month of the emergency that the ECC initially seemed to be effectively banned. Although it continued campaigning, a further crackdown in December 1986 made it clear that government would attempt to prevent the ECC from working publicly again.

The intensity of state action against the ECC is due to the SADF's central role in safeguarding minority rule both physically and ideologically.

The SADF became indispensable to the maintenance and defence of apartheid from the late 1970s. Between 1983 and 1984, 43 000 soldiers were used in 'ordinary police work' (*CT,* 19.05.84). In 1985, as black resistance entered a new phase that seriously threatened the government's civil control of black areas, 35 000 troops were deployed in over 95 townships.[10] The 1986 Defence White Paper stated that conscription, which provides about 70% of the SADF's manpower, is absolutely necessary for the army to play this role.

As a result, government perceives opposition to conscription and the SADF as a threat to 'the nation's physical capacity to survive', and automatically equates the ECC with 'the enemy'. According to the minister of law and order, the ECC is one of South Africa's 'four main enemies', along with the United Democratic Front, the African National Congress and the South African Communist Party.

War resistance fundamentally threatens state ideology. With the military's rise to power, 'total strategy' became official state policy. It is based on the belief that South Africa faces a 'total onslaught' that requires a 'total response' from all areas of society and every citizen. The response is broadly political rather than purely military, and places as high a premium on psychological and ideological struggle as on the physical dimensions of the conflict. The key task is to build morale and cohesion behind the state, and weaken that of the enemy.

The state has attempted to unite the white community through the military doctrine of 'national security': conflict is reduced to a struggle against 'communism' and the use of force is presented as the appropriate response. The SADF is projected as a unifying symbol, and military values of obedience and discipline are inculcated in civil society.

The very existence of the war resistance movement challenges these notions, casting doubt on the state's interpretation of society and conflict. The ECC is perceived as attempting to weaken the social cohesion of the white community and undermine its will to 'defend the country'. By doing this from within the ruling group, the ECC is seen by many white people 'not just as the enemy, but as traitors', as a Stellenbosch student leader once put it.

The future of the ECC and war resistance

The intensity of state repression of black resistance under the state of emergency is unlike anything previously experienced in South Africa. White extra-parliamentary organisations are relatively protected, but it is uncertain to what extent they will be able to campaign again. Ongoing police harassment and the emergency restrictions on opposing conscription make the ECC's future particularly precarious.

However, the ECC is determined 'not to ban itself'. At its 1986 year-end assessment, it felt strongly that 'democratic organisations have to challenge the government's ability and right to outlaw peaceful opposition'. It will attempt to continue raising public awareness about military issues and develop 'lower-profile and therefore less risky ways of reaching people'. It will also concentrate on the organisational issues that became priorities under the emergency: tight security without sacrificing democratic practices; a high level of morale and cohesion in the organisation; and support structures for ECC members in hiding or detention.

State harassment of the ECC may inhibit public opposition to conscription, but it cannot solve the crisis of war resistance. The ECC gave this resistance expression and direction, but did not cause it. Resistance is due to the material sacrifices involved in four years of compulsory military service and increasingly to moral abhorrence of the army's role in defending apartheid. Until government accepts the inevitability of fundamental change, the struggle will intensify and greater demands will be placed on the white community. As the physical, economic and psychological costs of the civil war rise, so will white resistance.

In 1974 Ds Beyers Naude, then head of the Christian Institute, commented on the likely effects of section 121 (c) of the Defence Act. His statement accurately predicted the future of the war resistance movement under more serious attack in 1987:

> The drastic penalties...will certainly act as a deterrent to individuals who have basic objections to military service to express their true feelings... But it does in no way resolve the crisis of conscience facing many young people who are utterly opposed to the unjust system which is ours, and who are called on to defend this system by force of arms.

Notes

1 'Conscript' refers to any white South African male liable for military service in the SADF, although not necessarily already in the army.

2 I have been a member of the ECC for the last three years and this article therefore reflects an ECC perspective of its history. It is not, however, an official ECC review.

3 All statistics and quotes in this section are taken from Catholic Institute of International Relations (CIIR), *War and Conscience,* London, 1982.

4 D Sandler, 'Plucking the Wings off Butterflies: a phenomenological investigation of the experiences of white SADF conscripts in the black townships', BA Honours dissertation, Department of Psychology, University of Witwatersrand, 1986.

5 According to Commandant Gary Whyte, 25% of national servicemen finishing their two years' service in 1985 had no employment (*Star*, 11.12.85).

6 CIIR, *War and Conscience.*

7 According to the minister of defence, 7589 conscripts failed to report for duty in January 1985 (*CT*, 13.03.85).

8 Court cases concerning conscripts failing to report for duty are described in 'The ECC's evidence to the United Nations Special Committee against Apartheid, 1986', unpublished, available from ECC.

9 Affidavits by township residents and soldiers' accounts of their experiences can be found in the ECC's evidence to the United Nations.

10 House of Assembly, parliamentary question no 878, 1986.

Reform and Resistance in South Africa's Bantustans[1]

Jeremy Keenan

The ten years since 1977 are frequently described as the 'reform era' in South Africa. However, it is not reform of apartheid, but its reformulation that is being witnessed. Nevertheless, as Wolpe warned, 'while it is clearly politically important to expose the shallowness of the so-called reforms, these reform policies have opened up new spaces of contestation'. What needs to be investigated, he said, is the extent to which these 'reforms' have transformed that political terrain, set up new bases of conflict and contradiction and paved the way for possible new alignments.[2]

The South African political terrain has been dramatically transformed in the last three years. One dimension of this involves the political struggles that emerged in the Transvaal bantustan areas of Bophuthatswana, Lebowa and Kwandebele in the past year.[3] Much that happens in the bantustans goes publicly unnoticed and unrecorded. Yet more than 50% of the country's African population is constrained to live in these areas under the most repressive conditions.

In the last 18 months or so most of the Transvaal bantustan areas, especially Bophuthatswana, Kwandebele and Lebowa, witnessed a dramatic escalation of popular resistance to the structures of the apartheid state. This was characterised by widespread state violence, most notably the Winterveld shootings in March 1986 and the fact that Kwandebele and much of Lebowa became 'no-go' areas. Heightened resistance was also marked by the emergence and proliferation of numerous local political organisations, most commonly regional crisis committees, action committees, civic associations, women's organisations and youth organisations.

The violence is not a result of emergence of these organisations. Rather their formation was usually a defensive reaction to intensified state control and repression. More often than not this involved the presence of the South African Defence Force, police or state-backed vigilantes, as well as indiscriminate use of violence and terrorism to stifle legitimate demands and quell the emergence of responsible and representative local leadership.

Local organisations in most cases originated as single-issue bodies which responded to problems like rent increases, boycotts or state violence, then broadened their scope to take on the general defence of the community and its organisation on a wider political front. The role of the youth was significant in this. The development of crisis committees, civic associations, women's and other committees in many cases followed or was precipitated by the formation of youth organisations. Not only did youth organisations help establish other bodies, but in most areas they took the lead in trying to link local organisations into regional and national structures.

There are a number of reasons why the youth played such an important part in the upsurge of bantustan resistance. The increase in state violence and disruption of education in urban areas caused many youths to move to the bantustans, even if temporarily, to attend school or to escape state violence in the townships. 'Reform' was accompanied by increased repression in the bantustans, together with a dramatic increase in unemployment in these areas. Both affected the youth most severely.

The South African government's public explanation for intensified popular resistance in the bantustans is that it is part of a concerted strategy. This, it says, is co-ordinated and directed externally by the African National Congress and its 'communist' masters, and internally by its surrogate forces, notably the United Democratic Front, in order to make the country ungovernable and overthrow the state.[4] This alleged grand conspiracy the state calls the 'revolutionary onslaught'.

Contrary to the state's explanation, this upsurge in resistance is fundamentally locally based and organised. Indeed, there is a danger of progressive forces themselves attributing too much centrality to the role of national organisations such as the ANC or UDF in these struggles.

In some areas, as in northern Lebowa, resistance may have been inspired by national organisations. But in many others popular resistance has been singularly localised. Often it appears that those involved had little or no knowledge of the UDF or other national organisations. In most cases local bodies affiliated to the UDF only after they had emerged from their particular local sites of struggle. Even then, the UDF has contributed more as an ideological than an organisational force. There are still some areas where key local organisations have not formally affiliated to the UDF or any other national organisation. These local struggles above all had a grassroots character and developed democratic and representative forms of organisation and leadership. These characteristics are their strength and ultimately the strength of the UDF as well.

In almost all cases local-level organisation in bantustans is a direct reaction to the state's 'reform' policies. Far from stabilising post-1976 South Africa, these policies escalated resistance to the apartheid state and its appendages in the bantustans. Four factors singly or in combination provoked much of the contemporary bantustan 'unrest'. These are:

* increasing poverty and unemployment;

* new forms of capital investment in both bantustan agriculture and industry, which led to increased land dispossession and more intensive exploitation;

* intensified control and repression; and

* burgeoning corruption in both central and local bantustan authorities.

While there is a clear overall pattern underlying the spread and escalation of popular resistance in the bantustans, their local manifestations cannot simply be read off from the national struggle. Indeed, where national organisations intervened directly in local struggles they sometimes misunderstood or ignored local conditions and the needs of the people, with detrimental results, as in the case of Winterveld.

Nonetheless, struggles in the bantustans are integral to the national struggle. Indeed, the latter is the sum of these many local conflicts and its strength lies in the type of organisation which underpins them.

Repression and control in the bantustans

The state's urban labour preference policy was designed to protect a supposedly more stable, affluent and privileged urban population. Job opportunities were offered primarily to 'qualified' urban dwellers, and unemployment was relocated to the bantustans. One study revealed that labour recruitment from the bantustans, as recorded by registrations of African workers, fell by 850 000 between 1975 and 1981.[5] Since then the number has declined still more steeply.

The allocation of jobs in the Pretoria region is an example of how the urban labour preference policy works to relocate unemployment. The border growth point of Rosslyn, some 25 km north-west of Pretoria on the South African side of the Bophuthatswana border, was established in the early 1970s to take advantage of cheap labour in Bophuthatswana. Following increased unrest in Pretoria's black townships of Mamelodi and Atteridgeville in 1985, the labour bureau in Rosslyn was closed. Workers from Bophuthatswana were unable to renew their annual contracts. Many were consequently dismissed and replaced by workers from Mamelodi and Atteridgeville recruited through the Pretoria labour bureau.

The state also actively increased relocation of 'illegals' to the bantustans. Influx control, contrary to official pronouncements, has intensified. In what many people naively interpreted as a gesture of conciliation, the state declared a moratorium on 'illegal' workers in the urban areas in 1979. Thousands of workers came forward and registered their employment contracts at the labour bureaux. At the end of the year most were refused contract renewals and forced out of the urban areas.

The 'reform' period also witnessed a heightening of forced 'black spot' removals into the bantustans, and the redefinition of bantustan borders to engulf many of the relocation areas or dumping grounds initially established on the South African side of borders. The current 'consolidation' of the Bophuthatswana border in the Marico and Moretele-Kwandebele regions is a particularly good illustration of this.

In the past the bantustans functioned primarily to reproduce a supply of cheap labour. Today their main function is to contain and control politically the rapidly increasing 'surplus' African population. The way such control is effected through bantustan structures is extremely complex and varies according to local and historical conditions. But there are a number of common mechanisms.

Security legislation, violence and intimidation

The bantustans, especially the 'independent' ones, introduced or were delegated security powers which often go beyond those of South Africa itself. The extent of these powers makes the introduction of a state of emergency in these areas unnecessary. Where there are legal safeguards against unbridled use of draconian powers, recourse to them is overridden by security legislation or brute intimidation.

The 'independent' bantustans have their own armies and police forces. The SADF and the South African police have free rein in the others. Where the state's forces are fettered by legal or other constraints, as in some non-independent bantustans, state-backed vigilantes are used to terrorise known and suspected opponents of the regime.

In most bantustan areas these forces maintain reigns of terror. They are usually permitted and encouraged to operate outside, or granted effective immunity from, the law. The state's support of such actions was well illustrated in Bophuthatswana in 1986. The police colonel who had ordered police to open fire on a public gathering in Winterveld, killing at least 11 people, was promoted before the token, publicly-rejected commission of enquiry into the shootings had even heard evidence of his role in the Winterveld massacre.

Intimidation, physical assaults and torture are now commonplace. In Bophuthatswana, for example, police have been using terrorist methods for several years now. These aim not only at suppressing opposition to the regime, but at deterring people from trying to exercise limited rights like defending themselves in court. Such action was demonstrated during the so-called 'squatter' trial of Bosplaas (Winterveld) residents which lasted from May 1984 to October 1985.

The effect of police intimidation in Bophuthatswana was also seen in the events leading up to and following the 1985 schools boycott. At the end of 1984 pupils began to boycott schools in Pretoria's black townships. The boycott continued into 1985 but did not spread to Bophuthatswana until July 1985.

In the first half of 1985, the Bophuthatswana police persistently intimidated and assaulted schoolchildren, accusing them of being 'comrades' and supportive of the Pretoria schools boycott. The police action, designed to deter Bophuthatswana children from emulating their peers in Pretoria, actually led to the spread of the boycott to the Garankuwa and Mabopane schools during the last two weeks in July and early August.

Police reacted to this boycott with more assaults. Pupils responded by forming the Garankuwa Youth Organisation (GYO) and trying to involve their parents in bringing pressure on the police. But parents failed to do much because of their own fear, largely a result of police brutality in the Winterveld area. Unchecked, the police were effectively out of control by the end of the year, beating, assaulting and torturing almost anyone they pleased. This indiscriminate brutality swelled the ranks of the GYO, making it appear larger and more organised than it was. Not until the end of January 1986, when the Metal and Allied Workers Union and the Catholic Church brought legal action against the Bophuthatswana authorities, exposing them to extensive publicity, did the beatings and torture ease.

Influx control and citizenship

South Africa claims to have abolished influx control. But other legislation concerning approved housing, employment, squatting and slum clearance will be deployed to control African entry into 'white' urban areas. Further, the influx of blacks to white areas has been, and will increasingly be effected by 'efflux control' imposed by the bantustans, especially 'independent' ones.

The abolition of influx control and restoration of citizenship legislation, in conjunction with the Aliens and Immigration Laws Amendment Act of 1984, will affect residents of 'independent' and non-independent bantustans differently. Residents of the latter bantustans may enter South Africa, though in practice their settlement will be governed by legislation concerning suitable accommodation and employment.

For citizens of the 'independent' bantustans the future is bleak. They make up about seven million of the total African population of 26 million. As 'foreigners', citizens of 'independent' bantustans can enter South Africa for 14 days. If they find work it must be approved by the Department of Manpower. Approval will only be given if no South Africans are available for the job. The contract of employment must be registered by an immigration officer of the Department of Home Affairs, then attested in the bantustan of residency. Few employers are likely to go to this trouble. This makes it almost impossible for citizens of these bantustans to obtain employment in South Africa.

Corruption

Systematic corruption in the bantustans is also a form of control. It has three distinct but interrelated forms. First is the large-scale embezzlement of public funds by bantustan political leaders and their accomplices. Much of this money, involving hundreds of millions of rands, finds its way into Swiss and other foreign bank accounts. The effect of such corruption is to deplete the budgets of various government departments, most notably in the fields of social security, health and public works, thus further impoverishing the bulk of the population.

A second kind of corruption is the result of the need to gain and maintain the political support of the petty bourgeoisie. This includes both 'traditional' tribal and community authorities and the many levels of the hierarchy of the ruling political party. This makes for an enlarged and more affluent petty bourgeoisie which is increasingly dependent on and necessarily supportive of the bantustan authorities.

A further manifestation of corruption is an extension of the second, and involves the maintenance of local administrative control, which is usually in the hands of tribal or community authorities.

Bantustan governments, dependent on the control of the populace maintained by local tribal or community authorities, turn a blind eye to members of these authorities enriching themselves at the expense of the local population. It is in fact recognised as a perquisite of the job. But corruption at central government, bureaucratic and party levels means that insufficient funds are available to maintain local-level control through tribal or community authority police and the local party machinery.

Local authorities are therefore encouraged to fund themselves. They do this by illegally levying numerous 'taxes', institutionalising bribes for work-seeker and other permits and by withholding and stealing social security payments. This 'self-funding' has led to resistance and opposition to the bantustan authorities by local populations.[6]

Such resistance requires intensified control and repression, usually by larger contingents of police drafted into the area. These in turn often have to be funded or provisioned at least in part by local funds, which requires more levies, bribes and theft. Most bantustan areas are now characterised by this vicious spiral of increased poverty and resentment, followed by more repression and greater extortion. The system is maintained, at least for the moment, by the other forms of control outlined above: physical violence and intimidation, the denial of legal rights and employment, withholding of social security, eviction and seizure of land.

Agricultural and industrial exploitation

Part of the positive picture of reform painted by both the South African government and business is that economic development in the form of industrial and agricultural 'development' has accelerated rapidly in the bantustans during the last few years.

Industrial decentralisation, a massive drain on state revenue, has created relatively few jobs. And most of these are characterised by very low wages, poor safety and health conditions and prohibitions on trade union organisation. There are a host of illegal practices involving false pension and tax deductions, non-payment of overtime, sexual harassment and denial of access to doctors of choice. Nearly all workers who experience such abuses clearly understand them and the system which makes them possible. They are a major cause of the increasing resistance to the bantustan system.

The situation in the agricultural sector is worse. In 1977 the Promotion of Economic Development of Bantu Homelands Act of 1968 was amended to remove all restrictions on the flow of capital into bantustan agriculture. As a result several millions of rands have been invested in commercial agriculture. This has had disastrous effects on local populations, as tens of thousands of peasants and subsistence producers have been dispossessed of their land. This process of land dispossession will almost certainly accelerate following the SA Development Trust's handing over of 4,5-million hectares of land to the governments of the six 'non-independent' bantustans at the end of 1986. These bantustan administrations are now empowered to use and allocate this land as they see fit. (For details of this, see the article by Keenan and Sarakinsky in section six of this *South African Review*). The transformation of bantustan agriculture is leading to the rapid elimination of the remains of an already impoverished peasant or tribal agricultural base. The process has been widely resisted, to the point where much commercial agricultural production in bantustans is protected by the military. Several of the cotton and citrus schemes in Lebowa, for example, are protected by SADF and/or SAP contingents. And at Champagne, also in Lebowa, three casspirs have been stationed at the project since May 1986.

Poverty

Relative and absolute poverty in the bantustans have increased dramatically over the last few years. Reasons for this are the overall decline of average African incomes since 1976, both individual and household; the urban labour preference policy and relocation of unemployment to the bantustans; denial of access to employment opportunities outside the bantustans in conjunction with high unemployment and low pay in the bantustans; extreme labour abuse and exploitation; the collapse of social security and health services; loss of land and consequent decline in agricultural subsistence income; and widespread corruption and extortion.

The effect of increasing poverty on political consciousness is difficult to assess. Most sections of bantustan populations are acutely aware of their greater poverty, understand the reasons for it, and are consequently more resentful of and opposed to the apartheid system that created and is exacerbating it.

But there is some truth in the adage that one cannot revolt on an empty stomach. Awareness of the causes of bantustan poverty can hinder the development of political organisation. In the Winterveld area, for example, many workers employed in the Bophuthatswana factories at Garankuwa, Babelegi, and across the border in Rosslyn and elsewhere, deliberately isolate themselves from worker and community organisations for fear that involvement will lead to their dismissal and the exposure of their families not just to hardship but to the real risk of death.

There is evidence that the development of political organisation and overt resistance is most muted in areas like Winterveld where survival is most precarious and where there has been a relatively long tradition and experience of poverty, social cleavage and excessive repression and control.

The Mapulaneng district in Lebowa

The most significant bantustan popular struggle in 1986 was certainly the resistance to Kwandebele 'independence'.[7] While this received national and international media coverage, the struggle of the people of Mapulaneng, where an estimated 60 people have been killed since the beginning of 1986, was never mentioned in the press and is almost unheard of in South Africa.

Mapulaneng is geographically separate from other parts of Lebowa. It is situated in the Lowveld where it shares a common border with the Mhala district of Gazankulu. The Mapulaneng magistrate's office is in Bushbuckridge.

Since March 1986 Mapulaneng has experienced widespread violence. The area is heavily patrolled by the SADF, police and state-backed vigilantes. The entire executive of the Mapulaneng Crisis Committee (MCC), which was formed by the people of the most affected communities, was detained and charged with terrorism.[8] The formation of the MCC had the direct blessing of Lebowa Chief Minister Phatudi and his Minister of Law and Order, and was specifically aimed at putting an end to the violence.

What lies behind this violence and the charges against the MCC? In the last few years the Mapulaneng region was subjected to several instances of land dispossession in favour of commercial agriculture as outlined above. Both the state, in the form of the Lebowa Department of Agriculture, and a private company, Measured Farming, were involved.

In the Dingleydale community in the area, the threat of further land take-over by Measured Farming stimulated wider organisation of the community's 'planning committee'. Its primary objective was to prevent the community's remaining productive land being taken over. The committee instructed lawyers and achieved some success. This increased the political awareness of people in adjoining communities and showed the effectiveness of organisation.

Although this land issue was not directly related to the violent events of 1986 it played a significant part in the politicisation of the area and in increasing the general resistance of communities both to the state and the agricultural company concerned. It also provided valuable experience in methods and benefits of organisation.

Violence began in March 1986. On 17 March a group of students gathered outside the bottle store of a certain Morema, chairman of the Shatale Town Council, and asked him for the third time to leave the township. Morema came out of his bottle store with a handgun and shot a student. In the ensuing fight he was killed and thrown into his bottle store, which was set alight. The houses of another five people who had heeded the students' requests to leave the township were then burnt down. In the aftermath of this incident police took about 30 children at random into detention. At least one of those detained and beaten by police was in Johannesburg at the time of the incident. Two teachers and two members of the Housewives' League were also detained.

Why did the students ask Morema and the five others to leave the township?

In the previous six months 14 residents from Shatale had mysteriously disappeared. Evidence pointed to a gang of six who were selling parts of human bodies to 'witchdoctors'. The increase in unemployment, poverty and general insecurity had caused more people to consult 'witchdoctors', leading to an increase in demand for human body parts that were an important ingredient in the medications of some 'witchdoctors'. This demand appears to have been met by this gang of six. The ringleader, Morema, was eventually arrested in early 1986. Several parts of human bodies were found in his refrigerator and taken to the police station at Bushbuckridge. Most of the township's students saw this as conclusive proof of Morema's involvement in the murder of the 14 missing people. Nevertheless, the prosecutor did not send the docket to the attorney general and Morema was released without charges being laid.

The children of Shatale, believing that Morema, the police and the prosecutor were in collaboration, decided to take the law into their own hands. They saw this as self-defence against further murders, and asked Morema and his accomplices to leave the area.

Children and teachers taken into detention after Morema's death claim to have been methodically sjambokked by the police until they passed out. At least five of the women claim they were raped by police. Members of Morema's family joined the police in assaulting the detained children. They have since been armed by the police and form the nucleus of a police-backed vigilante group which beats up and arrests any 'subversive' elements they find on the streets.

As a result of this police brutality and the emergence of vigilantes, the people of Shatale formed a crisis committee. Another branch of this committee was formed at Green Valley a few kilometres to the north of Shatale, where similar violence had broken out. Within a few weeks of the outbreak of violence at Shatale, each community had elected ten members who formed a committee of 20 - the Mapulaneng Crisis Committee. The elections were held in the presence of the member of the Lebowa legislative assembly for the area after he had asked the Lebowa minister of law and order what to do to put an end to the violence. The minister himself, having conferred with Chief Minister Phatudi, suggested the formation of a crisis committee and gave his permission for its election.

The MCC started by raising funds for a lawyer to bring a case against the police. It acted as a mediator between students and authorities in educational and other disputes, with the intention of restoring 'peace and normality' to the area. It had considerable success, at least for a short period. For example, when a bakery in Shatale was robbed, the owner, having no confidence in the police, turned to the MCC for assistance. The MCC requested the students to help in apprehending the thieves. The thieves were caught and handed over to the police.

In April students of Pilgrim's Rest, some 50 km away, who called themselves 'comrades', decided to remove their corrupt chief. He was embezzling money collected by the community for the school building, imposing an additional R10 tax to pay for his bodyguards, imposing excessive fines in the tribal court, accepting bribes, and working in close collaboration with the police. Student rallies in the area were dispersed by police teargas. The MCC intervened in the conflict. The students were organised into a branch of the MCC; the chief withdrew his bodyguards as there was no further need for them, and co-operated fully with the MCC.

The MCC was not able to stop so-called 'witch' killings. At Green Valley, for example, gangs consisting mainly of unemployed youths engaged in a spate of 'witch' killings. Many appear to have been politically motivated. Most suspects, like the Morema family at Shatale, were seen to be in collaboration with the authorities, or were traders or businessmen dependent on and hence supportive of the bantustan system. As a result the youth saw 'witches' and those people associated with them not just as evil but as political criminals. Many witch killings were justified as attempts to clean up criminal elements while ridding the area of government and police collaborators. At the same time, however, it provided an opportunity for hoodlum elements to loot and rob traders and others at will. At least 40 people labelled as 'witches' have been killed by these youth gangs.

The MCC attempted to stop these 'witch' killings. The committee's intervention in Green Valley reduced the number of killings but did not stop them. Similarly, at Marite about 15 km from Sabie, the MCC was unable to prevent two shopowners from being attacked and their shops burnt. The shopowners were suspected of involvement in child murders and the sale of body parts. It appears that the MCC and the students had little or no influence over the gangs of youths who were roaming the area.

Police did not seem eager to discourage these gangs. They certainly have been unable or unwilling to apprehend them. For example, one gang raped a young woman from Shatale. As police took no action the youths of Shatale took the law into their own hands. They pursued the gang onto a farm called Champagne where they caught one of its members. They interrogated this man as to the whereabouts of the remainder of the gang before handing him over to the police. They then burnt a butchery which belonged to the gang's leader. Police released the rapist without any charges being laid, but detained 168 of the Shatale students. One hundred of them, who were under 18 years of age, were flogged and released while the remainder were held for several weeks without bail before being given long jail sentences for public violence.

The MCC and the students came to represent a major threat to the state. The MCC is the democratically elected, responsible and legitimate leadership of the area and as such is the antithesis of the apartheid state. Such organisation and leadership rapidly undermine bantustan structures of control and must be neutralised and disorganised. The youth, especially when organised as in Mapulaneng, presents a similar threat. Not only is it politicised and conversant with the symbols, rhetoric and issues of the national struggle, but it acquires legitimacy by helping the community to clean up crime when the police fail. It was therefore convenient for the state to encourage and tolerate the presence of 'hoodlum' gangs, giving police reason to arrest and detain students - the 'comrades'.

Mapulaneng is now heavily patrolled by both the police and the SADF. Residents are arbitrarily arrested and tortured, and witnesses claim that at least two children have been shot by the security forces. Some also allege that the SADF has damaged and stolen property. The police and army presence has generated further hostility and resistance to the state, and increased support for the MCC and other organisations subsequently formed in the region.

The state reacted by detaining nine of the MCC in July 1986, including the entire executive and the two members of parliament for the area. They were subsequently charged with 'terrorism', but acquitted in mid-June 1987.

As a grassroots organisation the MCC is a threat to the state. No national organisation was involved in it, despite the state's claims of a conspiracy. Indeed, its members told 'comrades' who came into the area from the Reef at the beginning of 1986 that they did not want outside interference, and did not need to be told how to run their affairs as outsiders from Johannesburg would not understand the local problems. A reason some members gave for not having affiliated to the UDF or any other national organisation, even though they were broadly supportive of them, was that they feared being 'taken over' and losing control of their organisation and its affairs.

Bophuthatswana

The failure of 'outside' political organisations to understand specifically local problems and experiences led to a negative reaction by many Winterveld residents against national or external political organisations after the March 1986 Winterveld shootings.

The background to the 26 March shootings was touched on earlier. Notwithstanding claims to the contrary, there was little or no effective political or other organisation in the Odi-Moretele (Winterveld) districts of Bophuthatswana prior to the formation of the Garankuwa Youth Organisation (GYO) in 1985. The GYO was set up in response to the schools boycott and police action against pupils. Its membership was local and small, and organisational structures were scarcely developed. But as police intensified arbitrary and brutal assaults on young people and others, nearly all the youth in the Garankuwa area joined the GYO. Older people, too, were alienated from Mangope's regime by police brutality.

Police violence escalated further from November 1986 through the Christmas period in reaction to the consumer boycott. This was linked to the dismissal of some 1 000 Metal Box workers from the Rosslyn plant in November. Most of the dismissed workers were residents of Bophuthatswana. Their dismissal followed a strike which many Bophuthatswana residents and unionists felt had been very badly handled by the South African Allied Workers Union, an affiliate of the UDF. Nevertheless, the strike and subsequent dismissals gave the UDF a presence in the Garankuwa and Mabopane areas and a means of generating wider support in the area. The Metal Box issue and the UDF presence stimulated further unrest in the area over the November-January period.

Metal Box products like beer and soft drink cans are easily identifiable and boycotted. Moreover, the transport system between Bophuthatswana and Pretoria was easily monitored by those implementing the boycott, at Bel Ombre and Pretoria Central stations, the Pretoria bus depot, taxi ranks and the Shoshanguve entry to Bophuthatswana. The Congress of South African Students (COSAS) and other UDF affiliates were active in trying to organise and control the boycott.

But the boycott did not succeed in Bophuthatswana. The reasons for it were not clearly explained to the residents. Further, the Bophuthatswana police, able to get away with far greater atrocities than their South African counterparts, could hold political organisation in Bophuthatswana in check. And police brutality, in conjunction with most Bophuthatswana shopkeepers' support for Mangope, meant that many store owners were willing to break the boycott.

Finally, UDF affiliates, namely COSAS, the Shoshanguve Civic

Association and Youth Congress, as well as many who claimed to belong to these organisations, demanded money from Bophuthatswana residents as they passed through Shoshanguve to pay for the establishment of public parks, trails and other facilities. But they did not properly explain the reasons for these contributions. Buses and taxis were stopped, with people often forced to pay a minimum of fifty cents. This was a fundamental political mistake. It led to many Bophuthatswana residents seeing the UDF not as a liberator but as a further problem in their already difficult lives.

The legal action brought by MAWU and the Catholic Church against the Bophuthatswana police and Mangope in January 1986, along with the consequent media focus on the Bophuthatswana police, forced the police to limit their brutalities. As the violence subsided and things returned to some semblance of normality in February and early March 1986, membership of the GYO quickly dissipated. The public gathering in Winterveld on 26 March, when the police opened fire on the crowd, marked the end of this phase of political activity in Winterveld.

In the aftermath of the police shootings, Wintervelders looked back critically on the events of the preceding months. There was criticism of the UDF and its affiliates. Some argued that the political organisers entering the area from Pretoria had not understood the particular problems of Winterveld on which organisation should have been built. Many now see the organisers' mistake as trying to link the struggles of Winterveld and Bophuthatswana residents to national issues, rather than building organisations on the specific problems facing people in the area.

The outside political organisers can quite legitimately argue that their mistakes and the temporary failure of resistance to develop further in the Winterveld area are attributable to the intensity of police brutality and the intimidation of people living in the area. But the fact that people in Winterveld have been able to reflect analytically on such tragic events so soon after their occurrence is a positive indication for future political organisation in the area.

Bophuthatswana: the space for contestation

The fact that reform policies have opened up new spaces for contestation is nowhere better evidenced in the bantustans than by Bophuthatswana.

The ideology of Bophuthatswana - its Bill of Rights, justice, economic prosperity and freedom from apartheid - is crumbling as the reality becomes apparent: police atrocities, jungle justice, massive corruption, a myriad of foreign exchange and related frauds, and now insolvency.

Control in Bophuthatswana was based on this ideology, the support of a relatively large and affluent petty bourgeoisie (at least in comparison to South Africa), and the ability of the ruling clique to grease palms at various levels of political authority and control.

The governments of Bophuthatswana and South Africa are now on the horns of a dilemma. At the end of 1987 Bophuthatswana, in accordance with its constitution, has to hold elections. Although Mangope has repeatedly professed his desire for a healthy and democratic opposition, his ruling party had to rig the last elections held in 1982. According to government officials, this was done by distributing the votes cast by Tswanas living in South Africa among constituencies which were opposition strongholds. The minister responsible for organising these elections, Amos Gomongwe, subsequently died. The attorney general resigned shortly before the elections, saying to his former colleagues that he was 'not prepared to go along with arrangements for the elections'. As it is now common knowledge in Bophuthatswana that the last elections were rigged, it will be more difficult to repeat the performance next year.

It is necessary for Mangope to ensure that not a single opposition member of parliament is elected. Such a person could legally demand and possibly obtain access to state records and documents that would reveal the scale of corruption and embezzlement of public funds.

In the first half of 1987 the South African government refused to grant and renew a number of loans to Bophuthatswana. Bophuthatswana's insolvency was publicly confirmed in August 1986 when the Standard Bank of Bophuthatswana refused to honour government salary cheques. Salaries were paid only after negotiations with the South African government. These appear to have been a continuation of earlier talks between South Africa and Bophuthatswana, when Pretoria agreed to bail Bophuthatswana out on condition that it reclaimed control of its Department of Finance and Treasury. The 60% increase in South Africa's foreign affairs

budget, announced by Finance Minister Barend du Plessis on 3
June 1987, was largely accounted for by South Africa's financial
rescue operation in Bophuthatswana.

Bophuthatswana's parlous financial state, the consequence of
corruption and financial mismanagement, has dire political implications. Members of the civil service have become increasingly
disillusioned. A growing number can no longer be counted on to
support the government. The same is true of other elements of the
petty bourgeoisie. Funds are no longer as readily available to
grease the party machinery and allow the continued expansion and
relative affluence of the commercial petty bourgeoisie. In many
parts of Bophuthatswana alliances are forming between elements
of the working class, what is left of the peasantry and elements of
the petty bourgeoisie.

In one community, for example, many tribal councillors supported a tyrannical, corrupt chief and were responsible for and
beneficiaries of the seizure and reallocation of tribal land. They are
now realigning themselves with the people in the community,
legitimising their volte-face by saying that the community's ances-
tors are unhappy about what has happened and will not bring rain
until the land is returned to the people.

Bophuthatswana's (and Pretoria's) dilemma is only beginning.
Hitherto the 1,5-million non-Tswanas in Bophuthatswana have
been kept under control by being denied citizenship, reduced to
the status of 'illegals' and consequently denied legal access to the
labour market. Under the 'reform' legislation which restores South
African citizenship, though, the position of Tswanas and non-
Tswanas in Bophuthatswana will be reversed. South Africans living
in a foreign country, which includes non-Tswanas in
Bophuthatswana, can register their South African citizenship in the
nearest South African magisterial district to the border of that
country.

As a result non-Tswanas, currently denied access to the labour
market because of their 'illegal' status, will now be free to move
and seek work in South Africa. Tswanas, on the other hand, will
find it almost impossible to get work in South Africa under the new
legislation, and could find themselves sinking into the impoverishment now experienced by most non-Tswanas. The latter will not
need reminding that it was Mangope personally who decided that
Bophuthatswana should take 'independence'. Mangope has already

threatened that non-Tswanas who come into Bophuthatswana with South African documents will be evicted within 24 hours and will forfeit their property. Whether he can legally do this is debatable.

When non-Tswanas begin to realise their new-found rights they will be in a much more powerful political position. They will also realise that Mangope's threats of eviction are hollow. South Africa will certainly not tolerate over one million impoverished blacks being shunted over its border, especially when that border is close to the outskirts of Pretoria. Indeed, one obvious condition for bailing Mangope out of his present financial mess is that he does not implement his threat to evict non-Tswanas from Bophuthatswana.

Potential class realignments

Though South Africa will in all probability continue to prop up the economically unviable bantustan regimes, their state of economic crisis is precipitating and intensifying their political crises.

In Bophuthatswana, economic crisis has done much to open up political divisions and intensify political strains. An active realignment of class forces and interests is taking place. This is generating a more unified extra-parliamentary popular opposition to the current regime and the fundamental structure of the apartheid state. But it is dangerous to generalise from the Bophuthatswana case to all other bantustans. Bophuthatswana provides one instance of the political crises which are developing within the bantustans; the feuding between the ruling elites of Ciskei and Transkei is another manifestation of this process.

It is premature to predict the form and direction that these class realignments will take. But the alliances between disparate and formerly opposed class interests, as evidenced in the examples of Bophuthatswana and Mapulaneng, suggest that the political implications of current bantustan resistance for the national struggle should not be ignored or underestimated.

Notes

1   This paper was first presented at the Review of African Political Economy conference on 'Popular Struggle in Africa', Liverpool University, England, September 1986. This article is a substantially shortened version of the original paper, which has been rewritten and published in *Popular Struggles in South Africa*, James Curry, London, in press.

2   H Wolpe, 'Strategic Issues in the Struggle for National Liberation in South

Africa', mimeo, 1983, 2.

3   The comments in the first part of this paper are applicable to the other bantustans. However, the nature of the struggle in these territories can only be fully understood within their specific local and historical contexts.

4   This sort of explanation is not limited to what is happening in the bantustans. It is being used by the state in its attempts to 'explain away' and obscure the reality of all acts of resistance to it, no matter where or under what circumstances they may have arisen. A prime example of this is the current Delmas treason trial.

5   Marian Lacey, 'Feudalism in the Age of Computers', Black Sash Annual General Congress, 1983.

6   See Jeremy Keenan, 'Pandora's Box: The Private Accounts of a Bantustan Local Authority', *South African Review 3*, Johannesburg, 1986.

7   See Transvaal Rural Action Committee, *Kwandebele - The Struggle Against Independence*, Johannesburg, 1986.

8   They were initially held on unspecified charges which included treason, murder, attempted murder and arson, and finally charged with terrorism. In mid-June 1987 they were found not guilty and discharged.

Section 2:
States of Emergency

Introduction

Glenn Moss

The national state of emergency, proclaimed by State President PW Botha on 12 June 1986, was renewed on expiry for a further year. Major features of emergency rule have included:

* massive detentions;
* increasing curbs on reporting of both repression and resistance;
* brave, but ultimately very limited, attempts to challenge emergency rule through the courts;
* an ever-narrowing legal space for political opposition and the media.

As both David Webster and Amanda Armstrong point out in this section of the *South African Review*, emergency regulations built on a long tradition of already-existing repressive legislation. Provision for interrogative and preventive detention has existed in South African law since 1963. The media has been restrained in its reporting by a myriad of legislative restrictions contained in over a hundred statutes. Some of these made it difficult and dangerous to report accurately on the overtly repressive institutions of South African society, such as prisons, and activities of the police and defence force.

Yet by July 1985, when a partial state of emergency was imposed, government believed its daunting arsenal of repressive and controlling legislation was inadequate to deal with the growing challenge to its rule. Popular organisation and protest - particularly around schools, rents and consumer boycotts - had rendered a number of townships 'ungovernable', and government's attempt to impose black local authorities on African townships lay in tatters.

Eight months later, in March 1986, the partial state of emergency was lifted. David Webster calculates that almost 8 000 people were detained in this period, of whom 80% belonged to organisations affiliated to the United Democratic Front.

During and after the partial emergency, opposition tactics began changing. The development of alternative organs of power - particularly civic organisations, street committees and people's courts - became the focus of energy for many township activists.

This set the context for the reimposition of emergency rule in June 1986. The protest and popular resistance of the first half of the 1980s had developed into more challenging, if embryonic, organs of local power.

Government aimed to crush these developments through national emergency rule, while at the same time removing repression and resistance from public and media scrutiny. The four articles which make up this section of the *Review* detail elements of emergency regulations, the way repression has operated, and attempts to challenge emergency restrictions through court action.

David Webster's detailed analysis of emergency repression provides a comprehensive breakdown of detention trends, targets of emergency action, use of the courts, and bannings. These dynamics, including growing 'informal' repression involving vigilantes, are explored in Glenda Kruss's case study of the Western Cape under emergency rule. Kruss also demonstrates the different effects of the emergency on African townships, small towns and rural areas, and the coloured townships of the Western Cape.

A key question raised, but not answered in this section, involves the emergency's impact on organisation. Mass detentions and arrests, police and army raids, and the removal of different levels of leadership have obviously weakened the township structures which developed during and after the 1985-86 emergency period. However, the extent to which new forms of organisation such as street committees have been able to survive state attacks is not clear.

In many of the Eastern Cape communities which provided the cradle for the development of new structures of 'people's power', repression was most intense. In some townships, almost every person who had any involvement with street committees was detained. In Duncan Village (East London), for example, 256 street committee office-bearers were detained in June 1986. Almost a year later all but 19 remained behind bars.

In general, repression has been most intense in those townships where opposition political structures were most developed. In cases such as Alexandra (Johannesburg) and Duncan Village, the state has started upgrading projects after smashing popular structures of power.

Inevitably, the emergency is not only about attacking opposition. It also involves the promotion of interests more sympathetic to state initiatives. Thus, for example, the Inkatha-linked United Workers Union of South Africa (UWUSA) benefited when most leading COSATU trade unionists in Northern Natal were detained. This created more space for UWUSA's operations in that area.

In much the same way, government's upgrading programme in Duncan Village, which followed severe repression of the UDF-affiliated Duncan Village Residents' Association, aimed to create a basis of legitimacy for the state-sanctioned black local authority.

The most visible challenges to emergency rule have been fought out through the law courts. Nicholas Haysom and Steven Kahanovitz analyse the most important of these cases. But as they correctly point out, legal processes take place alongside and in response to much larger battles. Legal challenges to the emergency have limited, to some extent, the level of official terror which the emergency aims to allow. But in many cases technical challenges to the state have been met by a tightening up and more efficient drafting of emergency regulations.

This theme is taken up by Amanda Armstrong, who argues that legal challenges to media restrictions can be double-edged. Publication of material and information as a result of successful court applications is a victory for those resisting media control by the state. But these challenges have sometimes resulted in amendments to regulations and police orders involving harsher and more sophisticated forms of control.

As this *Review* is published, South Africa is well into its second year of a national state of emergency. Repression has obviously weakened organisation, although workers organised into trade unions have survived the onslaught thus far, and won some remarkable victories in a climate of repression and recession. But as David Webster argues, the emergency has not involved a successful policy of containment for the state. Any 'success' has been achieved at the cost of enormous repression, especially in the form of army and police street patrols. And its price has been the massive alienation of millions of township residents.

Repression and the State of Emergency

David Webster

South Africa's first state of emergency was declared in March 1960. In the following three months police detained 1 500 people and arrested 10 000 more, mainly on charges relating to acts of defiance and pass offences. Subsequently government banned the African National Congress and Pan-Africanist Congress.

In 1963 government empowered the police to detain people without trial for purposes of interrogation. In the years which followed, parliament granted greater arbitrary powers to the police, culminating in the Internal Security Act of 1982. Figures are not readily available, but at least 16 000 people were detained in the 22 years after the introduction of detention-without-trial.

During this period South Africa earned its place in the rogues' gallery of repression. While regimes in countries like Argentina and Chile went in for spectacular abuses of human rights, they lacked the stamina and steady concentration of South Africa's security police.

By 1985, the nature and tactics of repression in South Africa were ready for change. Two years earlier the United Democratic Front had been formed. Its affiliate organisations mushroomed across the country and soon became the major focus of security police activity. Popular organisation and protest, especially in schools, began to challenge many aspects of government policy.

Despite the powerful array of repressive laws already at its disposal, government imposed a state of emergency in July 1985 in an attempt to crush internal opposition to apartheid.[1] This emergency was partial, initially covering only 36 magisterial districts mainly in the Witwatersrand and Eastern Cape. It was later extended to the Western Cape. After eight months government lifted the emergency in March 1986; almost 8 000 people had been detained and over 22 000 charged with various offences, mainly public violence.

In the three months after the 1985 emergency was lifted, it became clear that emergency rule had failed in its goal of crushing popular opposition. While most progressive organisations were adversely affected by the first emergency, the Detainees' Parents Support Committee (DPSC) calculated that 84% of those detained belonged to organisations affiliated to the UDF. Repression forced opposition bodies to adopt new tactics; the politics of street committees became the focus of energy for activists.

Three months passed, during which organisations regrouped and political activity gained momentum. Republic Day on 31 May 1986 saw a presidential amnesty: a six-month reduction in sentence for all prisoners except those convicted of political offences. Bewildered but gratified convicts were released in their thousands from the overflowing jails. The vast majority released were black petty offenders with convictions for pass law offences.

With space available in the prisons, the state president informed the nation on 12 June that he was pre-empting a major insurrection by declaring another state of emergency. Minister of Law and Order Louis le Grange had tried to rush legislation through parliament giving police the equivalent of emergency powers which could be invoked locally or regionally. But a campaign to block Le Grange's bill delayed its passage.

The new emergency showed signs of lengthy and careful planning. On the night before it was declared, security forces swept through black communities detaining thousands. By June 1987, over 26 000 people had been detained. In eight months of this emergency, security police detained as many people as the total held under previous emergencies and security legislation for the past 26 years. Internationally, South Africa is now second to none on an index of repression.

Three phases of repression

Three significantly different phases characterised 1986. The first, from the beginning of January to 7 March, saw the 1985 emergency tail off. During this period, police detained 631 people at a rate of about ten a day. This was considerably fewer than during the first five months of the 1985 emergency, when 7 367 people were held at a rate of 46 per day.

The second phase covered the three-month period between emergencies, during which detentions and harassment increased. The main tool used was the Internal Security Act. The final phase began in June with the declaration of the present state of emergency.

The end of the 1985 emergency

The lifting of the 1985 emergency is somewhat puzzling. Various government officials claimed that it had succeeded and an acceptable level of 'normality' was restored to the townships. More probably, international pressure on government had reached an intolerable level and internal disquiet over the emergency was becoming a political burden. When the emergency was lifted the majority of those still in detention - mostly UDF leaders - had been held for the full eight months.

Most observers agreed that while opposition organisations had been severely hit by the emergency, they had survived. Some had learnt new tactics which were to stand them in good stead. Many civic associations, which before the emergency had large memberships on paper, had been forced to take up grassroots issues and forms of organisation; street committees became a reality, and persisted as a form of organisation.

The August 1985 banning of the Congress of South African Students (COSAS) was, however, a severe blow. COSAS was the largest mass-based affiliate of the UDF and maintained strong representation and discipline in the schools. It took some time for students to regroup, and an appeal against the COSAS banning failed in October 1986. After a brief hiatus, students began to organise themselves into town or regional congresses, with the long-term goal of forming a national body.

Phase two: business as usual

The second phase began on 7 March, when the emergency was lifted. This resulted in the mass release of detainees, but by no means ended repression. Instead of emergency powers, security police used the marginally weaker Internal Security Act. They continued to detain activists and harass organisations at a faster tempo than in the latter part of the emergency. When the emergency was lifted, there was a sudden leap in the number of those detained under section 50 of the Internal Security Act.

Section 50 bears some resemblance to emergency provisions. It is primarily a preventive detention clause, though there are many reports of interrogation and abuse of detainees held under its provisions. It empowers a low-ranking officer to detain a person for 14 days. The usual pattern is for the detainee to be held for less than the fortnight specified, then released. A significant number, however, are held for the full term, then further detained under a different provision, usually section 29.

The spectacular scale of the two emergencies tends to obscure the fact that the Internal Security Act was used throughout 1986. Indeed, the number of such detentions for the year, 3 989,[2] is almost twice the previous highest total - 2 440 in 1985 - and four times that of 1984, the next highest.

Le Grange's successor, Law and Order Minister Adriaan Vlok, revealed that 3 512 people were held under section 50 up to the June 1986 emergency. In those five-and-a-half months, an average of 639 were detained each month. Section 50 was used during the earlier emergency in non-emergency areas, but the vast majority detained under its provisions were held in the three months between emergencies. The minister reported that section 50 was not used after 12 June 1986.

The most notorious security provision is section 29 of the Internal Security Act. It empowers security police to hold a person indefinitely, specifically for purposes of interrogation. Detainees are kept in solitary confinement, and it is from those detained under this section that the vast majority of allegations of torture and abuse come. Unlike section 50, which was not used during the 1986-87 emergency, section 29 was used throughout the year. Under its provisions, 390 people were held.

Recently a pattern has emerged: police detain under section 29 if they believe they have a potential case against detainees. This is indicated by a much higher prosecution rate against detainees thus held - 104 cases, or 27%, compared with 159 prosecutions, or 5%, of section 50 detainees (*Cit*, 21.02.87).

The Internal Security Act has two other sections which empower detention. In 1986 police invoked section 28, a form of preventive detention, eight times. Detainees thus held generally serve long terms, ranging in 1986 from five to eight-and-a-half months (*Star*, 23.02.87), though all were first detained in 1985. The section is used to remove important leaders from their communities, as was done in earlier times to Matthew Goniwe, Fort Calata and other Eastern Cape leaders who were later assassinated.

Finally, section 31 empowers detention, not at the behest of the security police but of the attorney general. This is used to hold potential state witnesses incommunicado, and was invoked 79 times in 1986. It is a particularly controversial aspect of the law, and is shrouded in secrecy.

Table 1:

Internal Security Act sections used for detentions, 1985-1986

	1985		1986	
	No	%	No	%
Section 28	8	-	8	-
Section 29	406	17	390	10
Section 31	25	1	79	2
Section 50	1 924	82	3 512	88
	2 363	100	3 989	100

As the three-month period between emergencies drew to a close, the state cynically used the Internal Security Act to introduce the 1986 emergency. In 1985 the state president announced the emergency before it was implemented. Warned, many activists went into hiding and escaped the subsequent swoop. This time, more than a thousand activists were detained under section 50 of the Internal Security Act the day before the emergency was declared. Once held, they were switched to detention under emergency regulations the following day.[3] Nevertheless, a large number of activists had anticipated the new wave of repression and already gone into hiding.

A number of trends emerged in the use of the Internal Security Act throughout 1986. Some are familiar - for example, repression was greatest in the Transvaal and Eastern Cape, reflecting the fact that they are the areas where political organisation and mobilisation are strongest. Table 2 shows the geographical distribution of detentions under the Internal Security Act. The largest category is 'place unknown' - statistics gleaned from parliamentary questions, with the minister reluctant to disclose details. The figure includes those kidnapped from neighbouring countries.

Table 2:

Geographical distribution of Internal Security Act detentions

	1985		1986	
	No	%	No	%
Transvaal	262	36	323	42
Natal	100	14	104	13
Western Cape	197	27	66	9
Eastern Cape	75	10	256	33
Northern Cape	43	6	6	1
OFS	49	7	14	2
Known place				
of detention	726	100	769	100
Unknown	1 714		3 220	
	2 440	100	3 989	100

The categories of people police choose as targets of repression are revealing. The more politically active and effective a group, the more its members attract security police attention and become victims of detention. The numbers of people detained therefore serve as an index of political organisation. Table 3 breaks such figures down into five major categories of security police targets. The first two need further explanation: 'scholars and students' refers largely to school children and in fact this category is mainly made up of militant members of student organisations like COSAS, the various student congresses and the Azanian Students Movement (AZASM). 'Community and political workers' refers to members of civic associations and political groups such as the UDF, the Azanian Peoples Organisation (AZAPO) and the Cape Action League (CAL). The majority in this category are young people, generally members of youth congresses.

Table 3:

Known targets of Internal Security Act detention

	1985 %	1986 %
Scholars, students and teachers	27	30
Community and political workers	28	21
Trade unionists and workers	3	4
Clergy and church workers	1	3
Journalists	2	1
Other or unspecified	39	41

Both Le Grange and Vlok, as successive ministers of law and order, defended high levels of detention by claiming that many detainees had committed crimes and were a threat to the state. If this were so, one would expect detentions to be followed by a series of trials with high conviction rates. The emptiness of these claims, however, is shown in Table 4, which analyses the fate of detainees held under Internal Security Act provisions. The statistics are drawn from the ministers' own answers to questions in parliament and from DPSC records. Some 95% of those held under section 50 were not charged, and those who were had only a 14% conviction rate. Even the notorious section 29 produced only 104 charges, with a conviction rate of 27%. For all detainees, the chance of being put on trial is only 7% and the chance of conviction in court a derisory 1%.

Table 4:

Fate of known Internal Security Act detainees in 1986

	Detained	Charged		Convicted		Acquitted		Released without charge	
		No	%	No	%	No	%	No	%
Section 28	8	-	-	-	-	-	-	8	100
Section 29	390	104	27	-	-	-	-	286	73
Section 31	79	-	-	-	-	-	-	79	100
Section 50	3 512	159	5	37	14	226	86	3 353	95

The three months between the emergencies did, however, provide organisations with breathing space and time to regain emotional energy. Street committees gained new momentum, people's courts began to emerge, and although many schools were on boycott, student organisation grew. Above all, youth organisations and congresses flourished. Their birth stems from a COSAS decision in 1982 to form organisations for youth who were out of school and often unemployed. Members of these youth organisations, with little to lose and fired with the enthusiasm and idealism of the young, soon emerged as the vanguard of struggle in the townships. Their militancy was to exact a heavy price - in the emergency to follow, they were to be the main target of repression.

The turn of the screw: the 1986-87 emergency

Remarkably, in a year which saw Internal Security Act detentions reach double the previous high, four times higher than the norm, a second emergency was declared. In the short space of 12 months, security forces detained a further 26 000 people.

The declaration of the new emergency on 12 June 1986 took very few by surprise. The prologue consisted of increasingly desperate attempts by government to force through Le Grange's proposed Public Safety Amendment Act of 1986. These were temporarily thwarted by a concerted extra-parliamentary campaign led by the DPSC, UDF and opposition in the tricameral parliament. As the key date of 16 June approached, it was clear that government was determined to act before then. Activists, anticipating a clampdown, went into hiding some time before the anniversary. When massive raids were carried out on 11 June, most leaders escaped the dragnet.

The decision to impose the new emergency was no sudden whim. The raids showed evidence of extensive, detailed planning. It soon became clear that the police were working from lists. They had learnt the lesson of the previous emergency, and gave no prior warning - hundreds were detained under section 50 of the Internal Security Act the day before the state president officially declared the emergency.

At first, confusion reigned among organisations and monitoring groups. There was a strict clamp on news of detentions - on both numbers and identities of victims. The DPSC was particularly

___ Names indexed

___ Bibliog items noted

___ Notes marked, pp.

___ Notes taken, pp.

Other:

hampered. Only organisations with well-developed lines of communication like trade unions were able to release information about members who had been held. The Labour Monitoring Group, with its close links to the union movement, was able in this period to publicise the extent to which unions had been hit. Later, the Community Research Group began to investigate and publicise the degree to which political and community organisations had been affected, giving more balance to the overall picture.

One reason for the confused picture was that security policemen around the country were apparently instructed to 'clean up your own patch'. Accordingly they moved against individuals whom they regarded as 'problems'. The result was detentions throughout the country, from cities to small rural towns and villages. Often the individual dislikes of particular security policemen had free rein. In many cases this resulted in the settling of personal vendettas. One instance of this in Grahamstown caused the courts to order the release of a detainee. Strong regional trends developed, reflecting different strengths of organisation and varying styles of repression practised by local police chiefs and bantustan fiefdoms.

Initially police used trial and error in deciding who to detain. They made numerous mistakes, and a large number of people were released before the initial 14-day detention period expired. Senior activists whose names were on the lists, however, were destined to be held for a very long time - some will undoubtedly stay in jail for the duration of the emergency. Unlike the previous emergency when police released the names of all detainees, the authorities attempted to conceal the scale of repression. Names were periodically tabled in parliament, but only those held for 30 days or more appeared on such lists. Monitoring groups like the DPSC report that most detainees are held for less than a month.

The minister of law and order initially tabled over 13 000 names, followed in June 1987 with a further list of 1 400 names. A conservative estimate of the true figure is probably double this. The minister refused to give the total number of detainees, claiming that 'extra-parliamentary activists and radicals...misused information on detainees in the most dreadful way, to the detriment of South Africa and the majority of its peoples' (*Cit,* 18.02.87). He contested DPSC and South African Institute of Race Relations estimates of over 20 000 emergency detainees.

But monitoring groups' previous experience is that their estimates are too low. By February 1987, the DPSC had independent knowledge of a total of 9 000 detainees. When comparing its list with the names released by the minister, it found a 90% discrepancy: of the 13 000 names he provided, the DPSC knew of only 1 400. The combined total is about 21 000, which does not include the mass detentions of municipal workers in Tembisa, dairy workers in Johannesburg and whole church congregations in Elsies River and Graaff Reinet. These individuals' names are not known to monitoring agencies, and number roughly 3 000. There are also hundreds of detainees in small rural areas whose names are unknown.

Table 5:

Cumulative emergency detention total, June 1986 - June 1987

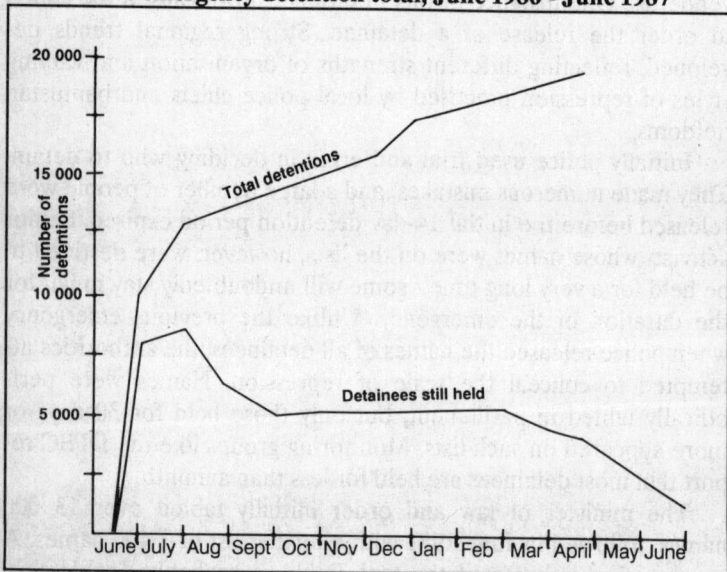

Geographical spread of detentions

As in the previous emergency, the Pretoria-Witwatersrand-Vaal (PWV) complex and the Eastern Cape have suffered most from security force activity. Detention figures for these areas reflect this (see Table 6). The 1986 emergency covered the entire country, not just selected districts. Nonetheless a remarkable feature of this period was the devastating scale of detentions in small rural towns, rural areas and bantustans. Of the latter, Lebowa was hardest hit.

This pattern reflects the widespread emergence of UDF structures in outlying areas, especially in the Eastern Transvaal where youth congresses sprang up and gathered large-scale support in a very short time. Mawhelereng Youth Congress (in a large rural area near Potgietersrus), for example, has a substantial membership; many members are in detention in Nylstroom. Namagale township at Phalaborwa likewise saw its youth congress decimated by detentions. The region has an umbrella organisation, the Lowveld Youth Movement, which has links with many smaller areas. In Table 6 these detentions are reflected in the 'Transvaal country' category. The Boland is another predominantly rural area which saw considerable repression.

Table 6:

Geographical distribution of 1986 emergency detentions

Area	No	%
PWV	1 799	24
Transvaal country	866	12
Eastern Cape	2 460	33
Western Cape	945	13
Northern Cape	241	3
Natal	680	9
OFS	405	6
	7 396	100

Targets of repression in the 1986 emergency

The youth and children: The most startling feature of the 1986-87 emergency is the number of young people detained. Children have frequently been the target of repressive action in the past, 1976 involving an earlier example of this. In the last two years, however, the severity of the price the young have had to pay for political militancy has intensified.

In 1982, only eight people under the age of 18 were detained; in 1984 nine were held. The 1985 emergency changed all that.

Approximately 2 875 children under the age of 18 were held - 25% of the total - of whom 2 000 were under 16. In the 1986 emergency, the DPSC calculates that about 10 000 aged 18 and under have been detained - 40% of the total. If one adds to this the youth (age 25 and under), the figure for detained youth and children totals 79% of all detainees, or 18 750. Some detained children are as young as 11 and 12.

Table 7:

Known targets of detention in the emergency as at December 1986

	No	%
Scholars, students and teachers	1 039	33
Community and political workers	1 450	46
Trade unionists and workers	475	15
Clergy and church workers	130	4
Journalists	19	0,5
Other	50	1,5
	3 163	100

The figures in Table 7 are drawn from DPSC analyses of detainees whose occupation and affiliation are known. While the data is incomplete, it nonetheless provides a significant sample and can be generalised to represent an accurate picture of the emergency.

Scholars, students and teachers: These make up the second-highest number of people detained in the current emergency. They accounted for 33% of detainees registered in the previous emergency. The prominence of this category of detainees is due to the continued militancy of school children. Although COSAS, the main vehicle for student demands and organisation, was banned, inferior education remained a burning issue and school boycotts and student militancy escalated rather than declined.

The 'war against children' in the 1985 emergency[4] has intensified. That roughly 10 000 children were detained since 12 June 1986 demonstrates police determination to smash student organisation. Tactics varied from detaining student leaders for lengthy periods to intimidation of rank-and-file students who were detained for shorter periods, but were reportedly often subjected to beatings. The tactic of intimidation appears to have backfired, as relief workers treating released detainees report that there has been a severe hardening of attitude and increased militancy among the younger ones.

If a single issue dominated 1986, it was education. School children suffered from the closing of schools and from South African Defence Force interference in schools. Many schools were virtually occupied by the SADF. In some cases, soldiers administered corporal punishment to pupils. Adults were not exempt from repression, and a Tumahole (Parys) school teacher brought a supreme court injunction against the security forces for their activities in his school. There were complaints of soldiers beating and humiliating teachers in front of school children - teachers claimed that this destroyed students' respect for them.

A consequence of the schools crisis was the formation of the Soweto Parents' Crisis Committee. Similar groups were launched in other centres. In late 1985 a resolution which led to the formation of the National Education Crisis Committee (NECC) was taken at a conference at the University of the Witwatersrand. This body played an important role, mediating between boycotting students and education authorities like the Department of Education and Training. Despite its mediating activities, the security police harassed the NECC executive, and many of its leaders, such as Vusi Khanyile, Molefe Tsele and Bill Jardine, were detained.

Political and community workers: As Table 7 demonstrates, by far the largest category of detainees known to the DPSC involves political and community workers. They comprise 46% of the total, and fall into four main organisational areas: civic or residents' associations; youth organisations or congresses; women's groups; and overtly political groups such as the UDF, AZAPO and CAL.

From the beginning of 1986, the UDF increased and consolidated its membership through civic and residents' associations. This was especially true in the Transvaal, Eastern Cape and Border. Inevitably members of such bodies became security police victims. The Port Elizabeth Black Community Organisation and the Duncan Village Residents' Association (DVRA) suffered body blows, as did the Alexandra Civic Association and Alexandra

Action Committee. The DVRA's street committee system, for example, was almost wiped out in June 1986 when 256 of its elected office bearers were detained. Nine months later, all but 19 were still languishing in East London's Fort Glamorgan prison. Alexandra Action Committee and Civic Association members were detained en masse and their leaders charged with treason, sedition and subversion.

In the police view, many civic associations which launched street committees and people's courts were implementing the M-plan. This blueprint, named after ANC leader Nelson Mandela, was first mooted during the 1950s. It aimed to set up small local structures to ensure full community participation in a larger organisation, in a way not unlike the trade union model.

Growth and development of present-day grassroots organisation is uneven, but is deeply rooted in some communities. Participants view these structures as democratic alternatives to ineffective and corrupt black local authorities. Police feared they would be used to make townships ungovernable. The security forces responded with twin tactics: intimidation by mass arrest and detention, and use of the courts.

The youth were consistently in the forefront of community struggles. Reports from around the country reveal that even in rural areas, communities which had been dormant were first galvanised by the youth. They emerged as the most militant resisters, the foot soldiers of the struggle.

National oppression is more effective in controlling parents than youth. Black parents are constantly aware that their jobs, homes and (in rural areas) their land, are under the control of apartheid functionaries. This exerts a cautionary influence on parents, who feel family responsibilities deeply.

The youth are less subject to such controls; they have far less to lose. Unemployment affects the young far more than their elders - the majority of the unemployed are young school-leavers who have never held a job. Even well-qualified young people have difficulty finding work, and consequently see no future for themselves under the present regime. The young have large reserves of energy, are idealistic, courageous and, unlike some of their parents, have not been cowed or defeated. Youth congresses consist largely of the young unemployed.

Women's organisations suffered to some extent in the

emergency, but were rather less hampered than other political groups. In the Transvaal, a senior executive member of the Federation of Transvaal Women, Sister Bernard Ncube as well as a few rank-and-file members, were detained. The Natal Organisation of Women was severely harassed. Six of its members were detained, but under section 29 of the Internal Security Act rather than the emergency. In all, women account for 14% of detainees, or 3 500 people - a surprisingly low figure considering the number of women activists.

Opposition political organisations attract security police attention as a matter of course. At the beginning of the emergency, AZAPO, AZASM and other National Forum-affiliated groups experienced a wave of detentions, with over 90 members detained in the first month. However, security police interest in these groups later tended to tail off. At the peak of detentions affecting these organisations, their activists accounted for 4,5% of detainees. This figure later declined to 3%. UDF-affiliated detainees constitute 79% of the total.

Trade unionists and workers: Two trends developed in detention of trade unionists and workers. First, individual unionists - usually organisers, shop stewards or union office bearers - were sought out and detained. Second was the mass detention of workers and rank-and-file union members. The former generally faced a lengthy spell in prison, while the latter were held for much shorter periods, sometimes only one day. The two trends reveal different aspects of police thinking and behaviour.

Individual unionists are usually detained in a deliberate security police tactic of singling out 'troublemakers'. A total of 529 unionists were individually detained. Apart from those taken in the first two weeks of the emergency, most fell foul of the police during strike or industrial action. At least four trade unionists were subjected to restrictions - a mild form of banning order restraining them from participating in certain campaigns and activities - after their release. A senior unionist of the Metal and Allied Workers Union, Moses Mayekiso, was first held under emergency regulations, then under section 29 of the Internal Security Act. He was finally charged with sedition and then treason.

Table 8:

Fate of trade unionists detained in 1986

	No	%
Released without charge	241	46
Charged	4	1
Released and restricted	4	1
Held under section 29	1	-
Still held, December 1986	279	52
	529	100

There were five major instances of mass detention. The most spectacular was in Tembisa, where 1 200 municipal workers downed tools in solidarity with a detained union leader. Police promptly detained all of them, but released most after only one day. The union involved, the South African Black Municipal Workers Union (SABMAWU), was involved in a second, unique event. It is unionising municipal police, and 150 of these unusual workers later went on strike, also on the East Rand, and were detained for a short time. SABMAWU is not affiliated to either of the large federations of labour.

COSATU members also experienced mass detentions. Food and Allied Workers Union (FAWU) workers at Nels and Clover Dairies struck early in the emergency, and police responded swiftly to management calls by detaining 740 FAWU members. The majority were released in a few days, but some served long periods in detention. In East London, 73 South African Allied Workers Union members were held within the first two days of the emergency, but it appears the police were more interested in their membership of the Duncan Village Residents' Association than in their unionism.

Table 9:

Mass arrests of unionists under the 1986 emergency

Union	No	Occupation
SABMAWU	1 200	Municipal workers
SABMAWU	150	Municipal police
FAWU	740	Dairy workers
SAAWU	73	General workers
	2 163	

The 2 163 detained unionists account for 7% of the DPSC total of 38 671 detainees.

The majority of those taken in mass detentions were members of SABMAWU. The remainder are members of COSATU affiliates. Individual detainees known to the Labour Monitoring Group display a revealing pattern. The overwhelming majority (78%) belonged to COSATU and its constituent unions, a very small minority to the Azanian Confederation of Trade Unions (AZACTU), and a few more to the Council of Unions of South Africa (CUSA), now merged with AZACTU in the National Confederation of Trade Unions. Unaffiliated unions, such as the Western Cape Teachers Union, the National Education Union of South Africa, Textile Workers Industrial Union and the Media Workers Association of South Africa, accounted for 9% of detentions.

Table 10:

Known detentions of individual trade unionists up to March 1987

	No	Percentage of known union detainees	Percentage of all detainees
COSATU	373	78	1,30
AZACTU	13	3	0,05
CUSA	48	10	0,19
Unaffiliated	45	9	0,18
	479	100	1,72

This reveals the severity of police action against COSATU, and no doubt reflects its organisational strength on the ground. The CUSA/AZACTU alliance suffered far less, probably due to lower membership and less militant and organised shop floors. Overall, in the full context of the emergency, detained unionists and workers amount to 9% of the total.

Trade union trends changed during the emergency period - different unions became militant at various times, often in response to factory floor issues; police generally intervened. Natal was a key area of union detentions and harassment. Unions opposed to the Inkatha-linked United Workers Union of South Africa (UWUSA) were severely repressed, which made space for UWUSA to gain a foothold. Independent unions, like other progressive organisations, were the victims of vigilante attacks. In one instance three Metal and Allied Workers Union leaders in the township of Mpophomeni were abducted and killed by vigilantes allegedly linked to Inkatha.

Clergy and religious workers: Religious leaders and workers have played a significant role in opposing apartheid for many decades, and in the 1986 emergency were in the forefront of a number of struggles. Many religious figures were detained, some were deported and numerous others harassed. Two entire congregations - one in Elsies River, the other in Graaff Reinet - were detained. The latter, it seems, was holding a prayer meeting to protest the emergency and accompanying repression, and was held for a considerable period. There were also numerous individual detentions, including those of Peter Kirshoff from Pietermaritzburg, Peter Hortop of KwaThema, Sister Bernard Ncube and Sister Catherine Obotseng of Kagiso.

Notable among religious groups affected by repression is the recently formed Call of Islam, a muslim group based in the Western Cape which supports the UDF. Many of its members and some of its Imams have been held.

In 1986 about 800 religious workers of all denominations and faiths were detained, 2,79% of the total.

Journalists: Journalists are particularly at risk under a coercive system trying to conceal the true extent of its ruthlessness. Those working with visual media like television crews and photographers came under constant attack, often of a physical kind. George De'Ath, covering clashes between witdoeke and comrades in the

Western Cape, was hacked and beaten by the vigilantes and died in hospital.

Journalists covering unrest incidents have been teargassed and sjambokked. In 1986, 89 media workers were detained, some for lengthy periods. Zwelakhe Sisulu, editor of *New Nation,* is the most prominent, but Mxolisi Fuzile and Phila Ngqumba of Veritas News Agency in King William's Town were detained on the first day of the emergency, effectively closing down their agency. Brian Sokutu of Port Elizabeth and Clive Stuurman, editor of the Oudtshoorn community newspaper *Saamstaan,* were also held from the early stages of the emergency.

Other formal repression

Detentions are but one of an array of weapons available to the state in its attack on popular organisations. Others include the use of the courts, bannings, listings, restrictions and deportations.

Use of the courts

In 1984 and 1985, the state attempted to conceal the true level of its onslaught against anti-apartheid groups by use of courts. Criminalising the opposition is an old tactic, but it reached new heights during this period. Before the two emergencies, government was still trying to clean up its image and could not afford to appear too repressive. This changed with the declaration of the first emergency on 19 July 1985, when government openly declared its defiance of both world opinion and internal resistance.

Treason trials: In 1986 there were eight treason trials involving 49 individuals. Six were completed, resulting in ten convictions and eight acquittals. Of the latter, three were accused in the as yet uncompleted Delmas treason trial. At the end of the year 31 people still faced charges of treason in two different trials.

Trials under the Internal Security Act and other legislation: The DPSC recorded a total of 96 political trials on charges other than treason which were completed during 1986. Methods of police interrogation generally result in statements or confessions from the accused. These are often contested in trials-within-trials when the accused allege their confessions were obtained by coercion. Despite this, the prosecution's success rate is remarkably low. Of the 672 people charged with political offences, 499 or 74% were acquitted or had charges withdrawn.

Table 11:

Internal Security Act and other political trials in 1986

Offence	No of trials	No of persons charged	Acquitted or withdrawn No	%
Terrorism	27	76	43	57
Furthering aims of a banned organisation	4	7	4	57
Subversion	6	32	32	100
Sedition	1	5	5	100
Internal Security Act contravention	8	12	8	75
Contravention of emergency regulations	2	2	2	100
Sabotage	1	5	-	-
Possession of firearms or explosives	5	7	1	14
Possession of banned articles	5	21	13	62
Breaking banning order	2	2	2	100
Quoting listed person	2	2	1	50
Attending an unlawful gathering	10	370	289	78
Demonstrations Act contravention	6	57	52	91
Police Act contravention	1	2	1	50
Prisons Act contravention	1	1	1	100
Refusing to testify	5	5	-	-
Harbouring a guerilla	3	8	5	62
Obstructing police	4	4	3	75
Intimidation	2	13	11	85
Public disturbance	1	41	26	63
	96	672	499	74

Public violence trials: In terms of sheer numbers, other trials pale into insignificance when compared to charges of public violence. Public violence is the most common charge arising from 'unrest incidents'. Offences can range from throwing stones at a bus or surrounding a councillor's house, to attacking armoured police or army vehicles. In reply to questions in parliament, Minister of Law and Order Adriaan Vlok revealed that 11 006 people were arrested for public violence in 1986, of which 7 710 were charged with public violence, malicious damage to property, arson, murder and assault (*NN*, 26.02.87). Vlok did not note the number of convictions, but experience suggests a very low conviction rate. The majority of cases end in the withdrawal of charges.

Banning of organisations

In March SAAWU was declared an unlawful organisation in the Transkei under the Transkei Public Security Act.

During September 1986, the Congress of South African Students challenged the validity of its banning in the Natal Supreme Court. On 1 October the court upheld the banning.

In October the UDF was declared an affected organisation under the Affected Organisations Act, thereby cutting off its access to overseas financial support. A subsequent appeal launched in Natal was upheld, but is in turn on appeal in the Appellate Division.

Banning of persons

Bannings under the Internal Security Act: At the beginning of 1986, ten people were living under banning orders issued in terms of sections 19, 20 and 21 of the Internal Security Act. On 11 March two Port Elizabeth activists, Henry Fazzie and Mkhuseli Jack, were served with five-year banning orders. Jack successfully challenged the validity of his banning order in the Port Elizabeth Supreme Court. As a result a number of other banning orders fell away. Others expired during the year, so that by the end of 1986 no one was restricted by these orders.

Restrictions under emergency regulations: During 1985 a new form of banning was introduced under the emergency. Certain emergency detainees were, on their release, served with an order restricting their movement, activities, occupation, utterances, attendance at educational institutions, access to designated buildings and presence at gatherings.

When the 1985 emergency was lifted in March 1986, such bannings had been served on 69 known persons: five in the Transvaal, two in the Eastern Cape and 62 in the Western Cape.

During the present emergency, this form of banning was more extensively used. Many released detainees were served with restriction orders in terms of regulation 3(6) of the emergency regulations. Reports indicate that the number of released detainees under restriction orders runs to several hundred, but the authorities refuse to disclose their names. The DPSC knew of 40 persons restricted in this way by the end of 1986.

In November a new type of restriction order was first served on persons other than those released from detention. This was issued in terms of regulation 7(1) of the emergency regulations. Persons served with these orders are forbidden to call for:

* Release of all emergency detainees and political prisoners;
* Lifting of the state of emergency;
* The unbanning of the ANC;
* Withdrawal of the SADF from the townships;
* Abolition of the tricameral parliament;
* Ending conscription.

They are also not allowed to participate in the Campaign for National United Action. These restriction orders only apply within the Johannesburg and Randburg magisterial districts. By the end of 1986 this form of restriction order had been issued to 36 Johannesburg residents.

In December the police commissioner for the East Rand prohibited *any person* from making the calls listed above if they participated in the activities of certain campaigns and organisations on the East Rand. A few days later the divisional commissioner in the Western Cape ordered the same restriction on all persons connected to 12 local campaigns and organisations. These orders, identical to those issued to individuals, effectively restrict the entire populations of the Western Cape and East Rand.

Listing: In July 1986 a list of 180 people was gazetted. The penalty for quoting any utterance of those on this 'consolidated list' is a prison sentence of up to three years. Of the 180, 27 are in South African prisons, 32 live in South Africa, 98 are in exile and 23 are dead. This list contains 20 fewer names than that of the previous year.

Banning of gatherings

The annual blanket ban on outdoor political gatherings was reimposed on 1 April under the Internal Security Act.

Ministerial bans were also imposed on indoor political meetings. All meetings concerning school or student boycotts, and work stoppages or stayaways, were banned from 1 April 1986 to 31 March 1987. All meetings of 74 organisations in 30 specified districts were banned from 31 December 1985 to 30 June 1986.

But bannings under the Internal Security Act were overshadowed by the numerous orders issued by police under regulation 7(1) of the emergency regulations, which banned and restricted many meetings and funerals.

Legal interventions

Table 12:

Cases brought on behalf of individual detainees

Area	No of applications	No of detainees
Johannesburg	15	36
Pretoria	11	51
Kimberley	1	3
Bloemfontein	1	2
Grahamstown	5	13
Pietermaritzburg	5	5
Durban	9	56
Cape Town	9	40
Transkei	1	1
Venda	1	1
	58	208

Of the cases listed in Table 12, 16 applications were granted, including those of detainees who were released while the application was in progress; 15 were refused; and 27 are still pending.

Some detainees also challenged the emergency regulations and thereby the validity of their detentions.

The long-term futility of legal intervention is indicated by the singular lack of enduring success in challenges to the emergency. Most cases fail, and the few which succeed are usually overturned on appeal. The state also produces amended regulations to cover legal loopholes almost as soon as they appear.

Legal challenges to emergency legislation

During 1986, several detainees, organisations and newspaper groups brought court applications which challenged the validity of the emergency regulations or of orders issued under them.

Table 13:

Court actions against emergency legislation

Area	Number
Johannesburg	4
Pretoria	1
Bloemfontein	1
Grahamstown	2
Pietermaritzburg	2
Durban	2
Cape Town	3
Appellate Division	1
	16

Seven applications challenged the validity of the regulation allowing for detention and three challenged regulations or orders which affected newspapers. Eight applications led to new rulings, seven were unsuccessful and one was withdrawn.

The first application to achieve some success was that of the Metal and Allied Workers Union in the Durban Supreme Court in July. It challenged the validity of the declaration of the state of emergency. The court ruled that the declaration was valid, but certain definitions of 'subversive statements' were wholly or partially void. It found that emergency detainees were allowed access to lawyers. The state is appealing against the ruling.

Also in July, a full bench of the Rand Supreme Court deleted the phrase in emergency regulation seven which authorised *any person delegated* by the commissioner of police to make certain orders. This made invalid an order by the Soweto divisional commissioner of police prohibiting 26 organisations from holding meetings in specific areas. This application was brought by the UDF.

In August, confusion arose in Natal as a result of two contradictory judgements made within days of each other by the Durban and Pietermaritzburg divisions of the supreme court. The Durban court declared invalid the first and third clauses of emergency regulation three, which concerned arrests by members of the security forces and the duration of detentions. In Pietermaritzburg, the court ruled that the same clauses were valid. Both applications were made by detainees, Solomon Tsenoli and Peter Kirshhoff respectively. In both cases, the rulings were appealed against. In September the Bloemfontein Appeal Court in a combined case confirmed the validity of the two clauses.

Several English-speaking newspaper groups combined to challenge six emergency regulations in the Natal Supreme Court. During the hearing the state conceded that two regulations concerning news reports about police conduct and the presence of journalists in townships and unrest areas were not binding because they had not been properly promulgated. The court ruled that regulations 7(1)d, 10b, 11 and 12 were invalid. This lifted several restrictions on the press and rendered void restrictions on funerals or other gatherings by a divisional commissioner of police.

Many of the judgements against the state have been negated by the redrafting of emergency regulations and promulgation of new rules under the regulations. This is discussed in greater detail by Armstrong, Haysom and Kahanovitz in their contributions to this section of the *Review*.

Action against the media

The emergency regulations placed considerable restraints on the media. The state has also acted against press organisations and individuals in a number of ways since the emergency was declared.

During 1986, the commissioner of police or one of the divisional commissioners issued nine orders imposing press restrictions under emergency regulation seven. Some affected the media nationally; others were directed at specific publications. Two of these orders were issued in June, one in September and six in December.

On three occasions the security police seized editions of newspapers. They inspected editions on four occasions and once questioned three journalists from one newspaper. In 1987, police threatened to seize any newspaper printing a DPSC advertisement for National Detainees Day on 12 March. They attempted to seize *The Star,* but the advertisement was amended and a court order obtained protecting the newspaper.

The state's onslaught against the media included intimidation of journalists. Four foreign correspondents were deported or expelled from South Africa in 1986 after the declaration of emergency on 12 June. Another journalist was issued with an expulsion order in December. At the end of the year he was awaiting a hearing on his appeal to the relevant authorities.

Four journalists were detained under security legislation and several under the emergency regulations. The editor of the *New Nation,* Zwelakhe Sisulu, was detained twice during 1986 and was still in detention in June 1987.

Extra-legal repression

Extra-legal repression covers a wide range of activities. Some appear to have official sanction, others tacit approval, and yet others appear to be fairly autonomous from the state apparatus. They include torture and abuse of detainees and attacks by pro-apartheid vigilantes against organisations and individuals supportive of the UDF or COSATU.

During 1986 there were a number of applications for restraining interdicts and other court actions relating to allegations of assault and torture of security and emergency detainees.

Table 14:

Court actions concerning maltreatment of detainees

Area	Number of court actions	Number of applicants
Johannesburg	3	3
Pretoria	1	1
Durban	6	29
Pietermaritzburg	3	3
Bloemfontein	1	38
Port Elizabeth	1	1
	15	75

Such legal interventions are merely the tip of the iceberg. Scores of allegations concerning maltreatment while in detention are made by released detainees. In November 1986 the DPSC produced a memorandum on children under repression[5] which detailed numerous cases of alleged abuse of children in detention. The DPSC also analysed the cases brought to its advice office during the emergency, and found that 135 ex-detainees alleged abuse or torture. These cases cover a small minority of detainees - they are drawn from records of an advice office which serves only the PWV. In addition, the cases are drawn from *released* detainees; thousands are still in detention.

Allegations of torture were substantiated by a panel of doctors of the National Medical and Dental Association (NAMDA) who treat released detainees. The panel has treated over 600 former detainees since July 1985. A sample of these cases revealed that 83% showed medical evidence of physical abuse. A total of 93% complained of physical abuse or injury at the hands of the security forces. The 10% discrepancy can be explained by the fact that the detainees were released a long time after injuries were incurred.

The doctors who examined detainees found that 60% of the patients were 'severely injured', while 85% complained of severe, symptoms. Detainees complained of various types of physical abuse, and 82,5% showed clinical signs compatible with their allegations. The majority of allegations were of being hit with a rifle butt, beaten with a heavy whip or stick, being punched, kicked or slapped. A total of 25% alleged sexual abuse, most commonly being forced to strip naked during interrogation, and suffering assault on their sexual organs.

Other extreme forms of torture which were alleged include electric shocks, suffocation and hooding with a canvas bag, causing partial suffocation and disorientation and making it impossible to identify interrogators. Many detainees were held in solitary confinement and suffered isolation and sensory deprivation.

The doctors found that the psychological stress of detention was very severe, and as important as the physical injuries. Fully 95% of those examined showed signs of post-traumatic stress syndrome as defined by the American Psychiatric Association. This included those who were detained for five days or less and not placed in solitary confinement. The syndrome has several components: existence of a major source of stress; re-experiencing of the trauma; numbing of responsiveness; hyperalertness; sleep disturbance; impairment of memory and concentration; panic attacks; and avoidance of activities which remind the victim of the traumatic event.

Some 30% of detention victims had sexual problems, including the inability to have orgasm, premature ejaculation, frigidity and loss of libido. Gastro-intestinal complaints were common, as was memory disturbance - many found it hard to read a newspaper, maintain a conversation and remember facts.

The detainees' ages ranged from 14 to 45: the average age was 23. The period of detention ranged from four hours to 315 days, with an average of 36 days. Most were held in prisons or police stations, but two were held in a temporary army camp with an armoured vehicle used as their prison. Only 33% saw a doctor during detention, despite the fact that this is required by the regulations and that 78% had asked to do so.

Deaths in detention or police custody

Given the level of torture and duress to which detainees claim they are subjected, it is not surprising that the number of deaths in detention rose. The DPSC distinguishes between detention and police custody. The former refers to those held under security or emergency legislation. The latter is a necessary category because police frequently conceal a detention by holding a person under criminal legislation, even though the motive for arrest is political.

According to DPSC records, 54 people died in detention up to the end of 1983. In the following two years a further four died, bringing the total to 58. In 1986 two men held under security legislation died in Lebowa. One was Peter Nchabaleng (59), Northern Transvaal UDF president; it appears that he choked on his vomit after being beaten unconscious by Lebowa security policemen on 11 April. The other was Makompo Kutumela (25) who died on 6 April.

Two people held under emergency detention regulations also died. They were Xoliso Jacobs (20) who died on 22 October in Upington and Simon Marule (20) who died on 23 December in Benoni.

The DPSC has been keeping records of politically related deaths in police custody only since 1984. In the first two years these records were kept 14 deaths were recorded.

In 1986 there were also several deaths in police custody of persons arrested in circumstances which appeared to be politically related. On 12 April 1986 Eric Ngomane (22) died in Hazyview. On

5 October 1985 Mbuyiseli Songelwa (29) died in East London. On 12 December 1986 Shadrack Maphumulo was shot and killed in Swaziland while being kidnapped by South African agents. Police refused to release his body, which resulted in a legal dispute with the family. On 15 December 1986 Benji Olifant (25) died in Klerksdorp.

Informal repression

Formal methods of repression like detentions and use of the courts are closely paralleled by a number of 'informal' practices designed to intimidate, inhibit, and on occasion eliminate political opposition to the government. Both formal and informal repression share one characteristic: their targets are anti-apartheid activists. They differ in that the former is carried out officially and openly by the security forces, the latter usually not - the link to the authorities is often shadowy or even untraceable.

Vigilante groups are most often responsible for informal repression. The relationship of such gangs and hit squads to apartheid's official structure is often clear. The bantustan leaders of Kwandebele, for example, made little effort to hide the fact that vigilante groups called 'imbokotho' were operating with official approval. In other areas vigilante groups have operated with official collusion. A case in point is Crossroads, where the 'witdoeke' operated against 'comrade' groups while security forces looked on without intervening. At times security forces allegedly did intervene directly, using teargas to rout 'comrade' defenders. In Natal the issue is more complex. Inkatha-supporting vigilantes operate with a great degree of autonomy, but with the same effect - the disorganisation of UDF and COSATU leaders and organisations.

The authorities are fond of depicting the struggle evoked by this unofficial repression as 'black-on-black violence'. It is implied that this is particularly savage and inexplicable violence between 'brothers' - bloodshed for which the regime is free from blame. In fact it is either designed to shatter resistance to Pretoria's rule, or else flourishes in the rifts and divisions which apartheid itself has created among the voteless majority.

Vigilante groups tend to be reactive, arising in areas where progressive organisations have made headway in mobilising communities. Their social composition is varied. Many are made up of migrant workers or the unemployed who feel alienated from slightly more secure, fully urbanised people. Inkatha and the Crossroads witdoeke are examples of this. Others, such as the Makabasa gang of Soweto, have deep urban roots. Vigilantes appear to have greatest impact in smaller communities, often rural towns.

Recently vigilante groups have been recruited into municipal police and trained for three weeks. This gave rise to their nickname of 'kitskonstabels' (instant cops). In many instances vigilantes appear to have been recruited primarily as bodyguards by unpopular community councillors. Thabong (Welkom) provides an example. In 1985 and 1986 a vigilante squad called 'Pakathis' (after the name of a councillor) emerged to 'scourge Thabong of rowdyism'. The mayor of Thabong, EB Tlali, acknowledged that 'under the guidance of council members patrols were organised and inspired by the old maxim "spare the rod and spoil the child". All meetings of potential stone-throwers were broken up with no more than the energetic use of sjamboks'.[6]

This apparently benign statement conceals the brutality to which he referred. So energetically were sjamboks used that 17-year-old Daniel Mabenyani died four days after being flogged by the Pakathis. The gang also shot and killed two 15-year-old boys. Hundreds more were kidnapped and thrashed, or attacked with pangas, sticks and kieries. The relationship between the vigilantes and the councillors was so close that the Pakathis used council offices as interrogation and flogging centres; council vehicles were used for street patrols, and several councillors were often seen among the attackers.

The case of Thabong has echoes in many communities around South Africa. Leandra in the Eastern Transvaal is another example. In such communities vigilantes have forced progressive anti-apartheid groups to operate underground and have banished their leaders. On the other hand, where progressive community organisations have deep roots, they have been able to resist vigilantes successfully.

The emergence of vigilante groups is no accident. They arise in predictable situations and are organised and behave similarly. Across the country, a great number have adopted the same name - the A-Team - even in rural areas where the only television sets are in the homes of community councillors or policemen. However, the planners who seem to be behind these groups are not working in a vacuum. Social conditions for the conflict between vigilantes and communities are often generational differences in political awareness and approach. Sometimes the rift is between rural or migrant people and permanent urban dwellers. Elsewhere the jobless and criminal elements provide fertile recruiting grounds.

The emergence of pro-apartheid vigilantes in all their various guises was trumpeted by the government mouthpiece, the Bureau for Information, which describes such unrest as 'black-on-black' and portrays security force action as mediating and keeping the peace. In this they are abetted, perhaps unwittingly, by the South African Institute of Race Relations, which releases reports on unrest deaths with a minimum of comment and contextualisation. In their March 1987 report, the institute noted that the main change in unrest-related deaths was that conflict within black communities had replaced security force action as the main cause of fatalities. In 1985, security force action had accounted for half the fatalities, and conflict within black communities for about one-third. In 1986 the positions had reversed. It is a pity the institute did not take its analysis the necessary step further: that this change reflected a shift in security force tactics.

Table 15:

Street fatalities in South Africa, 1984-1986[7]

1984		1985		1986	
		January	4	January	105
		February	35	February	112
		March	76	March	179
		April	46	April	145
		May	66	May	221
		June	45	June	212
		July	96	July	122
		August	163	August	76
		September	69	September	40
		October	86	October	16
September –		November	101	November	37
December	149	December	92	December	33
	149		879		1 298

Both the Bureau for Information and the Institute of Race

Relations have claimed that because death rates and other measurable incidents of unrest have declined, the state of emergency seems to be working. There is no doubt that the 1986-87 emergency has been a war of attrition between the authorities and anti-government organisations, with the former gaining the ascendancy. It is virtually impossible for extra-parliamentary organisations to hold public or mass meetings. While fewer leaders were detained in the second emergency, they have been forced underground, which is not conducive to the politics of mass mobilisation.

What fatality figures illustrate more than anything else is the level of control imposed on the militant youth who used the streets as their recruiting and mobilising grounds. They do not indicate a successful political policy of containment. The 'success' of the emergency has been achieved at the expense of enormous repression in the form of army and police street patrols. And it has been bought at the price of massively alienating township residents.

Notes

1   M Coleman and D Webster,'Repression and Detentions in South Africa', Southern African Research Service (ed), *South African Review 3,* Johannesburg, 1986.

2   These figures are gleaned from answers to parliamentary questions *(Star,* 23.02.87; *Cit,* 21.02.87). They came as a shock to monitoring groups such as the DPSC which, despite attempts at accuracy, only recorded 2 320 Internal Security Act detainees in 1986, which was 42% or 1 669 less than the official figure.

3   In detention statistics for all of 1986, therefore, there is some overlap between those held under section 50 of the Internal Security Act and those held under emergency regulations. The figure is difficult to calculate, but may be over 1 000 (Vlok told parliament that 1 060 Internal Security Act detainees were held for one day). Most of these detentions were probably on the eve of the emergency.

4   Helena Cooke, *The War Against Children,* Lawyers' Committee for Human Rights, New York, 1986.

5   Detainees' Parents Support Committee, *Abantwana Bazabalaza: a Memorandum on Children under Repression in South Africa,* Johannesburg, 1986.

6   *Abantwana Bazabalaza,* 36-37.

7   *Race Relations News,* December 1986.

The 1986 State of Emergency in the Western Cape[1]

Glenda Kruss

In declaring a state of emergency on 12 June 1986, State President PW Botha announced that radical and revolutionary violence had increased. This had occurred in spite of government's commitment to negotiation 'for a new South Africa in which the reasonable aspirations of all its citizens would be satisfied' (*Argus,* 13.06.86). After thorough consideration and with due regard to economic, political and security implications, the emergency was declared as the most effective security action to maintain public order.

Declaration of the first, partial state of emergency was government's response to escalating opposition in 1985. This took the form of school, rent and consumer boycotts, mass stayaways and the rise of people's power. In the 1985 emergency government seemed to have lost control; it acted wildly in all directions to crush opposition political activity.

When the first emergency was lifted in March 1986, the state appeared to have regained a measure of control. But opposition organisations interpreted the move differently:

> They lifted the emergency because they were forced to do so, because they were afraid of the united mass action of the people which they know is coming after March 31... In the meantime, the emergency in fact continues to exist throughout the country. There is little difference now from when the official state of emergency was in force.[2]

A second state of emergency was declared on 12 June, shortly before the tenth anniversary of the Soweto uprising of 16 June 1976. It began yet another phase in the state's continuing effort to crush resistance and restructure apartheid through its 'reform' programme.

Most of the information contained in this article was gathered from interviews with people from various townships, community and political organisations, monitoring groups, and lawyers working with those most affected by the emergency.

The emergency regulations

The 1986 emergency regulations provided sweeping powers in three main fields:

* they extended powers of arrest, detention and search to police, the defence force and transport police, limited their liability and the recourse to the courts of those affected;

* they provided for proclamation of orders controlling movement in and access to any areas, as well as prohibiting reports or comments on any security force action in connection with public safety; and

* they stringently defined 'subversive statements' in such a way as to produce a virtual press blackout.

In the Western Cape, the general regulations were supplemented by a series of orders issued by the SAP's divisional commander, Brigadier CA Swart. These aimed to control school boycotts and placed restrictions on funerals. Most significantly, 119 political and community organisations were prohibited from holding any meetings or public gatherings, from issuing any publications including stickers, pamphlets and posters, or disseminating the speeches of office-bearers. All community and political organisation was thus effectively gagged.

The emergency in the African townships

Compared with the 1985 emergency, security force action in Cape Town's African townships increased dramatically. Each area has its local dynamics, divisions and history of repression. But a general pattern was discernible: overall state strategy aimed to crush popular organisations - particularly the emerging street committees and civic structures - and to promote community councils or black local authorities. The state is striving for greater credibility and legitimacy by implementing 'upgrading' or improvement programmes under the control of these bodies and the new 'mayors'.

By the time the state of emergency was declared, the Crossroads-KTC crisis had already affected communities and disrupted organisations. The 'witdoeke' vigilantes, allegedly in collusion with the police, destroyed the Crossroads-KTC squatter communities in May 1986. This benefitted

> the community of Old Crossroads, the government - who have been trying for three years to get the squatters to move to its 'model' township of Khayelitsha, 30 km from the centre of Cape Town - and the police (*WM*, 13-19.06.86).

The land the squatters were forced to leave was to be used to upgrade the community of Old Crossroads under the leadership of Johnson Ngxobongwana. One fieldworker stated that in these areas,

> the emergency was in some senses an anti-climax, in that a lot of the pressures had already happened... The emergency helped to carry through the process. For example organisations were not around to rally people; but it would not have really made a difference.

As a New Crossroads woman observed: 'It is very difficult to say that the emergency is different... Nothing is better than the other one. The badness is just carrying on all the time'. For some people, the emergency meant intensification of already high levels of repression and domination. The extensive police powers and control of access to areas and information allowed a 'mopping up operation' to take place, and the state attempted to get the area firmly under control.

According to one resident,

> Maybe that was one reason to crush KTC and join up with the vigilantes - there was resistance. Police were being shot back at. It was impossible for them to enter KTC... It was too dangerous, they couldn't control KTC at all.

Thus, while attention focused on the nation wide swoop, the KTC squatter camp was destroyed despite a supreme court interdict restraining vigilante leaders, the police and SADF from launching an attack similar to that in Crossroads. A journalist described the scene:

> I watched as the police stood by and observed the vigilantes torching the
> Zolani Centre, which had previously housed more than 2 000 refugees. I
> watched later in the day as police Casspirs moved ahead of vigilantes, firing
> teargas and birdshot at KTC residents trying to defend their homes against
> the vigilantes (*WM*, 13-19.06.86).

Under cover of the emergency regulations, 'the most brutal
forced removal in South Africa's history' could be finalised. While
bulldozers demolished the remains of KTC in preparation for
upgrading, notices were served on churches and organisations shel-
tering refugees that such shelters were illegal and must be closed
down. The land was cleared and surrounded by barbed wire, and
emergency regulations were promulgated to prevent re-occupation
or re-establishment of squatter camps. Most refugees had already
moved to Khayelitsha; but those living in church halls, schools,
refugee centres, and those squatting on new sites, were now forced
to move to the desolate tent town. A group of some 250 squatters,
for example, who had erected shacks at Browns Farm, Phillipi,
were harassed by Divisional Council (DIVCO) officials aided by
the police. Some shacks were destroyed and plastic sheets confiscated. There were allegedly threats that the witdoeke would come
to destroy the shacks. Despite DIVCO's attempts to force squatters
to Khayelitsha, they resisted because 'there are too many leaders at
Khayelitsha and they will not find peace there'.[3]

Some emergency detentions seem to relate to the May 1986
Crossroads crisis. Many of those whose homes had been destroyed
were detained. They were allegedly separated from other
detainees, beaten and forced to sign statements denying police involvement in the destruction of the camps and police collusion with
the witdoeke. Some were charged with public violence. There is
evidence of a concerted attempt to cover up police involvement
with vigilantes.

Detentions were widespread. A lawyer believed that the state
was having a bad success rate with public violence cases, so

> it has been easier to simply detain everyone and keep them off the streets.
> Detentions have been indiscriminate... The police clearly had instructions to
> take in as many as possible and lock them away for extensive periods.

The Repression Monitoring Group estimated that 307 people were detained in the Western Cape between 12 June, when the emergency was declared, and 23 June. This was an extremely conservative figure, especially since detainee numbers in the 1985 emergency were underestimated by 50%. By January 1987, the Detainees' Parents Support Committee claimed there had been 20 000 detentions during the 1986 emergency. The situation was exacerbated by the complete ban on publishing the names of detainees and the refusal to confirm detentions - the era of 'missing' people was a stark reality. Many people, particularly executive members of civic, youth and women's organisations, went into hiding to avoid detention. Roadblocks at all entrances to the townships were a daily reality, 'but people are just used to it now'.

Use of informers or 'impimpis' was one of the most divisive and fear-provoking police tactics - particularly in Langa, a small township where community members are well known to each other. Langa residents described the operation of 'impimpis': at 3 or 4 am police visit a house and take the target person out to a car where the 'impimpi' waits, wearing a balaclava to hide his or her identity. If the target person is identified by the 'impimpi', he or she is immediately detained and taken away in a separate car. This happened before the emergency, but has worsened under its regulations. The detained person is usually from one of the community organisations and is often held and questioned for long periods, depending upon police information and his or her political importance. One person explained that 'the police have used the emergency to try to get people and information they were looking for. Politically active people were detained, as well as those involved in street committees'.

Asked why the state declared an emergency, many emphasised that it was intended 'to divide people, to break unity, to scare people, to discourage activists, because they are now banned from doing things, then they become discouraged and think "what can we do?"' To some extent this has succeeded. In some areas people have lost confidence, and 'a lot are sitting down because they are scared'.

Attempts to hold public meetings, even on bread-and-butter issues - for example to discuss ways of combating 'skollies' and pickpockets - are unsuccessful. There was greater willingness to support such initiatives before the emergency. However, organisations

continue to meet regularly, if more secretly, and there is greater
security consciousness. In some areas, although community meetings are banned, there are so many issues to be dealt with that
people continue to hold them. There is a strong spirit of defiance:

> People must do things while the state of emergency is on. They are giving dif-
> ficulty to the people in detention if they do nothing, because the government
> is saying that those are the troublemakers, and things will be fine now. We
> must resist, even forget that the emergency exists.

A recent development causes fear and threatens community
safety and individual lives. 'Kitskonstabels' (instant constables), the
township task force, are trained for three weeks at Koeberg. A
number of township residents were recruited by advertisements for
'security guards' which promised large salaries. Rumour had it that
once at Koeberg recruits were not allowed to leave. Some claim
that police recruited ex-detainees into these jobs, and continue to
attempt to recruit from community organisations.

A constantly expressed fear was that the kitspolisie, like the witdoeke, would cause war and divide people: 'Organisations are now
campaigning against these people and we are scared that it will
cause a war between us'. 'Even the children call the kitspolisie
witdoeke'. People fear 'another bloodshed'. Anticipation that the
kitspolisie would be introduced was enough to make a community
feel threatened and ready to act in its defence. Shortly after the
kitspolisie went into action, there were numerous incidents including attempts to disarm them; their homes were burnt and their lives
threatened. But as one woman phrased it: 'These are our people,
they are putting us to fight each other'.

Rent boycotts have received very little publicity. In New
Crossroads, a rent boycott has been under way since December
1984. The community appears well organised into street committees and very united. Houses are now being sold off in line with the
state's new urbanisation policy in what the community sees as an
attempt to break the rent boycott. Community members fear that
evictions by troops may take place. However, community organisations have agreed to refuse to buy the houses or to allow outsiders
to move in.

In Langa the boycott was broken through different methods: by
intimidation and by dealing individually with residents. One
method reported is to send inspectors from the administration

board, under police guard, to repossess the keys to the house in the early hours of the morning. Another is to take people to the police station, again in the middle of the night, and interrogate them as to why they are not paying rent, often forcing them to sign documents they cannot understand. Others were called to the administration board office and told 'Mrs So-and-so (a well-known leader) is paying rent, and she tells you not to pay; why not pay?' There is a strong fear of eviction and this is used to pressurise individuals to give in, pay arrears and resume payment.

The majority in Langa are now paying rent, but some continue the boycott which started in 1985. Hand in hand with the attempt to break the rent boycott is a concerted campaign to sell houses. A homeowners advice bureau offers free advice. A census is being conducted - particularly of backyard shack dwellers - to determine the number of inhabitants and who is employed. The purchase price of each house was quoted to the residents.. People fear that they will be moved to Khayelitsha if they do not take up the option to buy. The homeownership scheme appears to be under the control of the newly appointed mayor of the Cape Town townships, Ronald Njoli. However, neither Njoli nor the schemes to boost his legitimacy have much credibility among organised township dwellers.

The emergency in small towns and rural areas

Similar tactics have been used in the small towns and rural areas of the Western Cape, but there repression is far more brutal and overt, with very real threats of death or injury to the most innocent community members.

In Zwelethemba, Worcester, for example, there was a reign of terror. The township has a permanent SAP and SADF mini-encampment guarding its sole entrance and is constantly patrolled. Typically on weekends a curfew is announced over loudhailers, and people found on the streets are physically assaulted. One young man was sjambokked on his way to church and lost the sight of an eye. A 13-year-old boy was allegedly shot in his own backyard, then charged with public violence.

On the first Saturday of the emergency, police entered the Zwelethemba shops still patronised by residents during a consumer boycott and chased out those present with sjamboks. A mother was separated from her two children as a result. She eventually traced them to the police station, where a number of those present in the shops were being held. Later, after pressure was brought to bear, all those under 16 were released.

Various tactics are used in attempts to divide the community. A liquor hall which the community had demanded be converted to a community centre and which it had forced to close, was reopened during the emergency. In an attempt to sow division between political organisations, rumours of unknown origin circulated, linking the formation of an AZAPO branch in the township with the reopening of the beerhall. But as one woman phrased it: 'We don't want trouble and fights between the UDF and AZAPO to cause trouble for us'. But the community was concerned and unsure as to how to deal with these developments. However unfounded such rumours are, under emergency conditions they can be destructive.

The direct police aggression in Worcester is unusual. In other centres repression is mediated through vigilantes, allegedly with police or administration board assistance or collusion.

The residents of Zolani, Ashton suffer under the rule of vigilantes known as 'amosolomzi', or, as one of their opponents called them, 'vet katte'. The history of conflict goes back to school boycotts in 1985. A group of 'fathers' from the Langeberg Co-op - virtually the sole employer in Ashton, a town of high unemployment - clashed with school students in an attempt to force them back to school.

Since then this vigilante group has dominated township life. In a significant new development, vigilantes, as well as working at Langeberg Co-op, are employed by the development board as community guards for R56 per week. This was confirmed by Gilbert Matroos in court.[4] Residents claim that these 'community guards' are terrorising the local population.

Following a funeral in Zolani, a crowd stoned and burnt the homes and cars of some vigilantes. There is evidence that vigilantes went around with a list and arrested people late that night after the event. Most of those arrested were involved in civic or other organisations, or were individuals against whom vigilantes bore a grudge. For example, one woman was at home cooking when she heard the commotion, but did not even go to investigate, because 'the food was on the stove'. When she was in bed that night, she was arrested and kept in jail for three months awaiting trial. Some of those arrested were allegedly assaulted in the presence of police. All accused were discharged at the end of the state's case. Allegations of this nature are rife; but vigilantes apparently have free reign.

In Paarl, political and ideological differences in the community have been exploited to pit people against one another. Again the community is divided as the state works to bolster the bodies and initiatives it sponsors.

At the beginning of the emergency, many were detained - generally those active in civic, women's and youth organisations. In October, a number of leaders were called to a meeting of the local administration board to inform officials of grievances so that they could improve conditions. The group told the officials to come to the township and hear the grievances from the people themselves. A complication arose over the role of the mayor, BL Nobula. Evidently the officials wanted popular leaders to present Nobula to the community at this meeting, and so gain credibility for him. Not surprisingly there was great concern and dissatisfaction about this proposal.

A woman who refused to attend this meeting received death threats the following day, from someone calling himself Ngxobongwana. Ngxobongwana, the leader of Old Crossroads, is a name associated immediately with witdoek vigilantes. The voice, however, was a youthful one, obviously not that of Ngoxobongwana. The threatened woman was told to bring peace within the township because 'an African must not fight an African', and was warned to stop taking part in political activities or she would be killed.

Tragically, this threat was interpreted in terms of the ongoing conflict between the UDF and AZAPO in Mbekweni, a conflict with a long and complicated history.

Overall, in the words of a relief worker:

> The Boland areas are small and more organised. Since 1984, people have been strong... The police have taken exception to those areas, they are trying to crush them. For example, in Robertson resistance forced the community councillors to resign and join people's organisations. This has shown what a failure they are. The authorities are now hammering and trying to crush community organisations.

The emergency on the Cape Flats

Key activists and leaders in the coloured townships of the Cape Flats have gone into hiding or been detained. Mass detentions right at the start of the emergency were particularly effective. On Sunday 15 June, an entire congregation - 189 men, women and children - was detained at a prayer service in St Nicholas Anglican Church, Elsies River. On 16 June shooting and teargassing, followed by detentions, occurred after a prayer service at St Athan's Road Mosque. On 20 July, at Holy Trinity Catholic Church, Elsies River, some 500 people attending a service in support of the families of detainees were held inside the sealed-off church. The congregation was video-taped and eventually allowed to leave; whereupon departing congregants were teargassed. Residents of a nearby block of flats reported that 'police were firing rubber bullets at some of the congregation who were going home over the nearby bridge which leads to Modderdam Road'.[5] Three detentions were reported. For many people, this was sufficient deterrent against involvement in public protest.

According to one informant, 'The emergency gives that fear of mass detention. In 1985 people thought that speakers and leaders at meetings would be detained. Now they realise that even just going to a meeting they can be detained, even in church services'. In most areas, activists and organisations continue working secretly and under trying conditions, but it is difficult to mobilise the community on a large scale because people are too afraid to get involved.

High-profile and public organisation was almost impossible, especially in the first three months of the emergency. However, where an issue is important to people's daily lives, it is still possible to organise a united response. For example in Bo-Kaap, where a new housing scheme proved highly controversial, a joint committee was formed to meet with the council, hold meetings and attempt to solve the problem to the advantage of the community.

Disinformation campaigns also contribute to people's fear. Pamphlets circulated in the name of opposition organisations attempt to criminalise them. For example, a pamphlet circulated in Mannenberg before a commemoration service for the 1985 'Trojan Horse' killings portrayed the deceased as victims of UDF killings. The propaganda effect of television is also a real threat to organisations attempting to gain support.

The state's strategy of destabilising community organisation and attempting to co-opt people into approved channels is also in evidence. For example Bonteheuwel, which in 1986 was highly troubled and militant particularly in the schools, was apparently allocated large sums for upgrading schemes to improve living conditions.

But optimism remains:

> Despite all this (the emergency) things are changing - they are not what they were two years ago. People will pick up again, on the basis of the past year, when it is possible... May Day and June 16 were mass stayaways, which show that things are on the march.

The emergency and organisations

A broad range of organisations - political, community, worker, student and religious - have been effectively banned in the Western Cape. Orders prevent 119 organisations from functioning, from holding any meetings and publishing any statements in any form. It is too early to assess what the effects will be on their work and support in the long term.

But 'organisations have learnt the lessons of the previous state of emergency and are taking the time now as an opportunity for consolidation, education, and developing skills for future periods'. Finding new ways of working has been emphasised - the aim being to survive in a situation of semi-legality while fighting for the legal right to meet.

Attempts are made to find and exploit loopholes in the emergency regulations. One approach is through the courts and legal process. An application to the supreme court was brought by the UDF and the Western Cape Teachers Union for an order invalidating regulations and orders made by the divisional commissioner of police, at that time Brigadier CA Swart. These organisations were fighting for their right to hold meetings and to restrain 'the police from rendering lawful UDF and WECTU meetings inaccessible to people entitled to attend' (*Argus*, 01.08.86). Days before the matter was to come to court the relevant regulations were repealed. Almost immediately, new regulations were drafted, restoring the restrictions.

There is a general feeling that high-profile styles of organisation

are no longer appropriate. Almost all attempts to hold mass meetings have been thwarted. Three proposed UDF meetings were
banned: one to celebrate its third anniversary; one to plan a
response to the current crisis; and a memorial meeting for Samora
Machel. The End Conscription Campaign ran a 'Right to Speak'
campaign culminating in a rally. But a UDF 'Christmas of Concern'
campaign, intended to focus attention on detainees, was banned. A
People's Cultural Festival - music, plays, poetry and discussions -
planned for December was banned the day before it was due to
begin. A protest march was organised by the Muslim community,
following the Nederduitse Gereformeerde Kerk's declaration that
Islam is a false religion. Some 300 protesters congregated on the
Grand Parade in the centre of Cape Town. The crowd was dispersed by sjambok charges and a number were arrested, while
Saturday morning shoppers went about their business. The state
took tough action against any form of opposition, whether organised by youth groups, civic organisations or religious groups.

The emergency was also notable for the clampdown on trade
unionists, particularly those from affiliates of the Congress of South
African Trade Unions. COSATU itself was banned from holding
meetings and issuing publications in the Western Cape. Officially
most trade unions could continue functioning, but under constant
threat of detentions and harassment. Many unionists went into
hiding, offices closed down, there was uncertainty as to whether
meetings could be held or not, and offices were searched and
names of officials and office-bearers gathered. One unionist expressed it thus:

> It seems they were trying to look for persons perceived as 'political'; alterna-
> tively, detentions are a form of harassment, of scaring people by random
> detentions of unionists... They gave warnings, just to let people know that they
> were watching and could act, should they so desire or require.

By late August, the Labour Monitoring Group knew of at least
50 detentions of trade unionists in the Western Cape. The Food
and Allied Workers Union was particularly affected, with 20 members detained. Protest work stoppages among its members were
recorded at two fruit-packing companies in Grabouw. At the Sea
Harvest plant in Saldanha Bay, workers went on strike following
the detention of a fellow worker. This led to the closure of the factory for a day. The Transport and General Workers Union suffered

four detentions and held a number of protest strikes. A new type of
restriction order was served on one of its officials, Rae Lazarus, on
her release from detention. But

> although trade unions have been badly affected by the state crackdown and
> there can be little doubt that industrial relations in the future will be marked
> by this current experience, it is also true that unions have shown much more
> resilience under pressure than even the most popular of the political or-
> ganisations.[6]

Organisations legally able to continue working under the emergency included a range of crisis relief and monitoring groups. They
too were under extreme pressure - of time, limited resources in the
face of a massive demand, stringent emergency regulations and the
constant threat of detention.

The Advice Office Forum, a body co-ordinating resources, campaigns and strategies for a number of community-based advice offices, was one such body. Advice office workers were harassed or
forced into hiding, and their offices were constantly visited by the
security police or forced to close.

In Cape Town the Repression Monitoring Group runs a relief
office offering counselling and assistance to detainees, prisoners
and their families. It aims to help the families of detainees to take
action themselves despite a sense of confusion and helplessness.
This is done by confirming detentions, applying for visits, delivering
food parcels and pocket money, and so on. A second task is to
record information and compile statistics which are published in a
weekly fact sheet.

There is a great deal of co-ordination between groups. The
Dependents Conference focuses on assisting detainees, prisoners
and their families with legal and financial aid. It was responsible for
bringing 15 to 20 urgent supreme court applications for the release
of detainees. The present crisis has increased its workload enormously - members have had to work as far away as Knysna, as well
as in the Boland and Southern Cape, and have assisted with 550
legal cases from January to August 1986. They are helped by the
Black Sash Court Monitoring Group whose members monitor the
progress of political trials as well as providing support for
prisoners' families.

In the first days of the emergency, the Progressive Federal Party
warned government that it would use parliament to expose

excesses. Its Unrest Monitoring Action Group visits trouble areas, collects affidavits and passes this information to members of parliament so that questions can be raised. A research team monitors a computer listing of detainees' names - in effect a missing persons' bureau.

The effects of the emergency are continually changing. For the first two months people were very much aware of its restrictions and harshness on a daily basis. Since then, it has faded from the public's mind, and organisations have begun to find ways to function.

On 29 November 1986, an amendment published in the *Government Gazette* empowered police to ban indoor gatherings without first obtaining a magisterial order. Perhaps this was a warning to opposition organisations not to resume their work. The proclamation and the tone of four 'technical' amendments 'show that the state of emergency is certainly not dead' (*Argus*, 30.11.86). This was graphically confirmed by the still more stringent restrictions on 'subversive' publications promulgated in December 1986, and by the clampdown on re-emergent activists, organisations and campaigns since then.

The overwhelming consensus is that the 1986 emergency was an attempt to crush political resistance. The state is determinedly on the offensive to 'restore law and order'. But resistance has grown into a mass rejection of apartheid domination in all spheres of life. In assessing the effects of the emergency, it is important to understand it as just one particularly repressive historical moment in the struggle for liberation in South Africa.

Notes

1   Research towards this article was carried out under the auspices of the South African Institute of Race Relations (Western Cape).
2   Zwelakhe Sisulu, 'People's Education for People's Power', *Transformation*, 1, 1986, 97.
3   Unrest Monitoring Action Committee, 'Report on monitoring visit to Browns Farm', 20.08.86.
4   Evidence led by Gilbert Matroos, at the trial of State versus M Bakwana and 29 others, 20.10.86.
5   Unrest Monitoring Action Committee, 'Report', 20.07.86.
6   Pippa Green, 'Trade Unions and the State of Emergency', *South African Labour Bulletin*, 11(7), 1986, 75.

Courts and the State of Emergency

Nicholas Haysom and Steven Kahanovitz

For a period during 1985 and 1986 South African human rights lawyers could be forgiven for believing they were the central actors on the political stage. A November 1985 headline in the *Weekly Mail*, for example, proclaimed that 'Courts challenge the state'.

Daily newspapers frequently ran similar headlines: 'Major setback for government'; 'Judge's ruling brings new rights; 'Courts reverse apartheid'. This reflected the euphoria of human rights lawyers who believed that at last, 'their time had come'. And it generated a misplaced optimism that South Africa could take a civil liberties route out of its racial and political problems, as the United States had supposedly done 30 years before.

This optimism incorrectly encouraged the view that the courts, standing alone, were capable of awarding or returning democratic and civil rights to passive legal subjects, and that it was judges and lawyers who were the guardians and grantors of these rights. This perspective ignored the fact that the legal process takes place alongside much larger struggles and often in response to them.

Even so, many of the legal challenges to state policies and practices were impressive - even unthinkable only ten years ago. The new-found confidence in the courts reached a high point in August 1986 when Justice DP Friedman, using a line of reasoning which even his admirers found strained, ruled in effect that every emergency detention was invalid. After Friedman's judgment in the *Tsenoli* case was rejected by the Appellate Division in October 1986, the spate of legal challenges began to ebb noticeably.

This article addresses two associated questions. What impact did the courts have during 1985 and 1986; and why did they receive so much attention and political significance?

It is difficult to appreciate how marked the swing towards forensic activism was, without noting the doldrums the human rights industry had experienced in the previous 30 years. South Africa has long been noted for its obsession with law and legal institutions. This is manifested by a misplaced and remarkably persistent pride in the independence of the judiciary and the fairness of its legal institutions. It is also manifested in the government's propensity to couch extreme and authoritarian powers in precise legal form.

One must go back 30 years to find a period in which human rights litigation enjoyed its current level of support and enthusiasm, when judges were regarded as potential allies in the struggle for democratic rights. During the 1950s, when some believed that a liberal judiciary stood between the Nationalist government and the implementation of apartheid policy.

In the next two decades legal activism gave way to pessimism. The Nationalist government introduced legislation that explicitly provided for racial discrimination and replaced rights of legal redress with autocratic or discretionary powers in the hands of officials. These 'administrative' powers were open to judicial review on only the narrowest of grounds. At the same time allegations that appointments to the bench were made on political grounds were levelled. The judiciary developed what jurisprudents called an 'executive-minded' approach to legislation under the philosophical banner of legal positivism - parliament makes the laws, and judges merely apply them. A few lonely professors, notably Dugard, Mathews and Van Niekerk, pleaded for judicial and legal activism, for judges to make good laws through creative interpretation rather than apply bad ones.

The left responded to this jurisprudential debate with an understandably instrumentalist view of the courts and a cynical attitude to legal intervention. Many argued that the courts were unable to advance, defend or protect rights because they were the direct agents of the apartheid state and the dominant class interests which controlled it. Where the courts did advance 'rights' it was only to perform the function of legitimating the social structure to easily duped, powerless and rightless citizens. This 'no win' approach prevented any investigation of the tactical use of the courts.

Lawyers make a come-back

Legal pessimism in the 1960s and 1970s slowly gave way to a cautious optimism in the 1980s. Political organisations, trade unions and human rights lawyers began arguing for a tactical approach to the use of legal institutions and adopted a less instrumental view of the law. Left-wing jurisprudence acknowledged that law is necessarily a contradictory institution. Lawyers achieved victories in areas that could not be dismissed as insignificant. Rights to publish, to meet, to join trade unions, to freedom of movement and to job security, were patently important, even preconditions of political or trade union organisation. Several successes were achieved initially before tribunals such as the Publications Appeal Board and the industrial court.

Trade unions recognised that the use of the industrial court could secure significant rights to job security, and freedom from victimisation and a variety of unfair labour practices in an otherwise authoritarian and repressive society. The industrial court allowed disenfranchised employees to call a white employer to account. The National Union of Mineworkers' judicious use of the industrial and supreme courts contrasted markedly with its British counterpart, which learnt in the course of the bitter and lengthy strike of 1984-85 that ignoring legal institutions could prove disastrous and naive. While left unionists in the United Kingdom were debating whether the courts should be boycotted, their South African counterparts were engaged in the more advanced debate as to the proper circumstances in which issues should be resolved organisationally, or were capable of advancement through legal avenues. The focus had shifted from the pessimistic 'no win' position to an examination of the organisational impact of an over-use of legal avenues.

In the Publications Appeal Board a range of progressive publications - Grassroots, SASPU National and *Work in Progress* - repeatedly had prohibitions and banning orders set aside. They learnt quickly that refusing to participate in the censorship appeal machinery was a fashionable principle only poets and artists could afford.

The legal challenges in the law courts proper commenced from 1980 onwards with selective attacks on aspects of apartheid policy. Successes were achieved in challenging influx control laws and regulations (*Komani* and *Rikhoto*); forced removals (*Shadrack More*); group areas (*Govender*); and township regulations and land rights.

These cases played an important role in expanding what was legally possible and in the renascence of a civil liberties approach to statutory interpretation. Legal challenges in the cases referred to above rendered many aspects of apartheid legislation inoperable. The state was often prepared to countenance these challenges without introducing amending legislation. Government was in any event introducing cautious reforms in an attempt to restructure the contours of opposition politics.

But this 'reformist' period was also characterised by a high level of repression. And while the state could live with challenges to aspects of apartheid policy it was less willing to sacrifice its ability to control political developments. For lawyers the real test was whether government would tolerate a challenge to its ability to deal with black resistance, and more particularly to its seemingly impregnable citadel, security legislation.

The parameters of legitimate resistance

In the early 1980s rapid growth of above-ground political and trade union organisation was based on legal, organised opposition to apartheid. One reason why 1984, 1985 and 1986 saw challenges to legislation affecting civil liberties was this growth of popular extra-parliamentary opposition to apartheid. For example the United Democratic Front expressly sought to exploit the possibility of open and public opposition to apartheid and thus had to explore parameters for political movements operating outside constitution-ally-defined structures. It was logical that the UDF and emerging unions, concerned to remain within the confines of the law, would conflict with government over the parameters of legality, and that this conflict would be played out in the law courts.

The state itself attempted to use the courts to confine extra-parliamentary opposition. This was clearest in the prosecution of UDF, community and union leaders in the Pietermaritzburg and Delmas treason trials. In both cases the prosecution was primarily directed at the campaigns, meetings, speeches and publications of the UDF. The Pietermaritzburg case illustrated that a spirited and aggressive defence before a receptive judge could force the prosecution to crumble. In the second case an equally spirited defence before a less receptive judge has not had the same impact.

A 1984 attempt to pre-empt politically motivated worker stayaways by prosecuting MAWU leader Moses Mayekiso failed to get off the ground, and until recently the state has been more reluctant to prosecute worker leaders. Although the state has experienced legal difficulties in some treason trials, this has not been the case in charging youths and activists in the lower courts with a myriad of lesser offences, particularly public violence.

While this article highlights legal activism, particularly through supreme court litigation, it must be remembered that South African 'criminal justice' takes place mainly in the magistrates' courts. While the supreme court (albeit inconsistently) was opening areas of democratic opposition in this period, the lower courts were acting as part of the state's disciplinary machinery against a rebellious youth.

Challenging detentions and bannings

Supreme court litigation had some impact in challenging the implementation of security legislation and the exercise of police powers under the state of emergency.

Security legislation notoriously protected police officials from legal checks by ousting the jurisdiction of courts. It prevented legal access to detainees, and granted wide and unfettered discretion to police officials. Challenges to aspects of security legislation started prior to the state of emergency when opposition organisations challenged prohibitions on meetings under section 46 of the Internal Security Act (*UDF vs Acting Magistrate; UDF vs Theron;* and *State vs Mahlangu).* In two of these cases the UDF had succeeded in having a magistrate's prohibition on indoor gatherings set aside. In *Mahlangu's* case the ministerial ban on outdoor meetings, enforced since 1976, was declared invalid. (Shortly after the judgment the Minister of Law and Order issued a new and apparently valid ban on outdoor gatherings).

It was not until 1985 that lawyers seriously considered challenging the power to detain people under the Internal Security Act and the emergency regulations. In 1985 successful challenges were launched against refusals to grant political trialists bail. In *Ramgobin's* case a Natal court criticised the right of the attorney-general to refuse bail and prevent an application for bail being heard by a court. Justice Milne commented that he failed 'to see the purpose or necessity of this legislative curtailment of ancient and fundamental rights, nor can I see any occasion under which its use can be justified. I venture to suggest that serious consideration should be given to its repeal'.

In due course the courts upheld challenges to the attorney-general's refusal to allow bail applications. Next to be challenged were preventive detention orders. Section 28 of the Internal Security Act allowed the authorities to detain people in order to prevent them from committing suspected future acts which might threaten the security of the state. In *Gumede's* case the court declared the detention orders issued by the minister of law and order invalid as he had failed to give adequate reasons for them. The case involved a number of UDF leaders who had been detained on the eve of the Indian and coloured tricameral elections. The minister then issued new detention orders and these too were subject to a similar but unsuccessful challenge (*Nkondo*).

When these cases were heard on appeal, the Appellate Division ruled that the minister was bound to provide proper reasons for detaining people. As a result of this judgment, several banning orders were set aside on the same reasoning. But in 1986 government introduced a new form of preventive detention which did not require that reasons for the detention be given.

Finally a challenge was launched against detention in terms of section 29, which provides for indefinite detention in solitary confinement for interrogation. Few lawyers believed that this could be challenged. But in *Hurley's* case the detention of churchman Paddy Kearny was successfully challenged in both the Natal court and the Appellate Division. The police argued that it was not necessary for them to justify the detention and that the courts were prevented from setting aside detention orders. The court held that it was entitled to investigate whether the detention was proper in accordance with law, and accordingly whether there were proper reasons for the decision to detain Kearny. As the police had not placed any reasons before the court it was unable to assess whether proper reasons for the detention existed, and accordingly ordered the release of Kearny.

In these cases the two barriers which security officials had long been able to hide behind were opened. In certain instances police were now obliged to give reasons for their actions. And the courts could not be excluded from checking whether procedures laid down in legislation had been followed.

When a state of emergency was declared in terms of the Public Safety Act in August 1985 and again in June 1986, new regulations gave wide powers to police officials which extended the powers they possessed under the Internal Security Act. These allowed for broad powers of arrest and detention with the object of curbing civil revolt through mass warehousing of activists.

Emergency detentions were subjected to literally hundreds of challenges along similar lines to the Internal Security Act detentions. In September 1986 over 100 applications for emergency detainees were pending. Initially many of the successful legal challenges were technical or procedural in nature, asserting merely a failure to follow the proper procedures; or a failure to supply any or proper reasons for an arrest or detention or to follow the proper sequence; or a failure to allow detainees the right to make representations.

In *Nkwinti's* case it was unsuccessfully argued that the state of emergency itself was unlawful. It was then argued that the minister was bound to allow detainees to make representations about their detention. For this purpose the minister had to give reasons for the detention. Justice Kannemeyer accepted that this proposition (raised in cases before the emergency) also applied to emergency detainees. He held that unless the regulations specifically excluded an opportunity to make representations, this had to be given.

Shortly afterwards the regulations were amended. The right to make representations before the minister decided to extend the detention beyond 14 days was expressly withdrawn. In the cases of *Fanie* and *Omar* the courts took this amendment to mean that a detainee had no right to reasons for detention or to make representations. However in *Momoniat's* case the Witwatersrand Supreme Court suggested that the amended regulations excluded the right to make representations for the first 14 days only, thus suggesting that there was still scope for intervention through the courts. In *Bill's* case the court ruled that detainees were still entitled to reasons for their detention after the first 14 days.

Challenges were also launched to procedures followed by the police. In *Hlahla's* case the release of the detainee was ordered as he had been held in a prison different from the one indicated by the minister of law and order. In *Itsweng's* case the detainee was first held under section 50(1) of the Internal Security Act. His detention was then changed to fall under emergency regulations without his knowledge. This subsequent detention order was held to be invalid as it was not preceded by a valid arrest as required by the emergency regulations. The *Suttner* case subsequently held that a person already arrested need not be released but only informed of his re-arrest under emergency regulations.

In due course applicants challenged the actual decision to detain. In these cases the good faith of the arresting officer was queried. For example in *Dempsey's* case a nun was arrested for interfering with a police officer: the court decided it was not necessary for emergency powers to be used because an ordinary criminal procedure arrest would have sufficed. In *Radebe's* case the release of a reporter was ordered as the arresting officer, who had merely come across the newsman while involved in a raid, could not have come to the conclusion that it was necessary to arrest him.

In *Jaffer's* case, a Cape butcher had been arrested because posters advertising a 16 June meeting were found at his shop. His release was ordered as the court held that there was no reason why he should be detained after 16 June. A similar decision was handed down by the Eastern Cape court (*Bishop of Roman Catholic Church of the Diocese of Port Elizabeth*) when it was held that there was no reason for the continued detention of a priest after the 16 June service at which he was to have officiated.

As challenges to emergency detentions increased, the success rate declined. It became clear that the impact of technical or procedural objections was limited. Success was fairly simple when a police official refused to give reasons for a detention, or to allow representations from a detainee. But once reasons were given or representations made the detainee had little chance of success in an application for release.

Challenging the emergency regulations

The power of arrest and detention is only one of the powers the state of emergency facilitates. A second is a back-handed compliment to the legal initiatives of the past two years. For the regulations expressly insulate police powers and conduct from legal inspection, supervision or discipline, and allow the security forces freedom to operate on the margins of illegality.

Emergency regulations excluded legal access to detainees. They expressly stated that courts had no power to set aside, pronounce upon or monitor the conduct of policemen.

Just as revealing is the indemnity granted to members of the security forces against any civil or criminal proceeding brought against them as a result of reckless, negligent, or unlawful acts committed 'in good faith'. To succeed in an action against the police a litigant would have to prove malice or bad faith on the part of the police. Effectively this indemnity provided a licence for official lawlessness.

The state of emergency is thus an attempt to enforce order without law, to exercise power in its most naked form.

A number of legal challenges successfully undermined this attempt to throw a protective barrier around police conduct. MAWU successfully overturned the regulation preventing legal access to detainees. The union argued that the state president exceeded his powers in making the emergency regulations and had not followed the proper procedure in doing so. If successful, this argument would have declared the state of emergency unlawful. The court hearing the MAWU application rejected these arguments, but did strike out some regulations prohibiting publication of subversive statements because they went beyond the powers of the state president or were so vague that no precise meaning could be attributed to them.

The court also ruled that the state president could not make 'regulations that affect the administration of justice in general' and as a result of this certain regulations inhibiting access of detainees to legal advisers were struck out. This in turn allowed the treatment of detainees to be monitored.

This monitoring was clearly necessary, as shown in the *Wendy Orr* case, where a district surgeon brought an application alleging widespread and systematic assaults on detainees in the Port

Elizabeth/Uitenhage region.

Another feature of the regulations is the attempt to control the flow of information within and from South Africa. Regulations restricted the right to report on conditions of detention, activities of political organisations, unrest incidents and police conduct. A number of these regulations were lacerated in court applications more fully detailed by Armstrong elsewhere in this section.

The state's prohibition on reporting of unrest events, treatment of detainees and conduct of security forces supports the suggestion that emergency regulations were primarily designed to allow the police a free hand in dealing with black resistance. This 'free hand' entailed a high degree of official terror unconstrained by legal or public scrutiny.

Human rights groups and the media soon began using the courts to expose police abuses. But in January 1987 government prohibited the reporting of proceedings or allegations made in court until the court had issued a 'final' judgment. In effect this restriction meant that allegations of torture or assault of the kind contained in the *Wendy Orr* matter could never be reported, for this case was settled out of court and thus no 'final' judgment was given.

Legal challenges were also brought with varying degrees of success against police orders prohibiting a variety of actions including the wearing of T-shirts, attendance at funerals, and holding of union meetings. In addition applications were brought to set aside rules governing detainees, or to restrain the security forces. Many of these legal challenges did little more than inconvenience the police and force them to account for their actions. They may have constituted little more than the 'dogs of law' snapping at the feet of the security forces.

But some of the cases did threaten to pose severe problems for the state. Amongst these was the *Tsenoli* judgment. The effect of this would have been to secure the release of every emergency detainee on the ground that police did not have the powers of arrest they claimed. However the Appellate Division rejected Friedman's judgment and restored the authority of the security forces.

The empire strikes back

The state responded to these legal challenges in a number of ways.

Its draftsmen were sent back to the drawing board, and new regulations issued to meet the criticisms of the courts. Many of the legal challenges had related to technical and formal deficiencies in procedures. Adapting to these requirements was not always difficult, as the courts required only an appearance of fairness. The wide, discretionary powers themselves were seldom affected.

Challenges to the actual powers of the authorities or the conduct of security forces were rare because these powers are couched in such broad terms. For example, once the police had learnt the required formula for justifying a detention, they could and did advance legally acceptable reasons for detaining individuals. Those applying for the release of detainees were hamstrung in their capacity to contest police allegations because the courts were reluctant to allow oral cross-examination of investigating officers and refused to allow detainees to be brought to court to testify.

A policeman advancing reasons for detention could do so sure in the knowledge that these would not be tested. When courts ordered legal access to detainees, police and prison officials introduced and enforced administrative obstacles leading to delays of three to four weeks before a lawyer could visit a detainee.

The state seldom prosecuted alleged contraventions of emergency regulations. Armed with wide powers to arrest or seize, detention or confiscation was simpler and swifter than prosecuting suspected 'law-breakers'. Similarly, foreign journalists have been deported for stories which displeased the authorities rather than prosecuted for failure to follow the regulations. This power to act administratively had a powerful disciplinary effect on journalists who resorted to self-censorship rather than risk deportation or closure of their publications. Authoritarian caprice was as powerful an inducement to self-censorship as the inscrutable emergency regulations.

The *Tsenoli* judgment signalled a retreat on the part of the judiciary which may have become concerned that it had overstepped the bounds of reasonable judicial intervention. Thus a recent application for the release of a 13-year-old was turned down on the grounds that 13-year-olds were indeed capable of threatening state security.

Reducing the level of terror

Lawyers can claim with some justification that the flood of legal challenges to the emergency powers exercised some check on the conduct of security force officials and reduced the level of official terror that the state of emergency was designed to allow. In some cases these challenges have been significant in their own right but in others they have been more of an irritation factor to the state.

But those who argue that legal restraints are of little significance should note that the authorities have gone to considerable lengths to exclude legal supervision and create the capacity to act outside legal limits. Those who have faced the new forms of extra-legal violence - assassinations and right-wing vigilante actions - will testify to their frighteningly destructive potential, and are unlikely to dismiss legal restraints as unimportant.

The state of emergency was itself one of the conditions for the boom in the human rights industry. Mass campaigns were hindered, and the regulations hampered many organisations in their daily operations. One way in which these organisations sought to maintain their political profile was by engaging the state through litigation, which ensured both kudos and publicity.

But the question remains as to why some judges should now be showing concern for human rights issues. There are those who suggest that the judiciary's new approach arises out of a concern to establish human rights, including property and 'group' rights, prior to black majority rule. This is given force by the fact that the previously unpopular concept of a bill of rights has suddenly become fashionable in government circles.

A more likely explanation is some judges' realisation that the law and its institutions are facing a severe crisis of legitimacy. The law has lost its protective capacity and has mainly oppressive connotations. In these circumstances lawyers as well as judges are increasingly concerned to distance legal institutions from apartheid's laws. In this way they hope to recapture some of the ground that has been lost, for example, to the risky but expeditious and inexpensive forum of the people's courts.

'Hear No Evil, See No Evil, Speak No Evil': Media Restrictions and the State of Emergency

Amanda Armstrong

The media clampdown during the present state of emergency was not thunder and lightning in a previously blue sky. For the South African media had been severely restricted before the emergency was declared on 12 June 1986.[1]

The emergency introduced harsh and far-reaching restrictions.[2] But for a number of years prior to this, the media, and in particular the press, were already subject to severe legislative restrictions. These are contained in over a hundred statutes, the most important of which are the Defence Act,[3] the Police Act,[4] the Prisons Act,[5] the Internal Security Act[6] and the Publications Act.[7]

Media restrictions before the emergency

With few exceptions, the pre-emergency restrictions are contained in statutes or amendments promulgated since 1977. The clampdown on media is therefore largely a phenomenon of the past decade.[8]

In terms of the Defence Act, no person may publish

* information relating to the composition or activities of the South African Defence Force;[9]

* any statement relating to a member or activity of the South African Defence Force calculated to prejudice or embarrass the government in its foreign relations, or alarm or depress members of the public;[10]

* any secret information relating to the defence of South Africa.[11]

In terms of the Police Act, no person may publish

* anything untrue concerning any action by the police without having reasonable grounds to believe it is true.[12] In a prosecution the state does not have to prove that the allegations made are untrue; rather, an accused has to establish that he or she had reasonable grounds to believe that the allegations were true.

Under the Prisons Act, no one may publish

* any false information about the behaviour or experience in prison of any prisoner or ex-prisoner, or concerning the administration of any prison.[13] Again, an accused has to establish that he or she had reasonable grounds to believe that information published was true.

In terms of the above three Acts, no person may publish

* photographs or sketches of military premises or installations,[14] certain persons in police custody,[15] or any prison or prisoner.[16]

The Internal Security Act prohibits publication of

* speeches or statements of people who are, for example, prohibited from attending gatherings, or who are on a consolidated list drawn up by the Minister of Law and Order;[17]

* material which would cause feelings of hostility between different races;[18]

* a notice advertising a prohibited gathering.[19]

Furthermore, in terms of the Internal Security Act the Minister of Law and Order may ban a publication for a specified period by notice in the Government Gazette.[20] The Act also specifies that a wide range of acts, including publishing, could constitute the offences of terrorism,[21] subversion,[22] or promoting communism.[23]

In 1974 the Publications Act was introduced to 'provide for the control of certain publications or objects, films and public entertainment'.[24] The Act is directed at publications which are 'undesirable' morally, or on religious grounds, or because they are prejudicial to the safety of the state.[25] It gives substantial censorship powers to the directorate of publications and its committees to ban publications either for distribution, or for possession and distribution. [26] These bans may apply to a single edition, or to all future editions of a publication.

In the Publications Act, the definition of 'publication' excludes newspapers produced by members of the National Press Union (NPU).[27] Thus as far as newspapers and magazines are concerned, this Act is directed at the more alternative press.

State pressure on the media intensified during the early 1980s, and the Steyn Commission into the mass media recommended further statutory restrictions. In an attempt to avoid this, members of the established media formed the South African Media Council. Members of the NPU are bound by the Council's constitution and its code of conduct, and are subject to disciplinary procedures. The disciplinary function of the council essentially amounts to a form of self-censorship as opposed to state censorship.

The media clampdown of the past decade has involved a state response to changing circumstances. Alternative newspapers and magazines have developed alongside the commercial press, while the foreign media has increased coverage of events in South Africa. Both the alternative and the foreign media's coverage of political and economic developments has been critical of the South African state. There has also been increasing coverage of the nature and extent of extra-parliamentary resistance.

A further reason for this ever-tightening control over the media since 1976 is the escalating resistance to the state. The state's response has been one of increasing repression, including restrictions imposed on the flow of information and ideas.

The emergency regulations concerning the media are in many ways an extension of these earlier statutory restrictions. They do create substantially different and far-reaching restrictions, but are part of an on-going process of repression and control which started years before the emergency was declared.

Economic pressures also limit what is published, particularly with regard to the commercial press. The large publishing companies, in order to make a profit, have to sell newspapers to a primarily white public, and have to obtain revenue from advertising. From the point of view of these publishing companies they cannot afford to print material which would alarm or challenge their readership or advertising clients. The commercial media therefore tends to reflect the ideology of the ruling classes in South Africa. Thus in a country which contains an ever-increasing diversity of views and opinions, the commercial media represents only a fragment of these.

This is even more so in the case of radio and television. With the exception of Bophuthatswana television, which the South African Broadcasting Corporation (SABC) has prevented South African viewers from receiving, and M-Net, which prohibits the broadcasting of news or political comment, all television stations in South Africa are controlled by the South African state via the SABC. There is similar state control over all radio stations broadcasting from within South Africa and the 'independent' bantustans.

The initial press regulations

The regulations governing the earlier state of emergency, declared on 21 July 1985[28] and terminated on 7 March 1986,[29] contained virtually no provisions aimed directly at restricting the media.

However, the regulations that accompanied the present state of emergency introduced extremely severe and detailed provisions aimed specifically at restricting the mass media, including not only the press, but also radio, film, television, photographic material and various other forms of visual representation.[30]

The most important emergency regulations affecting the media were:

* Regulation 9, which prohibited the taking or the publication of photographic material or sound recordings of unrest situations or of the conduct of any member of the security forces;[31]

* Regulation 10, which provided that any person who publishes, distributes or displays a subversive statement would be guilty of an offence which would be punishable on conviction with a maximum penalty of a fine of R20 000 or imprisonment for a period of ten years, or to imprisonment without the option of a fine.[32]

The definition of 'subversive statement'[33] was so widely framed that its meaning and its limits were very difficult to determine. It included anything which was likely to have the effect of:

* promoting any objects of an unlawful organisation;
* inciting persons to take part in various activities including resistance or opposition to the government;
* engendering or aggravating feelings of hostility in South Africa;
* encouraging persons to commit any act which endangers the safety of the public, the maintenance of the public order, or the termination of the state of emergency;
* weakening or undermining the confidence of the public in the termination of the state of emergency;
* promoting disinvestment or the application of sanctions or foreign action against South Africa.

In terms of Regulation 11, the Minister of Law and Order, who is the official responsible for all emergency regulations, or a person authorised by him, could order the seizure of one or more or all copies of any publication which, in his opinion, contained a subversive statement or any other information which may be detrimental to the safety of the public.

On 13 June 1986 the Minister acted in terms of Regulation 11 and ordered police to remove that day's editions of the *Sowetan* and *Weekly Mail* from distribution points - presumably because they contained 'subversive statements' or other information which was detrimental to the safety of the public.

In terms of Regulation 12, if the Minister was satisfied, on examination of any publication, that the publication contained material of a subversive nature, he could authorise the seizure of all copies of that publication and all subsequent issues of such publication. This provision in effect enabled the Minister to ban a publication for the duration of the state of emergency.

Finally, two of the numerous orders issued by the Commissioner of Police in terms of Regulation 7 directly affected the media. The first amounted to a blanket ban on the reporting of any conduct of the security forces.[34] The second prohibited the presence of journalists in any unrest or black residential area for the purposes of reporting.[35]

This was not the first time in South African legal history that such regulations have been introduced. During the first state of emergency declared in terms of the Public Safety Act,[36] namely the 1960 emergency covering over 120 magisterial districts, regulations[37] were issued which prohibited the publication of subversive statements, provided for the seizure of publications, and allowed for the prohibition of future issues of a publication. These provisions, although not as detailed as the emergency regulations above, are surprisingly similar to the current regulations.

The immediate effect of these regulations and police orders was to severely limit what could be published. The wide framing of the provisions also made it very difficult to determine which reports or photographs contravened the regulations or police orders.

The penalties for offences in terms of these regulations, and the powerful weapon of seizing an entire edition of a newspaper, made both the commercial and the alternative media loathe to risk prosecution or the economically dire consequences of seizure. For these reasons the media adopted a cautious and often conservative approach to what could be published.

Challenges to the initial press regulations

Internationally and nationally, protest was voiced against these regulations. Insofar as they affected the media, they were challenged in two court applications. The first involved *Metal and Allied Workers Union and Another v The State President of the Republic of South Africa and Others*[38] (the MAWU case). Four issues arose in this case, one of which was a challenge to the validity of the definition of 'subversive statement'. Essentially the application relied on principles of administrative law.

MAWU's lawyers argued that statutes (in this case the Public Safety Act) do not empower the authorities (in this case the state president) to make regulations which are so uncertain that people will not know how to comply with them, or whether they are even subject to them. The definition of subversive statement was uncertain and vague, therefore the definition was void and had no force and effect in law.

A second argument asserted that the state president had strayed beyond the limits of the Public Safety Act, and had acted ultra vires (outside of the law): the definition of a subversive statement was therefore of no force and effect in law.

The applicants were partially successful in their attack on the definition of a subversive statement. Sections of the definition were set aside, thus narrowing it, and the remaining sections were clarified to some extent by the judgement.

The second application involved the commercial English-speaking press, namely *Natal Newspapers (Pty) Ltd and Others v. The State President and Others*[39] (the Natal Newspapers case). Here the applicants challenged all those emergency regulations and orders which restricted the media.

The applicants relied upon administrative law arguments similar to those in the MAWU case. But in addition they argued that the regulations and orders granted discretionary powers to the state president's delegates which were contrary to the provisions of the Act, and that the regulations and orders were unreasonable, ultra vires, and therefore of no force and effect in law.

The *Natal Newspapers* applications succeeded in a number of arguments. The full bench of the Natal Provincial Division set aside regulations 11 and 12 - the seizure and banning provisions - and also set aside the two police orders banning reporting of security force actions, and journalistic presence in unrest or black residential areas.

Although the two applications provided the media with some short-term space in which to operate, the state was quick to respond by closing any gaps which had been created. The state president promulgated a series of amendments to the emergency regulations, which attempted to eliminate any existing loopholes and made the regulations more sophisticated.[40]

The new regulations

On 11 December 1986, the state president promulgated regulations designed specifically to restrict the media.[41] These codified and replaced all pre-existing regulations and police orders which imposed restrictions on the media during the present state of emergency, and also created additional and harsher forms of media control.

Prior to the promulgation of these new press regulations, state pressure was brought to bear on the NPU to draw up its own code for 'responsible' reporting during the state of emergency. In return the newspapers subject to the NPU would have been exempted from the new regulations. The state thus intended only the more alternative press to be subject to the new regulations. However, this attempt to divide and rule failed when the commercial media refused to co-operate in what amounted to further self-censorship.

The prohibition on 'subversive statements' remained in the new press regulations. But this was now more widely defined.[42] Prior aspects of the definition were redefined in a more detailed manner. Additional aspects were added to the definition, such as any statement likely to have the effect of inciting people to exercise power through alternative structures of local government, eg civic organisations, or inciting people to prosecute and to punish people by way of people's courts.

A significant aspect of the new press regulations is the introduction of 'publication control', where news or comment in certain categories may only be published with the permission of the state.[43] Thus if a newspaper editor is of the view that an article may contravene the provisions of this regulation, but still wishes to proceed with the publication of that article, the full text of the article has to be telexed to the Bureau for Information accompanied by a request for permission to publish.

Most of the categories listed are also mentioned in the definition of a subversive statement, such as boycott action, unlawful strikes, civil disobedience and unlawful gatherings.

However, this regulation goes beyond the prohibition on publication of a statement likely to have the effect of inciting the public to participate in certain specified acts. It is a prohibition on the publication of any news or comment which falls into the list of categories.

Furthermore, the categories are wider than those provided for in the definition of subversive statement, and include a prohibition on the publication of any news or comment in connection with any security action (widely defined in the new press regulations); the deployment of security forces or security technology; the circumstances or treatment of a person detained in terms of the emergency regulations; and the release of emergency detainees.

The new press regulations re-introduced the seizure provision which was set aside in the Natal Newspapers case. The Minister may now without prior notice issue an order authorising the seizure of a publication.[44]

In this regard, the major difference between the new and old regulations concerns the process of seizure. The new regulations set out more detailed procedural requirements for the state when it seizes a publication in terms of this provision. It has to provide the person or organisation affected with a copy of the order, and the test of whether a publication contravenes the regulations has to be objective, not just subject to the Minister's opinion. The Minister therefore does not have an unfettered discretion, and his decision must be based on factual and legal enquiries.

The provision whereby the Minister is able to ban future editions of a publication, set aside in the Natal Newspapers case, also re-emerged in the new regulations.[45] Again there are differences between this regulation and the prior regulation, the most important being that the Minister has to give a warning prior to banning, and can only prohibit publication for three months at a time. Again the test in connection with the application of this regulation is objective and no longer subjective.

The provisions of the two police orders which were set aside in the Natal Newspapers case have also been re-introduced: publication control includes news or comment on any security action,[46] and a separate regulation prohibits the presence of journalists in unrest areas, at restricted gatherings and at the scenes of security action.[47]

There is a new prohibition on the publication of blank spaces, or deletions of part of a text to indicate the nature and degree of censorship imposed upon the press.[48] This is in response to attempts by newspapers such as the *Sowetan, Weekly Mail* and the *Star* to indicate that they were being substantially censored by state-imposed restrictions. The state is thus attempting to conceal rather than reveal the fact of censorship.

An additional prohibition prevents the publication of news or comment on evidence submitted in court either by affidavit or oral evidence relating to the circumstances of, or the treatment in, detention of a person who is or was detained in terms of the emergency regulations and in which the court concerned has not yet given a final judgement.[49] This limits the normal privilege attached to evidence presented in a court of law, and is an attempt to silence evidence of unlawful conduct by security forces such as unlawful arrest and detention, and assault or torture of detainees.

The definition of 'publish'[50] is altered in the December 1986 regulations. It is defined as any act whereby a publication, or television, sound or film recording is taken personally or sent out of South Africa by post, courier or any other means. Previously this prohibition only applied to photographic material. The widening of this prohibition aims to prevent news or comment on the situation in South Africa from reaching the international community, and thereby to minimise anything which could fuel international sanctions and boycott campaigns.

A related prohibition, although not specifically in terms of the regulations, is the prohibition on the publication of information on the ports of origin and destination of, and the cargo aboard, ships entering South African harbours. This is a response to international sanctions, and attempts to limit information revealing sanctions breaking.

The new press regulations pay more attention than before to defining the media other than the press - television, radio, and film. Each of these is defined separately, and referred to specifically in the text of the regulations. The state has therefore sought to control not only the press, but all forms of media whereby news and comment can be conveyed to the public.

Further police orders

Subsequent to these new regulations, the state promulgated a number of police orders to close those few remaining gaps which the press has tried to take advantage of.

The first set of these orders related to the prohibition of statements by certain organisations concerning specified campaigns, such as 'Christmas Against the Emergency'. The orders were directed at specific newspapers, namely the *Weekly Mail*, *Sowetan* and *New Nation*.

The second type of order was in response to an advertisement calling for the unbanning of the African National Congress, placed in a number of newspapers. In this order the state tried to restrict the publication of any report or advertisement which would throw favourable light on any banned organisation, or which would explain or justify any campaign or action of any banned organisation in resisting the state.[51]

The Argus and SAAN companies successfully launched an application to set aside this order. The state responded within 24 hours of the court's decision by promulgating a new regulation and by issuing a new police order which essentially nullified the victory the press had won in court.

The efficacy of legal challenges

Challenges of a legal nature to state control over the media and the public's right of access to information, and attempts by the media to exploit any remaining gaps, are a double-edged sword. Publication of material which newspapers could previously not have published, or a successful court application, is a defeat for the state and a victory for those who are resisting state control over the media. But at the same time such challenges prompt state amendments to the regulations and police orders, which result in harsher and more sophisticated forms of control.

The media control which the state seeks to impose under the state of emergency is similar to previous statutory control, involving a two-pronged prohibition on news about the conduct of security forces, and the nature of opposition and resistance.

But there are also substantial differences between the pre-existing legislation and the regulations: the latter prohibit publication of news and comment which could previously be published. Furthermore, the regulations grant extended powers to state officials. For example cabinet ministers or government spokespeople may authorise the publication of material which would otherwise be prohibited. The Minister decides whether to authorise the seizure or banning of a publication. There is thus a move away from law enacted by an admittedly undemocratic parliament to rule by state officials.

Additional restrictions on the media

The attack on the media under emergency conditions has not only involved the above-mentioned restrictions.

From the outset of the 1986-87 state of emergency, the Bureau of Information has operated as the state institution responsible for dealing with the media. Headed by Dave Steward, son of a National Party propagandist, and Leon Mellett, a former police public relations officer, the Bureau has been more concerned to suppress than provide information.

The press has encountered little co-operation from the Bureau in attempting to clarify what can and cannot be published. When making enquiries, newspaper editors were simply referred back to the regulations and their legal advisors by Bureau officials.

From 24 June 1986 the Bureau refused to answer questions unless they related to its 'news' briefing of the day, or were submitted four hours before the briefing. As a result of the various police orders and regulations which prohibited publication of news on the conduct of the security forces and unrest incidents, the Bureau's 'news' briefings became the only source of information about these two areas. Bureau briefings on security actions or unrest incidents were seriously biased. They often occurred long after an incident, making the information un-newsworthy. Information released by the Bureau was often inaccurate or incorrect. And information on major incidents was sometimes not provided at all, so that a 'silence' surrounded them.

On 25 June 1986, daily 'news' briefings were suspended and thereafter irregular briefings were held. According to the Bureau the incidents of unrest had declined to such an extent that it was no longer necessary to hold regular briefings. Finally, on 25 September 1986, the Bureau announced that it was closing its media centre in Pretoria, and would in future respond only to telex requests for information on security action or unrest incidents.

Repressive actions against journalists and other media persons whose reporting has been critical of the state have also increased. In June 1986 the Department of Home Affairs instructed all newspapers to submit lists of employees with foreign citizenship. Subsequently a number of foreign journalists have been deported or refused work permits, including Richard Manning, Bureau Chief for *Newsweek*, and CBS cameraman Wim de Vos.

At least 19 journalists have been detained during the present state of emergency. Newspaper offices have been raided and in many instances material confiscated. In July 1986 the offices of the South African Students Press Union were raided by security police. A few days later these offices were burned down by unknown forces.

Finally, journalists have been the subject of physical assaults and attacks, the most horrific of which was the fatal Crossroads vigilante attack on ITN cameraman George De'Ath on 10 June 1986.

The incidence of police serving section 205 subpoenas upon journalists has also increased.[52] These order the journalist in question to appear before a magistrate to answer questions relating to police investigation into an alleged offence. Journalists in this position are often pressured to disclose sources for a particular story or piece of information.

Journalistic ethics prevent disclosure. But journalists refusing to answer questions face sentences of up to two or five years, depending upon the nature of the offence being investigated. Furthermore, journalists who do reveal sources may expose them to criminal charges in which case the journalist could be called as a state witness against the source.

A related attack involves prosecution of journalists in terms of section 27(B) of the Police Act, which states that it is an offence to publish any untruths about the police without having reasonable grounds for believing them to be true. Thus, before journalists are able to make adverse allegations against the police, they have to conduct thorough investigations. This is often difficult in the present situation of unrest, and very time consuming.

The effects of a restricted media

Since 1976, the South African state has been faced with an increasing economic and political crisis. Responses included a programme of reform. But this met with little success and the crisis has deepened since the latter half of 1984. The state, confronted with a recession and widespread extra-parliamentary opposition, has resorted to greater repression in an attempt to regain control. This has included an onslaught against the media and the imposition of severe restrictions on the flow of information, news and comment, both inside and outside South Africa.

The state seeks to achieve three goals through these restrictions:

* to prevent the international world from knowing the extent of repression and atrocities perpetrated by the security forces, and the extent of opposition to apartheid. The state thereby hopes to avoid international sanctions, boycotts and other forms of foreign action.

* within South Africa, the state seeks a form of political and ideological control where those forces which keep it in power, namely big business and the white electorate, remain ignorant about the levels of repression and resistance. The state is attempting to manufacture evidence of 'normality' within South Africa, and prevent publication of anything which would have a detrimental effect on public morale.

* finally, the state seeks to silence individuals and organisations resisting apartheid. In this way their impact organisationally and politically will be minimised. Many of the campaigns of these organisations are adversely affected by the prohibition on subversive statements. Organising campaigns by way of pamphlets, word of mouth and mass meetings has often become unlawful.

Both the commercial and the more alternative media have, for different reasons and to different degrees, attempted to resist and limit the impact of these restrictions upon the free flow of information. But state strategy has nonetheless been fairly successful. Much security force conduct is not published, nor are statements and activities of resistance organisations.

This is not only because of state-imposed restrictions, but also due to a breakdown in the process whereby news is collected and published. Articles are often not written because journalists are intimidated by state repression, or not allowed into unrest areas or areas where the security forces are active. Members of the public are less willing to come forward with information than was previously the case, for fear of possible consequences. And in writing articles, journalists, overwhelmed by the battery of legislation facing the press, often succumb to self-censorship.

The white electorate and capital have been lulled into a false sense of security, and have become increasingly unaware of the degree to which they are ignorant of events within South Africa. To a lesser extent, organisations and individuals opposed to apartheid are deprived of information, and thus isolated from one another. This creates uncertainty and confusion.

The long-term effects of a restriction on the flow of information, news and comment are particularly alarming. South Africans will no longer be aware of political and economic realities in their own country. And at a time when South Africa faces fundamental change, it is essential that there is informed debate about the form which that change will take. Without this many will be unable to participate in and adapt to such change.

Notes

1   Government Notice No R108 of 12 June 1986.
2   This was in terms of the emergency regulations promulgated in Government Notice No R109 of 12 June 1986.
3   Act No 44 of 1957.

4 Act No 7 of 1958.
5 Act No 8 of 1959.
6 Act No 74 of 1982.
7 Act No 42 of 1974.
8 Examples of other statutes containing provisions restricting the media are: the Armaments Development and Production Act, No 57 of 1968; the Demonstrations In or Near Court Buildings Act, No 71 of 1982; the Inquest Act, No 58 of 1959; the National Key Points Act, No 102 of 1980; and the Protection of Information Act, No 84 of 1982.
9 Section 118(1)(a) of the Defence Act.
10 Section 118(1)(b) of the Defence Act.
11 Section 118(4) of the Defence Act.
12 Section 27(B) of the Police Act.
13 Section 44(1)(f) of the Prisons Act.
14 Section 119(1)(a) of the Defence Act.
15 Section 27(a) of the Police Act.
16 Section 44(1)(e) of the Prisons Act.
17 Section 56(1)(p) of the Internal Security Act.
18 Section 54(2)(g) or Section 6(2) of the Internal Security Act.
19 Section 57(1)(b) of the Internal Security Act.
20 Section 5 of the Internal Security Act.
21 Section 54(1) of the Internal Security Act.
22 Section 54(2) of the Internal Security Act.
23 Section 55 of the Internal Security Act.
24 Preamble to the Publications Act.
25 Section 47(2) of the Publications Act.
26 This is in terms of section 9 of the Publications Act.
27 Section 47(1) of the Publications Act.
28 Government Notice No R120. Note that the regulations were promulgated under Government Notice No R121.
29 Government Notice No R10119.
30 Definition of 'publication' in section 1 of the emergency regulations.
31 'Security forces' was defined in section 1 of the emergency regulations to include members of the South African Police, the South African Defence Force, the South African Railways Police and the Prison Service.
32 Regulation 14 of the emergency regulations.
33 The definition is contained in section 1(viii) of the emergency regulations.
34 This order was issued by the Commissioner of Police by way of a telex on 16 June 1986 under Regulation 7(1)(c).
35 This order was issued by the Commissioner of Police by way of a telex on 16 June 1986 under Regulation 7(1)(d).
36 Act No 3 of 1953.
37 Promulgated as proclamation 91 GGE 6403 of 30 March 1960.
38 1986 (4) SA 358 DCLD.
39 1986 (4) SA 1109 NPD.
40 Government Notice Nos 10293, 10329, 10348, 10357, 10382, 10542.
41 Government Notice No 10541.
42 The definition of 'subversive statement' is contained in section 1 of the new

press regulations.

43   Regulation 3 of the new press regulations.
44   Regulation 6 of the new press regulations.
45   Regulation 7 of the new press regulations.
46   Regulation 3(1)(a) of the new press regulations.
47   Regulation 2 of the new press regulations.
48   Regulation 3(3) of the new press regulations.
49   Regulation 4(a)(iii) of the new press regulations.
50   The definition of 'publish' is contained in section 1 of the new press regulations.
51   Government Notice No R102 of 8 January 1987.
52   Section 205 of the Criminal Procedure Act No 51 of 1977.

Section 3: Labour

Introduction

Eddie Webster

It is seven years since the state accepted the recommendations of the Wiehahn Commission and embarked on an attempt to incorporate black worker demands into the industrial relations system. How effective has the state been in shaping union development along the lines of pure collective bargaining? To what extent have the new unions been absorbed into the industrial relations system in a way that separates the economic and wider political struggles? The articles in this section suggest that the results of the Wiehahn reform strategy are contradictory.

In the immediate post-Wiehahn period significant gains were made in developing a system of collective bargaining along traditional industrial relations lines. An estimated 20% of the labour force now belongs to trade unions. Foundations for nation-wide industrial unions have been laid in all major economic sectors. As Jonathan Crush argues, this rapid growth has been facilitated in the mines by the stabilisation of the labour force. Although the Congress of South African Trade Unions (COSATU) failed to meet its ambitious deadline of one union per industry within six months of its launch, Alan Fine argues that the principle of mergers has taken hold. Perhaps more significant is the organisational depth of the new black unions. By the end of 1985, these unions were organised in 3 500 workplaces, had signed 450 plant agreements, had an estimated 1 500 shop steward committees or councils and over 12 500 shop stewards.

Management's unilateral power to dismiss has been curtailed by the emergence of a system of industrial legality which lays down a set of procedures to be followed in the event of dismissal or retrenchment. As Paul Benjamin shows, these procedures have been strengthened by the dramatic increase in trade union use of the industrial court - from an initial 20 in 1979 to 2 042 in 1986.

Strikes are becoming a normal part of the collective bargaining process. The six week strike by 18 000 SA Transport Services workers in March 1987 and the parallel strike by 8 000 postal workers indicate significant changes in the public sector industrial relations arena. Strikes are losing many of the sinister implications attached to them in the past. Workers are using a range of tactics, from go-slows and overtime bans to factory occupations and sit-ins. Although most strikes continued to concern wages, issues like dismissals, retrenchment, recognition and detention were also major causes of strike action. Of particular significance was the work stoppage of over 250 000 miners, called by the National Union of Mineworkers on 1 October 1986 over the Kinross mine disaster - the largest black worker stoppage in the history of South African mining, says Jean Leger.

During 1986, wage bargaining came to the fore. Many of the new unions have joined industrial councils and started to draw on the skills of professional economists in their negotiations. Although wage increases in unionised plants in 1985-1986 exceeded the average increase in black wages, they are still, Judy Maller argues, below the inflation rate.

Additional problems were experienced in other areas. Health and safety is one, as Ian Macun and Jonny Myers show. Here the legislative picture is contradictory, with some changes advantageous and some disadvantageous to labour. There is a strong move towards deregulation which poses a substantial threat to all working conditions, including occupational health and safety. For unions with a set of pressing demands, health and safety has tended to take a back seat, except in the case of a few unions with a track record of activity on these issues.

On the other hand an issue previously neglected, that of the conditions of women workers - see the article by Georgina Jaffee in the resistance section of this book - has now become an established part of industrial relations bargaining.

Significantly, the state is beginning to curb its interventions partially in two key areas of the labour market: statutory job reservation and the pass laws. The 'abolition' of the pass laws in June 1986 only established freedom of movement as a nominal right; residence in urban areas now depends on 'approved accommodation'. But job reservation, as Robyn Rafel outlines in her article, has been abolished in all occupations except mining.

The articles in this section make it clear that while the state has had a degree of success in incorporating black worker demands into the industrial relations system, it has seriously undermined its own reform programme. Historically, capitalist reforms have only been reasonably successful when collective bargaining concessions were backed by expanded political rights, as in nineteenth century Britain. Although Wiehahn foresaw the need for political rights, the South African state has been unable to move in a direction acceptable to the black majority.

The contradiction in the Wiehahn reforms is clear: it created the legal space for the rapid growth of industrial unions while failing to provide for their political incorporation. Instead of accepting universal franchise, which has always served as a useful integrating mechanism, the state has moved hesitantly towards a racially-based political restructuring that still excludes Africans and maintains white control. This has intensified the demand for national liberation. At the same time the recession has deepened, producing high levels of youth unemployment. It is this social category above all which - along with students - has led township resistance since 1976.

Since the present insurrection began in 1984, therefore, trade unions have faced a dual challenge: they have been forced to confront the question of national liberation, and have had to relate to the youth-led civil war in the townships. These pressures forced union leadership to think through the relationship between factory-based trade union struggles and the broader political struggle.

Rob Lambert's article traces COSATU's attempt to respond to this challenge. Fine feels that COSATU failed to meet the optimistic expectations raised at its launch and that it retains sharp ideological divisions. In contrast, Lambert believes that an alliance between unions and the youth, students and community groups has begun to emerge. He believes that the debate inside COSATU has shifted from whether or not alliances are in the interests of the working class to the form such alliances should take, and to the definition of socialism and its relationship to the national struggle.

The problems COSATU encounters in its attempt to develop this alliance are compounded by the complexities of a sharply-divided working class. These divisions encompass skill, religion, education, language, access to political power, ethnicity, region, migrant versus settled labour and, above all, race. They are expressed in many complex ways in working-class culture and are manifested in divided worker organisation and a divided political tradition.

The persistence of division, and indeed its promotion through legislation like the Group Areas Act, is a significant obstacle in the way of COSATU's attempt to promote alliance politics. This emerged most clearly from the October 1986 merger of the Council of Unions of South Africa and the Azanian Confederation of Trade Unions to form the National Council of Trade Unions. The new body claims membership of 350 000. Ideologically its emergence was a predictable development, as it reflects the alternative Africanist or black consciousness tradition in oppositional politics.

Powerful forces are determined to break COSATU's embryonic alliance. The entire security apparatus has been mobilised to try to contain the vigorous resistance that emerged after 1984. The Labour Monitoring Group's December 1986 report showed that 614 union leaders, about 80% with COSATU links, had been arrested in terms of the emergency regulations. More disturbing was the murder of at least four Metal and Allied Workers Union members and their relatives at Mpophomeni near Howick. These killings, on 5 and 6 December 1986, were carried out by vigilantes reportedly carrying Inkatha flags.

The most effective response to this onslaught is still being debated. Some argue for a return to 'collective bargaining unionism'. Significantly, National Union of Mineworkers president James Motlatsi, speaking at the union's annual congress in March 1987, chose not to retreat from alliance politics, but rather began to spell out what the union means by an alliance. 'We must', he said, 'build firm, disciplined and effective alliances with the democratic organisations'. Lambert believes that such an alliance, unlike that involving the South African Congress of Trade Unions in the 1950s, may succeed in the long run because of the greater strength and durability of the shop floor structures the new unions have established in the workplace.

This is the tactical and strategic choice facing the union movement - to retreat in the face of the state onslaught, or, on the basis of the shop floor gains in the post-Wiehahn period, to consolidate the embryonic alliance, take up the concerns of working people as a whole and engage directly with the national liberation movement.

Trends and Developments in Organised Labour

Alan Fine

If 1985 finally saw the creation of the Congress of South African Trade Unions representing the non-racial political tradition in the labour field, 1986 more or less completed the ideological rationalisation of the union movement.

While COSATU maintained its position as the most important South African labour organisation with little difficulty, expectations created in the euphoria surrounding its launch were decidedly not met. Faced with the effects of the economic crisis and the second state of emergency, COSATU's clear-cut political and economic victories were few. Ideological differences between the so-called workerists and populists are still far from resolved. In its experience of some stayaways, the organisation found it was not able to mobilise workers at will in all circumstances; it became apparent that a great deal of consolidation was needed.

The formation of the United Workers Union of South Africa (UWUSA) only served to highlight this need. Inkatha perceived a need to challenge COSATU on its own ground, and formally launched UWUSA on May Day, symbolically at the same venue as COSATU's inaugural rally six months earlier.

The Council of Unions of SA (CUSA) and the Azanian Confederation of Trade Unions (AZACTU) rejected non-racialism - a main feature of COSATU policy - and joined together in October to represent the black consciousness and Africanist traditions.

Finally, the Trade Union Council of South Africa (TUCSA) recognised its irrelevance on the labour scene and dissolved itself - unlamented by all except its last few remaining affiliates.

This led to a further increase in the number of unaffiliated unions. Their membership now represents more than half the total organised workforce. But any significant realignment of these unions into existing federations will be a lengthy process.

COSATU

The second state of emergency hit COSATU union leadership particularly hard for a time. Labour Monitoring Group (LMG) end-of-year statistics for 1986 show that 614 union leaders, about 80% of them with COSATU links, had been arrested in terms of the emergency regulations. More than half were still in detention. And more than 2 000 rank-and-file union members suffered the same fate. The two unions most affected were the Metal and Allied Workers Union and the Commercial, Catering and Allied Workers Union of South Africa. By mid-February 1987, at least another 150 striking OK Bazaars employees had been held.

But it was not only state attacks that caused difficulties for COSATU. It also faced ugly competition from Inkatha. At the same time ideological conflicts and tactical differences within COSATU are far from settled; attempts to deal constructively with them have come off the rails more than once.

COSATU's most successful endeavour was probably its May Day campaign, where it was the main force behind the mobilisation of 1,5 million workers in South Africa's biggest ever stayaway. Labour Day has consequently been accepted as a de facto public holiday by almost everyone except government, which has accepted a public holiday (Workers Day) on the first Friday of each May. In the second half of 1986 and in early 1987, hardly any agreement over wages and working conditions was made without including a deal on May Day. The most controversial aspect of such negotiations was usually whether 16 June should be granted as a paid holiday as well. COSATU participated in the effective 16 June stayaway in 1986, and by early 1987 most unionised firms were agreeing to this demand.

But a tendency to call stayaways indiscriminately was halted by

COSATU's failure to mobilise more than a relative handful of workers on 14 July in a protest against the state of emergency and widespread detentions of union leaders. Possible reasons were that COSATU had underestimated the extent to which its organisation had been weakened by detentions and had failed to gain the support of progressive organisations. But there were also complaints within COSATU, particularly from the Western Cape and Natal, to the effect that the views of regional structures and affiliates had not been adequately canvassed.

It seems the difficulty of effectively mobilising regular mass stayaways was recognised. As a result, apart from the unions directly affected, there were relatively low-key responses to two potentially explosive issues - the Kinross mine disaster in September 1986 in which 177 people died, and the police shootings which killed a MAWU member at the union's November annual general meeting in Durban. The calls on those occasions were merely for brief commemoration meetings at COSATU factories.

Individual affiliates, too, have on occasion embarked on doomed strike action apparently without properly assessing their chances of success. The most prominent example was at General Motors (GM), where about 450 workers were dismissed after a three-week strike over the nature of GM's disinvestment from South Africa. Several hundred others returned to work without having won any gains. The lesson learned was, to coin a phrase, that right is not necessarily might. Or as one COSATU union leader commented: 'Some just do not know the meaning of the word "retreat"'.

Another consequence of the GM strike was a partial rethink of the disinvestment issue. Thus far the disinvestment of some 80 US companies and a few European ones has done little to erode apartheid. While it seems unlikely that COSATU will go back on its conditional support for disinvestment, there is an acknowledgement that the issue is not as clear-cut as it once seemed.

A potentially self-damaging move was COSATU's vocal attack on Inkatha's Chief Mangosuthu Buthelezi from its first day of existence. While conflict between Inkatha and COSATU was always inevitable, it is generally conceded now that COSATU would have been wiser to consolidate its strength in Natal before taking on what is, after all, an extremely powerful force in that area. Indeed, the second half of 1986 saw a notable decline in COSATU's anti-

Buthelezi rhetoric.

Earlier in the year nine people died in conflict between UWUSA and the National Union of Mineworkers at the Hlobane colliery. In December the conflict reached a crescendo with the murder of four MAWU members at Mpophomeni, allegedly by Inkatha followers. There were further confrontations in Northern Natal before the year was out. It seems some kind of truce was eventually reached, but it is likely to be tense and temporary. Three workers died in December 1986 and January 1987 in conflict between the Food and Allied Workers Union and UWUSA at Jabula Foods in Springs.

The ideological debate within COSATU between so-called workerists and populists permeates the organisation. The first priority for COSATU and its affiliates is to prevent this becoming destructive - as it has threatened to do in a number of instances. The two positions have become less clear-cut, and so have their protagonists. It is no longer a case of the ex-Federation of South African Trade Unions and unaffiliated unions on the one side versus the former UDF unions on the other. Opposed views now exist within almost every affiliate, and will continue to do so as COSATU's merger programme proceeds.

At the heart of the debate is the nature of the present and future relationship between the union movement and the progressive political organisations. COSATU's assistant general-secretary Sidney Mafumadi, reflecting the populist view which has been dominant within COSATU, explained: 'Although the ANC is banned it enjoys substantial support. It is clear there can be no solution to South Africa's problems without its participation. COSATU is part of the mass democratic movement of organisations operating lawfully. But we do not want to ignore the coincidence of many of the perspectives of ourselves and the ANC'. He however rejected suggestions that COSATU is a front for the ANC, something a number of COSATU people found to be the focus of their interrogations in detention. Said Mafumadi: 'We are not their puppets and they are not ours'.

To the 'workerists' the trade union movement should maintain an independent political position. As one of its protagonists put it: 'The unbanning of the ANC is a long way away. In any event, close links with these organisations could mean that the unions will eventually become just another typical government-controlled labour movement'.

The debate has more immediate implications for COSATU. For example, among the unresolved issues discussed at the last central executive committee meeting of 1986 was the formal role of student and community organisations and the unemployed within the organisation. According to one participant the debate on this issue was tense. But 'at least the "workerists" came out and spoke their minds for the first time', he said. The conflict has caused a great deal of tension. Attempts to set up structures in some of COSATU's most populous regions - the Witwatersrand, Vaal and Eastern Cape - were delayed by walkouts and other ugly scenes. The conflict prompted MAWU to pass a resolution at its conference in July calling for freedom of speech. The resolution, directed as much at COSATU as at government, has been discussed at length by the COSATU executive.

The Witwatersrand regional structure was eventually constituted only in November. The 'workerists' won the crucial elections, but their margin of victory was extremely narrow. The fact that this time the results were accepted by all is, however, an indication of a greater tolerance for opposing views.

Conflict reared its head again in December when about 15 unionists perceived to be 'workerists' received letters from 'the internal wing of the national liberation movement' threatening dire consequences should they not cease their support for an independent political position. Exactly who the authors were is unclear.

Another serious ideological division during the year, and one of COSATU's biggest challenges, was the splinter-group breakaway from the National Union of Textile Workers (NUTW). The NUTW is reputed to be one of the strongest representatives of the workerist view. So when COSATU was invited to mediate it had to choose between the union and a splinter group representing an ideology closer to that of the COSATU leadership. However, to the surprise of some, COSATU took a strong stand against the newly-formed Textile and Allied Workers Union, telling it that if it wished to be part of COSATU it would have to rejoin NUTW and work out its differences from within. This, said NUTW general secretary Johnny Copelyn, 'shows a greater level of maturity than COSATU leadership is generally given credit for'.

On the other side of the coin is the resolution passed at the COSATU inaugural conference, which aimed at setting up one union per industry within six months. The organisation came nowhere near meeting the deadline. New amalgamated unions were formed at mid-year in the food and transport industries. Committees consisting of the appropriate unions have been set up in each sector and their proceedings led to varying degrees of progress. General unions have transferred some members to the larger industrial unions. A new construction union with 30 000 members was launched on 30 January 1987.

Plans to form a union for agricultural workers are in the early stages, and Chris Dlamini, COSATU's vice president, sees this lack of progress as one of the organisation's failures. Attempts to organise the unemployed effectively will doubtless also prove more difficult than initially imagined.

But though the over-optimistic merger deadline was not met, the principle of mergers has taken hold. There is increasing concern focused on the areas where progress has been lacking, and at least one general union has been threatened with expulsion from COSATU for not co-operating.

CUSA/AZACTU

The CUSA/AZACTU merger in October 1986 was precipitated by COSATU's refusal to fall into line with black consciousness opposition to white intellectual leadership in trade unions. The new grouping claims to represent about 350 000 workers.

Ideologically it was a logical development. This apart, there is as yet no sign that the merger will add much in the way of status or muscle to what CUSA already had. AZACTU has supplied only one sizeable union - the Black Allied Mining and Construction Workers Union, which says it has 75 000 members, though it has done little to demonstrate that it actually is one of South Africa's largest unions, as claimed.

Like COSATU, CUSA/AZACTU has not yet resolved differences between unions coming from its original two components. The AZACTU contingent, despite its smaller size, proved unwilling to be swallowed. One indication of this is the fact that the new organisation took until April 1987 to decide on a name for itself: the National Council of Trade Unions (NACTU). It seems CUSA representatives at the inaugural conference suggested that the name CUSA be retained, but the AZACTU group refused.

Indications are that ideological differences between the mildly black consciousness-orientated CUSA and Africanist AZACTU will still have to be dealt with. As with COSATU, the yardstick of real unity within NACTU will be its success in building single industrial unions. There are a number of small industrial and general unions in the AZACTU camp and, once again, they are likely to resist being swallowed. But this seems inevitable should mergers go ahead. Among CUSA's 11 former affiliates are some substantial unions. They are particularly prominent in the metal, transport, food, and chemical industries.

Both CUSA and AZACTU participated in the May Day and 16 June stayaways. However, CUSA and COSATU parted company tactically in their protests against the state of emergency and the detentions which occurred in its wake. Rather than taking the course of work stoppages (employed particularly by CCAWUSA and the Chemical Workers Industrial Union) as a form of pressure on employers to get involved, CUSA issued a joint statement with the Federated Chamber of Industries and the Associated Chambers of Commerce, condemning the emergency and calling for the release of detainees.

COSATU's communications with the major employer groups were limited to negotiating a deal on the non-dismissal of detainees and allowing time off for union members to take the place of detained officials.

UWUSA

The two main planks of UWUSA's policy platform are support for the free enterprise system and opposition to the campaign for sanctions against South Africa. This position is a direct challenge to COSATU's support for some sort of socialist economic programme and international pressure against South Africa.

Justifying the launch of a new union whose existence would inevitably be divisive, Buthelezi argued that COSATU had tended to neglect the economic interests of workers in favour of advancing the goals of the ANC-UDF political tradition. That assertion is debatable. Whatever may be said about COSATU's political programme, there is no evidence to suggest that its individual affiliates have softened up at all on their economic strategies.

Indeed, UWUSA is itself open to that very criticism. Despite denials, it is clear to all observers of the labour scene that the purpose of the organisation's existence is to strengthen Buthelezi and Inkatha's political position among workers. UWUSA's test will be whether it can demonstrate that it can be as successful at improving the working conditions of its members as it is at articulating Inkatha policy.

It is too early to make a final judgment. UWUSA appears to have built up a fairly sizeable membership in Natal. By April 1987 it was claiming 100 000 signed-up and 60 000 paid-up members countrywide with two-thirds of its strength in Natal. Its progress in the Transvaal, where it has also set up offices, is more difficult to gauge. Some Natal COSATU factories, or sections of them, have moved over to UWUSA. Overall, though, UWUSA seems to have been more successful in enrolling previously unorganised workers than in winning mass defections from COSATU unions.

The most worrying aspect of the battle between COSATU and Inkatha is the bloody toll it has exacted. This conflict is likely to escalate in the coming year.

Apart from a small number of former leaders of some COSATU affiliates, UWUSA leadership comprises top ex-Inkatha officials and members of the Kwazulu Legislative Assembly. This vital ideological struggle on Buthelezi's home ground is in their hands; most are businessmen. A union confederation headed by petty capitalists is an incongruous situation, which may in time precipitate a conflict of interest between members and the union hierarchy. Or it could evolve into a repressive structure of labour control.

TUCSA

The steady growth of the black union movement over the past 13 years slowly but surely eroded the importance of South Africa's long-established union organisations. The death of TUCSA late last year typifies this.

From a high point in early 1983, when TUCSA represented nearly half-a-million workers in 57 unions, a rash of resignations left the organisation with 32 affiliates representing little more than 150 000 workers. TUCSA's decline can be attributed to a variety of factors. In the late 1970s a number of large conservative unions joined the confederation. They had recently decided to open their ranks to workers other than whites, and the multiracial TUCSA seemed their logical home. Some, like the Artisan Staff Association, had previously belonged to the right-wing whites-only South African Confederation of Labour (SACOL).

The conservative unions did not take long to make their mark in TUCSA. Their leaders soon became leading TUCSA officials. At the same time, unions reputed to be in the centre and on the left of TUCSA began to move further left. This can be at least partially explained by the growth of the black union movement and the civil unrest in which many of their black and coloured members found themselves engulfed.

TUCSA proved ill-equipped to respond to these pressures, particularly with the growing influence of the right in the organisation. The result was disenchantment and the disaffiliation since mid-1983 of about 25 unions representing more than 300 000 members.

The independents

The rash of resignations from TUCSA over the last three years and the organisation's subsequent demise spawned a large group of unions at present unattached to any of South Africa's trade union federations. As can be seen on the accompanying diagrams, they now represent almost half of the entire organised workforce.

While many independents found TUCSA's approach too conservative and cautious, they are nevertheless incompatible with the relatively militant approach of COSATU, CUSA and AZACTU. It remains to be seen whether this grouping decides to establish a formal or informal alliance. The leadership of the South African Boilermakers Society - which led the exodus from TUCSA - is in the process of establishing a Labour Forum which is intended to provide various types of services to its members. These would include economic research for use in wage negotiations and joint representations on proposed labour legislation. But it is unlikely that the Labour Forum will ever become a political pressure group or a force in labour.

There have also been reports that some of the unions which were in TUCSA at the death are attempting to set up a federation to replace TUCSA but 'which will have none of TUCSA's shortcomings'. A limited number of currently independent unions may eventually decide to join COSATU or NACTU. The Motor

DISTRIBUTION OF UNION MEMBERSHIP BY CONFEDERATION DECEMBER 1985

MEMBERSHIP FIGURES (Thousands)

COSATU   TUCSA   CUSA   SACOL   AZACTU

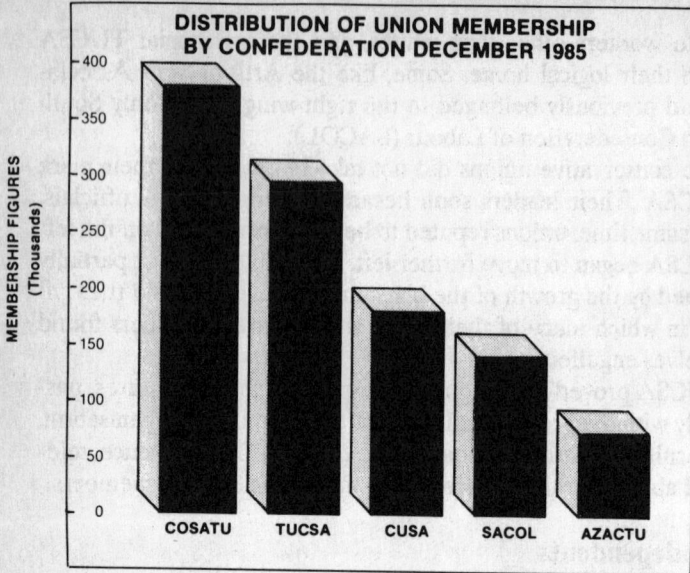

Source: Annual Report on Labour Relations in South Africa 1986-1987, Andrew Levy and Associates (Pty) Ltd.

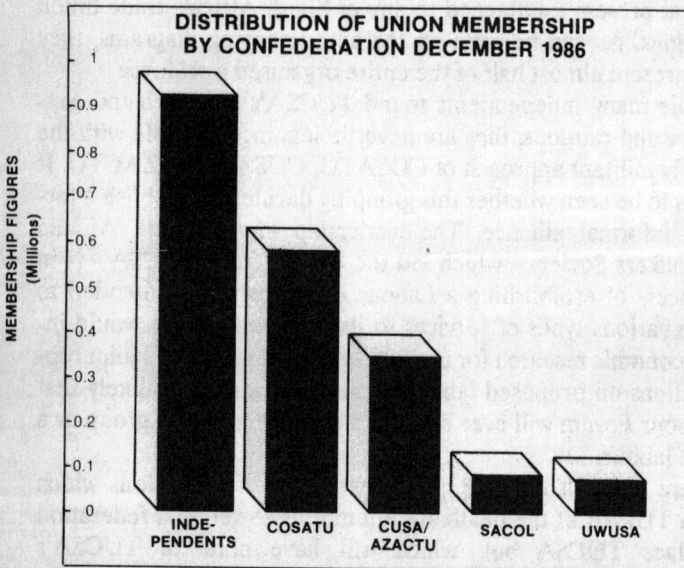

DISTRIBUTION OF UNION MEMBERSHIP BY CONFEDERATION DECEMBER 1986

MEMBERSHIP FIGURES (Millions)

INDE-PENDENTS   COSATU   CUSA/AZACTU   SACOL   UWUSA

Source: Annual Report on Labour Relations in South Africa 1986-1987, Andrew Levy and Associates (Pty) Ltd.

Industry Combined Workers Union, for example, merged with MAWU and the National Automobile and Allied Workers Union in mid-1987. The new metal union formed has affiliated to COSATU.

In another interesting development, the NUTW and six former TUCSA unions in the clothing, textile and leather sectors are engaged in talks aimed at setting up a combined organisation to represent the interests of their members in dealing with employers. A longer-term goal is a single union for the industry, but such a development is a long way away.

Strikes

The number of man-days lost due to strike action in 1986 again increased substantially over the previous year. This was not surprising, given the continuing growth in the organised workforce.

There are no definitive statistics of strike activity, and those that do exist are probably conservative. However, each source employs the same methodology each year and trends can thus be assessed. Statistics in this section are provided by industrial relations consultants Andrew Levy and Associates.

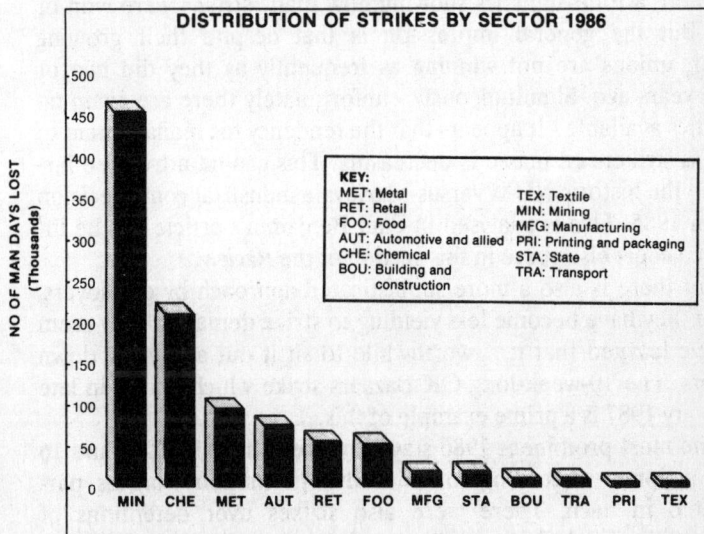

DISTRIBUTION OF STRIKES BY SECTOR 1986

KEY:
MET: Metal
RET: Retail
FOO: Food
AUT: Automotive and allied
CHE: Chemical
BOU: Building and construction

TEX: Textile
MIN: Mining
MFG: Manufacturing
PRI: Printing and packaging
STA: State
TRA: Transport

NO OF MAN DAYS LOST (Thousands)

MIN CHE MET AUT RET FOO MFG STA BOU TRA PRI TEX

Source: Annual Report on Labour Relations in South Africa 1986-1987, Andrew Levy and Associates (Pty) Ltd.

For the first time the number of man-days lost in 1986 due to strikes was more than one million, up by about 50% on 1985. As usual, the mining industry was most affected - almost half the man-days lost were in that industry. In second place was the chemical industry where both COSATU and CUSA/AZACTU have particularly active affiliates.

These statistics reflect only strike action due to shop-floor disputes. Politically-related industrial action accounted for at least another 3,5-million man-days, and possibly as many as 6-million. Wage disputes continued to be the most important strike trigger (37,4%), due to the generally low level of wage increases offered by employers during the recession. Grievances accounted for 14% of strikes, dismissals 13,4%, while other strike triggers accounted for 32,5%. Apart from strikes, there were numerous overtime bans implemented to enforce wage demands, particularly by MAWU. Disciplinary matters and grievances are relatively less prevalent as triggers than a few years ago, a reflection of the vastly increased workload of the industrial court, more use of private mediation and arbitration and, probably, the more efficient operation of procedures agreed to between unions and managements. A large number of the strikes categorised 'other' concerned retrenchment.

There are no statistics showing how many strikes were won or lost. But the general impression is that despite their growing power, unions are not winning as frequently as they did two or three years ago. Simultaneously - unfortunately there are again no statistics available - it appears that the tendency for management to dismiss strikers en masse is decreasing. This can be attributed largely to the historic NUM versus Marievale industrial court decision late in 1985. This is analysed in Paul Benjamin's article on the industrial court elsewhere in this section of the *Review*.

But there is also a more sophisticated approach by employers. While they have become less yielding to strike demands, they seem to have learned that it is worthwhile to sit it out and wear down strikers. The 10-week-long OK Bazaars strike which ended in late February 1987 is a prime example of this.

The most prominent 1986 stayaways were the May Day and 16 June actions - according to the LMG 1,5-million workers participated in each. There were also strikes over detentions of unionists, particularly in retailing and the chemical industry, soon after the declaration of the state of emergency in June. And up to

325 000 miners stayed away on 1 October to commemorate the deaths of the 177 miners at Kinross.

In addition, there were numerous localised stayaways called over a variety of issues, including funerals for the victims of police shootings. In some cases they were initiated by unions, in others by community or political organisations, and on occasion jointly. The vast majority occurred before 12 June 1986, and lasted for up to three days with varying degrees of success. The following are some of the areas affected: Soshanguve (two), Witbank, Mohlakeng, Garankuwa, Atteridgeville (two), Alexandra (three), Bele-Bela, Seisoville, Mamelodi, Ratanda, Langa (two), Port Elizabeth, the Vaal townships, Kabokweni, Nelspruit, Cradock, Port Alfred, Tembisa (two) and Tumahole.

Despite the pressures of recession and the state of emergency, union membership continued to grow in 1986, and worker militancy showed no sign of decreasing. Union campaigns on directly political issues went through something of a trough towards the end of the year, but appeared to be picking up as the white election, May Day and 16 June approached in 1987.

In early 1987, union wage negotiations were on the whole successful, as corporate profits began to rise sharply. This gave something of a boost to COSATU's living wage campaign. However, at the time of writing negotiations in two important sectors, mining and the metal industry, had just begun.

All signs in the first third of 1987 pointed to increased confrontation between the state and the union movement, with a constant police presence at union premises, particularly COSATU House, where there were two full-scale raids on affiliates in the building. During the run-up to the white general election, a number of cabinet ministers made threatening references to COSATU's political activities in speeches. Unions may well face intensified pressure to curb their political militancy.

Trade Unions, Nationalism and the Socialist Project in South Africa

Rob Lambert

The formation of the Congress of South African Trade Unions in November 1985 created the potential to strengthen the power of trade union organisation. COSATU brought together over half-a-million workers, making it the largest organisation of its kind in South Africa's history.

Yet size was only one element in the equation. COSATU had the potential to unite different tendencies between and within unions, provided democratic practices were adhered to. In the earlier situation debates had fractured and polarised between different union organisations. In essence, these debates involve the political role of the union movement in the national liberation struggle. This includes the precise nature of the relationship between economic and political forms of struggle, and between the struggle for a non-racial democracy and socialism.

The task of clarifying these debates will not be achieved without intense opposition from a state which intends to coerce COSATU into line with all the power at its disposal. It plans to enforce a more limited collective bargaining objective on the unions, thus pre-empting democratic debate, clarification, and strategic decisions on the movement's political role. The state has its own ideas of that role and does not believe these are issues working-class organisations should debate. Either COSATU fits into the postWiehahn industrial relations pattern, or it must pay the price for disruptive political activities and dangerous links with township organisations led by full-time agitators.

The state meant business, as the attacks on COSATU House and South African Railways and Harbours Workers Union (SARHWU) members indicated. Jay Naidoo, COSATU general secretary, captured the angry mood just after these attacks:

> Wednesday 22 April was our 'Bloody Wednesday'. A systematic campaign of smear, harassment and intimidation resulted in a brutal attack on SATS strikers which left eight workers dead and countless injured. As night fell, COSATU House was in a state of siege. Our building was stormed and the security forces moved systematically through each floor assaulting people indiscriminately, breaking down office doors and vandalising our union material and property. The army and the police then withdrew detaining hundreds and leaving in their wake a trail of blood and damage.
>
> 'Bloody Wednesday' was a signal from the regime. The onslaught against COSATU has been started.[1]

Some within the union movement, however much they oppose and abhor the state's violent actions, argue that the state's response is a logical reaction to COSATU strategy. They argue further that trade unions which flirt with national struggle are doomed, as the history of SACTU in the 1950s has proven. COSATU should instead consolidate its strength in the factories - the terrain proper to trade unionism. According to these critics South Africa has entered a reactionary phase of politics, and all that can be hoped for in the coming ten to 15 years is reform from above. Socialism is not on the agenda. Unions should therefore concentrate on bargaining for immediate economic gains for their members, rather than engaging in nationalist-inspired populist-styled campaigns that will only bring about their downfall.

Much current analysis provides intellectual support, intentionally or otherwise, for those articulating this position. A central thrust of these writings draws a parallel between the labour movement's 'discoveries' in the 1970s and 1980s and the failed politics of the 1950s. Steven Friedman, for example, argues that

> The present turmoil is...a repetition of the old and yet something entirely new. The difference between this and previous waves of resistance lies less in its

scale than in the nature of the tactics adopted by resistance groups. Many tactics and strategies which appear new are merely more dramatic attempts to revive an earlier resistance tradition.... A new approach began to emerge in the mid-1970s with the growth of the trade union movement, whose strategy was based on building tight grassroots and democratic organisation... The unions eschewed mass mobilisation and high profile campaigns in order to build a disciplined power base...and back demands with organised strength.[2]

Bill Freund reiterates this, arguing that the 'romanticisation of the 1950s' and the revival of ideas and practices which originated then, blind many in the anti-apartheid camp to the organisational and conceptual weaknesses of resistance in the 1950s.[3] Freund's central discussion is limited to a lucid analysis of the internal colonialism thesis, but Friedman has related his analysis to COSATU strategy:

Unions...find themselves under considerable pressure to aid political mobilisation rather than organisation and to surrender their control over political action to nationalist movements which command the symbols of resistance... (COSATU's) national leadership has moved increasingly closer to the UDF and to mobilisation politics.[4]

The implication is that despite the existence of countervailing tendencies, COSATU leadership has surrendered to the nationalists. The danger is that the political style this surrender entails may dominate as leadership shifts from steady, carefully planned organisation in the factories, to mass mobilisation launched at breakneck speed. Many critics view the two-day election stayaway on 5 and 6 May 1987 as a further example of the labour movement 'being dragged along by the nationalists' shirt tails'. The revival of these old practices is disastrous because 'the politics of that time were a total failure'.[5] Or, as Friedman argues, 'SACTU, in its attempt to evade the control of one nationalism, surrendered its priorities to those of another'.[6]

These theorists believe COSATU is courting disaster. By surrendering to nationalism it threatens not only the organisational gains of the 1970s and 1980s, but also the development of an independent working-class politics.

Revisions of history

Gramsci commented that 'history teaches, but it has no pupils'. In our context this can be rephrased: pupils are present, but they are fed on false histories. This does not mean there is *one* objective truth to be discovered provided correct procedures are employed. Any historical period will always be subject to controversy, debate and differing interpretations of the same events. This is particularly the case with the 1950s, given the intensity of those struggles, the extent of state repression, and the current tendency to adopt this experience as a constant reference point to evaluate the present.

Nonetheless, evaluations of the 1950s summarised above need to be challenged since many of the assumptions are half-truths: that SACTU represented the subordination of working-class politics to nationalism; that the 1950s are an example of mass mobilisation with little, if any 'tight grassroots and democratic organisation'; and that the period represented a *total* failure in dislodging or seriously challenging the state.

When debating tactics and strategies, history cannot be simplistically divided into the old and the new. While this may make for neater intervention and positioning in debates, it does not stand up to serious historical scrutiny.

The politics of the 1950s did represent a period of fairly widespread consensus on certain key issues: the need for socialists to solidify an alliance with the nationalists; the South African Communist Party's understanding of South African society in terms of the internal colonialism model; and the stages of change that this implied. Unity between the nationalists in the ANC and the SACP was welded during this period of intense struggle, but there were differences in emphasis, in the understanding of the possible course of struggle, and in perceptions of the relationship between organisation, mobilisation and resistance.

In some areas, organisational energy concentrated on building the national movement, while trade unionism tended to be neglected. It only needed emphasis during the second, socialist stage of struggle. Yet there was another position, dominant in some regions, and present in all, which viewed trade unions as the real base from which to build an effective national movement. This tendency placed as much emphasis on grassroots and democratic styles of organisation, both at a theoretical and practical level, as activists of the contemporary period do. Careful study of these practices reveals a real *continuity* between practices of the 1950s and the 'discoveries' of the 1970s and 1980s.

This emphasis on democratic styles of organisation meant the working class came to exert an increasingly powerful influence on the content of nationalist politics. Workers from the shop floor were elected to key positions in the national movement; SACTU leadership gave the Freedom Charter a socialist interpretation and SACTU itself did not rigidly differentiate between stages in the struggle for socialism. In its view a democratic revolution could immediately reach out to the next socialist stage if the working class was sufficiently well organised. And as mobilisation intensified, more sections of the leadership recognised the need to consolidate and extend organisation.

Not all 1950s practices were politically advanced. In the excitement of mass mobilisation attention paid to organisation was often scant. It was assumed the masses could be mobilised rapidly because they suffered the effects of racial discrimination. Within this perspective, it was believed the state would soon topple when faced with this pressure. There was also the liberal notion that national strikes could pressurise the state into democratic concessions. An alternate position did not view the strikes primarily in terms of protest politics, but as moments of politicisation, preparing workers for political struggle against the state.

Evidence indicates that SACTU grew most rapidly in those regions where its relationship with the national movement was closest. Nationalism did not detract from, but facilitated union growth in these areas. Workers identified with unions both as instruments for economic factory struggle, and as organisations with the potential for the wider transformation of society.

Evaluating the success or the failure of resistance against the state in this period is complex. Since the 1950s opposition movements did not dislodge the state, were they therefore *total* failures? Mistakes were made, some serious, but does this mean that nothing was gained from this experience? Subsequent events show this is not the case. Factory leaders trained during this period, for example, provided crucial continuity and played a significant role in the revivals of the 1970s.

These revisions are crucial. A more complex understanding of the 1950s can liberate contemporary strategic debates from romanticising the past, and from dismissing an entire experience as old, outmoded, protest politics.

The new union politics

During the 1970s Trade Union Advisory Co-ordinating Council (TUACC) unions in Natal focused exclusively on workplace issues and the need to build strong, democratically-structured unions and a class-conscious leadership. This strategy had an important positive impact on South African opposition struggles.

Its stress on democracy within the unions and the factories was a major contribution. These unions emphasised that leadership should be mandated by the members - an important element in ensuring democratic practices and avoiding many of the pitfalls of leadership corruption which had plagued unions in the past. The stress on factory issues was positive: it bound unions closely to their members by having to respond to immediate daily needs. The numerous battles fought for a living wage, against harsh and arbitrary supervision, and against unhealthy and dangerous working environments, all contributed to a style of unionism that is both democratic and responsive. The trade union strength so created, together with the political upsurge of 1976, forced a reform strategy on the state in the late 1970s.

In the post-1976 period the TUACC unions, most of which came under the umbrella of the Federation of South African Trade Unions (FOSATU) in 1979, tended to hesitate as pressures built up in the townships. Initially, they were concerned that township involvement might detract from their emphasis on strengthening factory-based structures and leadership. FOSATU did debate and at times engage in action outside of immediate industrial issues. But its leadership was limited by a negative evaluation of nationalism and dismissed much that was happening in the townships as populist. This opinion was partly based on the evaluations of the SACTU experience criticised above.

But in the early 1980s, rank and file workers on the East Rand took the initiative and formed shop steward councils in an attempt to respond positively to township problems.

Tactical and strategic shifts in the 1980s

During 1984, as resistance and repression escalated, particularly in Transvaal townships, leadership in some unions began re-evaluating union political strategies. This was a positive response to the township experience of factory leadership. A Sweet, Food and Allied Workers Union (SFAWU) shop steward recalled the early period of civil war in Tembisa township, and the new set of questions this posed for unions:

> The streets in the township are more or less flat with lots of people moving up and down all the time. Then the soldiers came carrying guns and raiding the houses. They would just come in without permission. When they tried to put the rents up from 1 August, pamphlets were distributed calling for a rent boycott. At night the SADF raided the houses of those not paying rent and took whole families to the police station. They would release one and tell him to go and get the rent.
> It was a terrible experience. We had no voice. All the community organisations had been banned. We had no platform to raise issues and we realised that the trade union was our only platform. We had to learn to use our power at the workplace on these issues.[7]

The same shop steward also referred to workers' experiences in organising the boycott of Simba Chips products. Township youth played a key role in the campaign and a new working relationship was forged:

> This was an eye opener to many in the unions who had not taken the youth seriously. For instance, I discussed with some of the youth in the townships and I was surprised to hear them talking in terms of class struggle and being clearer than many of the workers themselves.[8]

From these experiences SFAWU began to reformulate its political strategy. Its national executive committee (NEC) prepared a discussion paper and circulated it to other FOSATU unions, prior to the formation of COSATU.

The paper questioned what political role the new federation of trade unions should play and how the organised power of workers could be used to 'tilt the balance of forces in society as a whole', this being 'an urgent responsibility' that required 'absolute clarity'. It was argued that in the context of a deepening economic and political crisis, the country had entered

> a phase of uninterrupted struggle. It is the youth who are at the vanguard of that struggle. It is the youth that are demanding through their struggles fundamental change and a restructuring of society. In this flow of struggle the organised power of workers is crucial.

Therefore, argued the NEC , 'one cannot separate the struggle for national freedom from our struggle for our rights in the factory'. In the midst of this present crisis the working class 'should strive for maximum unity so that the politics of the working class can become the politics of our people'.

This necessitated 'seeking' alliances with other classes and organisations. Special note had to be taken of the fact that 'township struggles are being waged and determined by youth...who also constitute a major part of the masses of the millions of unemployed'. A move towards the politics of alliance would contribute in no small measure to the 'convergence' of workplace and township forms of struggle, rather than the existing situation where such struggles were being waged 'in parallel'.

SFAWU's NEC stated that such alliances should only be formed on a principled, disciplined basis: the union movement should spell out the terms upon which it was prepared to enter an alliance. Allies of the working class should understand that

> the struggle against apartheid must represent mainly the interests of the workers because we as workers produce the wealth in our country... Therefore it is the workers who must have the main say in running the society.

The NEC said that to further this goal 'it was important that such alliances take place on terms that do not subordinate the interests of the working class'. Other groups and classes should recognise the working-class's right to lead the struggle in such a way that the politics of the working class becomes the politics of the people. Other constituent groups in the alliance would have to accept a 'working class perspective' on issues which

> recognises the right of workers to control society in their interests and provides for a basic strategy that ensures that this is achieved and that consequently the interests of workers are advanced.

The emergence of a COSATU leadership position

Jay Naidoo, ex-general secretary of SFAWU and first general secretary of COSATU, developed the ideas of the SFAWU position paper. At the 1986 Grassroots Conference in Cape Town, in a talk entitled 'Building People's Power: A Working Class Perspective',[9] he argued that workers' power was an essential

element in the construction of people's power, as was the positioning of workers as 'the leading force in our struggle for national
liberation'. A key part of building workers' power would be 'the
democratic principles of worker control'.

In practice, said Naidoo, worker control meant members of the
trade union must have 'absolute control over all decision making in
the organisation'. This would be achieved through constitutions
which entrenched this principle; shop steward elections in each
department of a shop, factory or mine; leaders only acting on the
basis of mandates from membership and regular report backs; and
union structures which ensured a worker majority at all levels.

In Naidoo's view these principles have led to the consolidation
of worker power. Unions have been able to challenge 'the undemocratic control' management exercised over the lives of
workers in the factories.

> The power of the bosses in the factories began to erode. We began to push
> back their right to hire and to fire, to set production speeds and make their
> own decisions around retrenchments, wages and health and safety.

These gains, however small, gave the working class confidence
in its ability to bring about transformations in the wider society.
The Transvaal November 1984 stayaway, called in support of
democratic student demands, was the first decisive political action
by workers since the 1950s and reflected this growing confidence.
Naidoo believed the stayaway's most important effect was that it
'laid the basis for developing an alliance between students, youth
and worker-parents'. This was crucial in stimulating the growth of
'people's power', involving an alliance of classes, rather than the
working class striving on its own.

In turn 'people's power' required forms of organisation appropriate to the different terrains of struggle. These included student representative councils in schools, civics in townships, unions
in factories and a union for unemployed workers.. These spheres
had to be linked and not 'fought on isolated and individual fronts'.

The critique of COSATU politics from within

Although this new political direction is expressed in certain
COSATU resolutions, other strategies are also being posed within

the organisation. An alternative position advanced by sections of the NUTW leadership was developed as a critique of the SFAWU position paper.[10]

The critics charge that this new political direction is 'misdirected' and that the 'rush' to espouse 'alliance politics' might result in a situation where 'years of painstaking work can be swept aside and the working class again be without democratic mass organisation'.

The essence of this argument is that populism and nationalism, which have gained increasing support during the current crisis, stand in absolute contradiction to working-class politics. The organisational styles and political content of each are so fundamentally different that any involvement of the working class in such politics can only mean abandoning independence and with it working-class politics.

'It is ridiculous to suggest that this type of alliance politics will have any possibilities of leading to a society where workers have control', argue these critics. Rather, it will prevent an independent working-class politics from developing and prepare the ground for an alliance between a post-apartheid state and nationalism of every shade. This, they assert, will certainly debilitate and may even destroy individual member unions to such a degree that no working-class opposition to post-apartheid capitalism will be offered. The 'lessons of the 1950s' should have been learned, they argue: SACTU was 'decimated' in the 1960s precisely because of its alliance with and consequent subordination to the ANC.

As a result of this political direction unions built through years of 'painstakingly hard work' could be 'split into a thousand pieces virtually overnight'. Alliance politics stresses 'the people' and not the working class and is therefore a non-class-based politics which fails to prepare the working class for socialism. Unions will lose their organisational independence as they become embroiled in populist campaigns over which they have no control. They will be unable to maintain their independence because populist organisation is profoundly anti-democratic in character.

This scenario is based on the view that populist organisations have a profoundly different political style to working-class organisations. In the former,

leaders are leaders because they act as leaders, not because they are elected as leaders. The work of such a leader is to exhort whoever will listen to act. He is not limited by the size of his organisation. The organisation from which he comes often has no recognisable membership. It is an action committee that invites the masses to participate in actions as the occasion arises. It is the populist answer to vanguardism. You do not discipline such a leadership, you do not control their actions. On the contrary, you join their political style.

Engagement with populist organisations leads to 'rhetoric about socialism' only, and the constant compromise of the political and organisational practices of the working class. 'Far from widening the terrain of class politics, such attempts...simply neutralise workers as a class in their "communities"'.

Those arguing this position contend that jumping on the 'populist bandwagon' would cause serious divisions among organised workers. Populist failure to 'develop democratic organisational practices' would lock unions into 'unstructured organisations'. As a basis for action this 'could drag us into each and every adventurous action that is initiated'.

These 'confrontationist' practices would 'exhaust' unions rather than the state. Such practices also implied renouncing the challenge of widening working-class political initiative. To avoid this, COSATU should strengthen the local shop steward councils. But this did not deny that unions should be

> co-operating with other community organisations that are supportive of any programme on which we are working. Crucially, however, our right and ability to act on our own...must remain the cornerstone of our practices in such projects.

Towards the socialist project

The debates on questions of alliances and populism occurred soon after COSATU's formation. After 18 months' existence, COSATU has not only survived difficult conditions, but has begun to consolidate its base and extend the boundaries of the debate, despite multifaceted repression including extensive detentions of officials and members. In May 1987 COSATU House was bombed and the administration of all the unions severely disrupted; meetings around the living wage campaign and May Day rallies were banned, while the organisation itself was vilified in sections of the media. Despite this the leadership continued to encourage strategic debate among affiliates because of the complex and critical nature of the issues. According to COSATU's NEC, the federation

> is just over a year old. But our struggle is older than all of us. Today we are closer than ever before to the day when we - the workers and youth of our land - must free ourselves from the chains of poverty, hunger, exploitation and racism which bind us...

Differences we will always have. They are necessary in every democratic organisation to find the best ideas for the strongest way forward. That is what worker democracy means. But it also means that once we have decided we are loyal to that decision and we do our very best to carry it out in a disciplined way and comradely way.[11]

During 1986 the larger unions found little to attract them in the anti-populist stance. There was a greater concern to debate openly and critically the alliance principles, which had been put forward in abstract, generalised form by the COSATU leadership.

A number of issues had to be clarified. If unions accepted alliances as a vital element in developing working-class politics, which organisations should they align with? Could criteria that broke through the superficially-applied populist label be established to evaluate these organisations? How could the working class ensure that alliances were established on a disciplined basis so that working-class demands were not subordinated? Most importantly, what was meant by working-class demands? Was this a demand for socialism, and if so, what kind of socialism?

The Metal and Allied Workers Union and the National Union of Mineworkers played significant roles in extending democratic debate around these crucial questions. The July 1986 MAWU congress called for 'Unity in action, independence of organisations, and a commitment to socialism'. It argued that the essential task in the coming period was to 'begin to define what we mean by socialism':

> This is the responsibility of the working class. A document drawn up by workers would not have to replace other charters like the Freedom Charter. It would simply express what the working class was aiming to achieve under socialism. A working class programme is called for in the COSATU resolutions. But it cannot be imposed from above. It must develop out of the struggles and the experiences of workers themselves. This is the immediate task.[12]

During May 1987, in the immediate aftermath of the COSATU

House raids, Jay Naidoo outlined the broad objectives of the union movement then being debated in the affiliates:

> The formation of COSATU stamped very powerfully working-class politics on the agenda of the mass democratic movement.

One of the central aims of COSATU spells out our commitment 'to work for a restructuring of the economy that will allow the creation of wealth to be democratically controlled and its fruits fairly shared amongst the working class'.

It is an inescapable fact that socialism is firmly on the political agenda. It has been on the political agenda for decades. We face in South Africa, a brutal regime with its security apparatus fully intact. Apartheid, one of the world's most brutal capitalist systems, has the counter-effect of creating a very highly politicised and oppressed people.

For millions of workers and youth it is virtually impossible to extricate the tentacles of apartheid (regarding) hostels, migrant labour, township ghettoes etc from the brutalising and exploitative economic system.[13]

Commitment to socialism is explicit, contradicting those who have argued that, for tactical reasons, socialism cannot be placed on the agenda at this stage. The central question for the future then is: what kind of socialism? Although debates on this question are at an early stage, it will doubtless be socialism based on some form of workers' control.

This issue came to the fore at the March 1987 NUM congress, the theme of which was '1987, the year in which mineworkers take control'. In an address to that congress, Jay Naidoo stated that

> The theme of your congress comes at a crucial point in our history. At this critical phase of our struggle against apartheid, racism and capitalist exploitation, what is needed is political and organisational decisiveness.

We have seen intensified attacks against us by our enemies and their allies... COSATU fully backs the struggle of NUM to take control of the hostels and break the chains of tribalism that divide the working class in South Africa.

The Kinross disaster was for us last year a bloody reminder that the mine bosses put profits before workers' lives. NUM has subsequently led the struggle for workers control over health and safety.[14]

If socialism based on worker control is the labour movement's objective, what political strategy will realise such a programme?

COSATU's emerging political programme

Naidoo has argued that COSATU's political strategy is being fashioned by three factors: the historical context of the labour movement's development; an analysis of present objective conditions; and the way in which the working class can *lead* the present mass struggles.

To ensure leadership of such struggles COSATU resolved that 1987 would be a year of 'consolidation and decisive action',[15] and would include realising the slogan 'one union, one industry' by building

> powerful national unions, rooted in democratic shop-floor structures that can effectively challenge the power of monopoly capitalism, a dominant feature of South Africa's industrial society.[16]

Another task set for 1987 was to strengthen shop steward councils which are 'the pillars on which COSATU stands. We will make these councils the organised voice of workers' unity in every area'. The leadership also determined to strengthen worker solidarity action in every area, and thereby effectively implement the slogan, 'an injury to one is an injury to all'. COSATU also pledged to 'defend in action the gains we have won'. Campaigns such as those around a living wage and May Day would 'organise and unite our mass strength behind clear, co-ordinated, national goals'. Such campaigns would also provide 'the basis of organisation for our unemployed class comrades, millions of youth, students and other democratic allies'. Finally, COSATU committed itself to

> actively participate in the building of democratic structures in the communities where we live. In this respect we will take the lead in building street committees, and we will provide material assistance to youth, unemployed, farmworkers and women to build their own national organisations.[17]

COSATU leadership has stressed the need for criteria to assess organisations that unions seek alliances with in the struggle for

socialism. According to Naidoo, the clearest guide will be whether organisations adhere to the principles and policies the labour movement has forged over the past four years. These include:
* non-racialism;
* workers control and democracy;
* national organisation;
* a defined constituency;
* a proven record of mass struggle;
* involvement in mass struggle.

COSATU has determined various sectors which are vital components of the democratic movement and has identified organisations in each that, in differing degrees, meet the criteria listed above. These include:
* Youth - South African Youth Congress (SAYCO);
* Students - South African National Students Congress (SANSCO), and National Student Co-ordinating Committee;
* Unemployed - National Unemployed Workers Co-ordinating Committee (NUWCC);
* Women;
* Area committees and civics, at local and regional levels.

By taking these concrete steps towards forging alliances, COSATU was

breaking away from the theoretical clutches of intellectuals and organisations that excel in resolution writing, but who reduce all theory and practice to ideas that exist outside of mass organisation and struggle.[18]

It also represented the beginning of a

political programme through millions of workers and youth involved in mass struggle, rather than academically by a coterie of self-assured intellectuals tucked in the comfort of universities.[19]

Naidoo also warned against those intellectuals who interpret these developments as reflecting

a detraction from COSATU's commitment to the *leadership* of the working class and the building of a socialist society. It would be naive to interpret that (NUM's political) resolution implies the submergence of the interests of the working class and a backdown of the theme of its 5th annual conference, 'Mineworkers take control'.[20]

COSATU and the Freedom Charter

The Freedom Charter adopted by members of the Congress Alliance in 1955 has become an important element in the political resistance equation of the 1980s, as divergent groups identify with the broad aspirations the Charter represents. According to Naidoo,

> our biggest most powerful affiliate, NUM, representing 369 000 members adopted the Freedom Charter as the guiding document of our struggle for a democratic, socialist society. Just as the mines are the backbone of the South African economy, so NUM is the backbone of COSATU. The debates and the adoption of the Charter broadly reflects the debate of the labour movement as it seeks to more decisively position the role of the working class in the struggle for liberation from national oppression and economic exploitation. It expresses the need that has arisen to define the terms 'progressive', 'democratic' and the basis on which alliances are structured in the mass democratic movement.[21]

Naidoo went on to argue that

> The Freedom Charter is the most representative and democratic document of minimum demands formulated by the people of South Africa and it is clearly emerging within the ranks of workers as a rallying point to further our own class interests. In that context, a programme that cohesively unites and furthers our own interests needs to be systematically debated within our ranks.[22]

The adoption of a political policy that identifies fully with the national democratic struggle, while at the same time specifying a socialist direction, cuts through the sterility of the populist-workerist debate that is so all-absorbing to many. According to Naidoo,

> The interests of the working class can only be advanced by us locating ourselves in the hub of the struggle for democratisation of society, by building a working-class power as the foundation of the organs of peoples power.[23]

The Charter achieves this by blending transitionary socialist demands for nationalisation with generalised liberal-democratic demands. A dominant socialist interpretation will be imprinted to the extent that the working class dominates the democratic alliance. SACTU gave the Charter a socialist interpretation from the outset, saying that nationalisation would be established on the basis of workers' control. Even Mandela's liberal 1956 interpretation -

that realising the demands of the Charter would encourage a black petty bourgeoisie to flourish - was based on the notion that this would stimulate a more rapid capitalist development, strengthen the social base of the working class, and open the way to socialist transformation.

This position is of course based on the now controversial two-stage theory of change, rooted in the internal colonialism thesis. Notwithstanding the intense debate about stages, it is clear that this approach cuts through the knot of the populist-workerist debates. The adoption of populism in the Chartist sense solidifies the unity of the different groups comprising the alliance. The struggle of 'the people', led by the working class, towards the realisation of socialism is at once democratic because of the character of the labour movement itself. The political task is to attract those outside the factories and mines to the ultimate demands of workers.

This Chartist interpretation of the relationship between populism and socialist struggle is by no means universally accepted, as indicated by debates and resolutions at the launch of the National Union of Metalworkers of South Africa (NUMSA). The issue remains in the melting pot, and will only be clarified in the process of ongoing debate.[24]

This is not to say that populist *practices* should not be criticised if they are founded on a crude notion of mobilising the masses on the basis of their experience of racial discrimination, without sufficient attention to organisation and advancing the question of economic exploitation under capitalism. There is a tendency within certain, but not all, sectors of the UDF, for example, to argue that the question of socialism should not be raised on public platforms at this stage of the struggle. This is a far cry from the disciplined attempt by COSATU leadership to force the pace of industrial mergers during 1987 as the basis for consolidating *workers'* power, and thereby pushing the socialist project to the fore.

COSATU and the youth

COSATU leadership is searching for a viable strategy to deal with unemployment. To this end it has worked closely with the National Unemployed Workers Co-ordinating Committee. NUWCC organises unemployed workers in the townships, and seeks to make organised workers aware of the plight of the unemployed.

Youth, who comprise a large proportion of the unemployed, have been at the forefront of township resistance since 1984. Certain unions have attempted to establish constructive alliances with the unemployed, and this may ease the very real tensions between unemployed and unionised workers, tensions very common to industrialised societies.

In South Africa, racial oppression has compounded the generational tensions in township households. The attitude of youth is complex and contradictory: they recognise that their parents are victims of racial oppression and economic exploitation, and empathise with them; yet they blame their parents for not fighting this oppression with sufficient vigour:

> Our parents still have that old image they grew up under. They tell us that the white man is a white man, and that what he says is final. When we try to argue with our parents they will just say, 'What do you know, you were only born yesterday. You have got to listen to what we are telling you!' We are caught in a trap. What our parents don't seem to have is a desire for us to be better people... So now we do everything for ourselves without consulting our parents because it is useless to speak to a stone.[25]

This reinforces a potentially antagonistic relationship towards the unions:

> Many unions just ask for wage demands and the reduction of working hours. I know factories where workers just ask for boots and overalls...but do not find there's an importance in the struggle. But we are the highly politicised ones... We embrace one cause, we understand what the cause is, and we sacrifice, even our lives, because we understand what is actually happening. But workers, ha! If you only receive those boots and those boots are being torn up again, then you will start boycotting the factory and demanding new boots... That is why when we call for actions like stayaways they often don't understand the importance of the stayaway... They are often narrow, and just look at the disadvantages of stayaways. They just say, 'if we don't work for a week, we won't get money for that week'. So what they normally do is to take another route and walk through fences and jump those bridges to go to work... If individuals were highly organised and politicised their response would be positive enough. They would be able to sacrifice, even for the whole month, by staying away from the factories. It just depends on how the unions will operate.

Establishing an *organised* relationship with the unemployed will undoubtedly ease these tensions, as the youth come to understand trade unionism at a deeper level. It will also require a positive response on the part of organised workers. The youth gave an example of an East Rand shop stewards council whom they approached with the question,

> Will you tax your wage and put the money in a fund for the unemployed in the area? We have organised and prevented scabs from taking your jobs while you were on strike. Now, will you take this step and stand in solidarity with us?

These youth are still waiting for a reply, a sign that their views on the nature of trade unions are correct. They have engaged in developing township organisation such as street and area committees. These forms of organisation have the potential for surviving state repression and therefore allow for the fullest possible participation of township residents. However, the level of development of these structures between and within townships is extremely uneven.

Leaders of unemployed youth display a developed class consciousness and a sophisticated understanding of the differing currents of debate around the issue of national liberation. A major problem is the need for time and space to draw further layers of youth into this consciousness. This would allow them to gain control over what they describe as 'anti-social' township elements, that stratum which has lived off crime and ridden the tide of political upsurge. The uncontrolled and undisciplined violence they represent hinders the task of political organisation and consolidation in the townships. Each time the state represses organisation, it opens up further scope for the 'anti-social' elements and their anarchic and mindless activities: examples include the stoning and burning to death of two organisers of the Electrical and Allied Workers Union in Cape Town, and the destruction of the victimised Sarmcol workers' kombi in Soweto en route to present a performance of their play.

These are the challenges that COSATU, as a disciplined and organised force, will have to confront in the coming years.

Only one way forward

At the May 1987 congress of metal unions to establish NUMSA, COSATU leadership pointed out that it had no option but to confront political questions of national liberation. Because COSATU was a democratic organisation, its leadership had to respond to the demands and direction of its members. This commitment need not detract from the essential goal of the working class - the establishment of a democratic and socialist society where ordinary working men and women *participate* fully in the political decision-making processes, in the factories, mines and farms, in the areas where they live, at local, regional and national levels. Only on the basis of this radical democracy, can the cycle of exploitation be broken and the wealth that is created be distributed equitably in terms of human need.

These goals can only be realised within a commitment to national struggle, for it is the national struggle that has the greatest potential to unite different classes, and segments of classes, in a common liberation struggle. In taking the lead, COSATU has accepted the responsibility of imprinting working-class, socialist demands on the nationalist cause. This is the disciplined basis of the alliance, and those who do not accept this leading role of the working class will fall by the wayside.

Notes

This paper monitors leadership strategy in COSATU only. Because of the democratic character of COSATU, positions have not developed in a vacuum, but through continuous debate within the organisation. They therefore reflect significant shifts in the thinking of workers themselves. Currents of nationalist feeling or socialist commitment do not emerge simply as ideas from above, but derive from the lived experience of workers as they debate a way out of the impasse.

1   Jay Naidoo, 'COSATU - The Struggle for Socialism', paper delivered at the Western Cape Teachers Union Conference, May 1987.
2   Steven Friedman, 'The Struggle within the Struggle: South African resistance strategies', *Transformation*, 3, 1987.
3   Bill Freund, 'Some Unasked Questions on Politics: South African Slogans and Debates', *Transformation*, 1, 1986, 119.
4   Friedman, 'The Struggle within the Struggle', 66.
5   Freund, 'Some Unasked Questions', 119.
6   Steven Friedman, *Building Tomorrow Today: African Workers in Trade Unions, 1970-1984*, Johannesburg, 1986, 33.
7   Interview, 15.10.85.
8   Interview, 15.10.85.
9   Jay Naidoo, 'Building People's Power: A Working Class Perspective', paper presented to Grassroots Conference, 5 May 1986.
10 The paper was circulated during March 1986. The quotes that follow are taken from the paper.
11 Document, '1987 - The Year of Consolidation and Decisive Action',

February 1987.

12 MAWU position paper, 'Trade Unions and Political Direction', July 1986.

13 Naidoo, 'The Struggle for Socialism'.

14 Jay Naidoo, address delivered to the annual congress of the National Union of Mineworkers, 25 February 1987.

15 Naidoo, 'The Struggle for Socialism'.

16 Naidoo, 'The Struggle for Socialism'.

17 Naidoo, 'The Struggle for Socialism'.

18 Naidoo, 'The Struggle for Socialism'.

19 Naidoo, 'The Struggle for Socialism'.

20 Naidoo, 'The Struggle for Socialism'.

21 Naidoo, 'The Struggle for Socialism'.

22 Naidoo, 'The Struggle for Socialism'.

23 Naidoo, 'The Struggle for Socialism'.

24 Two political resolutions were put before the congress, one noting that the Freedom Charter is 'also a good foundation stone on which to start building our working class programme', and the other adopting the Charter 'as containing the minimum political demands that reflect the view of the majority of metal workers' vision of a free and democratic, non-discriminatory South Africa'. Both resolutions were adopted, indicating both a broad consensus and areas that still have to be debated. The relationship between populism and socialist struggle is by no means settled.

25 This quote and those that follow are taken from a workshop held in June 1986, involving unemployed youth activists from all regions of South Africa. They had been active in the Congress of South African Students prior to its banning. The workshop was organised by Ari Sitas, Moses Ngoasheng and Rob Lambert from the Community and Labour Research Unit, Sociology Department, Natal University.

Trade Unions and the Industrial Court

Paul Benjamin

A dramatic increase in trade unions' use of the industrial court took place in 1986. Over 2 200 actions were instituted, compared to about 800 the previous year. The Department of Manpower expects this figure to increase to 4 000 in 1987.[1] The vast majority of cases were brought by unions on behalf of dismissed members.

Increased use of the industrial court has had an impact on independent trade unions' patterns of collective bargaining. The background to this involves the recent reforms to the statutory system of industrial conciliation contained in the Labour Relations Act, until 1981 known as the Industrial Conciliation Act.

Wiehahn and after

South Africa's legislative framework for industrial conciliation has shown remarkable longevity. The two central institutions for negotiation and dispute resolution, the industrial council and the conciliation board, date back to the first Industrial Conciliation Act of 1924. Industrial councils - consisting of equal numbers of employee and employer representatives from a particular industry - are forums for negotiation over wages and other conditions of employment, as well as for resolution of disputes in the industry. In industries with no industrial council, the latter role is carried out by a conciliation board. This is a meeting between the parties to a dispute chaired by an official of the department of manpower. Many, but not all, of South Africa's major industries have industrial councils. Mining is the most notable exception.

By the late 1970s the statutory system which prevented participation by trade unions with African members was in crisis. The independent trade union movement had become a significant force in South African industrial relations, but its member unions could neither register nor use official structures to resolve disputes. The formal channels for representation of black workers were the works and liaison committee systems laid down in the Black Labour Relations Regulation Act. They represented an attempt by government to destroy black trade unionism and gave no recognition to trade unions. The Wiehahn Commission,[2] which was appointed in 1977 and reported in 1979, was instructed to investigate revitalisation and restructuring of the statutory system for industrial conciliation.

The strategy of emerging trade unions in the 1970s was to gain employers' recognition at plant level in factories with majority membership. This included negotiating collective agreements with employers which aimed at establishing the union's organisational presence. Such organisation was usually based on elected shop steward committees at factory level and involved setting up channels and procedures to resolve disputes and bargain about wages and other conditions of employment.

The Wiehahn Commission believed this growth of 'informal' collective bargaining could potentially undermine the statutory collective bargaining institutions. Plant-level bargaining was developing at the expense of industry-wide bargaining centred on the industrial councils. The commission's central recommendation, which became law in 1979, was to allow trade unions with African members to register in terms of the Industrial Conciliation Act and participate in the statutory conciliation system.

Registration would subject them to the controls in the Act. These are chiefly administrative, requiring that proper records and accounts be kept and regular elections be held. The only restriction on political activity was that unions could not fund or assist political parties. The commission assumed that independent trade unions would soon apply to join industrial councils and be absorbed into their activities. This system, the commission reasoned, had worked well for established unions; there was no reason why independent unions would not respond in the same way.

The next three years revealed the flaws in the commission's approach. Independent unions did not apply to join industrial councils, and made little use of councils and conciliation boards to resolve disputes. A number of trade unions did register, but as a tactical device in battles for plant-level recognition. Other independent unions refused to register and the 'registration debate' was a controversial issue in the early 1980s. Its significance subsequently declined. By April 1986, with the National Union of Mineworkers' registration, all major independent unions had registered.

In 1981, the controls in the Act were increased and extended to unregistered trade unions. This was as far as this aspect of state strategy could go. However, the policy had had little impact on the pattern of collective bargaining: the growth of extra-statutory bargaining at plant level continued unabated. The controls did not hamper the activities or growth of independent unions which kept their participation in the statutory framework to a minimum.

In 1982 the Labour Relations Act was amended for the fourth time since the publication of the Wiehahn report. The industrial court, created in 1979, was given increased powers. It took on a pivotal role in labour relations. Before 1982 few disputes had been referred to the court, which had not been able to use its unfair labour practice powers to develop a code of sound employment practice as envisaged by the commission.

But the 1982 amendment gave the court 'status quo' powers which allowed it to reverse unilateral actions in industrial disputes. Most crucially, it may order the temporary reinstatement of dismissed employees while the dispute over their dismissal is processed by the statutory conciliation machinery. The court can only order reinstatement if the dispute has been referred to an industrial council or a conciliation board for settlement.

These extensive powers to interfere with the exercise of management power for the first time made using the court an attractive proposition for trade unions. The procedure is relatively cheap and quick and offers a prospect of short-term relief for unfairly dismissed workers. While reinstatement orders are of an interim nature, a successful application frequently leads to an overall settlement favourable to the union and its members. The subsequent increase in cases enabled the court to develop its unfair labour practice jurisprudence and lay down a code of employment practice.

Dismissal and retrenchment

The first two areas in which the court developed guidelines were individual dismissals, and dismissal due to redundancy. Dismissal and disciplining of employees had caused considerable dissatisfaction and industrial unrest among black workers in the 1970s and 1980s, triggering over a third of strikes in some years. Black employees' desire for protection against arbitrary exercise of managerial power was a major factor in the rapid growth of the independent trade unions.[3]

Collective bargaining agreements negotiated by these unions contained clauses aimed at limiting the almost absolute power of employers to dismiss and discipline employees.[4] Such agreements required employers' consent to follow set procedures before dismissing workers, or to dismiss only where good grounds existed. Some agreements provided for an independent arbitrator to decide on the fairness of disputed dismissals.

The industrial court took its lead from the international standards that had been incorporated into these agreements and the more enlightened management codes. It held that, in the absence of a good reason, a dismissal is unfair. Minor disciplinary offences do not merit dismissal. This is in marked contrast to the previous position, when employers' ability to dismiss was limited only by their obligation to give notice and the fact that they could not dismiss for an employee's trade union activities. The court has also held that proper and fair procedures must be followed before a dismissal. Employees are entitled to a fair hearing at which they can dispute the case against them, question company witnesses and call evidence in their defence. At a hearing, dismissed employees can insist on being assisted by a representative of their choice, frequently a shop steward.

The continuing recession, as well as technological changes reducing the size of workforces, has resulted in a steady flow of retrenchment disputes. Since 1983 the court has attacked management's traditional approach to retrenchment as an opportunity to weed out 'bad eggs', unionists and other 'troublemakers'. The court stressed that it was important for employers to follow proper procedures when retrenching. It required them to consider ways of avoiding retrenchment, or of reducing the numbers retrenched. Management must give employees and their representatives, including trade unions, prior notice of its intention to retrench. It must consult with worker representatives and disclose information proving the need to retrench. Retrenchments must be conducted according to objective and verifiable criteria, particularly the 'last-in first-out' principle which recognises the seniority of employees.

In its judgments on both dismissals and retrenchments, the court stressed the importance of employees perceiving the actions of their employers to be fair. It sees this perception as playing an important role in preventing industrial unrest.

It is difficult to gauge the impact of the court's approach to dismissals and retrenchments on patterns of collective bargaining.

Available statistical evidence indicates a decline in the proportion of strikes caused by dismissal disputes. In 1985 and 1986 less than 20% of strikes were caused by dismissals, while earlier in the decade this figure was nearer 30%.[5]

The court's willingness to reinstate employees has had a profound impact on employers' behaviour. It made it clear that employers who did not follow the court's guidelines would have to reinstate unfairly dismissed workers. The court's stress on procedural fairness and employees' right to representation opened up a new area of organisational activity, with shop stewards becoming actively involved in representing employees at disciplinary hearings.

Retrenchments have in the past caused industrial unrest despite the difficulty of staging successful industrial action on the issue. The court's approach has been to require employers to bear the social costs of redundancy.[6] This has ensured that many employers do consult with representative trade unions. But the fact that many companies are in economic difficulties often limits the role of unions in challenging the extent of retrenchments and attempting to win better retrenchment benefits.

The court's approach emphasising procedure can be undermined by employers who consult with a union, but throughout the talks treat the retrenchment as a foregone conclusion. It can be extremely difficult for a union to prove this attitude, although the court has on occasion punished it. Employers who have relied on generally poor economic conditions to justify a retrenchment without showing a decline in their own business have been ordered to reinstate retrenched employees.

Employers and trade unions have shown a willingness to prevent dismissals erupting into collective conflict. This is demonstrated by the emergence of a private arbitration and mediation service, the Independent Mediation Service of South Africa (IMSSA), as a significant actor in South African industrial relations. In 1985 it arbitrated 23 dismissal disputes, and in 1986 the number rose to 68. In the first three months of 1987 there were 39 arbitrations. The vast majority of these were on the Witwatersrand, where IMSSA has its offices. When it expands to other major centres, use of its services is expected to increase. Arbitrators have no statutory authority, but company and union agree to comply with the decision of the arbitrator, who may reinstate dismissed workers.

A major advantage of arbitration is the speed with which a dispute can be resolved. Applications for temporary reinstatement are typically heard by the industrial court over three months after a dismissal. Final unfair labour practice determinations may not be made for over a year. The delays, which stem from the crowded court roll and other bureaucratic bottlenecks, can keep a dispute alive as a potential source of conflict. Arbitrations, on the other hand, are arranged at the convenience of the parties involved, and a final decision on the fairness of dismissal can be made within as short a period as two weeks after the dismissal.

Protection of strikers

Strike activity has been at a high level throughout the 1970s and 1980s. The majority of strikes were unlawful because the issue in dispute had not been brought before an industrial council or conciliation board. Participation in an unlawful strike is a crime, but there have been no prosecutions in recent years. The lawfulness of a strike does not protect participants from dismissal for breach of their employment contracts. An increasing number of disputes, particularly over wages, have been channelled through the statutory conciliation machinery. Unions have turned to the industrial court for support in reinstating employees dismissed for participation in lawful strikes in the last two years.

The most notable instance was in the mining industry, where in 1984, 1985 and 1986 unresolved wage disputes between the National Union of Mineworkers and the Chamber of Mines were referred to conciliation boards. In 1985 agreement on wages was reached with some mining houses at the conciliation board meeting. Lawful strike activity then took place at other mines where the dispute was not settled. This led to the swift dismissal and busing out of strikers. The union made a number of court applications for temporary reinstatement of its members.

Most notable was the Marievale case, where for the first time the court reinstated employees dismissed for participation in a lawful strike over wages. Its importance lies not only in the recognition of industrial action as an integral part of collective bargaining, but in the process by which the court arrived at its decision to reinstate the strikers. The court examined in great detail the merits and demerits of the conduct of the union, its members and mine management before, during and after the strike. It then concluded that the dismissal was unfair. The union had followed the conciliation procedures laid down in the Act, and had been willing to refer the dispute to arbitration or mediation. This offer was rejected by management. The court accepted that this left the union with no option but to call a strike. The strike did not last long, and the union distributed strike rules to its members, whose conduct was orderly. The court was critical of mine management's refusal to negotiate in good faith with the union, its paternalistic attitude to its employees and the fact that its sole concern had been the lawfulness of its actions. At no stage had it considered their fairness.

After the success of the application, the parties to the dispute reached a settlement; the dismissed employees were permanently reinstated. The Marievale judgment led to a marked increase in the number of wage disputes referred to conciliation boards or industrial councils. Lawful strikes, particularly over wages, also increased. The judgment does not give employees a licence to strike after exhausting the procedures laid down in the Act. It does, however, encourage parties in industrial disputes to legitimate their conduct. The court will not sanction precipitate or unreasonable conduct.

The impact of this decision on industrial relations is shown by the increasing use of mediation to resolve wage disputes. In 1986 IMSSA mediators conducted 130 mediations, mostly during negotiations on wages and other conditions of employment. The mining industry employers who had refused mediation in the 1985 wage dispute accepted the union's proposal for mediation the following year.

The Marievale judgment offers limited guidance to employers and trade unions involved in disputes, as the court was able to characterise the mine's conduct as unfair and unreasonable. It is not clear how the court will respond if both sides can show that they have bargained in good faith and that their final negotiating positions are reasonable.

The judgment's impact on industrial action is clearer. Wage disputes have become increasingly long and drawn out. The Commercial, Catering and Allied Workers Union - OK Bazaars strike lasted more than two months, during which the workforce was not given an ultimatum to return to work. The company did however try to restrict its economic losses by employing temporary replacement labour during the strike. Ultimately the dispute was resolved after lengthy negotiation in the presence of mediators.

An employer dismissing a striking workforce now faces being ordered to reinstate it at a later stage, and possibly having to pay up to six months' arrear wages. This quandary is illustrated by the litigation, still under way, over BTR Sarmcol's dismissal in May 1985 of its workforce of 800-odd employees. When the case concludes, more than two years will have passed since the dismissals. The drastic consequences of defeat in a case like this are an incentive for the parties to settle industrial disputes outside court.

Despite these developments, most strike action takes place before the conciliation machinery has been exhausted. The court was reluctant to help dismissed unlawful strikers, adopting the simplistic view that as they have 'taken the law into their own hands' they cannot expect protection from the court. This left employers with a free hand to dismiss striking workers and reconstitute their workforce as they chose. Strike activity was used to exclude trade union leaders and activists, and unsuccessful strikes often had dire consequences for trade union organisation. The court has now changed this attitude, holding that the selective re-employment of strikers can be unfair. Selective re-employment is only acceptable if carried out according to fair and objective criteria. The duty to consult with a union may extend beyond the dismissal to situations where the company is offering selective re-employment to dismissed employees.

This can make an employer's decision to dismiss a striking workforce hazardous. The employer who fires a workforce may have to choose between re-employing all his old workers or employing an entirely new workforce. This may have unpalatable cost implications, particularly where the workforce is skilled. Management must show an objective need to reduce its workforce to justify selective re-employment. This could be the case where the strike resulted in loss of business, creating redundancy. An employer wishing to dismiss employees for violent or intimidating conduct during a strike will have to approach such dismissals as it would any dismissal for misconduct, and offer each employee a proper opportunity to counter the evidence against them.

These decisions are in line with the clauses in a number of collective agreements which prohibit selective dismissal or re-employment of strikers. They greatly increase the bargaining power of trade unions during and after unlawful strikes, and effectively extend the sphere of negotiation to these situations. Strikes are no longer a gift-wrapped opportunity for a hostile employer to rid his business of a unionised workforce.

Collective bargaining

In the areas discussed, the court's decisions have, after initial uncertainty, shown a consistency and coherence that has influenced the conduct of industrial relations. The same cannot be said for the court's occasional ventures into the arena of collective bargaining. In a judgment like Marievale, the court severely criticised the old style of paternalistic management. But on other occasions the court has failed to appreciate the significance of the challenge to traditional forms of collective bargaining posed by the rise of independent unions.

This shortcoming is most evident in its response to the arguments of the Metal and Allied Workers Union that metal industry employers' refusal to bargain with the union on wages at plant level is an unfair labour practice. Until 1983 MAWU eschewed participation in the Industrial Council for the Iron, Steel, Engineering and Metallurgical Industries, the country's largest industrial council, which sets wages and working conditions for more than 330 000 employees. The union ultimately joined the council because it felt that its demands were being hijacked by parties on the council, and that the council negotiations would serve as a unifying focus for its growing membership.

After joining the council, the union continued to press for plant-level bargaining in the industry, a demand strenuously resisted by employers. The union argued that wage negotiations at the council are for minimum wages, while wage negotiations at plant level are for actual wages, which may be well in excess of the minimum. In the absence of plant-level bargaining, employers who are able to pay above the minimum levels are free to set wages unilaterally.

The court accepted the employer argument that there is no obligation on South African employers to bargain in good faith with trade unions, and that bargaining should be voluntary and not enforced on an unwilling party. Unfortunately, this argument is not based on analysis of the Labour Relations Act, but employer self-interest. Employers favour voluntary bargaining at plant level because they do not want to bargain at plant level.[7] The court's attitude offers little help to trade unions dealing with recalcitrant employers in these situations.

If an employer's reluctance to bargain at plant level provokes unlawful industrial action the court has no sympathy for dismissed strikers. If the dispute is channelled through the conciliation procedures found in the Act, the court is reluctant to compel the unwilling employer to bargain at plant level.

Proposed amendments to the Act

No amendments were made to the Labour Relations Act in 1985 or 1986. But in late 1986 a draft bill was published which attracted considerable comment. The amendments in the bill emerged from 1984 recommendations made by the National Manpower Commission (a think-tank operating under the auspices of the department of manpower without independent trade union representation). The most controversial of the proposed amendments would undermine the status and role of the industrial court.

These include the establishment of a special labour appeal court to hear appeals from the industrial court. It is feared that this could seriously reduce the status of the court. The bill also proposes major changes in the definition of an unfair labour practice. An unfair dismissal is defined separately from other unfair labour practices, and a separate procedure is proposed for obtaining relief in these cases. This innovation may make it more difficult to obtain reinstatement of dismissed workers.

The present definition of an unfair labour practice is open-ended. It allowed the industrial court to develop its guidelines for acceptable labour practices in response to developments in labour relations. The amended definition is more extensive, describing in detail conduct that would be an unfair labour practice. For instance, the bill proposes that any attempt by a trade union to prevent an employer dealing with another trade union is an unfair labour practice. This is in conflict with the concept of majoritarianism which is prominent in South African labour relations, according to which an employer would deal on collective issues only with the trade union with majority membership in a particular bargaining unit.

Employers' and trade unions' major criticism of this type of definition is based not on its incorrectness, but on the fact that its enactment would prevent the industrial court from responding to shifts in labour relations. The definition of an unfair labour practice would be fossilised.

Another proposed amendment worth noting simplifies application for the establishment of a conciliation board, removing the minister of manpower's current discretion on whether or not to appoint a board. This amendment would considerably simplify the process of channelling disputes through the statutory conciliation mechanisms in industries without industrial councils.

The industrial court and trade unionism

Overall, the industrial court has been able to offer effective responses in a number of areas of labour relations. This, coupled with its wide powers - particularly to reinstate dismissed employees - ensured it a central role in the expansion of trade unionism and collective bargaining. On issues like dismissals of individual employees and retrenchments the court has tried to use its unfair labour practice powers to remove such disputes from the arena of collective conflict and to provide procedures for their resolution.

The success of this approach is shown by the decline in the level of industrial action related to dismissal and retrenchment. Equally important is the willingness of employers, particularly with regard to dismissal, to subject their managerial prerogative to third party assessment through arbitration.

The court has recognised that the right to strike is essential to effective collective bargaining, and that statutory channels for dispute resolution will not be used unless strikers are afforded protection against managerial powers of dismissal. The court's attitude encourages employers and trade unions to resort to industrial action only where there is no other channel to resolve disputes. Trade unions are also encouraged to exercise control over their members during industrial action.

Notes

1. Speech by the director-general: manpower, to Labour Law Conference, University of Witwatersrand, January 1987.
2. RP 47/1979: 'Report of Commission into Labour Legislation', Part 1, 'Key Issues'.
3. See Eddie Webster, 'A New Frontier of Control: Case Studies in the Changing Form of Job Control in South Africa', report no 111, Carnegie Conference on Poverty, University of Cape Town, April 1984.
4. See Paul Benjamin, 'Collective Bargaining and the Managerial Prerogative', unpublished LLM thesis, Warwick University, 1987, chapter 5.
5. Statistics on strikers are from the Annual Reports of the National Manpower Commission and the industrial relations consultants, Andrew Levy and Associates.
6. See Clive Thompson, 'Retrenchments and the Law', address to Institute for Industrial Relations, 1985.
7. See Clive Thompson, 'On Bargaining and Legal Intervention', *Industrial Law Journal*, 1, 1987.

Job Reservation on the Mines[*]

Robyn Rafel

When parliament was prorogued in February 1987 for the white election, several bills had not been discussed. One of these paved the way for the abolition of job reservation in the mining industry, where the sole racially-inspired job bar is still entrenched in South African law.

The Mines and Works Amendment Bill was meant as the culmination of a process which began in 1981 when government accepted the recommendations of the Wiehahn Commission's sixth report. Parliament's failure to deal with the bill came as no surprise. The pre-election period was not a propitious time to tackle a matter which would add fuel to right-wing grievances. And South African history has graphically demonstrated that few issues have the capacity to inflame emotions more than the prospect of white miners losing long-entrenched privileges.

Job reservation is enforced on the mines through the discriminatory definition of 'scheduled person' in the Mines and Works Act. It disqualifies blacks for 13 certificates of competency necessary to perform key mining jobs. The certificates, issued by the government mining engineer, cover jobs ranging from rock

---

[*] This article is accurate to March 1987. Since then there have been several interesting developments relating to the mining job bar - the most important being the passing of the Mines and Works Amendment Bill in October 1987.

blasting to locomotive driver up to mine manager.

As far as mineworkers - as opposed to officials - are concerned, the blasting certificate is the one most crucial for black advancement. Possession of a blasting certificate not only forms the dividing line between black and white jobs, but is also a prerequisite for obtaining some, but not all the other 13 certificates. There are no black 'miners' as such, since the highest job level blacks can attain is that of team leader, which is just below blasting certificate level.

Behind the blatantly racist phenomenon of the 'scheduled person' is a fascinating, if repelling, history. It centres on white miners' fierce determination to establish and maintain their privileged position, their role in the making and breaking of governments, and mine owners' attitudes towards the utilisation of labour. These factors are as relevant today as they were earlier in the century.

Origins of the job bar in the mining industry

Job reservation is almost as old as South African industry itself. In the gold industry it was introduced in the 1890s.[1] Ostensibly it arose out of a concern to have safe working conditions. But the underlying reason was the determination of white workers (some of whom came from the northern hemisphere with strong trade union traditions) to protect themselves against being undercut by cheaper black labour.

Some early job reservation provisions made clear references to race. Others, no less discriminatory in intention, were not as blatant.

The Mining Regulations Law of 1896 was the first law covering blasting and made no mention of race. It merely held that persons doing blasting had to possess a blasting certificate of competency. The Crown Colony of the Transvaal's Ordinance 17 of 1907 contained the same provisions. But the 'competent person' was invariably a white man.

There was no attempt at obfuscation in the case of more skilled mining jobs. The Mining Regulations Law clearly stated that the positions of banksman and onsetter should be restricted to whites. The regulations of Ordinance 54 of 1903 extended this discrimination to the jobs of shift boss, surface foreman and mine overseer.

The same bluntness was apparent in laws covering supervisory jobs and jobs involving the operation of machinery. The Boilers and Machinery Law of the South African Republic (passed in the 1890s), for instance, provided that blacks could not qualify to become winding engine drivers. Later, in the time of the Crown Colony of the Transvaal, this restriction was extended to include the driving of locomotive engines underground.

The Mines and Works Act, which to this day is the most important statute governing mining, was passed by the Union government in 1911. It was largely based on the work of a Mining Regulations Commission appointed by the Transvaal government in 1907 to consolidate mining legislation and regulations.

The act itself did not contain a colour bar, but its regulations did. They specifically restricted the jobs of mechanical and electrical engineers, winding engine drivers, locomotive engine drivers, boiler attendants and miners entitled to blast to holders of certificates of competency. The telling bit came in Regulation 285 which stated that certificates could not be granted to blacks.

Defence of the colour bar

Despite these regulations, white miners' fears about being undercut by blacks were exacerbated during World War I. Many among their ranks who hailed from Europe left their jobs to go and fight. They were replaced by Afrikaner workers who, for the most part, had recently left the land and were less skilled.

These Afrikaner workers formed an intermediate band between unskilled black workers and skilled white workers. By the end of the war they formed about 75% of the white labour force, compared with about 40% at the beginning.[2] Inevitably, the exigencies of production led to blacks doing some semi-skilled work. This caused a great deal of disquiet among the new workers and ultimately resulted in the forging of the famous 'status quo' agreement of 1918. In it the Chamber of Mines undertook to maintain the existing status quo in the allocation of jobs among whites and blacks.

In later years, when production costs rose dramatically and profits dropped, the chamber came to regret that decision. The only solution, from its point of view, was to reduce white labour costs and extend the work and responsibilities of all workers.

At the end of 1921 the chamber proposed to white workers'

unions that: wages of the highest paid white miners be cut; the status quo agreement be abolished; and the job colour bar be restricted to skilled work only so that more blacks could be used in semi-skilled positions.

The unions rejected these proposals. The chamber's decision to implement them nonetheless led to the great strike of 1922. The Rand Revolt, as it was called, developed into a mini civil war and was only put down when the Smuts government called in the army and the airforce against the strikers.

After the strike, victorious mine owners instituted radical changes. The status quo agreement was abolished and in almost all semi-skilled jobs whites were replaced by blacks, numbers of whites were retrenched without being replaced, new technologies were introduced, and white workers' underground responsibilities were extended. Before 1922 white miners' duties had consisted of rock breaking and heading one gang of black workers. After the strike their duties included safety in the stopes and responsibility for a larger gang of black workers.

These measures suited mine owners' purposes. But because white miners were less able to cope with their duties, blacks took on some of their roles in contravention of mine safety regulations.

In 1923 this matter was taken up by the department of mines. It initiated a case in the magistrate's court against the manager of Crown Mines for allowing a black to drive an electric locomotive underground. The manager, a Mr Hildick-Smith, was acquitted on the grounds that the regulations were ultra vires (outside of the law) because they were discriminatory and the Mines and Works Act did not make provision for discriminatory regulations. The supreme court subsequently upheld this judgment.

The case was to have important repercussions. But one curious aspect was the chamber's attitude. If, as its actions demonstrated, the chamber was opposed to the colour bar, why did it not use the judgment to do away with the colour bar completely? Apparently mine owners were concerned only with reducing the scope of its application, not with abolishing it.[3]

Smuts's role in quelling the 1922 strike ultimately led to the downfall of his government. White miners got their revenge in the 1924 election when their votes were crucial in putting the Pact government into power. In 1925 that government, for whom protection of the white worker was a major concern, appointed a commission of inquiry to investigate contraventions of the job colour bar. The Hildick-Smith case finding that the Mines and Works Act regulations were ultra vires was a factor which influenced the commission. In 1925 it recommended that the job bar should be incorporated directly into the act.

The Mines and Works Act was amended in 1926 to incorporate the infamous 'scheduled person' definition which has been retained in all its subsequent revisions. The definition is unequivocal: the only workers eligible for certificates of competency are whites, 'Cape Coloureds or Malays, Mauritian Creoles or St Helenans (or their descendants born in South Africa)'. Johnstone summed up these events:

> The pendulum had thus come full circle. The state, which in 1922 had served as the instrument for the repression of white workers, was now in the hands of their representatives, and implementing a protectionist policy for them.[4]

Years later, in 1948 to be precise, Smuts was to learn the hard way about the power of white miners for a second time when they swung the election to bring the National Party to power.

Experiments on the mines

The 1922 strike and its aftermath had such an impact that it was not until the 1960s that attempts were made to change work practices on the mines. Ironically, this time it was the whites-only Mineworkers Union (MWU) which made the opening gambit.

In 1963, the MWU approached the chamber demanding that its members, some of whom were contract workers and others remunerated on a daily basis, should receive a monthly wage. After negotiations the Gold Producers' Committee announced it was prepared to give daily-paid men, but not contract workers, a basic minimum monthly wage.

Naturally, the chamber demanded something in return: an experiment to ease the colour bar on several mines to allow black workers greater responsibilities. This was achieved through temporary exemptions from mining regulations granted by the government mining engineer.

The MWU executive, under its then general secretary Eddie Grundling, received the green light for the experiment in a series of meetings with members. The experiment started in August 1964 and by June 1965 it was taking place on 12 gold mines.

In terms of the experiment, competent 'non-scheduled' persons (black 'boss-boys' with at least three years' experience) were permitted to:

* take a gang from the waiting area to the workplace;
* inspect the working place and make it safe, providing that no blasting had been done there;
* let the gang commence work, and supervise work in accordance with various instructions;
* exercise supervision of explosives in unopened boxes and convey them where required;
* ensure that every member of the gang had left the working place before blasting; and
* inspect the gang at the end of a shift and report to the miner in charge.[5]

The major advantage was that instead of wasting a great deal of time at the beginning of a shift while blacks waited for whites to 'make safe', work could be started far more quickly.

In many ways the experiment represented no change. There is considerable evidence that mine regulations were frequently breached and that the experiment was merely trying to achieve a legalisation of existing practices. But for many MWU members, the experiment represented the thin end of the wedge. Their fears stemmed primarily from the fact that most MWU members had no higher qualification than a blasting certificate. They would therefore be the first to feel the effects of black advancement.

This caused a split in the MWU. Anti-experimentalists formed an action committee and called for Grundling's resignation. Wildcat strikes erupted. Matters took a turn for the worse in March 1965 when Grundling stated publicly that white miners approved of their new status. He said collieries were to be included in the experiment. The action committee appointed Dr Ras Beyers, an arch-racist, as its legal advisor. Grundling responded by calling a 24-hour colliery strike in support of extending the experiments, as a result of which four collieries came to a standstill. There were further strikes on gold mines against the experiment and the malcontents attempted to seize control of MWU offices in some towns.

Government reacted by appointing a commission of inquiry. Its terms of reference were to report on the nature and purpose of the experiment and the wage proposals connected with it; the advantages and disadvantages of the experiment for miners and the mining industry; and economic, labour and other implications of the experiment.

In his evidence to the commission, Beyers made the following points:

* whites had been replaced by 'non-whites';
* the status of some 'non-whites' had been raised;
* the experiment made inroads into the traditional colour bar; and
* if the experiment was accepted, it would result in 'great unrest and formidable problems'.

In its report, the commission concluded that:

Although it is clear that the experiment has certain merits, the commission feels that it cannot be applied unchanged in its present form on a country-wide basis because of the harmful implications it contains.

Government subsequently called off the experiment in the interest of industrial peace.

For the MWU, however, matters did not rest there. Conflict between pro-experimentalists and anti-experimentalists continued, leading to Grundling's downfall. In his place Arrie Paulus and Cor de Jager rose to the positions of MWU general secretary and president respectively in 1967. Both men still occupied these positions at the beginning of 1987.

Government willingness to bend over backwards yet again to protect the white miner was the key factor in defusing tensions caused by the experiment. Black workers' aspirations had not yet become an urgent enough issue to persuade it otherwise. In later years, when the MWU and government began to part ways and black workers' demands became more pressing, government's attitude began to change.

Concession time

Rifts the experiment caused in the MWU were a telling reminder that white miners were still prepared to go to great lengths to protect themselves against the black threat. But as time passed, they became more pragmatic. Indeed, it was none other than the fiery Paulus who negotiated an agreement with the chamber in 1973 in which the MWU made significant concessions in exchange for higher pay.

In his 1974 presidential address, the president of the chamber reported:

> The annual negotiations with trade unions in 1973 brought about important changes in work practices and hopefully set a pattern for further agreed advances in the future. As a result of these changes both white and black employees on gold mines and collieries have enjoyed higher earnings, while contributing to higher productivity.

The MWU concessions consisted of permitting, with certain provisos, specially trained black team leaders to assume some of white miners' responsibilities for making work places safe and allowing work to start. To give effect to this it was agreed that the time needed by miners to cover working areas for the purposes of supervision could be increased.

Reliable persons without blasting certificates could also charge up for blasting, provided that this was done within sight of a miner (who had to be not more than 15 metres away). These reliable persons could, in addition, mark off positions for the drilling of non-blast holes (eye bolt or rock bolt holes but not holes drilled for support purposes).

In 1976, further changes to work practices were introduced which resulted in blacks assuming still more responsibilities.

Again, the major impetus came from the MWU. The mining unions had long demanded that the chamber reduce the six-day mine working week to five days. These demands had always been refused on the grounds that unless a reduced working week was accompanied by a major re-organisation of work practices, there would be an unacceptable loss of production.

In mid-1975, after inconclusive negotiations, the MWU declared a dispute as a result of the chamber's refusal to agree to a five-day week without any concessions regarding work practices. The parties reached agreement after joint discussions with the minister of mines: a five-day week would be introduced on gold mines. A separate agreement was clinched for collieries which involved the introduction of an 11-shift fortnight, progressing after two years to a five-day week.

Implementation of both agreements was, however, dependent

on the chamber and other mining unions concluding a satisfactory agreement on a five-day week. The process got under way, but subsequently came unstuck when the unions representing artisans withdrew their demand, declaring that the changes it would involve called for 'suicidal sacrifices'.

The MWU nevertheless continued pressing for a five-day week and in May 1976 declared a second dispute with the chamber. When the matter went to a conciliation board, deadlock ensued. In a MWU strike ballot the majority of its members voted in favour of downing tools in support of the demand. A number of meetings with the ministers of mines and labour followed in an effort to find a compromise solution.

At the last of these meetings on 14 August, the minister of mines, Fanie Botha, in the words of a mining source, 'read the riot act' to the parties, instructing them that there should be no reduction in mine production as a result of their discussions.

In September, the chamber and the MWU reached agreement on the introduction of an 11-shift fortnight on gold mines and collieries. The MWU agreed to changed work practices in exchange for increased remuneration for its members. Similar agreements had been reached beforehand with the artisan unions.

Concessions the MWU agreed to, and for which the government mining engineer granted exemptions, included:

* increasing the maximum distance at which white miners may supervise charging up from 15 to 30 metres, and allowing suitably qualified blacks to charge up two development ends (working areas in the stope) simultaneously;

* allowing white miners to instruct black team leaders to make working places safe, with certain provisos - primarily that blacks should have received instruction to this effect during the previous shift. Again, the key factor was that delays at the start of a shift were greatly minimised.

These exemptions still apply today, and the agreements of 1973 and 1976 to a large extent brought about what the earlier experiments failed to achieve.

The Wiehahn Commission

In 1977 government appointed a commission under Professor Nic Wiehahn to examine South Africa's labour legislation. This was widely expected to lead to the legal recognition of black trade unions and moves to end the mine job bar. In the period before the issue of the first Wiehahn report in 1979 these expectations intensified.

On 5 March 1979, MWU members at the O'Kiep copper mine in Namaqualand went on strike over management's decision to employ three coloured artisans. Shortly thereafter about 6 500 MWU members downed tools at 70 other coal, platinum, copper and gold mines throughout South Africa. As the strike progressed, the MWU threatened to expel members who did not join in. The union has a closed shop agreement with the chamber, and this implied that scabs would lose their jobs.

Commenting on the strike, Carole Cooper wrote:

> The importance of the O'Kiep issue in the sequence of events was that it directly and immediately affected white miners and thus became the catalyst for the mobilisation of workers on all mines on the job reservation issue. The fact that the workers went on strike also demonstrates, perhaps, that union fears regarding possible changes in the industry, post-Wiehahn, were not entirely allayed by the minister's assurances that the MWU would be consulted if changes were to take place.[6]

Employers reacted quickly. They stated that the strike must be aimed at the government since they were not aware of any dispute workers had with employers which could have given rise to it. The chamber said it assumed the strike concerned the imminent release of the Wiehahn Commission. On 8 March the chamber announced that strikers had terminated their own employment. On 11 March the chamber said the industry would take legal action to protect miners who continued to work or returned to their posts - thus giving them protection against the MWU's threat.

By 14 March it was all over. Paulus's attempt to organise a crippling general strike on the mines had failed. Several important lessons were learned: other mining unions had not called their members out to back the MWU - their members took over the strikers' work; and most importantly, government refused to interfere - a sure sign of disaffection between the National Party and the MWU.

Government had also learned its lessons. The Wiehahn Commission's sixth report, which was devoted to the mining industry, was released only after the 1981 election. The report dealt in depth with the issue of the 'scheduled person'.

Much to the dismay of the MWU, the commission found that the definition 'hampers production without necessarily improving safety'. It recommended the definition be deleted from the Mines and Works Act and its regulations and be replaced by a definition of 'competent person'. The commission also recommended that negotiations on the removal of job reservation should be linked to

> devising a more satisfactory future basis for the recognition of trade unions than that of the closed shop agreements in association with the allocation of occupations agreement.

In terms of these agreements, all mine workers who are not black, or learners, are obliged to join unions. The union they are allocated to depends on the nature of the work they perform.

Significantly, in its comments on altering the definition the commission noted:

> Apart from thereby regularising a de facto situation and promoting the development of better work practices, the consequent flexibility to organise work purely on the basis of competence will enable reduction of the work force when coupled with technological advancement and will enable the industry to utilise its available technical skills more effectively.

Government, in a white paper on the report, accepted the recommendations and ordered the chamber and the mining unions to come to a settlement within a 'reasonable time'. Mindful that there would be opposition, it laid down certain conditions as prerequisites:

* adequate measures should be taken to allay possible apprehensions about future job security on the part of white workers;

* work standards should be rigorously maintained;

* all workers should be required to achieve the same level of proficiency with respect to training and experience before being appointed to a post;

* employers should not introduce changes in work practices and conditions of employment unilaterally, but rather with due regard to the process of consultation and negotiation with affected employee organisations;

* adequate job security measures should be incorporated in collective agreements; and

* all groups should be provided with adequate provisions

against racial victimisation.

In 1981 negotiations began between the chamber and the mining unions to fulfil the white paper's directives. For several years nothing much was achieved. It was only in March 1984 that talks got under way in earnest. There had at that stage already been rumblings in employer quarters - notably Anglo American - that the 'reasonable time' stipulated by government for a settlement was running out.

To comply with the white paper's directives, the talks were structured so that two matters had to be settled before consideration could be given to changing the 'scheduled person' definition. These were: the future industrial relations structure of the mining industry; and establishment of a comprehensive security of employment agreement for white miners. The former was prompted by a concern to ensure agreements between employer and employee bodies in the mining industry could have the force of law and be monitored. In essence, this required the creation of an industrial council. Ironically, although the Industrial Conciliation Act, which made provision for the establishment of industrial councils, was introduced in 1924 specifically in response to the 1922 uprising, the mining industry has never had an industrial council.

Absent from the talks was Cyril Ramaphosa, general secretary of the black National Union of Mineworkers (NUM), which had been formed at the end of 1982. The chamber justified this on the grounds that NUM had not existed at the time the white paper was issued and could not therefore be regarded as a party to the negotiations. The chamber did, however, undertake to consult with NUM on the issues. This was not to come about for several years.

Talks between the chamber and the unions proceeded, with both sides agreeing they should not be discussed with the press. Consequently, it was only on rare occasions that outsiders were able to obtain glimpses into machinations at the negotiating table. Nevertheless, it was apparent all along that the major blocking agent was the MWU.

At the end of 1984 it was reported that the parties had made good progress on the concept of establishing an industrial council, although there were several points outstanding. But as time passed, it became clear the talks had bogged down. Pressures for something to be done intensified. In 1985 Danie Steyn, minister of mineral and energy affairs, announced in parliament that 31

December was the target date for concluding the negotiations. Steyn also said the Mines and Works Act would be amended to end job reservation during the 1986 parliamentary session.

It did not require great insight to realise that discord over the security of employment agreement was the sticking point. With time running out the chamber increased pressure on the unions. They in turn agreed to submit proposals as to what they would regard as adequate safeguards for white workers by 7 November. The chamber had made its suggestions on the question as early as March 1984. But unions failed to produce a proposal by 7 November.

Shortly before 31 December the extent of union squabbling over the issue became apparent when it was revealed that Paulus was insisting on inclusion of a demand for the abolition of closed shop and allocation of occupations agreements. This amounted to a declaration of war on the other unions. Abolition of the agreements implied a free-for-all for membership, with the MWU aiming at recruiting all whites opposed to changing the 'scheduled person' definition. Understandably, the other unions opposed Paulus's demand. The end of the year thus came with no agreement on security of employment in sight.

Government steps in

In early 1986 the department of mineral and energy affairs (DMEA) exercised its prerogative to step into the affair. But when the nature of its solution became known, it was greeted with almost universal condemnation.

The DMEA produced a draft amendment bill to the Mines and Works Act. It proposed the establishment of a statutory selection board which would have complete say over which workers were eligible to qualify for the bottom five of the 13 certificates reserved for 'scheduled persons'. Representation on the board was heavily weighted in favour of the MWU and two other unions known to have reservations about changing the definition - the SA Technical Officials Association (SATOA) and the SA Engine Drivers', Firemens' and Operators' Association. The suspicion was that Paulus had been doing some successful behind-the-scenes lobbying with government.

So adverse was the reaction to the draft bill by the chamber and the majority of the unions that the DMEA undertook to redraft it. The department's actions prompted the chamber and most of the unions to press on with their negotiations with a new sense of urgency.

Towards the end of March 1986, Danie Steyn received a letter outlining the results of their talks. In essence, it said the chamber and nine of the unions had reached agreement on establishing an industrial council. In addition, they had achieved a large degree of consensus on the terms for guaranteeing white workers' security of employment, although there were some sticking points.

One of these related to union fears that blacks would flood the market once the job bar was lifted. The unions had proposed that a board should be established to set labour complements for the industry and lay down entry requirements for jobs. The chamber, on the other hand, insisted that this was a management prerogative. Consensus had been reached that unions would be able to lodge a complaint with the proposed industrial council if they believed that overtraining was occurring. But the unions also demanded that a procedure be instituted whereby mines would have to advise the council of their training programmes in advance. The future application of the mining industry's closed shop was another point on which no consensus had been reached.

The two unions which refused to ratify this agreement were the MWU and SATOA.

Steyn was faced with a difficult choice. He could either leave it to his department to come up with a new bill to resolve the impasse, knowing that the chamber and some of the unions would probably oppose it. Or he could accept the chamber-nine union agreement, knowing that the MWU and SATOA were opposed to it, and make a decision on the outstanding points regarding security of employment. Luckily for Steyn he was given extra breathing space when the parliamentary session was cut short and government announced that it would only reconvene on 18 August 1986.

More talks between all the parties involved were held in the intervening months. In that time it became clear the DMEA now believed amendments to the act should permit Steyn to lay down minimum requirements - which would be non-racial - for entry into jobs requiring certificates of competency. Factors mentioned in this regard were educational and age requirements, and any others that the minister chose to impose. It is known that the chamber opposed this idea, arguing that government should play no role in determining the eligibility of candidates for certificates.

Early in August the chamber and the nine unions reached total consensus on the security of employment agreement. The last barriers fell when they concurred that the closed shop would in future be applied to all persons who qualified for certificates of competency, and when the chamber agreed that the industrial council should control training levels. The closed shop agreement was important as it was designed specifically *not* to be used as a job reservation mechanism by a union like the MWU which has a racially exclusive constitution. It is not clear, however, what implications the closed shop agreement would have had for members of NUM.

When parliament convened on 18 August the DMEA's fourth version of the bill was tabled. To the disquiet of the chamber and other parties, it provided for committees to be appointed to advise the minister on who should be eligible for certificates. It also made provision for the minister to set criteria relating to practical experience, command of language, physical health, security, age and educational and training qualifications which candidates must meet, although the exact nature of these requirements was not spelt out.

The bill provided that in instituting the advisory committees, the minister should consult with unions which, in his opinion, are representative of the majority of employees who are holders of the certificates in question, any other unions, as well as mine owners. This was taken to mean that a union like NUM could be involved in the process.

That same week the chamber, the MWU and NUM made representations to the parliamentary standing committee considering the bill. The content of the chamber's representations to the committee was not made public, but it is known that it had one major objection: that the bill amounted to real changes to existing practices, and that it was proposing a whole new set of preconditions in the form of advisory committees and selection criteria for candidates.

Current regulations to the Mines and Works Act hold that persons wishing to qualify for a certificate of competency have to pass a test administered by a commission of examiners appointed by the government mining engineer. They also stipulate the minimum requirements with which candidates must comply for each certificate.

These relate mainly to age, practical experience and the candidates' moral standing.

Since its inception NUM had demanded the abolition of job reservation. The issue was one of the points raised by its members in industrial action at Anglo's Vaal Reefs mine in 1985 when approximately 14 000 black mineworkers were dismissed. In its representations to the standing committee, NUM rejected the Wiehahn Commission's recommendations and the white paper because they were concerned mainly with protecting white workers. NUM also rejected the bill.

As Ramaphosa said:

> It is our view that the bill seeks to deviate from the recommendation accepted by the government by prescribing unnecessary requirements. Ultimately they add a discriminatory dimension to the standard requirement for attaining a certificate of competency, by failing to give adequate protection against racial victimisation, and also by introducing an outside body such as the contemplated committees that will purport to advise the minister to interfere in matters that should ordinarily be regulated through collective bargaining between workers and mine owners.

Despite Steyn's earlier undertaking, parliament prorogued in 1986 without the bill being debated. During the break the standing committee heard further representations and made some changes to the bill. The nature of those changes were revealed early in 1987. They were not significant: the words 'providing that no distinction shall be made on the basis of race or colour' were added to the subsection relating to the requirements certificate candidates must meet; the wording in the subsection dealing with advisory committees was amended to read:

> The minister shall consult with any employee's or employer's organisation in the mineral industry, as well as any other organisation or organisations, which in his opinion may have an interest in the institution and composition of the relevant committee.

Essentially the revised bill did not address the chamber's objections nor those of NUM.

The decision to prorogue parliament before the bill was debated meant the job reservation issue had been relegated to the parliamentary back-burner once again. But with Paulus standing as a candidate in Carltonville for the Conservative Party, it was sure to be a rallying point for the 6 May election.

Implications of the abolition of job reservation

There is a general perception that when job reservation finally does go, blacks will immediately move into more skilled positions. But, according to mining industry sources, this is far from the case. Indeed many practical points will have to be sorted out first.

In February 1987 it was estimated that 19 000 whites held various certificates of competency on the gold mines. Of that total, 12 000 held blasting certificates, the vast majority of whom (some 8 000) were members of the MWU. Industry-wide, it was estimated that there was a pool of some 50 000 blacks in job categories six to eight who had the potential to be regarded as eligible candidates for certificates. There are also many blacks in other positions on the mines, and others not engaged in mining, who might show an interest in obtaining blasting certificates once this possibility becomes available.

Clearly, not all these people can be accommodated immediately. Those who already hold blasting certificates will not leave the mines overnight. And even though the industry has a net shortage of blasting certificate holders, work is organised to ensure production is not hampered. The provision allowing the government mining engineer to grant exemptions for blacks to carry out certain tasks plays no small role in that process. In addition, industry sources makes no secret of the fact that violations of mine safety also contribute to the maintenance of production, although they stress that this is in no way seen as desirable.

Consequently, mine owners are anxious that the underground mining situation should be normalised when job reservation is abolished. This raises several questions. It is understood the government mining engineer has already indicated that when the job bar goes he would like to see those concessions granted when the 11-shift fortnight was introduced, phased out. But mine owners see it differently. They want the concessions written into the regulations of the Mines and Works Act, as this would give them flexibility to organise work.

Other issues would also have to be resolved. The commission of examiners for blasting certificates, for example, has up to now only been geared to cope with approximately 1 000 applications per

annum. Unless it adjusts to cater for larger numbers, a bottleneck
will develop.

More importantly, there are massive financial implications if
blacks acquire blasting certificates. They cannot be paid less than
their white counterparts - the chamber has already committed itself
on this point. If the number of blasting certificate holders grows, it
implies greatly increased wage and bonus bills. Moreover, questions of housing, pension and medical aid schemes, and social
mixing on the mines would also have to be thrashed out.

It will take time - and no doubt many disputes - before the matters raised here are resolved. But there is no doubt that once this is
achieved mining will be conducted in a safer and more efficient
manner. That alone should be sufficient motivation for the parties
in the mining industry.

Notes

1   Frederick A Johnstone, *Class, Race and Gold: a study of class relations and racial discrimination in South Africa,* Routledge & Keegan, 1976, 66.
2   Johnstone, *Class, Race and Gold*, 105.
3   Johnstone, *Class, Race and Gold*, 149.
4   Johnstone, *Class, Race and Gold,* 167.
5   Ari Sitas, 'Rebels without a pause: the MWU and the defence of the colour bar', *South African Labour Bulletin*, 5(2), October 1979, 38.
6   Carole Cooper, 'The mineworkers' strike', *South African Labour Bulletin*, 5(1), May 1979, 6.

Restructuring Migrant Labour on the Gold Mines

Jonathan Crush

Since the mid-1970s the gold mining industry has rapidly achieved one of its most elusive goals: a regular, predictable and controlled flow of labour between the mines and rural labour reserves. This has been achieved without recourse to the usual stabilising tactic of increasing the number of foreign workers in the workforce. Foreign labour was once especially valued for its steady flow, level of experience and longer-term commitment to working on the mines.[1] But the same can increasingly be said for the large number of local workers drawn into the industry in the 1970s and early 1980s.

In recent years there has been a consistent trend towards longer minestays and shorter homestays among miners from all areas. Most migrant miners now return regularly and repeatedly to mine employment, to the same mine and, in a significant number of cases, to the same job and work gang. The drop-out rate from the industry has hit an all-time low: many mines have return rates of over 90%.

One result is that a smaller pool of workers is now needed to maintain mine complements. Although the average size of the workforce has actually increased in the 1980s, the absolute number of workers engaged each year has shown a steady decline in almost all areas.[2] This has severely restricted opportunities for new or retrenched work-seekers to find (even temporary) work on the mines. The proportion of 'novice' or untried workers in the workforce has fallen from a high of 30% to 40% in the mid-1970s to its current level of less than 10%. Ironically, this causes concern in mining circles, leading to recent suggestions that all mines should be obliged to maintain a minimum number of novices 'to prevent the pot boiling over in the rural areas', as one official put it.

The large groups of unemployed work-seekers who daily congregate at rural recruiting points, and occasional violent attacks on TEBA (The Employment Bureau of Africa) offices, fuel this concern. In the current climate the mines have changed from an employment centre of last recourse to one of first resort for many rural migrants. TEBA recently calculated, without too much bravado, that it could supply an additional 250 000 to 300 000 workers if the jobs were available.

TEBA now does little or no active recruiting since new workers can simply be taken 'off-the-doorstep'. This constitutes a severe form of spatial discrimination for workers who do not live close to recruiting offices and who are financially incapable of making the daily trek in the hope of being engaged.

TEBA's current cost-cutting drive exacerbates the situation for the unemployed. In 1983, the Chamber of Mines took a major policy decision to close down its relatively costly northern Botswana operation.[3] In southern Botswana five more offices have been shut down since 1985, centralising recruitment around a small number of urban nodes. In South Africa, over 20 TEBA offices have been closed since the late 1970s.

On the mines, the experience levels of the workforce continue to rise appreciably. Fion de Vletter's recent analysis of Anglo American mines shows, for example, that over 50% of miners have five to ten years' service.[4] But his data also reveals that the number of workers with more than ten years' service is still at around 3%. De Vletter predicts that the foreign component of the workforce may fall dramatically in the next five years since two-thirds of foreign workers are now in the five to ten years' service bracket. This of course assumes foreign migrants will 'voluntarilyy' leave the industry in increasing numbers.

Traditionally many miners expected their sons to replace them as primary wage-earners as soon as they were old enough to join the workforce. But in the overcrowded labour market of the mid-1980s fathers may stay on at the mines since there is no guarantee that sons will secure the vacated space. In these circumstances there will be a slower pace of attrition of foreign labour.[5]

Migrancy and time-discipline

For the mines, the advantages of a more stable pattern of labour migration are obvious. Without having to spend the vast sums required to house the workforce permanently on the mines, the industry can lower costs of recruiting and training new workers. It can impose new standards of work organisation and discipline and further the formal and informal skilling of black workers. It can be confident of reducing drainage of skills and experience from the mines and controlling the flow of labour. Greater time-discipline is constantly being imposed on miners and the migrant labour system. This can be seen in at least three areas: elimination of recruitment incentives; computerisation; and transportation changes.

Elimination of recruiting incentives

Mines are phasing out recruiting incentives which provided workers with a degree of flexibility in the labour market. Workers who have made their own way to the goldfields are no longer signed on at mine gates. Industry recruiting schemes like the Assisted Voluntary Scheme, which encouraged mine-gate recruitment, have been discontinued. And there has been a decided shift in the contract lengths asked of mine recruits, as the mines mount a frontal attack on the shorter six-month contract.

At first this was a calculated risk, since so many workers preferred the shorter agreement. In the mid-1970s, for example, 75% of local workers were recruited on six-month contracts. But when it became clear that conditions were ripe this type of contract was phased out. In mid-1981, the eight Goldfields mines adopted this as group policy, moving to a standard nine-month contract. This was extended to one year in May 1985. In 1984, Rand Mines discontinued six- and nine-month contracts, placing all workers on a standard one-year contract. Anglo American introduced a standardised 40-week contract in 1985. Some urban recruiting offices, such as Durban, still receive orders for six-month recruits but it is only a matter of time before the shorter contract disappears altogether.

There has also been growing pressure in the industry to discontinue the Chamber's Valid Re-engagement Guarantee (VRG) incentive scheme. Such schemes - to encourage longer minestays, shorter homestays and regular return to mine service - have characterised the industry almost from its inception. In 1979 the Chamber introduced a simplified and standardised VRG system. Four different certificates were devised: TEBA 461, which guaranteed re-employment and an early return bonus to workers with more than nine months' continuous service; TEBA 460, which guaranteed re-employment to workers with six to nine months' service; TEBA 459, a stabilisation certificate issued to workers in upper job categories; and TEBA 458, a leave certificate issued for temporary absence from the mines.

By 1984 over 75% of the annual intake of labour was in possession of one or other of these certificates. In 1981, and again in 1983, the Chamber of Mines discussed summary abolition of the scheme, but decided in the end to allow it to die a natural death. The desire to discontinue VRGs arose from a conviction in the industry that the system, with all its rigidities, still gave migrant workers too much flexibility.

There have also been intensified conflicts with the National Union of Mineworkers about the disciplinary uses of the system. If a mine wished to get rid of certain workers they were simply denied VRGs thus restricting further access to the mine and, in some cases, to the entire industry.

The TEBA 460 and 461 VRGs are now being phased out as the mining groups move towards extended use of stabilisation and leave certificates for all workers. Their precise nature varies from group to group but the mines' intentions and the implications for workers are uniform. Anglo American dropped its use of 460s and 461s on all mines in late 1984. At present, leave certificates are issued to all workers in Patterson job categories 5-8, and stabilisation certificates to those in categories 1-4. Rand Mines has a 'stabilisation scheme' in which stabilisation certificates are issued to all workers with a minimum 12-months' service. Other mining houses are dropping all VRGs except the leave certificate. In 1984, Gencor introduced a 'paid leave scheme' for all employees. Goldfields and JCI have recently followed suit. Anglo American has recently introduced a 'leave stabilisation scheme' at President Steyn which is now being extended to all mines. At the outset of a contract, the mine and the miner enter an 'agreement' specifying an exact period of stay on the mine, departure date and period of leave.

All mines intend to work towards complete control over the periodicity of migrancy by placing all workers on standardised contract lengths, awarding fixed periods of annual paid leave and holding each worker to specific departure and return dates. TEBA is currently designing a 'negotiated leave certificate' to be used on all mines. Workers are faced with the dilemma of conforming to the industry's drive for total control over the timing of their migrant behaviour or of being excluded from further employment on the mines.

Computerising migrant labour

The last decade has seen the growing use of computer technology to regulate and control the flow of labour. In the 1970s, the Chamber of Mines and individual mining houses began to investigate the possibility of computerising the migrant labour system to improve its efficiency. The Chamber itself now has a Central Records of Service data base which contains centralised information on the personal characteristics and work histories of all miners. Terminals in TEBA offices in the field allow recruiting officers immediate access to the work records of all experienced miners.

For more detailed manpower planning and control on the mines themselves, mining houses have tended to adopt individual solutions. The most advanced of these is in place on Anglo American's massive Vaal Reefs complex, where over 40 000 black miners are employed. Human Resources Information Systems (HURIS) is a sophisticated application of computer technology which provides the mine with full and detailed data on the personal characteristics, work history and daily job performance of each worker. It allows tighter time and attendance control at mineshafts; short- and medium-term matching of particular workers with particular jobs; monitoring of labour needs, wastage and return in order to plan and regulate the rotation of labour; and identification and isolation of 'undesirable elements' in the workforce.

The benefits of labour control through HURIS are summed up by mine management as 'planned work on planned gangs in planned jobs'. Anglo's intention is to extend HURIS to all its mines. It is also a pilot project for the industry as a whole, and similar systems will probably be in place throughout the industry by the 1990s.

Transportation

The mines draw labour from a widely dispersed and fragmented labour reservoir. Efficient transportation systems have been deemed essential to reduce the period of unproductive labour-time spent travelling between home and workplace. Workers in transit to and from mines have traditionally been shuttled by rail and local bus services, supplemented since the 1940s by air services. In the last five years, the Chamber of Mines has rejected continued use of the railways in favour of mass busing of workers on South African Transport Services buses. The Transkei was the first area to be completely serviced by bus. Most other areas have since followed suit.

'Labour buses' serve the secondary purpose of insulating miners from the vulnerabilities of public travel. In 1984, for example, a highly-organised group of over a hundred women 'worked' the trains around Ladysmith carrying returning miners to Natal. Miners were plied with alcohol and drugs and then dispossessed of their belongings and pay packets. The host of 'con' men and women who accost workers outside TEBA offices in the rural areas have proved to be more difficult to avoid.

Implications of stability

The new reality of a stabilised migrant labour force has implications for workers themselves. An initial distinction must be made between 'insiders' and 'outsiders'. The latter include retrenched workers from other sectors, ex-miners, and new work-seekers with little prospect of alternative employment. The plight of these workers, whose traditional safety net of minework has now been removed, is seen in the atmosphere of despondency that pervades the grounds of TEBA offices in the rural areas.

Investigations of the survival strategies of these 'outsiders' have been conducted in Maseru (Lesotho) and Natal. They demonstrate the existence of a 'drift to despair' amongst a growing number of workers whose lives and expectations have been defined by migrancy. The situation is most critical in areas such as Lesotho where historical dependency on minework is so firmly entrenched that the alternatives to migrancy are very circumscribed. Many workers have resorted to creative strategies to secure mine contracts. Thus, for example, a massive clandestine trade in forged VRGs has sprung up. Recruits holding forged certificates, many of whom have never worked on the mines before, have been forwarded from as far away as Malawi and Mozambique.

The implications of stability for the 'insiders' are somewhat different. Historically, labour migrancy powerfully inhibited united worker action on the mines. The existence of an increasingly stable migrant workforce has provided NUM* with unprecedented opportunities for formal organisation.

NUM demands for a better deal on the job have included attempts to contest the mines' manipulation of workers' time. In negotiations with the Chamber, NUM has claimed with some force that the mines have no arbitrary right to withhold re-employment from workers who have failed to meet stringent leave regulations. The union has also fought with some success for more equitable leave regulations. Industry retaliation against NUM has tended to take place in the compound rather than the courthouse, through mass dismissal and selective re-engagement.[6]

The newly-stabilised migrant labour flow is probably a transitional phase in the downgrading, though not complete elimination, of the migrant labour system itself. In the mid-1970s an industry survey indicated that the proportion of the black workforce permanently settled at or near gold mines was only 1%, well below the 3% maximum allowed by law. A decade later, few mines were in danger of transgressing the official limit and have had to answer repeated charges that they are hiding behind government legislation. But in retrospect, 1986 may well be seen as a turning point in mine policy on stabilised labour.

A major test case here is Rand Mines' East Rand Proprietary Mine (ERPM) in Boksburg. Since 1981, when ERPM announced plans to increase its workforce by between 6 000 and 7 000, there has been an impasse between mine management and local white residents of Boksburg as to where the workers would be housed. ERPM planned to build new hostels close to the mine (and therefore to white residential areas). Local whites lobbied the state to

* National Union of Mineworkers (founded 1982)

have workers housed in urban townships 15 to 20 km away. The mine claimed this would cost them an extra R9-million a year in transport costs, and would lead to drastic cuts in mine efficiency. As a mine spokesman pointed out,

> nowhere in the South African mining industry are workers housed remote from their shafts. Long hours underground in hot humid conditions - together with varied shift times - dictate that workers be housed adjacent to the shaft.[7]

To defuse the situation, Rand Mines announced that it would try to increase its recruitment of urban blacks for ERPM, so that locally-recruited workers could live with their families.

In early 1986, TEBA embarked on an experimental recruiting campaign in the townships of the East Rand. ERPM received 2 000 applications for minework and 300 workers were recruited. At the end of 1986, however, less than 30 remained in service.[8] This experiment led Rand Mines to consider significantly increasing the proportion of permanent urban labour on its mines. At the very least this would eliminate the continuing costs and inefficiencies associated with migrancy as a system of labour mobilisation.

Other mining houses - particularly Anglo American - are moving in the same direction. One major constraint is the cost factor. One estimate puts the cost to the industry of providing permanent housing units for the entire mine workforce at R8-billion.[9] Another constraint is the significant number of foreign workers in the mine workforce (currently 40%). It is unlikely that the South African state would permit their permanent settlement at the mines. Foreign workers are disproportionately represented in the higher wage and skill brackets which the mines are most inclined to stabilise, though this too will eventually change.[10]

The favoured way around the cost constraint seems to be to shift the cost of providing married accommodation onto the workers themselves, through township and mine property home-ownership schemes. These were under discussion in the mining industry throughout 1986. In early 1987 several companies announced plans for a R700-million township development near Welkom. Of the 33 000 housing units to be built over the next five years, 16 000 are earmarked for Gencor and Anglo employees on the Free State goldfields (*BD*, 26.03.87).

Similar announcements may be expected during 1987, though it is doubtful that they will pacify NUM, which has recently 'declared war' on the mines' system of labour supply and control and demanded that the mining industry commit itself unequivocally to dismantling migrancy within two years.[11] Struggles within the context of the migrant labour system are now shifting to a struggle against the system itself. There can be little doubt that it will be bitter and protracted.

Notes

1 On the changing role of foreign labour in the mine workforce see J Crush, 'The Extrusion of Foreign Labour from the South African Gold Mining Industry', *Geoforum*, 17(2), 1986, 161-72; and D Yudelman and A Jeeves, 'New Labour Frontiers for Old: Black Migrants to the South African Gold Mines, 1920-85', *Journal of Southern African Studies*, 13(1), 1986, 101-24.

2 The major exceptions to this trend are several labour reservoirs actively being opened up by the mines: they include the rural areas of Bophuthatswana and Kwazulu, and resettlement sites such as Onverwacht and QwaQwa.

3 J Taylor, 'Some Consequences of Recent Reductions in Mine Labour Recruitment in Botswana', *Geography*, 1986, 34-46. Northern Botswana was once a fulcrum of the mines' recruiting operations: see A Jeeves, 'Migrant Labour and South African Expansion, 1920-1950', *South African Historical Journal*, 18, 1986, 73-92.

4 F de Vletter, 'A Comparative Analysis of Skills and Other Characteristics of Foreign Mine Workers on the South African Gold Mines', paper presented at a meeting of the Southern African Labour Commission, Blantyre, Malawi, 1986.

5 Both scenarios, of rapid or slow attrition, presuppose that the mines will continue to draw less than 5% of their novice labour from outside the country, and that there will be no political interference in the flow of foreign labour to South Africa. See, however, J Leger, 'Mozambican Miners' Reprieve', *South African Labour Bulletin*, 12(2), 1987, 29-32.

6 M Golding, 'Mass Dismissals on the Mines', *South African Labour Bulletin*, 10(7), 1985, 97-118. The most recent case was at Anglo American's President Steyn Mine in January 1987 when 2 200 workers were dismissed; see 'NUM Condemns Dismissal of 2 200', *Star*, 04.02.87.

7 SA Mining, February 1985.

8 'Migrant Labour Challenge', *FW*, 21.01.87.

9 'Migrant Labour Challenge'.

10 De Vletter, 'A Comparative Analysis'.

11 'NUM Vows to End Mines' Tribal System', *Financial Times*, 27.02.87.

From Hlobane to Kinross: Disasters and the Struggle for Health and Safety on the Mines

Jean Leger

The fire which killed 177 workers in the Gencor-owned Kinross mine on 16 September 1986 highlighted the important issue of work safety for workers and their unions, especially miners and the National Union of Mineworkers. The disaster - the worst in the history of gold mining - tragically emphasised the ongoing fatality and injury toll on South African mines.

While safety was previously assumed to be a managerial prerogative, the response to Kinross shows how unions are asserting worker rights in this sphere and how workers can take militant action to demand safer working conditions. In the three years between the 1983 Hlobane Colliery and 1986 Kinross disasters, NUM has taken up numerous safety issues and defended worker interests at fatal accident inquiries. Yet it took the Kinross disaster and a massive strike to shake management and government officials out of lethargic complacency and into a crisper approach to mine safety.

Hlobane: NUM's first disaster experience

NUM's harsh initiation into safety hazards involved the Hlobane Colliery explosion which killed 68 workers nine months after the union was founded in December 1982. NUM responded with its first national industrial action: a half-hour stoppage involving about

30 000 miners. At the joint inquest-inquiry into the disaster the union assembled a powerful legal and technical team and emerged as the industry's safety watchdog. For the first time since the Coalbrook disaster of 1960, black miners were represented by an independent legal team. Prior to Hlobane, a frequent practice was for an employee of The Employment Bureau of Africa (TEBA) - the Chamber's recruiting organisation - to 'represent' black workers at inquiries.

At the Hlobane inquest managerial safety practices were heavily attacked. Widespread neglect of safety precautions at the mine was revealed. Ironically, Hlobane had a rating of four stars (out of a maximum of five) under the Chamber's 'International Mine Safety Rating Scheme'. The mine and members of its management were subsequently successfully prosecuted for six breaches of the Mines and Works Act. But the small fines imposed - the company and five employees were fined a total of R1 200 - were negligible deterrents against managerial neglect of safety precautions.

NUM attempted to gain more equitable compensation for those injured and families of those killed at Hlobane. In June 1985 the Workmen's Compensation Commissioner awarded the union's claim for increased compensation (under section 42 of the Workmen's Compensation Act) because managerial negligence contributed to the disaster.

In terms of this decision, Rand Mutual, the Chamber's insurance carrier, will have to make up the increased compensation, equal to the full financial loss experienced by families of the deceased workers. Currently NUM and Rand Mutual are calculating the increased compensation, which is expected to range between R1-million and R2-million. This is the first increased compensation claim pursued by black miners since the Coalbrook disaster.

In an unprecedented but related move on behalf of four survivors, NUM is suing the mine manager, resident engineer and mine overseer for a total of R65 000 for 'pain, shock, suffering, loss of the amenities of life, disfigurement and general disability'. While the Compensation Act precludes suing the 'employer' for damages, workers have a common-law right to sue co-employees in their personal capacities if they were negligent. In the past managers were generally prosecuted in terms of the Mines and Works Act and faced small fines - as happened after Hlobane. But the costs likely to follow civil claims may be a greater deterrent against neglecting safety precautions.

Kinross and worker resistance

Three years after Hlobane, the Kinross fire shared many features of the colliery explosion: a horrifying fatality toll, a media outcry and alleged serious managerial neglect of recognised safety precautions. But three aspects of the Kinross disaster are significantly different. Firstly, NUM was able to take immediate actions to defend the interests of the dead or injured workers. Secondly, the union could override management control over information by revealing some of the events surrounding the accident. Finally, the union mobilised thousands of workers to protest poor safety standards exemplified by the disaster.

The accident occurred during a welding repair to a broken rail track in a level 15 haulage, some 1 600 metres below surface. At about 9.25 am on 16 September, sparks from one of the oxy-acetylene cylinders used for the welding operation ignited polyurethane foam lining the tunnel walls. The 50-200 millimetre thick layer of polyurethane had been sprayed along 600 metres of the tunnel walls in 1980 to limit corrosion of rock bolts used to prevent rockfalls. Fanned by the 25 km/hour ventilation current in the tunnel, the fire spread rapidly and consumed 400 metres of the polyurethane, producing huge quantities of carbon monoxide, carbon dioxide, cyanide and other toxic fumes. Of the 4 200 miners underground at the time, 177 died and 235 were injured. It is likely that the majority of the victims were overcome by carbon monoxide fumes.

Gencor, in breach of a long-standing agreement with the media's Conference of Editors to provide immediate details of disasters, delayed eight hours before announcing a death toll of 13. Management only revealed the full extent of the disaster early the next morning, nearly 24 hours after the first firefighting teams had descended underground.

Within hours of the first details being announced, NUM set about representing the interests of its members. The next day union officials joined the underground inspection by the government mining engineer. Shaft stewards and organisers started the crucial task of interviewing witnesses and collecting statements from survivors to establish the circumstances surrounding the accident. A week later an international expert on the use of polyurethanes in mining, Dr Herbert Eisner, arrived from Britain to investigate the accident on NUM's behalf.

Prior to unionisation, management controlled information simply by keeping the press off mine property, and ensuring accident details were not recorded from survivors living in mine compounds or recovering in mine hospitals. But the sheer scale of the Kinross accident resulted in extensive media coverage and pressure from the international press. Dozens of reporters descended upon the mine and for the first time a local mine accident was broadcast on television screens around the world. After the disaster the Chamber released a number of misleading press statements, claiming that 'polyurethanes and other products used in mines have until now been regarded by mines as safe'. This was untrue.

NUM members were among key witnesses present at the start of the fire. Union officials soon released first-hand accounts of what had happened. Starting with these accounts the press pieced together a picture of alleged neglect. In particular, the media claimed that:

* polyurethane foam, the fuel source for the fire, was a well-known fire hazard and its underground use was severely restricted in most major mining countries, including Britain, where it had been banned since 1968;

* permission was granted for open-flame welding to be carried out in an area coated with inflammable material;

* no fire extinguisher was present at the site where welding took place;

* polyurethane foam had led to at least one major fire on Gencor's Buffelsfontein mine in 1977 and to a fire which caused ten deaths at Anglo's Vaal Reefs mine in October 1983.[1] At the time NUM had approached Vaal Reefs' management to discuss the fire;

* in applying the foam the mine had ignored safety precautions prescribed by manufacturers, such as limiting the lengths of polyurethane coating to 10 metres, with 12-metre gaps in between to act as firebreaks;

* polyurethane foam had been used instead of shotcrete (spray-on cement) because shotcreting required heavy machinery in the haulage. Shotcreting machines would have blocked the haulage - a

critical ore transport route between the number 1 and 2 shafts of
the mine - and thus delayed production;

* no tests had been performed on the foam before it was used
underground;

* the mine had lost its five star 'safety rating' in June on account
of 'shortcomings' in planned inspections of operations such as
welding and fire control, planned observations, and rules and
regulations.

Within a week the Chamber issued further press statements
claiming that member mines had been warned of the hazards of
polyurethanes on several occasions since 1969. This contradicted
earlier statements. After defending Kinross management against
allegations of negligence, the Chamber now distanced itself from
the accident.

While the death toll was the focus of concern, NUM also sought
to defend the interests of survivors who risked developing chronic
lung damage, particularly asthma and restrictive lung disease.
NUM proposed a joint research study with Gencor to identify,
compensate and follow up survivors whose health had been affected. Eventually, two months after the disaster, a single meeting
was held. Although Gencor undertook to respond to the proposal,
this was not forthcoming. This raised doubts about the Chamber's
claim that it welcomed proposals for joint research projects from
NUM.

NUM called for a day of mourning on 1 October. In contrast to
Hlobane when the year-old NUM had about 50 000 members, by
September 1986 NUM had established itself as the biggest union in
Africa with over 300 000 members.

Gencor agreed that its workers could take the day off, but the
remaining mining houses refused, proposing five minutes of silence
instead. Between 250 000 and 275 000 miners supported the call
made at short notice, and several hundred thousand members from
COSATU affiliates in other industries observed the day, marking it
with special services and work stoppages.[2]

The day of mourning, 1 October, saw the greatest black worker
stoppage in the history of South African mining, involving half of
all black miners. Apart from Gencor, support came from all Anglo
American gold mines except for three shafts at Vaal Reefs and one
each at Western Deep Levels and President Steyn. Substantial
numbers stopped work at other groups. Many more miners

observed 1 October than May Day or 16 June, indicating the crucial importance of health and safety to these workers, and the
potential power of miners.

Kinross coincided with the final phase of the protracted 1986
mining industry wage negotiations. The Chamber had implemented
increases of between 17% and 22% on 1 July while NUM was holding out for 26% across-the-board, a paid holiday on 16 June and
'income security'.

Three days after the disaster, attempts to resolve the dispute
through conciliation board hearings deadlocked and the Chamber
ruled out mediation and arbitration. Worker anger over the Kinross fatalities heated up the wage dispute, pushing it towards a
strike. As NUM prepared to ballot its members, the Chamber
proposed mediation and offered a further 1% wage increase but
refused to agree to income security.

The massive support 1 October received was not lost on the
Chamber, which eventually conceded improved accident leave and
the novel 'security of income' clause. Accident leave was increased
from 42 to 56 days per year cumulative to 112 days. The final formulation of the income security clause grants miners, demoted to
lower paying jobs as a result of occupational injuries or diseases,
maintenance of their earlier higher wages for the first six months of
the new lower paying job.

The Chamber also undertook to help find more favourable re-
employment for disabled workers. For the first time, classic health
and safety issues were successfully negotiated during wage bargaining.

In the aftermath of Kinross several key issues were raised.
NUM demanded legislative provisions for union representatives
and technical consultants investigating the cause of an accident to
have access to the site. Currently the Mines and Works Act grants
worker representatives only the right to join the initial accident inspection. The interests of injured workers and those of the families
of deceased workers are severely prejudiced if their representatives
arc denied access thereafter. Mine management has much easier
access to the site and is often directly involved in assisting the mine
inspectorate in its investigations.

After the initial on-site underground inspection at Kinross,
senior Gencor mine management agreed that NUM representatives could make further visits to the accident site. In a similar

vein, President PW Botha responded to international criticism of South African mine standards by inviting 'responsible representatives of foreign governments and mining industries to visit and ascertain for themselves what our safety standards and mechanisms entail'.

When NUM put forward Dr Herbert Eisner, former director of the British Health and Safety Executive's Explosion and Flame Laboratory, Gencor reneged on its earlier undertaking, denying that it had received persistent requests from NUM for access. NUM general secretary Cyril Ramaphosa accused Gencor of 'hiding the information and getting rid of the evidence'.

Eventually Dr Eisner and other NUM representatives were allowed to visit the site two weeks after the accident. The visit proved of little use because of the time lapse, and repairs which had been undertaken in the interim. Moreover, instead of taking part in an accident investigation, the NUM team found itself part of a delegation of some 60 people visiting the site as part of an 'open day'. While restricting the number of NUM representatives, Gencor invited representatives of all the mining houses, artisan and white miner unions, the United Workers Union of SA, the Black Allied Mining and Construction Workers Union and marginal unions such as the United African Workers Union. Some of these unions had no members at Kinross or any of the neighbouring mines. The visit was hurriedly conducted and NUM representatives were not given time to take basic measurements. Legislation is clearly required to ensure worker representatives free access to investigate the site of an accident.

Although management is ultimately responsible for materials and methods used undergound, why did the government mining engineer not outlaw the use of polyurethane foams underground? Accounts of disasters and experimental research involving polyurethanes have been widely publicised abroad since the late 1960s. The government mining engineer's 1983 annual report recorded details of the Vaal Reefs polyurethane fire disaster.

A similar criticism can be levelled against the mining houses. The Chamber has frequently argued that it is not necessary to repeat overseas health and safety research. While this argument is perhaps plausible, reliable mechanisms are required to ensure relevant results are applied locally. Currently no adequate mechanisms exist. Nor has the Chamber suggested legislation to control polyurethane hazards.

In addition, the efficacy of the 'International Mine Safety Rating Scheme', the cornerstone of management safety efforts, has once more been thrown into question. According to a senior Chamber safety spokesman, in the case of the Hlobane disaster the colliery's 'four star' rating would not have been altered even if all the transgressions of the Mines and Works Act revealed at the inquest had been noted during a 'safety audit'.[3] At Kinross several years' use of the rating scheme did not reveal the polyurethane hazard present since 1980.

The inadequacy of workmen's compensation was also highlighted. Compensation up to a maximum of 75% of the deceased worker's monthly earnings for a widow with three or more dependent children appears equitable. However, the low wages paid to black miners and the extent to which compensation lags behind the inflation rate mean that within a few years the monthly sums paid become wholly inadequate. Compensation increases awarded by the commissioner have averaged 4% per year over the last seven years while the inflation rate has typically risen by 15% to 20% per year.

After the disaster Gencor executive chairman Derek Keys announced a R2-million trust fund in addition to the compensation payouts to ensure 'dependants suffer in no further way than in the irreparable personal loss for which there is no human remedy'. Gencor's establishment of the trust emphasises the inadequacy of compensation payments in periods of spiralling inflation.

State and Chamber responses to Hlobane and Kinross

At the Hlobane inquest NUM's technical consultants advocated the introduction of self-rescuers and methanometers for measuring methane. In a positive response, the government mining engineer introduced draft regulations for self-rescuers, methanometers and refuge bays. However, the dates set for their implementation lapsed. Originally self-rescuers were to be introduced in all collieries by the end of 1985, in gold mines by the end of 1986 and all other mines in 1987.

Until Kinross it appears the implementation of self-rescuers was being stalled, the Chamber arguing that 'unique' local conditions had caused the delay. While this is true of the gold mines, conditions in South African collieries are in many respects similar to those in foreign countries and should not delay the introduction of self-rescuers unduly. Shortly after Kinross the government mining engineer gazetted new regulations for self-rescuers, refuge bays and methanometers.

In response to Hlobane the Chamber revised the 'five star' rating scheme 'without losing the core principles of management input and control'.[4] The scheme was promoted afresh in a high profile media campaign.[5]

Days before Kinross the Chamber had triumphantly announced the lowest mine accident statistics ever recorded for a six-month period: for the first time the gold mine fatality rate had dipped below 1,0 to 0,88 per thousand workers in service. But the criticism around Kinross put the Chamber on the defensive with insiders describing the disaster as an 'organisational setback'. The Chamber moved quickly and set up a Hazardous Materials Unit to identify and reduce fire hazards of materials used underground. In addition an ad hoc 'task force' was established to analyse past major mine fires with a view to recommending changes, from introducing self-rescuers to improving mine layouts. A month later the Chamber finally recommended to member mines that safety boots with steel toecaps (and with metatarsal guards where appropriate) be issued to miners - a long-standing NUM demand. The Chamber also announced it would convene its first industry-wide health and safety congress in 1987.

A more sophisticated Chamber response to underground hazards also emerged. Dr Horst Wagner, the new director of the Chamber's research organisation, argued that the introduction of new, more mechanised technology was necessary for safer mining. He noted that

> Safety and environmental conditions on deep-level mines can be improved in the longer term only if the rate of production per metre of stope face is increased... Significant improvements in deep-level mining efficiency can result only from the mechanisation of stoping operations.[6]

An implication of this view is that a loss in employment is acceptable in striving for greater safety.

Ongoing health and safety issues

While Hlobane and Kinross stand out as disasters remembered by workers and the public alike, the day-to-day accident toll is staggering. Some 2 000 miners died and 45 000 were seriously injured in the three-year period between these two disasters.

This period was punctuated by a number of smaller disasters including several severe rockbursts at Blyvooruitzicht, ERPM and Western Deep Levels, a methane explosion at Middelbult which killed 33 miners, two more explosions at Vaal Reefs and Ermelo which killed seven and six workers respectively, a fire at Buffelsfontein which overcame eight miners, and many more. But the death toll mostly rose in ones and twos in smaller accidents seldom reported in the press.

Increasingly NUM is addressing itself to the issues these disasters raise. The union has represented workers at several fatal accident inquiries since Hlobane. Its experience at some of these inquiries in 1985 and 1986 is worth noting:

* as a result of an inquiry into a blasting accident at Rietspruit Opencast Colliery in which two blasting assistants were killed, the presiding inspector of mines found that the responsible miners, shift boss, acting mine overseer, acting production manager and acting manager had acted negligently. The two miners have been charged with culpable homicide.

* in the case of the Rietspruit pylon accident reported in *South African Review 3*, the compensation commissioner has awarded increased compensation to the dependants of the two workers killed in the accident. A foreman charged with culpable homicide for his role in the accident, was acquitted.

* an inquiry into the death of ten workers in another blasting accident at Deelkraal gold mine in August 1986 raised questions about the training given to black miners, particularly in relation to explosives. According to the evidence, the team leader and his workers had received their training 'on the job'. NUM's legal representative submitted that while this may have been adequate for routine blasting operations, it left them ill-equipped to deal with the dangers of non-routine situations.

* in cross-examination of management at an inquest into the November 1985 ERPM rockburst which killed 17 miners 3 300 metres below surface, NUM challenged the safety of conventional

tunnel support and the adequacy of current techniques for avoiding rockfalls and rockbursts in deep-level gold mines. Rockfalls and rockbursts together cause more than half of all mining fatalities.

* by February 1987 no inquiry had yet been held into the Middelbult explosion of August 1985 which killed members of the Chemical Workers Industrial Union. In early 1986 the government mining engineer referred the case to the attorney-general to decide whether a prosecution should be made and is awaiting this decision before holding an inquiry. The attorney-general informed mine management in December 1986 - 15 months after the accident - that he intended to press a charge of culpable homicide. The long wait means that lessons to be learnt from the disaster have been delayed and further lives may be lost in a similar accident.

A similar procedure appears to have been adopted for the Kinross disaster. The attorney-general is to bring charges of culpable homicide against mine management and has said that in view of this no inquiry or inquest will be necessary. This approach is regrettable. Evidence which may be important in preventing similar accidents in the future is far more likely to emerge in an inquest or inquiry than in a culpable homicide case.

Following the Kinross disaster the NUM head office has been swamped with requests to represent workers at fatal accident inquiries. It appears the mine inspectorate have taken an unannounced decision not to issue their inquiry findings. This is probably because NUM and other black mine unions like BAMCWU and CWIU (Secunda collieries) have paid so much attention to accident inquiries.

The accident inquiry finding indicates whether any persons may be held responsible for the accident and whether a breach of regulations led to the accident. The decision not to issue findings means injured workers and dependants of deceased workers now have little basis for deciding whether to attempt to claim increased compensation.

Another major NUM concern has been negotiating safety agreements and the recognition of safety stewards. The union has concentrated on mines owned by Anglo American and draft agreements are being tested out at the Elandsrand, Western Deep Levels and Freegold (Holdings, Saaiplaas and President Brand divisions) gold mines. Anglo management has approached negotiations constructively, recognising the need for safety stewards and agreeing that safety stewards should be elected to represent each level, section or department. While each draft agreement differs, features of the individual agreements include:

 * paid time off for safety and health training (two to ten days) given by NUM. Management has proposed that some way be established to ensure stewards are trained to a predetermined level. Currently the union is preparing a comprehensive 'miners manual' for training purposes. Several thousand safety stewards will probably attend week-long training courses over the next few years;

 * workers wanting to stop work in dangerous conditions are required to follow safety grievance procedures;

 * safety stewards are obliged to make regular safety inspections - at least once per month. Current management loss control checklists will be used as the basis for these inspections on some mines;

 * paid time off granted to safety stewards to caucus safety issues. At one mine two hours per month has been agreed to;

 * stewards and union-appointed technical consultants are to have full access for carrying out post-accident inspections;

 * safety stewards are permitted to take environmental measurements and samples.

Initial discussions on a draft health and safety agreement have been held with the Chamber. This is an important development: as recently as July 1986 Chamber representatives argued that safety and health issues should not be negotiated and that unions should only be consulted.

NUM regional and national safety congresses were held in the first half of 1987 and regional and national safety committees have been formed. NUM also commissioned surveys of occupational stress and hearing loss experienced by rock drill operators who are exposed to noise levels of between 110 and 120 decibels. In a fateful co- incidence, the union published an accessible version of an academic study into mine safety in the week of the Kinross disaster. It was entitled *A Thousand Ways to Die*.

Death remains part of the process

Disasters receive a great deal of attention but seldom account for more than 15% of all mining fatalities. Many believe mine safety improvements come about after major disasters lead to legal reforms and renewed concern for safety by mine management. Some writers have challenged this approach, arguing that only when disasters occur in periods of growing worker organisation and militancy will safety improvements be effected.[7] The accident experience in South Africa bears this out.

In 1960 at the Coalbrook Colliery 437 workers were buried alive in the worst-ever South African mine accident. The period following Coalbrook saw tough state repression of trade unions and political organisations. Despite a major government-appointed commission of inquiry into safety as a result of Coalbrook, mine fatality rates in the 1960s and 1970s did not improve significantly over those experienced in the 1950s.

In contrast with Coalbrook, the Hlobane colliery disaster co-incided with the massive growth of worker organisation on the mines. It also appears to be a turning point for accident statistics. While it may be premature to judge trends, the fatality rate on collieries has declined dramatically since Hlobane and currently is less than half of what it was before. Similarly on the gold mines, the benefits of worker organisation in resisting dangerous working conditions are reflected in the fatality rate. The rate declined steadily after 1983 until Kinross. But even while better organisation is the key to miners' struggles for greater safety, death will remain part of the process.

Notes

1 Government Mining Engineer, 'Annual report for the year ended 31 December 1983', Government Printer, Pretoria, RP 18/1984.
2 Labour Monitoring Group, 'Kinross stayaway', *South African Labour Bulletin*, 12(1), Nov-Dec 1986.
3 AJ Gill, 'Perspective', *Loss Control Survey*, 4(3), August 1985, 3.
4 Gill, 'Perspective', 3.
5 Anon, 'Comment', *Loss Control Survey*, 5(2), May 1986, 3.
6 Horst Wagner, 'The challenge of deep-level mining in South Africa', *Journal of the South African Institute of Mining and Metallurgy*, 86(9), 1986, 337-392.
7 Daniel Curran, 'Symbolic solutions for deadly dilemmas: An analysis of federal coal mine health and safety legislation', *International Journal of Health Services*, 14(1), 1984, 5.

Health and Safety Organisation: A Cape Perspective on Trends in State - Management Labour Relations

Ian Macun and Jonny Myers

Health and safety occupied a somewhat precarious position on the agenda of the independent union movement during 1986. This was due to several factors, including the reorganisation of unions in the wake of the formation of the Congress of South African Trade Unions, the effects of the emergency and the worsening recession.

Unions with a history of health and safety activity consolidated prior health and safety gains and the first two health and safety agreements in the country were signed in 1986.[1] The Chemical Workers Industrial Union and the South African Chemical Workers Union took important new health and safety initiatives. But in general there was little new health and safety activity from unions previously uninvolved in these concerns. Those unions involved continued these activities.[2]

Disasters like Kinross cast gloom once again in the mining industry and the National Union of Mineworkers continued its efforts to achieve representative health and safety structures. These could go some way to ensure adequate health and safety practices in the country's most dangerous industry, run by some very hostile managements.

While not many unions took up the issue, health and safety was relatively high on management agendas. By the end of 1986 Machinery and Occupational Safety Act (MOSA) safety structures were widely implemented in most sectors. This demonstrated compliance with the law, but, in most cases, no deeper commitment to operating these structures for the benefit of employees.

The state has been active in drafting new regulations. But at the same time compensation practices have been administratively altered behind the scenes. A contradictory picture has emerged: worsening conditions and practices alongside new regulations. This possibly reflects contradictory thinking within the state about deregulation, privatisation and the need to construct an acceptable industrial relations environment.

Trends in health and safety work

New groups

Two new groups working with unions in the area of occupational health were established during 1986. In January, the Industrial Health Unit was established at the University of Natal, Durban. This was the first of its kind in the Natal area. Later in the year, the Industrial Health, Safety and Education Project was formed in East London, with the aim of servicing unions in the Eastern Cape.

Research developments

The chemical industry: The South African chemical industry is dominated by multinationals and large conglomerates. While it has a high hazard-profile internationally there has not been extensive exposure about worker health and safety in the South African chemical industry. It is a highly profitable industry with complicated production processes involving many uncharted hazards.

As a result of strong shop-floor organisation, SACWU and CWIU have made inroads in raising awareness of chemical hazards and have challenged management in a number of cases. These unions have succeeded in obtaining access to plants for union officials and union-nominated health and safety consultants. As a result, known cases of chemical poisoning were systematically evaluated.

This process involved mass health screenings, industrial hygiene evaluations, followed by engineering changes and increased worker participation in health and safety organisation. Substances identified as poisonous included solvents, plastics, paints, inks and dyes.

Management response in the firms concerned ranged from attempts to pre-empt union investigations by engaging health and safety consultants of their choice, to more flexible positions such as agreeing to pay the costs of union-initiated investigations. In one case this led to engineering changes to improve safety and health in the firm.

Work organisation and conditions: Another union concern is shift-work. In 1986, unions like NAAWU and MAWU in the motor and components industry initiated a research project to investigate the effects of shift-work.

Research has been undertaken to establish the extent of shift-working in these and other industries.[3] Union members and officials are beginning to take up issues such as the length of shifts, breaks in rotating shift rosters, the amount of night work in shift rosters, as well as the traditional issue of shift premiums - a kind of inconvenience payment.

Negotiations around shift-work reflect union concerns about unemployment. Unions attempt to develop strategies to counter the insidious process of retrenchment by negotiating staffing levels and hours of work. Research to back up these demands has focused on the health and welfare aspects of shift-work, particularly the adverse effects of night work and strenuous shift rosters, and workrelated issues such as transport and meal arrangements for shift workers. This research has led to fundamental questioning of the necessity for shift-work in the first place. Some unions have taken a position against continuous shift-work in principle, although they have not been able to stop it in practice.

The need for industrial hygiene and safety engineering expertise

A noticeable trend in 1986 was improved access to plants characterised by strong shop-floor organisation. This meant it became possible for health and safety activity to progress beyond the basic level of providing workers with general information. As union health and safety experts have not had access to workplaces in the past, health and safety education has usually consisted of one-off sessions with little follow through. This has had limited impact on the improvement of workers' health and safety organisational skills.

With improved access to workplaces, joint inspections by labour and management have become integral to consultancy work by health groups for unions. This in turn has meant health consultancy groups have recognised that they need people with industrial hygiene and safety engineering expertise, and that safety representatives and shop stewards must be effectively trained. This need is likely to increase with time and indicates an important gap in the services available to trade unions.

Industrial hygiene evaluations are made problematic by poorly qualified personnel and inadequate laboratory facilities throughout the country. Where such facilities do exist, they are mainly in large multinational companies. All of these features raise questions of possible bias in determining the extent of hazards.

South African industry generally seems to be designed with little reference to safety considerations. In the future it is likely that the problem of how to improve safety, work design and control of hazardous processes will become more acute as legislative controls will probably increase. At present there is no formal safety engineering training available in South Africa. The few existing safety engineering personnel are invariably employed by management, and unions have little access to such expertise. And many factories still rely on relatively poorly-qualified technicians for safety design.

The importance of the lack of union-sympathetic expertise in industrial hygiene should not be underestimated. Worker health and safety initiatives frequently face management assertions that improving the situation is prohibitively expensive and impractical. This forces protection of workers into problematic and conflict-ridden routines involving personal protection.

Reliance on personal protection, often coupled with disciplinary measures, is a particularly common managerial attitude towards health and safety. Personal protective equipment is the cheapest means of dealing with this type of problem. It is also victim-blaming rather than system-blaming. In other words the system is left faulty while the worker exposed to the faults of the system is additionally burdened by ineffective and uncomfortable equipment, and becomes a target for disciplinary enforcement into the bargain.

Other problems related to safety engineering and industrial

hygiene emerged in 1986. These included management attempts to convince inadequately-trained shop stewards that there were no safety problems; and management bringing in consultants to show that no real hazards existed in particular plants.

In-plant health and safety organisation

Unions and safety representatives or safety stewards need an understanding of the complexities of production in order to effectively monitor and prevent hazards. For this, effective, independent health and safety training is necessary. But unions provided relatively little training in basic health and safety for their members in 1986. This is due partly to increased economic and political pressures on unions during the year, but also reflects the generally slow development of health and safety as a union issue. Progress in establishing worker-elected health and safety structures has also been slow, although more organised workers have expressed dissatisfaction with managerial domination of the health and safety area.

A factor underlying slow development in health and safety organisation appears to be the delay on the part of a number of unions in addressing the question and also in formulating a clear position on the options in MOSA regarding health and safety organisation.

Health and safety agreements

During 1986 the first two health and safety agreements were signed between Transport and General Workers Union and Turnall, an asbestos-cement manufacturer, and SA Allied Workers Union and Malcomess, a tractor part assembly company. Other unions like the Black Mining and Construction Workers Union and Paper, Wood and Allied Workers Union have agreements in draft form and still subject to negotiation. In some cases unions have pushed for these agreements so as to codify and consolidate health and safety gains made in a particular industry over time.

It is arguable whether the lengthy process involved in instituting a health and safety agreement is necessary in all organised factories, or mainly in those where there are particular hazards in the production process, such as the chemical, mining and asbestos industries.

But these agreements are still very important: they bind both parties to a set of responsibilities and obligations about health and safety in the firm, and to the principle of negotiation of health and safety matters; they establish a framework for management-labour relations which is far more acceptable than that in the relevant legislation; they fix previous gains made in this area and obviate repetitive struggles; and they raise union members' awareness of health and safety problems and the means for their resolution.

Legislation

Health and safety legislation has continued to embody contradictory trends, weakening workers' health and safety rights in certain respects but conferring some new rights in others. A feature of MOSA has been the continued emphasis on management responsibility to provide safe and healthy working conditions. However, MOSA's concern with regulating conditions should be seen in conjunction with recent moves towards deregulation.

New regulations: Three sets of regulations under MOSA were published during 1986. These are: the Facilities, the Electrical Machinery, and the General Safety Regulations. Only the latter have been passed. Regulations governing environmental conditions (noise, heat, etc), general machinery, driven machinery and asbestos are still pending.

Some of these regulations are new, others are updated versions of pre-existing regulations. Concerted management resistance to new control measures meant successive drafts of the regulations were weakened and took a long time to reach their final form. In some cases, notably the Facilities regulations, worker benefits have been substantially weakened when compared with regulations dating back to the 1960s or 1940s. But in the General Safety Regulations, industrial workers are given some important new rights and additional obligations are placed on employers.[4]

Deregulation: The Temporary Removal of Restrictions on Economic Activity Act (TRREA Act), gazetted in September 1986, represents a particularly disturbing development with potentially severe implications for health and safety, as well as for wages and other conditions of work.

In terms of this Act, the state president may suspend most laws in any geographic area. For example, specified employers may be exempted from all legal responsibilities in the field of health and safety. There is some limited protection of health and safety regulations: the president must act on the advice of a standing committee of parliament and in consultation with the minister of manpower. Protection could, however, only be exercised by union lobbying at this level.

This act aims to promote the unfettered development of free enterprise in all areas, and to promote small business in particular by removing 'restrictive legislation'. It is also likely that this act will be applied to the most vulnerable, namely unorganised workers, whose conditions are generally the worst.

Deregulation moves through legislative initiatives began before the TRREA Act.[5] These developments went together with great interest in privatisation, which is probably the dominant trend in state thinking in terms of economic change. Large sectors of the business community have supported these initiatives. For a more detailed discussion on privatisation and deregulation, see Duncan Innes's article in section 6 of this *South African Review*.

Compensation: Late 1985 saw a further blow to worker interests. The workmen's compensation commissioner changed the disability classification for workers with occupational chest diseases. Previously the lowest category was 35% disability. (This means the person is 35% disabled. The percentage is used to calculate financial compensation and bears some relationship to the degree of physical damage.) A 35% disability entitled those in this category to a lifelong pension. In November 1985 a new disability category of 20% was introduced and workers in this category now receive a lump sum payment only.

All those now classified as 20% disabled would previously have fallen into the 35% category and received a pension from the workmen's compensation commissioner. By revising the classification, many workers, perhaps the majority of compensation claimants, became ineligible for this pension. Most claimants would no doubt be those detected by screening systems in various plants and whose occupational disease could be in its early stages. In money terms, the value of the benefit, reduced from life pension to lump-sum payout, was altered to between a third and a half of its former value.[6] This disadvantageous revision was introduced with no reference to organised labour. Attempts to raise the matter directly with the commissioner, or indirectly via parliament, proved unsuccessful.

All state medical certification bodies immediately implemented the revision. Indications from industries like asbestos and cement are that virtually all cases of asbestosis certified since November 1985 now receive the lump-sum payment instead of the pension. In the past some companies, like Everite, contributed the balance to the workmen's compensation commissioner's pension to make pension payouts equal to the worker's last basic wage. They allowed workers with asbestosis to opt for voluntary retirement on these terms. These companies refuse to extend such conditions to those classified as only 20% disabled and these workers now receive only a lump sum from the commissioner.

Other legislation: During 1986, a bill was put forward proposing amendments to the notorious Mines and Works Act, one of the most explicitly racist pieces of labour legislation. The National Union of Mineworkers, which has long campaigned for deracialising laws and practices on the mines, decided to give evidence on their objections to the bill to the standing committee on mineral and energy affairs.

One of NUM's main reasons for opposing the bill was the wide-ranging discretionary powers granted to the minister of mineral and energy affairs. Although the bill attempts to remove racial criteria for skilled jobs, discrimination is still possible in terms of proclamations which can be issued. This concentration of legislative power is similar to that in the TRREA Act and represents a broadening of this disturbing trend.

Implications for the parties

Labour

Those unions already involved have continued to take up health and safety, and a few other unions have taken up these issues for the first time, despite a context of weakened union demands due to the effects of the recession and the emergency. In addition, union administrative resources have been depleted directly or indirectly by state action against union members and officials. Management has often used the recession and disinvestment and sanctions campaigns to place unions on the defensive in wage and other bargaining.

The separate effects of these factors are difficult to evaluate as they are very closely interrelated. This in turn illustrates the closeness of political and economic factors in the current South African economic downturn.

At a regional level, unions have held a few educational seminars involving worker representatives from firms in building products, mining or chemicals. Topics such as bonus schemes, work study and pensions were also discussed.

Some progress has been made in negotiating national health and safety conditions in the asbestos industry, while NUM has made important submissions on legislation in the mining industry to the parliamentary standing committee charged with redrafting the Mines and Works Amendment Bill.

At federation level, neither COSATU nor the National Council of Trade Unions (NACTU) has thus far developed a health and safety policy or programme.

This is not to say that there has been no federation-level responses to health and safety issues. The success of the COSATU sympathy action with NUM's day of mourning for the dead Kinross miners demonstrates the importance of health and safety issues at this level.[7]

However, moves at the national legislative level on regulation, compensation and deregulation should be noted. These could reduce the potential for union control over health and safety in the workplace. Thus, apart from overt disasters forcing health and saftey onto COSATU's agenda, there would appear to be good grounds for attempting to halt the less obvious disaster of regulation, and implementing new labour programmes and initiatives on health and safety at a national federation level. Furthermore, the legislative changes raise the question whether supposedly technical legislation being laid down now will be transformed in a new South Africa, or whether it will survive into the future relatively intact.

Understandably, one of the effects of the emergency has been to harden worker and trade union anti-state feeling. This could, however, reinforce a tendency to avoid dealings with the central state. This avoidance is not without its inconsistencies given that many unions are prepared to register, participate in industrial councils or deal with state departments on issues such as removals. The important question is whether unions will consider engaging with the state via national labour federations with the aim of influencing the legislative process, particularly in areas where direct and more participatory forms of worker action are very difficult.

For instance, it may be relatively easy to oppose and protest new influx control measures by refusing to apply for new identity books. But it is virtually impossible to take similar action when it comes to changes to the compensation procedure, or attempts at deregulating certain sectors of the economy. In these cases, direct labour input by a national federation may be the only way to avoid leaving labour vulnerable to the unadulterated designs of management and the state.

Management

During 1986 management complied with legal requirements so far as to implement the MOSA health and safety structures in most workplaces. However, working conditions in many factories are no doubt still contravening legal requirements, leading to the strong impression that MOSA has been extensively implemented in form rather than in depth.

The delay in passing draft regulations such as those on asbestos and noise seems to indicate deep-seated management opposition to major changes and improvement of health and safety. This is consistent with both government and capital's developing economic programme which comprises conservative measures like privatisation, deregulation and other anti-working class economic policies such as keeping social security minimal, preventing freedom of association or movement, and withholding political rights. These often represent a threat to safe and healthy working conditions.[8]

Management response to disinvestment and sanctions has been to shift economic costs onto workers and to wage an ideological campaign which portrays labour and other popular organisation as the root cause of disinvestment and sanctions. In the health and safety area, substitution of dangerous substances like asbestos has been halted on grounds of higher costs for imported materials. Poor exchange rates which are inextricably bound up with the political situation were blamed. In another case, management of a chemical factory, where a number of workers had been poisoned, claimed it could not afford effective protective measures as its foreign parent company had decided to disinvest.

State

Contradictory state thinking is borne out by a number of new legislative measures. These include new regulations which rely on management self-regulation. In some cases these are weaker than pre-existing legislation and deregulatory measures. Changes to compensation practices have been effected, disadvantaging workers with chronic lung disease in dusty industries.

Early indications that MOSA enshrined the principle of management self-regulation have been borne out by the method of implementing MOSA and proposed monitoring of new draft regulations. There is little evidence, contrary to some claims, of any increase in the activity or efficacy of the factory inspectorate. However, preparations do seem to be under way to expand the state's industrial health capacity through training programmes and establishment of laboratories in the technical colleges in major urban centres.

A coherent labour strategy on health and safety

In 1986 well-organised labour showed it can more than hold its own in the promotion of health and safety despite the effects of the recession and the state of emergency. But events of the year did highlight the striking need for a coherent national labour strategy to challenge state and capital's attempts to construct what they call post-apartheid capitalism. This threatens workers' long-term welfare in that it lays the groundwork for undermining hard-won gains in all areas, including health and safety. Judging by the state's successes in the health and safety arena during 1985 and 1986, this trend is likely to accelerate. Changes will no doubt affect workers across the board, whether organised or not.

Notes

1   General Workers Union, 'Health and Safety Agreement at Turnall. A First in South Africa', *South African Labour Bulletin*, 11(7), August 1986.
2   Published material in the *South African Labour Bulletin*, which has reflected developments in health and safety, decreased in 1986 when compared with previous years. See *South African Labour Bulletin*, 11(3), January 1986, 11-14; 11(5), April-May 1986, 40-44; 11(7), August 1986, 38-46; 12(1), November-December 1986, 11-14.
3   Taffy Adler, 'Shift work in South Africa', *South African Labour Bulletin*,

11(6), June-July 1986.

4   Technical Advice Group, 'MOSA General Safety Regulations', *South African Labour Bulletin*, 11(7), August 1986.

5   Debbie Budlender, 'Deregulation via the Back Door', *South African Labour Bulletin*, 12(1), November-December 1986.

6   J Myers, 'Changes in the compensation system for occupational diseases' (letter) South African Medical Journal, 68(11), 1985; Industrial Health Research Group, 'Workman's Compensation: changing the rules', *South African Labour Bulletin*, 11(2), October- December 1985.

7   Labour Monitoring Group, 'Kinross day of mourning', *South African Labour Bulletin*, 12(1), November-December 1986.

8   David Lewis, 'Capital, Trade Unions and the National Liberation Struggle', *South African Labour Bulletin*, 11(4), February-March 1986.

Perspectives on Productivity in South Africa

Judy Maller

During 1986 wage bargaining came to the fore in the industrial relations arena. Trade unions, successfully in many cases, demanded across-the-board cost of living increases for their members in response to the high annual inflation rate of approximately 20%. The Institute of Industrial Relations estimates that wages were the most common cause of reported disputes in 1986:

Cause of dispute[1]	%
Wages	28,8
Dismissals	18,5
Arrests/victimisation	12,0
Work conditions	6,5
Racial attitudes/assaults	6,3
Recognition	6,0
Retrenchment	5,4
Sympathy	4,3
Miscellaneous	2,0
Hours of work	1,1
Grievance/discipline	0,8
Tax/stop orders	0,6
Union rivalry	0,6
Bonuses	0,3
Unknown	6,8

In the context of a deeply-rooted economic crisis characterised by double-digit inflation and growing unemployment - recently estimated to be in the region of six million people nationwide - employers have limited wage increases to below the inflation rate. Workers in the industrial and retail sectors, for example, won average wage increases of between 15% and 19% during 1986. This meant most workers experienced a reduction in their standard of living.[2]

A survey by industrial relations consultants Andrew Levy and Associates found that 1985-86 wage increases in unionised plants exceeded the average increase in black wages but did not reach the inflation rate. And the South African Labour and Development Research Unit has shown that the average minimum wage expressed in real terms is at its lowest point since 1981.[3]

Despite their limited increases, wage levels have caused growing management and government concern about productivity. The steep increase in black wages since the early 1970s is often cited by productivity pundits as the primary cause of South Africa's relatively low productivity figures. The low 'quality' of the local labour force is also seen as a significant factor. And black workers' inability to appreciate the nature of the market economy results in a tendency to waste materials and time, neglect machine and equipment maintenance, and work inefficiently.

According to a National Productivity Institute (NPI) publication,

> Employees and trade unions based their wage claims on past and present rates of inflation and avoid settling for wage increases lower than their expectations of the inflation rate. It is time that labour exercised greater discipline in wage negotiations.[4]

Rising wages were partly a result of the rebirth of the black trade union movement following the Durban strikes of 1973. But the high inflation rate, which reached 10% by 1974, effectively nullified wage gains. Present wage rates started from a low base rate and are continuously eroded by inflation.

The present emphasis on labour costs is misdirected since it is wage efficiency which determines productivity levels. The output side of the equation is crucial and this involves the areas of purchasing, stock-keeping, distribution and sales, marketing, research and development, and indeed the management of production.

In conventional economic terms, productivity is expressed as a ratio of total outputs to total inputs; this indicates the efficiency of an enterprise. Products are fashioned through the interaction of various factors of production: land, raw materials, capital and labour. The process of their transformation into products determines productivity.

The recession of the 1980s, combined with the effects of the long-term economic crisis, provided the impetus for a resurgence of management interest in productivity improvement. This interest has largely taken the form of increased pressure on workers, thereby nudging it into the spotlight of industrial relations conflict.

Some case studies

Management concentration on productivity improvement has prompted a renewed interest in tried and tested techniques of work measurement and incentive bonuses as well as newer methods of intensifying work. Downward pressure on profits coupled with increasing demands for a 'living wage' from trade unions have caused business to look more carefully at the costs and effectiveness of labour. Often this has resulted in disadvantageous terms of employment for black workers and has provoked a rash of disputes.

A highly publicised case during 1985-86 was the Foschini- Commercial, Catering and Allied Workers Union of SA dispute. This involved converting 20% of the workforce from full-time to part-time status. The move was prompted by management's concern that falling profits were the result of low salesforce productivity. A work study exposed 'over-manning' which led to the part-time proposal. Management rejected CCAWUSA's counter-proposal of short time for all workers, and a six-month-long dispute began. Eventually, towards the end of 1986, the dispute was settled in management's favour but the affected workers received substantial compensation.

A number of other disputes highlighted the increasing significance of productivity in industrial relations terms:

* a stoppage occurred at the SASKO Pretoria flour mill when an industrial engineering team from the NPI entered the premises to conduct a productivity audit as part of a company-wide rationalisation programme involving extensive automation and 'slimming' (a euphemism for large-scale retrenchments). The significance of this dispute was Food and Canning Workers Union's attempt, albeit unsuccessful, to bring in its own consultants to contest the NPI's assessment of manning levels;

* Transport and General Workers Union declared a dispute with Everite, a manufacturer of asbestos cement products, over the in-house incentive bonus scheme for workers in the hand-moulded goods section. The union challenged management on its own terms and demanded modifications to the bonus formula to ensure higher remuneration for workers through bonuses. In a significant victory, workers won the right to earn bonuses prior to reaching standard performance level - which management claims is calculated on a scientific basis;

* the National Union of Mineworkers has made several demands that black miners be included in the bonus system. The gold mining industry is characterised by bonus payments for employees not directly engaged in productive pursuits. The rationale is that supervisors will ensure their staff work as productively as possible if their own take-home pay depends on output. The vast majority of NUM members occupy the lower job categories which are excluded from bonus earnings (or limited to a strict proportion between bonus and wage earnings in the case of team leaders);

* at Samcor, National Automobile and Allied Workers Union shop stewards negotiated to end a productivity agreement in force at the plant since 1984. The agreement involved a commitment by the workforce to raise productivity and reduce absenteeism and scrap rates in exchange for bonus payments. Bonuses were calculated weekly on plant-wide output figures. Workers felt bonus pay was consistently too low and that their individual contributions to productivity went unnoticed in this scheme because individuals could not significantly alter the productivity level. Instead they demanded and won straight wage increases.

These examples illustrate ambiguous trade union responses to management strategies for productivity improvement. However, where rationalisation has been the major objective, unions have been quick to realise the potential disadvantages and take up the cudgels on their members' behalf.

Management strategies

Managements have addressed productivity problems in a variety of ways. Possibly the most important strategy is automation, which has been responsible for the rapid rise in productivity in Japan, America, Scandinavia, West Germany and some of the newly industrialised countries, especially in South-East Asia.

However, South African managements have not made extensive use of computerisation or robotics. High interest rates on borrowed capital meant investment in machinery lost much of its appeal for South African managers. Extensive mechanisation and automation are only profitable in economies of scale and South African manufacturing is based on short runs, characterised by frequent set ups and machine changes. As one commentator put it,

> much of South African manufacturing industry does not enjoy the necessary economies of scale to optimise production costs. In some cases, this is because the market is just too small.[5]

Numerous sources have reported a decline in capital investment.[6] This is not to deny that South African industry is investing in new technology, numerically controlled and automated machinery and robotics. But it does mean the amount of capital invested in such technology is declining and buyers are exercising greater selectivity in their capital purchases. Significantly, one result has been a tendency for productivity-aware managements to focus on increasing labour productivity. The NPI points to 'the fact that producers do not care to monitor the productivity of capital as readily as they measure the productivity of labour'.[7]

The use of scientific management is increasingly evident, particularly as companies embark on extensive cost reduction exercises. Since arbitrary changes in production and large-scale retrenchments are no longer possible in unionised workplaces, work study provides a more systematic approach to rationalising and identifying 'unnecessary' labour. The effects on workers of retrenchment, work intensification and changes in payment systems have nudged work study into the trade union limelight.

Work study

Work study, including time and motion studies and method study, involves the setting of labour productivity standards. Time study determines the standard time required for a job, which all workers are theoretically capable of meeting without undue physical exertion. The standard time is then compared with the actual time taken to do a job. The comparison provides an indication of the productivity of the worker concerned.

This measurement is based on a limited conceptualisation of the nature of manual labour. It does not adequately consider the variety of factors contributing to effective completion of a task. It also does not address the social, cultural and ideological components of production. It remains at best a mechanistic measure of individual worker efficiency.

The work study techniques used by South African managements were investigated through a survey of 200 companies which employ members of the Work Study Association, the professional association of work study practitioners.[8] Their activities provide insight into the effects of work study on work practices and working conditions.

The surveyed companies encompass all major industrial sectors and range in size from five to 23 000 employees. The use of work study appears to be concentrated in large companies: 54,2% of respondents work in companies with over 1 000 employees. A Natal productivity consultant agrees, saying that 'measurement is largely confined to bigger companies of over 300 employees. The smaller companies have rudimentary control systems if any'.[9]

Of the surveyed companies, 72% have work study departments. But the size of the departments varies and bears no relationship to company size. It appears that the number of work study practitioners employed by a company depends far more on senior management support for work measurement and its historical usage in the firm. For example, the mining, municipal and metal industries pioneered South African work study and today remain its primary users.

Work measurement techniques remain largely traditional. Of the companies surveyed, 78% use stop-watch measurement, and 43% use synthetic or standard data to measure work. It was generally felt that the stop-watch is more accurate and consequently it is used most often in setting new time standards. Most work study departments in surveyed companies were established during the 1970s.

The Work Study Association survey showed that a high priority is given to work measurement and labour performance monitoring as opposed to addressing total enterprise productivity. Over a third of companies surveyed cited increased labour productivity as their most significant achievement. Substantially fewer companies (16%) listed increased plant and equipment utilisation in their achievements. This emphasis could lead to conflict as 'workers resent efforts being made to improve their efficiency while they can see glaring inefficiency on the part of management'.[10]

Time standards are generally applied to production workers. In 78% of surveyed companies, semi-skilled workers work according to time standards. This is probably because this category consists predominantly of machine operators whose standards are set according to machine speeds. Time standards have traditionally, both in this country and in others, been the subject of ongoing union- management disputes. Management claims to scientific measures are disputed, particularly around allocation of personal and relaxation allowances and the assessment of the pace and effectiveness of the workers being studied. Both these components are fundamental to the setting of standards and depend entirely on the work study practitioner's discretion.

A further union criticism of work study is that it often results in lowered employment levels because it continuously attempts to rationalise the organisation to reduce inputs, including labour. Of the companies surveyed, in 1985 and 1986, 45% have retrenched or laid off employees; 36% have reduced numbers by natural wastage; 21% redeployed excess employees. Only 7% actually increased employment levels and 16% reported unchanged numbers.

It is unlikely that these reductions can be directly attributed to the practice of work study. But a survey of trade unionists' opinions showed that work study is often used as the basis for planning retrenchments: unions are faced with proposals for retrenchment on the basis of the number of hours of work needed to complete existing orders. Trade unionists expressed belief in an association between work measurement and retrenchments.[11]

At its first congress in December 1985, the Congress of South African Trade Unions adopted a resolution on unemployment, resolving to

> fight as one united force to defend all jobs threatened by retrenchments; fight the closing of the factories; fight for participation in and control over...the implementation of any new technology; and fight all attempts by employers to make workers work harder and attempts to rationalise production because in the present system this always leads to unemployment.

Incentive bonus schemes

Management often tries to get around demands for wage increases by linking wages directly to increases in productivity. Incentive bonuses have thus become an important item on the negotiation agenda. In many cases unions accepted the implementation of incentives as the only way to achieve increased earnings for their members. But in many cases disputes were the result.

Approximately half the surveyed companies employ incentive bonus schemes (52%) and production workers are the primary targets. Foremen and artisans are often less suitable because their jobs are non-repetitive and therefore more difficult to measure, or because their salaries are high and do not respond to the motivation of incentives.

A frequently-used index of the effectiveness of an incentive scheme is the proportion of affected employees who reach bonus level. If too few workers achieve bonus, it no longer acts as an incentive because workers feel it is impossible to reach. A high proportion of workers should regularly earn bonuses for the scheme to be effective. In 27% of surveyed companies using incentives, less than a third of workers earn regular bonuses.

Although there are no authoritative guidelines as to the percentage of a workforce which should regularly earn bonuses, it may safely be concluded that motivation provided by incentives does not operate effectively in these companies.

The effectiveness of incentive bonus schemes has been the subject of extensive debate. One informant in the clothing industry pointed out that 'most South African firms only introduce incentives when things are going wrong'. A common result is that labour relations deteriorate when management discovers the increased costs involved and cuts the bonus rates. Incentives may even have a demotivating effect in situations where a constant work load cannot be guaranteed. 'People get used to bonus earnings and feel that their wage has effectively dropped when the bonus is not there' said a work study consultant.

It is becoming increasingly difficult for local managements to provide this guarantee in the context of the current economic recession. An expert consultant has proposed that a successful bonus scheme should generate between 25% and 35% of the basic wage. Increased payments should be in direct proportion to increases in work output.

The surveyed companies did not specify in detail how they calculated bonus payments but very few pay for output increments in direct proportion to the wage rate. Many use retrogressive systems:

workers are paid at successively lower rates for each production increment over and above their set target. Others use their own formulae for this calculation. One informant estimated that South African unions 'seldom demand more than 15% as the minimum average increase in earnings to arise from bonus'.

There are no authoritative international guidelines on the effective implementation of incentives. In the highly industrialised and unionised countries, managements increasingly opt for flat wage rates rather than incentives schemes. This is largely due to workers' successful manipulation of these schemes to derive maximum benefit and to worker opposition to variations in payments. For South African industry the incentive option is part of managements' search for non-capital forms of productivity improvement. They believe incentives have potential to improve worker productivity since they have not yet been applied systematically to the black workforce.

But unionists interviewed regarded incentives negatively: bonuses were often the cause of industrial relations disputes; they were also too low to effectively motivate workers and were often used to foster corruption and favouritism. Unionists felt wages should be linked to the cost of living rather than to productivity and many had attempted to negotiate for incentive schemes to be 'bought out'.

Unionists argued for a system where workers shared in increased company profits. CCAWUSA, the giant retail union, issued a statement during a highly publicised strike at Pick 'n Pay in 1986: 'Pick 'n Pay is a wealthy company. We want a share of those resources'. Of the unionists interviewed 25% supported the concept of profit-sharing, which they saw as a means to redistribute company wealth. A CCAWUSA spokesperson said that 'when the union states that it wants a share of the profits, it means it wants a bigger share of the total of revenue to go to the living wage' (*FW*, 22-28.05.86).

Unions are advocating novel ways of determining wages which go beyond traditional collective bargaining. The major demand is for a living wage to be determined jointly with workers and their representatives. The 1985 COSATU congress resolved that

> the central executive committee establish as soon as possible what workers regard as a minimum living wage; ...(and) fight for this minimum living wage to be automatically linked to the rate of inflation...

The initial momentum for this came from the Metal and Allied

Workers Union and the campaign was launched officially in early
1987.

COSATU officially rejected performance-linked bonuses when
General Secretary Jay Naidoo stated that

> Handouts from the company and other discretionary rewards will not impress
> the workforce. We want to be paid for the labour we put into our work, and
> this means wages which meet our needs (*FW*, 22-28.05.86).

Instead unions are advocating the allocation of company profit to
workers in the form of living wages. The potential for conflict over
payment systems has emerged quite clearly: management is pursuing
systems of performance-linked payment: 'You pay people for what
they do, rather than for how long they spend doing it. If you pay so
much per hour, you do not guarantee any work'.[12] Unions, on the
other hand, are clearly articulating the demand for wages linked to
the standard of living.

Other industrial engineering techniques

A number of new industrial engineering strategies are currently
being widely publicised as effective ways of improving productivity.
Some are:

Just-in-Time (JIT): a Japanese manufacturing system which aims to
reduce inventory so that stock arrives from the supplier directly onto
the shopfloor. The 'Kanban' - a system of moving work-in-progress -
ensures that work arrives at successive work stations 'just-in-time' to
be worked on. This eliminates costs associated with warehousing and
stock storage on the shopfloor. It also ensures that quality and maintenance problems are rectified immediately. Parts and products are
standardised as far as possible to allow for efficient change-overs and
minimal set-up times. Workers are 'multi-functional' under JIT and
perform work wherever they are needed in the factory.

JIT has recently been implemented by a number of South
African companies: General Electric Corporation, Toyota and some
of its suppliers, Fedmech, Tuberlaken of SA, Hulett Packard and
Wilson Rowntree. But JIT methods have not been adopted on a
wide scale primarily because it is risky to reduce inventories, particularly in times of wide market fluctuations and labour activity.

Materials Requirements Planning (MRP): assists planners to predict the demands for each element of a manufacturing process at any given time. The scheduling of labour, materials, machine time and other resources is estimated by extrapolating backwards from the delivery date of the finished product. MRP eliminates the need for large inventories of stock because each part is manufactured immediately before it is required. MRP is often used in a complementary fashion to JIT.

Maintenance Management has developed a third generation maintenance programme which makes possible different maintenance schedules for different types of technologies. Detailed analyses of patterns of equipment failure have generated different maintenance needs for each machine to ensure optimum performance.

Innovations in *Materials Management* include automatic storage and retrieval systems, automated sorting systems, production and inventory control, changes in conveyors and pipelines, and the use of computer-aided design in scheduling materials' transport.

It is difficult to assess how widely these systems are being used. South African industry has undergone extensive computerisation, particularly in large companies where economies of scale make it profitable. But the extent to which computers are effectively utilised is under-researched.

Participatory management

Lack of consultation on productivity-related issues appears to contribute to conflict over time standards, production schedules and rates of bonus pay. The surveyed work study practitioners usually do not consult workers or their representatives when changing work methods or time standards. In 48% of companies surveyed, workers are informed of proposed changes, but these are never negotiated. Most managers believe productivity is not a legitimate area of worker and union concern, and it is an area where management attempts to retain its prerogative.

Unionists interviewed believed work measurement and productivity were issues for negotiation. They felt workers and their organisations should be consulted about changes in work practices to effect productivity improvements, both to ensure that management was implementing acceptable changes and because workers would be able to contribute positively to this process.

According to a COSATU spokesperson,

> We are not interested in the kind of paternalism where a decision is taken, for example to introduce new technology, and management comes to the union to discuss the effects, ie retrenchments. We want to be consulted first (*FW*, 22-28.05.86).

This increasing worker interest in meaningful participation in the production process also emerged in a recent Market Research Africa sociomonitor survey which found that 'nine out of ten urban blacks believe workers should have some say in the running of their section of the company where they work' (*Star*, 14.06.86).

Inclusion of black workers in production decisions has not progressed beyond the current vogue of quality circles: 21% of surveyed companies have introduced some form of employee involvement, usually quality circles. Quality circles are small problemsolving groups of workers from the same department or work station. The groups meet regularly to solve production-related problems, like quality, bottlenecks and safety. The aim is to encourage workers to identify with the company objective, motivate employees and enhance their productivity.

Just under half the unionists interviewed were aware that quality circles operated in some factories they organised, but in no cases had they ever been consulted, and they remained suspicious of these structures. They did acknowledge that quality circles might provide workers with real benefits: recognition of their mental abilities; increased respect and greater involvement in their jobs. But unionists also felt quality circles might lead management to by-pass unions and use workers' brainpower to benefit the company alone. As one unionist said: 'Quality circles do take away some alienation of the job, but the net effect is to co-opt workers'. Unionists were sceptical about whether quality circles would work effectively in the context of low salaries and low standards of living.

Part of the 'participatory' initiative has been experimentation with forms of worker motivation which attempt to instil in workers an appreciation of and commitment to capitalist economic principles. An example is the NPI programme entitled '6M Simulation Training' which it claims is currently being used by over 500 companies in South Africa. The 6M programme illustrates to employees the function and interaction of the basic principles in Western industries. Understanding these principles, how they interact and what their influence is on the organisation, as well as on the employee, equips the employee to make a positive contribution towards company performance.[13]

Some business leaders have become increasingly vocal about other forms of worker participation in the benefits and responsibilities of the enterprise. This is to ensure a harmonious and productive working environment. Suggestions have included profit-sharing, worker share-holders and even worker directors. An industrial relations consultant articulated this view at a recent conference:

> We need to find new models which avoid out-and-out conflict in the workplace. We need to pursue both power and profit sharing and break down the distinction between management and workers.

Limited experiments in profit-sharing and worker shareholding have been attempted by a few South African companies, but with little public exposure or analysis of the effects.

Managing the profitability crisis

South African managements are using work study and quality circles extensively, often in complementary ways. This dual approach must be seen in the light of a crisis of profitability and increased workforce militancy.

There has been much publicity about the various productivity management techniques in recent editions of *Productivity SA, Financial Mail, Business Day,* and the *Foundry Welding Production Engineering Journal.* But it is clear these strategies are not in general use in South African industry:

* JIT techniques are practised in no more than 50 companies;

* quality circles operate in approximately 100 companies;

* work study, one of the most basic of industrial engineering techniques, is largely confined to factories with over 300 employees;

* participatory techniques are manifest mainly at the level of rhetoric on the part of business leaders.

South Africa's relatively low productivity has been isolated as one of the primary reasons for the country's low economic growth, namely 1% for 1986 with a negative capital growth. But at the level of the individual enterprise, lack of management skills and systems is a major contributory factor to the deteriorating situation. Rule-of-thumb management coupled with direct supervision of workers remains the order of the day.

It has been amply demonstrated worldwide that increasing worker involvement in an enterprise's decision-making process, particularly in relation to questions of production, has enhanced productivity, often dramatically. Local business leaders have recognised this process, hence their public calls for increased worker participation.

But trade unions have recognised mismanagement at the level of the economy as a whole as well as lack of management expertise at the micro level of the factory. The 1985 COSATU congress resolved to

> fight to open all books of every organised company, so that workers can see exactly how the wealth they have produced is being wasted and misused by the employers' profit system, and on that basis demand their full share of the wealth they have produced. Should the wealth not be there, then it will only prove the inefficiency of employer management and strengthen the case for worker control and management of production.

As a result, unions are putting forward far-reaching demands for participation. Their vision of worker participation extends to workers control in the context of a more democratic society. A resolution from the 1986 MAWU congress calls explicitly for a socialist future in South Africa. It remains to be seen whether business's initiatives regarding participation will become widespread - and even if they do, whether worker share-holders, or even worker directors, will satisfy the aspirations of the organised working class.

Notes

1   Figures supplied by the Institute of Industrial Relations.
2   Figures supplied by the Institute of Industrial Relations.
3   *South African Labour Bulletin,* 12(1), November-December 1986, 40-41.
4   National Productivity Institute, 'Annual Report, 1984-85', 7.
5   JC van Zyl, 'Industrial Strategy: Quo Vadis?', paper presented at Port Elizabeth Manufacturing Convention, 1986, 4.
6   National Productivity Institute, 'Annual Report 1985', 8.
7   National Productivity Institute, 'Annual Report 1985', 7.
8   A postal questionnaire administered to individual members of the Work Study Association achieved a 46% response. In addition, personal interviews

were conducted with a random sample of 20% of respondents to obtain qualitative data about their work study practices and productivity improvement techniques. See J Maller, *Perspectives on Productivity*, TAG/Sociology Research Programme, University of the Witwatersrand, 1986, for more detail.

9   Quoted in Maller, *Perspectives on Productivity*, 19.

10   International Labour Organisation, *Introduction to Work Study*, Geneva, 1973, 42.

11   A survey of South African trade unions organising workers in companies associated with the Work Study Association was conducted to complement the postal survey of work study practitoners. Trade union officials and shop stewards at concerned companies were interviewed.

The union survey indicates unionists' perceptions, which may be limited but remain of great importance since the way unionists perceive work measurement at present will form the basis of their systematic response in the future.

The union survey is incomplete. The primary focus was the emergent unions, because the established, ex-craft unions are under-represented in the sample. Over many decades the established unions have been involved in conflict over the measurement of work and the setting of time standards.

12   Interview quoted in Maller, *Perspectives on Productivity*, 40.

13   National Productivity Institute, advertising brochure.

Section 4: Relations With Southern Africa

Introduction

Joseph Hanlon

When South Africa wanted to sabotage the Commonwealth's Eminent Persons Group mission, its troops attacked the capitals of three neighbouring states. When there was a need to respond to US sanctions, Pretoria announced an end to recruitment of Mozambican miners.

South Africa's attacks on its neighbours are hardly new, but the brazen nature they have acquired recently surely is. During 1985, Pretoria maintained the pretence of not meddling in the affairs of its neighbours (other than Angola). But this ended with the January 1986 blockade of Lesotho, which eventually triggered a coup and brought to power a government more amenable to pressure from Pretoria.

South African attempts at maintaining regional hegemony previously involved economic dominance and a political and military cordon sanitaire of white-ruled states. With the independence of Mozambique and Angola in 1975 this began to break down. But it was majority rule in Zimbabwe and the victory of Robert Mugabe's Zimbabwean African National Union (ZANU) that directly threatened Pretoria's dominance. With the ZANU victory, nine majority-ruled states were able to form SADCC (the Southern African Development Co-ordination Conference). This loose economic association aimed to 'liberate our economies from their dependence on the Republic of South Africa, to overcome the imposed economic fragmentation, and to co-ordinate our efforts toward regional and national economic development'.

The South African regional dream was the creation of CONSAS (the Constellation of Southern African States), but even Pretoria's erstwhile allies, Malawi and Swaziland, ended up in SADCC instead.

Although South Africa invaded Angola and attempted various destabilisation strategies during the 1970s, it was largely content to support Rhodesia and its unilateral declaration of independence (UDI) during this period.

But in 1980 South Africa began waging full-scale war on its neighbours. Since the beginning of 1980, this war has cost nearly 750 000 lives and more than R50 000-million in destruction, lost production and other costs.

Wherever possible, South Africa aims to maintain economic dominance in the region. Its net profit on all dealings with the SADCC states is roughly R1 500-million per year (taking into account trade surplus, payments for the customs union and migrant miners, and all other transfers). The money itself is important, especially as sanctions loom, but Africa is also the main export market for manufactured goods (as distinct from minerals) and thus vital to the survival and expansion of South African industry. A Botswana economist estimated that 23% of the growth of South African manufacturing in the 1970s was accounted for by sales to Botswana, Lesotho and Swaziland. This figure is even higher if Malawi, Zambia and Zimbabwe are included. The South African monopoly groups have significant stakes in several of the neighbouring states, particularly Botswana, Zambia, and Zimbabwe, and this increases South Africa's interest in continued economic dominance of the region.

Economic power can be translated into military and political power. The more dependent neighbours are on South Africa, the more vulnerable they are to pressure. Transport is one of the most vital aspects of this dependency. In mid-1986, South Africa imposed transport sanctions against Zimbabwe and Zambia, and closed the border with Lesotho. The government also announced that it would no longer employ Mozambican miners. These actions were later withdrawn or modified, although in Lesotho only after the government fell.

Militarily, South Africa aims to ensure that the neighbouring states are not used as bases and access routes for anti-government guerillas. But in general, military power is used to enforce political and economic goals.

South Africa's main political goal is to demonstrate that majority rule cannot work. Much destabilisation is intended to create chaos, and South Africa will then claim that this is an inevitable result of majority rule. Alternatively, Pretoria aims to make the majority-ruled states dependent on, and subservient to, white-ruled South Africa.

There is extensive overlap between these economic, military and political categories. For example, there is no economic reason for Zimbabwe to send imports and exports via South African ports, when Mozambican ports are nearer and cheaper. But freight and forwarding in Zimbabwe is dominated by Renfreight, owned by Safmarine and thus by Old Mutual. Not surprisingly, Renfreight sends goods via South Africa. This is further encouraged when South African commandos and Pretoria-backed Mozambique National Resistance (MNR or RENAMO) forces are used to attack the railways linking Zimbabwe to Beira and Maputo. A mix of economic and military power thus gives South Africa a stranglehold over Zimbabwean shipping, making it much easier for South Africa to impose sanctions on Zimbabwe.

Sanctions

The South African government would dearly like its neighbours to oppose sanctions in the Commonwealth, United Nations and other forums. Internationally, it has proved extremely difficult for any South African to counter the outspoken calls for sanctions by statesmen like Robert Mugabe, Kenneth Kaunda, and the late Samora Machel. Thus South African regional policy is increasingly aimed at pressing leaders of neighbouring states to oppose sanctions, or at least moderate their tone. Destabilisation and South African-imposed sanctions often have this objective. The blockade of Lesotho in January 1987 made it clear that Pretoria was prepared to help overthrow its critics. In early October 1986 an unprecedented campaign of calumny and vitriol was launched against Samora Machel, and troops were moved to the Mozambican border. Just a few days before the plane crash which killed him, commentators in and outside Mozambique were publicly asking if South Africa was going to try to kill or overthrow Machel. Since then there have been warnings that South Africa might move against Mugabe.

So far this campaign has failed. Pretoria has not found any credible regional leader prepared, both publicly and privately, to oppose sanctions. But this remains a key element of South African regional strategy.

South Africa and its allies, particularly Margaret Thatcher and Ronald Reagan, make much of neighbouring states' dependence on South Africa. Sanctions, they argue, will hurt these states, and it is only fear of international criticism that prevents their leaders from speaking out against sanctions.

Three factors suggest this is not true. First and most important, dependence is created in large measure by South African destabilisation, or the threat of it. Goods flow through South Africa only because South Africa has blown-up or disrupted the alternative SADCC routes. 'We are already suffering. How much more can we suffer?' asked Robert Mugabe in a speech on 15 June 1986. 'We support sanctions because it will shorten the time that we must suffer'. In effect, destabilisation has worked too well. Its cost is so much higher than the impact of sanctions that the SADCC states see sanctions as a small price to pay for the end of apartheid.

Secondly, there is a profound misunderstanding of the nature of dependence, carefully cultivated by South African officials and businesspeople. For example, in an interview published in the (London) *Guardian* of 9 July 1986, Thatcher talked about Zimbabwean goods going through South Africa, and asked: 'Close Beit Bridge and how are you going to do it? That's the maize route. When there was drought, that's the route through which maize went to keep people alive'. But what Mrs Thatcher did not say (and perhaps did not know) was that the maize was moving south! Surplus Zimbabwean maize was feeding South Africans, not vice versa.

There is extensive trade between South Africa and its neighbours, but the main beneficiary of that trade is South Africa. SADCC members buy little from South Africa that they cannot obtain elsewhere, often at a lower price (although the collapse of the Rand has made South African industry more competitive).

Of the nine SADCC states, Angola and Tanzania have no trade

with South Africa, although both market diamonds through De Beers' central selling office. Zambia and Malawi have increasing trade with South Africa, but none is essential. Mozambique has little trade with South Africa, and South African sanctions against Mozambique have largely ended the once-profitable traffic through Maputo port. But Mozambique does earn nearly R100-million per year from migrant labour, and South Africa supplies half of the city of Maputo's electricity. Zimbabwe sells over R150-million worth of goods per year to South Africa - about half of its manufactured exports, but only 12% of total exports. Cutting those would hurt, but not fatally. Few imports from South Africa are vital.

For Botswana, Lesotho and Swaziland, the position is different because customs union membership integrates them totally into the South African economy. This relationship does not benefit the BLS states: gains from customs union payments are far outweighed by high prices caused by South African protectionism, and by the impact of a free market which means that new industry locates in South Africa and not BLS, thus hampering development. But pulling out of the customs union would be highly disruptive, which is why these three small countries have not done so. Botswana, which left the Rand monetary zone many years ago, has enough wealth from diamonds to cushion any move, and may soon leave the customs union. Such a move would be harder for Swaziland, although it is already benefiting from sanctions as firms like Coca Cola move there. Lesotho is totally dependent on remittances from migrant miners, and thus might be indirectly hurt by sanctions. Both Lesotho and Swaziland obtain much of their electricity from South Africa, which could cause problems. The BLS countries obtain all their oil from South Africa, but there is no reason (other than South African threats) to continue this.

The direct and indirect effect of sanctions on the neighbouring states, except Lesotho, would be relatively small, although there could be some temporary disruption.

The third point about sanctions concerns South African retaliation rather than the impact of Western sanctions. Commonwealth sanctions did not hurt Zambia or Zimbabwe; what hurt were the counter-sanctions imposed on their rail traffic by South Africa. US sanctions did not hurt Mozambique; but South African retaliation - cutting back on mine recruitment - did. Pretoria has made it clear that if sanctions are imposed, its neighbours will suffer. That involves retaliation, counter-sanctions, and destabilisation.

SADCC confronts sanctions and destabilisation

On the face of it, SADCC has failed to meet its central goal. Dependence on South Africa has increased. More cargo passes through South Africa than in 1982. Zambia, Malawi and Mozambique all have more trade with South Africa than before, although Zimbabwe is finally reducing its South African trade.

But this misses three central points. First, SADCC has succeeded in bringing the nine majority-ruled states together, despite their wide disparity of economic and political philosophies. Unprecedented co-operation is taking place at the levels of railway and electricity parastatals, ministries of agriculture, and so on. Officials and ministers now have a regional dimension to their thinking that was absent five years ago.

Second, SADCC has drawn unexpected support from international donors. In the past six years, more than R4 400-million has been secured for SADCC development projects. Many of these are already going ahead. Britain and the US are finally putting in significant amounts of money. Both were initially hostile to SADCC intentions to break links with South Africa, while the US is trying to overthrow the government of a member state (Angola).

Third, the most important SADCC projects are well funded and work is already well underway. They are the Beira and Dar es Salaam Corridors, which will provide sufficient railway, road, oil pipeline and port capacity to make it unnecessary for any SADCC state except Lesotho to use South African ports and railways. By 1988 these vital SADCC projects could end Pretoria's stranglehold over SADCC transport.

But will Pretoria allow this to happen? Since 1980, South African commandos have attacked oil, railway and port installations in Mozambique, Angola, Lesotho and Zimbabwe. These raids have disrupted traffic of the inland states of Malawi, Swaziland and Zambia which have not, so far, been hit directly. It is widely assumed by SADCC and its foreign partners that South Africa will try to hit both the Beira and the Dar es Salaam Corridors, to cut traffic and maintain its transport stranglehold. International military help to protect the Beira Corridor now seems assured. And with the relative success of the Beira project, there is now talk of trying to reopen the

Zimbabwe - Maputo and Malawi - Nacala links.

At the January 1986 SADCC annual conference in Harare, it became clear that South African destabilisation is now a unifying force. SADCC projects are explicitly geared to resisting destabilisation, and foreign donors are increasingly expressing support for SADCC in terms of resisting South African aggression.

Undoubtedly destabilisation has been a cheap and effective tactic for South Africa. It has crippled the economies of Mozambique, Angola and Malawi and disrupted others. It helped precipitate a change of government in Lesotho. And it may have tempered the anti-apartheid outbursts of some regional leaders. But destabilisation has also drawn world-wide support for the SADCC states, and that support seems set to grow in direct proportion to South African destabilisation of the region.

The costs of destabilisation

This section of the *Review* contains three articles covering specific aspects of South Africa's relations with its neighbours. Rob Davies, in an analysis of South African regional policy from mid-1985 until the end of 1986, argues that South Africa has adopted an increasingly ruthless and visible use of force against its neighbours. This differs from the period immediately after the Nkomati Accord, when South Africa acted against its neighbours mainly through surrogate forces like the MNR and UNITA.

Jeremy Grest explores the effects of South African regional policy on Mozambique. Detailing the changes which have taken place in Mozambican society since the Nkomati Accord, Grest shows how Mozambique's economy was placed on a war footing once it became clear that South Africa continued to support the MNR. Reorganisation of agriculture, industrial production, transport and the bureaucracy have all taken place in a war context, with a powerful neighbour intent on economic and military destabilisation.

Finally, Robert Edgar assesses the 1986 Lesotho coup. While they argue that the coup had its roots in a political conflict within Leabua Jonathon's Basotho National Party, they also demonstrate how South Africa's clamp on border traffic between the two countries brought Lesotho's political crisis to a head, precipitating a military coup.

In a report to the Organisation of African Unity, SADCC

estimated the cost of destabilisation during the five years 1980-84 to be $10,1-billion, broken down as follows:

$-million	
1 610	Direct war damage
3 060	Higher defence spending
970	Higher transport and energy costs
230	Lost exports and tourism
190	Smuggling and looting
660	Supporting refugees and displaced persons
800	Loss of existing production
2 000	Lost economic growth[1]
260	Boycotts, embargoes and sanctions imposed by SA
340	Trading arrangements[2]

In a January 1987 United Nations Children's Fund (UNICEF) paper, 'Children on the Front Line', Reg Green and others estimated the cost of destabilisation (using the same method as SADCC) to be $7-billion for 1985 and $8-billion for 1986, or roughly $25-billion (R50-billion) for the seven years 1980-86 inclusive. This is significantly more than all the international development assistance received by these countries during the same period.

Some 100 000 people died in a famine in Mozambique in 1983-84, these deaths being directly caused by actions of the South African-backed MNR. In *Beggar Your Neighbour*[3] I argue that it was conscious South African policy to starve people, in the hope of causing them to turn against FRELIMO. In addition, 50 000 people have been killed by South African and MNR military actions. And in Angola since 1980, roughly 100 000 people have died as a result of UNITA or South African raids, or from war-induced famine.

The UNICEF report also looked at the effects of destabilisation on health services. In Mozambique, for example, when MNR guerillas attack a village they often burn down the health post and try to kill health workers, vaccination teams, etc. By 1985, 25% of health facilities in Mozambique had been destroyed. There has been similar destruction in Angola. Both countries had developed highly effective immunisation programmes which are now severely curtailed. The effect is that child mortality (under five), which had been falling rapidly in 1975-80 in both countries, began to rise again. UNICEF estimates that without South African destabilisation, child mortality in Angola and Mozambique would have fallen to the level of Tanzania. That means that since 1980, 215 000 children under five in

Mozambique and 320 000 in Angola have died unnecessarily. Although not killed by bullets or machetes, they are still war victims.

On these calculations, the total number of deaths in Mozambique and Angola due to South African destabilisation (1980-86 inclusive) is 735 000:

Mozambique war	50 000
Mozambique famine	100 000
Angola war and famine	50 000
Mozambique children	215 000
Angola children	320 000
Total	735 000

These stark figures form the backdrop against which this section's articles on South Africa's relations with its neighbours should be read.

Notes

1   The calculation of lost economic growth is considered an underestimate by some authors. Reg Green and Carol Thompson put it at $4-billion in D Martin and P Johnson, *Destructive Engagement,* Zimbabwe Publishing House, 1986.
2   'Trading arrangements' refer to the estimated loses due to the BLS countries being forced to remain in the customs union with South Africa.
3   Joseph Hanlon, *Beggar Your Neighbours,* CIIR/James Currey, London, 1986. More details on the material costs of destablisation can be found in the appendix to this book.

South African Regional Policy Post-Nkomati: May 1985 - December 1986

Robert Davies

On 21 May 1985, a South African Defence Force reconnaissance commando landed in Angola's Cabinda province. Its members intended to destroy installations managed by the American Gulf Oil Company. As a military operation the raid was a failure. Angolan soldiers killed two members of the commando unit while a third, Captain Wynand Petrus du Toit, was wounded and captured.

The Cabinda raid marked the beginning of a new phase of regional relations. The attack visibly violated South Africa's 16 February 1984 Lusaka cease-fire agreement with Angola and was the first direct SADF assault on a neighbouring state since that agreement. It also went against the 16 March 1984 Nkomati accord South Africa had signed with Mozambique.

Pretoria never intended these accords to deter it from continuing its regional destabilisation, as the 'Gorongosa documents' demonstrate. Throughout the accord phase from 1984 to mid-1985, numerous violations occurred. But these were usually carried out clandestinely by proxy forces like UNITA and MNR. At the same time Pretoria attempted to project an elaborate image of 'good neighbourliness' and 'peaceful co-existence' in its relations with neighbours. The Cabinda raid signalled a strategic shift from this stance towards a regional policy involving increasingly ruthless and visible use of force.

Subsequent developments confirmed this pattern of escalating aggression against regional states. Some of the major incidents up until December 1986 included:

* 14 June 1985: SADF raid against residences in Gaborone: 18 killed;

* 1 July 1985: bomb attack outside ANC offices in Lusaka;

* August 1985: the 'Gorongosa documents' provided conclusive proof of continued SADF support for the armed bandits of the Mozambican National Resistance Movement (MNR or RENAMO) despite the Nkomati accord;

* 28 September - 3 October 1985: the first major SADF incursion into Angolan territory since the February 1984 cease-fire agreement; Pretoria later publicly admitted backing UNITA. Defence Minister Magnus Malan said support for UNITA would continue until 'all foreign troops left Angola' (*Paratus,* November 1985);

* November 1985: the State Security Council reportedly adopted a plan to retaliate against international sanctions by imposing counter-sanctions against regional states, including the repatriation of foreign migrant workers (*BD,* 11.11.85);

* December 1985: according to a Mozambican government communique, specialist SADF saboteurs working together with MNR bandits carried out a series of sabotage actions in Mozambique's Maputo province (*Guardian,* 07.12.85);

* 20 December 1985: the State Security Council issued a rare public warning to six neighbouring states threatening that if they did not stop 'the menace of terrorism' from their territories 'all the peoples of Southern Africa will pay a heavy price'. On the same day a clandestine hit squad killed six ANC members and three Lesotho citizens in Maseru;

* 2 January 1986: a blockade on Lesotho exacerbated acute internal conflicts which eventually provoked the overthrow of Prime Minister Leabua Jonathan's government in the coup of 20 January;

* 6 February 1986: according to Mozambican government sources, specialist units from South Africa, again working alongside the MNR, planted landmines on Maputo beaches (*Noticias,* 10.02.86);

* 21 April 1986: a car bomb planted by agents operating from South Africa injured 50 people in a residential area of Maputo (*Noticias,* 22.04.86);

* 19 May 1986: simultaneous SADF raids against Gaborone, Harare and Lusaka;

* Mid-1986 onwards: intensified MNR activity in the central provinces of Mozambique culminating in a large-scale conventional invasion of Zambezia and Tete provinces in September (*Star,* 12.09.86; *FM,* 24.10.86). A series of abductions and murders of alleged ANC sympathisers in Lesotho and Swaziland by clandestine

hit squads;

 * August 1986: imposition of restrictions on the movement of Zimbabwean and Zambian exports and imports through South Africa. Further large-scale SADF attacks on Angola;

 * 8 October 1986: a ban on recruitment of Mozambican migrant workers. Threats of military action against Mozambique followed;

 * 19 October 1986: President Samora Machel and 33 aides died in suspicious circumstances on South African territory;

 * 23 November 1986: two former Lesotho cabinet ministers, Desmond Sixishe and Vincent Makhele, together with their wives, were murdered by a clandestine death squad;

 * December 1986: more murders and kidnappings of alleged ANC members and sympathisers in Swaziland (including both Swazi and Swiss nationals). Foreign Minister RF Botha said he had prior knowledge of and approved these actions, and warned that similar operations would be carried out in the future (*Times of Swaziland,* 15.12.86, 16.12.86, 17.12.86).

Pretoria's regional strategy objectives during the accord phase

Although the Lusaka accord with Angola was a development of considerable significance, it was the Nkomati accord of March 1984 signed with Mozambique which really marked the beginning of the accord phase of regional relations. Nkomati was more comprehensive and far-reaching than the Lusaka agreement. Signed at a higher level, amidst considerable pomp and ceremony, it was a comprehensive non-aggression pact as distinct from a limited ceasefire agreement. It also sought to re-negotiate aspects of economic relations between the two states.

The accord did not mean the two signatories had come to share a common view on regional relations. Mozambique saw Nkomati as defining a new pattern of regional relations based on principles of international law. The accord was also to serve as a diplomatic instrument to isolate MNR armed bandits from their external backers. Though agreeing to live in 'peaceful co-existence' with South Africa, the Mozambican government hoped to compel the Pretoria regime to cease supporting MNR bandits. Failing this, Pretoria would be exposed as the regional aggressor. The price which Mozambique saw itself compelled to pay was withdrawal of transit facilities which the ANC had informally enjoyed. But Mozambique resisted South African pressures to withdraw all forms of support for the ANC, recognise the 'independent' bantustans and acknowledge the legitimacy of the Botha regime's reforms. FRELIMO reaffirmed its support for the struggle of the South African people and the ANC - although exclusively at the 'political, diplomatic and moral' levels.

The Botha regime saw Nkomati in a wholly different light. Pretoria's strategists did not see the accord itself as defining a new pattern of regional relations. For them it was to be a tactic: a device to remould regional relations in accordance with Pretoria's stalled 'constellation of states' initiative. The accord would be used as a means to generate the common approach on the economic and security fronts envisaged in the constellation strategy. Through this South Africa would emerge as the regional power in Southern Africa: the force with which all other interested parties would have to come to terms, whether they liked it or not. This in turn would open the gateway for South Africa to escape from its international isolation. At the Nkomati signing ceremony PW Botha pointedly referred to his vision of a 'veritable constellation of states in Southern Africa'. Partly with the benefit of hindsight, it is apparent that Pretoria's strategists hoped Nkomati could achieve the following strategic objectives:

* South Africa anticipated the accord would have a major impact on the liberation struggle in South Africa. By depriving the ANC of its alleged bases in Mozambique, it was hoped the armed struggle would rapidly wind down; ANC influence over the mass struggle would be weakened and the struggle as a whole would become divided and more easily containable. To a large extent this calculation was based on a view of the mass struggle as an externally directed total onslaught;

* Pretoria's strategists also believed Nkomati would create conditions for them to play a leading role in a process of political, economic and social restructuring in Mozambique which would undermine that country's attempted socialist transition.

A critical element in this was to be a Pretoria-sponsored political settlement between the Mozambican government and the MNR bandits. This was to be achieved through a combination of diplomatic and economic action with continued clandestine support for armed banditry. Such a 'settlement' would place the MNR bandits in a subordinate position in a 'power-sharing' government, where they would have sufficient influence to block any 'radical' programmes. The brokering of this Somali-type solution would allow Pretoria to exert influence and present itself as peacemaker. At the same time it could capitalise on the FRELIMO government's international recognition and prestige.

The Gorongosa documents and other evidence point to differences within the South African regime on the kind of tactics to deploy. But the same sources indicate high-level agreement over the central objective of achieving a South African-led political settlement between FRELIMO and the MNR. The Gorongosa documents record a meeting between South African Foreign Minister RF (Pik) Botha and an MNR delegation in September 1984. Also present were Defence Minister Magnus Malan and SADF chief, Constandt Viljoen. Botha told the MNR representatives that

> The fundamental objective of the RSA (is to) move the Soviets far from Southern Africa... Now the RSA is taking steps to...promote the distancing of Machel from Moscow, it seems that it is RENAMO which holds the key to peace in Mozambique... In recognising Machel as president of Mozambique, I am not demanding that you recognise the Mozambican government, but only Machel as president because it is he that is recognised internationally and you are not. The RSA does not have money to help RENAMO recuperate the economy if it wins the war... A cease-fire would benefit (the MNR). RENAMO would strengthen its position as a whole while that of FRELIMO would weaken. A cease-fire would mean the following for RENAMO: They would not be armed bandits. The international community would see you (RENAMO) in a good light... The investments being made would change the policies of Machel.[1]

At the regional level, South Africa saw Nkomati leading other states to enter into similar security agreements with Pretoria. This would immediately reduce support for the liberation struggle throughout the region. In the longer term, it would promote acceptance of Pretoria's hegemony by the other regional states, who would increasingly join South Africa in presenting a united front to the outside world.

At a wider international level, Pretoria planned to use Nkomati to break out of its international isolation, to claim recognition on the world stage as the de facto regional power in Southern Africa. External investors would then regard South Africa both as the regional power and as the natural route for channelling investments to all countries in the region. Foreign investment would flow in to boost South Africa's own crisis-ridden economy and South African firms would be guaranteed a stake in profitable ventures elsewhere in the region. Attempts by the Southern African Development Co-ordination Conference (SADCC) to reduce economic dependence on South Africa would also be thwarted.

Nkomati by mid-1985

By mid-1985, neither Mozambique nor South Africa had achieved the principal objectives they sought from Nkomati. The Pretoria regime continued to provide military support to the MNR and the Gorongosa documents, made public in September 1985, conclusively proved South African duplicity. As the Mozambican Security Minister pointed out, the documents provided evidence of a decision 'at the moment of signing the agreement not to observe it, but to maintain a climate of instability and war in the area'.[2]

If Mozambique failed to achieve its principal objective so did Pretoria. In many cases its position had worsened.

The internal struggle

Although Mozambique adhered rigorously to its side of the bargain and withheld transit facilities from ANC cadres, the armed struggle inside South Africa did not collapse. The first six months after Nkomati saw only a marginal decline in the number of sabotage and guerilla incidents. During 1985 there was a sharp increase. The number of actions in the period from January to mid-December was nearly three times the total for 1984 - 122 compared with 44 - and more than double the total for 1983. Moreover, ANC military strategy deepened from 'armed propaganda' to 'people's war'. An independent observer said the increase in armed actions in 1985 reflected a

> qualitative advance in (the ANC's) ability to conduct guerilla warfare... The attacks (had) been more extensive and show(ed) the ANC's increasing ability to operate from within the country... It (was) likely that most guerillas (were) based within SA and more attacks (were being) carried out by people who are trained here and have never left the country (*WM, 26.12.85*).

From the time of the September 1984 Vaal Triangle uprising it became widely recognised that there would be no solution to the crisis in South Africa without the ANC. A scramble of prominent personalities from the ranks of capital and even from some institutions of Afrikaner nationalism sought to meet with the ANC leadership, despite strictures from PW Botha about 'disloyalty'.

Relations with Mozambique

By late-1985, Pretoria's dream of a political settlement between FRELIMO and the MNR began to fade. Almost from the moment of signing the accord, Pretoria had made intense efforts to promote a negotiated settlement with the bandits. These reached a high point at the time of the October 1984 Pretoria declaration.

This four-point agreement signed by the FRELIMO government and the MNR declared that 'armed activity and conflict in Mozambique from whatever quarter must stop'; requested the South African government to 'consider playing a role in the implementation of this declaration'; and provided for the establishment of a commission 'to work towards an early implementation of this declaration'. The declaration also stated that 'Samora Moises Machel is acknowledged as the president of the People's Republic of Mozambique'.

Pretoria's strategists saw themselves on the point of making a breakthrough in which they would take a leading role in formulating and implementing the cease-fire and subsequent political accommodation. It was also anticipated that the SADF would be deployed in Mozambique. RF Botha told a press conference that

apart from monitoring a cease-fire, South African forces might be used in an emergency role to tackle socio-economic problems. This might include civic action programmes to help with agriculture, medical care, schooling and technical training.

The spectre of South Africa acting as 'peacemaker' in Mozambique would 'shake South Africa's enemies at the United Nations to the marrow', he said (*RDM*, 04.10.84).

However, the tripartite commission set up after the October declaration failed to produce a cease-fire let alone a political accommodation. FRELIMO indicated it was willing to discuss an amnesty to reintegrate MNR members into Mozambican society, but would not negotiate to share power with 'kidnappers, bandits and criminals' (*Herald* (Harare), 17.10.84). The MNR for its part, demanded all major ministerial posts in a provisional coalition government. It then reportedly almost agreed to a draft cease-fire agreement, and finally walked out of the commission on 17 October.

Pretoria was faced with a bleak situation. The Mozambican government was unwilling to accept coalition with the MNR, which in its turn refused to accept a relatively modest role in that coalition. Various subsequent attempts to resurrect cease-fire talks were unsuccessful.

Pretoria's failure to achieve a cease-fire agreement and to deliver the MNR, coupled with its increasingly evident duplicity, meant that it lost much of its credibility and potential influence. By June 1985 Mozambique no longer saw the Pretoria regime as acting in good faith to resolve the problem of armed banditry.

At a summit meeting in Harare, Presidents Machel and Nyerere and Prime Minister Mugabe discussed military support for Mozambique from Zimbabwe and Tanzania. This resulted in the joint Mozambique - Zimbabwe operation against MNR head-quarters at Gorongosa in August 1985. The documents captured at Gorongosa quashed any hopes, at least for the moment, that Pretoria would be an acceptable mediator in any negotiations with the MNR. When the evidence was presented to RF Botha in September, President Machel demanded the suspension of the Joint Security Commission set up by Nkomati, although the accord remains in force as far as Mozambique is concerned.

Regional relations

South African hopes withered at the regional level too. Nkomati did not lead other regional states to fall into line and enter into security agreements. This was despite intense pressure on a number of regional states, particularly in the period between Nkomati and PW Botha's trip to Europe in June 1984. Lesotho and Botswana were singled out, while Zimbabwe came under some pressure as well.

One of the notable features of this period was the resistance put up by these states. All refused to sign formal agreements, although they each reiterated that they would not permit liberation movements to operate from their territories.

The international level

There is no doubt that Nkomati offered South Africa a unique opportunity to enhance its standing among the major western powers. It made PW Botha's visit to Western Europe in June 1984 possible, an event which would have been inconceivable earlier. Botha's trip did not generate greater support among the peoples of the countries he visited, as the massive protest demonstrations showed. But he did achieve a significant initial breakthrough at the level of state officials and leading figures of Western European capitalism. The *Sunday Times* commented that

> Botha has cast himself in the only role open to him - not as the defender of apartheid nor as hesitant reformer, but as an African statesman, an earnest advocate of the nations which share the sub-continent with South Africa. This role would have been scarcely credible a bare six months ago. In these post-Nkomati days, however, not even the most hesitant European leader could fail to recognise Mr Botha's claim to the title, or the seriousness of his intentions (*ST*, 10.06.84).

By the end of August 1984 the Pretoria regime seemed so flushed with its own image that it directed its bid for recognition as the Southern African regional power at the superpowers, including the Soviet Union. In an important speech, headlined 'PW's new stand on working with the USSR', Botha attempted to define the forms of superpower involvement in the region. South Africa would not oppose the 'justifiable global interests' of the superpowers - including those in Southern Africa. In return the superpowers would not endanger South Africa's 'essential regional interests'. If the superpowers sought 'peace and prosperity' for Southern Africa, South Africa would not oppose their involvement and would even be prepared to co-operate.

The *Rand Daily Mail* saw this development as Pretoria's attempt to define the parameters of 'acceptable' links between regional states and the Soviet Union.

> Improved relations with Mozambique and the prospect of improved relations with Angola - both of which have close links with the Soviets - might have led the government to believe that the chances of including Soviet assistance in the economic redevelopment of Southern Africa are now strong (*RDM*, 01.09.84).

Pretoria had some limited success in its bid to make South Africa the natural route for capital investment during the initial post-Nkomati period. According to South African press reports, Portuguese businessmen showed great interest in tripartite ventures in Southern Africa, particularly Mozambique. These would involve Portuguese technicians in projects financed by Western European or North American concerns, and organised in association with South African firms or the South African subsidiaries of multinationals.

By the end of 1984, however, many of these earlier gains were being undermined. This was partly a result of the growing international perception of South Africa's duplicity over Nkomati. More fundamentally, it was a consequence of the deepening domestic crisis. By mid-1985 there was a massive 'loss of confidence' on the part of foreign capitalist investors, who saw the Botha regime as incapable of stabilising crisis-ridden South African capitalism. PW Botha's 'Rubicon speech' of August 1985 accelerated this trend as did the snowballing of the international disinvestment campaign.

South African regional policy in the post-accord phase

South African failure to capitalise on the accords profoundly affected state strategists' view of the regional environment. The Botha regime seems to have concluded that the time has passed when it could hope to break out of its international isolation by presenting a facade of good neighbourliness. Instead Pretoria judged it had little to lose by being seen to act more aggressively in the region. It seems to believe the level of sanctions will be determined more by the outside world's perceptions of domestic developments.

The regime's strategists still harbour their perception of the mass struggle, and particularly the armed struggle, as an externally-generated total onslaught. They believed continued armed activity after Nkomati had to do with alternative ANC infiltration routes. For example Professor Mike Hough, director of the Institute of Strategic Studies of the University of Pretoria, wrote in August 1985 that it was generally accepted that

the Nkomati agreement was a setback for ANC military actions in South Africa. Some ANC reactions suggested that they 'did not need' the frontline states to provide bases any more, and that 'internal bases' would be created in South Africa. It soon became clear however, that the ANC was attempting to establish alternative infiltration routes, primarily from Botswana, but also from Zimbabwe. And although the Nkomati agreement and the non-aggression treaty between Swaziland and South Africa resulted in a clampdown on ANC military activities in Mozambique and Swaziland, it did not imply that the ANC would not still attempt to use these two countries as transit routes to South Africa... Simultaneously, there are also indications of a larger ANC presence in Lesotho (*South African Foundation News*, 08.08.85, 11.08.85).

The shift towards a more aggressive stance may also be a consequence of growing military influence in government. The *Sunday Times* wrote after the important meeting of the State Security Council on 20 December that

> Hawks in the government - led by Defence Minister Magnus Malan - have in the past few months reportedly succeeded in swinging the pendulum back towards aggressive militarism in the Southern African region...(The) crucial State Security Council meeting (of 20 December) sealed what could become a new phase of regional militarism (*ST*, 22.12.85).

Objectives and instruments of current policy

At present the regime has defined two priorities for its regional policy. It has committed itself to striking decisively at the ANC and SWAPO presence in the region: plugging this perceived leaking sieve has become a South African preoccupation. Repeated allegations have been made against Botswana, Lesotho, Zimbabwe, Zambia, Angola and Mozambique: all are accused of permitting, or turning a blind eye to, the establishment of ANC bases on their territories. SADF raids were launched against Botswana (twice), Zimbabwe and Zambia. After the 19 May raids against Gaborone, Harare and Lusaka, PW Botha said that

> We will continue to strike against ANC base facilities in foreign countries in accordance with our legal right. We have only delivered the first instalment. We will certainly not be deterred by fanciful arguments that are being advanced here and abroad. South Africa has the capacity and the will to break the ANC. I give fair warning that we fully intend doing it (*Cit*, 22.05.86).

By mid-1986, death and kidnap squads, a regional variant of domestic vigilante gangs, were being deployed against alleged ANC members in 'friendly' states (Swaziland and post-coup Lesotho). At about the same time, South Africa claimed that ANC members in Maputo were responsible for a series of landmine explosions in the Eastern Transvaal (claims denied by both the ANC and

Mozambique). In early October, Defence Minister Magnus Malan said the SADF would permit no build up of 'revolutionary activity' in neighbouring states. This was followed by the announcement on 8 October of a ban on Mozambican migrant labour, two days after a landmine explosion in Kangwane had injured six SADF members.

There were other factors precipitating this ban: pressure by the frontline states on Malawi; and the US Congress's adoption of a sanctions bill. Nonetheless, there is no doubt that the ban was partly intended to pressure the Mozambican government to reduce, if not eliminate altogether, the ANC presence in Maputo.

By the end of the year South Africa became more open about its involvement in kidnappings and murders in neighbouring states, even those with whom it had signed non-aggression pacts. On the day of a meeting with Swazi Prime Minister Sotja Dlamini, Foreign Minister RF Botha told a television interviewer that he had known in advance of the raids which led to the deaths of two people (including a child aged five) and the abduction of Swazi and Swiss citizens in December. He approved of such actions and warned that they would continue.

South Africa's second regional policy priority has been to respond to the threat and reality of sanctions with coercive economic measures against regional states. 'Counter-sanctions' are intended to pressurise regional states into withdrawing support for sanctions and even into tacit support for Pretoria's campaign against sanctions. These threats are meant to support the assertion that the principal victims of sanctions will be black South Africans and neighbouring states.

Coercive economic measures against regional states are nothing new. Since the beginning of the 1980s at least, regional states have found themselves subjected to hold-ups of transit cargoes, delays in supplying essential commodities, manipulation of flows of migrant labour and customs union revenues, and even outright blockades. Pretoria's involvement in this kind of action belies its claims that it is opposed to all forms of sanctions. From mid-1985 plans were formulated to apply such measures as a specific response to international sanctions. By early August 1986 'senior South African sources' were quoted as saying Pretoria's reaction to sanctions would be 'graduated but potentially massive,...defensive and appropriate'. High on the priority list was a trade 'tit-for-tat' against neighbouring states. A new licensing regulation on Zimbabwean imports from

1 August was described as the 'opening shot' in the sanctions war. The 'second leg' would involve the repatriation of foreign 'refugees' and, if necessary, workers (*ST,* 03.08.86).

Other reports spoke of Pretoria distinguishing between different regional states. Some states (notably Swaziland and Lesotho) had explicitly opposed sanctions against Pretoria and could not be subjected to the same sorts of pressures as those which had vocally called for sanctions. More importantly, a number of regional states were to be used for sanctions breaking.

The press reported that Fred Bell, former executive general manager of Armscor, has been appointed to head a top secret 'sanctions-busting' operation. This would depend in part on 'facilities' in several regional states. In particular, Swaziland was being looked to as a possible base to 'launder' and re-document South African merchandise (*SStar,* 03.08.86).

At the same time, South Africa has decided to capitalise on its leverage against the SADCC countries arising from their dependence on South African ports and railways - a dependence created largely by the repeated sabotage of Mozambican facilities. As pressure for sanctions increased, Pretoria made it plain that it intended to use this leverage in its 'counter-sanctions' campaign. This was demonstrated by the hold-ups of Zimbabwean and Zambian traffic in August, and again in early October when Foreign Minister RF Botha threatened to respond to a US Congress vote for sanctions by blocking the trans-shipment of US grain to regional states. Pretoria wishes to prevent Mozambican ports from serving as an effective alternative.

The SADCC's January 1986 decision to rehabilitate the Beira Corridor to take an increased tonnage of SADCC cargo was thus seen as a threat. As the *Financial Mail* put it in August:

> There is...a real possibility that if Beira threatens to become a viable alternative, Pretoria will shift from economic warfare to the real thing, using its military power (or MNR surrogates) to disrupt the rail link and oil pipeline from Beira, on which Zimbabwe is so heavily dependent (*FM*, 15.08.86).

In the event the *Financial Mail's* prediction proved accurate. As rehabilitation work on the Beira Corridor advanced - faster than expected by many cynics in South Africa - bandit activity from Malawi was stepped up. Initially concentrated in Zambezia and Tete provinces, it was intended eventually to embrace the entire central region and cut the Beira Corridor. In December, MNR leader Alfonso Dhlakama acknowledged that this was a central objective, although he argued it was merely coincidental that it would benefit South Africa (*Star*, 16.12.86).

The regime's rhetoric speaks of it having taken 'the Israeli option' and not allowing diplomatic considerations or 'fanciful arguments' to stand in the way of its campaign to wipe out 'terrorism'. South Africa is open about support for at least one bandit movement operating against the government of a regional state - UNITA. It did not conceal its desire to see the overthrow of the Jonathan government in Lesotho (realised in the 20 January coup), nor its continuing ambition to bring about the downfall of the MPLA government in Angola.

Some of the rhetoric immediately preceding President Samora Machel's death suggests certain forces within the state had come to a similar conclusion about the FRELIMO government. The Mozambican president's death came at the time of a reported military build-up along the Mozambican border. At the very least President Machel's death in suspicious circumstances fuelled concern that assassinations of political leaders of 'difficult' regional states had become a part of South Africa's arsenal.

The current post-accord phase has seen a return to the familiar instruments deployed during earlier pre-accord phases of destabilisation. These include stepped-up military aid to UNITA and more direct SADF incursions into Angola; direct SADF raids against the capitals of three independent states; intensified bandit activity in Mozambique; the deployment of clandestine 'hit squads' in Swaziland and Lesotho; the imposition of restrictions on traffic from Zimbabwe and Zambia and a total blockade against Lesotho; and the expulsion of Mozambican migrant workers.

South Africa is also considering further punitive economic measures. These will possibly be applied in stages, depending on the progress of the sanctions campaign, as well as on regional and domestic developments. These 'economic disincentive levers' will probably include transport hold-ups and expulsions of migrant workers, withholding strategic supplies (food, oil and spare parts), manipulating the Southern African Customs Union and perhaps restricting regional investment by South African concerns. Border closures, transit traffic hold-ups and the manipulation of the ESCOM power supply to states drawing on the South African grid -

Mozambique and Lesotho - are other possible short-term tactics.

The limits and contradictions of regional militarism

However ominous these developments, regional militarism will not be without contradiction.

The regime's support base in monopoly capital is severely strained, and it can no longer mobilise unqualified support among monopoly capitalists for its political schemes. Opposition is inevitable when private sector economic interests might be adversely affected. This could blunt some of the economic disincentive levers. A new round of militaristic interventions will burden an economy already severely battered by the deepening crisis and recession. But previous suggestions that the economy would be unable to sustain a further militarisation have been dashed as military expenditure has increased without bringing down the economy.

The old adage that 'war is good for business' seems partially applicable to South African capitalism. According to Fred Bell, then executive vice-chair of Armscor, the Angolan and Mozambican 'peace initiatives' in 1984 had a traumatic effect on the South African arms industry. A number of state and private firms producing rifles, ammunition, shells and bombs were forced to close (*ST*, 08.12.85).

Nevertheless, there are signs that the costs of existing security force commitments are placing an increasing burden on the crisis-ridden economy. The cost of the war in Namibia has been steadily rising while mass action inside the country has led to the costly deployment of SADF troops in the townships, as well as to the announcement of a multi-million rand programme to increase police recruitment by 25%. This has taken place in an economy which has experienced four successive years of low or negative growth (*ST*, 27.10.85).

Notes

1   *Gorongosa Documents*, (extracts), (two volumes), Maputo, 30 September 1985; *Gorongosa Documents*, (extracts): '1984 Desk Diary', facsimile of handwritten entries in page marked 'September 1984 Week 39', translated by author.
2   Press Conference on Gorongosa Documents, Maputo, 30 September 1985.

Mozambique since the Nkomati Accord*

Jeremy Grest

When Mozambique signed the Nkomati Accord in March 1984, the Mozambican government believed this would provide the breathing space necessary to defeat the Mozambican Resistance Movement (MNR) militarily and start the process of reconstructing the country's severely damaged economy.

FRELIMO strategy in the 'accord phase' - from March 1984 until about September 1985 - assumed that the war with the MNR would wind down rapidly after the termination of South African support for the 'armed bandits'. But the 'Gorongosa diaries', found at MNR headquarters in 1985, marked a turning point for FRELIMO. The documents provided irrefutable evidence that South Africa continued to direct the MNR, and had never intended to honour the accord. Instead, Pretoria had tried to use Nkomati to force FRELIMO into an accommodation with the MNR.

FRELIMO did not renounce the accord, although the Gorongosa documents showed South Africa's leaders up as regional aggressors and aided the campaign to isolate the regime internationally. However, FRELIMO was forced to re-evaluate its assumptions

---

*   I would like to thank Rob Davies and Alan Whiteside for their comments on an earlier draft of this paper.

concerning the solution of Mozambique's military and economic problems. This re-evaluation was conducted in a context where Pretoria abandoned any pretence of 'peaceful co-existence' in the region and engaged in more overt military and economic destabilisation.

President Machel's death in October 1986 came at a time of rapidly escalating regional tension and robbed Mozambique and the frontline states of a leader whose clear-headedness was badly needed. That FRELIMO has survived the loss of such a leader at a time of grave crisis is an index of its strength and durability as a party.

International response as the war escalates

By late 1984 the MNR had carried the war to all ten provinces. It virtually paralysed economic life in the countryside with systematic attacks on transport and communications networks, schools, clinics and shops. In August 1985 FRELIMO captured the main MNR base at Gorongosa with the help of Zimbabwean troops. (The 'Gorongosa diaries', referred to more fully in Davies's article in this *Review* section, were found in this exercise.) But in early 1986 the MNR intensified its attacks in the central provinces of Sofala and Zambezia, capturing the Marromeu-Luabo sugar complexes on the Zambezi river, and a number of small towns. Mozambican armed forces were unable to hold the Gorongosa base and it had to be retaken with Zimbabwean help. By mid-1986 the war was going badly for FRELIMO in the Zambezi Valley, with the MNR increasingly based in and supplied from Malawi.

Mozambique's armed forces were hampered by lack of logistical back-up in the field. Soldiers have often faced the MNR without regular supplies and some sources have pointed to an almost total lack of military organisation. The armed forces total about 15 800 active personnel, of whom 10 500 are conscripts. Estimates of MNR strength go as high as 15 000 troops, of whom 6 000 may be trained.

Because of the growing MNR threat, Zimbabwe increased its troop commitment to Mozambique from around 1 500 in mid-1984 to 12 000 in 1985. Military duties expanded from guarding the Beira-Mutare oil pipeline and the road through Tete to Malawi to a more generalised combat role in support of FRELIMO. For a brief period, high-level ZANU officials expressed doubts about Zimbabwe's deepening involvement. But since it had made a strong commitment to the Beira Corridor project, Zimbabwe's leaders felt that in an era of sanctions and counter-sanctions, a presence in Mozambique was not simply an act of solidarity but necessary to defend Zimbabwe's vital strategic interests.

Malawi's expanded role in supporting the MNR had its roots in the close ties between elements of its ruling class and Portuguese interests before Mozambican independence. These groups helped create one of the MNR's components after independence. South African strategy was to use Malawi as a platform for attacks aimed at cutting Mozambique in two, and establishing a unified MNR permanently in Zambezia province. But a joint Mozambique-Malawi security commission has been set up in an attempt to ensure that Malawi is not used as a launching pad for the MNR, and that transport routes through Mozambique are opened.

In the 'accord phase' after Nkomati, when continued South African backing for the MNR was not fully evident, it became clearer that the MNR had an international support network with a strong European connection based in Portugal. This support enabled the MNR's external leadership to continue its propaganda and support activities as before. South Africa has expended much effort in creating a political profile for the MNR, presenting it as a legitimate internal resistance movement with popular support.

FRELIMO has offered surrendering MNR members amnesty. But it refuses to enter political negotiations with an organisation which, it argues, is externally led and backed, and seeks to establish neo-colonial social relations in Mozambique. The MNR lacks a popular base, but may have support in some areas by virtue of its physical control, and may benefit from peasant alienation from FRELIMO due to past neglect of family-based agriculture. The MNR 'declared war' on Zimbabwe in 1986, signalling the possibility of an extension of its operations to include that country.

Only South Africa gives the MNR public legitimacy. Internationally, it is widely regarded as a South African surrogate force likely to grow as South Africa becomes more aggressive in its regional destabilisation.

Tanzanian troops are actively involved in support of FRELIMO, and Julius Nyerere has committed Tanzania to providing rear bases for FRELIMO to continue its struggle should this become necessary.

United States policy towards Mozambique has shifted since Nkomati. Mozambique is now perceived as having a key role to play in creating stability in the region, and the US state department is un-equivocal in its view that the MNR is a South African-backed terrorist organisation. In November 1985 Mozambique's new relationship with the United States was formally cemented by President Machel's official visit to America.

As conflict in the region intensified after Nkomati, British policy shifted to the point that in 1986 it began to provide direct military support for Mozambique. It also supplies Mozambique with materials, and trains officers in Zimbabwe. A private British security company with Special Air Services (SAS) connections is now involved in training a rapid-reaction counter-insurgency force in Mozambique.

British and American policy changes are based on the failure of previous policies towards South Africa. These countries realised their long-term political and business interests were better served by strengthening ties with the rest of Africa and taking more seriously the goals of regional organisations like the Southern African Development Co-ordination Conference (SADCC). They also probably believe Mozambique is ripe for 'turning' away from socialism.

Nigeria has proposed a Pan-African force to help defend the region against South African aggression, and has been approached by Mozambique for defence aid.

Mozambique occupies a key position within the SADCC regional economic alliance by virtue of its transport routes to Zambia, Malawi and Zimbabwe. The war being fought by South Africa through the MNR is aimed at preventing the development of these routes as alternatives to dependence on South Africa. A second crucial MNR activity has been to disrupt Mozambique's economy in order to obstruct development and any attempts at a transition to socialism.

The war economy

Mozambique's economy has been placed on a war footing since it became apparent that the MNR was not going to 'wither away' after Nkomati. Defence expenditure in 1986 accounted for nearly 42% of the budget. In March 1986 the politbureau assumed direct control over the economy as it attempted to halt the economic and military decline. Between 1982 and 1985 Mozambique's gross social product declined by 33%, largely due to MNR activities but also due in part to serious shortcomings in economic management as well as the accumulated effects of the war against the Rhodesian regime. FRELIMO leaders have recognised that Mozambicans will have to survive in a state of war for as long as the apartheid regime exists, and have placed the battle against the MNR as a top priority.

FRELIMO economic strategy, involving centralised state planning and emphasis on large-scale capital intensive projects, was seriously questioned within the party in the 1980s as the costs, both economic and in terms of political support, became evident. At FRELIMO's fourth congress it was argued that Mozambique possessed neither the capital nor the skills for a forced march to socialism which appropriated a peasant surplus as a base for rapid industrialisation. The fourth congress marked a political and economic reorientation towards small projects using locally available raw materials: production was aimed at goods for local consumption, and policy shifted towards increased state support for peasant producers and private agriculture. But this came too late to reverse Mozambique's economic decline, an important factor in pushing FRELIMO into the Nkomati Accord.

Reorganising the bureaucracy

Since the fourth congress, FRELIMO has attempted to restructure the bureaucracy involved in economic management. Planning has been decentralised to district level, where it is supposed to relate more closely to economic realities. Key officials have been sent out of Maputo into the countryside to oversee the process. But Mozambique inherited an anarchic Portuguese bureaucratic style. This, blended with a post-colonial infusion of East European central planning methods, has created some intractable problems for FRELIMO.

The government has taken measures to make state enterprises accountable for their profitability. It has also introduced productivity incentives and penalties into employees' service conditions. At the same time it announced an austerity programme aimed at cutting government spending. Government has attempted to hold down spending on imports to limit the growth of its foreign debt, which at the end of 1986 was about US$3 000-million, owed mostly to governments rather than private banks. These debts are mainly soft loans sought over the last five years to compensate for loss of income caused through South African action.

In October 1985 Mozambique reached agreement with its creditors on debt rescheduling and will begin repayments, spread over 11 years, in 1990. In 1984 Mozambique, having signed the Lome III agreeement with the European Economic Community (EEC), joined the International Monetary Fund and the World Bank. These moves have brought the economy much more directly into the orbit of capitalism's major world financial institutions.

This reorganisation was accompanied by a move to open up the economy to foreign investment. The new 1984 Law on Foreign Investment was designed to provide the necessary incentives to attract foreign capital. And an office for the promotion of foreign investment has been opened, signalling Mozambique's serious purpose.

Foreign exchange allocations have been altered so that companies may now retain a proportion of their earnings for ordering supplies instead of submitting the total to the central bank and then requesting a reallocation. A related trend since Nkomati has been the channelling of US and West German aid and donations towards the private sector. Early in 1987 a new law on domestic investment was passed aimed at encouraging 'local business' and joint ventures with foreign capital.

The anticipated influx of investment from South Africa after Nkomati did not materialise, nor did Mozambique gain better terms in respect of revenues from transit traffic through Maputo, migrant labour, or tourism. South African Transport Services, in breach of a previous agreement with Mozambique, undercut Maputo's competitiveness with South African ports by offering special contract-rate discounts on goods which had historically travelled through Maputo.

In October 1986 the South African government implemented a threat to expel Mozambican workers from South Africa in retaliation against Mozambique's support for sanctions and alleged harbouring of ANC guerillas. The Chamber of Mines subsequently negotiated an amelioration of the original decision which will result in skilled workers keeping their jobs. But unemployment in southern Mozambique will still be aggravated, since the ban precludes recruitment of novices, and is designed to phase out Mozambican migrant labour. South Africa's use of its economic leverage over Mozambique has intensified since Nkomati, making Maputo a prime target of Pretoria's counter-sanctions.

In January 1987 the Mozambican metical was devalued by over 400% - from a little over 40 meticals to the US dollar down to 200 meticals to the dollar. This was an attempt to bring its official value, pegged against a basket of other foreign currencies, in line with its actual buying power. Since Nkomati the government has been attempting to re-establish control over trading circuits inside Mozambique, and to combat a black market which has grown so large that it has virtually displaced official circuits.

The metical is reported as trading on the black market at figures as low as one-fortieth of its official value. Given the extreme shortage of consumer goods and the low value of the metical, a form of barter economy has reasserted itself in large areas of the country. Peasant producers in particular have been reluctant to accept cash knowing there is little to be bought with it. The black market is so widespread that it could not operate without official connivance at fairly high levels. But in the periodic drives against the black market, only the smaller operators are usually netted.

The state has moved to deregulate prices of fresh produce in the main urban centres to provide greater incentives for producers. But many producers lack the transport necessary to bring goods to market directly, and rely on transport owners who are often themselves stallholders. In many cases stallholders have formed cartels, and trade at astronomical prices, ensuring profits from mark-up rather than turnover.

A wider range of consumer goods is available to those with access to foreign currency in special stores in the major urban areas. But neither peasants nor urban workers have benefited from the state's deregulation of markets. For them the new prices in the shops to which they have access are out of reach.

Urban workers' standard of living has been eroded over the last few years and the state is currently reviewing its wages and prices policy, including urban housing rentals.

The agricultural picture: war, food and famine

Although Mozambican agricultural policy underwent important shifts at the fourth congress, problems have remained intractable. They are aggravated by the continued war; drought; and in 1985 serious flooding of all major rivers. Agricultural production has dropped dramatically in recent years in war-torn sectors, but has stayed the same or in some cases improved where the security situation is better. Export crops such as cashew nuts, cotton, copra, tea, sugar and sisal have been particularly badly hit, resulting in substantial loss of foreign exchange earnings. This in turn has limited Mozambique's ability to import the fertilisers, pesticides, fuel and spares necessary to keep the export sector going. Crops produced for the internal market such as rice, maize and beans have also fallen in volume, but not to the same extent.

In September 1986 the government appealed to the international community for urgent food aid to avert famine facing almost four million Mozambicans. The natural disasters office reported that the three southern provinces of Maputo, Gaza and Inhambane were again suffering from severe drought. The situation in Maputo province was aggravated by banditry. The security situation in Gaza and Inhambane had improved, but further north in Manica, Sofala and Tete banditry was the determining factor in the emergency, although poor rainfall had affected parts of these provinces.

In December 1986 in Zambezia, Mozambique's richest agricultural province and major export earner, it was estimated that 1,5-million people were suffering from shortage of food and clothing due to South African aggression from Malawi. The MNR destroyed food stores, crippled the transport network by destroying trucks capable of moving food, and also caused less land to be cultivated.

Mozambique therefore faces a refugee problem of staggering proportions. Around 250 000 people have been displaced into Zambia, Zimbabwe, South Africa and Malawi. More than a million peasants have fled their homes for districts less beset by war, placing a further strain on the already-stretched capacity of the receiving areas.

Transport has become a serious bottleneck in relief operations. Apart from a shortage of trucks, fuel is extremely scarce and access roads have gone without maintenance for so long that many are impassable. Hunger-related deaths have been reported in Gaza, Inhambane and Tete, and malnutrition is rampant in much of the country.

Some fourth congress decisions on agriculture have been implemented. Further investment on large-scale projects and state farms has been curtailed, and the largest state farm in the Limpopo Valley has been broken up into ten separately managed farms of between 1 000 and 1 500 ha each. State farm managers have been made accountable for the economic performance of the units under their control, and credit facilities are being carefully monitored through the central bank. A certain amount of redistribution of under-utilised state farm land has also taken place with peasant co-operatives being the main beneficiaries.

The state has committed itself to providing more aid to the peasant sector, and to creating firmer links between co-operatives and the agricultural extension network based on the state farms. It has also acknowledged that part of the reason for the decline in marketed peasant output lies in its neglect of the rural trading circuits. It has raised producer prices on agricultural commodities and is giving attention to providing better access to the basic consumer goods needed by peasants to reproduce the household economy. The state is also turning its attention to improving the quality of locally produced hoes and other production tools. Low quality of tools has been a source of complaint in the past.

Where peasant production has recovered from drought and MNR activity, surpluses have been produced. These have not been marketed, partly because of transport and security problems and partly because of a lack of consumer goods on which peasants can spend their earnings. Greater attention has been paid to production of food in the 'green zones' around the major cities. Defence of these areas has meant increased amounts of fruit and vegetables available for consumption, but as mentioned earlier, their cost has been subject to speculative mediation by transporters and stallholders.

Much of the foreign aid formerly marked for state farms is now being redirected towards co-operatives and small private farmers, reinforcing the shifts in state policy since Nkomati.

The state's 1986 agricultural recovery programme aims to concentrate resources in priority areas of high agricultural potential. These are known as agrarian regions for integrated development. Within these regions state farms continue to occupy a central position. They produce for both the internal and export markets and organise a rural extension network for the peasant sector. Current agricultural strategy seems to reflect a compromise between the peasant line which emerged strongly at the fourth congress and the large projects favoured by sections of the party and the bureaucracy.

Attempts to boost industrial production

Industry in Mozambique has also been affected by the crisis in the countryside. In 1985 production was down to 42% of its 1981 level. This decline is largely the result of an acute shortage of foreign exchange needed for machinery, spare parts and raw materials. This in turn is a direct consequence of the drop in export crop production. The war has reduced supplies of agricultural produce to the processing industry, and has also disrupted mining activities.

In May 1985 the government announced a series of potentially far-reaching economic measures to boost production. Since food production by peasants and private farmers was a priority, consumer goods had to be made available to support the state's agricultural marketing campaigns. Current industrial policy aims to provide consumer goods for the rural population without using precious foreign exchange.

This policy encouraged the development of small-scale local industries using local resources to meet local needs. Much of the funding for this development came from non-government organisations. The government also aims to refurbish existing plant producing consumer goods, inputs for light industry and agricultural machinery and tools. Plant has become badly run-down due to lack of spares and maintenance. The World Bank has loaned $45-million for industrial rehabilitation to be spread over a number of industrial sectors producing consumer goods as well as the transport and agricultural sectors. The World Bank and the United Nations Development Programme are jointly sponsoring a major study of Mozambican industry which will have policy implications for future strategy.

The May 1985 measures were designed to intervene in the whole production circuit at the level of costs, prices, wages, taxes, bank credit, foreign exchange management and marketing. The government is aiming at greater efficiency in the state business sector and has placed more emphasis on management norms, which include defining responsibility, ensuring profitability and maintaining quality standards.

The state is redefining its role in the economy. Current strategy emphasises market-related performance by the state sector and encourages the growth of private capital in selected areas as a 'new economic policy' unfolds. The state is revising taxation norms to establish incentives for businesses producing food, basic consumer goods, construction materials and export products. Producer prices were raised on a range of agricultural commodities to stimulate production. This went together with a rise in consumer prices.

The Programme for Economic Recovery announced in January 1987 contains stiff austerity measures to reduce the budget deficit which stood at about US$250-million at the end of 1986. The aim is to balance the budget by 1990: the budgeted deficit for 1987 is 30-billion meticals. Those no longer needed in the civil service and workers in unproductive companies are to be relocated to productive work in the countryside as part of the programme. The secretariat of labour has been upgraded to a full ministry to carry through the rationalisations envisaged, and to deal with increasing unemployment as miners return from South Africa for the last time.

Strategic transport networks

The rehabilitation of Mozambique's transport networks is the government's second priority after agriculture. This assumes particular importance in the face of South African destabilisation and Mozambique's key position in the SADCC regional transport network. The ports of Maputo, Beira and Nacala are most important for the landlocked SADCC members and provide potential alternatives to dependence on the southern routes.

Transport routes have become a prime target for South African attack. This reflects its strategy to maintain regional economic dominance and prevent frontline states from disengaging economically and applying sanctions.

Since 1985 SADCC has made the Beira Corridor project its top priority. The aim is to maintain a strategic corridor from Beira to Mutare which will prevent the economic strangulation of Zimbabwe and Zambia. Having secured the road, railway and oil pipeline militarily, SADCC plans to upgrade the port and railway facilities to increase their carrying capacity and efficiency.

In 1985 Mozambique established the Beira Corridor authority to manage the project. The authority has substantial financial backing from the EEC, the Scandinavian countries, the USA and the GDR, as well as support from the Zimbabwean private sector. The ten-year plan outlined in April 1986 envisages construction of specialised handling facilities at the port, deepening of the port's channel and rehabilitation of the telecommunications and civil aviation network.

The corridor project is central to the SADCC's viability. The EEC, recognising its political importance in Southern Africa, is committed to the corridor project as part of a general shift in approach towards Southern African problems. A viable SADCC alternative poses a threat to South African transport dominance: keeping the corridor open will become a measure of SADCC's resolve and organisational capacity.

When MNR activity closed the Malawi-Nacala rail link, the frontline states pressurised Malawi to act against the MNR or face closure of its southern routes to South Africa through Tete and Zimbabwe. The combination of economic pressure and the military defeat of the MNR in Zambezia has made Malawi's rulers fall back into line with SADCC. There are also plans to reopen the Maputo-Zimbabwe rail link which has been closed to international traffic for the last three years by the war.

The war economy is FRELIMO's strategy for survival in the face of catastrophic economic decline brought about by South African aggression, natural disasters, the impact of the international economic environment and poor management. FRELIMO has begun to open the Mozambican economy to foreign investment and new forms of accumulation, as well as to reorganise the state economic apparatus in an attempt to halt the decline. This process has also signalled a new phase in the class struggle within Mozambique.

Party, state and people

FRELIMO's 1983 fourth congress was held as Mozambique's political and economic crisis deepened. Congress debates on the crisis were open and critical. Resolutions which emerged in response to pressure from the base signalled a shift back towards a 'mass line': greater emphasis on small-scale local initiatives and the peasant agricultural sector. Advocates of the large-scale, technocratic approach to planning and development were placed on the defensive politically as the congress resolutions redefined priorities and laid down the new boundaries for struggle within the party and the state.

Since the congress, FRELIMO strategy has been to strengthen party structures to facilitate better leadership in the time of crisis, and to reorganise the state apparatus for greater efficiency. Key FRELIMO officials were sent out of the capital to take charge of the provinces. Here they gained direct experience of daily conditions and saw the results of central government policy at first hand. The focus of these initiatives was a more effective war against the MNR and reviving peasant agriculture.

There have been several cabinet reshuffles since Nkomati. In June 1984 the internal affairs, security, and mineral affairs ministers were dismissed. No reasons were given at the time, but at the new incumbents' swearing-in ceremony Machel spoke about situations of illegality and injustice in state structures causing great damage to the economy. Powerful individuals were held responsible for the developments mentioned by Machel; and disciplining them was a potentially dangerous move as it threatened the cohesion of FRELIMO's politbureau.

In a politbureau reshuffle of May 1986 the minister of defence, Alberto Chipande, was brought back from Cabo Delgado where he had been sent as governor in 1983. Whilst there he had retained his portfolio but in practice President Machel had taken increasing charge of defence. Armando Guebuza, the interior minister dismissed in 1984, remained a member of the politbureau with responsibility for agriculture and food until January 1987 when he was made minister of transport, an important technical portfolio.

After the fourth congress, Planning Minister Mario Machungo was sent to Zambezia as governor where his experiments with peasant marketing were important in influencing FRELIMO to create partially free markets for certain produce. An economist by training, he had held the key portfolios of agriculture in 1978 and planning in 1980 and had been responsible for the implementation of the unsuccessful ten-year plan.

In July 1986 Machungo was appointed as Mozambique's first prime minister since independence. The post was designed to allow the president to concentrate on Mozambique's defence, while the prime minister took charge of the council of ministers, provincial governors and the state apparatus. Prime Minister Machungo was also placed in charge of economic policy.

President Machel's death in October 1986 was a severe blow to FRELIMO. The central committee chose Joaquim Chissano, the foreign minister, member of the politbureau and a founder member of FRELIMO, as his successor in a transition that was marked by its disciplined unity. His appointment reaffirms current FRELIMO policy and signifies the continued political dominance of the leadership team headed by Machel.

Chissano has reiterated FRELIMO's line on the MNR: there can be no compromises whatsoever in the struggle against the banditry used by South Africa as an instrument of regional destabilisation. He has also reaffirmed the currency and validity of the economic and social directives from the party's fourth congress, and is likely to pursue them vigorously as president.

The state apparatus is an arena of intensified struggle. Leadership and both local and foreign capital perceive the bureaucracy as too large, inefficient and unproductive to remain untouched by Mozambique's grave fiscal crisis. Both party leadership and local and international capital are closely scrutinising sectors of the economy under state jurisdiction. The state's partial withdrawal from economic management and the leadership's drive to re-establish conditions for accumulation on a market-oriented basis mean that the bureaucracy itself is a site of intensified struggles.

Current state strategy to encourage the growth of the 'private sector' follows a period of widespread black-market trading which saw some traders making large illegal speculative profits. In the countryside, war, drought and the collapse of trading circuits have combined to accelerate social differentiation. Countless peasants have been displaced from their land. Those who still have access to migrant employment are advantaged. In the south, goods and vehicles brought back by returning migrants have reinforced the position of wealthier families within peasant society. They have been able to grow and market a surplus independently of official trading circuits, thus benefiting from the high black-market prices paid for food crops, and have expanded their holdings.

The state's commitment to the 'family sector' in agriculture does not clearly distinguish between competing forms of production. In the 'green zones' around Maputo, production has increased dramatically in recent years in response to the state decontrolling consumer prices. Here there was a struggle between co-operatives and small capitalist farmers over access to land, with city officials favouring the latter as 'more efficient'.

Statements by party leadership on the 'class struggle' inside Mozambique refer to 'the people' standing with FRELIMO against foreign aggression, while 'reactionary elements' and 'infiltrators' who take advantage of current difficulties and attempt to recreate feudal society and revive tribalism, regionalism and racism. These developments have been facilitated, it is said, because FRELIMO has dropped its guard and its members have drifted away from their revolutionary traditions in work and lifestyle.

Official statements, understandably, do not elaborate on the internal balance of class forces, nor do they focus too deeply on contradictions between them, since the principal contradiction is still largely defined as being between 'the people' and imperialism and its local allies. At issue within FRELIMO is the development of a 'patriotic' political line will enable the war to be won, peasant support to be regained, and new conditions of accumulation based on an alliance of foreign capital, private capital and the state to be created.

At the level of political representation attempts have been made to broaden FRELIMO's support base. The people's assembly has been given greater weight, aiming to make it a more active organ of popular representation which exercises supervision over the state. At the July 1986 session the new prime minister presented an account of government activities for the first time ever.

National elections were held in Mozambique between August and December 1986. They were heralded as an opportunity to consolidate national unity in the face of MNR threats. The election was held in phases, and was supervised by a national elections commission, which organised brigades to run the process at the local level on the same basis as used in 1977.

Direct elections were held at local level where candidates presented themselves at mass meetings. District level and administrative post candidates were elected indirectly by electoral conferences, and provincial and national candidates were elected by secret ballot based on an approved list of candidates drawn up by FRELIMO's central committee. Individuals barred in 1977 from participating for being compromised through association with the colonial regime were permitted to participate.

Electoral meetings in rural areas were linked to drives to increase peasant production of cotton and cashew nuts. A feature of the elections was the rejection of candidates in various parts of the country on the grounds of corruption, most notably the mayors of Beira, Nacala and Quelimane. FRELIMO's ability to conclude elections under war conditions, and the level of participation achieved, reinforces an image of a party committed to broadening participation and strengthening support - and struggling successfully to achieve these aims - at a time of profound crisis.

The mass democratic organisations - the Organisation of Mozambican Women (OMM) and the Organisation of Mozambican Youth (OJM) - have been mobilised behind FRELIMO since Nkomati. An extraordinary conference of the OMM was held in November 1984, preceded by an intense period of mobilisation and discussion which revealed great potential for the organisation of women around gender-related issues. A study of Mozambican women drawn up during the preparation for the conference found that over 42% of women are economically active, and of these 97% are involved in agriculture. Apart from agricultural workers only 10% of the rest of the working population are women. However, some observers have argued that FRELIMO's stress on women's emancipation through participation in production has ignored the long-term question of transforming gender relations.

The OJM held its second conference in March 1986, more than eight years after it was founded. Much of the discussion revolved around the war and military service, with particular attention given to the poor logistics of the army. Irregular supplies of uniforms, food, equipment, wages and information were criticised, as well as corruption involving the diversion of military supplies onto the black market. The 'arbitrary recruitment' of young people found without proper identification documents was also a cause of dissatisfaction, as was the virtual absence of whites, people of Asian origin and of mixed race from the army. Women delegates asked why so few women were being drafted.

Commitment to a socialist future

In the three years since Nkomati, Mozambique has withstood the most sustained military attack ever launched by the MNR, and the tragic death of President Machel. Much of the population has been displaced by war and is facing starvation. Key sectors of the economy are in a virtual state of collapse, and future rehabilitation lies in mortgage with the World Bank and the International Monetary Fund.

Faced with these multiple crises FRELIMO is trying to win the war, reorganise its own structures and support base, and assert control over the crippled economy. The spread of the war in Mozambique has increasingly drawn in its neighbours, as it has become clear that Mozambique's security is vital for the frontline states in their attempt to withstand Pretoria's aggression.

Knowing that there will be war as long as apartheid survives, FRELIMO aims to contain the damage by strengthening its own defensive capacities and developing a Southern African strategy which increases pressure on Pretoria and raises the cost of its support for the MNR.

An important gain for FRELIMO since Nkomati has been the shift in the regional and international political climate. Western capitalist states have shown much greater interest and involvement in Mozambique's problems. Their search for an end to apartheid is leading to the development of a regional approach which leaves Mozambique far less isolated than before. Mozambique has successfully argued that the problem of the 'armed bandits' is in effect the problem of apartheid.

Mozambique's 'war economy' is designed to create the material base from which to win the battle with the MNR both militarily and politically. Increased production, greater efficiency, more support for peasants, greater foreign investment and private accumulation are all aimed at strengthening the economy and gaining support from key strata in the population.

FRELIMO is well aware that important battles have to be won in the countryside if it is to maintain its legitimacy as a ruling party. Strengthening political participation at all levels in society has been one of FRELIMO's most important weapons in the struggle to maintain cohesion and isolate the MNR.

FRELIMO remains committed to a socialist path, the precise form of which remains a matter for continuing struggles. Some of the contours have been sketched out above, although questions of sheer survival have become uppermost in this phase of Mozambique's history. Most of FRELIMO's energy and political ingenuity is currently aimed at creating a region without apartheid and war. If the programme for economic rehabilitation is effective, and the emerging Western regional strategy succeeds in creating more space for Mozambique to defend itself, then there is reason to hope that the corner has been turned.

The Lesotho Coup of 1986

Robert Edgar

'I myself believe that I am in firm, complete control. I have never in all my political career of more than 30 years been so accepted, not only within the (military) force, but within the country at large.'
- *Leabua Jonathan speaking to a group of journalists on 19 January 1986.*
'The Military Council of Lesotho under the direct command of Major General JM Lekhanya has taken over the affairs and administration of the country with His Majesty King Moshoeshoe II as head of state.'
- *announcement on Radio Lesotho on 20 January 1986*

The year 1986 opened with a major success for South Africa's destabilisation policies. On 1 January, Pretoria announced a clamp on border traffic with Lesotho until the Lesotho government moved to expel African National Congress activists. Almost three weeks later, the Lesotho Defence Force (LDF) staged a coup against Prime Minister Leabua Jonathan. This ended the 20-year rule of Lesotho's only head of state since independence, who had proved to be a major irritant to South Africa.

Because of the timing of the two events, many observers have concluded that they were not unconnected and that there was direct South African involvement in the military coup. While the extent and importance of South African interference in Lesotho's domestic affairs cannot be minimised, this interpretation is not borne out by the facts. For the coup resulted from a political conflict within Leabua Jonathan's Basotho National Party (BNP), which was brought to a head by the South African-generated border crisis.

Events leading up to the coup

Jonathan's deteriorating relationship with the South African government and the deepening splits within his ruling BNP were central to the events leading up to the coup. For some time Pretoria had put extensive pressures on the Lesotho government to neutralise the ANC presence. The border restrictions of January 1986 were one of these pressures. Others included a ban on British weapon shipments from passing through South Africa, sponsorship of the Lesotho Liberation Army (LLA), slowing down payments from the Southern African Customs Union, encouragement and money to political opposition parties such as the Basotho Democratic Alliance (BDA), a 1982 raid into Maseru that killed 42 people, and several border slowdowns in mid-1983.

The earlier border restrictions were trial runs to determine precisely which economic pressures would squeeze the Lesotho government most effectively. These mounting pressures kept Lesotho on the defensive and created a significant group of people inside and outside the government who believed that a confrontational policy with South Africa could only jeopardise Lesotho's precarious existence.

The second major problem facing Jonathan was the increasing factionalisation of his ruling elite. After almost 20 years of rule, the BNP was riven with internal schisms as factions tried to secure positions from which to operate when Jonathan finally left the scene. And Jonathan made few preparations for an orderly succession, which accentuated rivalries.

The key contest was between the Lesotho Defence Force and the BNP Youth League (YL). In recent years, the LDF's prestige declined markedly, largely because it was unable to deal effectively with the LLA's sporadic, but disruptive guerilla warfare. The YL on the other hand, had acquired power at the military's expense. Its leaders had immediate access to Jonathan and, most importantly, YL followers received arms and training from the North Koreans, who had been resident in Lesotho since diplomatic relations commenced in late 1983. Military officers suffered one humiliation after another and complained bitterly of their loss of status as the YL rapidly developed the potential of becoming a parallel military force.

The YL's power became evident in its confrontation with students at the National University of Lesotho. The university had long been one of the few centres of opposition to Jonathan's regime, and YL leaders saw it as a battleground where they could flex their new-found muscles.

In 1984, they backed a faction that took over the Students' Representative Council (SRC) in a disputed election. They also organised speakers and thugs to disrupt the campus. A counter-SRC group called the All-Academic Societies Federation was founded in March 1985. When a new academic year began in August, YL sympathisers made their presence felt by intimidating and beating up Federation members. The YL reign of terror reached epidemic proportions by October, and the Federation called a protest strike which was supported by virtually the whole student body.

The strike lasted for almost three weeks. Few student demands were met, but their defiance forced the YL to back off and leave the university alone after students went back to classes. However, YL power was clearly demonstrated during the confrontation. For instance, YL officials arrogantly issued deportation orders to some South African students without the knowledge of relevant government ministries. By comparison the authority of the military and the police was feeble.

Another indicator of YL influence was seen in the run up to the abortive elections called by Jonathan for September 1985. The first elections since Jonathan usurped power in 1970, they were designed to give him legitimacy in the eyes of the international community and to deflate internal criticism.

Election rules were weighted in favour of the BNP. Candidates had to lodge R1 000 deposits and bring 500 supporters to nomination meetings. Opposition supporters feared reprisals if they showed themselves openly at nomination, so their parties either denounced the election process from the outset or pulled out. In the end, only BNP candidates filed for nomination.

During the period before nomination day, Youth League members actively intimidated their opponents, especially inside the BNP. The YL was implicated in the killings of several BNP stalwarts in rural districts, who were replaced by YL candidates. After the election fiasco, the YL increased its influence even further by lobbying successfully to have some of its members appointed to a newly-created post in most government ministries, minister of state.

By the end of 1985, the Youth League triumvirate of Desmond Sixishe, minister of information; Francis Matholoane, minister of co-operatives and fisheries; and Vincent Makhele, foreign minister, had developed a considerable power base in Jonathan's government and were poised to take on the military. They called for the sacking of key military officers, including the LDF's commander, Major-General Justin M Lekhanya, and won over a group of disaffected officers. These included Lekhanya's deputy commander, Brigadier BM Ramotsekhoane, and Colonel Sehlabo Sehlabo.

The border crisis at the beginning of 1986 heightened Lesotho's domestic crisis and brought the inevitable confrontation to a head.

The build-up to 20 January

On 1 January 1986 the South African government imposed severe restrictions on the flow of goods and persons through border posts with Lesotho. The rationale for the border slowdown was the Lesotho government's unwillingness to clamp down on ANC activists who, South Africa claimed, were increasingly using Lesotho as a launching pad for bomb attacks inside South Africa. On 19 December 1985, South African soldiers had attacked several houses in Maseru, killing six ANC members and three Lesotho citizens. The South African government then demanded that Lesotho hand over ANC members named on a list prepared by Pretoria. The Lesotho government strongly denounced the raid and this may have contributed to Pretoria imposing the border restrictions.

The border clampdown was not total, but traffic slowed to a standstill as about one vehicle per hour was allowed through at each border post. Cars and trucks were subjected to extensive searches and some took several days to get across the border. The South African authorities did not explain why they were searching vehicles leaving South Africa when the declared aim was to prevent the infiltration of ANC cadres from Lesotho.

Some foodstuffs and goods did make it into Lesotho, but most trucks carrying perishable cargo turned back rather than wait. South African border guards did not allow key items such as hospital supplies and petrol to move across the border. Within a few days the Lesotho government had to restrict petrol sales to essential vehicles only.

Notably exempted from border restrictions were mineworkers, who travelled through on foot. This was a familiar pattern. In 1983, when similar border restrictions prevailed, mining houses successfully lobbied Pretoria not to hinder the flow of mine labour, and so this time there were no disruptions.

As the border restrictions began to bite, the leaders of five opposition parties decided to send a joint delegation to meet with Pik Botha in Pretoria on 10 January. These parties advocated a rapprochement with Pretoria and expressed sympathy for the pressures being exerted on Jonathan's regime. The delegation included CD Molapo, a former foreign minister in Jonathan's government, who led the Basotho Democratic Alliance, a party openly funded by Pretoria; Gerald Ramoreboli of the United Democratic Party, a former minister of justice; and BM Khaketla of the Marematlou Freedom Party. On the day after their return, Jonathan had them and several others detained.

The coup

Precisely when the military officers decided to make their move against Jonathan is not clear. Their coup was slow in developing and marked by indecision. At around mid-day on Wednesday, 15 January LDF units surrounded the prime minister's offices and the BNP headquarters. The sudden appearance of well-armed soldiers in downtown Maseru shocked many people, and contributed to a rumour that the 'Boers' had invaded the country.

Almost immediately panic set in and thousands of people and cars began streaming out of the capital. When the rumour hit outlying areas, some people responded with shock and resignation, while others began to take up crude weapons, sticks and stones to confront the enemy invasion.

Meanwhile LDF soldiers cleared government workers out of the prime minister's offices and took Jonathan to the king's palace. In front of King Moshoeshoe II they presented him with a set of demands. The first was that Jonathan should disarm and disband the Youth League. Jonathan prevaricated and asked that several of his colleagues, including Peete Peete, investigate LDF grievances and present a report.

On Friday, 17 January, LDF commander Lekhanya and a six-person delegation from the government set off for Pretoria to discuss the border crisis. The discussions achieved nothing. Neil van Heerden, deputy director-general of foreign affairs and spokesman for the South African team, which included officials from the military, intelligence and security police, reiterated South Africa's position that unless the Lesotho government expelled ANC activists, it would not lift the border restrictions.

In Lekhanya's absence, the showdown between the LDF and the YL began. The major confrontation took place on Friday afternoon at the main army barracks near Maseru where soldiers loyal to Lekhanya and those supporting the YL fought a fierce battle, with dozens of casualties. The Lekhanya faction won and they moved out to raid YL homes, arrest its leaders and confiscate arms caches.

On Saturday, the LDF attacked the home of a leading YL sympathiser in the military, Colonel Sehlabo, near Masianokeng about 10 kilometres southeast of Maseru. Sehlabo's men were routed in a shootout lasting much of the morning and early afternoon. Sehlabo was not present as he had already turned himself in to King Moshoeshoe.

By Saturday's end, the LDF contingents were firmly in control of the situation. They had not yet decided on Jonathan's fate, but it was increasingly obvious that they could not turn back.

In the meantime, Jonathan had gone to his Kolonyama home about 50 kilometres north of Maseru. From there he put up the appearance of being firmly in control. And there must have been an air of unreality when on Sunday afternoon he hosted a group of international journalists for a rare personal interview. He belaboured Western nations for abandoning Lesotho in the face of South African pressure and raised the possibility that he might appeal to socialist-bloc countries for assistance. He also berated his political opponents in Lesotho and contended that he had never been more popular in all his years in office.

That evening, LDF ringleaders met to decide their next move. Lekhanya, who had been closely associated with Jonathan all of his military career, was apparently still reluctant to topple him. His junior officers had no such loyalties, and said they were going ahead with the coup with or without Lekhanya's participation. He threw in his lot with them.

On the morning of 20 January, Radio Lesotho announced that a military council under the command of Lekhanya, and with the participation of King Moshoeshoe, had ousted Jonathan and taken control of the country. Almost immediately, jubilant crowds poured into the streets of Maseru, hailing the coup and feting the soldiers as liberators.

Because of the military's close identification with the man they overthrew, they were conscious of the need to broaden their appeal. One of the first steps was to give King Moshoeshoe a visible role, hoping that he could provide a symbol of national reconciliation and unity.

The king undoubtedly welcomed the turn of events since he had been relegated to a ceremonial function under Jonathan. On the day of the coup, he was seen driving without protection through the crowded streets of Maseru enjoying the celebrations. Whether the king had a direct hand in Jonathan's overthrow is still open to question. Two of his close relatives, Colonels Sekhobo and Thaabe Letsie, were among high-ranking military officers who masterminded the coup. While it is doubtful that he was an innocent bystander, there is no evidence to suggest that he actively plotted with the military to depose Jonathan.

Under the terms of the order suspending the old regime, Moshoeshoe was given the power to select a council of ministers drawn from long-time confidants and members of opposition parties. There was only one carry-over from Jonathan's cabinet: Evaristus Sekhonyana, who had been removed as foreign minister in 1984 after he advocated signing a security pact with South Africa. The military also took over four cabinet posts as well as creating a military council, which has had considerable say over government policy during the past year.

Post-coup developments

In the aftermath of the coup, many observers believed the new government would deal severely with leaders of the disbanded YL. Fuelling this view were reports that the YL had been planning its own ruthless coup and that some of Jonathan's cabinet had stolen millions from the treasury. Certainly the military showed no mercy to soldiers who had sided with the YL. Ramotsekoane and Sehlabo died in prison in early March, but YL leaders were initially let off fairly lightly. They were not brought to trial, although former ministers such as Matholoane, Sixishe and Makhele were periodically detained for questioning. But certain elements wanted the Youth Leaguers to be severely punished, and in mid-November, Makhele, Sixishe and their wives were abducted from a home in Roma and brutally murdered in the mountains.

Leabua Jonathan was rusticated to his Kolonyama farm. He and several of his associates did not stay inactive and the new government warned him on occasion to keep quiet and not hold meetings.

On 7 September he was placed under house arrest, but released on 23 September after challenging his detention order in court. He also gave frequent interviews to journalists and expressed his bitterness against his ousters. Jonathan attributed the coup to many things, but dissension within his own government was not one. He also called for democratic elections to prove his popularity. He may have longed for a return to the political arena, but he died of cancer in a Pretoria hospital in March 1987.

The South African connection

While South African footprints can be seen all around the coup, it would be a mistake to conclude that Pretoria engineered the military takeover. However, there is no question that since the coup the South African government has pressed home its advantage and has been able to develop a harmonious relationship with Lesotho's new leaders.

Immediately after the coup, Pretoria still had reservations about the character of the new regime, and continued border restrictions until ANC activists were expelled. It is likely that Jonathan would also have sacrificed some ANC members as he had done on previous occasions, but the zeal with which the new government acted against ANC (and PAC) members who were on a list produced by South Africa was extraordinary. About 50 people were rounded up, detained and then flown out of the country on Saturday 25 January. There was some question as to whether these people would be handed over to South Africa, but after a flurry of communications between the United Nations High Commission for Refugees, ANC headquarters, the Lesotho government and Pretoria, it was agreed that the ANC members would be airlifted to Lusaka on a chartered plane.

The expulsion of ANC members was overseen at the Leabua Jonathan Airport by members of the South African security police, who checked people in and photographed them, a procedure repeated in subsequent expulsions. A few hours after the ANC plane took off, the border restrictions were lifted and have not been reimposed.

The new cabinet includes a few individuals with progressive credentials such as Michael Sefali and Khalaki Sello. The presence of these people and King Moshoeshoe II's populist leanings have led some to believe that the new government would never really move into Pretoria's camp even if it did accommodate Pretoria in the short term. But it is apparent that the real power in the new government rests with the military and, in a number of ways, Lekhanya and his military council have tipped their hats decisively in Pretoria's direction.

They have continued with the expulsion of ANC members at South Africa's request. ANC members have been periodically rounded up and expelled on short notice. Some had lived in Lesotho for many years and had no chance to close down businesses or sell off possessions. There have also been rumours that the Lesotho government has signed a security accord with South Africa, but even if this is not so, the security arrangement between the two countries has been working effectively.

The new Lesotho government closely followed key elements of the South African propaganda line, including opposing disinvestment and economic sanctions. The American press reported that Lekhanya offered to visit Washington to add his voice to those opposing sanctions legislation. Lekhanya has also regularly attacked the National Union of Mineworkers, claiming that the union politicises Basotho mineworkers and arguing that mineworkers should not involve themselves in South African politics. This concern is probably related to continued South African threats to repatriate Basotho miners, who number more than 100 000. Lesotho citizens (including NUM president James Motlatsi) have been very active in NUM and mineworkers have historically been a key source of support for the opposition Basotho Congress Party.

Another disconcerting sign of close Pretoria-Maseru relations was the visit of Kaiser Matanzima, the former president (but still very much the kingpin) of the Transkei. Attending the funeral of a judge of the high court of Lesotho in May, he took the opportunity to meet with officials of the Lesotho government and was feted at a banquet attended by Lekhanya. The king was noticeably absent, sidelined by diplomatic influenza. Although Lesotho government sources claim that the talks were aimed at halting LLA units operating from Transkei, there is no question the Transkei government saw the meetings as an opportunity to open the possibility of diplomatic recognition. An invitation was extended to the king to pay a state visit to Umtata, but he has not accepted it.

In return for Lesotho's accommodating stance, South Africa has finally moved forward with the much-delayed Highlands water scheme. On 24 October Pik Botha travelled to Maseru to sign an agreement authorising the implementation of the $800-million project. It will bring much-needed water to industrial areas in South Africa and generate an estimated $100-million in income for Lesotho when it is built over the next decade.

Whether or not South Africa contributed to Jonathan's downfall, the 1986 Lesotho coup is a major triumph for South Africa's policy of regional destabilisation. A regime that had proved troublesomely independent was replaced by one more in line with South Africa's vision of regional co-operation. But because of Lesotho's unique geographical situation and her acute vulnerability to South African coercive measures, one cannot predict that what happened in Lesotho will be duplicated elsewhere.

South Africa has deftly wielded a wide range of economic and political pressures over a number of years to bring the Lesotho government to heel. South Africa has also been able to exploit long-standing political divisions and has offered its backing to virtually every Lesotho political group at some point in return for their promise to neutralise the ANC if they took power. And it has shown no hesitation - as in the case of the BPC/LLA - to drop clients when it sees a chance to cultivate a more promising relationship. At the beginning of 1986 South Africa seized on the opportunity to deepen the fissures within Jonathan's ruling clique. Rather than intervene directly in a Grenada-style invasion, Pretoria orchestrated an economic crisis which helped to bring the YL/LDF conflict to a head and made a coup possible. Pretoria could not pull strings to ensure that the new government would be to its liking, but it can be argued that South Africa prefers a government with a measure of legitimacy to a puppet regime. As one analyst, writing in Eduardo Mondlane University's 'Southern African Dossier', put it, this 'removes the necessity of having to provide the support that would probably be necessary to sustain unpopular, unrecognised puppet regimes in power'.

In the future, Lesotho may be allowed to follow an independent line on some issues unconnected to its relationship with South Africa. But as the events of 1986 have shown, the distinction between the Lekhanya regime and the 'independent bantustans' has become very fine.

Section 5: State Restructuring and Policy

Introduction: Ruling Groups and Reform in the Mid-1980s

Daryl Glaser

It may seem perverse in 1986 and early 1987 to write about the South African state's reform strategy. The country is under a nation-wide state of emergency; and government enthusiasm for further reforms appears to have waned considerably over the past year. Internal instability and growing international isolation have left South Africa's rulers looking increasingly directionless.

Nonetheless, it is premature to dismiss 'reforms' as a thing of the past or too insubstantial to warrant attention. The state is continuing, however unevenly, to restructure its institutions, policies and legitimating ideologies in ways that are, according to a certain definition, 'reformist'. Contributors to this section draw attention to initiatives of this kind in the fields of mass transport and housing, the informal sector, influx control, removals, residential segregation, and local and regional government.

The state, however bruised by the fractiousness of white politics, still has considerable support among the white population. It commands economic and military resources that outweigh those of domestic opponents and regional neighbours. This could allow it to buy enough time to restructure the terms of the confrontation between itself and its opponents and relaunch a more far-reaching restructuring programme at some future point when conditions are more favourable.

But there is little doubt that the pace of restructuring has slowed; much of its coherence and sense of purpose have been lost. Articles in this section also document the hesitations and enduring conservatism of the reform process.

Other papers, notably Hyslop's on the Afrikaanse Weerstandsbeweging (AWB) and Maré's on the KwaNatal Indaba, look at the reform process from a different direction. They explore the divisions and realignments Botha's limited reformism has generated in the white bloc and among bolder reformist groups outside the central state.

The articles in this section do not provide a comprehensive account of the politics of restructuring in the mid-1980s. But by examining evidence of both momentum and inertia in the reform enterprise, they help unravel a few of its complexities.

Depoliticising power

The state's awkward attempt to combine technocratic state intervention with a commitment to the 'free market' has been a signal feature of the Botha administration's reformism. It has a single overriding purpose: to depoliticise state interventions affecting the black population.

A number of contributions to this section illuminate the ways this concern is impinging on particular policy areas. Platzky notes the increasing use of racially neutral legislation to enforce 'orderly urbanisation'; McCaul discusses the ostensibly apolitical, technicist provisions proposed for regulating conflicts in the transport sector; Hendler and Parnell note the growing free-market rhetoric accompanying housing provision. But free-market language is more than simply a facade for interventionism in new forms. Concern to depoliticise the state's role also stems from a recognition that it cannot deliver goods to its black subjects on the scale necessary to co-opt them.

In these circumstances it makes sense for government to present provision of goods and services to the underprivileged as the responsibility of the private sector and impersonal market forces beyond the state's control. This is despite the fact that there is considerable resistance *within* the state to the market emphasis, especially among officials concerned with influx control. Contributions in this section of the *Review* provide concrete examples of actual or proposed state withdrawal from service provision and regulation.

Rogerson explains efforts to deregulate small business activity (with its potentially detrimental impact on worker health and safety); McCaul investigates state proposals for phasing out subsidies to users of mass transport; and Parnell and Hendler, suspicious of notions of state withdrawal, nonetheless note the privatisation of housing and the growing use of site-and-service schemes as opposed to state-provided dwellings. This trend is obscured by the counter-cyclical reflationary measures now in force: but these in no way alter the state's commitment to resolving an increasing proportion of future social welfare problems via the market.

Decentralisation

A central component of the depoliticisation drive is the state's goal of political and economic devolution. While earlier literature commenting on the state's 'Total Strategy' noted attempts to incorporate blacks in more effective local government organs, its main focus was the *centralisation* of power in organs like the executive branch and state security council. This has gone hand-in-hand with wide-ranging efforts to restructure and vest new administrative and planning functions in metropolitan and regional levels of the state. These are typically multiracial but non-elective bodies like regional services councils, provincial executive committees and regional liaison committees.

In certain respects these initiatives will centralise rather than decentralise: they devolve administrative functions rather than real powers. They will emasculate local municipalities. The central state will continue to appoint and regulate many of the new regional bodies. But they are also part of a serious central state attempt to offload the responsibility for contentious decisions about resource allocation onto regional and metropolitan organs. This, in theory at least, will depoliticise the role of the central state and decentralise conflict.

The significance of this trend is amplified by non-official reformist initiatives to draw blacks into multiracial regional settlements - witness the Kwazulu-Natal Indaba - and by the efforts in some reformist circles to promote the reorganisation of South

Africa into a federation or confederation based on semi-autonomous regional units.

Contributions to this section show how the state's concern to devolve functions to regional and local bodies is affecting specific policy areas. McCaul indicates that regional services councils will probably be handed responsibility for subsidising commuter fares and refereeing conflicts in the transport sector; Platzky warns of decentralised administration of influx control; Parnell and Hendler, as well as Rogerson, note the importance of local and regional bodies in shaping housing and transport policies on the ground.

The black middle class

Efforts by the ruling groups and dominant class to nurture and forge alliances with an emerging black middle class go back to the 1970s. Several papers in this section illustrate the state's continuing pursuit of this objective and shed light on some of the social strata that make up the amorphous middle class of urban blacks. Rogerson details official efforts to promote informal sector manufacturers and, to a lesser extent, street hawkers and shebeen owners. McCaul illustrates the state's belated but growing infatuation with black taxi entrepreneurs. Maré offers insights into the reformist politics of Natal's pro-Inkatha trading elite. And Hendler and Parnell discuss provisions for an upwardly mobile home-owning stratum in the townships.

Only Gottschalk's article begins to address the growing political significance of the black middle class. But key questions remain unexplored in this collection: How effectively and with whom have these middle strata forged alliances? How conservative or radical are they? To what extent are they buffeted by political storms beyond their control, as opposed to actively generating a distinctive or potentially hegemonic politics?

Insiders versus outsiders

Earlier critical writing on 'Total Strategy' exposed state attempts to nurture divisions between permanent urban 'insiders' and 'outsiders' - those without urban residential rights in 'white' South Africa. According to those accounts, 'insiders' would be granted more effective local government participation and a range of material privileges - job and occupational mobility, property rights, improved amenities

- while 'outsiders' would be consigned to political marginalisation and material deprivation in the bantustans. Quite clearly this was the purpose of the Riekert Commission's proposals, various subsequent administrative tightenings of influx control, and the notorious Koornhof Bills.

But the neat logic of this interpretation never quite captured the whole picture. Even while the Riekert-Koornhof offensive was underway, the state embarked on its most ambitious attempt ever to relocate industry to the periphery, including parts of the bantustans: the so-called Good Hope plan. While conceived, like industrial decentralisation programmes before it, as an extension of influx control, its implementation does not fit easily with the picture of bantustans deliberately consigned to permanent deprivation.

More importantly, earlier literature on restructuring over-estimated the degree of agreement within and between the state and capital over the trade-off between the co-option of insiders and exclusion of outsiders. By 1984-85 intense interdepartmental struggles, domestic and international political pressures, and signs of growing union strength despite a severe recession, produced a consensus around the opposite: the need to lift at least some influx control restrictions, allowing outsiders to settle in 'white' South Africa. By opening the floodgates to increased numbers of work-seekers, reformers hoped to silence the regime's local and overseas critics while undermining the bargaining strength of urban-based unions already hampered by high unemployment.

This influx will probably still be regulated by the Group Areas Act, as Pirie shows, and, as Platzky indicates, by a host of other legislation. Housing provision for the newly urbanised would largely take the form of site-and-service and self-help schemes, issues touched on by Hendler and Parnell.

Moreover, new urbanisation would as far as possible be channelled to deconcentration points - sites in the region of, but well away from, the metropolitan heartlands. It is increasingly towards these points that the Good Hope regional development plan seeks to direct new industrial job creation as well. By taking jobs to the newly urbanised in this way, McCaul argues, planners hope to reduce the long travelling times between work and home that currently bedevil long-distance commuting.

The present state approach to social restructuring does not so much abandon efforts to divide insiders from outsiders as attempt to redraw the boundaries between them and to change the terms of their relationship. Instead of a rigid insider-outsider division, the state is encouraging a diverse range of urbanisation patterns. The most 'inside' will be those legally resident in established formal black townships on the edge of white cities; the most 'outside' will be migrant-peasant households, the unemployed and those in resettlement camps deep in rural areas where recruiting of migrants is slower.

In between will fall a number of categories with different levels of privilege and access to rights and facilities: those in informal settlements in 'independent' bantustans (for example, Winterveld); those informally settled in 'self-governing' bantustans; those in formal townships in 'independent' bantustans (such as Mdantsane); those in similar townships in 'self-governing' bantustans (like Kwamashu); those in various 'deconcentrated' townships in the outer orbit of the main urban centres (Khayelitsha, Botshabelo, Ekangala); and those illegally clinging to sites closer to the urban cores (as in Soweto or the East Rand).

There is, as the architects of orderly urbanisation fully recognise, enormous potential for conflict and division between these various categories as they compete for scarce urban resources or struggle to defend positions of relative privilege against the more recently urbanised. Recent clashes at Crossroads and between Pondos and Zulus near Durban illustrate this new divide-and-rule danger.

Whither the reforms?

The remarkable scaling-down of government's commitment to and ambitions for reform since the Eminent Persons Group visit in May 1986 is consistent with its generally faltering and equivocal approach to change. Far from having a clear conclusion implicit in its origins or a linear forward momentum, the restructuring process has been marked by an ad hoc rhythm of forward leaps and backsliding, peaks and troughs.

The articles in this section attest that the reform process is currently in a trough. Reforms are being dropped from the agenda or are introduced inordinately slowly, amid a welter of qualifications and hedging. Pirie documents Pretoria's current schizophrenia about the Group Areas Act; Platzky the resurgence of old-style apartheid in forced removals; Rogerson the state's lack of decisiveness in cutting through the red tape binding some informal sector entrepreneurs; McCaul the state's vacillation between a pro- and an anti-black taxi stance. Hendler and Parnell stress the extent to which the own affairs-general affairs division is still influencing the provision of housing.

Why has the National Party leadership not been able to formulate and push through a more advanced programme of reform? Part of the answer is that it lacks the political imagination. Few of its members, even of its more advanced verligtes, envisage the salvation of South African capitalism through universal franchise and a unitary state. Most of the party remains wedded to 'power-sharing' and 'group self-determination'.

This may be because, as Hyslop concedes, the party has not become fully bourgeois. Supporting a universal and unitary franchise is not necessarily the litmus test of embourgeoisement. Such a solution is viewed even by most businessmen as a threat. But the NP's continuing racial and ethnic preoccupations do suggest it is still trapped to a surprising extent in the dynamics of Afrikaner political mobilisation.

This may be why, as Hyslop argues, the far right is able to exercise a continuing power by proxy. However successful the NP has been in winning English supporters (witness the 1983 referendum), and however seriously it takes the forging of alternative support bases in the black population, it continues to see a real threat in the defection of the party's Afrikaans support base to the far right. Until now that threat has been expressed mainly in electoral and parliamentary terms. But Hyslop's contribution on the AWB shows how the far right has also begun to acquire a sinister extra-parliamentary cutting edge.

It is not only the far right which exercises a degree of power by proxy. Extra-parliamentary, mainly black, political organisations - youth, student and pupil bodies, civic associations and trade unions - have demonstrated a remarkable capacity to veto state initiatives, especially those that affect the black community. The list of reform casualties in the 1980s is long: the South African Indian Council, black local authorities, the tricameral parliament, the National Statutory Council and others.

While such successful episodes of resistance do not challenge state power as such, they deliver massive setbacks to a regime more preoccupied with legitimacy than its predecessors. Popular resistance provides the backdrop to a number of articles in this section. McCaul discusses the politicisation of transport; Hendler and Parnell refer to the paralysis of black local government; Hyslop views the rise of the far right as a response in part to the growing assertiveness of the black majority; Platzky shows how the state has used forced removals to break the back of resistance in highly organised communities; and Maré documents the bitter struggles between black groups for the future of Natal and their impact on the KwaNatal initiative.

Faced with vetoes from the right and extra-parliamentary left, lukewarm imperialist backing for its reform efforts and a shrinking capacity to deliver material goods at home, the NP leadership has increasingly taken refuge in a strategy of repression. Against this backdrop, Pretoria's steady progress towards a capacity to manufacture nuclear weapons - illustrated in the Koeberg Alert article - assumes a particularly terrifying significance. It also exposes the responsibility of Western powers and multinationals for facilitating this regime's capacity to launch a Southern African holocaust.

Militarisation and repression have been constant companions of the South African state's top-down reform programme. But now, for the first time, they appear to have taken centre stage at the expense of reform. This may be a way of buying time. The government has clearly decided that further restructuring will be futile until it brings society under effective control once more.

Realignments and de-alignments

Growing numbers of establishment political forces, both inside and outside the state, are not only dissatisfied with the ruling party's pace of reform, but had, until recently, lost faith in its capacity to bring an acceptable measure of stability to the country.

The list of the disaffected is long, ranging from the 'New Nats' in the ruling party and cabinet, through various co-optees in black local government and the bantustans, to the Natal provincial administration. Outside the state (though in a period of corporatist representation, not entirely outside) is the most important of disaffected establishment forces: organised capital.

After big business enthusiastically backed the Botha regime in the late 1970s and early 1980s, and as late as November 1983 supported the tricameral constitution, the business-state honeymoon came unstuck. The agent was the hammer blows of township rebellion and its economic consequences: the declining rand, the debt standstill, disinvestment and low investor confidence. Sections of organised business began to breach what has suggestively been called the Carlton Contract - the 1979 agreement by business to leave constitutional restructuring in Pretoria's hands. After 1985 the Association of Chambers of Commerce and the Federated Chamber of Industries began to spell out their own constitutional proposals, and prominent businessmen visited the ANC in Lusaka.

In fact, business became directly involved in formulating constitutional models much earlier, but only at the regional level: the Kwazulu-Natal initiatives which began under capitalist sponsorship in 1980. More recently, with Pretoria's reformist fortunes declining and 'moderate' black leadership facing a growing challenge, business advocacy of KwaNatal has become much more up-front.

Maré explores these and connected issues in his contribution on Natal. The central issue in the Natal struggles, he suggests, is nothing less than the future economic direction of South Africa: capitalism or socialism, expressed in the showdown between the United Workers Union of South Africa and the Congress of South African Trade Unions, with business's money on the former.

Organised capital has not abandoned Botha - the most recent business-state têtc-à-tête in November 1986 proves as much - nor has it formulated a coherent alternative politics; it has little taste for an all-out battle with government. But it has begun to open up lines of communication, and thus explore the possibility of future deals, with as many social forces as possible. The possibility of a much more serious capitalist defection from the status quo, and its embracing of the ANC for instance, cannot be ruled out absolutely. But right now the politics of organised capital, though fluid and breaking fresh ground, remains cautious. Business is still investing money in the Worralls and Buthelezis and still wistfully hopes that Botha himself would give a bolder reformist lead.

Can South Africa be reformed?

One urgent question not directly addressed in this section is whether successful capitalist reform is possible in South Africa. Gottschalk's vivid polemic on the contradictory consequences of the ruling class's restructuring leads one to seriously doubt the capacity of the present regime to effect such reform.

But water flows quickly under the bridge in South Africa today. It is still not inconceivable that a substantially reconstituted (perhaps even predominantly black) reformist regime could at some stage reach an accommodation with the liberation movement that leaves the essential features of capitalism intact. Youth radicalisation, the UDF-COSATU rapprochement and ideological competition from the far left are pulling the liberation movement towards a more resolutely anti-capitalist stance. But other powerful forces - above all the awesome power of the state and its capacity to unleash genocidal destruction - may in time have the opposite effect. These questions have still to be addressed explicitly.

The Impact of the Ultra-Right on South African Politics

Jon Hyslop

An improbable figure strutted to the centre of South Africa's political stage in 1986: Eugene Terre'Blanche, leader of the Afrikaner Weerstandsbeweging (AWB). Terre'Blanche's rallies attracted thousands of white voters across the country. His followers broke up meetings conducted by National Party leaders, and the AWB and Conservative Party emerged as close allies. Paramilitary units organised by the AWB were a controversial issue and a threatening force; and the right-wing upsurge which Terre'Blanche symbolised became a threat to the National Party's reform strategy.

What accounts for the AWB's rise to prominence? What role has it played in the contemporary political crisis? How should it be politically characterised? And how important will its future role be?

The AWB's rise was the product of a conjunction of features in South Africa's political and economic crisis: the political fragmentation of the NP; government's shift toward a greater element of free market orientation in its policies, resulting in less state protection for the white working and lower-middle classes against black economic competition; the deteriorating economic position of the lower white social classes after the collapse of the 1980-81 boom; and the development of mass resistance to the existing social order in the townships.

These factors created a situation in which large numbers of white workers, small businesspeople and civil servants felt abandoned by their traditional NP leaders, and threatened by economic change and black insurgency. In these circumstances, they increasingly turned to the forces of the ultra-right.

During the 1940s, DF Malan's leadership reconstituted the Afrikaner nationalist movement as a populist alliance of white workers, the petty bourgeoisie and emergent capitalists. This alliance was cemented by a common commitment to checking the power of Anglo-South African economic dominance, and to countering the threat of job competition posed by black labour.

The alliance came to full flower during the 1950s, but by the 1960s problems had set in. The NP had been so successful in promoting the growth of Afrikaner capital that by the mid-1960s a powerful Afrikaner capitalist class had emerged. This class became increasingly influential within NP circles, tending to press for pragmatic modification of Verwoerdian apartheid doctrines in the interests of economic expansion.

By the end of the 1960s the few trivial moves which the Vorster leadership had made in this direction and the more bourgeois and less populist new style of the regime were alienating groups on the party's extreme right. This led to the breakaway of the Herstigte Nasionale Party (HNP) in 1969. But this party did not attract a great following, and for a long time remained a rightist gadfly on the rump of the Nationalist elephant.

The rise to power of PW Botha in 1978 marked a sharp shift in the NP's internal conflicts. Botha's policies sought to draw significant sections of the black population into a defence of the 'free market system'. This could only be accomplished by reducing the economic privileges of white workers and the lower-middle class, and allowing some blacks more access to the political system.

As a result the late 1970s and early 1980s saw a headlong retreat from job reservation, attempts to restructure local government and social services for blacks, acceptance by the state of the permanence of black urban populations and black trade unions, and a strong effort to strengthen the black business class. Politically, the process culminated in the attempt to incorporate coloureds and Indians in the new tricameral parliament.

The white populist alliance collapses

These departures from the NP's traditions of strict segregation, protection of white economic privilege and exclusion of blacks from national political processes precipitated another revolt of the faithful. The NP moved away from its traditional populist posture, following a path mapped out by the SADF's technocratic generals and Afrikaner big business. This led towards the creation of an authoritarian but deracialised capitalist social order.

When Andries Treurnicht and his supporters split from the NP and formed the Conservative Party (CP) in March 1982, they immediately drew the support of thousands of Afrikaner workers, minor civil servants and farmers who felt the NP had abandoned 'the white man'.

Since then there has been great erosion of NP support in these sectors, with the NP base remaining firm only among the urban middle strata of employees and professionals, as well as Cape agriculturalists and Afrikaner big capital. In the 1987 white election even the latter began to show dissatisfaction with the NP, but that was because many of them wanted a more reformist policy. Thus by 1982 DF Malan's great populist alliance had finally been torn in two. This generated the political crisis within Afrikanerdom which was the first condition of the AWB's emergence.

A second factor contributing to the rise of the far-right was the growth of free market and privatisation policies, logical corollaries of the NP's new direction. South Africa had rightly been described as a 'welfare state for whites'. Now the NP was to be the Thatcherite executioner of the welfare state which it had itself created.

For example, 1986 saw moves toward introduction of school fees in white state schools *(BD,* 18.11.86). The workplace became increasingly integrated as job reservation disappeared; the number of registered African apprentices increased more than eight times between 1981 and 1985,[1] while automation further undermined the traditional position of white artisans. Some inner-city areas which had previously been whites-only became 'grey', undermining the segregated housing market which had benefited less well-off whites.

Above all, the period since the 1981 boom saw the worst economic setback for white workers since the Great Depression. In 1981 there were just over 6 000 registered white unemployed;[2] by 1985 this figure had soared to over 25 000;[3] and by April 1986 it stood at over 32 000.[4] There were significant drops in the real wages earned by whites in mining and manufacturing between 1984 and 1985.[5] The recession also dealt a heavy blow to the position of white small businesses: the annual number of insolvencies rose nearly four times between 1981 and 1985.[6]

The political and ideological formation of the white working class and petty bourgeoisie over a century of industrialisation was largely structured by racist political leaderships and institutions; and the upheavals facing these classes coincided with the great challenges to the state from black township communities in 1984-86. So it was not surprising that those sectors of white society whose position was most dependent on institutional racism swung hard to the right.

Terre'Blanche's rise to prominence

Until 1984, Eugene Terre'Blanche had followed an obscure career on what were, even in South Africa, the outer fringes of ultra-right politics. A former policeman who subsequently became a farmer and part-time author, he founded the AWB in 1973. The organisation first came to public attention in 1979 when he led the tarring and feathering of a Pretoria academic who had dared to cast doubt on the sanctity of the Day of the Covenant. In 1982-83, Terre'Blanche and some of his followers were detained and charged with terrorism in connection with stockpiling of arms. He was found not guilty on the terrorism charge, but given a suspended sentence for illegal possession of weapons.

In 1984, however, the AWB started to become a more significant force. It was then that Carel Boshoff, the former Broederbond leader, engineered the formation of the Afrikaner Volkswag as a 'cultural' umbrella organisation uniting the Afrikaner far-right. The CP, HNP and AWB were all drawn in, and Terre'Blanche was able to play a dominant role in launching the organisation.[7] This allowed the AWB to move into the mainstream of Afrikaner politics, and to seize its moment when it came.

The ideology which Terre'Blanche puts across in his public pronouncements gives centrality to the concept of the Afrikaner volk (people/nation). The volk, he asserts, has the right to govern itself in an all-white state. Afrikaners should be able to exercise this self-determination in the 'old Boer republics' - the Transvaal, Orange Free State and Northern Natal. Other racial groups will have to find their future outside these areas. In Terre'Blanche's world view, Botha's reforms have led to the present political instability; only the AWB is capable of effectively putting down the ANC 'threat'.

Terre'Blanche rejects any form of parliamentary government - his volksstaat (people's state) would not contain any political parties, being based instead on representatives of occupations and professions in government, a scheme reminiscent of Mussolini's 'corporate state'. He denounces foreign investors, demanding that they be excluded from control of South African mineral resources (*VL*, 01.05.86; *Star*, 15.05.86; *Star*, 02.09.86).

Terre'Blanche's ideology thus differs considerably from that of the CP and HNP, which aim 'merely' for the restoration of the pre-

Botha apartheid order. The AWB position is not merely racist-populist, but essentially neo-Nazi. It emphasises the use of para-military forces in attaining power and crushing opposition; it centres on a messianic leader who will bring about a millenarian restructur-ing of society. It appeals to the disgust felt by its constituency for its existing situation, and includes demagogic attacks on party politics and big business. That the AWB has attracted the most militant of Botha's right-wing opponents is evidence of the depth of division within Afrikanerdom.

Strategically, Terre'Blanche has played an extremely shrewd game. He has, especially during 1986, promoted the image of the AWB through mass rallies, to which his spellbinding oratory draws thousands (*Star*, 26.04.86; *VL*, 01.05.86). Clever use is made of the symbolism of Afrikaner history, and especially the Boer War, on these occasions.

Defender of white against black and red

AWB influence on the broader right-wing movement is promoted through joint discussions and co-operation with the other far-right parties, and by widespread joint membership between the AWB and CP (*SStar*, 13.04.86). This allows the AWB to act as the hard edge of the far-right, with the CP its parliamentary face.

The AWB places great emphasis on building paramilitary units. This at once enables it to pose as the defender of whites against black and red 'threats', and to sow doubt about government's physical ability to defend white interests. During 1986 these units appeared to have been organised in two ways: there was the *Stormvalke*, a uniformed military corps of the AWB (*SStar*, 13.04.86), and the seemingly more broadly based *Brandwag*, supposedly defending white areas (*Cit*, 03.09.86). The AWB established 'citizens' councils' to recruit for the *Brandwag* (*FM*, 04.04.86). There were allegations that AWB units were engaged in vigilante activities. The AWB's hardline positions seem to have found a certain resonance in the police and the SADF, and there was evidently con-cern at cabinet level about AWB sympathisers in the police force (*Star*, 24-25.05.86; *FM*, 04.04.86).

Terre'Blanche was astute in the means he used to challenge NP leadership. During the first part of 1986 panic was spreading among whites about what then seemed to be government's inability to control township uprisings. The AWB chose this moment to attempt to disrupt NP political activity. In April an NP public meeting at Brits, at which Deputy Minister of Information Louis Nel was to have been the main speaker, was broken up by right-wingers led by the AWB (*Star,* 25.04.86; *Cit,* 25.04.86). A confrontation then shaped up over a May public meeting where Foreign Minister Pik Botha was to speak in Pietersburg. Despite the NP bringing in squads of bouncers to keep order, the meeting was successfully disrupted by Terre'Blanche's followers. For the first time police fired tear gas into a white crowd (*WM,* 23.05.86).

These actions seriously destabilised white politics: for a time it looked as if the NP would not be able to mount successful public meetings in its old Transvaal heartland. But imposition of the state of emergency in June 1986 rescued the NP, enabling it to answer far-right charges that it was responding softly to radical challenges. In October PW Botha restored the party's credibility somewhat in the Transvaal when he held a public rally in Potgietersrus behind a massive security screen (*Star,* 17.10.86). Nevertheless, the extent of the security precautions was a reminder of how the NP's confidence had been shaken.

The mark of the beast

AWB activity targeted issues which could be used to advance the claim that the NP was not defending white interests. One focus was on areas where they could exploit white fears that the government was backsliding on the segregation issue. For example in Krugersdorp, where residents of the new white suburb of Dan Pienaarville were anxious about the proximity of the black township of Munsieville, the AWB organised a petition for the removal of the township (*FM,* 04.04.86).

Another focus was the economic difficulties of poorer whites. The AWB involved itself in collecting and distributing food and clothes to poor white families (*Star,* 02.09.86). Culturally too, the AWB showed a keen grasp of what would strike a chord with its followers. It benefited from the growth of extreme evangelical Christian sects, many of which advanced interpretations of reality combining right-wing conspiracy theories with warnings of a coming apocalypse. So widespread were these ideas that the minister of finance felt constrained to deny in parliament that the electronic bar codes on supermarket goods were the Mark of the Beast mentioned in the bible's Book of Revelations (*Star,* 12.04.86).

Terre'Blanche taps directly into such thinking. The AWB's banner, he told a reporter, comprises three sevens, which counters the biblical 'number of the beast' - 666 (*Star*, 15.05.86). Thus the AWB brilliantly mobilises irrationalist popular ideologies for its own ends.

The AWB is a qualitatively different political movement from other currents within Afrikaner nationalism. The NP of the 1940s and 1950s and the HNP and CP of today are within a broadly populist tradition, mobilising supporters to take power through constitutional channels. Today's NP is an authoritarian technocratic party, expressing largely capitalist interests and gradually divesting itself of the baggage of its populist past.

The AWB differentiates itself from these traditions by its emphasis on mobilising physical force to smash its opponents as a strategy for taking power, and by the intense demagogy against capital and the party political system which it uses to draw support. In these ways it displays distinctively fascist political characteristics, placing it in the tradition of politics descended from the Ossewa Brandwag.

The distinction between that tradition and the more populist, legalist nationalist tradition is an important one. Those who want to argue that the NP is a 'fascist' formation are necessarily at a loss to explain how trade unions, a critical press, or scope for legal opposition organisations can exist under such a regime. In international perspective the AWB bears a strong resemblance to movements such as the National Front in France or the MSI in Italy, which managed to translate a message from the 1930s into a revival of the ultra-right in contemporary style.

In the 1987 white election campaign, Terre'Blanche further strengthened his credibility on the far-right by promoting himself and the AWB as 'honest brokers' trying to bring about unity between the divided CP and HNP. Policy differences between the CP and HNP are limited, involving such issues as whether Indians should have a 'homeland' (CP for, HNP against) and the role of Afrikaans in a right-ruled South Africa (the CP is for bilingualism, the HNP for Afrikaans as sole official language).

However, much deeper differences account for the extent of right-wing division. The HNP strongly resents the CP leaders who stayed in the NP for so long after the 1969 split; they are seen as having failed to oppose liberalisation of apartheid from its beginnings. Thus the HNP considers itself the historically legitimate leader of the whites.

Though no adequate data on the difference between the social bases of the HNP and CP are available, they are probably fairly distinct. Moves to liberalisation of apartheid threatened white workers through erosion of job reservation, before they threatened the economic and social position of the Afrikaner petty bourgeoisie and lower strata of salaried employees. The HNP has had links with prominent right-wing unionists since its inception. It is possible that white working-class interests have proportionately greater weight in the HNP than the CP. Ideologically the HNP seems more attached than the CP to parliamentary institutions within a racially exclusive democracy; the HNP shows far greater wariness of the AWB. Many on the far-right find the CP-HNP conflict frustrating, and the AWB has strengthened its position by advocating the need for the parties to overcome their squabbles and unite.

The AWB was able to act during 1986 as the cutting edge of the far-right, feeding into and reinforcing the growth of the more parliament-orientated CP. Through its violence and dynamism it has been able to dictate the pace of events to the other organisations of the far-right.

Access to political power

However, it is extremely unlikely that the movement can attain political power. While it can pull in the most hardened far-right militants, it seems that the white electorate's swing to the right will mainly take the form of the growth of electoral support for the CP, rather than the expansion of the AWB as an organised force. The best outcome that the AWB can with any degree of realism hope for is to become the junior partner in a CP government. But even this seems unlikely. It is improbable that the CP could raise sufficient support to take power in a general election. And constitutional restructuring may mean that the 1987 election was the last based on a purely white electorate; this again could prevent the CP from having its crack at power. Further, it is doubtful whether the authoritarian reformers of the SADF would countenance a Verwoerdian restoration. As for big business, it has shown more taste for negotiating with Tambo than with Terre'Blanche.

The CP, let alone the AWB, seems destined never to come to power. But that does not mean they cannot have a major political impact. The threat of the ultra-right has had an inhibiting effect on the NP's implementation of its reform strategy. NP leadership is torn between two considerations: on the one hand, it wants to implement a strategy of opening up 'free markets' and deracialising social institutions, but without any democratisation of national political power; on the other hand, it is concerned that the changes involved in this strategy will be too great for conservative white voters. The rise of the CP and the AWB have intensified NP concern about the latter point. As a result the pace of implementation of NP strategy has slowed. The far-right has played a 'spoiler' role: unable to take power itself, it has been able to exercise power by proxy, inhibiting the NP's scope to act to restructure society in the face of the political crisis.

The role of the ultra-right in establishing paramilitary and vigilante organisations poses a real threat to trade unions, community organisations and opposition activists. In the long term, a transition to a non-racial society will be made more difficult by groups prepared to use force to express their political disaffection. The case of the OAS in Algeria demonstrates how a small core of reactionaries can slow down the end of the old order and make far more costly in terms of lives.

The AWB's activities raise an important issue for those who look toward a non-racial future: the role of the white working class. Far-right organisations have been the only ones capable of articulating a politics to which white workers have responded. Given the extent to which all whites have benefited from the apartheid order, it is extremely difficult to get a hearing for a non-racial point of view amongst the broad mass of whites. Nevertheless, the white working class is a permanent feature of South African society: it will still be here even if the upper and middle classes leave en masse for Australia. A non-racial society will not be able to stabilise until it can learn to talk a political language to which white workers can respond.

Notes

1 Central Statistical Services (CSS), *South African Labour Statistics, 1986,* Pretoria, 1986, 3.2.3.
2 CSS, *Labour Statistics,* 2.6.1.
3 CSS, *Bulletin of Statistics, Quarter Ended September 1986,* Pretoria, 1986, 2.5.2.
4 CSS, *Bulletin,* 2.5.2.
5 CSS, *Labour Statistics,* 4.1.1.
6 CSS, *South African Statistics, 1986,* Pretoria, 1986, 15.23.
7 S Gastrow, *Who's Who in South African Politics,* Johannesburg, 1985.

Deconsecrating a Holy Cow: Reforming the Group Areas Act

Gordon Pirie

During its 36-year history the Group Areas Act, which dictates where people of different races may live and own or rent property in urban South Africa, has been subject to considerable criticism. But unlike the many amendments designed to strengthen the law, objections have generally been ineffective. By 1985 the rigidly, often inhumanely applied Group Areas Act had been used to confine coloured, Indian and white people to 1 700 or so racially exclusive residential areas. This racial zoning involved relocating upwards of half-a-million people, affecting coloureds and Indians particularly badly and leaving scars like Cape Town's District Six.

Against the background of accumulating resentment, frustration and guilt in South Africa, 1986 was exceptional for the hope it gave that the despised group areas legislation would be substantially modified, if not repealed altogether. Belief was widespread that scrapping both the Prohibition of Mixed Marriages Act and section 16 of the Immorality Act made changes in the Group Areas Act inevitable, if only to enable spouses of different races to live together in places of their own choice.

Alterations to the act affecting businesses[1] in 1985 made it plain that it could be changed without causing havoc. Indeed, midway through 1986 further legislative reforms were gazetted.[2] Restrictions on where black managers, executives and professionals could work were lifted; black and white students were allowed to share hostel accommodation without first obtaining permits; black domestic workers were no longer required to have separate entrances to their sleeping quarters and their own toilets. The Group Areas Act, along with the Separate Amenities, Slums and Housing Acts, was under scrutiny by the constitutional committee of the President's Council with a view to possible consolidation and revision. Under the Botha government this procedure had been established as the first step toward repealing apartheid legislation.

Government promises and denials

Government statements during 1986 raised expectations of group areas reform. At an international news conference in April, to announce the end of the pass laws and influx control, Constitutional Development and Planning Minister Chris Heunis remarked that he was not wedded to the Group Areas Act. And, though he later claimed to have been misrepresented, Heunis also reportedly told a National Party gathering that those who relied on group areas legislation to prevent miscegenation were 'not worth staying white' (*STrib*, 27.04.86). Also in April, State President PW Botha announced that the Act was 'no holy cow' (*ST*, 27.04.86).

Shortly afterwards, Botha spelled out a package of non-negotiable principles in a televised speech to the President's Council. Though he would not budge on protecting minorities and their cultures, he did not make any direct reference to the Group Areas Act as such, or to the principle of racial residential segregation (*WP*, 17.05.86). Later, the state president informed the NP federal congress that what flexibility there was in group areas legislation could be enhanced, enabling it to be applied 'with more understanding'. Though vague, Botha seemed to be opening the way for more compassionate treatment of blacks when it came to housing selection.

While he was prepared to allow housing market economics free rein in wealthier residential areas, he was anxious to protect poorer coloureds, Indians and whites by retaining some control over who was allowed to bid for homes in areas which blacks in general would find more affordable. Finally, it appeared that Botha intended to make it possible to apply group area restrictions to areas smaller than entire suburbs, for instance street blocks or individual blocks of flats (*Argus*, 15.08.86; *BD*, 02.10.86).

Reinforcing its declarations with several positive actions, government made it clear by the mid-1980s that it was becoming more sympathetic to requests from blacks that they not be consigned to remote and increasingly violent townships. Ninety percent of the 2 716 applications for exemption from group area restrictions during 1985 were granted (*CT*, 10.05.86), though between August 1985 and July 1986 only 280 applications were made, of which 40% were granted.[3] At least twice in 1986 government showed tacit approval of racially mixed areas. In March it announced that 20-year-old plans to turn Durban's mixed suburb of Clairwood into an industrial estate had finally been shelved. A single-race group area was not contemplated in its place, although property transactions between house-holders of different races were prohibited (*ST, Rapport,* 09.03.86). Subsequently, a government committee proposed that Indians as well as coloureds be allowed to live in a new township planned for Greytown in Natal (*ST,* 12.10.86).

Group areas prosecutions decline

During 1986 it appeared that the provincial attorneys general had been instructed to cease prosecutions for infringements of the Group Areas Act (*BD,* 03.09.86; *NW,* 04.09.86). This was in all probability a response to practical circumstances rather than a reform gesture. The sheer scale of racial integration in certain suburbs made it unlikely that all offenders could be brought to book. As the Conservative Party was quick to point out, by turning a blind eye to the estimated half-a-million blacks living in white-designated group areas, the Nationalists had made their own law look an ass (*SAO,* 29.06.86).

It was well known that inner-city districts such as Woodstock in Cape Town, and Hillbrow, Berea, Joubert Park, Doornfontein, Yeoville and Mayfair in Johannesburg, hosted thousands of blacks. In Hillbrow alone an estimated 40%, or 20 000, of inhabitants were black. An unknown but growing number of elite blacks were purchasing or occupying luxury homes along Durban's beachfront, in affluent Sandton near Johannesburg and in Constantia and Newlands in Cape Town (*DN,* 31.01.86; *Sow,* 15.05.86; *Argus,* 27.06.86; *Star,* 06.12.86). It was not only blacks as prominent as Archbishop Tutu who refused to apply for permission to live in white group areas (*Argus,* 06.05.86; *Star,* 04.09.86).

In addition to the bureaucratic and logistical difficulty of tracing and prosecuting the thousands of blacks contravening the Group Areas Act, the severe and inequitable housing problem also helped end prosecutions. As delegates heard at a conference on the future of group areas, the nation-wide shortage of houses in black townships totalled well over half-a-million, while there were approximately 37 000 vacant units in white areas (*BD,* 16.05.86). In the light of this, it was significant that in 1982 the supreme court had ruled that persons guilty of contravening the Group Areas Act could only be evicted if there was alternative accommodation available for them (*Cit*, 04.09.86).

Although there were encouraging signs about possible change in racial residential policy, it also became clear during 1986 that government was reluctant to grasp the nettle. For example, the three new black members of the Transvaal provincial executive committee were not automatically exempted from group area restrictions (*Star*, 04.07.86). And couples who had fallen foul of the Group Areas Act before prosecutions were officially ended were not reprieved. This was confirmed by convictions in the Cape areas of Maitland, Ysterplaat and Uitenhage, and in Roodepoort in the Transvaal (*Argus*, 25.07.86; *Rapport*, 12.10.86). Evictions continued, as in the case of four coloureds removed from a block of flats in Durban. In Graaff-Reinet an elderly Indian woman was forced to leave her home of 38 years, after being unable to renew her group areas exemption permit (*DN*, 31.10.86; *WP*, 20.09.86).

Adding to the atmosphere of intolerance, the powerlessness of the courts and public confusion, Heunis's deputy reminded estate agents and churches that in terms of the Group Areas Act, government could confiscate property acquired illegally or under false pretences (*Star*, *Cit*, 04.09.86). The state president made it plain that whereas he could conceive of the Group Areas Act becoming more humane, the principle of racial residential segregation was not about to be discarded. After telling the Cape NP congress in August that he thought Woodstock should become a coloured group area, an intransigent Botha reiterated that as long as he was in office, the Group Areas Act would remain on the statute book (*Afrik*, 24.06.86; *BD*, 02.10.86).

Pressure from press, business and political parties

Nonetheless, 1986 was a time of unprecedented activity and discussion about group areas legislation. Reflecting and in part shaping this, research by the press and other bodies found that experience of racial integration generated racial tolerance. Opinion polls were cited to show substantial and growing preference among blacks and whites for reform of group areas legislation, if not its abandonment (eg *Rapport*, 18.05.86, 24.08.86; *PN*, 02.10.86; *Cit*, 13.06.86; *Star*, 15.08.86, 14.11.86). Not all polls and surveys accorded, of course.

Catering for conservative tastes, one newspaper reminded its readers that in 1984 a scientific investigation had found that 77% of Afrikaners favoured retention of the Group Areas Act. The same mouthpiece trumpeted evidence, derived from two surveys, of a dramatic move away from preference for racial integration among Hillbrow residents. Unfortunately, the second survey sample was 16 times smaller than the original one, making the findings a trifle dubious. Finally, the right-wing South African Bureau for Racial Affairs (SABRA) reported anxiously on the anticipated geographical spread of Indian settlement (*Afrik,* 24.06.86, 08.10.86; *Pat,* 07.11.86).

In addition to presenting research findings, press headlines, reports, editorials and correspondence helped express a substantial body of opinion in favour of eliminating the scourge of group areas. In alternating outbursts of despair and encouragement, a profusion of stern leader-articles dismissed the Group Areas Act as 'irredeemably rotten' and a 'poisonous piece of misguided social engineering'. In its application of the act, the government was slated for its 'bungling, shortsightedness, prejudice, waste and greed on a grand scale in pursuance of sheer stupidity'. Its timid flirtation with residential desegregation was criticised as a 'heartless charade', a slide from a 'callous past to a burlesque present' (*Leader,* 07.03.86; *Argus,* 15.08.86; *NW,* 25.02.86; *ST,* 16.11.86).

Several cartoons (eg *NM,* 25.04.86; *PN,* 09.05.86) underlined the prominence of the group areas reform issue and highlighted the tragicomedy of the legislation. In a climate of putative reform, reports of absurdities and hurtful incidents were otherwise left to speak for themselves. A case in point involved an Indian woman who won a house in a competition but was obliged to accept money instead because the house was in a white group area. The practice of whites artificially inflating the asking price of their homes so as to exploit the coloured and Indian housing shortage was spotlighted (*Leader,* 07.03.86; *Star,* 28.10.86). There were also reports of unlawful building maintenance charges on illegal black tenants (*Star,* 15.05.86, 20.09.86; *Rapport,* 24.08.86). In a vicious circle, landlords of rent-controlled flats were disqualified from applying to the rent board for rent increases if the building accommodated blacks. Illegal black tenants on the other hand had no right to complain to the board about exploitation (*BD,* 04.09.86).

Finally, at a time when a moratorium on racially exclusive housing estates could have been expected, the creation of the first Indian townships in the Orange Free State at Harrismith, Virginia and Odendaalsrus was publicised (*Star*, 06.10.86; *FT*, 10.10.86). Confusingly, since the establishment of racially specific mass public housing schemes cannot be equated with housing desegregation, the press also feasted on white hostility to government proposals for black settlements next to white group areas. The announcement of new coloured townships near Umkomaas in Natal and Durbanville in the Cape, of extensions to the Katlehong African township near Germiston and of a second Soweto ('Norweto') north-west of prosperous Sandton rapidly galvanised protest (*ST*, 02.02.86; *Afrik*, 16.07.86; *Burg*, 08.10.86; *SStar*, 17.08.86).

The press was not alone in agitating for either revision or scrapping of racial residential zoning. Other prominent private sector establishments which followed suit were the South African Property Owners Association, the Institute of Estate Agents, the Trade Union Council of South Africa, the Association of Chambers of Commerce and the Dutch Reformed Mission Church (*ST*, 25.05.86, 23.10.86; *Cit*, 08.10.86; *Star*, 12.09.86, 23.10.86).

Knowing that the United States congress had stipulated repeal of group areas legislation as a precondition for lifting sanctions, business leaders also spoke out in favour of eradicating the Group Areas Act. They proposed to confront the state president on the issue at his November summit with them (*Star*, 30.10.86, 09.12.86; *PN*, 10.11.86). The Urban Foundation, emphasising the necessity for a rapid end to all discriminatory legislation, named group areas reform as 'the most critical issue facing business today', and urged that it be placed at the top of capital's 1987 agenda (*BD*, 21.11.86).

Nor were political parties tardy in pressing for eradication or modification of group areas legislation. The act came under repeated fire in the houses of assembly, delegates and representatives. In the house of delegates, where race zoning was dubbed 'legalised robbery', a member urged defiance of the law: 'to hell with group areas'. The act attracted continuous attention at Labour Party congresses during 1986, with the threat that failure to remove the legislation from the statutes would end the party's participation in the tricameral parliament (*WP*, 11.10.86; *Star*, 30.12.86).

In addition to clamouring for repeal of the act, the Progressive Federal Party launched a neighbourhood resistance campaign in Woodstock and spoke out against moves to establish yet another coloured group area to accommodate overflow from Pretoria's

Eersterus township (*Argus*, 10.10.86; *PN*, 24.10.86). The Transvaal secretary of the New Republic Party labelled the law 'morally indefensible', and at its Cape congress the NRP resolved to oppose the creation of any more group areas in the Peninsula.

If proceedings at its regional congresses are any guide, NP opinion was not entirely opposed to group area reform. Motions in favour of group areas were forthcoming from delegates to both the Free State and Cape gatherings. But delegates from the university town of Stellenbosch moved for the second year in succession that a more lenient policy be adopted towards racially mixed areas (*Cit*, *Afrik*, 24.09.86). Demonstrating that this attitude was not simply parochial, a number of letters and comments in the Afrikaans press expressed distaste for group areas (eg *Rapport*, 04.05.86; *OL*, 22.07.86; *Burg*, 07.09.86). Conversely, some letters in the English-language press rejected group areas reform on the grounds that the tranquillity of white suburbia would be shattered by overcrowding, vagrancy, discourteous street-corner businesses and disruptive recreation (eg *Star*, 15.08.86, 28.10.86, 29.11.86).

During 1986 conservatives to the right of the NP continued to be implacably opposed to changes to group areas policy, even if these were cosmetic. Much was made of government's hypocrisy, allowing importation of unrest into white areas, misleading voters and naivety about the extent to which extended families would live with couples exempted from group area restrictions.

Government was also criticised for inattention to white ratepayers' representations about black residential penetration into their suburbs. The favourite example was Mayfair/Homestead Park, Johannesburg, where white residents had for years been struggling to have the authorities expel unwelcome blacks (*Star*, 30.04.86; *Afrik*, 27.08.86, 01.10.86; *Pat*, 12.09.86).

The CP, playing on the same claims of neglect, accused the PFP MP for Hillbrow of being out of touch with his constituents' wishes. As evidence, the party collected 6 000 signatures from white residents who associated racial integration with high crime rates. The CP also announced that in the absence of effective policing in Hillbrow, it intended helping establish a residents' association to act against illegal tenants (*Cit*, 05.09.86; *Pat*, 03.10.86). Elsewhere, embittered whites resorted to racial harassment and ridicule. In Foreign Minister Botha's constituency, a Mauritian couple were taunted about their dress, called derogatory names, had their car tyres slashed and were confronted with an impaled pig's head (*Star*, 20.09.86).

Urban authorities urge practical reforms

By far the most acute political pressure for group areas reform came from local urban authorities. Beginning in March 1986, both the East London and Durban City Councils passed motions for change in race zoning. In East London the mayor's casting vote set the city on a collision course with government when the council determined unilaterally to open all residential areas to all races (*STrib*, 02.03.86; *EPost*, 04.03.86). As East London had no authority to implement its decision this was effectively a gesture of protest, but a significant one. In a political ploy involving less confrontation and more chance of success, the Durban City Council approved by a large majority a motion that government be requested to make available to all races a vacant stretch of land (block 'AK') near Greyville. Twenty years earlier Indian homes there had been bulldozed. Since then the city council was estimated to have lost R300-million in rates (*DN*, 03.03.86; *WM*, 13.03.86).

On the heels of these challenges to government, Pietermaritzburg voted to establish a non-racial suburb near Scottsville in an effort to relieve the shortage of 2 000 homes for Indians and 800 for coloureds (*NM*, 30.04.86). Later, the Sandton Town Council petitioned the state president to abolish the Group Areas Act (*BD*, 03.10.86). In another example of local government initiatives, Bloemfontein City Council gave permission for Indian factory owners at Botshabelo to live in Bloemfontein's white residential areas (*Cit*, 03.05.86).

Although it did not follow Durban or East London, as a local newspaper had suggested, the Kimberley City Council did respond to pressure from its coloured management committee and moved tentatively toward racial residential desegregation. It applied to have a portion of the town's 'white' west end proclaimed a coloured group area (*DFA*, 15.07.86, 10.11.86).

In Johannesburg the PFP almost obtained a majority city council vote to dump the Group Areas Act, but failed because it refused to accept the NRP's local option clause which would have allowed suburbs to practise racial exclusion if a third or more residents voted against desegregation (*Cit*, 23.10.86; *Star*, 23.10.86).

In other steps toward a more flexible approach to racial residential exclusion, the municipalities of Durban, East London, Port Elizabeth, Uitenhage and Sandton gave unqualified support to black people applying for government consent to live in areas of their choice (*WP,* 06.09.86; *DD,* 07.10.86; *NM,* 10.10.86; *Star,* 25.11.86). But not all local authorities conducted themselves similarly. In one notable instance, Zeerust Town Council responded to group area infringements by resolving to terminate water and electricity supplies to houses occupied illegally (*Afrik,* 10.09.86). And in Westville near Durban, the town council was unable to decide whether or not to approve an Indian professor's application for group areas exemption (*ST,* 15.06.86); the dilemma resolved itself on his appointment as South African ambassador to the European Economic Community.

Hopes for change dashed

Towards the end of a year of considerable activity around group areas legislation and implementation, a large part of the South African public eagerly awaited the recommendations of the President's Council enquiry into racial residential zoning. Leaks in August suggested that the constitutional committee was critical of racial curbs to the point of acknowledging that equal treatment was no longer possible in housing because whites had already availed themselves of the best ground and facilities. Indications were, however, that the report stopped short of advising complete elimination of the Group Areas Act. Instead, it was rumoured, town planning schemes and title deeds would become devices to regulate residential racial division in conjunction with the wishes of residents and property developers (*CT,* 22.08.86; *FM,* 29.08.86).

After some delay, the constitutional committee's recommendations on group areas were due to be tabled in the President's Council late in November 1986. In the end, however, the report was referred back to the constitutional committee for elaboration of awkward procedural issues. For one, there was doubt about how to entrench locally approved non-racialism so that subsequently elected municipal governments could not reverse it. Nor had it been decided how to avoid desegregating state schools and voters' rolls in racially mixed suburbs. Amid suspicion, disappointment and anger, which included threats by all opposition parties to withdraw from the NP-dominated President's Council, debate on the Group Areas Act was effectively postponed for six months. Since it was likely that the state president had ordered the delay, critics were quick to infer that government was playing for time with imminent by-elections and the 1987 white general election in mind (*SStar*, 05.10.86; *Cit*, 24.11.86; *WM*, 28.11.86). The time had passed when government might have confounded its critics and won votes away from the PFP-NRP by tackling the Group Areas Act boldly. Instead, it resorted to warding off right-wing gains at its expense.

Delayed reform to the Group Areas Act underlines the explosive ramifications which any meaningful change would have. There may be room for argument about the scale and geography of black residential relocation and its impact on property prices. But government has by implication conceded that in terms of its effect on educational and electoral policy alone, changing the Group Areas Act has implications which go far beyond the colouring of the residential quilt.

Although few in South Africa or elsewhere would agree with the SABRA chairman that residential desegregation would be tantamount to 'national suicide' (*Star*, 19.09.86), the Group Areas Act is undeniably a pillar of apartheid. The state president himself has said that the Group Areas Act is 'the cornerstone' of minority rights in South Africa (*DD*, 02.10.86), although he failed to define what he meant by 'rights'. Perhaps the president's statement is true insofar as these rights are conceived and exercised at present. But it is another question whether limiting housing options by legislation is the ideal or the only way of preserving minority entitlements, or whether privilege or equality acquired in that manner is worth treasuring.

Unwilling or unable to confront this issue, government may be expected to persist with its search for an ingenious constitutional escape from an imaginary conundrum. Since it hesitates actually to slaughter its holy cow, government's dilemma is first to yoke the bloated beast and then to eject it from apartheid's Augean stable without wrecking the entire edifice.

Notes

1 See G Pirie, 'More of a Blush than a Rash', *South African Review 3*, Johannesburg, 1986, 186-194. By July 1986 retail ownership in the main shopping precincts of 14 cities and towns had been desegregated and 80 further applications had been made (*FM*, 11.07.86).

2 *Government Gazette*, 10296, 27.06.86.

3 *Hansard*, questions and replies, col 2575, 05.09.86.

The State and the Informal Sector: A Case of Separate Development

Chris Rogerson

Promoting small business and upgrading the informal sector have generated an almost religious fervour among agents of the apartheid state during the 1980s. The introduction of a series of programmes to encourage or develop the small-scale informal sector in South Africa marks a remarkable volte-face from policy attitudes of a decade earlier.

Until at least 1976, both the national and local state considered the informal sector a social evil, a threat to public health or order and a blot on the urban landscape. Particularly in metropolitan areas, the growth of the informal sector was curbed by an impressive array of measures designed to preserve the facade of a modern city modelled on North American or Western European traditions. Amid the planned 'order' of the city beautiful, there was no place reserved for the common hawker, street barber, backyard industrialist or shebeener. Their operations were relegated to the darker nooks and crannies of South Africa's urban areas.

Under the new economic religion of Botha reformism, attitudes to the informal sector changed dramatically. Suddenly in the 1980s small-cale enterprise was to be tolerated if not actively promoted. One crucial event in the change was the 1981 launch of the Small

Business Development Corporation (SBDC), whose mandate was specifically to stimulate and assist the small entrepreneur.[1]

Further notable steps in upgrading the small-scale sector include the extension in 1982 of regional development incentives to small-scale industries;[2] the commitment in 1984 in a report of the National Manpower Commission to evolve 'a comprehensive policy to encourage small business enterprise;[3] and the state's acceptance in the White Paper on a Strategy for the Creation of Employment Opportunities that 'measures at any government level that might restrict the development of the formal and informal small business sector should, where at all possible, be relaxed'.[4]

The importance of developing the informal sector and small business was once again reaffirmed in both the 1985 President's Council report on a new urbanisation strategy for South Africa[5] and the subsequent 1986 White Paper on Urbanisation.[6] A host of other initiatives have been mounted over the past five years to 'normalise' or 'formalise' the position of certain informal sector operations, especially urban ones. These trends bear examination, as do the prospects for the state's designs for promoting the informal sector.

The informal sector in South Africa is far from homogeneous. It covers the economic spectrum from retail distribution, transport, personal services (such as child-minding, shoe-shining or hairdressing) and production, tothe lumpen-proletarian sphere of begging, scavenging, prostitution and crime.

Not surprisingly, concern to regularise and upgrade the informal sector is confined to that part of it which is deemed socially acceptable. Accordingly, our focus narrows to 'formalisation' developments in the three informal-sector niches increasingly viewed by the state as more or less acceptable: small-scale manufacturing; shebeens; and street trading.

Small-scale manufacturing

Programmes to generate new work opportunities in small-scale and informal-sector productive enterprises assume special significance against the background of recent trends towards de-industrialisation and the decline of large-scale formal sector manufacturing.[7]

Since 1981 employment in secondary industry has dropped alarmingly from a peak of 1,5-million jobs to a current total of 1,3-million, a loss of some 200 000 jobs. This sets formal sector manufacturing employment in South Africa back on a par with 1976. To foster an economic climate conducive to the blossoming of small-scale informal sector industry, the state has intervened both directly and indirectly.

One development with alarming implications for workers was the move in 1986 to accord wide powers to the state president to deregulate economic activity. It seems the competitiveness of small-scale industry in South Africa is to be assured by abolishing minimum standards for small firms with respect to wages, working hours, industrial safety and other conditions. Legislation such as the Temporary Removal of Restrictions on Economic Activities Bill will buttress efforts by the SBDC, the Urban Foundation (UF) and the bantustan development corporations, among others, to galvanise informal and small-scale industry.

The SBDC, UF and bantustan development agencies have been at the cutting edge of programmes to formalise existing informal sector or backyard manufacturers. Spearheading the drive to formalisation are offers of direct financial assistance, advisory services, and most important, the initiation of a series of new industrial park and factory flat developments ostensibly geared to the requirements of small-scale producers.

Geographically, the major efforts of the SBDC and UF have been directed at new industrial ventures in urban black townships inside the so-called common area. Examples are the establishment of industrial parks or factory flats in Soweto, Atteridgeville, Mamelodi, Katlehong and Kwazakhele. In the bantustans, SBDC initiatives at GaRankuwa, Mdantsane, Kwadabeka and Kwamakutha are undertaken only with the prior approval or co-operation of the relevant development corporation. The *raison d'être* of these industrial schemes is to afford space both for expansion of informal industrial enterprises operating in cramped backyard premises and to encourage new productive enterprises.

The schemes under the aegis of the SBDC and UF differ in certain striking respects. The SBDC perceives its role as principally to furnish pioneer industrial facilities in areas where these are lacking, so it concentrates mainly on construction of industrial parks and factory flats. These are rented to prospective township industrialists. Since 1982, however, the SBDC has permitted the gradual sale of factory premises to a few of its better-established manufacturers.

At the UF scheme in Katlehong the emphasis is exclusively on ownership rather than rental of factory premises. At the Batho Industrial Park in Mangaung a UF innovation enables producers to construct their own factories or workshops on an incremental self-help basis. Typical products at these township parks are clothing and knitwear, curtaining, furniture, tombstones and burglar-proofing, a mix of activities which mirrors the relative poverty of township markets. In the bantustans, a notable additional dimension is the emphasis on stimulating rural handicrafts as well as manufacture of school and nurses' uniforms.

Some insight into the workings, organisation and problems of formalising urban small-scale industry is afforded by studies conducted at the Orlando West estate in Soweto and at Katlehong. The Orlando West park hosts a typical collection of urban small-scale manufacturers, mainly producing clothing, furniture and metal goods. Most of these were clandestine backyard producers before the estate was established. Significantly, capital for their formalisation came almost exclusively from personal or family savings rather than from the SBDC, because of the high interest rates and restrictions associated with its loans. The workforce included both family labour and a high proportion of 'illegals', persons without legal residence in urban areas.

These enterprises commonly produced one-off custom-built items such as security fencing, or goods in small batches marketed through informal distribution channels (hawking) in the townships. The pattern of input linkages for production underlines the fact that these small-scale industries are not a separate economy divorced from the formal sector: inputs were procured mainly from wholesalers in Johannesburg.

A further highly significant finding: township manufacturers are not unsuccessful job-seekers; rather they tend to be relatively skilled, well-educated workers who voluntarily left their previous employers. Many new township industrialists, however, appear to become part of a network of relationships which binds them as sub-contractors to larger enterprises in white industrial areas.

This is exemplified by the case of one small industrial enterprise founded at Katlehong by a former employee of the United States multinational, 3M South Africa. During 1982 he was encouraged to start an 'independent' business enterprise at an industrial park to sub-contract for 3M, cutting and packaging certain of the company's products.

For this small enterprise, growth and capital accumulation depend crucially on paying employees on a piece-work basis and denying them the benefits secured by trade unions for workers in formal sector enterprises in the common area. Indeed, the history and operation of this particular enterprise may be indicative of the structures emerging in township industries as a result of the process of formalising small-scale industry and given new impetus by the march towards deregulation.

Shebeens

The shebeen trade provides an excellent example of an informal sector activity interlocking with the structures of the formal economy.[8] It would be wrong to view the typical township shebeener as an 'independent' business operator divorced from the formal economy. Since the end of liquor prohibition in August 1962, a network of linkages has evolved connecting the fortunes of South Africa's major brewing and distilling concerns with the humble township shebeen.

Because of the illegality of shebeens, these bonds were forged covertly. Nevertheless, as far back as 1972 liquor wholesalers were with state blessing fielding teams of full-time personnel to visit shebeens and promote their wares. Today the estimated 15 000 shebeens - the vast majority of which are still deemed illegal - are a crucial part of the distribution channels of corporations such as South African Breweries, Gilbeys Distillers and Stellenbosch Farmers' Wineries. Rough estimates suggest that the shebeen trade may account for as much as 40% of all liquor business in South Africa.[9]

In light of this, it is scarcely surprising that behind-the-scenes lobbying by liquor capital was critical in decriminalising shebeens and in the move towards legalising and formalising township taverns.

Starting to formalise shebeens was integral to the state's broader initiative to cultivate the support of a township petty bourgeoisie.[10] Between 1977 and 1980 a major enquiry was launched into liquor consumption and distribution in black residential areas, with a special focus on the possible legalisation of shebeens.

During this period, the country's largest liquor concerns openly supported formalisation. For example, in the wake of continuing police raids on shebeens and seizure of vehicles, goods and refrigerators, South African Breweries made an urgent appeal to the state in January 1980 for unconditional licensing of shebeens. But only in May 1980 did the state finally announce its acceptance of formalisation, opening up the prospect of the illegal shebeen being transformed into licensed township tavern.

Crossing the Rubicon from illegal shebeen to legal tavern is, however, fraught with difficulties. Procedures for shebeen licensing have proved highly complex and often contradictory. In contrast to the simplification and deregulation of small-scale manufacturing, a labyrinth of regulations and controls was put in the way of formalising shebeens. For aspirant taverners the major impediment to legalisation is the need to comply with a plethora of recommended minimum standards before a licence is finally issued.

For a township residential site to be rezoned for business purposes, the regulations require that living quarters be separated from the business area by a dividing wall. Other minimum standards include a lockable serving hatch between the kitchen and public area, separate toilet facilities for males and females, suitable storerooms for full and empty liquor containers and a two-metre wall around the perimeter of the site housing the tavern.

To satisfy what state officials describe as these 'practical and reasonable'[11] standards for tavern licensing, conversions costing at least R15 000 are needed, and this sum is way beyond the means of the vast majority of shebeeners. Not surprisingly, the major consequence of such lofty and restrictive requirements was that the number of shebeeners able to qualify for a tavern licence was severely curtailed.

The first step in obtaining licensing is to secure approval from the relevant black community council and the liquor board for a 'conditional authorisation' or 'provisional licence' to trade. But the reluctance or inability of some community councils to concede such approvals as well as the collapse of local authority structures in many townships is an impediment to the pace of conditional authorisation.

The next obstacle is the need for adequate assistance from financial institutions to enable the applicant to comply with the minimum standards required for the final granting of the tavern licence. Generally the provisional licence expires after 12 months, though extensions may be granted. Until 1985 the speed of formalisation could only be described as glacial.

There were energetic efforts by several liquor companies to help aspirant taverners navigate the complicated procedures and clear the legal fog which surrounds the lodging of licence applications. But the record of formalisation fell far short of state officials' wildly optimistic predictions that at least 50% of shebeens would eventually be legalised.

In Soweto, the official guinea-pig area for working out national shebeen licensing procedures, of an estimated 4 000 regularly operating shebeens less than 40 had received all the necessary rezoning clearances by 1985. Only three had met the strict conditions for dividing the drinking area from the licensee's residence.

During 1986 regulatory authorities displayed greater flexibility and willingness to assist in the change from shebeen to licensed tavern. The momentum of formalisation has undoubtedly picked up, with an estimated 300 conditional authorisations and some 200 full tavern licences granted nationally by the end of 1986.[12]

The new legal taverns are a far cry from the usual township shebeen which has existed for almost a century. A tavern often has specially constructed premises and fixed hours of trade, selling exclusively on a cash rather than credit basis and meeting strict age regulations governing the admittance of patrons. Above all, the new breed of legal taverns is distinguished most clearly by the fact that they are run by successful petty capitalists rather than financially struggling elements of the township working class. Indeed, the great bulk of shebeens remains untouched by the moves towards formalisation. They continue to function precariously and face police raids on their illegal businesses.

Street trading

Formalising street traders' activities has far closer parallels to the saga of shebeen licensing than to the open blandishments offered by the state to small-scale producers.[13]

Again, it is evident that street hawkers do not function as a separate economy; they remain inextricably woven into the broader economic fabric. For example, many street vendors operate as commission sellers or dependent outworkers for downtown city retailers, wholesalers or manufacturers of clothing, cosmetics or plastic goods. Indeed, striking advertisements that proclaim 'Attention Hawkers' or 'Hawker Specials' appear almost daily in the township press.

Despite the network of ties to formal sector enterprises, the street trading community has had considerable problems in securing rights to trade legally in urban areas. Because of objections to hawkers on grounds of 'unfair trading' or hygiene, in many urban areas (such as Johannesburg) authorities have sought to limit licences issued to some perceived 'optimum' level; in others (such as Port Elizabeth and East London) street traders were banned.

In common with the shebeen business, the hawkers' licence application procedure is extraordinarily and unnecessarily complicated, involving for example the need to advertise an application to trade in at least two newspapers in both official languages. The estimated cost of lodging applications and press advertisements is about R150 a year for an ordinary licence to trade as a hawker in Johannesburg.

Johannesburg appears to be the laboratory for experimental relaxation of the strict controls which traditionally suppressed widespread street trading in South African urban areas (*Star*, 27.07.84, 02.08.84). Johannesburg by-laws still provide for a defended space within which hawking is not permitted, and defended times when even licensed hawkers may not ply their trade. But slightly more tolerance and even limited promotion is emerging. One small but notable relaxation affected the archaic restrictions called the 'move-on' regulations, which required hawkers to move their pitch a set distance every 20 minutes.

Further improvements in Johannesburg hawkers' operating environment include introduction of four 'free hawking zones' where fixed stalls are provided for trading (*Star*, 12.12.86, 18.12.86). On offer at these hawker markets are a variety of goods such as fresh fruit and vegetables, paper bags and a range of soft goods. The SBDC in particular has offered active support for the experiment in formalising street trading by allocating fixed stalls in specially designated hawker areas.

That said, optimistic visions that today's street hawkers will become the shopowners of tomorrow must be tempered by the findings of several studies. These attest to the generally low returns on street trading because of its dependency on large formal sector businesses. In the final analysis, enthusiasm for the limited improvements offered to hawkers in Johannesburg must be offset by the fact that only a tiny fraction of the street trader community is allowed to participate in these schemes. Current developments in Johannesburg should not be interpreted as the foundations for a dramatic growth of street trading on the scale of many cities in Latin America, South

East Asia or West Africa. There is only a marginal shift towards formalising street trading. Undoubtedly, in 1986 the planners and gatekeepers of South Africa's major metropolitan areas still retained a general bias against street hawkers as 'acceptable' constituents of the urban fabric.

Policy overview

In examining current state attitudes and policies towards the informal sector it is evident that there is a long way to go toward genuine and widespread promotion of the informal sector.[14] At best, the situation reflects a new attitude of grudging tolerance toward limited informal sector enterprise, rather than wholehearted implementation of a set of promotional policies. A tradition of repression of the informal economy remains deeply rooted in various levels of the state apparatus. Advances to formalisation have been markedly uneven across the spectrum of the informal sector, perhaps mirroring the varying degrees of 'social acceptability' of the different segments.

Not surprisingly, given falling rates of employment in formal manufacturing, small-scale informal production has been especially favoured. Under pressure from liquor capital, however, lukewarm approval has been accorded to shebeen formalisation. There has been least progress in the social acceptance and promotion of the common street hawker, who is still widely perceived as antithetical to a 'modern' urban environment in South Africa.

There are certain contradictions in state policy towards the array of activities that comprise the informal economy. Most notably, the move towards deregulation of small-scale manufacturing has not been paralleled in the cases of hawking and shebeening. The latter is distinguished by a new bureaucratic morass militating against rather than promoting formalisation.

Nonetheless, the general direction of state policy towards the development of the 'separate' informal sector is beginning to crystallise. The informal sector is increasingly perceived not as a problem but as a possible element in the solution to the contemporary economic crisis engulfing the state.

For the foreseeable future, formulation of strategies for upgrading elements of the informal sector will remain high on the policy agenda of the apartheid state. Accordingly, it is essential that progressive organisations and the trade union movement reflect carefully on their responses to the state's initiatives towards the separate development of the informal sector.

Notes

1 Small Business Development Corporation, *SBDC Activities: a Five Year Review, 1981-1986,* Johannesburg, Small Business Development Corporation, 1986.
2 Republic of South Africa, *The Promotion of the Development of Small Industries as an Element of a Co-ordinated Regional Development Strategy for South Africa,* 1984.
3 Republic of South Africa, *Report of the National Manpower Commission on Investigations into the Small Business Sector in the Republic of South Africa, with Specific Reference to the Factors that may Retard the Growth and Development Thereof,* 1984, 1.
4 Republic of South Africa, *White Paper on a Strategy for the Creation of Employment Opportunities in the Republic of South Africa,* 1984, 10.
5 Republic of South Africa, *Report of the Committee for Constitutional Affairs of the President's Council on an Urbanisation Strategy for the Republic of South Africa,* 1985.
6 Republic of South Africa, *White Paper on Urbanisation, 1981.*
7 The discussion on small-scale manufacturing draws upon the following sources: HM Jagoe, 'A Study of the Operating Features and Problems Relating to the Formal Manufacturing Sector in Soweto', unpublished MBA dissertation, University of the Witwatersrand, 1984; AW van der Willigen, 'Marketing as a Limiting Factor in the Growth Potential of Urban Black Industries', unpublished MBA dissertation, University of the Witwatersrand, 1984; A Black and J Stanwix, 'Crisis and Restructuring in the South African Manufacturing Sector', paper presented at the Workshop on Macroeconomic Policy and Poverty in South Africa, Cape Town, August 1986; CM Rogerson and M da Silva, 'From Backyard Manufacture to Factory Flat: The Industrialisation of South Africa's Black Townships', paper presented to the International Geographical Union Commission on Industrial Change Conference, Madrid, August 1986; and M da Silva, 'Small-scale Industry in Black South Africa', unpublished MA dissertation, University of the Witwatersrand, 1987.
8 Discussions of recent developments in the shebeen trade draw upon the following material: W Scharf, 'The Impact of Liquor on the Working Class (with particular focus on the Western Cape): the implications of the structure of the liquor industry and the role of the state in this regard', unpublished MSocSci thesis, University of Cape Town, 1984; W Scharf, 'Liquor, the State and Urban Blacks', in D Davis and M Slabbert (eds), *Crime and Power in South Africa,* Cape Town, 1985, 48-59; CM Rogerson and DM Hart, 'The Survival of the "Informal sector": The Shebeens of Black Johannesburg', *GeoJournal,* 12, 1986, 153-166; CM Rogerson, 'Consumerism, the State and the Informal Sector: The Formalisation of Shebeens in South Africa's Black Townships', paper presented at the International Geographi-

cal Union Working Group on Urbanisation in Developing Countries, Madrid, August 1986; and various issues of *eSpotini*.

9   Data on numbers of shebeens and their share of the liquor trade are drawn from J Gordin, 'The Illicit Sector', in M Fridjhon and A Murray, *Conspiracy of Giants: The South African Liquor Industry*, Johannesburg, 1986, 271-272.

10 A good introduction to the state's cultivation of an urban African petty bourgeoisie is provided by P Hudson and M Sarakinsky, 'Class Interests and Politics: The Case of the Urban African Bourgeoisie', in *South African Review 3*, Johannesburg, 1986, 169-185.

11 RWJ Simpson, 'The Origin and Future of the Shebeen', *Fidelitas*, July-August 1984, 28-29.

12 Personal communication with Lucky Michaels of the National Taverners Association, 26.01.87.

13 Material on street trading is discussed in detail in KSO Beavon and CM Rogerson, 'The "Informal Sector" of the Apartheid City: The Pavement People of Johannesburg', in DM Smith (ed), *Living Under Apartheid: Aspects of Urbanisation and Social Change in South Africa*, London, 1982, 106-123; RE Tomaselli, 'The Indian Flower Sellers of Johannesburg', unpublished MA dissertation, University of the Witwatersrand, 1983; KSO Beavon and CM Rogerson, 'Aspects of Hawking in the Central Business District of Johannesburg', *Proceedings, Geographical Association of Zimbabwe*, 15, 31-45, 1984; and RE Tomaselli and KSO Beavon, 'Johannesburg's Indian Flower Sellers: Class and Circumstance', *GeoJournal*, 12, 1986, 181-189.

14 Suggestions for promotion of urban small-scale enterprise are discussed in CM Rogerson, 'Late Apartheid and the Urban Informal Sector', paper presented to the Southern African Economy After Apartheid Conference, Centre for Southern African Studies, University of York, September--October 1986.

Land and Finance under the New Housing Dispensation

Paul Hendler and Sue Parnell

Throughout the 1980s the question of who pays for residential shelter has become increasingly charged as a theme of social change in South Africa. Common problems in the provision of housing, both by the public and, to a lesser extent, the private sector, are insufficient land and allocation of finance. This discussion will attempt to define the trends in land-use patterns, and public and private financing of housing, which have determined the housing experiences of the segregated working-class populations.

To approach housing from a standpoint which cuts across colour-divides is not to deny the real and continuing importance of racial segregation in housing policy. From 1979 the funding of all housing in urban areas was conducted through the National Housing Commission (NHC) and the National Housing Fund (NHF). But by 1987 most of the duties and powers specified in the Housing Act had been transferred to the housing departments of the houses of assembly, representatives and delegates, as well as to the department of constitutional development and planning. At that juncture the NHC and NHF ceased to exist.

The racially separated public housing departments mean that land and finance policies have differing effects on the segregated townships. Yet policy changes have not simply been made in terms of a neo-apartheid formula, but are the consequence of an interweaving of racist and economic considerations. The overall shift in policy that apparently endorses privatisation and encourages state divestment from the politically sensitive housing arena has been as important as the reshuffling of 'general' and 'own' affairs. And the effects of recent land-use and fiscal policy changes apparently cut across the experiences of some working-class residents, regardless of their race.

The land crisis

A major factor in the persistence of urban overcrowding is the shortage of land where blacks can live legally. Throughout this century restrictions such as the Gold Law (1885), the Natives Urban Areas Act (1923) and the Asiatic Land Tenure Act (1946) have limited the geographical spread of certain working-class and other residential areas. One glaring consequence of racist land pegging is the increasing overcrowding in black group areas of major urban centres.

In contrast, poorer sections of the white population have been privileged by the same legislation. Historically the clearance of 'black spots' from urban areas made land available in prime locations. On some occasions the state intervened directly to establish housing in these areas, while on others the removal of the competing population gave white tenants easier access to cheap accommodation. Since the reintegration of some inner city areas, however, land acquisition for poorer white workers has become increasingly problematic.

In the last decade, developments in the housing market have undermined poor whites' traditionally privileged access to cheap but convenient land. The gentrification of historically working-class suburbs, like Westdene in Johannesburg or Observatory in Cape Town, has pushed out tenants who could no longer afford rent in these upwardly mobile areas. In Mayfair in Johannesburg this trend was accentuated by the influx of middle-class people classified as Indian, whose greater purchasing power inflated housing demand in areas abutting the new Indian group area.

Until recently the state practice of turning a blind eye to group area violations, particularly in inner-city areas such as Hillbrow, and the policy of some of the large property owners of letting to black people in white group areas, have reduced available reasonably-priced shelter traditionally reserved for whites. Landlords also often prefer to let to blacks from whom they can extract a higher rent. This is particularly true in older rent-controlled buildings where illegal tenants are not in a position to challenge unofficial rent increases. Paradoxically, this has eased the situation for a minority of black people who would otherwise have had to live in overcrowded township ghettos.

Increasingly unaffordable housing and the general decline in white working-class living standards could have significant political effects as these people reassert demands for privileged access to housing. The Progressive Federal Party's loss of the Hillbrow constituency in the 1987 white election over the group areas issue is an example of the potential direction of white response to the housing crisis.

The pressure on residential land in townships classified African, Indian and coloured has been even more intense than in white suburbia. The extent of many existing townships has been practically frozen since their initial proclamation. Attempts to extend these residential locations have been thwarted by bureaucratic obstacles. And the push for industrial deconcentration has in many instances resulted in housing being located in outlying areas far from the urban cores. It is not simply racist group area provisions which have limited the establishment of additional housing sites in the townships. General restrictions on land use have been the result of a combination of group-area, industrial concentration and bureaucratic imperatives.

The Guide Plan for the Central Witwatersrand, based on industrial decentralisation, envisaged the allocation of a relatively large black group area north of Johannesburg to build the township of Norweto. But pressure from white land owners has stymied this plan for the moment. The latest Guide Plan for the Eastern Witwatersrand envisaged extending existing black group areas to utilise white farm land between Katlehong, Tokoza, Natalspruit and Vosloorus, as well as between KwaThema and Ratanda. Yet, at the same time, general state policy guidelines specify that new black residential development should be located near the Bronkhorstspruit-Springs deconcentration area.

Local authorities and land-use patterns

No investigation of regional and local land-use patterns would be complete without a discussion of the land allocation practices of local authorities. Legislation in the late 1970s and early 1980s transformed the mechanisms of site allocation by certain arms of local government. After the 1982 devolution of local government powers onto black local authorities, and until the phasing out of the development boards during 1986, local town councils increasingly assumed the duties of site allocation. The changing powers of black local authorities brought them more in line with the functions of established local governments administering white group areas.

But the transformation of local government was not an even process. Political conflicts between development boards and the then fledgling black local authorities tended to obscure the precise role these institutions played in the procedure of stand allocation. Local councils assumed the formal right to allocate sites to private developers and others, while the boards retained ownership of government housing stock as well as the function of processing 99-year leasehold applications.

With increasing numbers of violent attacks on local councillors and the subsequent demise of the boards, the very existence of some black local authorities has been placed in jeopardy. Police and military action under the current state of emergency is intended, in part, to re-establish the authority of local government structures. At present the armed might of the state appears to be a pre-condition for the resumption and development of the site allocation powers of the town councils.

A similar convergence between the powers of the black and white local authorities occurred in the Indian area of Verulam, which now has its own independent local authority. And on the Eastern Witwatersrand the Actonville and Bakerton management committees already play an important part in allocating sites for building houses. Whether the management committees will be ceded full local government powers is a moot point. Yet judging by the proposal for an independent municipality for Rynsoord and Modderfontein (East Rand), it would seem that some architects of state policy have accepted this option.

Against this background, the political sensitivity of the land question for both blacks and whites becomes apparent. Government's back-pedalling on the abolition of group areas in the light of the 1987 white election, combined with the involvement of discredited local authority structures in site allocation, indicates that the authorities have yet to establish a workable procedure for the speedy provision of residential sites. In contrast, the government has a precise policy for the financing of home ownership.

State housing finance

The official response to the housing problem has been the state's publicly announced withdrawal from housing provision. But this does not mean it has stopped all involvement: rather, trends during the past few years indicate that government is reshaping its role regarding housing.

Although government housing functions are increasingly being divided between the various houses of parliament, the poorer working classes of all residential areas are confronted with the financial implications of policy changes: limited subsidisation of conventional and self-help home ownership schemes; the removal of rent controls on private landlords; and the selling off of relatively cheap government-leased housing stock.

The new state housing policy announced in 1983 had two major thrusts. The first, which attracted by far the most attention at the time, was the sale of 500 000 state housing units. Although the 'great sale' was aimed predominantly at creating a home-owning class in the townships, houses in all areas were available for sale. Despite an unimpressive start, sales increased and by June 1984 18 876 units had been sold nation wide to black residents. A further drop in price recently increased this number to 50 000.

The second aspect of the new policy was the introduction of a subsidy for first-time house purchasers. Like the 'great sale' the subsidy was open to all, though the targets were primarily white residents. Concerned about the growing number of mainly young people who, because of rampant inflation and escalating building costs, had little prospect of ever owning their own homes, the state extended its existing subsidy on the purchase of houses.

Provisions for state housing assistance to whites have existed since the first Housing Act of 1920 when money was lent to individuals. Since then the number benefiting from government funding has steadily increased. In 1930 the growth of slums prompted the establishment of sub-economic housing schemes, and returning soldiers received priority in post-war housing reconstruction. Despite this, a white housing crisis persisted. In 1956 the civil service, which employed many of the residents in question, introduced a housing subsidy.

The 1983 extension of the housing subsidy to those not already receiving state assistance is significant for a number of reasons. Although officially colour-blind, the new measure clearly benefited whites most: and mainly, though not exclusively, whites in regular employment with incomes that would justify bond repayments on a R40 000 mortgage. And despite state rhetoric about minimising its intervention in housing, the new subsidy increased the state's role.

So while the state aimed to depoliticise the tense housing issue by withdrawing from its function as landlord, it continued to exert direct influence over allocation and subsidisation. This was most notable in white group areas, but the subsidy's significance in encouraging the emergence of a home-owning stratum in the population at large should not be underestimated. Between 1980 and 1985 an average of 1 700 new houses were built annually for private home owners in the black townships of the Witwatersrand alone.

In recent years the building rate for private home owners has increased, and an increasing number of black residents became eligible for the subsidy. Between October 1986 and February 1987, 3 141 first-time home owners in townships nation-wide received this subsidy. Subsidy legislation could therefore protect some of the politically sensitive middle-income white residents, while at the same time bolstering upwardly mobile township dwellers, whom the state sees as an important constituency.

Public subsidisation of home ownership has not been restricted to middle-income earners, for whom owning a house has become an increasing possibility. Equally significant has been the investment in township infrastructure and the encouragement of site-and-service schemes. The 'orderly urbanisation' strategy aims to replicate self-help and controlled squatting, such as that which occurred at Inanda (in Natal) - though it is debatable whether many of the unemployed and low wage earners will be able to afford monthly site-and-service charges. Yet for employed residents living in overcrowded conditions, serviced sites (such as those available in Holfontein near Daveyton, and Protea North in Soweto) plus a R5 000 building materials loan have made self-help home ownership a viable option.

Recent policy changes involve more than simple encouragement of home-ownership schemes. Despite deprioritising rented public shelter, official policy shows a continuing commitment to providing for the housing needs of at least some of those who cannot afford to buy their own homes, especially the aged and pensioners. In recent years a limited number of rented units have been delivered, albeit under strictly segregationist conditions: between 1982 and 1985 the state built 42 395 units in black development areas; between 1982 and 1986, 26 356 units in Indian; 42 606 units in coloured; and 11 862 units in white group areas. Despite the moves to privatisation, in order to finance these houses, the state retained the fiscal resource structures which formed the logistical backbone of the mass housing estates of past years.

After the inauguration of the tricameral parliamentary system, the National Housing Fund (NHF) continued to be responsible for all funding of state-built units. During 1984 the NHF was transferred to the control of the multiracial executive cabinet, and located in the department of public works and land affairs. This department was responsible for allocation of finance and setting building standards.

However, housing is regarded as an 'own affair' for communities with voting rights, and is therefore the responsibility of the ministers concerned in the respective houses of parliament. African housing is a 'general affair' under the jurisdiction of the department of constitutional development and planning. The NHF has been fragmented and its funds shared out between the respective 'own affairs' departments and 'black' housing organs.

Theoretically the state treasury will still provide capital for these separate funds. However, judging by the small amount (R8-million) appropriated as a direct contribution to the NHF during the 1984-85 financial year, and given the policy emphasis on privatisation, it is likely that housing funds will be forced to rely more and more on the capital and interest redeemed from township residents themselves.

Central government policy to rid itself of financial commitments to housing funds is further indicated by government's preference for financing infrastructure and services installation - for which R1-billion has been set aside between 1985 and 1990. In fact, since the early 1980s the trend has been to invest more treasury funds in infrastructure and building material and housing loans in the black townships than in the other group areas.

The latest developments in housing financing may localise conflicts, but are unlikely to end social strife over affordable shelter. The extent to which the central state withdraws from financing housing provision will determine the degree to which regions will be forced to draw on their own resources. It is doubtful whether local and regional state bodies will be able - or willing - to take on the full financial load being shed by the central state.

The regional services councils (RSCs), due to commence operation in July 1987, are meant to channel money to poorer working-class areas. But these bodies are fraught with their own contradictions, not least their control by the wealthier municipalities. The implication is that money will be directed to vested interests in wealthier areas. In addition, RSC taxes are expected to be recouped through price increases. The effect of the new financing policy on different occupational classes and income earners is likely to be uneven, but the lowest paid manual workers of all residential areas will suffer most.

State officials have argued that they have little or no money for housing, and the central government clearly does not have unlimited finance. But, among non-welfare states, South Africa already has one of the highest tax rates in the world and there is considerable resistance amongst both the business community and the white electorate to any increase in their tax burden. State spending on housing has also been constrained by rapid inflation in the prices of building materials (over 100% since 1980), as well as by the state's own economic growth strategies which minimise public intervention in the market place.

However, as important as the amount of public money available, is how that money is allocated. Of the R37 447,19-million budgeted for government expenditure during 1986-87, only R651,58-million (or 1,74%) was allocated for housing. Yet R5 123,28-million (13,7%) was spent on maintaining the SA Defence Force. In addition, millions of rands were earmarked for the tricameral parliamentary bureaucracies and their staff (the chairpersons of the 50-odd RSCs will together draw more than R5-million in annual income).

The downgrading of state investment in housing thus reflects not only rising inflation and economic recession, but also the need to strengthen the neo-apartheid system against the widespread resistance of recent years.

The politics of shelter

State reluctance to fund the building of dwelling units, and problems in allocating serviced sites and new tracts of land, have resulted in a large-scale housing shortage for the lowest income earners in all working class areas. Rising prices of building materials have escalated the costs of maintenance and provision of infrastructure and services as well as new dwelling units. Accordingly, a substantial number of working-class residents of all colours cannot foot the bill for newly constructed, serviced shelter.

At the same time there has been a concerted drive to subsidise the newly-built stock of first-time home owners, substantial reductions in the prices of existing government-owned houses and the extension of subsidisation to all state employees. This has enabled thousands of black residents to become home owners. And the emergence of a fledgling private market in places such as Soweto is another consequence of the new housing finance policy. Although it cannot address the needs of the lowest income earners, private sector involvement in the provision of houses is a growing trend.

Yet the provision of land where it is most needed for housing is hamstrung by political constraints such as the Group Areas Act, which remains firmly intact. Scrapping this law would not benefit poorer black working class people, who are without the financial wherewithal to afford 'white' real estate. But the act has put a brake on the expansion of a black home owning class by effectively cutting them off from the oversupply of housing in white group areas.

The growth of a class of home owners represents a new kind of township person for whom financial commitment and fixed employment become a necessary part of life. And state logic has been that such people will perhaps think twice before taking part in a general strike or consumer boycott.

The affordability problem has contributed to a political crisis in most of the country's townships. The collapse of black local authorities and burgeoning rent boycotts are the clearest indications of the critical heights to which conflict between the state and its adversaries has risen. Political struggles have not been confined to a single community, but have mushroomed nationally. Government response has been to intervene in all areas, the most blatant being military and police actions under the emergency powers established last June.

State intervention then, has included both repressive and co-optive measures; the latter including the attempt to depoliticise housing through home-ownership subsidy and the less obvious financing of infrastructure, services and some dwellings.

Contrary to a popular political wisdom - and the ideology of privatisation - public finance still contributes substantially towards national investment in housing. Yet the form of government intervention has changed since the 1970s. More dwelling units are being erected in townships near the major cities, and more public capital is being used to fund installation of infrastructure in these parts of the country.

At the same time, traditional forms of policing access to shelter in major urban townships have undergone substantial change. The emergence of a fledgling private market in places such as Soweto is one consequence of the ending of development board control over black local authorities. The new housing policy has heralded the demise of the old department of community development's strategy of a conventional housing delivery system. But at the same time - notwithstanding some parallels between current schemes and programmes of the 1950s - it is not entirely clear what the long-term goals of this policy are. One noticeable effect of the state's newly found role has been increasing subsidisation of home ownership to a few select inhabitants in residential locations in all group areas.

The availability of land and finance have thus emerged as critical issues for community organisations and establishment bodies alike. The strategy of providing financial subsidies clearly contains the possibility of co-opting a limited number of residents from the more privileged occupational classes. Yet due to the shortage of black residential land, the vast majority of township residents - including some of the wealthier inhabitants - will continue to suffer overcrowding and oppressive living conditions. Tensions within the state's new housing policy could thus contribute both towards unifying and towards dividing communities.

Crisis and Restructuring in the Passenger Transport Sector

Colleen McCaul

The state is poised to restructure the passenger transport sector over the next few years. It is doing so in response to serious crises and contradictions in the enormous task of moving more than two million African commuters between home and work each day.

The National Transport Policy Study (NTPS) is a key document in this process of restructuring. Several crises have made it necessary: these include battles waged by workers in the past and present around the conditions of their transportation; the ever-burgeoning costs, borne largely by the state, of providing a sub-economic transport service to workers; and struggles between transport operators themselves.

The proposed restructuring aims to devolve responsibility for the sector with its numerous problems to the regional services councils (RSCs). But it fails to address basic issues, such as the unduly large distances between home and workplace in apartheid South Africa, and the unaffordability of long-distance commuting to large sections of the African working class. As a result, the state will, in the process of addressing some difficulties, exacerbate others, and give rise to new crises.

A brief history of apartheid transport

The conditions of worker commuting in South Africa derive from apartheid's spatial engineering, with its artificially wide separation between home and workplace. Some 80% of African commuters currently spend an average of 2,5 hours travelling to and from work each day. About 20% spend between 3,5 and 7 hours, an average of 4,5 hours.[1] This extraordinary system dates back to the mid-1950s, when massive group area removals began. Many African freehold settlements were destroyed and tens of thousands of Africans moved from central city areas to new townships on the borders of metropolitan areas.

Adoption of severe influx control measures from 1952 limited and displaced African urbanisation. This was accompanied by the creation of bantustans for the residential, political and social accommodation of Africans not allowed to settle in the urban areas. During the 1960s and 1970s hundreds of thousands of Africans were moved into bantustans from 'black spots', white farms and the towns.

From 1967 residents of any African township within 50 km of a bantustan border could be relocated to that bantustan, and would be expected to commute up to 160 km daily to and from work. From this time, the state prevented the expansion and development of townships in such areas. Some 670 000 people were moved in this way between 1968 and 1980.[2]

As a result of the 3,5-million removals since 1960, the redrawing of bantustan boundaries to include African towns, urban relocation policy since 1967 and urbanisation within the bantustans themselves, 20% of South Africa's estimated 7-million urbanised Africans now live within bantustan borders.[3] Accordingly, an increasing proportion of the national workforce commutes from bantustans to work in 'white' areas. This bantustan-based commuter population has increased by about 150% since 1970, and numbered 773 000 in 1982. The remaining 1,4-million African commuters travel daily from townships on the borders of towns and cities to adjacent business and industrial areas. An estimated 54% of commuters travel to work by bus, 38% by train and 8% in kombi taxis.[4]

From 1952 the state intervened to support commuter bus transport financially. This was a result of the demands of its residential policies, the transport struggles in Alexandra in the 1940s and the monopolisation of the bus industry by private companies at that time, which decreased competition and enabled fare hikes.

The Bantu Services Levy Act of 1952 imposed a levy on employers who did not house their workers. The levy was 25 cents for every six days worked by each employee, five cents of which could be used to subsidise transport services. This was supplemented in 1957 - in the wake of a boycott of Putco buses in Alexandra related to a fare increase - by the Bantu Transport Services Act which empowered the state to increase the transport portion of the levy by ten cents per week, enabling an increase in subsidies to bus companies.[5]

Since 1957 the department of transport has subsidised the weekly or monthly bus tickets of genuine employees who cannot afford fares equal to the cost of their transportation - economic fares - from a fund of employers' contributions and the treasury. Further legislation in 1972 provided for subsidisation of transport for coloured and Indian employees.

The number of African worker-passenger journeys carried by the state-owned South African Transport Services (SATS) has increased from about 100-million in 1950 to almost 600-million in 1981-82, when figures peaked.

The first sub-economic rail passenger fares for African township dwellers, according to Pirie, were introduced in 1905 by the Cape Government Railways between Cape Town and Ndabeni and between Port Elizabeth and New Brighton. From the 1920s the state-owned South African Railways (SAR) sought financial guarantees and protection from competition for township services from the relevant local authorities. Only from the mid-1950s, with the intensification of residential racial segregation, did the state replace municipal guarantees with state compensation for railway losses, when it accepted the report of a high-level committee of inquiry called the Interdepartmental Committee for the Conveyance of Coloured, Indian and Black commuters, which studied rail transport to dormitory townships.

In 1963, the state eventually agreed to compensate the SAR for losses. It covered its losses retrospectively for 1957, and provided annual advances from 1963 onwards to cover estimated losses. In 1974 it was agreed that the SAR would absorb a proportion of operating losses annually.[6]

Crisis and conflict in the passenger transport sector

A series of crises and conflicts have emerged within the passenger transport sector over the years: the ever-escalating costs to the state of financing a sub-economic commuting system; workers' struggles around transport conditions; and conflict between suppliers of transport services.

The expense to the state of subsidising bus and train commuter costs has escalated dramatically since the 1950s. It has become an unwanted fiscal burden to the department of transport, the treasury and SATS.

Although employers in certain areas are obliged to contribute to bus transport subsidies through levies of up to R3 per month per employee, their contributions make up only about 13% of the economic tariffs of bus commuters (compared to 52% in 1970-71). The weekly cash fares paid by commuters amount to about 50% of the economic tariff, while the treasury, through an allocation in the department of transport budget vote, contributes about 37%.[7] The National Transport Commission is responsible for deciding whether the economic tariffs submitted by bus operators are justified, determining what percentage the passenger can afford and what percentage will be subsidised. The weekly tickets bought by bus passengers are therefore already discounted by the amount of the subsidy, and bus companies recover the balance from the treasury.

Longer-distance commuters receive a proportionately larger subsidy. Commuters living more than 50 km from their workplace can be subsidised by up to 80% of the economic tariff. On average the state pays about R200 per bus commuter per year. This figure can reach about R1 500 annually for a person travelling more than 90 km to work.[8]

While bus subsidies cost only R2,3-million in 1966-67, the state paid out R209-million in the 1984-85 financial year.[9] In addition, provincial administrations subsidise school bus services, municipalities cover deficits on their bus services through cross-subsidies and the department of development aid covers about half the ticket cost of people travelling within bantustans. If these amounts are added to the subsidies paid to private bus companies, the total is considerable. It was estimated at some R250-million in 1981-82 by the Welgemoed Commission of Enquiry into Bus Passenger Transportation.

The state-owned SATS, which carries 38% of African commuters, suffers enormous losses on its passenger services. These must also be taken into account in considering the total subsidy bill. Third class commuters pay only 37% of the actual cost of their journey.[10] The remaining 63% is only partially covered by the treasury. The rest of the losses are covered by cross-subsidisation within SATS itself. Thus SATS conveys certain manufactured goods at enormously inflated prices and uses these profits, as well as those on its harbours and pipelines, to cover losses caused by conveying passengers (and certain agricultural and mining products) below cost. This has caused a great deal of conflict within the transport industry and draws widespread criticism from the private sector.

During 1984-85 SATS lost a total of R767-million on all its passenger services (first and third class, mainline and commuter). The state contributed 53% of this and SATS cross-subsidised the remaining 47%.[11] Of this R767-million, R269-million (35%) was lost on third class commuter services.[12]

In other words, the total subsidy bill for working-class African commuters by bus and train was approximately R500-million in 1984-85. It continues to burgeon and SATS estimated a loss of R1,1-billion on passenger services in 1986-87. The department of transport budgeted R256-million in the same year for bus subsidies.[13]

The state has made clear its increasing reluctance to shoulder these huge bills. It seems ready to offload them, firstly onto capital - both in the form of a higher wage bill and through the forthcoming RSC levies - and then onto workers. But resistance by workers and township communities on the one hand and by capital on the other seems likely to be a considerable impediment to this.

Township communities have waged struggles around transport conditions, usually sparked by fare increases, since at least 1940. This led the Welgemoed Commission to comment in 1983 that: 'It is an unfortunate fact that in South Africa, public transport, particularly public bus transport, is highly politicised'.[14]

There have been some protracted struggles around transport provision, lasting for months and in some cases years. These struggles have often mobilised large numbers of people. While the major bus boycotts of the 1940s, 1950s and 1960s were waged by residents of metropolitan townships like Alexandra, Evaton and those of Pretoria, many of the major transport struggles of the 1970s and 1980s have involved bantustan-based commuters - KwaNdebele, Mdantsane and Empangeni commuters are cases in point - as a result of the growth since the late 1960s of this section of the commuting workforce.

Transport struggles are among the most significant forms of protest in some bantustan commuter areas. They create problems not only for the state, but for the bus companies. The latter are forced onto the defensive and may rely on state repression to coerce commuters back into their vehicles, which further polarises the situation. During more protracted struggles, companies have been forced to sell certain areas of operation, and write off huge losses.

Township unrest since September 1984 has seriously heightened the crisis of transport politicisation for both the state and transport operators. Buses (and increasingly trains) have been frequent targets of attack. Hundreds have been petrol-bombed, burned, stoned or hijacked. Many bus companies have withdrawn their vehicles to the outskirts of townships for short or long periods to avoid damage losses. Nonetheless, bus companies' unrest losses have been high, running into tens of millions of rands.

These crises of finance and politicisation exacerbate each other. Fare increases to extract greater cost recovery from commuters are often met with resistance. Losses incurred during such struggles cause further profitability problems for bus operators, who in turn apply for further fare increases and larger subsidies from the state. (The state has, for example, agreed to compensate Putco in part for its unrest-related losses).[15]

Conflict in the passenger transport sector has not been confined to that between commuters and the suppliers of their transport and the state. Conflict also rages between transport operators themselves, and revolves around competition to capture greater shares of the transport market. The major passenger transport-related battles are between kombi taxi operators and the bus companies, and between SATS and private sector freight hauliers. The Welgemoed Commission in particular has addressed itself to, and aggravated, the taxi-bus war, while the NTPS and the private sector have been particularly concerned with the conflict between SATS and the freight companies.

The kombi taxi-bus conflict emerged after 1977 when the state allowed African taxi operators to use eight-passenger kombis as opposed to four-passenger sedans. Since then, a substantial portion of the short-distance passenger market has been captured by these operators. Some 7,5% of the African commuting population travels to work by taxi.[16] The Welgemoed Commission's final report in 1983 launched a fierce attack on kombi taxis, arguing that

> the kombi taxi is in many cases a particularly strong competitor for the existing bus or train services because it does not operate in the spirit of the permit of a taxi and is used as a small bus along bus routes when it suits the owner. Bus companies are subject to strict controls and need to be protected from these people (*Frontline*, 03.84; *FM*, 10.02.84).

The report virtually recommended that kombi taxis be phased out. Some have seen this as the commission's compensation to the transport monopolies for its recommendation that bus subsidies be abolished in the long term.[17]

A draft bill based on the Welgemoed recommendations was circulated in late 1983. It proposed that taxis again become four-passenger sedans, that kombi taxis be phased out over four years, and that small 25-passenger buses with fixed routes, tariffs, and timetables be phased in. The bill was never debated in parliament, and met with a barrage of criticism, particularly from the private sector.

However, it appeared that from 1984 these proposals were being implemented administratively by the National Transport Commission (NTC) and the ten local road transportation boards (LRTBs) without benefit of legislation. It seems that these bodies began issuing new taxi licences for only four passengers and that insufficient numbers of permits were issued.[18]

Taxi operators are also subject to coercive control by the police, who frequently arrest and fine operators for lacking proper permits or overloading, and impound vehicles. This is done particularly during bus boycotts, when the taxis have an instantly expanded market.

In addition to state assistance in competing with the kombi taxi operators, many bus operators, both municipal and private, began introducing their own version of taxis - 25-seat midibuses - in open competition with African operators.

In the course of township unrest it appeared - from allegations by bus drivers, bus companies, the police and the minister of transport affairs - that the kombi taxi-bus conflict had become openly violent. Accusations, often fiercely denied by taxi operators, were that the latter had had a hand in arranging attacks on buses in a number of townships to ensure that bus routes terminated on the outskirts of townships, which left taxis with an expanded market.[19]

While the Welgemoed Commission and certain state bodies sought to protect the major bus companies against kombi taxi competition, the kombi taxi industry appears to have withstood the pressures and continues to expand rapidly. (Estimates of the number of legal and pirate taxis in the market vary widely, but range up to 120 000 vehicles). The NTPS found that the number of pirate (illegal) taxis had increased by about 28% between 1982 and 1985 and the number of legal vehicles by 11%. Over the same period the passenger loads of all other forms of public transport decreased considerably.[20]

A new range of vested interests in the kombi taxi industry has emerged. This is no doubt partly responsible for the fact that taxis may get a better deal in the new transport dispensation than they would have received if the Welgemoed Commission's recommendations had been formally implemented. Legal operators are organised under the banner of the Southern Africa Bus and Taxi Association (SABTA), which claims to represent the 40 000 legal operators. Its patronage is courted by the ailing motor industry (an estimated 300 new kombi taxis are purchased monthly), by financial institutions, and by insurance and oil companies.

Nissan and Toyota have seized most of the minibus market; Volkswagen is seeking to increase its 5% share. Wesbank offers special financial deals through SABTA for new buyers; South African Eagle Insurance Company offers large insurance discounts; oil companies have designed new oils specifically for taxis, and some - such as Shell - are collaborating in SABTA's plans to set up scores of discount service stations countrywide. SABTA claims its 40 000 members alone spend R1-billion annually on cars, spares, tyres, fuel and insurance (*ST,* 19.10.86; *FW,* 11.09.86).

The taxi industry has not only won the support of significant sections of capital, but has forged successful alliances in certain township communities. While such relationships are ambiguous - workers have on occasion boycotted taxis - residents and taxi operators sometimes share a common enemy in the bus companies, particularly during bus boycotts. Some taxi operators belong to United Democratic Front (UDF) affiliates. In Port Elizabeth townships and Pietermaritzburg's Sobantu, for example, community bodies organised boycotts of the midibuses introduced by bus companies in 1985. During the West Rand boycott of Greyhound Bus Lines in 1986, commuters demanded that the company's midibuses be withdrawn from the townships, that the company stop blocking residents' applications for taxi permits, and that it refund taxi operators fined during the boycott for overloading. Greyhound agreed to the second of these demands (*Sow,* 07.04.86; *Star,* 07.04.86; *DD,* 05.04.85; *EPH,* 11.04.85).

Bus companies have been forced to acknowledge the kombi taxi industry's strength. Putco recently recognised it as a 'permanent competitor', a factor to be taken into account when planning future services.[21] In February 1986 the South African Bus Operators Association, representing the interests of the major private bus companies, invited SABTA to liaise with it and negotiate co-operation and co-ordination of their respective services. It also announced that bus companies were considering moving into the taxi market. SABTA followed this up a few months later with a 'target sanctions' campaign calling on international companies to sell their workers SABTA taxi coupons at a discount to woo passengers away from 'government-owned trains and white-owned bus companies' (*Star*, 28.02.86; *BD*, 28.02.86; *Sow*, 03.10.86).

A second major conflict in the transport sector, directly related to providing commuters with a sub-economic transport system, is between SATS and the private freight hauliers about the former's policy of cross-subsidisation. In order to cover passenger (and certain other) losses SATS set rail freight tariffs for certain manufactured goods at anything up to 200% above cost. To prevent undercutting by the private sector SATS uses its own police force, the NTC and the ten LRTBs which issue road permits.

In 1981-82, for example, SATS objected to 30% of all permit applications by private road carriers; the NTC and LRTBs upheld 95% of its objections.[22] Private sector freight hauliers who operate illegally because they cannot get permits (about 22% of freight traffic on the roads is unauthorised) have their vehicles impounded by railways police at roadblocks and are fined.[23] The permit system costs the country an estimated R60-million annually.

The Public Carriers Association and other freight carrier and private sector bodies have called for an end to SATS's cross-subsidisation policy. They argue that financing SATS's losses should be government's responsibility, as sub-economic transport is a social service. The private sector is also critical of high harbour and pipeline charges, profits from which are also used for cross-subsidisation.

Restructuring the passenger transport sector

Faced with crisis and conflict in the passenger transport sector, over the past five years the state has been preparing to embark on wide-ranging restructuring.

Apart from the Welgemoed Commission of Enquiry into bus passenger transportation which reported in 1983 and 1984, the major state investigation was the NTPS, which was set up in 1981 by the NTC to assist in formulating recommendations to rationalise transport policy in South Africa. The NTPS focused on four major policy areas:

* development of a public passenger transport policy;
* development of a freight transport policy;
* rationalisation of the transport administration's organisational structure; and
* co-ordination of 'Southern' African transport policy (that of South Africa and the four independent bantustans).

The NTPS reports are couched in a technocratic discourse of deregulation and rationalisation which reflects a concern that the transport sector be exposed to competition and the free market.[24] The investigation was concluded on 31 March 1986, but the government white paper - along with three new transport bills - was only scheduled for the 1987 parliamentary session. The white paper will also deal with the Welgemoed Commission recommendations. Minister of Transport Affairs Hendrik Schoeman said essential legislation would be passed in 1987 and implemented over the next three years, and by 1991 all NTPS recommendations acceptable to government would be instituted.[25]

How the passenger transport sector is restructured depends not only on such investigations, but on the state's broader constitutional and reform initiatives. These feature political and administrative decentralisation, fiscal devolution, regionalisation, deregulation, privatisation and deconcentration. The NTPS has to a large extent incorporated these concerns in its proposals.

If they are implemented, RSCs will become the lynchpin of the new passenger transport deal. Already, a criterion for delimiting the boundaries of an RSC's sphere of jurisdiction is that it should embrace all commuter transport within that area.[26] Further, the Regional Services Councils Act of 1985 stipulates that RSC revenue can be used for payment or part-payment of transport services capital and running costs for commuters working in the relevant region, whether they live inside or outside the 'independent' bantustans.[27]

The major NTPS proposals for passenger transport that concern RSCs are:

* subsidies should be phased out in the long term;
* where they are necessary they should be paid by RSCs;

* all passenger transport policy decisions should be devolved to the lowest level of government;

* the permit system (in terms of which operators need permits or certificates from the NTC and LRTBs to operate on particular routes) should be abolished and replaced with a new system concerned with safety and quality;

* the 'operating authorities' required by operators in terms of such a quality control system should be issued by RSCs; and

* RSCs should establish regional transport plans, using contractors to service the transport needs of their regions.

The central state retains overall policy control, however, and will issue national policy guidelines for RSCs. The proposed new Transport Act, for example, will contain national guidelines on norms and standards for subsidising bus services.[28]

The NTPS proposal to remove the fiscal burden of subsidies by phasing them out in the long term is not new. The Welgemoed Commission recommended that a select parliamentary committee should draw up a timetable for phasing out subsidies, with due regard to economic, social and political consequences. It argued that employers should pay workers enough to enable them to bear their own transport costs, and that subsidies could be phased out as worker incomes rose. Transport Affairs Director General Adriaan Eksteen reiterated this view in mid-1985 (*FM*, 07.06.85). The proposal that RSCs pay subsidies where necessary is in line with the central state's general desire to devolve its fiscal responsibilities to the local state.

In terms of the NTPS proposals, RSCs will also decide which operators supply transport in their areas. They will enter into short-term contracts with bus companies, SATS and taxis, possibly after calling for tenders on fares for certain routes. All operators will require RSC authorisation to operate, and this will depend on their complying with the requirements of a road passenger quality system (RPQS) which will be incorporated in a new Road Traffic Act. This RPQS will specify certain technical safety and quality requirements. (A similar quality control system will regulate freight transport).

RSC transport contracts will stipulate service levels, fares, subsidy requirements and the boundaries of an exclusive area of operation within which an operator will be granted protection against competition. This will replace the present controversial permit system run by the NTC and its ten LRTBs, which are to be abolished. The new system is thus designed to deregulate the passenger transport sector and open it up to competition: remaining regulations will be technical - operators will have to comply with safety and quality requirements only - and in theory operators will compete equally when they submit tenders to RSCs.[29]

Carving up each region's passenger market between taxis, buses and trains - thus taking on the taxi-bus conflict - will be the RSCs' responsibility. The NTPS proposals, if implemented, will offer considerably less protection to bus companies than the Welgemoed Commission proposed. The NTPS's approach is more accommodating to taxis: it recommends that 16-seater kombi taxis be permitted. Meanwhile, before the NTPS recommendations are implemented, LRTBs will be asked to consider taxi applications more favourably and the present number of permits may be doubled. The NTPS also recommends that central government stipulate the minimum number of kombi taxis each RSC would have to allow.[30] This more favourable approach to kombi taxis - at the expense of the bus operators if RSCs choose to limit their current spheres of operation - is consistent with developments since the Welgemoed report.

The 1985 President's Council reports on urbanisation and on a strategy for small business development and deregulation recommended that taxis be encouraged. They recognised 'so-called pirate taxis' as a 'vital element' in the transport system which created opportunities for many entrepreneurs. The latter report suggested that permits be made more readily available to operators.[31]

The department of transport has already instructed the LRTBs to grant 15-passenger permits to larger vehicles. In 1986 it also established a committee so that SABTA representatives could meet senior departmental representatives to discuss problems between the government and the taxi industry (*Sow*, 18.09.86).

The NTPS provides for a transport tribunal - a sort of specialist court - to settle anticipated disputes about administrative practices and the new operating licence system, which will be administered by the RSCs. It stresses the proposed tribunal's impartiality and independence of vested interests or political concerns. A further shock-absorber for transport sector conflicts is the NTPS-proposed transport advisory council, a forum for consultation between private and public sector (with 70% and 30% representation respectively). It will recommend national transport policy to the minister of transport affairs and to parliament. In choosing private sector representatives the minister must consider the interests of all population groups and all users, operators and participants in the transport sector. The council will deal with all forms of transport.[32]

In dealing with the conflict between SATS and freight hauliers and the fiscal problems of SATS's enormous passenger losses, the NTPS completely concurs with the solutions SATS has proposed during the past few years. SATS is very keen to rid itself of the burden of cross-subsidisation - but only if it is relieved of its statutory obligation (as outlined in the South African Transport Services Act of 1981) to render sub-economic services. Another SATS condition is that road hauliers contribute more to road infrastructure, as SATS does to rail, thus placing them on an equal competitive footing.

SATS feels it must be compensated for commuter services losses from a source other than cross-subsidisation. It also wishes to operate commuter services as an agent on behalf of another authority which will compensate it for losses. SATS Assistant General Manager Barry Lessing said 'ideally the sources of these funds (loss compensation) should be within the areas that benefit most from the provision of these services'.[33]

The NTPS accepts that the road transport permit system, which historically protected SATS, should be abolished and that SATS ought to reduce freight, harbour, and pipeline tariffs to realistic, cost-related levels. To compensate SATS it advises that passenger losses be carried by the Treasury, RSCs or increased passenger fares.[34]

In order to put road operators on what it regards as an equal footing with SATS, the NTPS has considered ways of quantifying the cost of the road infrastructure so that road users can be made to pay more towards its maintenance and provision.[35] This is expected to raise an additional R253-million annually.

These proposals reflect the state's desire for SATS to operate on more businesslike, free market lines. The state is keen to shed some of its transport responsibilities; in 1985 the department of transport began an investigation into the merits of privatising SATS-owned services.

The solutions the NTPS seeks to the crises in passenger transport do not address the underlying structural causes - long commuting distances and workers' low wages. The 1985 President's Council report on urbanisation, however, recognised that phasing out subsidies would cause upward pressure on wages and political unrest. An important solution it proposes to costly long-distance commuting is that new urbanisation take place closer to cities. Where communities are established far from employment opportunities, industrial deconcentration should provide closer jobs. The committee in general favoured encouraging employment around peripheral residential towns or deconcentration areas like Ekangala or Botshabelo. It proposed to do this by means of disincentives aimed at discouraging employers from staying in metropolitan areas.

In 1985 the state showed some sensitivity to the spatial dimensions of its transport crisis when it reversed its urban relocation policies, reprieving residents of more than 50 townships under threat of removal to the bantustans. Deputy Minister of Co-operation Sam de Beer remarked at the time that a reason for the policy change was that what in 1967 were regarded as acceptable commuting distances were no longer so.[36]

The new policy proposals: an analysis

Restructuring the passenger transport sector is most unlikely to resolve the fiscal and politicisation crises confronting it. The RSCs' proposed partial takeover of the state's subsidy burdens will be severely constrained by their fiscal limitations: they are expected to raise only R1,3-billion annually in the four major metropolitan areas from levies on capital. The transport subsidy for working-class commuters alone is more than a third of this.

And as Constitutional Development and Planning Minister Chris Heunis warned employers in May 1985, RSCs cannot be expected to use their funds mainly for commuter transport as they must allocate the bulk to urgently needed infrastructural development. The state accepts the need to assist RSCs with the subsidy bill, but to what extent is still unclear - this indecision is reportedly a factor delaying introduction of RSCs. Ultimately, though, the state appears committed to phasing out subsidies in the long term.[37]

Phasing out subsidies will require commuters to bear the full costs of their transport, creating widespread demands for wage increases which will put pressure on capital to bear an even greater share of fiscal burdens. Used to bearing only a quarter of transport costs, capital is clearly reluctant to shoulder the whole load.

Organised industry and commerce have registered fierce protest at the new taxes on payrolls and turnovers - the proposed sources of revenue for RSCs - arguing that the system would fuel inflation, exacerbate unemployment and increase bankruptcies.[38] They expressed particular concern at the proposal that RSCs fund urban transport services. The Cape Town Chamber of Commerce, for example, said shifting the cost of transport subsidies onto the Western Cape region would undermine its prospects for economic growth. It argued that central government had an obligation to accept fiscal responsibility for the transport system because of its spatial policies. The former senior member of the executive committee on the Natal Provincial Council, Frank Martin, warned that if the third tier had to assume responsibility for subsidies, commerce and industry in some areas could be 'crippled' (*CT*, 07.07.86; *Star*, 28.08.86).

Forcing capital to finance urban reproduction in metropolitan areas may, as the President's Council urbanisation proposals anticipate, be an effective disincentive to stay in the cities, driving some sections of capital to deconcentration points. This would go some way towards addressing within apartheid structures the problems which necessitate restructuring the transport sector.

But forcing commuters to shoulder higher transport costs without concomitant wage increases will exacerbate the politicisation crisis, particularly in far-flung residential areas in bantustan commuter belts such as KwaNdebele, where up to 80% of the economic fare is subsidised. An indication of the potential for conflict: both times KwaNdebele fares were hiked, the entire daily commuting workforce - some 20 000 people - congregated to demand that the increases be cancelled. They were successful: on both occasions central government was forced to increase its subsidy.

Evidently the state is investing in the RSCs its hopes for depoliticisation of passenger transport. Asked how he intended depoliticising transport, Transport Affairs Director General Eksteen said the RSCs were 'an attempt to do just this' (*FM*, 07.06.85).

Devolution to RSCs is in theory depoliticising because it allows the central state to insulate itself from resistance by deflecting and localising conflict. It hopes too to insulate local bodies from resistance by legitimising them through a system of multiracial representation and by allocating them a redistributive role. They will also theoretically be protected from direct political pressures by their system of indirect representation.

However, Cobbett et al argue that their redistributive and legitimising role is unlikely to succeed because the third tier in African townships has been all but destroyed by mass resistance. Further, RSCs are extremely undemocratic, leaving township communities politically powerless. And South Africa's economic crisis will constrain their ability to redistribute resources, and therefore their ability to manage urban reproduction.[39]

Abolishing the permit system for freight transport and lifting the burden of cross-subsidising sub-economic services from SATS may resolve conflicts with freight hauliers and blunt private sector criticism. Some road hauliers, however, reject the suggestion that they contribute more to road infrastructure, as they regard the fuel levy as sufficient for this purpose. And of course this resolution of SATS's problems exacerbates the fiscal crisis, since losses formerly subsidised within SATS must be covered from new sources.

While SATS looks set to emerge unscathed if the NTPS proposals are implemented, bus companies, which have enjoyed a mutually beneficial relationship with the state since the 1950s, have expressed considerable anxiety. Their long-standing protection by NTC-issued route certificates guaranteeing stable markets may be undermined by the proposed RSC contractual system. Protection against kombi taxis - which RSCs may favour as they need no subsidies - is no longer guaranteed. And short-term contracts are unviable for bus operators with huge capital investments in assets geared for long-term markets.

Two major companies, Tollgate Holdings and Putco, reportedly saw the RSCs posing 'terrific practical problems for them'. They proposed to government in late 1986 that RSCs in whose areas they operated buy their assets (worth some R340-million), then appoint them public utility companies to manage the services on the RSCs' behalf.

Meanwhile Putco has frozen all new investment in rolling stock pending greater clarity about the RSCs. Its managing director Albino Carleo believes RSCs may eventually have to choose between 'killing' either the bus or the taxi industry (*FM*, 07.11.86). When government produces its white paper it will be seen which set of vested interests holds sway, as the Welgemoed Commission and the NTPS have put forward a very different solution to the taxi-bus conflict.

The RSCs, to which the state will deflect and devolve its passenger transport burdens if it implements the NTPS proposals, will be financially and politically unable to resist the resultant strains. Since the restructuring process will meet resistance from both workers and sections of capital, and as solutions to certain difficulties will exacerbate others, the transport passenger sector seems about to lurch into a new phase of crisis.

Notes

1 Of SA's 2,1-million African commuters, 29% spend 55 minutes travelling one way to work; 52% spend 90 minutes on a one-way journey averaging 20 km; and 19% travel 45 km for an average of 140 minutes on a one-way journey. Report of the Committee for Constitutional Affairs of the President's Council on an Urbanisation Strategy for the Republic of South Africa, PC3/1985, 94.

2 Laurine Platzky and Cherryl Walker for the Surplus People Project, *The Surplus People - Forced Removals in South Africa,* Johannesburg, 1985, 118.

3 Francine de Clerq, 'Some Recent Trends in Bophuthatswana: Commuters and Restructuring in Education', *South African Review 2,* Johannesburg, 1984, 272.

4 PC3/1985, 94.

5 Jeff McCarthy and Mark Swilling, 'Transport and Political Resistance', *South African Review 2,* Johannesburg, 1984, 27; Udo Witulkski, 'Black Commuters in South Africa', *Africa Insight,* 16(1), 1986, 17-18.

6 GH Pirie, 'African Township Railways and the South African State, 1902-1963', *Journal of Historical Geography,* 1987, forthcoming.

7 McCarthy and Swilling, 'Transport and Political Resistance', 28.

8 PC3/1985; Department of Transport, National Transport Policy Study, *Final Report on Stage 3.*

9 *Report of the Department of Transport and of the National Transport Commission for the period 1 April 1984 to 31 March 1985,* RP97/1985.

10 Barry Lessing, 'The Future Role of Rail in Commuter Transport in South Africa', Annual Transportation Convention (ATC) paper, August 1986.

11 Information provided by South African Transport Services, 22.01.87.

12 *Hansard (A),* 4, cols 239-240, 27.02.86.

13 *Hansard (A),* 4, cols 1208-1209; *Estimate of the Expenditure to be Defrayed from the State Revenue Account during the Financial Year ending 31 March 1987,* RP2/1986.

14 McCarthy and Swilling, 'Transport and Political Resistance', 32.

15 Putco Annual Report 1986.

16 PC3/1985.

17 McCarthy and Swilling, 'Transport and Political Resistance', 33.

18 South African Institute of Race Relations, *Race Relations Survey 1984,* 431-433.

19 *Star,* 09.05.85; *CT,* 31.01.85; *NW,* 06.02.86; *Hansard (A),* 11, col 8676, 1985; *Hansard (R),* 10, cols 1953-1954, 1986.

20 South African Institute of Race Relations, *Race Relations Survey 1985,* 223-224; Central Statistical Services, *Statistical News Release,* P.26.1, 13.11.86.

21 Putco Annual Report 1986; Putco, *The Unaudited Consolidated Results of Putco and its Subsidiaries for the Six Months ended 31 December 1985.*

22 NTPS, *Final Report on Stage 3.*

23 Momentum, 1(3), 1985.
24 M Wiechers and IB Moss, 'The Transport Advisory Council Act and the Transport Tribunal Act', ATC paper, August 1986.
25 *Star*, 13.10.86; *Hansard (A)*, 10, cols 3357-3359, 1986.
26 MJ Vermeulen, PJM Corbin and LMGP Luyckx, 'The NTPS Proposals for a New Passenger Transport Policy', ATC paper, August 1986.
27 Regional Services Councils Act of 1985, *Government Gazette*, 9868, 31.07.85.
28 Vermeulen et al, 'The NTPS Proposals'.
29 Various ATC papers.
30 Vermeulen et al, 'The NTPS Proposals', 16-17, 21-22.
31 PC3/1985.
32 Wiechers and Moss, 'The Transport Advisory Council Act', 5-7.
33 Lessing, 'The Future Role of Rail'.
34 Vermeulen et al, 'The NTPS Proposals', 24.
35 *Star*, 13.10.86; NTPS, *Final Report on Stage 6*, 154.
36 *Hansard (A)*, 13, cols 4867-4869, 1985.
37 *Star*, 28.08.86; Vermeulen et al, 'The NTPS Proposals', 19-20.
38 William Cobbett, Daryl Glaser, Doug Hindson and Mark Swilling, 'South Africa's Regional Political Economy: A Critical Analysis of Reform Strategy in the 1980s', *South African Review 3*, Johannesburg, 1986, 150.
39 Cobbett et al, 'South Africa's Regional Political Economy', 151.

Restructuring and Apartheid: Relocation during the State of Emergency

Laurine Platzky
for the National Committee Against Removals *

The South African government continues to expand and entrench apartheid as it tries desperately to control the direction and pace of change. Despite much talk of 'reform', the state uses classic apartheid strategies, like forced relocation and depriving blacks of South African citizenship, and continues to pursue bantustan 'independence'.

For the government to maintain power and privilege in white hands, it is crucial to restructure the society. One of the methods to achieve this has been the introduction of an 'orderly urbanisation' strategy in urban areas. 'Orderly urbanisation' is officially defined as 'direct and indirect means of control'.

Two concurrent trends are evident: old-style apartheid, accompanied by restructuring. In rural areas selected black spots have been reprieved, but the process of incorporating land and people into the

---

*   The National Committee Against Removals comprises AFRA (Association for Rural Advancement), GRC (Grahamstown Rural Committee), SPP (Surplus People Project (Western Cape)) and TRAC (Transvaal Rural Action Committee). The article is not a review of all instances of removals or orderly urbanisation but rather reflects the areas in which NCAR has been or is becoming active.

bantustans continues. There has been privatisation of both coloured and African communally-held land. In both urban and rural areas the state is trying to decentralise control in order to make local authorities and their security forces responsible for the maintenance of 'law and order'.

Recent legislation

During the January to September 1986 session of parliament a number of acts affecting the lives of the black majority of South Africans were passed. The Abolition of Influx Control Act repealed 34 pieces of legislation which curtailed freedom of movement for Africans. This was not insignificant. More than ten million blacks who are not linked to one of the four 'independent' bantustans of Transkei, Bophuthatswana, Venda or Ciskei are in theory now able to live and work anywhere in South Africa. But the plight of the TBVC residents is much more serious as they do not automatically qualify under the Restoration of South African Citizenship Act to live and work in the land of their birth.

The passage of various local authority bills, as well as the proposed amendments to the Criminal Procedure Act of 1977, are cause for concern. In line with the recommendations of the President's Council Report and the White Paper on Urbanisation, more financial and coercive teeth are granted to black local authorities. Known to most communities as 'puppet' bodies, these ex-community councils, now called town or village councils, have their own armed and formally recognised enforcers of 'law and order'. In the past 18 months the rise of right-wing vigilantes has all but crushed resistance in townships across the country. Now many of these same vigilantes are being employed as 'community guards', commonly known as 'amstels' or 'green beans', by former community councils, or as 'kits-konstabels' (black policemen with six weeks' training) by the South African police.

Legislated freedom of movement may have been granted to many people, but almost as many have been permanently excluded from the common area through the Aliens Act. Wide-ranging controls have been delegated to black local authorities and public resources such as housing and communally held land are to be privatised. This means that those blacks with resources to buy into privatisation schemes will be able to get rich at the expense of those without.

Since the present state of emergency was declared on 12 June 1986, government's removals programme has been back on the map in a big way. Emergency regulations have been used to crush resistance and render communities leaderless. It seems that the state is deliberately expediting removals under cover of the emergency. The timetable for threatened removals has been speeded up. Until recently the authorities negotiated with threatened communities, such as Oukasie at Brits, to get them to move 'voluntarily'. But in other areas they are now simply resorting to the old bulldozer tactics: disestablishment of townships, eviction notices and detention of resisters.

Orderly urbanisation

The new policy endorsed in the government's White Paper on Urbanisation is being implemented. From all over the country come reports of new site-and-service schemes, and people are forced to move from 'one squatter camp to another', re-erecting their homes at huge personal cost. With the present high level of unemployment, the average family cannot afford to build a new home and travel long distances in search of work and household necessities.

Trespass and anti-squatting laws are increasingly used with the same effect as the old influx control provisions, along with the Slums Act as recommended in the President's Council report.

Cape Town: The destruction of Crossroads/KTC was the biggest single forced removal in the last decade. This was accomplished when the interests of a repressive local committee dovetailed with government determination to reduce the numbers of 'squatters' on the site.

Between 18 and 22 May 1986, vigilantes - known as 'witdoeke' - loyal to Johnson Ngxobongwana, the chairperson of the Old Crossroads executive committee, attacked and set fire to homes in the parts of Crossroads known as Nyanga Bush, Nyanga Extension and Portland Cement. An estimated 100 people were killed in the clashes. In uncontested affidavits prepared for a supreme court interdict to prevent a similar attack on the KTC squatter camp, residents and outside observers recorded that they had watched members of the state's 'security forces' assist witdoeke and set fire to shacks.

Despite the interdict, between 9 and 11 June KTC was also

destroyed. Some 70 000 people were left homeless in the wettest Cape winter in years. Welfare agencies fed, clothed and sheltered the refugees. The only option government offered them was a site-and-service scheme at Khayelitsha. The people objected. They wanted to return to the area they had previously occupied and were unwilling to move to an area controlled by witdoek commander Mali Hoza, a leader similar to Ngxobongwana.

For years government has been trying to get rid of Crossroads. All attempts failed, and the number of African squatters in the Cape Peninsula rose from 25 000 in 1978 to an estimated 250 000 in 1986. All along government has been determined that if it could not destroy Crossroads entirely, it would only accommodate the 'original' residents, some 25 000 people. Now at last the authorities have managed to get Crossroads under control. Ngxobongwana has been installed as 'mayor' with a 'town council', and the army presence at the clinic goes unchallenged.

On the burned-out Crossroads area 1 400 widely spaced, serviced sites are ready to be occupied. There are high-mast lights and streets wide enough for casspirs to patrol. Criteria according to which people will be allowed into the scheme have not been announced. This is a highly contentious issue as at least half of those chased off that land a year ago are determined to return there and leave the refugee camps in the townships.

Khayelitsha: Meanwhile at Sites B and C, the site-and-service schemes at Khayelitsha, orderly urbanisation is under way. The leaders of the five groups which moved there from Crossroads in 1985 have formed an executive committee which allocates sites to newcomers. It is alleged that refugees from Old Crossroads have to pay R25 to get a site, but are given receipts which state that they have paid only R13. The department of community services of the Cape Provincial Administration, which took over development board functions after 1 July 1986, claims it cannot stop this fraud.

The new executive reportedly collected R17 000 from the people to pay consultants to advise on development for the area. Using money from Sullivan Code companies, the committee is building eight brick houses. This was lauded as an entrepreneurial initiative by an official and is consistent with government policy that the people themselves should pay for their own development rather than be dependent on the state. Meanwhile welfare agencies have queues of destitute people needing food. When asked why they cannot buy it for themselves, they reply that they have to pay their dues to the leaders.

Another 400 former residents of Nyanga Extention, which is part of the Crossroads triangle, moved out of backyard shacks and refugee centres to Browns Farm. This is unoccupied land planned for industrial expansion on Lansdowne Road, south of Nyanga and New Crossroads. However, on 27 August divisional council workers demolished their shelters. The refugees were charged with trespass and taken to Khayelitsha.

Most of these people returned to the townships. They joined other refugees and started new informal settlements on vacant ground. One of these is Mpetha Square, named after Oscar Mpetha, the jailed veteran trade union leader, whose house stands opposite the settlement. There are also settlements next to the Nyanga Development Centre and in the dense bush along the N2 national road.

Residents are constantly harassed by police who threaten to set the witdoeke on them if they do not move to Khayelitsha. Community Services officials are currently 'surveying the area for planning orderly urbanisation which has replaced influx control', according to spokesperson Sampie Steenkamp. Evictions seem imminent.

Refugees would like to return to Crossroads but officials have wired off the area and are building roads. Until they can return to the land they claim was allocated to them by development board officials, they say they will stay and risk witdoek attacks. As one woman commented:

> We don't know what the witdoeke want because they said Crossroads was theirs and we must go. They fought us and we left, so why must they come here now? They say they want our old area for upgrade. Now we've left. Now we are upgrading our own area here. Next they will want this area too.

Another resident claimed that

> the government hired the witdoeke to do a forced removal but we will not go to Khayelitsha. There the witdoeke are strong and we do not want to fight. We will build here and live in peace.

On Christmas Eve 1986 a temporary supreme court interdict (which was later made permanent) restrained leaders Mali Hoza,

Sisa Nyandeni, Mncedisi Maqhula and the witdoeke from attacking anyone or damaging property in Sites B and C. Hoza reportedly said:

> You are the comrades from Crossroads. We attacked you in Crossroads and we are going to continue attacking you here... Here you have to listen to the rules, if you can't do that, you have to move out.

The KTC camp was a target of police repression in 1986. Raids on residents were frequent and 'kitskonstabels' became an unpleasant feature of townships and informal settlements.

The future of the refugees is uncertain. They have no option but to move to Khayelitsha, yet they continue to try to organise themselves with no recognition and little outside support under a state of emergency.

At Lwandle hostel near the Strand in the Western Cape 177 people were arrested in May, and on 16 September several women were arrested at the Mfuleni hostel in nearby Kuilsrivier - all under trespass laws. The Kuilsrivier women were found guilty and sentenced to R50 or 50 days, penalties similar to those under the old pass law system.

Duncan Village, East London: This East London township has long been threatened with removal. In 1985 all but 'illegal squatters' were reprieved. Now the authorities have announced that more than 40 000 people will have to move because the area is too overcrowded to upgrade. They will be moved once sites are available, presumably near Mdantsane in the 'independent' Ciskei, where they will have no chance of regaining their South African citizenship.

Red Location, Walmer: In Red Location, part of the fenced-off New Brighton area, the Ibayi Town Council (ITC) issued 450 of the 1 400 households with eviction notices in terms of Section 3(b)(1) of the Prevention of Illegal Squatting Act of 1951. They were to move to the site-and-service scheme at Motherwell, more than 20 km away from Port Elizabeth, by 23 November 1986.

'It will not be a forced removal, but let's call it a semi-forced removal. There are many unruly elements in the area', said ITC manager Edward Pullen. Residents sent a petition to State President PW Botha, appealing to him not to move them or divide the community of 10 000 people. As a result of their protests, the ITC backed down and announced it would upgrade the area. But residents fear the same 'weeding-out' fate as Duncan Village.

The Witwatersrand: In Soweto, hundreds of squatters living in backyards and on vacant sites throughout the township have been evicted and their shelters destroyed, with no alternative accommodation offered. In raids on the Roodepoort hostels in the Transvaal, people were convicted under the Prevention of Illegal Squatting Act

'Orderly urbanisation' has clearly replaced influx control removals. In the words of one trade unionist, 'We no longer have to carry a *dompas,* this is the age of the *slimpas*'. For the past ten years the state appears to have been working towards a new policy for urban control, known as orderly urbanisation. The Crossroads/Khayelitsha case could be seen as a pilot study for this new process. The tactics outlined in the President's Council report are only just beginning to be implemented in other areas, particularly the Eastern Cape.

Informal settlements

Kabah (Langa), Uitenhage: In an attempt to control the population and disorganise resistance, the state has dealt particularly harshly with one of the most articulate and organised communities: Langa. On 12 June 1986 members of the Langa Co-ordinating Committee, the only body representing residents in their refusal to move, were either detained or went into hiding.

In mid-July, while the fate of 426 shacks between 4th and 9th Avenues awaited a Port Elizabeth Supreme Court judgment, Kabah residents were subjected to midnight-to-dawn evictions by officials of the Kwanobuhle Town Council. According to a Black Sash report:

> At midnight the trucks started coming into the township, telling the people to start pulling down their homes, calling to them from loudspeakers that either they demolished their own shacks or the bulldozers would do it for them.

By the end of August about 20 000 people had been moved from Langa, which is a ten-minute walk from the centre of Uitenhage, to the tent town in Kwanobuhle, 15 km southwest of Uitenhage. While Barry Erasmus, the council administrator, claimed the council only moved people at their own request, residents said men in green uniforms not only harassed and intimidated people into demolishing their shacks, but carried out the first removals. One victim, Frederick Stegman, 25, said:

> At about 7 pm on the night of 21 July officials came to my house in 13th

Avenue and demolished it. We (four adults and a two-year-old child) spent the night sleeping outside. It was midwinter and very cold.

On 29 July the Port Elizabeth Supreme Court declared all structures between 4th and 9th Avenues illegal. This was two weeks *after* the removals began. The next day Black Sash and church workers collected statements from 150 residents gathered to complain about the removals. Not one of them wanted to move.

Their reasons:

* Kwanobuhle is too far from town to have reasonable access to work, shops and hospitals - the last are particularly important to pensioners. The cost of transport is way beyond most people's means;

* Rents are considerably higher in Kwanobuhle. In fact, a number of Kwanobuhle residents had moved to Langa because they could not afford the rents;

* Kwanobuhle schools are too far away for primary school children to walk; and

* People are afraid of vigilantes and municipal guards in Kwanobuhle.

Removals continued night after night until Langa was cleared in November. Residents reported to the Black Sash that every night:

> The loudspeakers reiterate their call to 'Break your shacks'. It is no longer even necessary for them to continue 'or we will do it for you'. It would take more than ordinary courage to withstand that midnight knock on the door.

Africans are also being cleared out of Blikkiesdorp, an area of Langa on the edge of the coloured township of Rosedale.

Despatch: On 22 September 1986, African residents of Despatch, a small town between Port Elizabeth and Uitenhage, were given 24 hours notice to move to Kwanobuhle. Eight hours later trucks, accompanied by armed municipal police, arrived to move them. No one in the community had been consulted about the move and community leaders were all in detention. More than 500 families have been moved.

By the end of December 50 000 people had been moved to Kwanobuhle tent town. So far six people have died, poisoned by carbon monoxide as a result of lighting fires in the tiny tents in an attempt to keep warm.

Conditions in Kwanobuhle tent town are very poor. Initially water had to be trucked in from outside. Now water is supposed to be delivered daily and stored in large plastic containers, but women report that two or three days may go by before water is delivered. 'People go to sleep thirsty', they said.

Transportable chemical toilets are available; each one serves eight families and is emptied only twice a week. There are no shops and people have to walk long distances to Kwanobuhle settlement or to Uitenhage for provisions. This is 'site and service' and 'orderly urbanisation'.

On 18 September a British diplomat who saw the tent town said, 'Hiroshima must have looked like this after the bomb'. One resident, asked whether he had moved voluntarily, said: 'I feel I was a coward to move, but we were all so afraid. They treat us like animals so how can we behave like human beings?'

On 4 January 1987 a Crossroads-style 'witdoek' raid was conducted by about 1 500 men marching 'calmly' through the streets at 4 am, according to Major Eddie Everson, a police liaison officer for the Eastern Cape. He said that

> the marchers wanted a return to normality and a return of the children to school. They had tried to get hold of the trouble-makers, removed the furniture from specific houses and set it alight. Houses were left untouched.

When the men encountered opposition, the two groups 'thrashed it out' and 'the youngsters fled into neighbouring koppies'. Four hours later the police dispersed the group. At least two people were killed and many injuries were reported.

Lawaaikamp, George: On 3 April 1986 the George Municipality began demolishing homes in the informal settlement of Lawaaikamp and moving its people to the site-and-service scheme of Sandkraal. Residents have been allocated serviced sites with toilets and taps, and have to pay a R21 monthly service fee. The few who can afford between R7 000 and R9 000 have opted to buy knock-down wooden bungalows without knowing what the monthly repayments will be. The rest have to build their own houses again.

The George Municipality issued the 2 000 remaining residents of Lawaaikamp and the 1 000 African residents of the nearby coloured townships of Borchards and Urbanville with eviction notices for 31 December 1986. Until recently these people were frightened to resist, but then began to organise and publicise their plight. With legal help they won an extension beyond 31 December but were told they would have to move when more plots at Sandkraal became available.

At Lawaaikamp the service fee was R25 a month. Services include four taps (of which only three work) and irregular refuse and night-soil removal. The camp is marshy and dirty and has been deliberately neglected. However, on 13 March 1987 the community won one of their demands: the monthly fee was reduced to R19,08.

The first official reason for the removal was that, according to the municipality, Lawaaikamp was a health hazard. Later members of the Cape provincial executive committee said the land had been allocated to coloureds so Africans must move. The community appealed to the Labour Party to support them in their bid to remain on the land, but no reply has yet been received.

The George town clerk said Africans were living in a coloured group area. Members of the executive committee added that the land belonged to the municipality and they were entitled to allocate it for coloured housing should they so wish.

Although Sandkraal is only 1 km beyond Lawaaikamp, people do not want to move to a site-and-service scheme because they were promised 770 brick houses at Lawaaikamp. They might be prepared to move to better housing but not 'from one squatter camp to another'. In the 1950s and 1960s they were moved from Blikkiesdorp, Rosemoor, Blanco and other areas in the George vicinity. Many people have lived in Lawaaikamp since the 1940s, while others were told by officials to move there more recently. Now once again and at their own expense they are expected to rebuild their houses from scratch at Sandkraal: wooden houses, unlike those made of corrugated iron, cannot be easily dismantled and little of the material can be re-used.

On 15 November the first community meeting since the declaration of the state of emergency was held. The people refused to be moved. They demanded that Lawaaikamp be upgraded, that those who wanted to return from Sandkraal be allowed to, that their leaders be released and that the service fee be reduced. Since then they have met regularly.

Sandkraal is the first proclaimed area for Africans in George. The old Coloured Labour Preference Area policy was strictly enforced in the region. So although Africans have lived in Lawaaikamp since the 1940s, until the proclamation of Sandkraal they had no security in the area.

The removal of the African people from Lawaaikamp to Sandkraal is a clear example of how mass detentions under the state of emergency have facilitated the state's relocation of communities. In George 180 people were detained. Two members of the civic association were in detention for eight months, 15 are under restriction orders and some are in hiding.

The next steps in this 'voluntary' removal are the eviction of 'unregistered' residents and those in arrears with payment of service charges, and the introduction of a community council which would be likely to agree to a removal. Residents do not want a community council, and say they are quite content to be represented by the George Civic Association, which is accountable to them, not to the authorities.

Natal: Action has also been taken against residents of informal settlements in Natal. The Pietermaritzburg City Council served eviction notices on 70 African families who had been squatting in the Indian area of Northdale since 1985. The council then demolished their homes in January 1987. At least one resident was deported to the Transkei and the rest are expected to move to relocation areas in Kwazulu. The evicted families are living in the bush surrounding the sites of their demolished homes in an attempt to maintain their casual jobs in the area.

Township removals

Oukasie, Brits: The 10 000 residents of the Old Brits Location (Oukasie) are still determined to remain where they have lived for the past 55 years. On 17 October 1986, after ten months of negotiations, Constitutional Affairs Minister Chris Heunis announced proudly that the township had been dis-established and its people would be moved to Lethlabile, 20 km away on the Bophuthatswana border.

Most members of the Brits Action Committee (BAC) were detained on 12 June. That was the day the Brits people buried one of their most loved residents, Joyce Modimoeng, wife of Metal and Allied Workers Union (MAWU) organiser and BAC member David Modimoeng. Mrs Modimoeng was killed by a hand-made bomb in a pre-dawn attack on her home.

Oukasie residents are angry about the dis-establishment and determined to stay. Residents, the unions and employers in Brits have tried to negotiate with the state. At the request of the BAC and local branches of MAWU and the National Automobile and Allied

Workers Union, planners and engineers compiled a well-researched report showing that it is feasible to upgrade Oukasie for R3-million. The state has not accepted the report and has refused to reverse its decision to dis-establish the township.

Tshikota, Northern Transvaal: Over the past 14 years the 6 000 residents of Tshikota township, 3 km from Louis Trichardt, have been moved. The North Sothos were sent to Indermaak and Seshego over 100 km away, the Tsongas to Waterval and the Vendas to Vleifontein. Waterval and Vleifontein are approximately 30 km from Tshikota.

Two of the remaining 47 North Sotho-speaking families left at Tshikota moved to Vleifontein after being intimidated by the local superintendent. They were told to move or their houses would be knocked down with their possessions inside.

The remaining 45 families do not want to move. Residents have petitioned government to no avail. Deputy Minister of Land Affairs Ben Wilkens continues to insist that they should move 'for development'. But residents do not want to move 25 km from their conveniently situated Louis Trichardt homes to Vleifontein in a bantustan.

Vleifontein was incorporated into Venda on 1 April 1986, despite promises to the people moved from Tshikota that this would not happen. Although the 5 000 people who moved to Vleifontein over the past ten years never chose to renounce their South African citizenship, they are now all 'foreigners' with no rights to live or work in South Africa - or even to enter it.

Waterval is part of Gazankulu. However, because Gazankulu is not independent, Waterval residents may now live and work anywhere in South Africa if they are able to find jobs and accommodation.

Eastern Cape: In the Eastern Cape, both the townships of Kenton-on-Sea and Cathcart are threatened with removal to site-and-service schemes further from the white towns.

Natal: The future of Umbulwane outside Ladysmith is not clear. Its people have been told that the area may be developed as an extension of Steadville township. Whether Umbulwane landowners and their tenants will be able to stay in the upgraded area, or whether the land will be expropriated for township development for the overcrowded area of Steadville is not known. The uncertainty is causing Umbulwane residents deep concern. They wish to remain on their land and upgrade the township, and yet retain its rural character. They have sunk their own boreholes and built pit latrines but want to improve the roads and build community facilities.

The bantustans

In 1986 government embarked on an intricate legislative process of extending and entrenching grand apartheid. This involved an attempt to allow bantustans to administer the residents of scheduled and released land outside the borders of the bantustans, a move since abandoned. The schedule to the National States Constitution Act was also amended. This vastly extended the powers of bantustan's in effect enabling them to take major decisions without reference to Pretoria. Also passed was the Borders of Particular States Extension Amendment Bill, which provided for the addition of substantial areas of land to the 'independent' bantustans.

Communities living in these areas will join the permanent residents of 'independent' bantustans who are not automatically eligible to benefit from the recently passed Restoration of SA Citizenship Act. Now, like some seven million Xhosa-, Venda- and Tswana-speaking people, they are defined as 'aliens' who may not move freely within South Africa. Their lives will be governed by the Aliens Act of 1937.

The penalty for employing an alien without permission is a R5 000 fine or two years' imprisonment, or both for a second conviction. Employers have been instructed to give priority to employing South Africans.

Bophuthatswana: Residents of communities such as Braklaagte, Leeufontein and Machakaneng in the Western Transvaal, and Bloedfontein and Geweerfontein in the central Transvaal, have successfully resisted physical removal. Now Pretoria will go ahead with incorporation in terms of the Borders of Particular States Extension Amendment Bill. The government of Bophuthatswana has been consulted, but not the affected communities.

With the reality of forced denationalisation becoming clear, not only have a number of communities in the Transvaal and Eastern Cape expressed resistance to incorporation, but some already included in Bophuthatswana and Ciskei are discussing secession. This is no idle threat. They know Bophuthatswana President Lucas Mangope has already rejected dual citizenship. Bophuthatswana now provides that anyone taking out South African citizenship automatically loses Bophuthatswanan citizenship. Such people may face loss of their right to land, property and residence in Bophuthatswana.

Ciskei: At Thornhill in the Ciskei 20 000 people want to secede. They say they were promised land ten years ago when they fled from Herschel because of the impending independence of the Transkei. They are still living in poverty-stricken conditions on small plots, with no land for ploughing or grazing.

Kwandebele: As a result of near-insurrection, the Kwandebele Legislative Assembly backed down on its 1986 'independence' plans. Widespread resistance to independence was launched by civil servants, youth and traditional leaders such as the royal family, after a mass meeting of some 10 000 people at the royal kraal on 12 May 1986. Between then and 12 August, when it was decided not to take independence, at least 160 people were killed. However, in May 1987 the legislative assembly again voted to request 'independence' from South Africa, asking that it be 'backdated' to December 1986. But by late 1987 the Kwandebele authorities had shown no signs of meeting the South African government's preconditions for the granting of independence. However, building of showpiece projects continues and the threat of further attempts to foist 'independence' on the people remains.

On 11 November 1986, two leading anti-independence members of the royal family, Prince James and Prince Andries Mahlangu, were detained in Siyabuswa, 'capital' of Kwandebele. Since then there have been widespread detentions of anti-independence leaders in Kwandebele, with leading members of the royal family constantly harassed.

QwaQwa: Moves to make QwaQwa independent are also rumoured. Some 23 000 hectares were recently added to Onverwacht, now known as Botshabelo, the sprawling rural slum of more than half-a-million people 50 km east of Bloemfontein. This is to be incorporated into QwaQwa. More land near Golden Gate National Park has also been granted and will be be added to the only piece of QwaQwa near Harrismith.

On 3 July 1986, 179 Sotho-speaking families originally from Herschel in Transkei were dumped in Botshabelo. Their land was first incorporated into Ciskei, then into Transkei in 1976. In 1981 the chief minister of QwaQwa, TK Mopeli, and the then minister of co-operation and development, Piet Koornhof, promised them compensatory land in the Harrismith district. But like the Thornhill people, they are still waiting.

Land added to QwaQwa in the Harrismith district was not allocated to the Herschel residents who had fled to Phutaditjhaba, capital of QwaQwa, where they were given rent-free housing for two years while they waited for their promised land. When they were told to pay rent, they refused and were trucked to Botshabelo. All their cattle and the rest of the Sotho people (some 28 000) are still in Herschel, waiting for the promises to be fulfilled. If Botshabelo is incorporated into QwaQwa, they say they will 'trek'. They are no longer prepared to live in bantustans.

Black spot removals

Natal: The Mentz (formerly Tempel) Commission on consolidation of Kwazulu has still not reported, although on 19 January 1987 it announced some amendments to the plans for the Vryheid district. Some 240 000 people in Natal are threatened with removal as a result of the commission's interim report, published in September 1985.

Transvaal: In the Transvaal no further reprieves have been announced. At Mathopestad residents' optimism was heightened by success in their application for a telephone, which was granted after a wait of 15 years. However, they remain worried because in a letter dated 21 November 1986 to the people of the nearby black spot of Motlatla, Deputy Minister Wilkens stated that while people would not be 'forced to move, negotiations on a future move were envisaged'.

Eastern Cape: During the 1986 session of parliament Wilkens announced that Eastern Cape black spots would no longer be incorporated into the Ciskei. However, a visit to the black spot of Lesseyton near Queenstown in June, after the announcement, revealed that South African and Ciskeian officials had recently advised both landowners and tenants that they must move. The headman appeared to support the community in its unwillingness to move. But there is tension between landowners and tenants as a result of official promises to tenants that they will be given land in Whittlesea North.

Newlands, near East London, has not received official notification that it will not be incorporated into the Ciskei. The headmen in the area still fulfil their official duties but have joined the residents' association.

In Kwelera, another black spot in the 'white corridor' between Ciskei and Transkei, residents continue to be confused and threatened by removal. Although Pretoria has acknowledged its responsibility for administration of the area, it took months for pension payments to be transferred from Ciskeian to South African control. Pensioners have applied for back payments for the period between January 1982 and May 1986 during which the Ciskei paid out pensions amounting to nearly one-third less than those Pretoria pays.

Farm removals

People continue to be squeezed off the land. In Natal fieldworkers report that hundreds of farmworkers and former labour tenants are evicted each month. Local magistrates do not appear to have been informed of the repeal of Chapter IV of the 1936 Development Trust and Land Act, and there are reports of people still being prosecuted under this non-existent law.

In the Weenen district, for instance, a farm manager served 300 people with hand-written eviction notices ordering them to 'clear of' (sic) the farms Bloukrantz, Hopewell and Zwagershoek by 9 October 1986. Before the labour tenancy system was outlawed in 1981, these people used to work six months of the year for the farmer in exchange for being allowed to live on the farm and graze their cattle. If a farmer or company owned a number of farms, as in this case, one was often used as a 'labour farm', given over to labour tenants in exchange for free labour for half the year.

In most cases, too many people have been forced to scratch a living from such labour farms. As a result the land is eroded and most recent evictions are prompted by conservation laws. But evicted tenants are forced onto even more overcrowded and eroded land in Kwazulu.

One evicted former labour tenant, Ndlala Zungu, aged 61, had worked for the last 40 years for the Bloukrantz farmer. Bent double with a spinal disorder, he said he and his extended family of 18 members had nowhere to go. The farmer had dismissed them because he could no longer work. He could not provide sons to work the fields as his sons had left to seek better jobs on the Witwatersrand.

On 20 October, when the eviction notice expired, Zungu was found guilty of unlawful squatting and sentenced to three months' imprisonment or a R150 fine. He spent one month in jail before his family could muster the money needed. Zungu was convicted under Section 26(1)(b) of the 1936 Land Act which had been repealed by Section 17 of the Abolition of Influx Control Act on 1 July.

This is not the only case of repealed legislation used to evict farmworkers in Natal. However, under the Prevention of Illegal Squatting Act even harsher measures can be taken against former labour tenants. They can be dismissed from their jobs, their homes can be demolished without notice and a magistrate can transfer them to any other district.

The only option for evicted farmworkers and labour tenants is to move to the distant 'closer settlements' in Kwazulu. There they would have no access to land and would not be able to keep livestock. Stringent anti-squatting laws prevent them from moving to 'white' towns. Although the pass laws have theoretically been abolished, no land has been set aside in Natal for people evicted from white-owned farms who may wish to establish themselves in urban areas, as the 1987 demolitions of Northdale shacks illustrate.

In the Eastern Transvaal ex-farmworkers unsuccessfully took legal action in an attempt to regain their right to live on white-owned farms. The law offers no protection against eviction, even if a family has lived on a farm for generations. The increase in landmine explosions in the Eastern Transvaal, the drought and increasing numbers of farm bankruptcies have resulted in widespread evictions over the past 18 months.

Rural dispossession

Both in bantustans and in the 20 'coloured' reserves, relocation is quickening. In line with the government's policy of privatisation, thousands of people are being squeezed into tiny plots on the already overcrowded 13% of the land set aside for blacks.

Communal land is being surveyed and leased to individuals. The policy is that not everyone can have access to land, that 'bona fide' and 'viable' farmers must be encouraged. This excludes the most destitute because they have no regular cash income to invest.

Leliefontein, a 'coloured' reserve in Namaqualand, has been divided into 47 economic units, 30 of which have been allocated.

Some 4 000 people will lose access to grazing and crop land as school teachers and shopkeepers take up leases on the recently fenced units. As a result of local resistance to this exclusion, the house of representatives has set up an internal commission of enquiry into the issue. The results are expected during 1987.

In Natal 100 Doornkop families wait for Kwazulu officials to decide their future. They do not want to move from the formerly white-owned farm which was consolidated into Kwazulu and sold to a black entrepreneur who has served the people with eviction notices. Residents were promised that when the farm was incorporated they would be allowed to remain. Now they are subject to Pretoria's idea of reform: removal carried out by blacks rather than whites under the same system of private land ownership.

The state's 'reform' programme has enabled it to restructure its means of repression, and to decentralise to local bodies the responsibility for carrying out the abusive population relocations demanded by its programme of social engineering.

This combination of restructuring and repression is deliberately confusing. Lack of control over their own lives and growing impoverishment will continue to cause deep resentment and resistance among the majority of South Africans.

The central state is attempting to keep its hands clean by blaming 'black-on-black' conflict for the ongoing violence, rather than its own refusal to change fundamentally. A more cynical development in the attempt to maintain power and privilege in white hands is hard to imagine.

The Power of the State
and the State of Power:
Recent Developments in
South Africa's Nuclear Industry

Koeberg Alert Research Group:
Thomas Auf der Heyde, David Fig,
Andrew Stoddart, John Venn and Peter Wilkinson

In the last three years South Africa has undertaken a significant expansion of its nuclear industry. Two nuclear power reactors have come into operation at Koeberg; a nuclear waste dump has been opened in Namaqualand; and a uranium enrichment plant is nearing completion at Valindaba.

Certain of the technologies needed to make the local nuclear industry self-sufficient have not yet been developed. But major research efforts are directed towards closing the remaining gaps.

The development of South Africa's nuclear programme has become increasingly difficult to justify on the grounds of economic rationality. Nor does it represent an appropriate response to the country's energy needs, and mounting evidence of nuclear disasters around the world has undermined the industry's claims to provide safe, clean energy.

Despite this, grandiose plans have been drawn up to extend South Africa's dependence on nuclear power. Current research and development funding dramatically reflects the priority the state attaches to the nuclear option.

This anomaly - the apparent irrationality of further nuclear development on the one hand, and the state's determination to proceed with its programme on the other - must be explained. An important factor is the inextricable bond between the so-called civilian nuclear industry and military applications of nuclear power. This provides a possible motive for the state's interest in further expansion of its nuclear programme. The emergence of a nuclear bureaucracy with a vested interest in the drive to develop this country's nuclear capability also plays a part.

Even if the political and military implications of the nuclear power programme are discounted, it is important to debate other issues which surround it. How energy resources are to be supplied and distributed most equitably is too critical a question to be left unexplored at this stage in South Africa's history. To develop these arguments, it is important to have some knowledge of the technologies and processes which constitute the nuclear fuel chain.

The nuclear fuel chain

During the last decade it has become a commonplace in circles which critically address the nuclear issue in all its dimensions that civilian and military uses of nuclear energy are inextricably linked. The nature of the link - more specifically the origin of the nuclear weapons proliferation problem in the export of ostensibly civilian nuclear technologies - has been explored in considerable detail by Amory and Hunter Lovins for the environmentalist group Friends of the Earth.[1]

More recently, particularly in the wake of the disaster at Chernobyl, recognition of this relationship appears to have spread to the European peace and disarmament movements.[2] Rob Edwards, in a pamphlet published last year by the Campaign for Nuclear Disarmament, vividly articulated this growing awareness: 'Nuclear power and nuclear weapons are like Siamese twins, conceived together, joined at birth, and now inseparable'.

To understand how this has come about, it is necessary to grasp the fundamentals of how nuclear energy is produced, beginning with the material which is the central element of the nuclear fuel chain.[3]

Nuclear fuel

Uranium oxide, or less commonly uranium metal, is used to fuel the vast majority of nuclear reactors. (The few so-called fast breeder reactors built so far use a mixture of uranium and plutonium oxides). Uranium is used because one of its forms is readily capable of undergoing nuclear fission and occurs naturally in significant quantities. This form, the isotope uranium-235, has chemical properties virtually identical to other non-fissionable forms of uranium but with a slightly different atomic structure.

Fission is the process in which the nucleus of an atom is ruptured into two fragments (or 'fission products') by the impact of a sub-atomic particle called a neutron. Splitting the nucleus releases further high-energy neutrons, one or more of which may collide with and cause fission to occur in other nuclei. Nuclear reactors are simply the means by which the energy released in the process of 'chain reaction' may be controlled and made available to boil water to produce steam, which is then used to drive turbines and so generate electricity. Nuclear bombs, on the other hand, are devices in which the chain reaction process is forced instantaneously and explosively out of control, with devastating consequences.

The nuclear fuel chain - or, as advocates of nuclear power prefer to call it, the nuclear fuel cycle - describes the circulation of uranium fuel material through a series of discrete but interlinked processes. Diagram 1 provides a highly schematic and simplified representation of the complete chain, showing how its various components relate to one another.

Uranium mining and milling

The chain begins with the open-pit or underground mining of uranium ore and its milling and chemical processing to produce a mixture of uranium oxides called yellowcake. Naturally occurring uranium, however, contains only 0,7% of the fissionable (or 'fissile') isotope, uranium-235, as against 99,3% of the more stable isotope, uranium-238. To sustain a relatively efficient nuclear reaction, the uranium fuel material generally has to be enriched so that it contains a certain minimum (usually 2%-3%) of uranium-235.

Hex production and enrichment

Enrichment can be undertaken through a variety of technologies, the most common of which (gaseous diffusion, gas-centrifuge and jet-

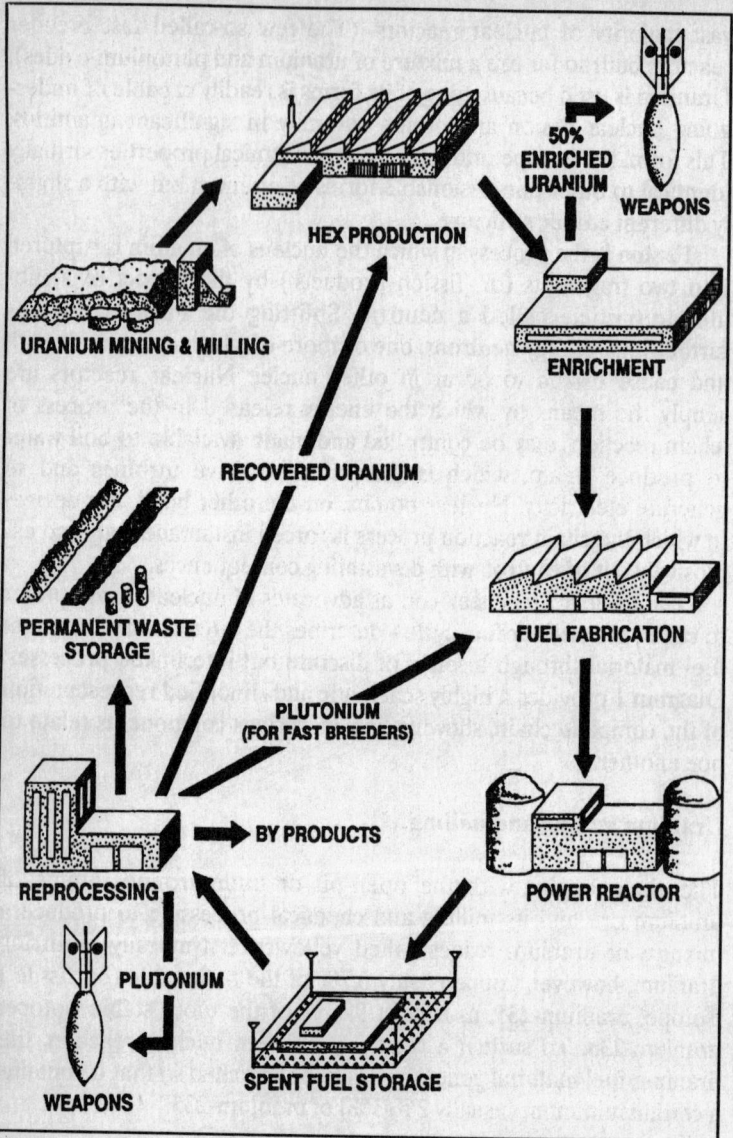

Diagram 1: The Nuclear Fuel Cycle

nozzle separation techniques) all require conversion of the solid uranium oxide mixture into a compound, uranium hexafluoride or 'hex', which can be relatively easily vaporised. In essence the process involves the progressive concentration of hex molecules containing uranium-235 - which are slightly lighter than the more numerous molecules containing uranium-238 - until the required proportion of fissile material is achieved.

Though the costs involved would escalate rapidly, the technologies in common use in theory do not preclude the continuation of the enrichment process to produce weapons-grade material, that is uranium with a fissile content high enough to be used in the manufacture of relatively efficient nuclear explosives. A crude and unpredictable bomb, for instance, could be constructed with material enriched to a uranium-235 content of 50%.

Fuel fabrication

In the conventional civilian fuel chain, uranium enriched to a 2%-3% uranium-235 content is transported to a fuel fabrication plant. There it is processed chemically into a uranium dioxide powder. This is formed into the required shape, usually high-density pellets or rods, and assembled into metal-clad fuel elements. These elements are then inserted into the core of a nuclear reactor in a quantity and configuration which enable controlled nuclear chain reaction to be initiated and sustained.

Reactor operation

A wide range of designs for nuclear power reactors have been developed, but details and variation of reactor design and operation need not be addressed here. The significant point is that the spent fuel elements produced by all reactor types in the course of their normal operation contain what is classified as valuable fissile material (plutonium-239 and unused uranium-235), as well as other highly radioactive, but unusable, waste materials. Reprocessing involves the separation and recovery of the former from the latter.

After a predetermined period of operation, spent fuel elements are extracted from the reactor core. They are then stored for some years, usually under water, to allow the more short-lived radioactive fission products to decay, spontaneously breaking down through certain nuclear processes which eventually produce elements that are more or less stable and hence less radioactive. Even after a storage period of five years, however, the irradiated reactor fuel remains intensely radioactive, and its transportation and reprocessing require stringent safety precautions.

Spent fuel reprocessing

Reprocessing is a complex and dangerous operation which uses various chemical procedures first to separate the recyclable uranium and plutonium from the other fission products in the spent fuel elements, then to separate the uranium and the plutonium from one another. The recovered uranium may then be returned to the fuel chain by passing it through the enrichment and fuel fabrication processes. The plutonium may be recycled to produce the mixture of plutonium and uranium oxides used to fuel fast breeder reactors. Alternatively, it may be employed directly in the manufacture of nuclear weapons.

Permanent waste storage

The high-level (highly radioactive) waste materials which remain after the recovery of uranium and plutonium from spent reactor fuel require permanent and safe disposal. The problem is that these materials include certain elements which decay to relatively low levels of radioactivity only over extremely protracted periods, in some cases several millennia. Despite the claims of the nuclear industry, none of the elaborate disposal methods proposed so far can guarantee total containment of the waste material over such periods.

As a result, representation of the nuclear fuel chain as a clean (non-polluting) and very largely self-contained cyclical process has in recent years been exposed as, at best, misleading.

Civilian-military linkages

There are two major routes to the production of nuclear weapons. Both are tied directly to the nuclear fuel chain and employ technologies central to the 'peaceful' application of nuclear power in the generation of electricity.

The so-called front-end route uses enrichment technology to produce weapons-grade enriched uranium and therefore diverts fuel material from the chain before it enters the reactor. Conventional methods of enriching uranium to this grade are very costly in terms of both capital and energy. But experimental laser techniques currently being developed promise to be both highly efficient in energy terms and relatively inexpensive. Their application can only exacerbate the problem of proliferation from the front end.

The rear-end route, on the other hand, involves reprocessing spent reactor fuel to separate out plutonium. Because of its dangers, reprocessing is perhaps the least widespread of the various processes which make up the nuclear fuel chain. So-called quick-and-dirty reprocessing plants are, however, within the technological capabilities of many nuclear countries. They could allegedly separate sufficient plutonium from spent reactor fuel to make a crude but functional bomb every week. Because of this possibility Amory and Hunter Lovins refer to power reactors as 'bomb factories'.[4]

That civilian and military uses of nuclear technology are indivisible was unequivocally demonstrated in 1974 when India detonated what it called a peaceful nuclear explosion using plutonium produced by a reactor which had originally been supplied by Canada under the 'Atoms for Peace' programme.[5]

The linkage was further underlined in 1979 by Israel's decision to attack and destroy a power reactor under construction in Baghdad, on the assumption that its completion would sooner or later enable Iraq to develop a nuclear weapons capability.

Clearly the acquisition of such a capability is directly underpinned by the degree to which a country has managed to import or develop self-sufficiency in those processes which constitute the central components of the nuclear fuel chain.

The development of South Africa's nuclear programme

From its beginnings in the immediate post-war period, the nuclear industry in North Atlantic Treaty Organisation (NATO) countries sought to incorporate South Africa into its activities. This was largely due to Southern Africa's abundant deposits of uranium, a commodity essential to the nuclear fuel chain.

The payoff for providing uranium to NATO countries was a gradual transfer of nuclear technology, at first enabling South Africa to set up elaborate nuclear research facilities, but in more recent times enabling it to forge virtually every link in the nuclear fuel chain.

It is this systematic acquisition of the entire chain which is of particular concern, since it has implications for South Africa's

capacity to manufacture nuclear armaments. The technology
associated with the fuel chain has been obtained regardless of the
fact that South Africa has shown reluctance to sign or ratify the 1968
Nuclear Non-Proliferation Treaty (NPT). The NPT was designed to
prevent the spread of nuclear weapons technology to non-nuclear
countries.

A number of the principal signatories of the NPT, including
Britain and the United States, helped South Africa to close the gaps
in the fuel chain. South Africa has also collaborated with other non-
signatories. At various times these included Argentina, Brazil,
France, Iran, Israel and Taiwan. The last two in particular remain in
close contact with the South African nuclear programme. Link by
link, South Africa obtained the technology it needed.

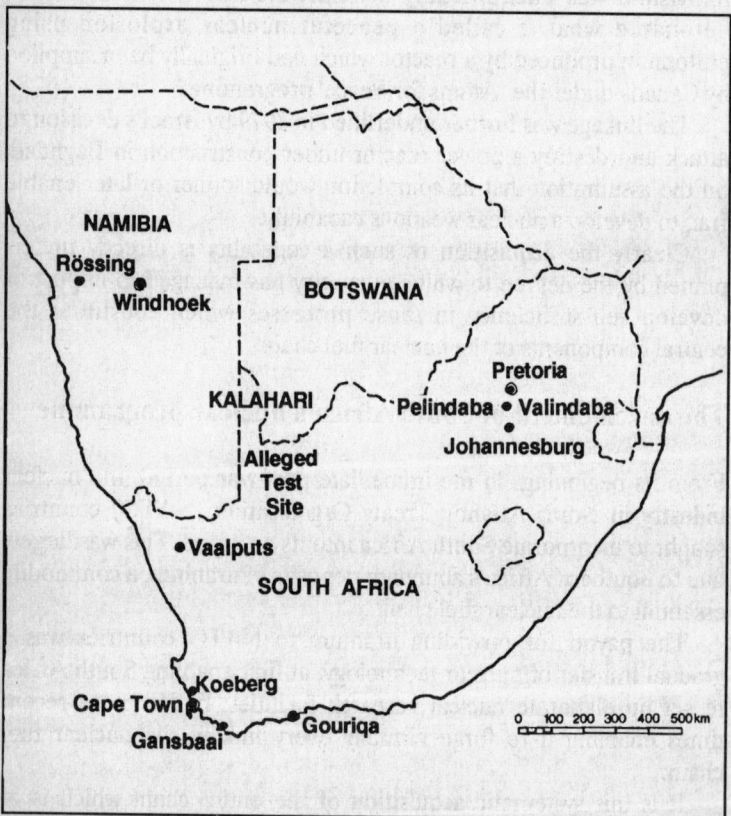

Figure 1: Sites of nuclear facilities in South Africa

Uranium mining

South Africa is one of the world's largest producers of mined uranium and has significant reserves of the mineral. Its continued colonial administration of Namibia has ensured South African control over the natural resources of the territory. Since 1976, when the giant open-cast Rossing mine started operations, South Africa has been able to market uranium mined beyond its borders. (In terms of the Nuclear Energy Act of 1982, it is an offence - punishable by the imposition of a R20 000 fine or a 20-year prison sentence - to reveal information on quantities of uranium mined and exported and on estimated reserves available.)

Not only is this uranium an important source of foreign exchange for South Africa, but it also helped lay the foundations for the development and expansion of a domestic nuclear industry.

British and US involvement in South Africa's nuclear development was initiated after the Manhattan Project, the secret wartime programme to build nuclear weapons, had conducted an intensive survey of geological literature in an attempt to locate global uranium supplies.

In their efforts to develop their own nuclear armaments industries in the post-war period, Britain and the US formed a joint procurement enterprise called the Combined Development Agency (CDA). The CDA established a close working relationship with South African nuclear scientists and encouraged the formation of a uranium research committee in 1946. In 1948, the South African parliament passed the Atomic Energy Act, which led to the appointment of the Atomic Energy Board (AEB) in 1949. The AEB was charged with sole control over the extraction, processing and sales of uranium.

The CDA encouraged South African gold producers to mine uranium as a by-product, and scarce capital was provided for this task. In 1952 the first uranium was sold to the CDA. In the 1950s, British and US capital facilitated the opening of 27 mines and 17 uranium oxide plants. By 1958, uranium production was adding 50% to the profits of the gold mines.

Apart from the Witwatersrand gold mines, other major sources of uranium included the Phalaborwa copper mine, Namibia's Rossing, reprocessing of gold ore tailings on the East Rand and the large Beisa uranium mine near Welkom. The Karroo also contains rich, but as yet unexploited, uranium reserves.

Rossing is the largest source of uranium in the sub-continent, adding 50% to the deposits under South African control. This naturally has implications for South Africa's continued presence in Namibia. The legal strictures of the South African nuclear legislation also apply in Namibia, insulating the operating company, Rio Tinto Zinc (RTZ), from having to reveal full information about Rossing's production, health standards and environmental impact. The recently formed Mineworkers' Union of Namibia might develop sufficient thrust to challenge RTZ on these issues.

Foreign investment in many uranium mines has meant that South Africa is deeply integrated into the international nuclear industry. This integration is sealed by extensive exports of uranium oxide to many of the nuclear countries of the West, thus underwriting the possibility of South Africa obtaining nuclear technology as a quid pro quo.

Hex production

Mining companies have invested enormous amounts of capital in processing technologies, as well as in research and development for the future. For example, in 1967 locally based uranium producers set up a consortium, the Nuclear Fuels Corporation (NUFCOR), which spent enormous sums on improving the purity of the uranium oxide to enable South Africa to produce its own uranium hexafluoride ('hex').

Originally all hex production occurred in Britain, whose Atomic Energy Authority (UKAEA) had first option on processing NUFCOR's uranium oxide. In 1970 the British government had to decide whether to transfer the technology of hex production to South Africa. The decision was not publicised, but in October that year the AEB claimed South Africa was now in a position to build its own hex plant. It seems likely, therefore, that the technology was provided through the UKAEA. A pilot plant was opened in June 1975, and production on an industrial scale began at Pelindaba in early 1976.

Enrichment

Transfer of enrichment technology to South Africa has been a matter of great controversy. Despite claims in 1970 by then Prime Minister

John Vorster and the president of the AEB, Dr Ampie Roux, that South Africa had developed a unique enrichment process, it is now widely believed to have been a modification of the jet nozzle technique developed as a result of US training and West German assistance. Documents stolen from the South African embassy in Cologne in 1975 revealed a high degree of West German collaboration in securing this technology.[6]

In 1970 the AEB set up a special agency, the Uranium Enrichment Corporation (UCOR), to run a pilot enrichment plant. Three years later, UCOR obtained a licence from the West German firm STEAG to develop the enrichment process for commercial use. The pilot enrichment plant at Valindaba was completed in 1976, and a medium-scale commercial enrichment plant was developed during the 1980s. Now nearing completion, it is estimated that two-thirds of its output will be required for power generation in South Africa, and the remainder will be exported.

Enrichment is an extremely expensive process. The value added to uranium by its enrichment makes its export in this form far more lucrative. If South Africa activates clauses in supply contracts enabling it to export enriched uranium rather than uranium oxide, foreign exchange earnings will rise dramatically. Acquisition of the enrichment technology has also made it more feasible for South Africa to produce weapons-grade uranium by repeated processing of the material.

With the expansion of the South African nuclear programme and especially with the start of power reactor construction, new legislation was drafted to reflect the increased sophistication of the industry and to provide the measures needed to cover its operations in a blanket of secrecy. In 1982, the Nuclear Energy Act replaced the Atomic Energy Act of 1948. It allowed for the formation of the Atomic Energy Corporation (AEC) into which were incorporated UCOR and the Nuclear Development Corporation (NUCOR), which took over the functions of the former AEB. NUCOR, based at Pelindaba, is responsible for nuclear research and development in fields other than enrichment technology, which is the province of UCOR at Valindaba (see Diagram 2 below).

Fuel fabrication

To become independent of its foreign suppliers, South Africa sought to develop the ability to manufacture its own fuel elements for insertion into its reactors. In 1982 NUCOR undertook a project aimed at manufacturing fuel elements for the SAFARI-1 reactor. The project is code-named ELPROD, presumably derived from the words 'element production'.

Experts believe that considerable efforts are being made to manufacture fuel elements for the reactors at Koeberg nuclear power station as well. It is widely known that hafnium-free zirconium, needed for the fuel element cladding, is being produced at the RTZ-run Phalaborwa mine.

Reactors

Under US President Dwight Eisenhower's 'Atoms for Peace' programme, the United States supplied South Africa with a research reactor and the heavily enriched weapons-grade uranium with which to fuel it. This reactor, known as SAFARI-1, began operating at Pelindaba in 1965. Two years later a second research reactor, apparently designed and built by South African engineers, was commissioned. This has been known as Pelinduna-Zero or SAFARI-2.

The decision to build commercial nuclear power stations linked into the national electricity grid involved both the AEB and the state power-generating monopoly, the Electricity Supply Commission (ESCOM). It seems that ESCOM had reservations about putting into action plans initiated by the AEB. Nevertheless, ESCOM commissioned the construction of two 922-megawatt[7] power reactors.

The tender for construction was awarded in August 1976 to a French consortium led by Framatome. The French were favoured over a US-Dutch consortium because of the activities of the anti-nuclear lobbies in these countries. France was not unduly perturbed by such pressures and had, for example, been willing to supply South Africa with conventional military equipment when other countries were extremely reluctant to break the arms embargo. Moreover, France, like South Africa, had not signed the NPT and was therefore not subject to its strictures.

The site ESCOM chose for the reactors was a farm 27 km from central Cape Town, the heart of South Africa's second-largest metropolitan area, with a population of over 1,8-million. Despite vigorous public objections, the Koeberg reactors were commissioned in March 1984 and mid-1985.

Questions to the minister of mineral and energy affairs in parliament revealed that estimates of the capital costs of the Koeberg reactors leapt from R600-million in 1975 to R1 827-million in 1984. The latter figure excluded the costs of considerable damage to secondary switching equipment as a result of an ANC attack in December 1982. Repairs and delays on interest repayments amounted to R68-million, a significant contribution to the cost overrun of R519-million since 1975. In ESCOM's 1984 annual report, its chairman, Jan Smith, referred to Koeberg as a three billion rand project.[8]

ESCOM's central argument for locating the reactors in the Western Cape was the escalating costs of coal-fired power in the region. Yet ESCOM's own figures indicate that nuclear energy is fed into the national grid at a cost of 5,6 cents per kilowatt-hour (c/kWh) as compared to 1,89c/kWh for electricity produced by the Transvaal coal-fired power stations.[9]

The high capital costs of producing nuclear power added considerably to the debt burden faced by South Africa and the consequent escalation of energy prices in recent times.

Not willing to learn the economic lessons of the Koeberg installation, ESCOM has embarked on a R13-million search for a new coastal site for further nuclear power stations. Of 19 possible sites, the most favoured is near Gansbaai, where the AEC opened an office in January 1987. ESCOM initially announced that construction could begin in the mid-1990s, and the new plants would go into operation early in the next century. But, more recently, ESCOM's chairperson John Maree stated that 'it is highly unlikely we will see another atomic power station after Koeberg much before 2025' (*FM*, 08.05.87). This can be attributed to the reduction in the growth of electricity consumption and the difficulty in obtaining new foreign loans experienced after South Africa's debt repayment moratorium.

ESCOM's financial troubles have forced it to moderate its belief that South Africa's future energy requirements would be almost exclusively met by nuclear power stations from about 2030. On the other hand, the AEC's long-range plans incorporate the assumption that South Africa's nuclear future depends on fast breeder reactors, which would extend its dwindling uranium resources.

The development of fast breeders has run into serious technical and economic problems, to the extent that the United States has abandoned its fast breeder programme. At the same time, the apartheid state is having increased difficulty in raising international finance and buying sensitive foreign technology. This combination of factors casts a great deal of doubt on the ability of the local nuclear industry to realise its grandiose vision of a highly nuclearised South Africa.

Reprocessing spent fuel

After energy is produced in South Africa's reactors, the spent fuel contains both waste and products which can be re-used in the fuel chain, such as plutonium.

The existence of the Koeberg reactors means considerable amounts of plutonium, one of the most toxic substances in existence, are being produced. In addition, the reactors produce a spent form of uranium which needs to be upgraded or reprocessed before it can be re-used in the fuel chain.

The problems associated with reprocessing are considerable. One has only to refer to the disastrous history of the Sellafield reprocessing facility in Britain, with its consistent breaches of international safety standards and constant allegations of severe environmental and genetic damage.

This phase is the least developed in the local fuel chain.

In 1986, the state announced plans for a nuclear research facility in Gouriqua, at the mouth of the Gouritz River in the south-eastern Cape. Despite the considerable costs entailed, it seems likely that reprocessing is one of the areas of research which this facility might undertake.

To date, no spent fuel has left Koeberg. The storage pools there, which were due to become saturated in 1989, will be reracked so that they will only be full by 1995. Thereafter it may be decided to place the spent fuel in so-called dry storage at Vaalputs, transporting it there in casks. Alternatively, according to agreements with the Koeberg contractors, reprocessing of the spent fuel may occur in France, unless a local reprocessing facility has been developed by then. It is clear, however, that without its own reprocessing facility, South Africa remains dependent on foreign collaboration for the completion of its nuclear fuel chain.

Waste disposal

Despite the nuclear industry's claims, no solution has been found to the problem of the safe and permanent disposal of high-level nuclear waste. But whether reprocessing eventually occurs in France or locally, the waste products will end up in South Africa.

Meanwhile ESCOM faces the problem of disposing of low- and intermediate-level waste, which ranges from contaminated gloves and clothing to piping and water used as a coolant in the reaction. The low-level waste is compressed into steel drums, while intermediate-level waste is solidified by combining it with a sand-cement mix poured into steel-lined concrete drums.

ESCOM has purchased a 35-hectare farm at Vaalputs in Namaqualand for use as a disposal site, claiming it was suitable on geological grounds and because of low population density. The executive director of the AEC's nuclear fuels division, JP Hugo, referred to Vaalputs as the 'Rolls Royce site for low- and intermediate-level waste'.

At Vaalputs the drums are stacked in 10-metre deep trenches before being capped with soil layers which are then revegetated. ESCOM claims this will suffice for the 300 years it takes for the waste's radioactivity to decay.

Transport of the waste began in November 1986 under AEC licence. The 800 km nine-hour journey is undertaken by truck, and red-faced ESCOM officials confessed that the truck carrying the third shipment of waste suffered a broken axle.

A senior ESCOM physicist, Dr Hermann Rohm, speaking at a conference on radioactive waste disposal held in Cape Town in September 1986, stated that there was a good possibility that high-level waste might also be stored at Vaalputs. Working groups have been initiated to investigate this possibility, but it would take up to 20 years to establish a high-level disposal site at a cost of hundreds of millions of rands (*Argus*, 09.09.86).

Sanctions

Despite the fact that in recent years South Africa has obtained sufficient foreign technology to complete virtually the entire nuclear fuel chain, its degree of dependence on foreign loans, blueprints, technology and know-how is still considerable.

At the same time the supply of uranium on the world market has been fairly plentiful, exceeding demand during most of the past decade. Not only has this adversely affected the world price and the amount of foreign exchange South Africa earned from uranium, but it has also meant that potential buyers are no longer so dependent on deals with South Africa.

Many countries with nuclear industries have ceased dealing with their South African counterparts. This received legal sanction in the US, for example, whose Comprehensive Anti-Apartheid Act of 1986 outlaws any nuclear collaboration. This trend is likely to increase as pressures from grassroots anti-apartheid movements force their governments to act. South Africa's continued failure to sign the NPT and the strong international suspicion of its capacity to produce nuclear weapons put this kind of sanction high on the list.

Yet the confidence of the local nuclear industry, the continued drive to complete the entire fuel chain, the huge budgets allocated to nuclear research and the fulfilment of international uranium contracts, all indicate that sanctions will be resisted.

The South African nuclear industry, although at a crossroads, has developed a degree of self-sufficiency which strengthens the capabilities of the present state to extend its strategic options in the provision of energy as well as in military terms.

The international nuclear track record: a dream gone sour

There are currently about 370 civilian nuclear power plants worldwide, generating more than 55% of the electricity supplied in Belgium, France and Taiwan, between 30% and 40% of that in Bulgaria, Finland, Sweden and the Federal Republic of Germany, and between 10% and 20% in most of the remaining industrialised countries. The two units at Koeberg together supply 10% of the electricity generated in South Africa. It certainly seems as if nuclear power has become firmly entrenched in the energy policies of most advanced industrialised states, and possibly even some newly industrialised states.

When recent, obstinate commitments to further nuclear development by nuclear and governmental agencies in France, the Federal Republic of Germany, Britain, Switzerland, South Africa, Japan, and the USSR are added to this picture, it is difficult to avoid the conclusion that nuclear power is here to stay.

However, at least since the late 1970s, the gap between the rhetoric of the pro-nuclear camp and the actual thrust of nuclear development has been steadily widening. For example, between 1978 and 1982, cancellations of nuclear power plant orders in the US more than offset all new orders in member-countries of the Organisation for Economic Co-operation and Development (OECD).[10] New orders totalled 42,7 gigawatts,[11] as opposed to the cancellation of 53,1 gigawatts worth of plant. In fact, with the notable exception of France, which contributed the bulk of the new orders within the OECD, nuclear power programmes have been delayed, slowed down and cancelled altogether.

The demise of the global nuclear industry is also reflected in its own diminished projections of nuclear generating capacity. By 1983, for example, the OECD's projection for 1985 was only one-third of what it had been 13 years earlier in 1970.

Although the decline in the fortunes and the future of the nuclear industry has been particularly dramatic in the West, it is also apparent in non-capitalist countries. Thus the Comecon[12] 1979 ten-year programme envisaged a total of 147 gigawatts of generating capacity in member countries by 1990, while more recently the target has been reduced to 96 gigawatts, and even this looks unreachable in light of a present capacity of no more than 25 gigawatts.

This downturn in international nuclear development is a result of numerous factors. They include the uneconomic nature of nuclear electricity and popular opposition to nuclear installations. Further, a worldwide reduction in industrial energy consumption was brought about by energy conservation programmes in the aftermath of the oil crises of the 1970s, and by the slide into global recession.

Cooked books: the economics of nuclear power

If the economics of nuclear power are to be evaluated objectively, the generation of nuclear power must be seen in the context of the nuclear industry as a whole. The costs of mining and milling, enrichment, fuel element fabrication, reprocessing of the spent fuel, long-term storage of waste products, transportation and security at each of these stages and the decommissioning of the highly radioactive remains of the reactor must all be included in any comprehensive economic analysis.

The earlier euphoria over nuclear power as a new source of energy 'too cheap to meter' was based on faulty analyses which failed to incorporate its hidden costs. These were absorbed by massive state subsidies in the form of research and development budgets and the use of nuclear facilities originally developed for military purposes. This false perception led electric utility companies to undertake massive investments in nuclear power. Instead of functioning more smoothly as it developed, however, it became increasingly plagued by cost overruns. These were largely caused by design modifications forced on the contractors by nuclear licensing bodies.

Thus, for example, construction costs for the first US commercial nuclear power plant, Oyster Creek, were $100 per kilowatt (kW) in 1963. By the late 1960s, these had risen to $300/kW, and in the mid-1980s, construction costs had soared to $2 000/kW. Similarly, the Grand Gulf 1 plant was originally planned at $300-million, when commissioned by the Mississippi Power and Light Company; but when it started up in 1983 its cost had skyrocketed to $2,5-billion and it was years behind schedule.[13]

These figures are remarkable not only in themselves, but also because they reflect the state of the nuclear industry in the US, the world's leading nuclear nation with almost 100 nuclear power plants. More important, the cost of nuclear electricity has risen much faster than the cost of electricity produced from coal, its main competitor. Thus while the average annual increase in construction costs of nuclear plants was 13,5% between 1971 and 1978, that of comparable coal plants was only 7,7%.[14]

SD Freeman of the Tennessee Valley Authority, a major utility company, concluded in 1983 that 'the cost of nuclear power isn't just high, it's unpredictable. No sane capitalist is going to build something for which he can't derive a cost:benefit ratio because the cost is unknowable'.[15]

Indeed, since the true costs have become more apparent, nuclear power programmes have only been able to flourish in countries with centrally planned economies, such as the USSR, and in countries like Britain and France where electricity utilities are protected from market forces by substantial direct and indirect state subsidies.

France is often held up by nuclear advocates as a textbook example of how to make nuclear power work. However, the utility Electricite de France (EdF) had to incur a heavy debt in order to finance its ambitious nuclear programme - in 1986 it owed $33-billion, one quarter of France's foreign debt.[16] It has been calculated that the EdF consumes nearly one-quarter of the nation's industrial capital and yet contributes only one-twentieth of the value added to national industrial output.[17]

The global nuclear industry has reached a crisis in its development. In some countries, such as the US, its further expansion has been seriously curtailed or stopped altogether in response to the grave difficulties it faces. In others like France, undaunted nuclear development may have disastrous economic consequences.

South Africa's commitment to further nuclear development

Nuclear development in South Africa is unlikely to escape the problems confronting the industry worldwide. In addition, it is likely to face specific difficulties, for example, the imposition of sanctions.

The officially acknowledged cost of nuclear electricity from Koeberg is substantially more than that of electricity from a comparable modern coal-fired power station fitted with pollution control equipment.[18] It does not reflect reprocessing of spent reactor fuel, which could run to R240-million annually. Nor does it include the cost of eventually decommissioning Koeberg, which could amount to as much as a quarter of its initial construction cost. Neither have the very substantial amounts spent on nuclear research and development over the past 25 years been taken into account.

Both coal and uranium are finite, non-renewable energy resources. South Africa possesses one of the world's largest known reserves of coal. Given the present uncertainty surrounding the development of fast breeder technology, this reserve represents four times the energy equivalent of South Africa's uranium resources. This reserve will enable the country to meet its energy demands until renewable energy technologies are adequately developed, without resorting to nuclear power.

In view of this, there seems to be no clear rationale for the country to develop its nuclear capability further. The nuclear bureaucracy, however, seems intent on such a course.

This is evidenced in a number of ways. First, despite the present oversupply of enriched uranium on the international market, the AEC has carried through its project of constructing a commercial-scale enrichment plant at Valindaba. Secondly, funds are being channelled to nuclear research on a massive and unprecedented scale. In 1987 the AEC's budget totalled R775-million, as against R68-million spent by the AEB and UCOR in 1976.[19] In addition, the AEC plans to develop a further nuclear research facility at the Gouritz River mouth near Mossel Bay, at a budgeted cost of R500-million.

Thirdly, a recent statement of the AEC's long-term perspective on energy planning in South Africa reveals an alarming vision of the role that nuclear power might play. The AEC chairman confidently assumes that 'a large-scale nuclear programme will commence in 2000, and increase so that no more coal stations will be built after 2080'. This will involve construction of some 30 light-water reactors of the Koeberg type, as well as commitment to the use of breeder reactor technology.[20] More concretely, ESCOM has started site investigations for further nuclear power reactors.

In view of the dismal track record of nuclear power as a cheap and safe energy source, the anomaly of South Africa's commitment to further development of its nuclear programme raises questions about the real motives which underlie it.

There have been persistent allegations over the last ten years that South Africa is involved in development and testing of nuclear weapons. In 1977 the USSR informed the US that one of its spy satellites had detected a nuclear test site in the Kalahari desert. It is believed that the site was eventually dismantled after secret negotiations between the US and South Africa. On 22 September 1979, the double flash characteristic of a nuclear explosion was recorded over the South Atlantic. It was subsequently claimed a nuclear cannon had been tested by a combined South African-Israeli task force.[21]

South African responses to these allegations have been ambiguous. On the one hand, the state has never openly admitted that it has acquired or intends acquiring a nuclear capability. On the other, it refuses to become a signatory to the Nuclear Non-Proliferation Treaty. Moreover, the safeguards represented by International Atomic Energy Authority inspections of those South African nuclear facilities open to them have elsewhere proved ineffectual.

The thinly veiled military implications of South Africa's nuclear capability were perhaps most clearly revealed in 1977 when the then minister of finance, Owen Horwood, asserted at the opening of the National Party's Natal congress: 'We'll have the A-bomb if we want'. He was reported as saying that South Africa had given the assurance that its nuclear programme was aimed at the peaceful use of nuclear energy and stood by that assurance. But if South Africa decided to use its nuclear potential in any other way it would do so according to its own needs and it alone would make the decision (*Star,* international edition, 03.09.77).

On balance, therefore, it seems not improbable that South Africa might possess nuclear armaments. The acquisition of enrichment facilities and power reactors as well as the production of plutonium have certainly provided the capacity to produce weapons-grade material.

Even if one were to discount such speculation, there are other grounds for the continuation and elaboration of South Africa's nuclear programme.

Since 1959 when the AEB set up twelve research committees, the nuclear industry has spawned a sizeable official bureaucracy and a highly specialised group of technocrats utterly dependent on the industry for their present and future livelihoods.

The structure of the industry was extended after the creation of the AEC and the Nuclear Development Corporation (formerly the AEB). To these enterprises must be added the Uranium Enrichment

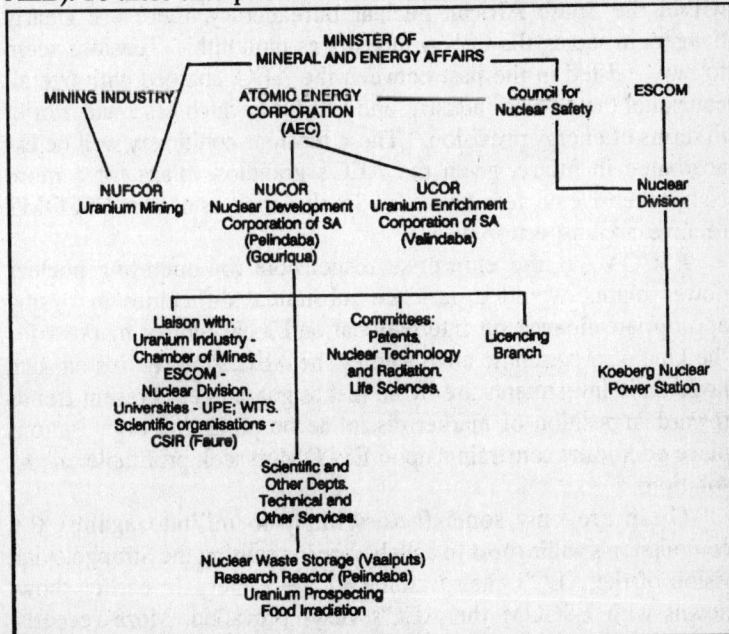

Diagram 2: The South African Nuclear Industry

Corporation, the Nuclear Fuels Corporation, the nuclear division of ESCOM, the Council for Nuclear Safety, and three university-based nuclear research institutes.

(Diagram 2 does not reflect the alleged involvement of Armscor and the SADF in the nuclear industry, nor the newly announced research institute of the Medical Research Council which will deal with radiation pollution.)

Taken together, all these enterprises constitute the South African nuclear bureaucracy. Pringle and Spigelman have shown how nuclear development tends to generate, and in turn is sustained by, a nuclear elite linked to a substantial military-industrial complex.[22]

Like all bureaucracies, nuclear elites have a vested interest in perpetuating their existence and extending their power. In South Africa, the nuclear bureaucracy has secured its interests by projecting the continued development of the nuclear industry as vital to the state's strategic interests. This has revealed itself in the advocacy of a highly problematic technical fix for the country's energy requirements.

Although from the outside there appears to be general consensus within the South African nuclear bureaucracy, there are clearly dangers in seeing the energy industry as monolithic. Tensions seem to have existed in the past between the AEC, charged with overall control of the nuclear industry, and ESCOM, which has a wider brief in terms of energy provision.[23] These tensions could very well be exacerbated in future, given the AEC's grandiose plans for a more comprehensive nuclear future for South Africa, as against ESCOM's relative circumspection.[24]

ESCOM, as the enterprise responsible for operating nuclear power plants, would experience substantial difficulties in raising appropriate finance on international and local money markets for the kind of programme envisaged by the AEC. And returns on such large-scale investments are by no means guaranteed. Present trends toward imposition of market discipline on parastatal organisations place additional constraints upon ESCOM to seek profitable energy solutions.

These are only some factors likely to militate against the commission's willingness to collaborate in realising the Strangelovian vision of the AEC's chairperson JWL de Villiers. In earlier showdowns with ESCOM the AEC's views prevailed. More recently, though, the AEC has been forced to cut its staff by 700 members across the whole spectrum of its programmes, affecting an estimated 10% of its scientists, technicians, artisans and administrative personnel (*BD*, 22.05.87). This indicates that its unbridled and dramatic growth cannot be sustained under conditions of financial recession. Yet even if the AEC's budget is cut or remains stagnant, rationalisation does not diminish the fact of the state's enormous and continued commitment to its nuclear industry.

Opposing nuclear development

The South African nuclear industry has encountered relatively little public opposition. However, in many other countries opposition to the nuclear industry has grown dramatically and moved towards the centre of the political arena. This opposition manifests itself at both a parliamentary and an extra-parliamentary level, the latter characterised by mass mobilisation and militant confrontation.

This kind of popular response is new, insofar as it is based on the realisation that technical choices reflect social relations and affect relations with the environment. This has been expressed in attempts to democratise control over technology and the use of the environment.

Such popular opposition has not been confined to the advanced industrialised countries, but has also emerged in developing countries undergoing rapid social change, such as the Philippines.[25]

Yet, insulated by law and isolated from any social forces which might have posed a challenge to it, the nuclear industry in South Africa pursued its continued expansion with impunity.

A post-apartheid South Africa will inherit an economy already to some extent dependent on the nuclear industry. While there appears to be consensus within the democratic movement that specifically military applications of nuclear power should be eliminated, Koeberg Alert believes there are sufficient grounds for rejecting the use of nuclear technology altogether.

This view is not the result of any fundamental opposition to new technologies in themselves. What we argue is that this particular technology poses substantial problems irrespective of who controls it, and that these will persist in the post-apartheid context.

The substantial issues which will require resolution are:

* the risk of catastrophic reactor failure, which cannot be eliminated, as the accident at Three Mile Island and the disaster at

Chernobyl have shown;

* the risk of contamination arising from accidents in other links of the nuclear fuel chain, as happened at the reprocessing plant at Sellafield;

* the problem of the regional agricultural, environmental and evacuation crises arising from any serious accidents in the Western Cape;

* the lack of a safe and permanent solution to the global problem of waste disposal, belying the claim of the industry that nuclear power is a 'clean' technology;

* the severe misallocation of scarce development resources which could be employed more productively and efficiently elsewhere;

* the secrecy inherent in the nuclear industry's highly centralised power structure, which would be beyond the reach of popular and democratic controls;

* the inability of nuclear power, because of its highly centralised nature, ever to meet the energy needs of over 60% of South Africans who do not yet have access to electricity.

Koeberg Alert, committed to a democratic future for this country, argues that one must go beyond simple opposition to the presence of nuclear reactors or rejection of nuclear weapons. We argue that any vision of a democratic future has to encompass energy planning which will ensure energy equity and popular control over the decisions of energy planners. We reject the argument, often raised by activists, that to debate these issues is inappropriate, or too narrow a concern at this time.

In any transitional period, it is vital for the democratic movement to take up questions of future planning, whether this concerns the legal system, issues of land tenure, education, foreign policy, urban settlement or employment. Accepting this perspective, Koeberg Alert argues that South Africa's future energy policy needs to be placed on the agenda of the democratic movement right now. We argue further that given sufficient information about the nature and history of nuclear technology, and within a framework of democratic decision making, the people of South Africa should reject the nuclear option.

Notes

1   Amory B Lovins and L Hunter Lovins, *Energy/War: Breaking the Nuclear*

Link, a Prescription for Non-Proliferation, New York, 1980.

2 See *New Socialist,* 42, October 1986, Nuclear Supplement, 3.

3 In large part the following outline is drawn from Walt Patterson's clear account in *Nuclear power,* Harmondsworth, 1983 (second edition), chapter 3.

4 Lovins and Lovins, *Energy/War,* 19-22.

5 See Peter Pringle and James Spigelman, *The Nuclear Barons,* London, 1983, 374-379.

6 See Zdenek Cervenka and Barbara Rogers, *The Nuclear Axis: Secret Collaboration between West Germany and South Africa,* London, 1978, chapter 1.

7 Megawatt - see glossary.

8 Electricity Supply Commission, Annual Report 1984, 14. See also the comments of ESCOM senior general manager Ian McRae, 'ESCOM's lightning conductor', *FM,* 29.03.85.

9 Hansard (A), 25.03.86, cols 688-689.

10 The OECD is an intergovernmental organisation made up of the major industrialised capitalist countries. Key members include the United States, Britain, the Federal Republic of Germany, Italy, Japan, Canada and France.

11 Gigawatt - see glossary.

12 Comecon is the Council for Mutual Economic Assistance. Its members include the USSR, Poland, Czechoslovakia, Hungary, Rumania, Bulgaria, the German Democratic Republic, Mongolia, Cuba and Vietnam.

13 Christopher Flavin, *Nuclear Power: The Market Test,* Washington, 1983, 12.

14 Flavin, *Nuclear Power,* 14.

15 Flavin, *Nuclear Power,* 19.

16 'The Price of Europe's Love Affair with Nuclear Power', *Business Week,* 28.04.86.

17 Jim Harding, 'The French Nuclear Debacle', *The Ecologist,* 14(3), 1984, 101.

18 *Hansard (A),* 25.03.86, cols 688-689.

19 JG Venn, 'Nuclear vs Renewables: A Misallocation of Resources?', paper presented at the Conference on Renewable Energy Potential in Southern Africa, Energy Research Institute, University of Cape Town, September 1986, 44.6-44.7.

20 JWL de Villiers, 'The Role of Nuclear Energy in the Supply of Electricity in South Africa', paper presented at a conference organised by the South African National Committee of the World Energy Conference, Pretoria 1986, 3.2-4, 3.2-5.

21 See *Washington Post,* 16.09.80, A25; also James Adams, *The Unnatural Alliance: Israel and South Africa,* London, 1984, 195; and Peter Pry, *Israel's Nuclear Arsenal,* Boulder, 1984, 46.

22 Pringle and Spigelman, *The Nuclear Barons.*

23 See for example the comments of ESCOM's Western Cape information officer Andre van Heerden to the Institute of Citizenship, *CT,* 27.10.83.

24 See comments of senior ESCOM physicist Hermann Rohm, *Argus,* 09.09.86.

25 See publications of the Nuclear Free Philippines Coalition, particularly Toby Dayrit, *Bataan Nuclear Power Plant: The Technical Basis for Rejection,* Quezon City, 1985.

Glossary

Power is the amount of energy used per unit of time. Electrical power is measured in watts (W).

1 kilowatt (kW) = 1000W (used by small electric room heater)

1 megawatt (MW) = 1000 kW (used by a large office block)

1 gigawatt (GW) = 1000 MW (used by a major city)

Electrical energy is measured in kilowatt-hours (kWh), equivalent to the use of 1 kilowatt for one hour. A typical middle-class family in South Africa uses roughly 600 kWh every month at a cost of about R60. In early 1987, this electricity was supplied at a cost of 7,6c/kWh.

State Strategy and the Limits of Counter-Revolution

Keith Gottschalk

The trends and conflicts of the final decades of apartheid seem set: mass unemployment; social engineering aimed at changing South Africa's demographic patterns; sanctions and subversion by foreign powers; and a generation of urban blacks in revolt. The investor class is disaffected, the intelligentsia alienated, and the working class insurgent. The state's bureaucratic-police-military machine oscillates between reform and repression as its power base shrinks.

The government flounders among tactics and strategies riddled with self-defeating contradictions. Long-term structural changes in South Africa's social order, and in the global balance of power, make these contradictions increasingly unstable.

In the social order, blacks form an ever-increasing majority of the working class, and an ever-increasing minority of the white-collar, professional and managerial strata. This potentially strengthens black resistance politics with human, financial and organisational resources. The changing colour of classes aggravates the crises of legitimacy and hegemony of a civil society based on racism.

The global balance of power demonstrates the shift from the world of 1910, dominated by racist ideology and colonial empires, to a globe dominated by anti-racist and anti-imperialist rhetoric. Right-wing Western governments impose creeping sanctions. Centrist social democrat governments subsidise the African National Congress. African and communist governments give the ANC military aid. Most states try to uphold the United Nations arms embargo on South Africa. Both major world powers, the United States and the Soviet Union, are increasing their opposition to apartheid, albeit in different ways.

The Chinese People's Republic and India will assert themselves as two additional superpowers by the end of this century. Already regional powers with nuclear and rocket industry capacities, they both have anti-racist and anti-colonialist foreign policies.

By the start of the next century, the global balance of power will no longer be bi-polar and white, but polycentric and multiracial. The slowness of this shift in the international environment from 1910 to 2000 should not blind us to its implications for Pretoria - and apartheid's lifespan.

The state's political dilemmas

Several factors ensure that repression almost invariably has a counterproductive aspect for the state. Present levels of political mobilisation and colour polarisation ensure that state violence and vigilante terror anger as much as they intimidate. The growing size and self-confidence of the black petty bourgeoisie, African, coloured and Indian alike, reflects its knowledge that it has world sympathy on its side. This occurs on a continent where every other settler colony is today under majority rule.

Whenever government closes boarding schools, colleges and universities to suppress boycotts, and orders students to return home, it disperses an increasingly revolutionary intelligentsia throughout rural South Africa. But if it leaves tertiary education institutions open, they serve as centres for dissemination of radical ideology and mobilisation of a national intelligentsia.

The curricula of 'Bantu', coloured and Indian education fail to reproduce the ideology of the dominators among the dominated during this epoch of rebellion and repression. For consciousness arises from social being.

Similarly, police assaults and killings of black youth during the insurrections of 1976-77 and from 1984 onwards had two major results. Police repression recruited larger numbers of volunteers for the ANC military wing, Umkhonto we Sizwe, than the underground itself had managed in the previous ten years. And police brutality ensured mass support for trained insurgents returning to start operations.

The government faces the same no-win dilemma with white youth. If it grants military conscripts deferment to attend universities, they encounter liberal and radical thought which produces an increasing number of conscientious objectors. The SADF-state security council response has been to phase out deferments. This means that demobbed conscripts will enter campuses and intellectual life with the same traumatic experience of civil war as French conscripts did during Algeria's War of Independence.

This is likely to increase polarisation: on the one hand it gives rise to increasing receptivity to the issues raised by organisations like the End Conscription Campaign, and heightened political awareness of the military-police underpinning essential to apartheid's survival; on the other hand it is also likely to produce more youthful supporters for the far-right parties which are eroding the state's power base.

Either way, if government continues to rely on conscripts, especially white conscripts - artisan, white-collar, professional and management alike - then civil war increasingly means disruption of production. It will also cause further polarisation of white youth and the middle-aged from the decision-making establishment.

If, however, the state security council chooses to rely on expanding the permanent force, financial constraints on salaries dictate that career infantry brigades and divisions will be, as in Namibia, overwhelmingly black. Colonial askaris, from Arab *harkis* in French-ruled Algeria to the African Rifles in settler Rhodesia, remained loyal to the end. Nevertheless, this strategy has unpalatable implications for the South African state. Even with few desertions and no mutiny, an overwhelmingly black army demonstrates the way blacks can wield military muscle to both the white electorate and the black majority.

The national security management system also faces the dilemma of deployment. If the government does not saturate every ghetto with troops and police, minimally-patrolled neighbourhoods may at some point become 'liberated zones'. If the government does saturate every township, an increasing proportion of its troops remain pinned down in small, isolated groups. Dispersed to every farmhouse and suburb, the armed forces are weakened and their patterns of deployment become predictable to the opposition.

Above all, the cumulative effect of government 'reforms' is to antagonise the majority. Each grudging half-reform prised out of government is invariably hedged about with qualifications largely annulling its pre-publicised benefits. Each reform is only extracted under immense and sustained pressure. Each reform is not seen as merely a one-off, ad hoc concession, but as part of a process of restructuring. Thus all reforms granted fuel a revolution of rising expectations.

In South Africa's history *kragdadigheid* by intractable bureaucrats, rather than revolutionary conspiracy, precipitates each rebellion.

In 1960, the Pan-Africanist Congress planned a passive resistance campaign at Sharpeville to protest against passes. Police shooting of demonstrators precipitated the state of emergency which culminated in the banning of the ANC and PAC, driving them underground - and so starting the armed struggle.

In 1976, the 'Bantu' education bureaucracy rejected all black student demands that certain subjects be taught in English: 'If you want to learn in English, go to England'. This triggered off the next major rebellion, which it took government 18 months to suppress.

The Vaal Triangle rent boycott of September 1984, and its attempted suppression, is taken by many commentators as the start of the current uprising. But even before that, a series of stonewalling actions by the state escalated specific campaigns into general insurrection. Political killings marked the start of the 'low-level civil war' for at least six months prior to September 1984:

* On 13 February 1984 a police van drove into school grounds in Atteridgeville. It knocked down and killed 15-year-old Emma Sathekge.[1] In the subsequent unrest the police detained 97 pupils, injured 102 and education authorities suspended 69.[2]

* Similarly, the dismissal and detention of Matthew Goniwe, headmaster at a Cradock school, led to riots and deaths. From Thabong at Welkom to the East Rand and Mabopane East these spreading demonstrations resulted in eight further killings. The dead ranged from a six-year-old pupil to a technikon student demonstrating over poor food;[3]

* From July and August 1984, protests against the tricameral parliament elections spread dramatically to those classified 'coloured'

and 'Indian', including 630 000 pupils. The demonstrations, and accompanying police repression including assault and detentions, spread from Cape Town to the rest of the country.[4]

The September 1984 rent boycotts in the Vaal Triangle marked a quantum leap in resistance; state violence in suppressing the boycotts fanned resistance further. The demonstrative *kragdadigheid* of the police, down to routine public floggings of demonstrators and subsequent actions banning even petitions to free detainees, is well known.

It is safe to predict that the government will suppress the current rebellion, but that the actions of Pretoria's hardline bureaucracy and armed forces will trigger off the next uprising within a few years.

The state's supremacy in the resources of coercion and military hardware slowly enabled it to regain temporary dominance during 1986-87, in the sense of physical control. But its lack of legitimacy means that it can only suppress organisation, not govern through consent of the governed. Its tactical errors, and the ongoing structural changes of a maturing industrial social order, sooner or later provide spaces for the renewal of contestation between government and the people.

The state's economic and fiscal blunders played an essential role in precipitating the current revolt. Ask any security police detective or joint management centre committee which ideology and organisation is the biggest cause of revolution in South Africa. They are unlikely to reply 'monetarism and the Reserve Bank'. Yet James Davies's theory of revolution[5] supports Duncan Innes's analysis in *South African Review 3*. The government imposed its catastrophic austerity policy in August 1984. Interest rates of 26% for producers and 32% for consumers caused massive rises in company bankruptcies, black unemployment, and the current depression.[6] Community councils then imposed precisely the rent increases the Riekert Commission thought had such merit.[7] The industrial proletariat of the East Rand and Vaal Triangle, hit by massive retrenchments, had little alternative but to fight back. The police offensive against community organisations in South Africa's largest rent boycott escalated a local civil disobedience campaign into national insurrection.

Foreign policy: the limits of destabilisation

The government's aggressive reflex reactions to international and regional events demonstrate Pretoria's inability to foresee how its aggression and destabilisation can boomerang. The state security council, despite its national intelligence service, military intelligence, security police and disinformation committees, rarely perceives that actions may have unintended consequences.

Foreign policy towards Lesotho is an instance. In 1964, South Africa's prime minister of the time, Hendrik Verwoerd, worked through the Broederbond and the SABC to provide funds to Chief Leabua Jonathan and his Basutoland National Party in the Lesotho election. Later, under Prime Minister John Vorster, the South African government supported Jonathan's 1970 coup to thwart the election victory of the Basutoland Congress Party (BCP).

But in the decade that followed, Jonathan's government assumed as many rhetorical and diplomatic postures against apartheid as its BCP opponents could ever have, in an attempt to win international legitimacy and aid. Jonathan's increasing hostility to Pretoria was also sharpened by the South African government's crude emphasis on Lesotho's economic dependency and political powerlessness. Jonathan's engagement with the Non-aligned Movement and the fact that he generally turned a blind eye to ANC activists in Lesotho were the last straws for Pretoria. The South African government began to back the BCP's sabotage wing, the Lesotho Liberation Army, against Jonathan. In the end, as Robert Edgar describes in section 4 of this *Review,* Pretoria's actions encouraged the coup that deposed the Jonathan government in January 1986.

The same scenario would possibly follow if South Africa gave UNITA sufficient military backing to seize power in Angola. A UNITA government, far more than Jonathan's, could only obtain diplomatic legitimacy and rid itself of the image of being a 'boer puppet' by adopting an increasingly anti-apartheid stance.

If, on the other hand, Pretoria abandoned UNITA, this would shake the confidence of all its remaining clients, whether Namibian, bantustan or tricameral.

The South African government's regional destabilisation policies have three aims. First, to limit Umkhonto we Sizwe's ability to use neighbouring states as springboards for insurgency in South Africa, and to demonstratively inflict high costs on those states offering the

ANC sanctuary. Secondly, to play for time in Namibia by sustaining the ongoing UNITA insurrection, so weakening Angola's ability to aid SWAPO. Thirdly, to exhibit enough military muscle to deter global powers from local adventures.

The consequences of government's destabilisation of frontline states have been equivocal, to say the least. Pretoria has attacked the ANC repeatedly and had it expelled from country after country, but ANC insurgency inside South Africa has attained an unprecedented level.

The South African government's destabilisation policy has asserted its dominance over the region. But it has provoked the internationalisation of the conflict. It forced a Soviet and Cuban commitment, unprecedented south of Ethiopia, to build up Angola's defences, with token military aid also coming from Portugal, France and Brazil.

It forced the United States to exempt Mozambique from its usual destabilisation of third world Marxist governments. Britain's Conservative government now provides military training and other assistance to three neighbouring states: Botswana, Mozambique and Zimbabwe. The US is starting to retrain the Lesotho armed services and Portugal and other European Common Market members are supplying increasing aid.

This aid is nowhere near enough to turn the tide against South African regional domination. But it indicates that further extension of Pretoria's destabilisation policy will attract the superpower intervention the South African government wishes to deter.

Structures, strategy and ideology

In its attempts to alter both ideology and institutions, government's strategy is a hesitant rehash of the policy it imposed on Namibia from 1974. In Namibia, this policy failed to provide more than a transparent facade to the reality of coercion and patronage. As far back as 1977, the government restructured its Namibian policy to constitute its bantustan and other ethnic clients as the Democratic Turnhalle Alliance (DTA), reconstituted and broadened again in 1985 as the Multi-Party Conference.

Government also first published its constitutional proposals for South Africa in 1977. But it has not yet included its bantustan chief ministers in the tricameral parliament to form a South African variant of the DTA - ten years after its counter-revolutionary prototype in Namibia. Here, the erosion of its power base with each reform, cosmetic or not, has compelled hesitation.

Government claims 'apartheid is dead'. But it neither replaces it with any other ideology, nor rescinds the constitutional and social order based on statutory ethnicity. Government purported in 1985 to have returned to the concept of one citizenship. In reality, government still persists in its apartheid ideology of 'identity' and separate ethnicities. It has so far restored citizenship to only 2 000 of the 7,5-million South Africans whose citizenship it revoked.

The state seems to have no clear set of goals. Technocratic efficiency is a means rather than an end. 'Total Strategy' is similarly not a political goal, but merely the state security council's ideological alibi to justify government's violation of human rights and the constitutional restrictions on its power.

Episodic attempts to replace or supplement ethnicity with Christianity in state ideology, as in Namibia, are even less likely to succeed. Unlike Namibia, South Africa has an increasingly militant Muslim minority, not to mention smaller Hindu and Jewish minorities. And apartheid has polarised christianity. Government appeals for christians to support its goals and policies provoke derision, and create controversy rather than submission. In any case falling back on religious appeals in an industrialising and secularising society is, in the longterm, a self-defeating strategy.

Demography and strains on the bourgeoisie

Herman Giliomee perceptively noted that 'one of the perennial ironies of history is man's search for security from his anxieties in terms that make its attainment impossible'.[8]

White racists fear most of all the 'swart gevaar': being outnumbered or 'swamped' by the black majority. So for a century, South Africa's racist, labour-repressive political economy had three cornerstones: black families should remain poor; the pass laws should force them to live in the countryside; and they should labour only as migrant workers.

This strategy ran counter to established demographic principles: other factors being equal, poor families have more children than rich families; rural families have more children than long-urbanised families; couples separated by migrant labour have more children than families living under one roof.

The result is that the white proportion of South Africans fell from its all-time high of 22% in 1921[9] to 15,6% in 1985.[10] The ongoing population explosion - half of all South Africans are now under the age of 18 - will reduce whites to less than 10% of the population by the year 2000.

These trends have consequences for political and class power. Radical analysis which theoretically stresses class above race has itself thus far used race-centred concerns. For example, debate over the rise of the black bourgeoisie focuses on the extent to which it might politically polarise the black majority, and provide the state with a collaborative stratum.[11]

But a class-centred analysis would invert this conceptualisation. To what extent will an ever-increasing black proportion -and eventually a black majority - of the white-collar, professional and managerial strata politically polarise the petty-bourgeois and bourgeois *classes*?

The class organisation of South African capitalism follow the polarisation of the political terrain: there is a three-way split between Afrikaner nationalists, Anglophone white liberals, and black nationalists. The local bourgeoisie remains unable to fuse its Afrikaanse Handelsinstituut, the Sakekamers, Federated Chambers of Industry, Association of Chambers of Commerce, National African Federated Chambers of Commerce and Western Cape Traders' Association.

They cannot agree on any political issue, from racial manipulation of the market through group areas statutes to the state offensive against COSATU and its member unions. The class unity of the bourgeoisie, and even more so that of the petty bourgeoisie, remains subordinate to more directly political alliances.

Such bourgeois political disunity, in the face of a relatively unified revolutionary mass movement, creates a situation rarely seen in modern times, except in China in 1949 and Nicaragua in 1979. In these countries, the rapacious parasitism of the Chiang and Somoza families raised expropriations and levies on corporations to a level undermining profitability, so polarising a 'national bourgeoisie' from a 'compradore bourgeoisie'. Major sections of the national bourgeoisie, politically alienated from the regime, remained neutral or formed alliances with the insurgent movement.

In Africa, family strategies to accumulate capital usually follow one of two trajectories: expanding trading or bus companies; or black professionals rising into management in multinational corporations, and then acquiring multiple concessions, franchises, directorships and other interests.

In South Africa, government policy imposed every possible restriction on the rise of a black bourgeoisie and petty bourgeoisie from before 1924 to after 1976. Statutory and administrative discrimination barred Africans from property ownership in the towns, prohibiting them from accumulating the collateral which banks and building societies insist upon as a prerequisite for mortgages and commercial credits. The state barred African businesses from incorporating companies, from making significant share purchases and even from renting more than one business premise. They could not employ non-African staff, thereby barring them from managerial posts in non-African corporations.[12] Monopoly concessions to white-owned bus companies froze out black cab and bus owners.

Both the colour bar and discriminatory education budgets effectively barred blacks from most professions and white-collar posts, with a few historical exceptions such as teachers and nurses servicing 'non- whites'.

Currently, government equivocates. It pays ideological lip-service to building up 'a strong black middle class' with vested interests in capitalism. But its police neutralise this by actions like the detention of most members of the KwaThema Chamber of Commerce, and the forced closure of shops owned by blacks in Cradock, Worcester and elsewhere to break black consumer boycotts of white shops. Confining the black professional and managerial strata to group areas where they must pay vastly higher prices than whites for plots, flats and houses both angers them and reduces family capital for business investments.

The combination of rising black bourgeoisie and middle class experience of racism, gratuitous police assaults against blacks of all classes and monetarist-inspired depression, bankruptcies and retrenchments, all go to make a most explosive set of catalysts for revolution.

Who are the managerial and middle classes? Matriculation, and university and college education delineate the other major trajectory of entry into these classes.

In 1960, 28 Africans obtained the matriculation exemption necessary for university admission. At that time, blacks - African, coloured and Indian - comprised 11% of university students.[13] Since 1984 blacks have constituted the majority of all successful matriculants, over two-thirds of all teachers' training college students, and over one-third of university students.[14]

Before 1994, blacks will constitute the majority of university graduates. The majority of new entrants to the professional strata and junior management will be black upwardly-mobile professionals. They will begin climbing company hierarchies into the boardrooms of class power.

Obviously blacks will not own significant proportions of listed shares in the foreseeable future; but in the corporate epoch the managerial strata are the agents and decision-makers of bourgeois economic power. The changing colours of the professional strata and management cannot but sharpen the present polarisation of the bourgeoisie. The founding of alternative professional associations amongst doctors, entertainers, lawyers, social workers and teachers reflects this structural shift at the petty-bourgeois level.

This trend, where blacks become the majority of entrants to particular strata, is far more advanced in the working class.

In 1887 white artisans wielded a monopoly of skills at the point of production; in 1987 they are a blue-collar minority, encreasingly encircled on the mines and parastatals such as SASOL and SATS. First job fragmentation and dilution, and subsequently erosion of the colour bar itself, accelerated their declining importance in both absolute and relative terms. Increasingly, whites man the agencies of coercion and state power, rather than operate the means of production.

Political consequences follow. In 1922 the ICU and other African unions tended to be short-lived and peripheral to the white-dominated labour movement. Today the Congress of South African Trade Unions and the smaller National Confederation of Trade Unions set the pace for the organised working class. The demise of the Trade Union Council of South Africa and marginalisation of the South African Confederation of Labour reflect the relative decline in importance of blue-collar whites in the working class.

In summary, 1922 saw a working class racially and politically divided, and a corporate bourgeoisie racially united. The year 2002 will see a working class marked by overwhelming political and racial unity, but a managerial class politically and racially divided.

At its height in 1985-86, the present insurrection temporarily weakened the political bonds between the state and major segments of the establishment. Some judges reversed their interpretations of repressive statutes in order to uphold the rule of law. Editors of the commercial press demonstrated greater readiness to risk breaking the law.

The economically dominant segment of the bourgeoisie - English-speaking white businessmen - mostly vote for the Progressive Federal Party and oppose many of the state's economic and fiscal policies. The PFP and leading corporations, Afrikaner journalists, the Broederbond, clergy and university vice-chancellors have all visited the ANC in Lusaka, London or New York.

This demonstrates that, given a sufficient level of organic crisis, ruling class alliances constituting the hegemonic bloc start to come apart at the seams. More and more members of the establishment, when under pressure, dissociate themselves from the present government, and start to negotiate the costs of operating under the ANC.

Within a decade blacks will form the fastest growing segment of our professional, managerial and business classes. A quarter of a century after the dismantling of the colonial empires, it is unlikely that they will submit to being the only national bourgeoisie to remain dominated in their own state. As with every national bourgeoisie from Egypt to Zimbabwe, they will no longer seek to join the settler bourgeoisie, but to displace it: to enjoy the power and patronage of hegemony.

This, and the growing muscle of the working class in Africa's most industrialised state, raises the price for state legitimacy to at least majority rule. The settler colonial social order and its racial ideology make it more difficult for the South African government to become a viable neo-colonial regime than other third world oligarchies. However successfully it manages to suppress one or other specific insurrection, the present state remains intrinsically unstable, and further insurrection is inevitable.

The government found it more difficult to suppress the revolt of 1976-77 than that of 1960. It has struggled for three years to suppress the insurrection which started in 1984. The next spiral of revolutionary struggle, may be even more difficult to contain. As these cycles recur, and more and more elements of the establishment become disaffected, the time will come when the present state is confronted by insurrection it cannot suppress.

Notes

1   South African Institute of Race Relations, *Race Relations Survey 1984,* Johannesburg, 1985, 69, 789.
2   *Race Relations Survey 1984,* 69.
3   *Race Relations Survey 1984,* 70.
4   *Race Relations Survey 1984,* 70-71.
5 · 'Revolutions are most likely to occur when a prolonged period of objective economic and social development is followed by a short period of sharp reversal'. J Davies, 'Towards a theory of Revolution', *American Sociological Review,* 6(1), 1962, 5-19.
6   D Innes, 'Monetarism and the South African Crisis', *South African Review 3,* Johannesburg, 1986, 291.
7   Carole Cooper and Linda Ensor, 'Summary of the Riekert Report', *South African Labour Bulletin,* (5)4, November 1979, 12-13.
8   H Giliomee and L Schlemmer, *Up Against the Fences: Poverty, Passes and Privilege in South Africa,* Cape Town, 1985, 324.
9   Republic of South Africa, *Statistical Year Book 1965,* Pretoria, A-11.
10 South African Institute of Race Relations, *Race Relations Survey 1985,* Johannesburg, 1986, 2.
11 For example, P Hudson and M Sarakinsky, 'Class Interests and Politics: The Case of the Urban African Bourgeoisie', *South African Review 3.*
12 These restrictions flow from the then Natives Land Act, 17/1913; Natives (Urban Areas) Act 21/1923; Group Areas Act 41/1950, their amendments, and decrees promulgated under their powers.
13 South African Institute of Race Relations, *Survey of Race Relations in South Africa, 1961,* Johannesburg, 1962, 234, 255.
14 South African Institute of Race Relations, *Race Relations Survey 1985,* Johannesburg, 1986, 379, 384-5, 401.

'Mixed, Capitalist and Free': The Aims of the 'Natal Option'

Gerhard Maré

Future political commentators may well focus on 1986 and 1987 as the years during which the South African state abandoned all pretence at hegemony - at maintaining the moral and political leadership essential to state control in most capitalist societies. Instead of meaningful reform came a series of measures and scenarios relying on rejected approaches and bankrupt ideas, on naked repression and the privileges of white domination.

But in Natal, under the umbrella of a state of emergency, a direction emerged to provide hope to those who believe that 'real reform' is still possible in South Africa. Under the banner of 'Together we all win', the Natal-Kwazulu Indaba started selling the idea, if not the content, of negotiation, multiracialism, federal options, and a bill of rights. With the approval of fragile alliances from the 'political middle ground', proposals for a single majority-rule legislature for the province were unveiled during November 1986. They were the fruit of about eight months' work towards consensus.

The extension of national political violence to the region on a scale equalling that of the rest of the country preceded the Indaba and continued during its deliberations.[1] Natal ceased to be a special, less turbulent case. Despite a massive state clampdown, or in the course of it, conflict became endemic. Trade unionists and workers, political organisers and sympathisers, police and innocent bystanders were killed. In Natal, violence has been directed at and has arisen from three directions: the state and its 'security forces'; unions and progressive organisations, including the ANC; and Inkatha.

Not all conflict was organisational or political. As in the rest of the country, gang warfare, looting and true mob violence characterised much of the social unrest. A noteworthy aspect of social instability in Natal is the prevalence of cattle theft, robbery of food delivery vehicles in rural areas, stoning of passing cars, robbery of motorists who break down on the road, and 'faction fighting'.

Despite allegations of active or passive collusion between Inkatha and state apparatuses, it is an oversimplification to see Inkatha as a mere direct extension of the state. On some levels it undoubtedly is, especially through the bantustan structures it controls, such as the Kwazulu police force. However, in important areas it reflects a different and specific dynamic: Inkatha represents different class interests and aspirations to those most strongly expressed through the state.

'Real reform' or capitalism without racism

There is a direct relationship between the dynamics of 'real reform' in Natal and the violent struggle between those espousing different directions and agendas for the country as a whole. Social turbulence in Natal is driving the moderate 'real reformers' to a concrete reform programme, and is at the same time driving them into the arms of Inkatha which is perceived as having the power to control dissident elements in the region.

'Real reform' differs from the state's discredited fumblings in that it proposes to restructure South Africa politically, moving from blatant racial discrimination and racial allocation of rights and resources to their distribution according to social position and privilege. The only restructuring the state has undertaken with any vigour and success involves methods and means of repression, such as setting up joint management centres and appointing a new minister of law and order. 'Real reform' on the other hand proposes to ensure that capitalism survives without racism. As Chris Saunders, head of the Tongaat-Hulett group and probably the most influential capitalist in the region, told a United States-South Africa Leadership Exchange Programme (USSALEP) conference in 1983:

On the demographic proportions facing Natal-Kwazulu it is obvious that by
the year 2000 the choice of the road which we follow is simply between being
mixed, marxist and dominated, or being mixed, capitalist and free.[2]

Capital has attempted to promote movement in this latter direction, and to ensure that its achievement does not depend solely on
the state. This was undertaken through the Lombard Commission, a
non-state investigation appointed by sugar capital to propose alternatives to the state's consolidation programme for Kwazulu, which
reported in 1980;[3] and most strongly through the Buthelezi
Commission (1982)[4] and the Indaba (1986).

The 'Natal option' is born

As the crisis in South Africa intensified, it became clear that the
state had only repressive power without the moral confidence and
ability to reform South Africa out of trouble. In this light, initiatives
by capital increasingly became political interventions rather than
mere suggestions to the state. Already capital had moved into areas
like public housing (through the Urban Foundation) and education
(through the New Era Schools Trust). The Indaba marks capital's
most comprehensive political intervention to date, along with the
visit by businessmen to the African National Congress in Lusaka.

Two factors are important in making sense of the 'Natal option'.
The first is the existence of a real political constituency that owes
allegiance to a conservative African leader. The combination of conservatism and a constituency is rare in contemporary South Africa,
and is probably the main characteristic of Natal's much-vaunted uni-
queness. The second is the presence of an organisation, Inkatha, representing the self-conscious striving of an African petty bourgeoisie
for integration into the capitalist system. These two factors had a
range of implications which affected events of the past 18 months.

Because of the availability of a moderate constituency, Natal was
perceived as the most suitable region in South Africa for political
experimentation (possibly in the knowledge that the state could
always put the lid on it if things went wrong). Chris Saunders called
Natal 'a model' in 1983, while Frederick van Zyl Slabbert spoke of
the region having 'all the necessary ingredients...to make such an
Indaba a political laboratory for the rest of South Africa to look up
to' (*NM*, 25.05.85).

This was probably the first public use of the term 'Indaba' to describe the envisaged 'convention'. The region's perceived suitability is based on Buthelezi's ability to deliver a constituency, and hence stability. This is essential to consociational political engineering, which depends centrally on achieving elite consensus rather than on mass political mobilisation, consultation and education.

The Indaba process carries the approval of conservative US political scientist Professor Samuel Huntington, architect of a cynical 'reform' strategy.[5] He said after a visit to Natal in 1986 that the Indaba, rather than the state's performance, offered hope for reform because of Buthelezi's presence: he was a leader who could bring along a constituency. Buthelezi's value as 'deliverer' was also publicly acknowledged by Bruce Forssman, president of the Durban Metropolitan Chamber of Commerce (DMCC), and Tony Ardington, chairperson of the SA Cane Growers' Association. The latter called on Natalians to act quickly 'to ensure the asset (Buthelezi) and the opportunity were not lost'.

It is not surprising that this aspect of Buthelezi's role, through the Inkatha movement, should have been so appreciated in 1986. There were fresh memories of the previous year's violent disruption centering on Inanda, and of the successful stayaway and consumer boycott in support of the Sarmcol strikers near Pietermaritzburg. Capital knew the options were either greater long-term state repression, with its own costs, or the role Inkatha seemed willing to assume which made direct state repression unnecessary.

So a mere week after trouble broke out in Inanda, Inkatha Secretary General Oscar Dhlomo could claim that Inkatha was in complete control of the township;[6] and Inkatha central committee member Winnington Sabelo, whose wife was killed in one of several attacks on Sabelo himself, threatened to evict all UDF members from Umlazi township. While Dhlomo refuted this threat, Buthelezi praised Sabelo in May 1986 for his work in 'protecting the community' (*Ilanga*, 19-21.05.86). In addition, COSATU's November 1985 launch in the heart of Durban, with an explicit commitment to socialism, was followed in May 1986 by the formation of Inkatha's pro-capitalist, pro-investment, anti-COSATU United Workers Union of South Africa (UWUSA).

The reluctance to be publicly associated with Inkatha in political ventures which followed the debacle of the Convention Alliance in

1985, when both the Progressive Federal Party (PFP) and Inkatha withdrew from their founding association with the National Convention Movement, was gone from Natal in 1986. Ardington, for example, was a member of the Convention Alliance and has subsequently been closely associated with the Indaba.

Inkatha - a key factor in the Indaba process

Politically Inkatha represents to capital a potential for control of the regional African population, through force if necessary and through the allegiances of politicised ethnicity if possible. It also represents desirable political sentiments and has an impressively wide range of international contacts with conservative governments and the funders and agencies associated with them.

But the economic dimension is equally crucial in making sense of the 'Natal option'. Inkatha's economic agenda is becoming clearer daily. While the fact that Inkatha delivers a constituency is important, the economic direction it gives this constituency is critical.

In 1974, a year before Inkatha was formed, Prime Minister John Vorster announced that 'white' capital would be allowed into the bantustans under conditions decided on by bantustan governments. By mid-1975 it was reported that the Checkers supermarket chain would, if allowed, operate within Kwazulu under a scheme whereby 51% of shares would be retained by Checkers (this proportion to be reduced in time). The remainder of the shares would be held by 'Kwazulu citizens' and the Kwazulu Development Corporation.

This capital penetration into bantustan ethnic enclaves involved tripartite agreements which set up tripartite companies (tripcos). It caused a flurry of economic and political activity in Kwazulu. Those traders who would either not benefit or would be detrimentally affected by the tripco agreements organised against Buthelezi and then against Inkatha. They tried to use the political figure and tradition of the Zulu king. But Inkatha, from the start of its activities in 1975, allied itself with those members of the regional petty bourgeoisie who had managed to link their fortunes to monopoly capital operating in Natal and Kwazulu.[7]

Buthelezi and Inkatha won the confrontation on behalf of the section of the petty bourgeoisie subordinate to monopoly capital, and consolidated that hold over the next ten years. A clear indication of this victory came at the end of 1985, when trade unions and popular organisations attempted to extend the successful boycott of white-owned retail outlets sparked off by the Sarmcol strike and dismissals[8] into solidarity with the national campaign against the state of emergency and for the release of political detainees. Details of Inkatha's involvement in events are not clear. Early in August Buthelezi told the BBC that while he was against violence, consumer power could be used to achieve political ends. So it would have been difficult for Inkatha to attack the boycott call publicly. And apparently the Federation of South African Trade Unions (FOSATU) called a meeting with Inkatha where both sides agreed to avoid violent confrontation. However, Inyanda (the Natal and Zululand African Chamber of Commerce, an affiliate of Inkatha) threatened boycotters and refused to give the campaign its blessing because of the harm it would do to its members' benefactors within the white business community. As Inyanda president PG Gumede said:

> At a time when I am busy appealing to the white private sector in the name of Inyanda to assist in the rehabilitation of black businessmen in KwaMashu and Umlazi, I cannot on the other hand be seen to be condoning the actions of FOSATU and all those who join them in advocating the consumer boycott.

He called on members, some of whom initially supported the FOSATU call out of sympathy or because of the potential increase in local trade, 'to obey and co-operate, particularly in Natal and Kwazulu, under the leadership of the Kwazulu Chief Minister...' (*NM*, 02.09.85).

It would appear that, initially at least, shops and shopkeepers perceived to be linked to large-scale capital or to Inkatha became victims of arsonists and looters during the violence of August 1985. They therefore could not benefit from a boycott of white-owned shops, and at the same time depended on grants from the DMCC to restore their businesses. In Inanda itself the destruction took on the racial form of Zulu-Indian conflict.[9]

FOSATU was forced to call off the boycott in the region because of the real threat of violence and division within the African community. Gumede spoke of a 'war' between FOSATU on the one hand and Inyanda and Inkatha on the other. The boycott was called off despite earlier success where 'black custom at white businesses in Pietermaritzburg dropped by an average 60%-70%' (*DN*, 02.09.85).[10]

A struggle for regional supremacy

The concern to avoid potentially violent conflict which seemed to characterise contact between FOSATU and Inkatha during the boycott did not last long. It died when FOSATU was replaced by the wider unity of the Congress of South African Trade Unions in November 1986.

While there is little value in trying to determine who verbally attacked whom first after the COSATU launch, the reasons for the mutual, open antagonism between the two organisations are important. It is best understood as a clash between two directions, or two visions of a future South Africa. In Natal it is unmediated (or less mediated) by the state's political intervention and the politics of apartheid. Elsewhere in South Africa, the absence of Inkatha equivalents forced the state to depend on its own forces or on transparently manipulated vigilante activity and ethnic violence. The reason conflict did not flare up as clearly earlier in Natal lies partly in the relationship between the 'new' unions of the early 1970s and the Kwazulu authorities, and the relative absence of popular ideas of a socialist alternative in South Africa at that time.[11] A crucial implication of COSATU's formation was that it shifted the political centre of gravity to the Transvaal and the ideological centre of gravity towards the unions, and towards a leadership with less concern for the idiosyncracies and concerns of political life in Natal with its pockets of fanatical Zulu ethnicity.

The UDF's formation earlier had had tremendous impact on the national and international political strategy of the Inkatha movement. However, it would appear that Inkatha's loss of the image of a 'revived ANC' in 1983 has since been overshadowed by the challenge, both organisational and ideological, from COSATU.

What if Inkatha loses the constituency it promises the 'real reformers', along with the economic direction it injects into that constituency? It then promises to become no more than the Muzorewa option, a role which is sometimes, inaccurately at least for the present, ascribed to it.

The position taken by Inkatha and its appendage UWUSA is pro-capitalist, pro-investment, and anti-socialist. In the past 18 months this has resulted in continual attacks on and defensive action by COSATU members; direct organisational involvement by Inkatha in the labour field through the formation of UWUSA (a move termed 'a serious mistake' in that Buthelezi's 'cleverest move would have been to remain solely on the political terrain with which he was already familiar');[12] organisational clashes between UWUSA and COSATU and other unions; the involvement of capital in Natal in political structures and campaigns; and the sealing of a conservative alliance. This has been compared, probably with unintentional aptness, with the Namibian Democratic Turnhalle Alliance, which is also an alliance of pro-capitalist interests designed to exclude a popular left-wing movement from power.

After the violence following the assassination of lawyer Victoria Mxenge in early August 1985, the violence associated with the Inanda area from August, and the formation of COSATU at the end of November, the 'real reformers' saw the acute need for stabilising action, and events succeeded one another rapidly.

Indaba initiatives

Following months of intense speculation and years of groundwork, an 'Indaba' to write a legislative structure for the region was announced. Invitations were sent out early in 1986. Because of the long-term and recent political antagonism between the organisers and some of those invited, and because of the mode of operation of the Indaba, it was clear from the outset that progressive organisations would not participate. Ultra-conservative groups also declined. This left the field open to a conservative political 'middle ground'.

The Indaba, meeting for the first time in April 1986, can be divided into four groupings, each comprising about nine members:[13] the first represented capital - *as it operates in the region*. This distinction is important as it is no longer possible to speak of a regionally distinct capital in terms of *ownership*. However, capital (in this case especially sugar capital) is tied to a site of production where stability has to be ensured.

The dominant partner here is the Tongaat-Hulett group under Chris Saunders, who was no doubt also making up for his publicly confessed sin of support for the 'yes' vote in the 1983 referendum. He personally headed the Indaba's 'image management committee' until the fury of the far-right within the Indaba led to the committee being disbanded. With some truth, the right wing accused Saunders's committee of manipulating the direction and public image of the

Indaba prior to consensus.

While Tongaat-Hulett has diversified extensively into food, clothing and shelter,[14] its base is still the sugar industry. For example, within this Anglo American-controlled group sugar contributes 41,6% to turnover, as compared to 11,4% by foods and 20,7% by building materials.[15] Tongaat employs more than 40 000 workers.

Also part of the capital grouping in the Indaba are the SA Sugar Association, the Natal Agricultural Union, the Kwazulu Cane Growers' Association, and industrial and commercial bodies (divided into ethnic sub-categories). Significantly, sugar and some other business interests were behind setting up the Lombard Commission eight years earlier.

The second group is composed of political representatives of the region's dominant and peripheral economic interests. These organisations all, with one inconsequential exception (the Reform Party of Yellan Chinsamy), participate in state-created structures - either the tricameral parliament (in the case of Solidarity and the National People's Party, the Labour Party and the New Republic Party) or the bantustan (Inkatha). Here the New Republic Party (NRP), in limbo after the demise of its provincial home with the abolition of the Natal Provincial Council in 1986, was of necessity the most imaginative in its proposals that the 'middle ground' be given political form.

It appears that the PFP, by playing party politics and claiming the Indaba too much as its own, forced the rejection of the Indaba proposals - a response by no means inevitable - by Home Affairs Minister Stoffel Botha. The PFP's claim probably made its difficult pact with the NRP even more unpalatable to the more conservative members of that doomed political party. And the fact that the Indaba was an essential point of agreement in the NRP-PFP pact for the 1987 white election probably weakened supporters of this regional option within the state camp at least temporarily. They were represented most strongly by ex-ambassador Denis Worrall, who with great insight declared that 'one of the virtues of the Natal Indaba is that it could bring Chief Buthelezi into national politics' (*NM*, 31.10.86; *DN*, 04.12.86). Worrall gave government's rejection of the Indaba as a major reason for his defection from the ruling party.

The third group of Indaba participants is made up of local and regional administrative bodies. The Indaba was convened by the Natal Provincial Administration's Frank Martin (an NRP member) and the Kwazulu government's Oscar Dhlomo (who is also secretary general of Inkatha). Thus together they represented the *de jure* - administrative division of the region.

There was no Indian or coloured representation at this regional second-tier level until the establishment of appointed provincial government in 1986. There was no regional structure for providing services and patronage by and for Indians and coloureds between 'Cato Manor and Cape Town', between local and national government. As a result, parties and individuals representing these population groups were not involved in provincial-level practical co-ordination that preceded the Indaba. But they had to take their seats in the Indaba in order to ensure participation in a future non-racial or multiracial Natal and to compensate for the waning prospect of real power at a national level.[16]

The importance of these administrative bodies in the Indaba (they had not been involved in the deliberations of the Buthelezi Commission, whereas capital had) indicates that the Indaba set itself the task of constructing an alternative way of running the province - but one still based on the previous components of government. This aim of retaining previous structures is to be seen in the recommendations of the Indaba. After all, the Indaba was the third phase of a process which in its first phase had already achieved commitment to co-operation between the Kwazulu Legislative Assembly and the Natal Provincial Administration. Phase two was the establishment of a Joint Executive Authority between these two bodies. This had to gain parliamentary approval, but Natal Administrator Radclyffe Cadman said that by April 1987 the joint authority would be operating. But by mid-1987 nothing had been finalised yet.

The fourth and final grouping in the Indaba consists of a motley array of religious bodies, women's organisations (such as the Women's Bureau), the only workers' organisation (the Black Allied Workers Union) and so on.

A bill of rights, a constitution and a two-tier parliament

These then are the groups who worked towards consensus in secret (despite many leaks) to bring forth a bill of rights. The bill of rights has its share of internal faults and an ultimate weakness: it would apply in only one region of a country still controlled by a central state with its own agenda of discrimination and repression.

Also revealed was the outline of a constitution for the region. While many details are not known and others may not yet have been thought of, the Indaba proposals involve a 'parliament' of 100 members for Natal (the name to be retained for the region including Kwazulu). Sixty-six members would be elected within 15 constituencies (the greater Durban area would be divided into three) made up of 15 economic development regions within the province and Kwazulu. The remaining 34 members would be allocated in proportion to the number of votes cast in the elections for parties or individuals (so 3% of votes would ensure three representatives in the first chamber). All people over 18 resident within the region would be able to vote.

There is, however, to be a second chamber of 50 members, of whom ten would be elected by each of five 'background' groups, constituted ostensibly by 'voluntary association'. In other words, individuals could choose to belong to the 'Afrikaans', the 'English', the 'Asian', the 'African', or the 'South African' (or 'at large') group. However, an 'African' would not be able to choose to belong to the 'English background' group, for example. The South African group would be there for those who did not want to belong to any group! As little as a fortnight before the proposals were released, Dirk Kemp of the Indaba Support Group (set up outside the Indaba structures by the Tongaat company) denied that these 'background' groups would have any powers other than over cultural, religious and language rights. But the second chamber will, in effect, be able to veto any legislation except financial bills passed in the 'parliament'. Guardianship of each group's cultural rights will be exercised by a proposed 'cultural council'.

Not surprisingly in the light of the importance of tribal authorities and chiefs in Kwazulu administration and control, a 'council of chiefs' is proposed. Its powers have not been touched upon in the reports on the Indaba proposals. However, existing tribal authorities will continue to function as local government structures. It is also suggested that there be a governor general, to be appointed by the state president.

These then, in brief, are the proposals on which Kemp commented as follows:

Unfortunately the public has not had the opportunity of arguing through all the alternatives in the way the Indaba delegates have. So they will simply have to rely on the word of their representatives in the Indaba that what emerges from it as the final proposal is really the best, if not the only, acceptable option that is available (*DN*, 17.11.86).

A few days later Frank Martin, co-convenor of the Indaba, said the final agreements of the Indaba would probably be disliked intensely by most people:

> But if that were to be so, then we have done a good job, as in our complex society what pleases one person will displease another... What Natalians should be asking themselves is this - can they live with it? (*DN*, 26.11.86)

It is clearly not intended that Natalians will have the opportunity to decide, *after informed discussion and along with all other South Africans,* on this 'Natal option'.

As the Indaba continued, many people died in less publicised and formalised areas of the struggle for control over the region. Central to that struggle were trade unions affiliated to COSATU, and UWUSA and Inkatha.

Inkatha/COSATU clashes continue

Clashes between the 'Inkatha line' of racial reform and an alternative vision of South Africa are central to the future political and economic direction of the country as a whole. This is not to deny that there were incidents which fell outside this central conflict. Violence, deaths and destruction of property have occurred: between Inkatha factions; in 'faction fights'; between youth groups and Inkatha; between ANC members and sympathisers and Inkatha members; and between localised gangs and economic interests protecting their turf or attempting to extend it. And, of course, there was conflict between the 'security forces' and many of these groups or individuals. However, the dominant organised incompatible interests within the region are represented by Inkatha and the trade unions.

For example, after COSATU members refused to drive buses from Pietermaritzburg and surrounding townships to the 1986 'May Day' launch of UWUSA at Kings Park in Durban, frequent clashes erupted. By October 1986 three people had been injured. At the end of June the Sizanani Mazulu Transport workers involved in the dispute went on strike in protest at a fellow driver's UWUSA recruiting activities; the person in question subsequently left and became a full-time organiser for UWUSA (*Echo*, 23.10.86).

Pippa Green has written of the attempts by the Inkatha-controlled Esikhawini township council to ban a 1986 COSATU May Day rally in the township,[17] and about the concerted campaign against COSATU unionists in northern Natal generally - a campaign that cannot but help UWUSA in its attempts to establish itself in that part of the province.[18]

Two notable events of 1986 occurred at the Hlobane Colliery and in Mphophomeni township. At Hlobane, close to the heartland of Zulu ethnic mobilisation, the National Union of Mineworkers has had an organised presence for several years. Here too the warning signs were visible in the form of clashes after the formation of UWUSA, as an aggressive ethnicity was dragged into the workplace and used to attack members of COSATU affiliates.

On 23 May 1986 the Zulu king, Goodwill Zwelethini, addressed the official opening of the Zululand Anthracite Colliery. Present were the minister of mineral and energy affairs, mine management and, importantly, chiefs and their councillors, reflecting a trend of extending the influence of 'traditional' authority into spheres other than those of rural administration and control. The king claimed to 'rise above politics' in his public pronouncements, then attacked COSATU president Elijah Barayi and NUM members who 'are intent upon destroying the economy and attacking the free enterprise system'. He accused some mineworkers of making 'a habit' of insulting Buthelezi and warned 'other blacks who come to work here' that while they were welcome 'they must behave themselves and respect black leadership of this region'.[19] A shop steward who lives in Zululand was subsequently accused of having denigrated the king, and forced to apologise.

Early in June, a few days after the king's speech, NUM members at the Hlobane Colliery (owned by ISCOR, whose Newcastle plants have historically been the scene of intrigue in favour of Zulu royalty) went on strike over mine management's refusal to allow a NUM organiser onto mine property and over the closure of the NUM office. Newspapers immediately reported the clashes that followed in terms of inter-ethnic 'faction fighting', but from later reports and affidavits it is clear that the violence took place between NUM members on the one hand and UWUSA members supported by mine management and outsiders alleged to belong to Inkatha on the other. Mine management went so far as to say that Inkatha did not like the

NUM presence, leading one miner to ask, 'Are we employed by Inkatha or are we employed by the mine?' At least 11 people died in the clashes and many more were injured. Hundreds left the mine.

Equally horrifying was the violence in the township of Mphophomeni. On the night of Friday 5 December 1986 three Metal and Allied Workers Union trade unionists and the daughter of a striking Sarmcol worker were abducted from Mphophomeni, a township close to Pietermaritzburg and home to many of the strikers from the plant at Howick.[20] In a secluded spot three of those abducted were shot and killed. They were: Phineas Sibiya, chairperson of the shop stewards' committee at BTR Sarmcol, a MAWU branch executive member and leader of the 1 000 striking workers from Sarmcol sacked by the British multinational in 1985; Simon Ngubane, a fellow shop steward; and Flora Mnikathi, daughter of a Sarmcol worker. The fourth member of the group, Michael Sibiya, escaped when the shooting started.

These deaths followed a concerted assault on COSATU unionists throughout Natal at the end of 1986. In the Isithebe industrial area in Kwazulu, for example, MAWU had to vacate its offices after its landlord was threatened and potential members were intimidated by carloads of people (*BD*, 02.12.86). A woman was killed, allegedly because she was mistakenly identified as a COSATU supporter; at Empangeni workers wearing COSATU or MAWU T-shirts were assaulted; at the Mandini township 'busloads' of people, allegedly from Lindelani, stronghold of Inkatha central committee member Thomas Mandla Shabalala, beat up COSATU supporters while shouting pro-UWUSA slogans (*DN*, 10.12.86); another report suggested Kwazulu police involvement in the attacks and harassment (*DN*, 10.06.86); in Chesterville two MAWU members were killed with pangas; at Hambanati members of the National Union of Textile Workers were prevented from travelling to their union's annual general meeting.

It is probably inaccurate to suggest that a *massive* regional conspiracy is afoot in Natal, involving Inkatha, its trade union, capital and organised political interests. It is true though that these parties are benefiting from each other's strengths, exploiting others' weaknesses, and forging a non-apartheid future that will probably involve unhealthy doses of mobilised ethnicity, regional 'stability' of the oppressive variety, and a minimum of redistribution through social and public services.[21] This alliance will also mean that the interests most directly represented within Inkatha - those of a petty bourgeoisie striving for the security seldom possible for this class - will benefit from the extended and solidifying relationship with big business as well as from the relaxation of social segregation to which their relative wealth will entitle them.

Probably because of the threat this poses for racial privilege, certain right-wing interests in Natal have opposed the Indaba. In northern Natal towns such as Newcastle which are marked by economic depression and white unemployment, such limited class reshuffling can only pose a threat. Aksie Blanke Natal, the far-right group formed to oppose the Indaba, has a potential for mobilising artisans, small traders, clerical staff and white small agricultural interests. The 1987 white election gave an indication of the extent of right-wing rejection of the Indaba proposals. But if actualised these proposals will probably mean little change in terms of economic redistribution or political freedom for the vast majority of the regional population.

Notes

1 Heather Hughes, 'Violence in Inanda, August 1985', *Journal of Southern African Studies* (forthcoming); Ari Sitas, 'Inanda, August 1985: "Where wealth and power and blood reign worshipped gods"', *South African Labour Bulletin*, 11(4), 1986.

2 CJ Saunders, 'The future of Natal-Kwazulu: the pursuit of non-racial capitalism', opening address to USSALEP Conference on Development and Employment, Tongaat, 1983.

3 JA Lombard et al, *Alternatives to the Consolidation of Kwazulu: progress report*, Bureau for Economic Policy and Analysis, University of Pretoria, Pretoria, 1980.

4 Buthelezi Commission, *The Requirements for Stability and Development in Kwazulu and Natal*, Durban 1982.

5 Gerhard Maré, 'The New Constitution: Extending Democracy or Decentralising Control?', *South African Review 3*, Johannesburg, 1986.

6 South African Institute of Race Relations, *Race Relations Survey 1985*, Johannesburg, 1986.

7 Gerhard Maré, 'Class conflict and ideology among the petty bourgeoisie in the "homelands": Inkatha - a study', *Conference on the History of Opposition in Southern Africa*, Development Studies Group, Johannesburg, 1978.

8 Labour Monitoring Group (Natal), 'Monitoring the Sarmcol struggle', *South African Labour Bulletin*, 11(2), 1985.

9 Sitas, 'Inanda, August 1985'.

10 Also Pippa Green, 'Northern Natal: meeting UWUSA's challenge', *South African Labour Bulletin*, 12(1), 1986.

11 Gerhard Maré and Georgina Hamilton (forthcoming), *An Appetite for*

Power: Buthelezi's Inkatha and the politics of 'loyal resistance' in South Africa, Ravan Press, Johannesburg.

12 Michael Morris, 'Lessons from May Day: UWUSA, Inkatha and COSATU', *Work in Progress,* 43, 1986.

13 For more detail see Gerhard Maré, 'Kwazulu/Natal Indaba: regional rule for Inkatha?', *Work in Progress,* 46, 1987; Daryl Glaser, 'Behind the Indaba: the making of the KwaNatal option', *Transformation,* 2, 1986.

14 *The Condenser,* Tongaat-Hulett group publication, 1970, 1-2.

15 Robin McGregor, *McGregor's Investors' Handbook,* Grabouw, 1986, 553.

16 Jo Beall, Jeremy Grest, Heather Hughes and Gerhard Maré, 'The Natal Option: regional distinctiveness within the national reform process', Association for Sociology in Southern Africa Conference, Durban, 1986.

17 Pippa Green, 'May Day courage in northern Natal', *South African Labour Bulletin,* 11(6), 1986.

18 Green, 'May Day courage'.

19 'Official opening of the Zululand Anthracite Colliery, speech by His Majesty King Goodwill Zwelethini', 23.05.86.

20 Debbie Bonnin, 'From labour tenant to industrial worker: the case of the Sarmcol strikers', unpublished mimeo, Industrial Sociology, University of Natal, Durban, 1986.

21 It is remarkable how publicly adamant regional economic interests have been to downplay or deny the practicability of meaningful redistribution - for example, Saunders, 'The Future of Natal/Kwazulu'; DMCC president Brian Hill (*ST,* 18.01.87); JA du Pisanie, Senbank economist (*DN,* 29.12.86); Afrikaanse Handelsinstituut (*Rapport,* 14.12.86). The drawcard of 'rewarding' the region through investment and aid has been equally frequently advanced by the business and political communities.

Section 6:
South Africa's Political Economy

Introduction

Beyond the Indicators: A Perspective on the South African Economy

David Kaplan

This section of the *Review* outlines the principal economic developments of 1986. It argues that in terms of overall economic performance there was no departure from the trend evident over the last decade or so - in brief, that the economic crisis continued unabated. It suggests some elements of an explanation for the continuing crisis, examines some of its consequences and critiques some proposals that have been advanced to resolve it.

In 1986, the South African economy confounded the economic pundits. Their predictions were frequently incorrect and, more often than not, offered widely differing interpretations of the state of the economy.

In the third quarter of 1985, there was an 'upturn' in the economy which many expected to be maintained through 1986. In early February, for example, following PW Botha's reformist address at the opening of parliament, Gerhard de Kock, governor of the Reserve Bank, declared that '1986 now seems set to be a year of rising income, output, trade and employment. The time for another "prepare to meet thy boom" statement may not be far off'.

However, the first half of 1986 saw economic growth falter with substantial declines in remunerations, fixed investment and company profitability. In the third quarter there was a pronounced upsurge in business confidence. With a rise in the gold price the value of the rand improved, retail sales increased and company profitability rose. The governor of the Reserve Bank, in his annual address at the end of August, forecast 'a renewed cyclical upswing in the short-term and a considerably higher real average rate of growth in the medium and long-term'. And yet once again, by the year-end it was evident that the 'economy was running out of steam' and the pundits rapidly revised their forecasts downwards.

Periods of economic recession have historically been characteristic of the South African and other economies. But in contemporary South Africa, recession uncharacteristically no longer gives way to significant and sustained economic growth. Since 1974, South Africa has experienced a number of 'upturns' (1975, 1980, 1983, 1985 and again in 1986) but each of these has entailed limited growth and has rapidly petered out. Moreover, historically the normal pattern was for the prior recession to condition the following upturn, such that generally more severe recessions would be succeeded by more substantial upturns. But the economic 'upturns' at the end of 1985 and that which commenced in the second half of 1986 show all the signs of being very limited and of very short duration - and this after a lengthy recessionary period punctuated only by short periods of revival. Recessionary conditions have become the South African norm and periods of expansion only limited and temporary aberrations. It is these exceptional features which justify the term 'crisis'.

In such circumstances, the usual economic indicators on which the pundits base their forecasts give a confusing and sometimes downright misleading picture. To take an example: share prices are seen as one significant indicator of the prospects for the economy. Share prices on the Johannesburg stock exchange rose significantly throughout 1986. However, the booming stock exchange was not an indicator of business confidence but rather the reverse. The rise in share prices was principally a consequence of investors' reluctance to undertake productive investments given their lack of confidence in the longer-term prospects for the economy. Short-term liquid financial investments were preferred to longer-term fixed investments and resulted in booming financial markets but a diminishing capital stock.

In the 1980s, aggregate new fixed investment has declined at an average rate of 4% a year and 1986 saw further declines (see Cassim's contribution in this regard). The decline in fixed investment in the key manufacturing sector was particularly pronounced in 1986 and the total was less than half that for 1983. Preliminary indications are that the downward trend will continue in 1987. This downward trend in fixed investments has occurred despite the increases in company profitability registered in the second half of 1986 and the substantial reductions in the borrowing (overdraft) rate. Clearly, fixed investment is proving impervious to the usual inducements and reflects a more fundamental pessimism as regards the economy on the part of business.

A declining and aging capital stock is not just a symptom of the crisis. It in turn contributes to the crisis in many ways, resulting in a reduction in the productive potential of the economy and adversely affecting labour productivity. It has had a particularly devastating effect on those industries which produce new plant and equipment (the capital goods sector). The decline in manufacturing output has been most pronounced in the transport equipment and machinery sectors. The severity of the recession and its long duration have wreaked havoc in these sectors and 1986 saw a continuing decline. These are, of course, precisely the sectors of industry where South Africa is weakest and most import-dependent. Development must occur here if the traditional foreign exchange constraints that have operated on the South African economy, as a consequence of the reliance on imported capital equipment financed through the export of primary commodities, are to be relaxed. It is in these sectors that many other countries at a stage of development comparable to South Africa, the so-called newly industrialising countries (NICs), have since the mid-1970s shown such spectacular growth. Thus, South Africa's relative position in this respect has deteriorated considerably.[1]

With a diminished capacity in the production of capital goods, so that an ever-higher proportion of imports consist of vital capital goods (now running at around half of all imports), the South African economy is ever more vulnerable to external 'shocks'. This has occurred at the same time as the world economy has become far more unstable. In particular, with the ending of the Bretton Woods system of fixed exchange rates, the price of gold, responsible for about half of all South Africa's export earnings, has been subject to wide fluctuations. This has, in itself, imparted considerable unpredictability to the South African economy.

However, even where there have been substantial rises in the price of gold, this has not provided the impetus for a sustained and major economic 'upturn'. That a favourable external stimulus is incapable of generating a sustained economic 'upturn' is a further indication of pronounced structural deficiencies in the internal organisation of the economy, what Cassim here calls the social structure of accumulation. Indeed, the higher gold price and the accompanying 'upturn' commencing in 1980 saw major borrowings abroad by South African companies and parastatals. This was encouraged by the state's relaxation of exchange controls. As a result, when the price of gold declined, the ratio of South Africa's debt to GDP rose markedly - and much of this debt was of a short-term nature. To service the debt, and in the absence of new sources of foreign loans, severe austerity measures had to be implemented, so exacerbating the subsequent recession. For the first time in some 40 months, the price of gold began to rise steeply after July 1986. But, once again, the rise in the gold price is having little lasting effect on domestic investment and thus the impetus to economic expansion is likely to be weak.

The private sector's unwillingness to respond to the normal incentives and increase its productive investments has resulted in government impatience and criticism. In his 1986 annual address, the governor of the Reserve Bank, while in true banker style calling for caution, went so far as to raise the spectre of government compelling the private sector to invest. De Kock said that 'the government has every right to expect the private sector to show more confidence in the future'.

But the policies actually implemented by the government in order to promote economic expansion were far more orthodox. Cassim has outlined the government's monetarist-inspired policies, namely a liberalisation of financial markets together with a reduction in the rate of growth of the money supply. He points to some of the negative consequences - the severe contractions in certain industries, the dramatic rise in bankruptcies and unemployment, and the declines in fixed investment. Moreover, the declines in profitability hastened the process of disinvestment and facilitated the ever-increasing concentration of economic power as the larger firms with more financial reserves and muscle expanded through acquisitions of disinvesting foreign firms or of firms strapped for cash. Government policies thus only compounded the problem of economic uncertainty, while the lowering of interest rates and the mildly inflationary 1986 budget did little to restore confidence on the part of investors.

The second set of policy panaceas designed to correct the economic malaise revolves around the government's announced intention of giving a greater scope to the private sector through policies of privatisation and deregulation. As yet the state has not spelt out the precise content of these policies, but the principle has already been enthusiastically supported by many in the private sector and academia. Innes discusses the declared motivations for such policies, both as an economic strategy designed to increase efficiency and as a political strategy designed to depoliticise society. As a political strategy, he argues that privatisation is elitist and will widen the gap between the haves and the have-nots. Since the lines of cleavage correlate closely with race, this will be racial discrimination under another name. In regard to economic strategy, the argument that the private sector is necessarily more efficient than the state in the provision of a wide range of services rests heavily on the presence of competition in the market place. But in South Africa, as is now widely acknowledged, there is a very high level of economic concentration, with relatively few companies dominating most market sectors and with the large conglomerates all operating in a large number of sectors. Moreover, as we have already noted, the trend towards concentration has been gathering momentum given the recession and disinvestment.

Privatisation and deregulation as strategies of economic growth are being heavily promoted by many governments in the advanced capitalist countries (and indeed by a number of 'socialist' countries) and in the Third World by the international aid agencies such as the World Bank. Whether or not such policies will facilitate economic growth, and especially at what social cost, is presently the subject of considerable debate. But two particular factors in the South African case cast doubt upon the efficacy of these measures. Firstly, as noted above, the high and increasing level of economic concentration will severely limit competition. Secondly, and more fundamentally, a greater economic role for the private sector can only ever be advantageous if the private sector is willing to productively reinvest its newly acquired profits. As we sketched out above, business is presently extremely reticent to invest in productive assets. Indeed, only expanded investments by the state and the public corporations have prevented the capital stock from declining even further. Thus, under the present malaise, a greater role for the private sector may be counterproductive.

Many of the key features of the contemporary crisis besetting the South African economy can be discerned in the particular plight of the agricultural sector. Cooper's article in this *Review* explores this area. The agricultural sector has been faced with falling prices on export markets and rising import prices. As with the economy in general, agriculture's terms of trade have declined steadily since 1975. A series of widespread droughts over the last four years has exacerbated the problem. While the crisis in agriculture has been partially cushioned by extensive state subsidies and price supports, underscored by the political significance of white farmers, farm income has fallen nonetheless since 1980 and the sheep and cattle herds are about 10% down on 1982. Capital investment has declined significantly over the last four years and further declines were recorded for 1986. In unit terms tractor sales declined by 80% between 1981 and 1986, while fertiliser sales declined by 40%. Despite reductions in capital expenditure, the debt position of farmers worsened considerably and stood at over R13-billion in 1986. The burden of the debt also increased as a result of higher interest rates. Many farmers have sold up and the concentration of land ownership has increased markedly. A significant penetration of the agricultural sector on the part of the large conglomerates is underway. By way of conclusion, Cooper broadly outlines some of the policies that would need to be followed in order to rationalise agricultural production, including land reform.

By the end of 1986, the immediate prospects for agriculture were more promising. The rains had been good and interest rates and fuel and fertiliser prices were lower. Farm incomes are predicted to rise significantly in 1987 and make a major contribution to the economic 'upturn'. However, a number of factors should be taken into consideration. Firstly, there is the government's commitment to ensuring more market-related farm pricing. Secondly, there is the threat of sanctions. Finally, the world food trade in basic grains is at a very low level and the price of maize internationally is expected to decline. These factors suggest that the rise in farm incomes will be limited, even in the short term, while in the longer term the industry faces severe constraints of a structural nature.

While agriculture presently contributes only 7% of South Africa's GDP, it provides employment to 14% of South Africa's workforce - an index of the sector's low level of productivity. Moreover, 47% of South Africa's population is in the rural areas, and this underlines the vital importance of agricultural production. While there are significant variations within agriculture - according to region, product and type of employer - generally farm work compares unfavourably with urban employment: working conditions are very harsh and remuneration (in money and in kind) has always been extremely low. As Keenan and Sarakinsky show, the situation on 'white farms' has, if anything, deteriorated over the last decade. As the crisis in agriculture intensifies, severely indebted farmers are likely to respond by squeezing their workers even harder. In 'bantustan' agriculture, the situation of farm workers is even worse. Moreover, in many cases the spread of commercial agriculture is accomplished by the dispossession of communities. At the year-end, the control over land in the six 'non-independent' bantustans was transferred to the administrations of these areas. These administrations are known to favour the further spread of commercial agriculture. Ironically, since many of these agricultural schemes are aimed at the export market, the imposition of sanctions on South African agricultural products may provide a glimmer of hope by retarding the spread of commercial agriculture.

There are two particularly evident omissions in this review of the South African economy - disinvestment and sanctions. Only the briefest discussion of these highly contentious issues can be entered into here.

The number of companies disinvesting from South Africa increased massively in 1986. Moreover, a larger number of those companies disinvesting had a significant stake in the South African economy. For example, at least 20 US companies each employing more than 100 persons disinvested in 1986. The two most significant were General Motors (3 056 employees) and IBM (1 484 employees). Other significant US companies included GEC, Eastman Kodak, Coca-Cola, Eaton Corporation and Marriott Corporation. In fact, the overwhelming majority of firms disinvesting from South Africa (probably 75%) were from the US. However, there were significant disinvestments on the part of firms from elsewhere, and the largest was that of Barclays Bank from the UK.

In only a small minority of cases were the operations of disinvesting companies actually liquidated. Where this did occur, the companies were generally small. Thus, disinvestment has meant a transfer of ownership - sometimes to another foreign firm (eg Bata) but, in most instances, to local concerns. In some cases local management bought the shares (eg IBM and General Motors), but in many cases, especially where the firms were large, the beneficiaries tended to be the larger local corporations (eg Anglo American's purchase of Barclays).

A debate has raged in the press as to whether this or that company is disinvesting for commercial reasons or because of political pressures. In many cases, eg General Motors, the decision to disinvest was, at least in important part, a result of the fact that the return on investments by overseas companies has fallen dramatically and many have made no profit for a number of years. But in other cases, especially companies for whom the South African sphere of their operations generated a significant share of world-wide company profits - despite their denials to the contrary - political pressures seem to have been the key motivation behind disinvestment, eg Barclays. With no solution to the recession in sight and pressures on companies with investments in South Africa unlikely to cease, we can expect to see disinvestment continuing.

But, given that disinvestment rarely means any cessation of production and is confined to a change of ownership, will this necessarily affect the South African economy adversely?

In most cases where a change of ownership has taken place, the new (generally local) owners have signed franchise agreements and technical contracts with the disinvesting company. These ensure that they have access to the products and, most critically, the technology of the disinvesting company. 'In terms of our agreement (with IBM)', explained the managing director of the now locally owned IBM operation, 'we will continue to obtain systems engineering support facilities, support from international centres and we will continue to have the right to attend IBM education courses'.

The local companies therefore continue, after disinvestment, to produce essentially the same commodities as before, utilising the same production techniques. The products of General Motors, IBM and Coca-Cola, for example, will still be available in South Africa. (Eastman Kodak is exceptional. It closed down its local operation completely and has stopped any sales of its products to South Africa.)

In the short term, therefore, disinvestment will have little adverse effect upon the local economy. However, in the longer term local companies' access to the products and technologies of the parent is by no means guaranteed. Many high technology companies, in particular, have shown themselves very reluctant to 'trust' important parts of their technological know-how to any company other than a direct subsidiary. In the case of a direct subsidiary the use of and access to the technology can be directly monitored and controlled. Moreover, if additional international action against South Africa embraces the export of certain products and technologies, local companies will find it more difficult to evade these restrictions than would direct subsidiaries. Finally, if the economic crisis is not resolved, the significance of the South African market for overseas firms will decline and the advantages of licensing products and technologies to South African producers will decrease.

In the period under review disinvestment has therefore had little effect on the economy, and this is unlikely to change in the immediate future, but the longer-term implications are likely to be more profound.

Very broadly, the same can be said in regard to sanctions. In October 1986, the US congress adopted the Comprehensive Anti-Apartheid Act. Sanctions measures have been adopted by a number of other countries, most significantly members of the European Economic Community and Japan. The principal South African exports now subject to sanctions include coal, steel products, pig iron, agricultural products, textiles and sugar. Moreover, some countries, notably the US and Japan, have placed restrictions on exports of some computers and other advanced technology to South Africa. This is in addition to the prevailing embargoes on oil and arms.

The experience of Rhodesia under the Smith regime (and indeed

South Africa's current experience with the arms and oil embargoes) strongly suggest that as long as countries have the wherewithal to pay, they will be able to import. Except for some items at the technology frontier, and South Africa needs few of these, almost anything can be obtained from a variety of willing sources. Thus exports hold the key. As presently constituted, something in the order of 5% of South Africa's total exports are subject to sanctions. Moreover, there are significant loopholes even here. Firstly, in most cases existing contracts are being allowed to run their course. Secondly, there are considerable possibilities for 'back-door' entry. In this regard, a number of South Africa's trading partners are crucial. Taiwan may well be South Africa's door to the Far East, while Israel (and possibly Portugal) are excellent entrees into the EEC. Israel's easy entry into the US markets (often requiring little documentation) may be of particular significance. Thirdly, completely new markets for South Africa's sanctioned exports are being investigated, notably in South East Asia. Again, the Rhodesian experience would suggest that these loopholes are of much greater importance where the commodities being exported are in short supply on the world market. If the market is 'firm', importers are more likely to turn a blind eye or accept more complex and lengthy importation through third parties. The possibilities for exporters of negotiating effective discounts are also increased. However, in the case of many of South Africa's exports presently subject to sanctions the world market is currently weak, eg coal, iron and steel. With slow growth rates in much of the developed world, raw material prices are presently very low and tending to decline even further. Raw materials make up some 90% of South Africa's exports (gold, 50%+; other minerals and metals, 25%; agricultural and food products, 10%). The impact of sanctions on South Africa's exports will therefore depend critically on the conditions that prevail on the world market.

Estimates of the potential impact of sanctions upon the South African economy vary widely. However, there have been few estimates that have calculated the likely inter-industry effects of sanctions, eg, a decline in say steel exports will adversely affect production of coal for use in the making of steel. One exception is a study done by the Federated Chamber of Industries (FCI).[2] Using a sophisticated macro-economic model of the South African economy, this study calculated the likely net impact of sanctions, incorporating the inter-industry effects. Based on the scenario of the sanction measures presently applied by the United States being extended to all countries trading with South Africa, the FCI study concluded that, over a period of 18 months to 2 years, sanctions will reduce the Gross Domestic Product by 1,7% and result in the loss of approximately 49 000 jobs. However, many of South Africa's principal trading partners, eg in the EEC and Japan, have far weaker sanction packages, while others, eg in Southern Africa and Taiwan, have yet to announce any sanction measures. In addition, no account was taken of the capacity to evade sanctions. The likely impact of sanction measures, *as presently constituted,* is thus limited. Of course the scenario could change. If mandatory United Nations sanctions were applied so as to result in an 80% export loss for most commodities (strategic minerals exempted), the FCI calculated a decrease in Gross Domestic Output of about 30% and the loss of over 1,1-million jobs.

But, for all their potential significance, sanctions did not have any measurable impact upon South Africa's economic performance in 1986. As with disinvestment, the extent of sanctions and therefore their effects on the South African economy will only become apparent with the passage of time.

The crisis of the South African economy pre-dates sanctions and disinvestment. It is a structural crisis and as such will require fundamental changes over a broad front. Not only is the present regime incapable of providing a solution, but its attempts at crisis management have, if anything, exacerbated the problem. This, very broadly, is the common thrust of the contributions to this section of the *Review.*

Notes

1 For a specific example see D Kaplan, 'Machinery and Industry: The Causes and Consequences of Constrained Development of the South African Machine Tool Industry', *Social Dynamics,* 13(1), June 1987.
2 Federated Chamber of Industries Information Services, *The Effect of Sanctions on Employment and Production in South Africa. A Quantitative Analysis,* South African Federated Chamber of Industries, 1986.

Economic Crisis and Stagnation in South Africa

Fuad Cassim

South Africa is in the midst of its most serious depression since the 1930s. All the signs of a deepening economic and political crisis are present. Unlike earlier crises, which served as catalysts for renewed growth and development, the present one has eroded some previous advances such as the growth of new industries. So far it has not generated any creative responses. The alternative to rapid structural change in the economy is stagnation, but changes required to alter the direction of development are blocked. A new political alignment is needed without which creative economic solutions cannot be found or implemented.

The current crisis in South Africa is not simply another in the series that have characterised apartheid and capitalism. It is different because it is part of a larger international crisis, in particular the slowdown in growth experienced by the Western economies. It illustrates the way the South African economy is dominated and distorted by subordination to the world economy. The South African economy will remain weak, both internally and externally, in the foreseeable future. Any temporary recovery will not resolve the problem. The economic structure which emerged in the post-war period, with the high growth rates of the 1960s and early 1970s, is no longer tenable. Moreover, the imposition of economic liberalisation policies has had a disastrous impact, precipitating the most serious regression of both economy and society.

To consider the current impact of economic policies it is

necessary to examine the nature of the long-term economic decline that faces South Africa. The aim here is to offer a brief characterisation of the economic crisis, and to look more particularly at the consequences of aspects of the government's economic programme implemented from 1980 to the present, and the contradictions and pitfalls of these policies.

Growth and a new 'social structure of accumulation'[1]

There have always been economic and political tensions in the structure and growth patterns of the South African economy. But with the present declining growth rate these tensions have become more acute. The existing 'growth model' - the relatively stable pattern of economic advance within the specific institutional framework of apartheid - is beginning to break down. The rapidly growing economy of the 1960s reached the limit of its potential in the early 1970s. In the periods 1962-72, 1972-81, and 1981-86, the average annual growth rates were 5,5%, 3%, and 1,1% respectively.

The South African policy response to the international recession of 1981 strengthened the recession's effects locally. In fact the current recession, which started at the end of 1981, shows no sign of being followed by self-sustaining economic recovery. The only restructuring that has been achieved is negative - the closing down of companies, retrenchment of labour and outflow of capital.

The current recession marks a turning point because it is superimposed on long-term economic decay. Fundamental problems impede the normal functioning of the prevailing type of accumulation. This calls for a change in context, or a new type of accumulation. Hence the state is attempting to develop a new social structure of accumulation (SSA). This is evidenced by changes in economic policy, in particular the turn towards neo-conservatism. During recent years, the economic thinking that is shaping policy-making in South Africa has been identified with supply-side and monetarist economic doctrines.

Capitalist economies experience periods of relatively rapid and stable growth once the set of socio-economic institutions which make up a social structure of accumulation are in place. White monopoly of land ownership, controls over the movement of the black population in general and black workers in particular, and political disenfranchisement are key elements of apartheid's SSA. But any such structure is subject to internal and external stresses which undermine the effectiveness of institutions in promoting profitability, investment and growth. The economy then enters a period of economic crisis during which political struggles develop around the nature of institutional changes that will be made in an effort to reestablish conditions for successful accumulation.[2]

The contemporary South African economy provides an apt example of such a situation. To what extent the current economic crisis will produce a new and successful SSA remains an open question. Determined state intervention and the intensification of apartheid policy in the post-war period, coupled with a growing international economy and availability of foreign funds, led to growth. However, with the onset of the oil crisis in 1973 and the deflationary policies of the latter part of the 1970s, the economy began to be characterised by low investment and productivity, and a declining industrial structure. Any domestic growth was immediately followed by a deterioration in the balance of payments, reduced economic growth and unemployment. This meant that balance of payments equilibrium could only be achieved at the cost of domestic unemployment and stagnation.

The growth model involving a high level of state regulation of the economy through extensive import substitution, state-protected industries, and a highly regulated and racially segmented labour market had run into difficulties by the 1970s, a result in part of a narrow domestic market which inhibited the development of economies of scale. Equally important was the foreign exchange constraint on accumulation, coupled with the rising popular pressure on wages and social expenditure generated by industrialisation. Thus South African industry became less competitive in world terms. More fundamentally, the state was increasingly unable to meet the growing costs of implementing apartheid policy and its consequences, such as the narrow domestic market. The growth pattern of apartheid and capitalism was called into question, and faced with a systemic dysfunction.

The social structure of accumulation which gave rise to high growth rates under traditional apartheid in the 1960s and early 1970s was supported by tight control of the labour force and of labour market institutions such as influx control, which reduced the cost of labour. However, by the late 1970s the effectiveness of this process was exhausted, and a new social structure of accumulation was called for. It was against this background that neo-conservative policies began to shape the agenda of state policy makers, to develop a new SSA.

As it became evident that the apartheid state was impeding the further development of capitalism, the need arose to uncouple the economic and political spheres, ie to separate racism from capitalism. More specifically, it became important to lessen the role of the state in the economy. This did not mean an end to state intervention, but a change in its direction. Hence, neo-conservative policies are being used as ostensible political and economic justifications for this exercise, which involves privatisation and deregulation. Although comprehensive steps towards privatisation and deregulation have yet to be taken, they have been adopted as policy by the state, and moves have been made towards their implementation. More recently a strategy of 'inward industrialisation' has been proposed, given the limits of import substitution and export growth. The real reason for these economic and political transformations is the maintenance of the core elements of apartheid domination together with new conditions for growth and profitability.

The rapid deterioration of the economy is manifest in several areas, and worsened by the horrific impact of monetarist policies. One is the changing balance of the various sectors - the shift of investment from productive to financial and service sector activity, usually referred to as de-industrialisation. Another is the fact that South African capital goods production, both relatively and absolutely, lags behind the newly industrialised countries in the third world, which are major manufacturing centres for the multinational corporations.

South Africa's economic development remains vulnerable to fluctuations in international markets. Capital stock (machinery and equipment) is being run down, hence future productivity is less likely to grow. This renders manufactured goods less competitive in the world market. The concentration of industry and the international orientation of the economy have combined to generate an economy characterised by low investment, low growth in living standards and a weakening industrial base.

Economic policy

Many of the negative trends of recent years were not simply induced by changes in economic policy, but are the result of deep-rooted problems of economic structure. The constraints on policy stem from the dissolution of an established pattern of economic growth because of racial control and regulation, structural imbalances and the restricted domestic market.

Government's new free-market monetarist economic model attempts to establish policies that allow the market a more important role. The stated objective of this policy shift away from the highly interventionist stance inf the late 1970s was to defeat inflation. More fundamentally it can be seen as a response to the general crisis that plagues the economy. Hence government's macro-policy focused on controlling the money supply and the deficit before borrowing. This macro-strategy was coupled with a focus on improving the supply side of the economy, ie reducing taxes. This involved increasing the role of market forces, lowering taxation and reducing government intervention, to stimulate private sector economic activity.

Financial reform resulted particularly in abolition of deposit rate controls and ceilings placed on bank credits to facilitate greater control over money supply. By 1983 the foreign exchange market was also deregulated, causing the financial rand to disappear temporarily and resulting in an open-door financial policy. This process of financial reform was taken further with the introduction of monetary targeting in the 1986-87 budget speech, the basis for which was laid in the De Kock commission. Since the De Kock commission accorded priority to fighting inflation through monetary policy measures, it is argued that control over growth in the money aggregates is logical. The impact and role of the financial and banking system have changed radically. From a highly regulated system subordinated to the state, it changed to an open system with freer interest and exchange rates. New mechanisms of regulation came into operation. But this liberalisation of financial markets, together with a restrictive monetary policy, had adverse effects on the economy.

These policies, despite their technical nature, amount in simple terms to a programme of economic austerity. Their high point was the austerity package imposed in August 1984, when the prime overdraft rate was raised to 25%, increasing interest rates in an attempt to curb spending and thus inflation. Contrary to what government says, evidence indicates that these policies failed and have been substantially reversed. However, inflation has not abated, output and investment have declined, and an unprecedented foreign debt crisis severely constrained the balance of payments.

The South African government's adoption of such policies owes much to the resurgence of monetarist ideas internationally. But domestic forces also played their part. For example, neo-conservatism was entrenched in the two major documents submitted to the meeting between the cabinet and senior businessmen on 14 November 1986. These involved proposals by the economic advisory council of the state president on a long-term economic strategy; and a proposed framework for a discussion of privatisation with a view to a white paper.

These policy changes also tie in with the changing nature of state formation in this country. The regime needs a repressive political and institutional setting in order to implement its new policies, and policy changes should be seen in this context.

Both the regime and its growth model exhibit intrinsic contradictions. The impact of deflationary policies on the lives of workers (unemployment and declining income) and on local capital (credit squeezes and bankruptcies) provoked generalised instability. Not only is current government policy unlikely to meet its objectives, but it will only reinforce the factors responsible for South Africa's economic decline.

The promotion of exports was emphasised in the white paper on industrial development strategy (1985) as an attempt to re-orientate industrial strategy, through export incentives and government assistance to certain industries. The recent dramatic decline of the exchange rate, whilst increasing exports to some extent, has not had a significant investment impact on export-oriented production. Given the economy's limited achievements, policy-makers have proposed a strategy of 'inward industrialisation' as a solution to the stagnation of the manufacturing sector.[3] In the context of external constraints tightening through sanctions, disinvestment, and access to foreign markets and capital, 'inward industrialisation' is more likely to be guided by the dictates of a 'siege economy' than by attempts to expand the domestic market and redistributive measures.

Domestic macro-economic effects

South Africa's current recession (since 1981) is characterised by a decrease in annual growth rates of gross domestic product (GDP), ie total output produced in the economy, which has had a devastating effect on the level of demand. This, in turn, has had a horrific impact on the entire macro-economy. Overall unemployment rose to its highest level of 22,5% in 1982.[4] Current African unemployment is as high as six million, according to some estimates.[5] The co-existence of negative growth rates, rising inflation and increasing unemployment means that per capita income is falling rapidly.

The objectives of government economic policy, the measures used to achieve those objectives as well as the effects on companies in South Africa need to be grasped to understand why demand decreased in the economy.

Financial reform can be placed at the heart of the crisis. The process of monetary restraint or regulation of the economy resulted in a contraction of demand. The state's economic managers expected that the liberalisation of the domestic financial market, along with the gradual discontinuation of controls on foreign finance, would lead to an increase in saving and investment. The result was markedly different.

The strongly depressive effects of monetary policy resulted in a crisis for local industrial capital and the economy in general. The immediate result of attempting to reduce the growth rate of money supply was a rise in the cost of borrowing. The bank rate rose from 9,5% to 17% in the course of 1981, and reached an unprecedented 25% in August 1985. In the latter part of 1986 the Reserve Bank began to lower interest rates in order to relieve the recession, but as yet this has had no impact on investment. Investment in plant and equipment is not likely to recover easily from its drop since 1981, 25% in real terms for the overall economy and 55% in manufacturing.

High interest rates had a further deflationary impact on output, employment and profitability. A large number of commercial and industrial companies were unable to cope with the impact of interest rate increases on their cost structure. In particular, inventory demand in the company sector fell dramatically. At the same time, companies faced increased salary and wage costs. With costs rising fast something had to give: company profits. According to the Frost Sullivan Agency, the rate of return on US investments in South Africa declined from 30% in 1980 to 7% in 1983. Many firms began making losses. Between 1980 and 1985 bankruptcies increased by 500%. The total number of insolvencies for 1986 shows an increase of 31,9% over 1985.

Firms responded by reducing current output and stocks in order to lower running costs and bank debt. The effect was to worsen the already weak growth of productivity and output. The index of the physical volume of manufacturing production decreased from its peak of 106,4 in 1981 to 95,4 in 1986. In private manufacturing real investment continued its decline, along with considerable under-utilisation of industrial capacity (in 1981 capacity utilisation was 86,3%, whereas in 1986 it was at 80,9%) and a drop in private consumption expenditure.

The decline in output was rapidly reflected in employment levels. This amounts to a process of de-industrialisation, associated with a long-term decline in industrial employment and increasing overall unemployment in the economy. The manufacturing sector, the economy's key generator of employment, has shown a net decline in employment. So a significant development is underway in the South African economy: a process of relative decline is turning into an absolute contraction of the industrial base. From 1980 to 1986, little more than 150 000 jobs were created whereas the labour force swelled by an estimated 1,5-million. While 185 000 jobs were created in the public sector, around 30 000 jobs were lost in the private sector.

The Bureau of Economic Research (Stellenbosch University), in its 1985 manufacturing survey, showed that nearly half the country's manufacturing sectors were operating at lower production levels than ten years ago. The only industries which remained relatively buoyant were beverages, the food sector, paper and basic metals. Retail sales dropped to a six-year low in 1986. The building industry hit rock-bottom in the middle of 1986. Car sales slumped from a high of 32 500 in 1983 to a ten-year low of 12 500 in 1986.

The crisis of recent years has seriously undermined the growth potential of the economy. Many sectors and regions have still not recovered from the severe recession of 1981, mining being the only major exception. Revenue levels rose strongly, due to export growth because of the weak rand. As a result wages are depressed, which de-mobilises sectors of the working people and results in a spiral of greater insecurity and control. The combination of the decline in real wages with unemployment appears to lay the basis for higher profitability by reducing labour's share of income in the national cake. The gap between wages and inflation appears to be widening. While inflation rose to 18,6% in 1986, average wage and salary payments rose by only 13,6%, making income distribution more unequal.

The problem of deficient demand is compounded by the fact that high interest rates did not result in a capital inflow. This was because the austerity measures, with their squeeze on company liquidity and profits, had shaken investor confidence. The impact on saving and investment was equally severe. A key structural feature of the economy, the rate of capital formation, has been steadily declining since 1980. Real gross domestic fixed investment was R17,6-billion in 1981, but in the third quarter of 1986 it was as low as R12,8-billion.

Economic growth can only be sustained if there is a recovery in investment. Despite the recent turn-around in interest rates, investors are still faced with a classic crisis of confidence. Capital expenditure on new assets in the manufacturing sector fell by nearly a quarter between 1983 and 1985, from R5,3-billion to R4,1-billion. This suggests that despite talk of a recent recovery, investors are reluctant to commit themselves to long-term projects. The long-term economic decline is likely to continue.

By the end of 1986 the mild expansionary budget of 1986-87, coupled with additional funds for employment creation, had not made a dent in the problem of increasing unemployment. Public corporations like SATS and ESCOM have cut back on capital expenditure. Nor does the Mossel Bay project mean that investment will immediately pick up. Even the likely turn in residential construction is a long-term phenomenon, in so far as growth is concerned.

Thus capital was drawn away from the industrial sector towards financial markets, a process to which the stock market boom bears testimony. There was a shift in the balance of the economy as investment was pumped into financial assets which provided a higher rate of return than the productive sector. As a result, the value of financial assets soared at the expense of the real sector. Industrial capitalist ventures with strong banking and financial connections have been able to survive, and have acquired plant and equipment from firms that have gone bankrupt. But they are either operating way below capacity, waiting for an economic recovery, or have in some cases transferred funds to higher-earning investments overseas.

Two trends emerge as characteristic responses to the crisis: the rise in speculative activity, and the rising numbers of takeovers and mergers that increase the concentration and centralisation of capital.

This involves a process of increasing domination of the market by large firms within a particular industry, and growing control over ever-larger numbers of firms by a few huge financial groups. The effects of this 'restructuring' force firms to rationalise their production, involving the closure of plants and/or retrenchments. The government has chosen to enforce this transformation through market pressures, ie high interest rates and deflation, and this forces less efficient firms out of business. It is a process which inflicts enormous hardship on the working people. Increased unemployment and political coercion represent an attempt to weaken the bargaining power of trade unions, in the hope that real wages will decline further and domestic profitability be restored.

As the market becomes dominated by fewer and larger firms, price stability becomes more difficult as firms are able to pass on greater price increases than would be the case under more competitive conditions. Hence, as markets become increasingly characterised by large conglomerates, the notion of the 'market' itself becomes an abstract one.

With total economic output falling since 1980, most financial demand has been for funds to purchase assets in the stock exchange. This resulted in an unprecedented expansion of the financial sector, as reflected in the booming turnover in equities and gilts - aptly termed 'casino capitalism'. Such financial activity largely involves speculation with existing assets rather than the creation of new ones through productive activity.

While some sectors of the economy remain profitable fields for investment - particularly mining with its improved revenue levels because of the low rand - investor uncertainty is still a key factor.[6] As a result, there have been a large number of divestments. Foreign corporations are selling the assets of less profitable subsidiaries to streamline their operations, or divesting to raise cash and reduce their commitments to the domestic economy. These moves are a reaction both to low domestic profitability and intense overseas political pressure. Between the beginning of 1985 and June 1986, 51 United States firms ceased operations in South Africa or sold their equity in South African subsidiaries.

The unique relationship of gold to the South African economy is an important factor. The benefits accruing from gold do not arise from the productive potential of the economy, but are an effect of the present international financial disturbances. As a result of uncertainty in international markets and the growing budget deficit in the US, investors have always showed a preference towards speculative trading in gold. While income from gold has protected South Africa from the full consequences of its weak national economic performance, it cannot compensate for the economic decline.

The decline in output, profitability and employment accompanying the monetarist stabilisation measures was expected by the policymakers. Most disheartening for them is the fact that despite the great social sacrifices demanded by the measures, the macroresults have been dismal.

External macro-economic effects

Foreign capital and technology have always been central to South Africa's economic growth and development, though the pattern has changed over time. In the 1970s the proportion of portfolio and direct investment declined while loans increased. A high and increasing number of short-term international bank loans to South Africa were incurred in the 1980s. While domestic savings consistently fell and reached historical lows, this was made up by external borrowing. Since these loans were concentrated in short-term lending, and the real economy was eroding, it meant a more expensive burden in carrying costs for the future. External debt jumped and new loans were obtained at substantially higher rates than normal. Such a framework spelt trouble.

The weakening of the South African gold-mining and manufacturing sectors, which are most sensitively linked to the world economy, explains the deteriorating financial position to some extent. In the first half of the 1980s the gold price dropped drastically from a record of $850 per ounce to well below half that by 1986. This, coupled with a severe decline in manufacturing production, meant that the balance of payments was badly in deficit for most of the first half of the 1980s.

Moreover, the manufacturing sector has become a net user of foreign exchange, since it is unable to export as much as it needs to in the face of competition from the newly industrialised countries. The implication of this is that further expansion and development of new branches of industry will have to contend with the swings in both demand and price of all minerals in world markets. Hence South Africa's exports provide an insecure basis for future growth.

Though the balance of payments current account moved into a substantial surplus in 1985, this was achieved by austerity measures which resulted in a decline in imports. Capital account flows, on the other hand, made a negative contribution. The huge outflow of portfolio and direct investment made South Africa's international financial position more vulnerable than ever to external dynamics because of the very open nature of the economy.

The 1983 measures of trade liberalisation and deregulation of the foreign exchange market did not have the desired impact. The rand shifted from an overvalued to an undervalued position, and the structural problems facing external trade were exacerbated. The terms of trade (the ratio of imports prices to export prices) declined from 4,2% in 1983 to -0,5% at the end of 1986. The decision to liberalise the capital account had adverse effects, creating political uncertainty and high rates of interest abroad. In introducing the 1983 measures government was too anxious to establish its credentials with the financial world, and rendered the economy vulnerable.

In February 1983 government abolished foreign currency controls on non-residents, as part of the De Kock commission's broader objective of deregulation and more market-related interest and exchange rates. The financial rand disappeared. Non-residents reacted quickly by selling stocks and shares and transferring to higher-earning investments in America and elsewhere.

Demand for the US dollar rose and the rand fell against the dollar. While the falling rand helped to increase export volumes, the costs of imported raw materials, capital goods and services all increased, as did the rand value of overseas loans and interest payments. From mid-1981 to late 1985 real GDP fell, while foreign debt increased 30% from $18-billion to $23,7-billion. Since 1980 the ratio of foreign debt to GDP has more than doubled, to about 45%. A high proportion was short-term bank debt, incurred by local companies and the Reserve Bank in the early 1980s.

The debt structure thus became highly unstable and more difficult to sustain. Debt instability, coupled with the Reserve Bank's policy toward the foreign exchange market, increased the volatility of the rand, with disastrous consequences for external trade. Despite the recent debt agreement, concerning $1,4-billion of standstill debt over the next three years, approximately $10-billion of foreign debt was not affected by the moratorium. Of this, $3-billion matures this year and could have a detrimental effect. In particular, debt repayment can constrain any economic recovery by limiting the amount available for domestic investment. The increasing vulnerability of the South African economy to international factors is directly related to its growing domestic economic problems.

In early 1985 intensified political resistance and falling overseas confidence resulted in the temporary closure of the foreign exchange and stock markets. On 20 July 1985 government declared a state of emergency. As investors began pouring funds out of South Africa, government imposed a debt freeze and a return to a two-tier exchange rate. These measures are an indication of the vulnerability of the South African economy to the world economy. Though South Africa's foreign debt is much lower than that of Brazil or Mexico, a huge amount of it is short-term. Furthermore, though the government complied with International Monetary Fund austerity economics, the fund is reluctant to make any loans. Political reform is the price demanded by international capital for loans.

There is a recent pattern of low growth and structural change in the South African economy. This is associated with imbalances in the domestic economy and lack of foreign capital, and entails a new form of insertion into the world economy. The imbalance between the major sectors of agriculture, mining and manufacture has resulted in growth being constrained by the balance of payments. The South African economy historically had almost continuous balance of payments deficits, which were alleviated by large capital inflows. The fact that the manufacturing sector became larger than mining and agriculture in relation to contribution to GDP, but failed to expand exports, meant that it became a net user of foreign exchange. This adversely affects the balance of payments.

South Africa is basically a semi-developed country, highly dependent on foreign capital and technology. Thus it must export to finance such imports. Manufacture, which was the dynamo of post-war growth, is currently not meeting the needs of a growing population, with output and employment levels declining. Because of its high import coefficient, any expansion of the manufacturing sector would certainly exacerbate balance of payments problems, particularly as foreign finance will be less forthcoming. And the restricted size of the domestic market remains an inherent problem.

Against this background, structural adjustment brought about by the deflationary stabilisation policy has accentuated the decline of South Africa's political economy by choking the industrial base.

Political and economic stalemate

Political factors are usually blamed for the new levels of resistance which have developed in South Africa. But the economic trends outlined have also acted to intensify political conflict. The stabilisation policies had a profound destabilising effect on the structure of production, social inequalities, political mobilisation and the insertion of South Africa into the world economy. Policies aimed at contracting the economy tended to depress industry and heighten social tension, while increasing the level of government coercion.

As the screws tightened, mass unemployment became a reality. Millions are out of work and will not hold jobs of any kind in the foreseeable future. It requires no great leap of imagination to understand why South Africa has seen unprecedented levels of unrest. To government, the issue is one of 'law and order', and this attitude justifies the expansion and increased use of its repressive arms. The crisis of the economy is also a crisis for the wider society.

Lack of investor trust in an increasingly coercive government must be added to the economic contradictions outlined above. This is reflected in the poor performance of gross investment. The political contradictions generated by government's model of growth have surfaced.

Business is increasingly vocal in its protests against the government. The links forged between business and government at the Carlton and Good Hope conferences have become tenuous, as indicated by the glaring absence of key business actors from the November 1986 Tynhuis meeting. How far the captains of business can go in distancing themselves from the regime remains uncertain. Big business desperately needs reforms both to restructure capitalism in the long term and more immediately to restore confidence.

Without the effective support of business and with rifts within its own ranks, government cannot hope to maintain a political economy in which control is increasingly based on coercion. The possibility of offering higher profitability to speed up growth is not politically feasible. This may well be the basic contradiction facing the apartheid government today. Because of its inability to resolve this contradiction, changes in the regime may be expected.

One possible course of development may see attempts to further increase coercion, to demobilise the popular classes. Hence the declaration of the second state of emergency on 12 June 1986, the detention of thousands of political activists, and harsher press censorship, all of which aim at eliminating legal political opposition.

South Africa's economic problems and constraints are deep-rooted and widespread. They arose from the structure of apartheid capitalism and have been exacerbated by destructive policies. To a large extent the current slight expansion in the economy is based on the switch of investment from production to finance, from long-term investment to short-term security. This must in the end deepen the recession and prolong adjustment. Present-day South Africa does not present a persuasive prospect for long-term stability and sustainable growth. In spite of the beginnings of a limited revival, it is unlikely that the economy can be redirected towards sustained development. Any improvement must be measured against the backdrop of a depressed economy.

The present economic crisis is the direct outcome of the application of financial and economic liberalisation policies. Deflationary policies, while necessary in some instances, generally solve short-term balance of payments problems at the cost of restricting development and further worsening the contradictions underlying the crisis. The application of neo-conservative policies to South Africa is simplistic and naive, in that they ignore the historical and structural contexts of capitalism and apartheid. At a deeper level, the 'restructuring' of the economy arising from these policies has made it more vulnerable to external control, as evidenced by the fact that the balance of payments remains unduly reliant on volatile mineral exports. At the same time it imposed a higher human cost. Economic regulation via the 'anarchy of the market' inevitably loads the dice against those most vulnerable and usually leads to a head-on collision.

The abysmal historical record of deflationary economic policy, with its effect of imposing stagnation, has tightened the constraints on South Africa's political economy. Contemporary political structures and their underlying socio-economic relations can only be sustained at higher social and economic cost. There has never been such an urgent need to develop a strategic conception of alternative policies that can replace the stagnation of the present. The immediate challenge may be to offer an alternative to the economics of neo-conservatism. But there is an equally important and deeper task of formulating alternatives to those economic and political structures which have created the long-term crisis of the South African economy.

Notes

1   DM Gordon, R Edwards and M Reich, *Segmented Work, Divided Workers: The Historical Transformation of Labor in the US,* New York, 1982.
2   Gordon, Reich and Edwards, *Segmented Work.*
3   Focus on Key Economic Issues, 36, May 1985.
4   M Sarakinsky and J Keenan, 'Unemployment in South Africa', *South African Labour Bulletin,* 12(1), November-December 1986.
5   C Simkins, 'Structural Unemployment Revisited', South African Labour and Development Research Unit, Cape Town, 1982.
6   D Kaplan, 'The Current Crisis and the Unions', *South African Labour Bulletin,* 12(1), November-December 1986.

Privatisation: The Solution?

Duncan Innes

The growing political and economic crisis in South Africa led last
year to world-wide demands for reform. Leading lights in South
Africa's white business community were among those who raised
their voices in support of reform. Caught in the crossfire between
government 'kragdadigheid' and militant black opposition, and with
the threat of sanctions becoming a reality, sections of the white
business community began pressurising the government for reform
as well as taking reform initiatives of their own. These included the
much-publicised visit to meet ANC leaders in Lusaka, and the
launch of the Business Charter and Project Free Enterprise.

While visits to Lusaka, overseas meetings and television debates
between white South African business leaders and representatives of
the ANC seem to be part of the business community's strategy of
feeling out the opposition, the Business Charter and Project Free
Enterprise represent attempts by sections of the business community
to put forward their vision of a post-apartheid South Africa. An
especially interesting feature of the vision sketched in the Business
Charter (which has been adopted by the Federated Chamber of Industries) is how close it is in certain respects to the ANC's Freedom
Charter.

Both charters stress that all are equal before the law, that the
authority of government must be based on the will of the people, that
there should be protection of family life, cultural freedom, equal
opportunities, equal education, freedom of movement and an end to

arbitrary arrest and detention. Both support the principle of universal franchise. And on the employment front, both charters support
the right to work, the right to equal pay for equal work and the right
to form trade unions.

Where the two charters differ markedly is around the issue of
future economic policy. The Freedom Charter is committed to state
intervention in the economy through nationalisation of the mines,
banks and 'monopoly industry', as well as through demands for (unspecified) controls over 'other industries and trade'. The Business
Charter, on the other hand, points in a different direction. Individual
property rights are emphasised, as is the individual's 'right freely to
employ labour and to own or manage a business'. The action
programme which accompanies the Business Charter is even more
explicit, demanding 'curbs on the share of government in the total
economy' and calling for 'privatisation and deregulation especially in
the areas of housing, health, transport and education'. These
demands are incompatible with the Freedom Charter's call for rent
and price controls, free medical services and free education.

Two very different strategies for economic reform are embodied
in the two documents. The Freedom Charter, committed to a
programme of major social reform, seeks state control over the most
important means of production and distribution so as to directly
appropriate and redistribute the wealth generated in these areas of
the economy. The Business Charter and accompanying action
programme seek to further 'both the scope and the incentive for
private entrepreneurship' so that, through the trickle down effect,
wealth which accumulates in private hands will gradually benefit
wider sections of the population.

The difference between these two approaches is broadly
expressed in the distinctions between social democracy and free-
market capitalism. This article critically examines the free market
position, particularly as expressed in the demands for privatisation
and deregulation made by the private sector over the past year.

The privatisation philosophy

Privatisation refers to the process by which the state either sells
assets to the private sector or hands over or sub-contracts certain
public services to the private sector. The overall effect of privatisation is to reduce the state's share and influence in the economy and

to increase the private sector's involvement by a corresponding amount.

Deregulation is often coupled with privatisation, since it is another means through which state intervention in the economy may be reduced - this time by cutting back on the regulations governing the activities of private companies and entrepreneurs in the market place.

It is important to examine the concept of privatisation in general terms before looking at it in relation to South Africa. For this purpose the ideas of Leon Louw, who is the self-proclaimed leader of the privatisation movement in South Africa, will be focused on. Not only has Louw co-authored a book on the topic, which has sold particularly well, but as executive director of the Free Market Foundation his influence is widely felt within the business community. Furthermore, Louw is not without ambition:

> I have set myself the task of providing an overview of what I call the First Global Revolution. There have been countless major and minor, peaceful or violent revolutions throughout history... (N)one have, to my knowledge, been global in magnitude.
> Great episodes such as the Enlightenment, French Revolution, Industrial Revolution, Christianity, Marxist revolution, etc have been confined - at least at the time they occurred - to relatively small parts of the globe or percentages of humanity. The more modern and far-reaching revolutions, such as the information, technological and medical revolutions, have not reached vast populations or entire countries. Perhaps the two most extensive revolutions have been Christianity and Marxism... However, probably well in excess of half the world's population remains relatively untouched by them. There is no revolution that seems to have been nearly as extensive and as potentially far-reaching and profound as what is becoming known as the 'Privatisation Revolution'.[1]

According to Louw, the privatisation revolution is 'essentially a near-universal acknowledgement that policies such as interventionism, central planning, socialism, welfare statism, communism, nationalisation, et al, have been comparative failures'.

Privatisation is diametrically opposed to what Louw refers to as various forms of 'statism'. But the difference runs deeper than this, encompassing an alternative world view: '(T)he root of the free market or what I prefer to call the libertarian view, is an essentially benevolent world view or view of humanity. Conversely, statists of all complexions, whether left wing, right wing or centrist,' seem to have an essentially malevolent world view'.

These competing world views express themselves differently in everyday life:

> When a libertarian and a statist observe the same transaction, they see two entirely different things occurring. If A and B transact voluntarily with each other, the libertarian is delighted. To the same degree, the statist is appalled. This seems curious.
>
> Any transaction between A and B can be imagined. Let us suppose that it is a contract of labour. A and B agree that B will work at manufacturing widgets which A sells for a profit. In return for his labour and skill, B is paid a wage. To the libertarian, both A and B have made a profit from their transaction. Were that not the case, they would not have transacted voluntarily with each other. They and society are better off. It is a win-win situation, or a 'positive sum game'.

However, it is just not true that those whom Louw refers to as 'statists' are 'appalled' by every voluntary transaction. Voluntary transactions are fine as long as they are mutually beneficial. The point which Louw obscures is that some transactions seek to benefit one party at the expense of the other. It is those kinds of transactions which many libertarians and statists alike are appalled by.

Louw, on the other hand, is 'delighted' by the above transaction even though he knows nothing about its content. It could be that A is employing B for 14 hours a day in return for a wage of 50c. It could be that while B earns 50c a day, A earns a profit of R50 per widget and B alone makes 20 widgets a day; it could be that B has to work in unsanitary and dangerous conditions. Even if this was the case, Louw would still be 'delighted' because what concerns him is not the content of the transaction, but the fact that it is 'voluntary'.

Louw could respond that if B does not like the terms of employment which A is offering, then B does not have to enter into the transaction. But this places a particular meaning on the word 'voluntary'. Louw uses the term to mean that B is not enslaved to A or forced to work for A as part of a prison sentence. But what about other social pressures which B might be under and which might limit his/her degree of freedom or bargaining power? For instance, the economy might be in a massive recession in which six million people are unemployed; B might have been out of work for a year; or B's daughter might be dying of malnutrition or his/her son might need money for school books and uniforms. No matter: Louw remains 'delighted' with the transaction because, in his terms, B is under no compulsion.

Regardless of the conditions, according to Louw, both A and B are 'profiting' from the transaction: A will be making a profit of a thousand rand a day; B will be earning a wage of 50c a day - which is, after all, 50c more than B would be earning if unemployed. The massively unequal distribution of income is of no concern to Louw. As he says:

> The libertarian is for an unequal distribution of wealth. When there is inequality emerging from a just and free volitional order, the libertarian sees some people prospering more than others. The statist sees prosperity for a few at the expense of the suffering masses.

Thus Louw returns to the notion of two different world views. But according to Louw, this does not imply two competing ideologies. While to him the so-called statist view is clearly ideological, his own view carries the stamp of eternal truth: 'The privatisation revolution then is a largely unarticulated admission of failure in statistic ideologies. The return to free or near-free markets is not an alternative or new or old ideology. It is, indeed, a non-ideology'.

It is tempting to dismiss such arguments as intellectual nonsense. How, for instance, can it be argued in one breath that one is 'non-ideological' and in the next state unequivocally that one is 'for an unequal distribution of wealth'? But despite its illogicality and insensitivity to basic humanitarian concerns, the privatisation argument has to be taken seriously and answered. There are two reasons for this. The first is because privatisation has become eminently respectable. As Louw himself points out, the views of the Free Market Foundation (of which he is an executive director)

> used to be denounced as 'pie-in-the-sky', 'too idealistic' or even 'the lunatic fringe'. Today we are typically complimented on how much more reasonable and moderate we have become. Actually we have become more purist and radical, but the climate of opinion here and around the world has swung so dramatically towards the positions we have been advocating that our even more radical position today seems moderate to the casual observer.

The 'privatisation revolution' has to be taken seriously because it is the spearhead of a major international campaign to recapture for the capitalist class many of the resources won over generations of struggle by working people.

Secondly, this campaign has now reached our doorstep. As Louw puts it, 'A point that is not entirely new but is nonetheless seldom recognised is the potential privatisation holds for helping to resolve the crisis in South Africa'. Both the Business Charter and Project Free Enterprise are committed to privatisation in this country. Major employer associations like the Federated Chamber of Industries, the Association of Chambers of Commerce and the Building Industries Federation of South Africa also support it, as does every commercial newspaper in the country. Even the government is showing some sympathy for the idea. But while privatisation may help to resolve the crisis in South Africa, it will do so in a way necessarily detrimental to the interests of working people and the poor in general.

The politics of privatisation

The specific claims that the privatisation lobby makes for pulling the South African economy out of crisis are varied and include the following: privatisation will accelerate growth, reduce inflation, provide more entrepreneurial opportunities, promote small business and reduce corruption. 'But', according to Louw, 'there is a benefit of much greater significance' to South African society: 'Privatisation is not just an efficient economic strategy, it is a political strategy which depoliticises society'. Louw argues that

> Whoever governs in a country such as South Africa will find that government ownership or control politicises issues and provokes conflict. If such things as housing, education, transport and labour (the four most conflict-ridden areas in South Africa) were privatised/deregulated, the major problems would be solved. These areas would be depoliticised.

This leads into the crux of the political argument:

> In a depoliticised South Africa, resolving the ultimate constitutional questions will be a great deal easier. Whites, justifiably, fear a potential black majority government if government is presumed to be omnipotent - controlling or owning virtually everything. Equally justifiably, blacks resist a white omnipotent government. However, if government were less powerful and less important in the course of events, white fears would be diminished and black demands defused.

Privatisation is thus presented as a non-ideological political strategy aiming at allaying white fears and defusing black demands. But how would white fears be allayed and black demands defused? The strategic thinking behind the privatisation argument runs as follows: The present white-controlled state has immense power and influence in the economy partly through the large share of the means of production and distribution which it directly owns and partly through the myriad of government regulations which control economic behaviour. If the majority government would inherit this power, including direct control over important sections of the economy and influence over the private sector currently owned by white capitalists. Thus white capitalists will suffer a double blow: not only will their influence over the state be diminished but their economic interests will be threatened.

The privatisation strategy seeks to reduce the threat which a transfer to majority rule poses to white capitalists: first, by handing to the private sector many of the assets currently owned by the state; secondly, by reducing if not removing the regulations which govern the economic activities of the private sector; and thirdly, the state itself will be broken down into ineffective cantons and stripped of many of its key functions, such as responsibility for defence, the police, housing, education, transport, and the economy as a whole.[2] By stripping the state of crucial economic resources, of the power to regulate the economy and of the physical power to defend the majority of the population and by transferring these economic and political resources into the hands of predominantly white capitalists, the privatisation lobby hopes to defuse the democratic demands of the black majority. If democracy means the transfer to the people of a state which has been stripped of all its major economic and political assets, then democracy itself will have been emasculated.

Privatisation has strong support among the business community and the commercial press. However, many people are lulled into supporting privatisation, not for cynical reasons, but because they find themselves in agreement with its attack on government mismanagement of the economy or because they see it as a way of extricating the state from the fiscal crisis. The privatisation campaign is presented in such a way as to appeal to legitimate grievances or fears the public may have.

The way 'depoliticisation' is used in the campaign to privatise education provides a clear example of this strategy.

'Depoliticisation' and deregulation

Since at least 1976 black school children have fought vigorously to remove apartheid ideology from the content of school subjects. There is wide support for this demand, even among the white public. The privatisation lobby focuses on this issue and argues that if the state hands over certain state-run services to the private sector, such as education, these will be depoliticised. They will no longer be run according to the dictates of apartheid ideology and nor will the content of school courses be ideologically determined. Instead, the private sector will allow parents to voluntarily decide which schools their children should attend. And the content of courses will be decided not in terms of racial ideology but by the manpower requirements of the free market economy. According to this argument, the whole system will thus be shifted from a racially determined base to a 'non-ideological' one. Consequently, the battle in the schools will cease.

What the shift to parental choice actually involves is a shift from a system in which choice is restricted by race to one in which choice is restricted by wealth. No peasant or working-class family will be able to send its children to an elite private school. In an effort to get around this problem, the privatisation lobby suggests a system of vouchers. This involves the state issuing every parent with an equal grant or voucher, but leaves the parents free to decide which schools their children should be sent to. Since some schools will offer better facilities and resources, and more qualified teaching personnel than others, parents can shop around and buy the best education for their children.

But the better schools will also be more expensive and the grant/voucher will be inadequate to meet the full fees, so parents will have to pay in extra to buy the better education. Since it is only the richer parents who will be able to afford the extra amounts for the better schools, inequality will be retained - this time by means of access to wealth. And since the better schools will attract the richer parents they will make more money than the poorer schools, which in turn means they will attract the best resources away from the poorer schools. Through this system inequalities in education will not only be maintained, they will be increased. And given that the existing inequalities are largely racially determined, the effect of the elitist 'free choice' system will be to reproduce racial inequality - though now in the name of 'free choice'.

While any proposed shift away from racial ideology in course content is to be welcomed, the alternative - that course content should be related to the manpower requirements of the free market economy - is by no means non-ideological. The concept of the free market, like that of socialism, is ideologically loaded. One cannot assume that substituting one ideology (that of the free market) for another (that of race) will automatically bring peace to the schools. To achieve this requires a course content which offers pupils a wide range of choices and develops their critical faculties.

But this flies in the face of the stated aim of the privatisation group: to depoliticise the schools. Placing a wider range of ideological choices before pupils and developing their critical faculties will contribute to the greater politicisation of pupils, but on a sounder intellectual platform than is currently the case. This is surely more desirable than the depoliticisation of school children. For if children are depoliticised by privatisation, who will take political decisions for them - private enterprise?

This attempt, through privatisation, to increase the power which private business exercises over the education system, is not confined to the schools. A report by Syncom, the private sector 'think tank' on privatisation, argues that 'syllabus design and teaching' at universities should be conducted with the involvement of the private sector.[3] The private sector thus seeks to gain direct control over what is taught in schools and universities, and over how it is taught. And privatisation will develop clear class divisions in the education system, with the best schools reserved (in terms of financial access) for the children of the upper classes.

A similar attempt to impose a clear-cut class - as opposed to racial - system of differentiation is found in the campaign to privatise health care, especially hospitals. Not only does the privatisation lobby want the state to sell off its hospitals, but it also proposes that these hospitals should be differentiated in much the same way as hotels currently are: in terms of the services they provide. The best hospitals, which will naturally be the most expensive, will be awarded five stars and the worst one star. According to this proposed system, members of 'the public' will then be 'free' to decide whether they want the very best, mediocre or worst medical care. According to its proponents, this system will encourage competition among hospitals, which will bring out the best in them.

Arising out of the inequalities of wealth in our society, this system will ensure the best medical care (five stars) for the richest section of the population, mediocre medical care (three and four stars) for the middle classes and the worst medical care (one and two stars) for the working classes and poor. And since the five star hospitals will get the most income, the gap between them and the poorer hospitals will grow over time.

Deregulation is another area in which depoliticisation is emphasised. According to the privatisation lobby, deregulation involves ending racial restrictions which inhibit the development of black businesses and entrepreneurial activity. Guy Woolford of the Small Business Development Corporation (SBDC) argues that

> You cannot expect business to be normal in a society where movement, property rights and entry to markets are restricted. There has been a marked increase in the politicisation of blacks because they cannot see any significant gain from active participation in the South African economy. Government should be making it easier for all races to go into business (*BD*, 14.01.87).

Deregulation in this context has a twofold aim: to build up a black middle class which will be committed to the preservation and expansion of capitalism in South Africa; and to ease the massive unemployment problem by allowing the development of an informal sector, especially among the black community. There are already over 650 000 informal sector businesses in South Africa, defined as 'unrecorded, unlicensed, mostly non-taxpaying, providing non-fixed salaried employment' (*BD,* 14.01.87). The number of these businesses is growing, as is their contribution to the economy: in 1986 the number of informal businesses was estimated to have grown by 10% compared with the previous year; there was also an estimated 10% growth in employment provided by the informal sector; and the sector's contribution to GNP rose by an estimated 5%.

However, the issue of deregulation is not straight-forward. One would support the call for the removal of all regulations which discriminate against people on racial grounds: the movement of people, their rights to property and entry to markets should not be racially determined. But the campaign for deregulation goes beyond this, including such areas as trading licences, business hours, health regulations, safety regulations and minimum wages. Deregulation in these fields may pose major problems for working people and for consumers.

The abolition of regulations governing minimum wages allows for the greater exploitation of employees. The abolition of regulations governing safety conditions at the workplace puts the lives of workers at risk and increases the likelihood of accidents. The abolition of health regulations could lead to unsanitary working conditions and encourage the spread of disease among workers and consumers. The abolition of regulations governing business hours could lead to employees being forced to work longer hours without adequate remuneration. Under the vaguely defined banner of a campaign for deregulation, which includes progressive demands for the abolition of racially discriminatory regulations, other regulations are included, the removal of which could worsen the position of working people and consumers.

Government is currently acting to implement deregulation in some of these areas. The competition board is in the process of submitting reports to the minister of economic affairs and technology dealing with the deregulation of black trading, trade licensing, business hours, health regulations, industrial parks and taxis. Stef Naude, chairman of the competition board, has already noted that shopping hours should be extended and that health regulations are too tight. In addition, the government recently introduced a white paper outlining its plans to deregulate the massive transport sector.

Deregulation in some areas could help the unemployment crisis by expanding the informal sector, but unregulated expansion is likely to lead to the expansion of sweat shops and Dickensian working conditions. With unemployment as high as it is, the capacity of employees to struggle against these conditions will be restricted. While the state deregulates the capitalists, it simultaneously creates the industrial reserve army which regulates the working class.

Privatisation and the economy

The privatisation strategy aims to 'depoliticise' society by transferring social regulation from the state to market forces which regulate both the economy and social life. Privatisation and deregulation are the means by which market forces will be freed to carry out regulation. Underlying the privatisation strategy is a model of a free enterprise system which, according to Louw, may be defined as one 'where the government plays little or no role in the economy. They do not inhibit workers or privately owned businesses with regulations and they themselves do not own or control any business'.

Because privatisation and deregulation increase opportunities for private capitalist activity, it is not surprising to find the private sector, and those sections of the media to which it is closely linked, strongly in favour of these policies. But this does not mean the policy is necessarily in the interests of the population as a whole.

Zac de Beer, a director of the Anglo American Corporation, feels it is: 'The more freedom we (private business) have in the economy without government interference, the better the chances for economic growth and rising standards'. The private sector claims it can carry out virtually any business undertaking 'cheaper, better and faster' than the state. By privatising and deregulating, the state paves the way for more wealth to be generated, which in turn means there is more to go around.

But why should the private sector necessarily do business 'cheaper, better and faster' than the state? The answer given by the privatisation lobby is: competition. To quote Louw: 'There is virtually an open and shut case now that when something is done by the private sector it is virtually always cheaper, provided there is private sector competition or at least the threat of competition'.[4]

But if the key issue is competition then it makes no difference whether something is done by the state or the private sector. As long as competition prevails, the alleged effects of competition (cheapness, etc) will be the same regardless of who owns the companies concerned. Conversely, if competition does not prevail, then the reverse effects (high costs, poor quality, slowness) will presumably occur regardless of whether the companies are owned by the private sector or the state. The issue of ownership has no bearing on this particular argument.

The privatisation lobby replies that state ownership precludes free competition because the state makes use of anti-market mechanisms such as monopolies and subsidies. But here the privatisation brigade is guilty of turning a blind eye to the multiplicity of anti-free-market mechanisms which prevail within the private sector as well. Monopolies are not the prerogative of the state - and neither are oligopolies, price-fixing agreements, market-sharing agreements and a wide variety of other monopoly practices which contribute to higher prices.

Against the 'open and shut case that when something is done by the private sector it is virtually always cheaper' one must consider:

* last year's 30% increase in the price of tyres - implemented simultaneously by the three private companies which dominate the tyre industry;

* the four closely synchronised price rises carried out in 1986 in the supposedly competitive privately-owned motor industry. If this industry is as competitive as many commentators claim, then how do the motor companies all manage to raise their prices by about the same amount and at about the same time?

* the price hikes for cigarettes announced simultaneously in January 1987 by the two companies which control the local cigarette market: the Rembrandt group and United Tobacco;

* the fact that South Africa's five largest retail companies between them control at least 74% of total turnover - a situation which Checkers MD, Clive Weil, says has led to 'structural inflation' from which return is virtually impossible (*BD*, 29.01.87).

There are literally hundreds of examples which counter the claim that the private sector is 'always cheaper'. Clive Weil sums up the argument well: 'This highly concentrated, pseudo free-enterprise capitalist environment has within itself a pent-up cost-push component which must in future lead to greater inflationary pressures' (*BD*, 29.01.87).

At issue is the high level of concentration and centralisation of capital within the South African economy - among the highest in the world. Where such concentration and centralisation occurs, where relatively few companies dominate a particular market or sector, they will seek to combine in one way or another to overcome competitive pressures and drive up prices. The privatisation lobby either ignores this argument or seeks to counter it by pointing to the 'threat of competition': where cartels or price-fixing agreements occur, these can be broken by the threat that if prices are driven too high, someone else will enter the market to undercut those prices. While this argument certainly had relevance in the early years of the industrial revolution in Europe, it is out of place in South Africa today. Much of industry in this country is highly capital intensive, relying on expensive imported machinery and equipment. It is not possible for the 'little person' with limited resources to take on cartels by undercutting prices.

In the provision of social services, the issue of rising prices within the context of privatisation becomes pernicious. In 1986 medical aid societies rejected demands by the private hospitals to increase their scales by 20%. Instead, they agreed to a 7% increase from the beginning of 1987, which follows last year's 12% increase. This ensured that the provision of medical care remains below the inflation rate and therefore relatively cheap.

However, for the private hospitals the issue is not one of providing cheap medical care: it is profit. Dick Williamson, chairman of the Representative Association of Private Hospitals, says that because of rising costs 'returns on capital are declining and margins are coming down substantially' (*BD*, 15.10.86). The importance profit assumes within the private hospital structure is clear from Williamson's comment that although the private hospitals are still profitable, declining profits do not attract investors: unless private hospitals can increase their profits they face a shrinking future. The way they are seeking to increase their profits is by raising prices. The private hospital sector is dominated by three groups: Rembrandt, Afrox and Clinic Holdings.

Where there is a high level of concentration and centralisation of capital there is a tendency towards the continuous upward movement of prices. Privatisation in South Africa will encourage the further concentration and centralisation of capital which in turn will probably lead to even higher inflation.

The privatisation lobby argues that privatisation will enable 'the public' to take over existing state corporations. But which sections of 'the public' will have the financial resources to buy up the major share of state enterprises like ISCOR, ESCOM and SATS? Which sections of 'the public' will have the technical resources to run them? Only the handful of giant private companies, like Anglo American, Barlow Rand and Rembrandt, which currently dominate the private sector. These are the sections of 'the public' which stand to benefit most from privatisation.

Where concentration and centralisation involve mergers or takeovers, there is a marked tendency towards increased retrenchment of employees. Last year's merger between Ford and Sigma, following which two plants were shut down and over 4 000 workers lost their jobs, is a case in point. Takeovers enable management either to rationalise production or, because of greater economies of scale, to employ new machinery. In either case the tendency is to retrench sections of the existing labour force in order to improve productivity. But the effect on the workforce is to produce so-called surplus employees who subsequently find themselves out of jobs.

Questioned on how managements should deal with the problem of 'surplus employees', Leon Louw replied that they should 'pay them to leave, buy them out, bribe them to leave'. When asked what these surplus employees should do once they had been bribed to leave, he replied that 'these able-bodied and productive people can then go out and do productive things in society and the market place. So you win all round. It's a win-win situation. There are no losers'.[5]

With black unemployment estimated at between three and five million - and rising - one wonders what 'productive things' Louw suggests these 'surplus employees' should do. And in the absence of regulations stipulating that 'buy outs' must take place, management can simply rid itself of 'surplus employees' without any financial compensation. Privatisation is likely to throw even more people out of work, leaving them without any alternative prospects.

Finally, the issue of democracy needs to be addressed. Although the present South African state is undemocratic, the concept of state ownership is more democratic than the concept of privatisation. A democratic state is, theoretically at least, responsible to the nation as a whole; a private company is, also theoretically, responsible only to a group of shareholders.

In practice, the vast majority of shareholders, especially small shareholders, play little or no role in the running of private companies with decision-making being concentrated in the hands of a few powerful individuals. Similarly, state-owned corporations, as well as the state itself, tend to become bureaucratised and unresponsive to democratic practices and demands. But through the greater politicisation of the population and through campaigns to democratise the state it may be possible to increase popular influence, if not control, over public corporate activity. However, when once these corporations pass into private hands they pass beyond the reach of public accountability.

Privatisation and racism

This discussion has examined aspects of privatisation and sought to expose its weaknesses, as well as indicated the broad social changes which privatisation is likely to bring about. Many important areas have not been adequately dealt with, such as the social implications of phasing out subsidies, especially on certain foodstuffs and in transport, education, etc. The issue of privatisation in housing has not been addressed nor have various theoretical issues been fully tackled.

This article has located the privatisation debate within a class perspective, showing how privatisation serves the interests of powerful elements among the capitalist class and offers very little in the way of advancement for working people. Some might argue that although this is true, it is nonetheless an improvement on the existing system of racial inequalities. But this ignores the fact that racial inequalities in South Africa already correspond closely to inequalities of social class. Privatisation will offer a relatively small number of black capitalists and entrepreneurs access to the ranks of the white middle and upper class. But for the vast majority of the black population privatisation offers no real respite from their existing situation. Indeed, in some instances it is likely to worsen that situation.

Although the privatisation strategy is not explicitly racist, it is elitist and, on the admission of its own protagonists, seeks to promote social inequalities. In the South African context this makes it racist in practice. Privatisation will not redistribute wealth in an equitable way. It will enable those who already have wealth, who are mostly white, to acquire more wealth and will leave those who are currently poor, who are mostly black, at the bottom of the social structure. Privatisation will alter the form of racial discrimination in South Africa, but will leave the substance largely untouched.

It is a strange irony of history that one of the major obstacles in the way of the privatisation lobby achieving its objectives is the current South African state. The roots of this irony lie in the racist social-democratic character of that state: it acquired a high degree of servicing and regulation functions to protect and promote the interests of poor white workers and farmers, and to promote Afrikaner capitalism. While the Freedom Charter calls for many of these services and regulations to be extended to promote the interests of black people, the Business Charter calls for the cutting back of such services and regulations. It is no coincidence that the campaign for privatisation arises at precisely the moment that black people are intensifying their demands on the state.

The South African state has so far shown a marked reluctance to move towards privatisation. Although the department of trade and industries has set up a commission evaluating activities in all state departments to identify where privatisation can be justified, the commission's activities are unlikely to be completed before the end of 1989. Furthermore, although the cabinet has already approved 11 state functions for privatisation, not one has so far been released to the private sector. As Harry Schwartz of the PFP has noted, there is a lot of talk within state circles about privatisation, but very little action (*BD*, 26.05.87).

The problem for the state is that it cannot fully concede either to demands from the popular movement or to demands from the privatisation lobby without causing its own destruction. To concede to the demands of the popular movement means handing over power to the majority of the population. To concede to the privatisation lobby - whose leading figures are mostly identified with English-speaking business interests - means voluntarily handing over many of its powers to the white English-dominated private sector. The crisis is not sufficiently advanced, nor the threat to the state serious enough, for such drastic action to be considered at the moment. The state still seeks to defend itself through a combination of *kragdadigheid* and limited reform, while making only minimal concessions to the privatisation lobby.

Only when the state's current strategy is no longer viable will it be forced to make major concessions to the private sector, releasing the full power of capital to confront the popular opposition. No doubt privatisation will then form an essential part of capital's arsenal.

Notes

1 Leon Louw, 'Privatisation: the Global Revolution', *Star*, 15.12.86. All subsequent quotes in this and the next section, unless otherwise specified, are taken from this source.
2 Leon Louw and Frances Kendall, *South Africa; The Solution*, Amagi Publications, 1986.
3 Quoted in Leon Benade, 'Syncom's schools plan is misdirected', *Star*, 03.02.87.
4 'Microphone-in', *SABC*, October 1986.
5 'Microphone-in', *SABC*, October 1986.

Ownership and Control of Commercial Agriculture

David Cooper

In the past few years large sectors of South African agriculture - particularly grain and livestock farming - have been severely affected by drought. As a result farmers are deeper in debt than ever, and an increasing number are being forced to sell out. Agriculture is also in trouble because its terms of trade have worsened in recent years. This reflects imported inflation and is in part a result of a world glut of agricultural commodities, especially grains and sugar.

As the rural economy slips into deepening recession there is a great deal of hardship in such areas. This process is accompanied by increasing centralisation of ownership of land and capital in the hands of a decreasing number of farmers in the white agricultural sector. As a relatively small number of white farmers come to control the more productive sector of the agricultural economy, white agriculture is becoming more and more dualistic in character.

Its productive core is capital intensive and employs wage labour. Over the past 20 years, it has shed a high proportion of its workforce. Those workers who remain in jobs enjoy better working conditions and wages, though in comparison with skilled workers in other sectors their situation is still poor.

By contrast, the large (in terms of land area) backward sector of white agriculture suffers from lack of capital investment and is becoming less productive. Generations of bad farming have resulted in it occupying the most ecologically damaged land. It relies less on wage labour; practices like labour tenancy and rent-paying squatters are still common, though they were illegal until 1986.

Government policy has promoted this division in white agriculture since the 1970s. The stated policy of the department of agriculture is to maximise the number of farmers. But since the time of the 1970 Marais-Du Plessis Commission better farming has been equated with richer farmers. The concentration of productive land in fewer hands was encouraged by granting richer farmers access to Land Bank loans, to tax incentives and outright subsidies within a framework of a 'freer market' policy. Commercially successful private farmers have a great deal of political and economic influence on agricultural and marketing policy.

But South African agriculture is dependent to a considerable degree on imports of machinery and chemicals, and on exports for its income. Sanctions, if successfully implemented, could have a strong impact on commercial farming, rendering agricultural investment unprofitable and causing workers to be retrenched.

Since urban and industrial South Africa is so greatly dependent on the commercial agricultural sector for food and raw materials, land redistribution policies in a post-apartheid South Africa will have to be carefully considered. The dualism in white agriculture is a factor that must be taken into account, and its implications for a future agricultural policy need to be spelled out.

White farming

White farmers are remarkably well represented in the white parliament which governs South Africa. Both the ruling National Party and opposition parties have a large number of farmer members in parliament. Since the NP came to power in 1948, farmers have been an important source of its support, and constituencies were delimited in such a way as to over-represent them significantly.

In recent years some of this bias in favour of rural constituencies has been corrected. Farmers became less important in the power structure of the ruling elite as industrial capital gained ascendancy, and in the late 1970s government began to cut off the flow of subsidies to marginal farmers. These poorer farmers, who lost most in the subsidy cuts, became responsive to the promises of government's far-right opposition. They are now a major power base for the far-right, especially in less productive farming areas like the Northern Transvaal and the Orange Free State, where the position of farmers has been significantly worsened by drought in the last five years.

During the period when they were an important part of the ruling alliance, farmers were well placed to demand a high standard of living in return for their allegiance. The state was only able to provide this through generous subsidies. Despite the stated aim of

decreasing agricultural support, subsidies continued to increase as
the political penalties became apparent. In 1985 the total agricultural
subsidy was R500,1-million, whereas five years earlier it was R174,6-
million. This represents an increase of 287%, which even in a period
of high inflation is a substantial rise.[1] In 1987 government announced
an additional R134-million subsidy to boost the maize price 'and
save farmers from ruin' (*Star*, 25.04.87).

Government's stated policy is to maximise the number of farmers
on the land, while conserving water and soil resources. From the
1930s subsidies were ostensibly designed to help poor farmers
survive as well as increase the commercial viability of the sector as a
whole. Farmers were offered cheap credit, loans or grants to
conserve soil and water resources, loans to improve farm workers'
conditions, and subsidies to encourage production of maize, wheat
and dairy products.

The Marketing Act of 1936 provided for the establishment of
marketing boards to promote sale of produce and to protect farmers
from dramatic price fluctuations. The boards became a way of
providing price support. In years of surplus, government subsidised
exports instead of allowing local prices to drop. The boards were also
responsible for promoting export markets and received substantial
subsidies to do so.

In 1970, government appointed a commission of enquiry into
agriculture. This commission, known as the Marais-Du Plessis Commission after its successive chairmen, noted that the subsidisation
policy had failed. Subsidies provided 20% of average farm income.
Rather than helping agriculture as a sector, subsidies had retarded its
productivity by keeping poor, 'unscientific' farmers on the land.

It would be better, argued the commission, for a smaller number
of more efficient farmers to control agriculture. Not only would
agriculture then be more productive, but efficient farmers would require fewer workers to live on the farms, achieving a second government objective - the displacement of Africans from the white rural
areas.

In some instances, Marais-Du Plessis rubber-stamped policies
already in effect. For example, from the 1960s government specified
the maximum number of farmworkers who could live on any white
farm. These numbers were generous enough for mechanised
production, but were designed to enforce production based on wage
labour on all farms, ending tenancy agreements and squatting, which

still persisted on less capitalised farms.

The Marais-Du Plessis recommendations, when given the force of law, effectively subsidised richer farmers with generous tax concessions and freer access to Land Bank loans, previously restricted to poorer farmers. As richer farmers mechanised they were able to buy up more land and bring it under capital-intensive production, displacing thousands of workers. In general the process of centralisation of farm ownership involved richer farmers buying out their neighbours rather than public companies moving into agriculture, although this happened to a limited extent.

Farmers are represented by the South African Agricultural Union (SAAU), which is made up of delegates from Namibia and the four provincial unions on the one hand, and the large co-operatives on the other. Politically the SAAU is very close to the ruling National Party.

The richer commercial farmers dominate the SAAU, and it consistently promotes their interests. Although at odds with some government policies like the use of land for industrial purposes, the union generally supports government policy, including favouring accumulation of wealth in the hands of a smaller number of farmers. The SAAU has worked closely with government on issues opposed by many poorer farmers, like abolition of labour tenancy and consolidation of the bantustans.

Most farmers belong to at least one co-operative. These are the major source of their economic power. Farmers are shareholders in co-ops which are their main supply of short-term credit as well as machinery, seed and chemicals, and the major buyers of their produce. There are 294 farmers' co-ops, but 18 central marketing and 26 large trading co-ops represent 63% of farmers, and are dominant. Co-ops' share of sales is rising, and the proportion of short-term credit supplied by them rose from 8% to 23% of the total between 1970 and 1981. They are funded by the Land Bank which provides them with capital at below commercial rates. Until recently, co-ops enjoyed special tax concessions enabling them to consolidate their dominant position in the agricultural economy.

Farmers are also represented on marketing boards. These are dominated by producers and control the sale of 86% of all produce. The 26 boards set the terms of sale for most agricultural produce to a greater or lesser degree. South African marketing policy is in flux at present. Government seems to be trying to reduce subsidies by linking agricultural prices to market demand. But with a glut of produce on world markets it faces opposition from many farmers who continue to expect some price protection. Freer marketing practices have been encouraged in recent years, but the state still subsidises losses and controls marketing to a considerable degree.

The concentration of farming production in fewer hands has been accompanied by increased use of commercial inputs such as machinery, pesticides and fertilisers. Farming is now big business. A large part of this commercialisation was bought with credit from co-ops, the Land Bank and commercial banks, whose loan exposure has increased rapidly in recent years.

From 1970 until the drought years of 1982-85, farmers used this finance to intensify production, particularly cultivation. Expenditure on inputs into agriculture increased dramatically, as farmers bought more tractors, equipment, fertiliser, herbicide and seed. Between 1980 and 1985 expenditure rose 155%, after increasing by 627% in the previous ten years.[2] Capital expenditure on tractors, buildings, cars and irrigation equipment increased rapidly, by 387% between 1970 and 1980, but fell back to 110% between 1980 and 1984.[3]

As agricultural expenditure increased, land values rose despite the fact that drought and high interest rates ought to have depressed prices. This was because the prosperous commercial sector was expanding its land holdings and maintaining demand. In fact, the largest single expense farmers incurred was interest and repayments on loans for land purchases. Even during the drought years of 1982-85, land values continued to rise ahead of inflation, by 151%. The biggest rise in land prices was in the ten years after the Marais-Du Plessis Commission: from 1970 to 1980 prices rose by 308%.[4]

Land values in all sectors were not equally affected, as Table 1 below shows. Values of land used for export crops - grapes and wool - rose most rapidly.

Table 1:
Index of value of land in different sectors, compared with index of producer prices[5]

	Land	Maize	Wheat	Land	Grapes	Land	Cattle grazing	Land	Sheep grazing
1975	100	100	100	100	100	100	100	100	100
1980	159	185	202	128	135	145	232	219	157
1983	267	294	258	259	175	217	256	252	220
1985	330	343	303	425	217	270	344	425	283

In the process of this commercial centralisation of agricultural resources, white farmers' debt rose to all-time record levels.

Table 2:
Agricultural debt, in R-millions[6]

	Land Bank	Commercial Banks	Co-ops	Agricultural credit	Private persons & other	Total
1970	278,0	281,8	113,4	136,2	574,6	1 384,0
1975	394,7	384,0	197,8	148,2	665,7	1 790,4
1980	675,6	801,5	866,9	180,0	1 314,6	3 838,6
1984	1 923,0	2 968,8	2 233,7	443,3	1 926,5	9 495,3

Since 1980, farmers have been squeezed both by high inflation - with input prices rising faster than producer prices - and by high interest rates. In an attempt to control inflation, the Reserve Bank set high interest rates, which contributed greatly to farmers' debt burden. After 1984, the collapse of the rand against other currencies resulted in greatly increased import costs for agriculture, which relies heavily on imports of machinery and chemicals. Even with the 1986-87 fall in fuel prices, inflation caused by expensive imports into agriculture is considerable. The agricultural sector's income from exports after the value of its imports is deducted was R1 893,6-million in 1980. In 1984 this dropped to R988,7-million.[7]

So far, agriculture has been examined in overall terms. Production has stagnated over the past five years, food imports have become necessary and farmer debt has increased geometrically. However, the position does not affect all farmers uniformly.

Land ownership and productivity

South African agriculture is divided into a productive core sector, and a large, unproductive periphery.

The periphery

This periphery exists partly because of ecological factors: in lar[ge] parts of the country, especially the arid west and north-west, farm[ing] is uneconomic except on very large units. These areas are the [most] ecologically damaged in South Africa, with extensive overgr[azing] and ploughing of grazing land leading to widespread erosion. Stricter state conservation measures aimed to improve the situation by placing a ban on new ploughing without permission, and stricter control of livestock numbers. Any gains have, however, been offset by the severe drought.

The problem is a structural one - private ownership has fostered a system of agriculture unsuitable to the ecology. An open, pastoral system as practised by pre-colonial farmers did not put as much pressure on grazing areas around watering points and took more account of ecological variations over a wider geographical area. Private tenure of land means that individual entrepreneurs are forced to exploit to the maximum a fenced-off, limited area, often with disastrous ecological consequences. This may simply mean grazing too many animals, or attempting to cultivate land suitable only for grazing.

Up to the time it was declared illegal in the 1960s, farms could be divided and redivided until they became commercially unviable. Speculators were able to use subdivision to profit from rising land prices. In some arid areas, like the north-western Transvaal, units are too small for farmers to earn an income equivalent to town income. So they abandon their farms to look for work in town. In other cases, farmers try to grow crops in ecologically unsuitable areas in the attempt to make a living. Because they do not take account of the long-term consequences, this leads to soil erosion, and makes the land uneconomic for farming.

In some areas, regional underdevelopment is responsible for lack of agricultural viability. Farms may be too distant from markets, or there may be a lack of storage or transport infrastructure. These backward regions are widespread - in the Northern Cape, the south-eastern and Northern Transvaal, Northern Natal, the Southern Free State and part of the Eastern Cape. In these areas, farmers tend to rely on less capital-intensive methods of production; cattle and sheep ranching predominates.

In many of these areas, farms are not occupied by their white owners. As early as 1960, 24% of Free State farms were unoccupied, as were 42% in four districts of Northern Natal.[8] Though no later figures are available, government's present concern to reverse this trend indicates that absenteeism is still a problem. On such farms, Africans survive by subsistence farming, or manage the farms for white owners living in towns.

In the border areas particularly, government perceives white owner absenteeism as a security threat, and offers substantial incentives for white farmers. These include living allowances, subsidies on boreholes, stock feed, rented grazing and security measures. A subsidy of R822 000 was paid to the Northern Transvaal Co-operative (*Star,* 16.06.86). And in 1980 alone, government provided interest-free loans totalling R20,9-million to 212 farmers and companies starting farms in border areas.[9]

Another unproductive sector is part-time farming. Around most major cities there are a number of small farms whose owners work in cities, their urban income subsidising the farm. The state discourages part-time farming, so no financial, advisory or marketing services exist, and these farms produce very little. In some cases, they are occupied by a large number of African tenants, some paying rent. Unlike larger farms, these peri-urban areas have seen an increase in the black population over the past 20 years.

The productive core

In the past ten years the number of farming units has steadily decreased, while capital value and debt have risen sharply, as table 3 indicates.

Table 3:
Aggregate capital value and debt in white agriculture[10]

	No of units	Capital value R-million	Debt R-million	Net value R-million
1976	75 562	250 741	30 407	220 334
1980	69 372	422 516	55 334	367 182
1985	59 088	728 490	184 334	544 156

Net farm income increased sharply between 1975 and 1980, but since then has declined sharply in real terms, as a result of drought and high interest rates. But this aggregate does not show the distribution of income within the sector.

According to a 1983 study:[11]

* 1% of farmers, or 590 units, contributed 16% of gross farm income, a projected average of R2,62-million per unit in 1985;

* 6% of units produced 40% of gross farm income at a projected

average of R1,09-million per unit in 1985; and

* 30% of farmers, or 17 700 units, produced 75% of income or a projected R409 500 per unit in 1985.

In 1970, the Marais-Du Plessis Commission also studied distribution of gross farm income. It found that 2,2% of farms produced 21% of gross farm income, 9% of farmers produced 49%, and 40% of farmers 87%.[12]

One government economist[13] correctly argues that the reason 18 000 farmers produce 75% of agricultural output is because they control 80% of South Africa's agricultural resources. This tendency toward increasing centralisation of production is largely the result of bias in financial policy, marketing practices and pricing policies. In years of good harvests, grain farmers in particular can earn very large amounts, and this is translated into large-scale land acquisition.

The tendency to large-scale mechanised farming has been accompanied by a move away from diversified agricultural production. Maize and wheat production is increasing at the expense of other grains. The reasons for this are complicated. Maize, wheat and now sunflower production can be mechanised to a greater extent than other crops, and this is attractive to large-scale farmers. Crops like groundnuts which should be favoured because of their high price are rejected because they are labour intensive. The dry bean price is not controlled to the same extent as maize and wheat, so over-production could result in a fall in price. It is also not possible to use herbicides as effectively on beans, which means a higher labour requirement. Sorghum is not price controlled to the same extent as maize, so it is not as favoured, even though it is a hardier crop and can be mechanised.

Such monoculture tends to result in gluts, so the state must continue subsidies to protect farmers from the economic consequences. It also requires less labour, has created substantial unemployment and is more vulnerable to crop failure because of drought. A diversified crop system, with crops growing at different times of the year, provides some protection against drought.

With the increasing size of commercial farms, production per hectare has not necessarily improved. It appears that production in the major farming sectors has stayed the same over the last ten years, while the costs of production have risen rapidly.[14]

Commercial agriculture in South Africa is remarkable for its degree of private as opposed to corporate ownership. But in recent years a number of large corporations have diversified from mining and industry into agriculture. These include:

* Anglo American Corporation. Through its Soetevelde farms, it runs megafarms in the Eastern and Southern Transvaal, Northern Free State, Northern Natal and the Rhodes Fruit Farms in the Western Cape;

* Kanhym Estates. A beef and maize company partly owned by Gencor, it has farms in the Eastern Transvaal;

* CG Smith Foods. A subsidiary of Barlows, it owns sugar farms in Natal;

* Tongaat-Hulett. Owned by Anglo, it has sugar and vegetable farming interests;

* Poultry companies like Farmfare and Stein Bros, owned by the food industry companies; and

* In forestry, SAPPI and Mondi - an Anglo subsidiary - are major planters.

These companies, along with the suppliers to agriculture and five food processing conglomerates (CG Smith, Premier Foods, Tiger Foods, Federale Foods and the co-ops), are investing in agriculture as part of a process of vertical integration. Their various subsidiaries supply farming requisites, are involved in production, are buyers and processors of agricultural products, and do packing, wholesaling and retailing. Despite stagnation in the aggregate agricultural income, these highly capital-intensive producers have maintained their profitability.

Sanctions and agriculture

Ownership of commercial agriculture is in the hands of a relatively small number of richer farmers or corporations. Farmers' income has risen most steeply in those sectors which derive a substantial part of their income from exports, mainly wool, fruit and sugar. This is because in rand terms the prices of exports have increased sharply since 1983. But costs of imports have increased even more rapidly, so import-intensive agricultural sectors such as grain have suffered the sharpest losses in recent years.

Effective sanctions could have a profound impact on agriculture. It has been estimated that in the Western Cape alone, a million people could lose their jobs as a result of sanctions on farm and related exports. Not only would commercial farmers suffer, but there would also be a 'knock-on' effect to the other sectors of the economy involved in agriculture.

Land values could fall dramatically and banks, already over-extended in their credit to farmers, could suffer heavy losses. Suppliers of capital equipment such as tractors and farm machinery are already in a severe recession. The effect on pesticide and fertiliser sales would be similar, further damaging the agricultural supply industry. Even partial sanctions could lead to a major pull-out by multinationals which supply agriculture, such as Shell, Massey-Ferguson and Ciba-Geigy. Multinationals manufacture the bulk of agricultural requisites used in South Africa. Tractor companies are already faced with heavy losses on the world market, and could be the first to decide to rationalise their operations.

Sanctions could lead to a glut on the local market if South African exports are boycotted. But a local food surplus is unlikely to lead to cheap food. Going by past experience, government would support prices through the marketing boards, propping up farmers' income for political reasons. Local food prices would in fact rise, as happened when the world sugar market collapsed.

Agricultural reform

Some rationalisation of South African agriculture is desperately needed. Farmers need to be more selective about the land they use for arable agriculture, and should be less dependent on the imported materials which are the hallmark of commercial agriculture today. A more rational farm policy would encourage a diversity of crops and a greater integration of livestock and arable production. Such a policy would not solve farmers' problems, but would dramatically reduce input costs. At the same time it would ensure more consistent, if not higher, net income per hectare, because the dangers of total crop failure as a result of drought could be significantly reduced by planting diverse crops suited to the local bio-climate and by ceasing to plough the worst soils.

At present private white farmers are unable to intensify production in this way because monoculture is simpler to manage. Some of the best-managed private and corporate farms are profitable because they do diversify and maximise their land use. But it is highly unlikely that such a policy will become widespread while the present pattern of ownership in agriculture continues. In the next few years, penetration of big business into the agricultural sector is likely to increase. Big business relies on capital-intensive agriculture, and while we may see more rational land use, its agricultural practices are unlikely to differ greatly from those of the rest of the commercial sector.

What of land reform? At present, the liberal call is to abolish the 1913 Land Act and open up land ownership to all South Africans. This will do little more than maintain the present high prices of farmland, allowing white farmers to leave agriculture with their accumulated capital. And the land clause in the Freedom Charter, which specifies that 'the land shall be shared among those who work it', is very general.

Land reform is a highly complex issue. Real land redistribution presupposes a government willing to expropriate land on a large scale and allow millions of people access to it. Such a policy would arouse a storm of white opposition and a flight of capital. Its economic and political costs to the state would be high. Many of the highly productive farms, which involve the use of considerable fixed and movable assets, are production units that would be very difficult to divide without damaging their productivity. They require large amounts of capital to manage as they are run at present. A simple policy of returning land to the tiller may be impractical.

One approach to land reform could take advantage of the dualistic way the industry is structured at present. The productive core sector could be left intact. This would allow agriculture to continue to provide for the food needs of the urban population and the raw material needs of industry, and to generate export revenue.

Redistribution would focus on the less productive land of the white periphery. Subsistence-based agriculture could be encouraged in these areas. It would be less dependent on capital inputs and the resident population could become self-reliant in terms of food and fuel. Given proper support, especially proper marketing and distribution mechanisms and appropriate extension and credit facilities, this sector could even contribute to the surplus produced by the agricultural sector.

But such a simple solution is likely to prove unsatisfactory. The productive core controls so much production because it owns such a high proportion of agricultural land and capital. Leaving the periphery, with its poor land base and limited resources to provide for the majority of rural South Africans, will in effect extend the bantustans without substantially changing the pattern of poverty found there at present. Resettlement in the periphery could make a significant contribution to land distribution, because of the area of land involved. But it will be essential to tap the resources of the productive core for any land redistribution policy to succeed.

An expropriation policy must therefore concern itself with the organisational forms - collectives, state farms or co-operative ventures - that will be appropriate in the productive core. Such a policy would involve intensive settlement of people from unviable areas in the thinly-populated agribusiness areas. Care needs to be exercised to prevent a breakdown in the course of such a transition, with its attendant spectre of large-scale agricultural failure.

Managerial, organisational and technical skills will be essential for success in restructuring core production. Because of the present division of labour between farmworkers and managers, the skills of the former alone will not be enough to maintain production. Any future state engaged in radical land reform will have to take extreme care to provide the inputs of capital, techniques and organisational skills to make it work. If such reform is not to have disastrous consequences, it will have to be planned with meticulous care. If a future government lacks the political will for such an undertaking, it may be best to leave agricultural production in the hands of its present owners.

Notes

1 Republic of South Africa, *Abstract on Agriculture,* Pretoria, 1986.
2 *Abstract on Agriculture.*
3 *Abstract on Agriculture.*
4 *Abstract on Agriculture.*
5 W Kassier, 'Tendense in die Landbou', paper presented at Lanvokon '86, Pretoria, 1986.
6 *Abstract on Agriculture.*
7 *Abstract on Agriculture.*
8 S Greenberg, *Race and State in Capitalist Development,* Yale, 1980.
9 Department of Agriculture, *Annual Report, 1982,* Pretoria, 1983.
10 H Hattingh, 'Skewe Inkomsteverdeling...', paper presented at Lanvokon '86, Pretoria, 1986.
11 Hattingh, 'Skewe Inkomsteverdeling'.
12 Republic of South Africa, *Second Report of the Commission of Inquiry into Agriculture,* RP 84, Pretoria, 1970.
13 Hattingh, 'Skewe Inkomsteverdeling'.
14 *Abstract on Agriculture.*

Reaping the Benefits: Working Conditions in Agriculture and the Bantustans

Jeremy Keenan and Mike Sarakinsky

At the end of a decade of PW Botha's 'reform' initiatives, conventional wisdom has it that general conditions of African labour have improved. This is allegedly due to the granting of trade union rights and increased wages which resulted in an overall improvement in black living standards. But on the contrary, African unemployment has increased massively and levels of poverty are devastating.[1] What improvements in working conditions and wages have come about were won by trade unions, not granted by reformers.

In those sectors or regions where unions are prohibited or not recognised - inter alia white agriculture and the bantustans - conditions have deteriorated considerably in the last decade.

Employment on white farms

About 834 000 Africans are currently employed as farmworkers in South Africa.[2] This represents a decline from about 1,4-million in 1971. According to Petrus Meyer, member of the house of delegates, 'many farmers treat their animals and implements better than their workers' (*Star*, 13.12.86).

In 1982 the minister of manpower requested the National Manpower Commission to investigate, inter alia, conditions on white farms and the desirability of introducing new legislation to regulate the relationship between white farmers and farmworkers. The investigation was duly completed and the report submitted in November 1984. It has not yet been publicly released.

The minister claims that he is still consulting with 'interested parties'. By this he clearly means the South African Agricultural Union (SAAU) and other organisations of white farmers.

When the commission was established in 1982, the minister of manpower assured farmers that no changes in the conditions of farmworkers would be made without the co-operation of farmers (*DD*, 10.03.87).

The purpose of the commission was to clarify conditions in agriculture and to protect farmers from 'unfair and malicious attacks'. According to the minister:

> There is, and always has been, a very sound relationship between employer and employee in agriculture... Employees in agriculture also enjoy a whole package of privileges which are hard to quantify. This includes, inter alia, free housing, free food, water, firewood, medical care, and in many instances free grazing for animals and land to cultivate.

This is not the case. Much of the evidence given to the commission of enquiry showed the lie behind the minister's claim, and emphasised the need for legal reform to bring the position of farmworkers onto a par with that of workers in other sectors. It is an open secret that the commission recommended reforms to the legal status of farmworkers. However, the government is afraid of alienating right-wing farming constituencies and therefore has not released the report.

Nothing has been done to improve conditions on white farms.

The legal position of farmworkers[3]

Farmworkers are excluded from South Africa's industrial relations machinery, including the Labour Relations Act, the Wage Act, the Unemployment Insurance Act, and the Basic Conditions of Employment Act. Accordingly,

* they cannot form registered trade unions, and are not protected from victimisation for union activities with unregistered unions;

* they have no access to the industrial court, and therefore no redress for unfair labour practices;

* they cannot enter legal agreements on work conditions;

* there are no regulations regarding minimum wages, conditions of service, health and safety standards, unemployment insurance, working hours, overtime pay, sick pay, sick leave, maternity leave and holidays.

Farmworkers are dependent on their employers for accommodation, schooling for their children, and their continued residence on the farm when they grow old. Many farmers run stores through which they extend credit, thereby increasing workers' dependence and indebtedness. The institutionalised alcohol dependence caused by the 'tot system' prevalent in the Western Cape is another form of labour control.

Farmers have control over workers outside of the work situation, including the power to demand that workers' wives and children also work on the farm. Farmers can enforce this through their power to terminate the employment contract, dismiss the worker concerned and evict the whole family from the property. This deprives them of their only available accommodation.

Where protective legislation does exist, there are too few inspectors to enforce its implementation. In 1971 it was reported that 34 labour liaison officers inspected 10 796 farms. Each officer was, on average, responsible for about 29 180 workers.[4] In 1980 there was only one inspector for every 1,4-million farm employees. During 1979 and 1980 no farms were officially inspected.[5]

Wages

A government survey referred to in parliament in 1981 showed that real wages and living conditions of farmworkers had deteriorated over the last 20 years. Average wages for farmworkers were between R25 and R35 per month in most regions (*Star*, 10.09.81).

The Farm Labour Project claimed that 'it is common to find employees who are not paid at all, or are paid sums such as R2, or R6 a month'.[6] Numerous cases show that more recently wages have not increased (see for example, *RDM*, 21.02.85; *BD*, 27.05.86; *WM*, 27.03.87).

Farmers justify these low wages by pointing out that workers also receive 'payment in kind' - rations, accommodation, access to land for subsistence, crops or cattle grazing. However, Mandla Seleoanc has shown that 'supplies made by the farmer do not necessarily meet the demands they are supposed to satisfy. It is not uncommon that they run out before their scheduled time'.[7]

Conditions on white farms

Employment conditions on white farms are deplorable as evidenced by the number of assaults on farmworkers, the rates of agricultural poisoning and accidents, the standard of housing, the levels of cash wages and 'payment in kind'.

An average of 60 hours per week are worked.[8] There is currently no limit to the number of hours workers may be required to work without a break and without overtime pay.

Most farmers regard leave as a privilege and not a right. All leave is arbitrary and at the discretion of the farmer. There is evidence that some farmers grant their workers no annual leave at all, or that all leave is unpaid (*Echo*, 18.12.80; *Star*, 16.06.86).

Assaults on farmworkers are common, but prosecutions and convictions are few. Farmers who are convicted of assault usually receive very lenient sentences (*BD*, 06.06.86). As a farmworker in the Sekhukhuneland/Steelpoort area said in an interview, 'For fear that we would lose our jobs, we never reported these incidents (assaults) to the police' (*BD*, 27.05.86).

Use of prison labour is widespread on white farms. These prisoners, working allegedly as part of their rehabilitation, are used as cheap labour. The conditions under which they work are deplorable, and assaults are common. Use of prison labour is outlawed under the General Agreement on Tariffs and Trade, to which South Africa is a signatory. Recently it was announced that prison labour was to be phased out as of September 1986, a decision unfavourably viewed by many farmers (*Star*, 16.06.86).

Farmworkers are excluded from most legislation concerning health and safety conditions. Where such provisions are applicable they are 'seldom if ever enforced... The current position is not much better than having no minimum standards at all'. The observance of these standards is left to the individual farmer, and consequently 'there is no bottom line as to how low the standard of health conditions on farms may be'.[9]

The 1961 Liquor Amendment Act outlawed the payment of alcohol as part of the wage, but it did not prevent the 'free' dispensing of alcohol. Alcohol is now provided as a 'perk'. In 1986 it was estimated that over 70% of workers on wine farms were either compulsive or very heavy drinkers, consuming as much as two litres of reject wine a day.[10] Not only does the 'tot' system affect the labourers concerned, it also affects their children, many of whom are born with foetal alcohol syndrome, or are stillborn.

There are some legislative provisions in regard to accommodation but few are enforced. On many farms workers have no toilets, running water or washing facilities. Most huts have earth floors, no glass windows, and metal sheets for roofs. Electricity is rare and overcrowding is common. The threat of eviction prevents farmworkers from demanding improved accommodation. Adult workers are tied to the same employer, as a change of employment leads to the eviction of relatives from farm housing.

The poor living conditions on white farms have given rise to outbreaks of tuberculosis, cholera, typhoid, polio and various skin, eye and water-borne disease. The situation is exacerbated by the lack of rural clinics. In addition employers fail to grant sick leave and sick pay, do not provide regular medical check-upsand refuse workers time off to visit clinics or district surgeons.

Data provided in 1976 by the National Occupational Safety Association showed that more than 300 farmworkers were killed in accidents each year, and some 2 000 permanently disabled (*Argus*, 05.05.76). Most of these accidents occurred because of lack of skill and training in the use of implements and machinery.

In addition to the usual diseases found amongst farmworkers in the United States and Britain, South African workers also suffer from anthrax-glands, Malta fever, tetanus and poisoning. Very few of the diseases linked to agriculture are covered by the Workmen's Compensation Act.

Poisonous substances are found in most insecticides, fertilisers, fungicides, herbicides and dipping chemicals. It is difficult to find exact figures for poisoning because most cases are treated privately and not reported. However, an expert wrote in 1984 that the rate of agricultural poisoning in South Africa is at least 20 times that of the United States or Britain, and that this is related to the use of unskilled labour and the failure to follow safety procedures when using poisonous substances.[11] Another specialist in the field estimated that 'several thousand' agricultural poisonings occur annually in South Africa.[12] An International Labour Organisation report claimed that an average of 1 600 South African farmworkers die each year from pesticide poisoning and related diseases (*SStar*, 18.05.86).

Compensation for work-related diseases and accidents is covered by the Workmen's Compensation Act. But many farmers fail to submit wage returns or pay assessments to the accident fund. Farmers also discourage claims by their employees so that they can claim a rebate from the fund at the end of each year. Many workers are ignorant of the existence and the workings of the fund. No diseases specific to agriculture are included in the act's schedule. And compensation is paid out on a formula dependent on wage levels and is therefore very low.

The only regulation controlling the use of child labour is the Black Labour Relations Regulation Act. Consequently the use of child labour on farms is widespread. It is common practice for children to be taken from farm schools during school hours to work. In 1981 only 31% of farm children attended farm schools, most of which only taught up to Standard Five. Of this 31%, only 13% of schoolgoers reached Standard Five (*Star*, 16.09.84).

Other factors work against the education of farmworkers' children. Schools are often distant or inaccessible; extra wages and food are needed by the family, so children have to work; school uniforms, books and fees are expensive; and teachers are forbidden to teach or lead extra-curricular activities outside formal school hours.

In March 1984 there were 5 331 farm schools employing 11 113 teachers and catering for 468 619 students.[13] Teachers are almost always underqualified and have minimal teaching aids. Classes are commonly overcrowded. There are usually no facilities for children to study at home - no space, books or electric lights. The drop-out rate is very high: of the 126 000 sub-A pupils who started school in the rural areas in 1978, only 19 000 reached Standard Five by 1984, ie 15% of the initial intake (*Star*, 16.04.85).

Farmworkers are covered by the Pensions Act but not the Unemployment Insurance Act. Many workers in the rural areas entitled to benefits do not receive them, because of the difficulty of navigating bureaucratic provisions and the inconvenient location of district pension offices.

The 1913 Land Act prevented Africans from buying, hiring or leasing land outside of the bantustans. The Development Trust and Land Act of 1936 made share-cropping, half-share farming and cash tenancy illegal. With the more recent abolition of labour tenancy in

1964, the number of people expelled from white farms increased. They have not only lost their homes and crops, but have been forced to sell their cattle at a fraction of the value. Those expelled are removed to the bantustans.

The unemployed and landless in the bantustans are forced to seek wage employment but denied the opportunity of choosing where they work. They must therefore accept the conditions on white farms.

In effect, farmworkers are 'indentured' into agricultural labour. The much-heralded Abolition of Influx Control Act, introduced in 1986, does not substantially change this. For while the labour bureaux system and the 'dompas' have been abolished, new mechanisms to facilitate 'orderly urbanisation' are being introduced.

Lack of access to both employment and approved, and therefore costly, accommodation will act against a mass influx to the urban areas. The levels of poverty and unemployment, as well as the acute housing shortage, are important mechanisms which control urbanisation. The state has the Prevention of Illegal Squatting Act, the Slums Act and various health and municipal regulations to control the movement of blacks into urban areas. The Group Areas Act has not been repealed, and blacks therefore remain subject to its restrictions. And the Aliens Act prevents the majority of denationalised blacks from regaining their South African citizenship under the Restoration of South African Citizenship Act, and therefore from benefiting from the 'abolition of influx control'.

Because of low wages farmworkers cannot afford housing in the urban areas. Their lack of educational qualifications and training makes it unlikely that they will find approved employment in the towns. Even if they did find employment and accommodation for themselves, their families would be evicted from the farms with nowhere else to go.

Despite the abolition of the labour bureaux, farmworkers are still effectively trapped in farm labour.

Forced removals from white farms[14]

There were over 1,1-million removals from white farms between 1960 and mid-1983, and at least 150 000 people are still under threat. This constitutes the largest single category of forced removal, about a third of all removals during the period.

The 1964 amendment to the 1936 Land Act abolished labour tenancy on white farms, and led to the eviction of 34 325 'squatters' between January 1964 and September 1969.[15] Those evicted from white farms were removed to the bantustans.

Farmworkers are not entitled to more than one calendar month's notice, unless they are on a special contract. Farmers are not compelled to give reasons for dismissals and evictions. Very often no notice at all is given.

The more than one million people evicted from white farms over the last two decades have not been free to move to the cities in search of employment in mining or manufacturing. They have been shunted into remote relocation areas inside bantustans where influx controls prevent all but a small minority from moving to the urban areas as migrant workers.

The authorities have an abundance of laws to ensure that dismissed or former farmworkers who continue to live on farmers' property are driven from the land. Even if evictions are not carried out lawfully, farmworkers cannot appeal to the courts to stop or suspend unlawful actions because of the Black Prohibition of Interdicts Act. All they can do is apply for compensation for any damages wrongfully suffered after the eviction or demolition of their dwellings has been carried out.

Although legislation prevents the registration of farmworkers' trade unions, it does not prevent their formation. Nor does it prevent farmworkers joining other unions. But farmers are not compelled to recognise or deal with such unions, which makes union activities difficult. Farmworkers have no protection from victimisation for union activities, or from any other unfair labour practices. This, together with the use of trespass laws, makes union access to them extremely difficult. Only religious representatives and teachers are allowed access to workers on farm property. The only telephones are in the farmers' homes, and workers have no access to them. The general prohibition on outdoor gatherings, and the lack of indoor venues on farms, act against union organisation. The absence of a farmworkers' union which employers are compelled to recognise and negotiate with means that farmers can unilaterally determine conditions of employment.

The Farm Labour Project speaks of a 'vicious cycle' - beginning with bantustan poverty:

Because conditions of employment are so poor blacks are reluctant to undertake farm labour. Because blacks are reluctant to undertake farm labour the farming community has asked for greater legislative intervention to ensure a captive labour supply. Because there is a captive labour supply the conditions of employment remain poor and uncompetitive.[16]

Most white farmers have been experiencing a sustained crisis of profitability. The drought, recession, debt, and increasing competition on the export markets from Latin America, Spain and Israel have forced farmers to reduce labour costs, either by paying workers less or becoming more capital intensive.

The role of the white farming community in the emergence of Afrikaner nationalism and apartheid after 1948 is well known. This sector has traditionally been one of the most racist and repressive in South African society. Parts of it have, since the 'reform era' began, become a major support base for the extreme right-wing parties. This does not bode well for labour organisation or the conditions of farmworkers.

Employment in bantustan agriculture

Agriculture in the bantustans has changed dramatically during the last decade. The main reason for this is the accelerated penetration of large-scale commercial agribusiness interests into the bantustans. This was facilitated by a 1977 amendment to the Promotion of Economic Development of Bantu Homelands Act of 1968, which effectively opened the gates for the inflow of investments. The capital that has been invested in many of these recent commercial agricultural schemes is of both state and private origin. The terms of this act make it virtually impossible to identify the source and degree of penetration of private, as distinct from state, capital into agricultural projects in the bantustans.

The bantustans are attractive to large-scale commercial agriculture for several reasons:

* ground rents, whether on tribal or state/trust land, are minimal or non-existent;

* many of these schemes provide guaranteed markets for agribusiness and its 'high-tech' agricultural inputs. A feature of these markets is trader pricing agreements;

* agricultural capital investment in the bantustans receives many forms of subsidisation.

Capital is able to transfer the risks of production to the nominal 'owners' of or participants in these agricultural projects, a process which has resulted in most of them being burdened with heavy debts. This has taken place, for example, in Bophuthatswana's agricultural corporation (Agricor) scheme at Bethanie.

Most private projects, as well as state projects, are guaranteed against absolute financial collapse by the political/ideological support 'subsidy' provided by the South African government. One reason why the state has encouraged and invested directly in so many schemes has been to give a semblance of economic viability to the bantustans. Agricultural development projects consequently cannot be seen to have failed. Most schemes, as well as the bantustan administrations themselves, have been able to rely ultimately on the South African government to bail them out.

Many of these projects were developed for political and ideological rather than financial and agronomic reasons. Bailing out has accordingly been on a large scale. The best example of this is the Bophuthatswana administration, which by 1986 had become insolvent. The long-term liability of Agricor was estimated at R200-million, while the indebtedness of its biggest project in the Ditsobotla region is nearly R100-million. The South African government has been forced to intervene directly and take control of Bophuthatswana's department of finance and treasury, a move reflected in the 60% increase in the budget of South Africa's department of foreign affairs.

The 'reform' era has been characterised by the intensification of repression, especially in the bantustans. This has been achieved through a combination of stringent security legislation; an escalation of state violence; various controls relating to influx into 'white' South Africa, notably the Aliens Act, and to 'efflux' from the bantustans; the systematisation of corruption at both central and local government levels; and the imposition of legislative regimes which deny workers in the bantustans all but the most minimal of rights.

Labour legislation in the bantustans is discussed more fully below. Here it is enough to say that capital investing in commercial agriculture in the bantustans is provided with systems of labour legislation which have no minimum wage provisions and which effectively deny workers any say in their working conditions, prohibit their freedom of association, outlaw strike action and deny any effective legal rights of redress other than those provided under common law.

The militarisation of bantustan agriculture

Champagne and Dingleydale are two adjoining farms in the Mapulaneng (Lowveld) district of Lebowa. Both are irrigated by a canal system. A portion of Champagne was originally established as a citrus farm managed by the former department of bantu administration. Dingleydale was replanned in the early 1960s on the principle of 'betterment'. The farm was divided into a residential area, grazing zones, and an agricultural section irrigated by canals. The population of Dingleydale today numbers 10 000.

Until recently the majority of households were allocated irrigated agricultural plots on which they were able to produce reasonable quantities of subsistence and marketable goods. That part of Champagne not under citrus cultivation provided additional grazing for the people of Dingleydale. Only about 10% of the potentially economically active population was totally unemployed, compared with a figure well in excess of this in most other bantustan areas.

At the end of 1983 the management of the Champagne citrus scheme was transferred from the Lebowa agricultural department to a private company, Measured Farming. Measured Farming's management contract was linked to the profit return it could make on the scheme. Measured Farming immediately extended the working week from five to six days, and the working day from five or six to 12 hours, but kept the wage rate the same. Workers, almost exclusively women, were put on a ticket system. To fill a ticket, the almost impossible quota of 200 trees a day had to be cleared. If the ticket was not filled, the worker was not paid.

After much resistance and the alleged intervention of the Lebowa government the ticket was reduced to 150 trees and the working day eased slightly. Workers were paid per 12-hour shift, pay which amounted to a little more than R3 per shift, or about 25c to 30c per hour. There were many illegal deductions from wages - for tax, unexplained pension contributions, firewood and other essential items, with the result that some workers received as little as R25 per month, or 8c per hour.

Under Measured Farming's management the Champagne citrus scheme has been expanded to take over the grazing land on Champagne and most of the grazing land on Dingleydale. The community at Dingleydale has good reason to believe that Measured Farming, in collaboration with the Lebowa government, is manipulating the situation with a view to taking over the irrigated plots of the people of Dingleydale.

Measured Farming's practices, like those on dozens of other similar projects in other bantustans, have been met with resistance. At Champagne this initially took the form of deliberate destruction of mango and citrus crops. Since May 1986 Measured Farming has been protected by a heavily armed detachment of South African police stationed on its land. The 'defence' of Champagne and many other projects by the security forces demonstrates the militarisation of agricultural production in these areas, and indeed the bantustans in general.

In 1986 the community organised itself further and appointed a firm of lawyers to protect its interests against the designs of both Measured Farming and the Lebowa government.

Agricultural workers in the bantustans are now probably even more exploited than those on white farms. Workers have little or no recourse to protection by law. There are many instances where workers who have attempted to seek protection in the law have been physically assaulted by the police. In Bophuthatswana, for example, squatters who tried to defend themselves against charges brought under Bophuthatswana's Land Control Act were physically assaulted by police. The police told passers-by that they were demonstrating what happens to those who get lawyers to defend them in court. This type of practice has become common in most bantustans.

A 'free market' in bantustan land

Bantustan communities upon whom agricultural development schemes have been foisted are often doubly exploited. Not only are they subjected to various forms of labour exploitation but in many cases they are also dispossessed of their land in the process. The labour practices and land dispossession accompanying most commercial agricultural developments in the bantustans have been a major cause of the popular resistance that has arisen in bantustan regions over the last two years.

But this is only a foretaste of what is to come. On 31 December 1986 the South African government transferred the control of 4,5-million hectares of land which had formerly fallen under the control of the South African Development Trust and other administrative bodies to the administration of the six 'non-independent' bantustans.

A South African government spokesperson explained that this meant the governments of these six bantustans could now decide in what way, and to whom, the land will be awarded, and how it will be utilised.

Strong pressures to introduce a 'free enterprise' economy into the bantustans and establish a 'free market' in land underlie this transfer of control.

Bophuthatswana's constitution commits the region to an economy based on a 'free enterprise' system. In the Ciskei far-reaching legislation, namely the Tribal Land Reform Bill, the Deeds, Registries Amendment Bill and the Local Authorities Bill, is designed to clear the way for the privatisation of land. Most other bantustans, including Kwazulu, have been advocating the privatisation of land, particularly land which is suitable for cash crops.

The establishment of a 'free market' in bantustan land will have devastating consequences. Relations in the market are inherently unequal. The abolition of regulatory controls in favour of market forces reinforces these pre-existing inequalities. 'In a society where legal and political institutions give land, capital and labour of the working class to one section of the population, the market forces will only consolidate that power'.[17]

The privatisation of bantustan land based on free market principles will lead to an escalation of landlessness and an intensification of poverty and inequality in access to economic resources. Since the transfer of power on 1 January 1987, there have been reports of people long-settled on trust land being evicted, with the land being sold or leased privately to individuals.

These moves will lead to a transfer and accumulation of economic power in the hands of supporters of the bantustan administrations. They will also give bantustan administrations more economic power and therefore more support.

The transfer of land is a carrot to the bantustan leaders, which, along with the transfer of greater powers of repression, may be enough to entice them to move towards acceptance of PW Botha's proposed national statutory council.

Industrial job creation in the bantustans

The South African government claims that the primary motivation behind its industrial decentralisation policy is to create jobs in the bantustans. This aims to reduce the high levels of unemployment and assist in economic development. Neither of these claims is true.

The South African government's notion of 'development', as far as the bantustans are concerned, is economistic and technicist. It is oriented to the production of meaningless national economic statistics such as GDP, and the construction of government buildings and other grandiose symbols.

The high rate of unemployment in the bantustans is primarily the consequence of the South African government's policy of relocating the unemployed to these areas. Indeed, one of the primary functions of the bantustans is to contain and control this growing surplus population.

Many of the jobs created in the bantustans are not new but relocated from the metropolitan areas. The government admits that 20% of these jobs are relocated from the metropolitan areas. The real figure is very much higher.

Jobs created in the bantustans are nearly always at a lower wage rate and under more oppressive and exploitative conditions than the job that was relocated or could have been created in the metropolitan areas. The number of jobs actually created in the bantustans has been insignificant in affecting unemployment. During the period 1982-1985 inclusive, the decentralisation programme as a whole, according to the government, approved 3 183 applications with a total capital investment of R4,8-billion and the potential for the creation of 212 742 jobs.[18] But approved applications are not necessarily taken up, and the number of jobs created (mostly relocated) is substantially less than government claims.

The figure of R4,8-billion is also misleading as it includes R1-billion spent on Sappi's new Eastern Transvaal plant, which was capital intensive and created only a few hundred jobs. And the figure is lower than the amount spent on subsidies to induce capital to locate or relocate in the bantustans.

The primary motivation behind the government's industrial decentralisation policy is to legitimise the existence and functions of the bantustans. The aim is to show that the bantustans are viable, and that they have their own successful economies which can attract capital.

The measures which attract industrial capital to the bantustans involve a comprehensive system of allowances, rebates and subsidies, and the provision of a controlled and cheap labour force.

Decentralisation subsidies

The precise nature and amount of subsidisation varies between development points and between bantustans. In general, attractions include rental, interest and power subsidies, employment incentives, relocation and training allowances, transport rebates, housing subsidies, personal loans, road transport permits, extraordinary insurance, GST exemptions and lower company tax.

In 1985 the highest subsidies available in Bophuthatswana, which is typical of the other bantustans, were:[19]

Rental subsidy on 70% of the value of land and buildings in respect of a project not exceeding R7-million. At 1985 interest rates this was about 12% (ie R36 000 cash grant on a building of R300 000);

Interest subsidy on 70% of the investment in land and buildings and on 50% of the balance of assets. In 1985 this was also about 12%;

Employment incentive: 95% of total wage bill or up to a maximum of R100 per worker per month, whichever is lower (ie a company with a wage bill of R20 000 may receive a non-taxable cash grant of R19 000);

Relocation allowance: up to R500 000 plus a further 20% of costs;

Training allowance: 40% of 125% of expenses;

Electricity subsidy: rates charged are equal to the tariff in the Eastern Transvaal - the lowest in the country;

Transport rebate: 40% on rail, or road if no rail exists;

Housing subsidy: 40% of ruling building-society rates, subject to a minimum of 6%;

Tender preference;

Personal loans;

GST exemption;

Lower company tax: in the Ciskei, company tax has been abolished altogether.

These incentives make it possible for inefficient and badly managed companies to make substantial profits. And many companies cream off substantial amounts of cash by fiddling the subsidy system, by illegally deducting and pocketing tax, pension and unemployment insurance payments from workers' wages and by withholding overtime pay and allowances.[20]

Controlled labour

Since 1960 labour legislation in the bantustans has increasingly diverged from that applicable in the remainder of South Africa. The bantustans are now covered by legal regimes which deny African workers nearly all the rights and benefits that have been won by their counterparts in South Africa. While workers in South Africa have won a number of significant rights since the late 1970s, those in the bantustans have been restricted to the provisions of the archaic Black Labour Relations Regulation Act of 1973, or its predecessor, the Black Settlement of Disputes Act of 1953. Both have been repealed in South Africa.

Workers in the bantustans are worse off now than they were before 1970. They are effectively denied the right to strike legally, excluded from all machinery that affects their wages, and not even protected by minimum wage determinations.

These restrictions are reinforced by bantustan security legislation and other repressive laws. Those bantustans that opted for 'independence' - Transkei, Bophuthatswana, Venda and Ciskei - have shown even greater determination than the others to crush trade union or worker organisation. Transkei and Venda have introduced labour legislation which makes no provision for trade unions and restricts employee collective bargaining machinery to an in-house liaison committee system. The same restrictions exist in the Ciskei through the retention of the Black Settlement of Disputes Act.

Bophuthatswana, supposedly the most successful and enlightened of the 'independent' bantustans, introduced comprehensive legal repression of workers in the form of its Industrial Conciliation Act. Prior to the introduction of this act, legislation allowed for nothing more than an in-house committee system of consultative status. Workers had no right to participate in the machinery dealing with conditions of work. Nor was there any legislation covering minimum wages, or legal protection against unfair labour practices.

Bophuthatswana's takeover of its own unemployment insurance fund and workers' compensation system resulted in the denial of these forms of social security to most workers.

Even before the introduction of its own labour legislation the Bophuthatswana government's determination to prohibit any legitimate and representative worker organisation was manifest in its brutal response to strikes that had broken out at Babelegi and elsewhere since 'independence'. A good example of the attitude of the Bophuthatswana government and most employers there to trade unions was given by the general manager of Sun City, Peter Wagner, following the dismissal of six employees in 1983.

The dismissals were the culmination of a labour dispute at the hotel complex. A number of employees, none of whom were members of trade unions, formed a committee called 'Delegation 21' which brought various grievances to the hotel management and to President Mangope himself. On the instructions of Mangope the six 'ringleaders' were dismissed.

When interviewed about these dismissals nearly two years later, Wagner stated that

> We were getting infiltrated by agitators from South African trade union organisers... I can prove that every single member of the '21' was a member, and the government also (can prove), was a member of a South African Union - and that is why the six got fired. But the average guy doesn't know that.[21]

The introduction of the Industrial Conciliation Act in 1984 (made retrospective to July 1983) was a direct response to the increasing presence and activity in Bophuthatswana of South African trade unions such as the National Union of Mineworkers, the Commercial, Catering and Allied Workers Union of South Africa and the South African Allied Workers Union.

While Bophuthatswana was going out of its way to attract foreign and South African companies, the Industrial Conciliation Act explicitly forbade the presence and activities of 'foreign' (that is South African) trade unions in Bophuthatswana, and precluded legal strikes.

This legal regime, reinforced by Bophuthatswana's security legislation and its disregard for its own Bill of Rights and due process of law, provided capitalists wishing to invest there with a cheap, readily available and compliant labour force.

The situation is similar in the other bantustans, both 'independent' and 'self-governing'. As a result, several hundred businesses have established new plants or relocated existing ones to take advantage of a system of labour control and exploitation that denies workers anything more than the most minimal rights.

These legal regimes, in conjunction with the security legislation and violence used by the bantustan and South African authorities against trade unionists and other organisations seen as a political or economic threat, have the following consequences:

* workers, not being protected by any minimum wage legislation, are paid exceedingly low wages;

* overtime is often not paid, or is paid as time off in lieu of wages;

* workers allege that sexual abuse is common. At the industrial centres of Babelegi, Garankuwa and Mogwase, in Bophuthatswana, women have claimed that they are sometimes forced to submit to sexual abuse, both to obtain jobs and to keep them;

* there is little legislation covering safety and health in plants. Workers have little recourse to workers' compensation or legal action for damages resulting from unsafe or unhealthy working - conditions, or negligence on the part of employers. An example is provided by Turnall, a subsidiary of the British company, Turner and Newall, which manufactures asbestos products in Bophuthatswana. Turnall workers claimed that going to doctors of their own choice, as distinct from the company doctor, led to dismissal. This has been corroborated by a doctor in the area;

* there is little recourse to legal protection against victimisation and unfair labour practices;

* police harassment and intimidation of workers, especially those suspected of being trade unionists or union sympathisers, is commonplace. In Bophuthatswana, 1986 began with a brutal campaign by Bophuthatswana police against members of South African trade unions living in the bantustan and commuting to South Africa to work. Many of these trade unionists, as well as innocent passers-by, were severely beaten or whipped, taken into police detention and tortured. They were only released after strong legal intervention by the catholic archbishop of Pretoria, the Metal and Allied Workers Union, and a team of Johannesburg-based lawyers;

* employers, safe in the knowledge that workers are too intimidated to bring action against them, engage in numerous practices relating to excessive working hours, illegal wage deductions, physical assault, and other forms of punishment and victimisation that are unlawful even within the bantustans.

Reformist claims made by the state are misleading and false. What improvements there have been in working conditions and wage levels are due to the pressures exerted by unions. In those economic sectors and regions of South Africa where unions do not exist or where they are prohibited, conditions and wages have not

improved during the 'reform' period. They may even have
deteriorated over the last decade.

Notes

1 M Sarakinsky and J Keenan, 'Unemployment in South Africa', *South African Labour Bulletin*, 12(1), January 1987; and J Keenan and M Sarakinsky, 'Poverty in South Africa', *South African Labour Bulletin*, 12(3), May-June 1987.

2 This figure is calculated from data provided in various editions of the Central Statistical Services Quarterly Reports.

3 This section is based on N Haysom and C Thompson, 'Farm Labour and the Law', Carnegie Conference, University of Cape Town, paper 84, 1984.

4 D Bachmeyer and W Vogel, 'Farm Labour in South Africa with specific reference to child labour', unpublished community medicine project, 1983.

5 J Baskin, 'Farmworkers and the National Manpower Commission', *South African Labour Bulletin*, 8(2), November 1982.

6 The Farm Labour Project. Submission to Manpower Commission on Farm Labour, Johannesburg, 1982, 11.

7 Mandla Seleoane, 'Conditions on eight farms in Middelburg, Eastern Transvaal', Carnegie Conference, University of Cape Town, paper 29, 1984, 46.

8 Farm Labour Project, 14.

9 Farm Labour Project, 20.

10 P van Ryneveld, 'The Crop and the Dop: Farm Life in the Western Cape', *Indicator South Africa*, 44, 1986, 73.

11 The head of the poison information centre at the Johannesburg hospital, Dr Pincus Catzel, in the foreword to HD Fourie, *Poisoning by Chemicals in Agriculture and Public Health*, Pretoria, 1984, vii.

12 Fourie, *Poisoning by Chemicals*, ix.

13 Hansard, col 302, 26.02.85.

14 This section is based on information drawn from The Surplus People Project, eds L Platzky and C Walker, *The Surplus People: forced removals in South Africa*, Johannesburg, 1985.

15 Minister of Bantu Administration and Development, *Hansard*, col 618, 10.12.70.

16 Farm Labour Project, 45. Such 'legislative intervention' paradoxically usually means the absence of any legislation.

17 Fuad Cassim, 'Criticising Conventional Economics', *Work in Progress*, 26, April 1983, 38-45.

18 South African Institute of Race Relations, *Race Relations Survey*, Johannesburg, 1985, 111.

19 See *Doing Business in Bophuthatswana*, Price Waterhouse, South Africa, July 1985.

20 See William Cobbett, 'Industrial Decentralisation and Exploitation: the case of Botshabelo', *South African Labour Bulletin*, 12(3), March-April 1987, 95-109.

21 Verbatim transcript of interview with P Wagner, managing director of Sun City, 11.12.84.